To Scott
& A like—
minded skeptical
colleague. Thanks
so much for the
visit and the
ingaging talk.
Best,
Kelly Lambert
Nov 30, 2007

Clinical Neuroscience

We are honored that a creation of Katherine Sherwood, an artist on the faculty of the University of California at Berkeley, graces the cover of *Clinical Neuroscience*. Katherine's paintings convey the essential union of the clinical and neurobiological worlds of mental health. This union is the basis of our book.

Katherine survived a devastating stroke in her left hemisphere that paralyzed her right side and left her unable to speak. The image of her own brain's circulatory system, viewed during a follow-up carotid angiogram, reminded Katherine of an ancient Chinese landscape and inspired in her a renewed creative spirit. Following considerable rehabilitation, Katherine embarked on a new artistic journey, painting with her left hand and incorporating the image of her angiogram in every new work. Today Katherine paints and teaches painting as well as courses about art and healing. Her experience is the featured Case in Point in Chapter Three.

Clinical Neuroscience
The Neurobiological Foundations of Mental Health

KELLY LAMBERT
Randolph–Macon College

•

CRAIG HOWARD KINSLEY
University of Richmond

WORTH PUBLISHERS

KGL: For my mother, Glenda Arnold Pitts (1942–1996), whose valiant fight against a terminal illness inspired me to learn more about the resilience of the human mind.

CHK: To my family, past and present, for molding me and for defining joy for me.

Senior Sponsoring Editor: Laura Pople
Assistant Editor: Danielle Storm
Development Editor: Barbara Brooks
Media and Supplements Editor: Danielle Pucci
Senior Marketing Manager: Carlise Stembridge
Associate Managing Editor: Tracey Kuehn
Art Director/Cover Designer: Barbara Reingold
Text Designer: Lissi Sigillo
Senior Illustration Coordinator: Bill Page
Illustrations: Matthew Holt
Photo Editors: Patricia Marx, Meg Kuhta
Photo Researcher: Nigel Assam
Production Manager: Sarah Segal
Composition: TSI Graphics
Printing and Binding: R. R. Donnelly and Sons Company

Cover art by Katherine Sherwood

ISBN: 0-7167-5227-1 (EAN: 978 0716752271)

Second printing

Worth Publishers
41 Madison Avenue
New York, NY 10010
www.worthpublishers.com

About the Authors

Kelly G. Lambert received her B.A. in psychology and biology from Samford University and her M.S. and Ph.D. in biopsychology from the University of Georgia. She is currently Professor and Chair of Psychology at Randolph-Macon College in Ashland, Virginia. She is the recipient of the 2001 State Council of Higher Education in Virginia's Outstanding Faculty Award. Her research focuses generally on the topic of behavior-induced neuroplasticity and more specifically on the areas of brain/behavior responses to chronic stress and the multifaceted neurobiological effects of maternal and paternal experience. Reports of her research have been published in journals such as *Stress, Nature,* and *Physiology and Behavior*. She lives in Mechanicsville, Virginia, with her husband, Gary Lambert (an industrial/organizational psychologist), her two daughters, Lara (11 years) and Skylar (7 years), and a menagerie of pets.

MRI SCANS OF AUTHORS' BRAINS: JEFFREY LORBERBAUM, MEDICAL UNIVERSITY OF SOUTH CAROLINA
K. LAMBERT PHOTO: GARY LAMBERT
C. KINSLEY PHOTO: GENNIFER LOVE

Craig H. Kinsley is Professor of Neuroscience in the Department of Psychology and Center for Neuroscience at the University of Richmond. His B.A. in psychology is from the California State University, Sonoma. His Ph.D., from the University at Albany, State University of New York, is in behavioral endocrinology. After receiving his Ph.D., he was a postdoctoral fellow and instructor in neuroscience and neuroendocrinology in the Department of Cellular Biology, Laboratory of Human Reproduction and Reproductive Biology, Harvard Medical School. His research, published in such journals as *Brain Research Bulletin, Developmental Psychobiology, Hormones and Behavior,* and *Nature,* focuses on the manifest changes that occur in the maternal brain and dictate the most important of mammalian behaviors, parental care. He is happily married to Nancy, and they have two children, Devon Alyse (13 years) and David William (9 years). His hobbies include his family, fishing, and music and stereo equipment.

Brief Contents

Contents

Disruptions of Homeostasis: Representative Clinical Disorders

PART III

Maintaining Homeostasis

PART IV

Preface

At a recent Society for Neuroscience meeting, nearly 30,000 neuroscientists gathered from across the world. They presented research on a range of topics, including evidence that

- The brain reward system in adolescents is more active compared to that of adults (Berns, Pagnoni, Zink, Martin-Skurski, & Capuron, 2004);

- The human mother's brain shows differential responsiveness to the sounds of crying infants and more activity than fathers' brains (Lorberbaum, Kose, Dubno, Horwitz, Newman, Sullivan, Hamner, Bohning, Arana, & George, 2004);

- Inner city residents may suffer from memory deficiencies related to stress effects on the hippocampus (Farah, Savage, Shera, Brodsky, Giannetta, Malmud, & Hurt, 2004).

These are fascinating findings, culled from literally thousands of interesting and rigorously gathered data presentations (and this is just one year's worth of new information!). The question is, what do we do with them all? How can we synthesize these data and apply them?

THE NEED FOR CLINICAL NEUROSCIENCE

A major challenge for neuroscientists today is the integration of basic research findings, like the ones above, into applied clinical approaches to treating brain disorders. At the same time, mental-health practitioners—those on the front lines of mental health delivery—must acquire broad-based knowledge of neurobiology, behavior, and environment if they hope to understand how brain mechanisms work, and when they do not work as they should. Molecular outcomes of drugs with equal clinical efficacy, for example, sometimes employ very different modes of action, depending on the underlying systems affected. Given the possibility that everyday stressors associated with living in a large city could affect one's neurobiology and memory (Farah et al., 2004), does it make sense to apply the same clinical psychological therapies aimed at treating depressed people from other populations? Is that counterintuitive? Only if one completely understands the mechanisms involved. We are, however, a long way from that day.

Recently the National Institute of Mental Health (NIMH) called for translational research grants to encourage collaboration between neuroscientists and mental health professionals. Such collaboration would create a "clinical neuroscience" that would translate into quicker results for in-need patients.

By 2025, depression is forecast to become the second leading illness in the United States (McEwen & Lashley, 2002). A meta-analysis published in *Psychological Science in the Public Interest* explores the response rates of depressed patients to various treatment modalities. Consider the treatment implications of these results. Interpersonal therapy rates are equally as effective as antidepressant drugs in reducing typical symptoms associated with depression. Further, 30 percent of respondents who received a placebo treatment reported improvement; see Figure 1.1 on page 6 (Hollon, Thase, & Markowitz, 2002). Considerable research in clinical neuroscience will be required to fully understand these results.

THE GENESIS OF THIS BOOK

As we designed a new course called Clinical Neuroscience for our students, we found several impressive general interest books and edited volumes, but we found no suitable textbook that integrated neurobiological mechanisms of mental health into the coverage of disorders that was readable, affordable, and comprehensive. We decided to write that textbook.

We have conducted extensive reviews of all the subject matter in this book and include novel interpretations and explanations. *Clinical Neuroscience* is a resource for anyone interested in an integrative, empirically based approach to mental health and for anyone who seeks to draw connections among courses offered in departments of psychology, biology, and neuroscience.

Initially, we envisioned the courses that we were designing within a psychology curriculum, specifically for upper-level undergraduates who had a prerequisite in basic biological psychology. In teaching the course, though, we discovered that students benefited from a unit on neurobiology and neurochemistry, and we have added that unit as Part II of the book. With this addition, a biological psychology prerequisite is not necessary, but it may be complementary. Because of more basic neurobiological information, this book may also be used as a nontraditional biology or psychology course.

AND THE AUDIENCE

As momentum gathers to prepare clinicians for the possibility of gaining prescription privileges (a practice already approved in New Mexico and Louisiana and likely to spread to other states) *Clinical Neuroscience* will be of value to upper-level undergraduate courses in clinical and counseling psychology. Further, the chasm separating psychology from biology—especially as it relates to brain regulation of mental activity—is growing smaller. The current volume will introduce even the most diehard dualist to evidence that the brain must be considered in all discussions of clinical treatments.

In addition, conversations with our neuroscientist colleagues at conferences and while researching this text over the past seven years have convinced us that clinical neuroscience is emerging not just as a course, but as a burgeoning field. Reviewers have elucidated the need for both separate courses and advanced seminars in clinical neuroscience. We believe this book will benefit neuroscience students as a reference as they navigate through their coursework and can also help them to keep an eye on applications—how neuroscience can benefit its subjects—thereby increasing the likelihood of translating the basic research into positive real-world outcomes.

As another example of speeding treatments from labs to clinics, medical students also can benefit from the book's integrative approach to mental health. That approach is appropriate for post-graduate audiences (such as internship-level faculty) as they prepare to move into mental health careers. By allowing instructors to draw connections between basic neuroscience and mental health applications, *Clinical Neuroscience* is equally appropriate for biology and neuroscience students. Building bridges between and among formerly disparate subdisciplines will hasten beneficial applications.

FORMAT OF TEXT

Because clinical approaches are an emerging area within the broad field of neuroscience, we put considerable thought into the identification, organization, and categorization of the topics covered in the text. Although diagnostic criteria from the *Diagnostic and Statistical Manual* (DSM) *IV-TR* were included as a reference for students for some conditions, we do not always follow the DSM categorizations (in part, due to their inherent vagueness). The structure of the text is as follows:

PART I: Introduction
Chapter 1   Emergence of Clinical Neuroscience
Chapter 2   Research, Treatment, and Points of View:
            Historical Perspectives

The introductory chapters include historical and contemporary overviews of theories and therapies in the mental health field. They establish a need for the more integrative, empirically based discipline of clinical neuroscience. Various disciplines (e.g., psychology, psychiatry, neurology, basic research) and their unique perspectives are also addressed; it becomes increasingly apparent that their once unique boundaries are becoming less distinct. Finally, a description of these many perspectives, or levels of analysis, in *Clinical Neuroscience* sets the stage for the multifaceted approach in the text.

PART II: Fundamentals of Clinical Neuroscience

Many students may already have some experience with the basics of neural structure and function. These early chapters will allow for a brief review for those students and for initial exposure to the basics of nervous function for the uninitiated. The inclusion of pedagogical components that relate directly to the field of clinical neuroscience will enable students to see direct connections between the basic information about the underlying "wet" tissue, and its regulation and dysregulation in the manifestation of the human's so-called "mental health and life." For example, neurodegenerative and cognitive processing disorders (such as Alzheimer's and attention deficit hyperactivity disorder) are included in the neurodevelopment chapter to show a direct link between basic mechanisms and the overt conditions they produce.

PART III: Disruptions of Homeostasis: Clinical Disorders

Mental disorders are viewed as disruptions of homeostasis, departures from endogenous averages, in this text. As the internal milieu is disrupted, the nervous system's attempt to compensate sometimes leads to extreme conditions that are classified as mental disorders. We have included obsessive-compulsive disorder and Tourette's syndrome in Chapter 7 (Disorders of Anxiety), major depression and bipolar disorder in Chapter 8 (Mood Disorders), and, as implied, schizophrenia and addiction are the sole disorders for Chapters 9 and 10, respectively. Although other disorders fit in these categories, a decision was made to include in-depth coverage of representative disorders within the categories rather than skim over every disorder included in the DSM. As mentioned, other disorders are presented in various chapters; for example, phobias are discussed in Chapter 1 and post-traumatic stress disorder (PTSD) is covered in Chapter 11. If instructors want to include disorders not covered in this text, supplemental readings can be used or, as we do in our classes, these disorders can be assigned for student papers and presentations.

PART IV: Maintaining Homeostasis: Balancing the Mind–Body Equation

Chapter 11   Stress and Coping
Chapter 12   Psychoneuroimmunology
Chapter 13   Eating Regulation and Associated Disorders

We place an emphasis in *Clinical Neuroscience* on the importance of maintaining mental health, or mental health homeostasis. There is overwhelming evidence that stress is a major factor in many mental disorders, prompting us to include stress and coping as a separate chapter (11) in this section. Terms such as *psychoneuroimmunology*, the topic of Chapter 12, convey the interdisciplinary relationship inherent in psychological processes, neurobiology, and immunology. It is important for students to understand this network and its interactions early in their academic careers. That the nervous system intermingles with the immune system provides compelling evidence that the immune system may play a critical role in mental health. Finally, the body's various foods serve as the brain's fuel and as the source of its raw materials; consequently, eating and the food we ingest are also intertwined with physical and mental health. We therefore cover the neurobiological mechanisms of hunger motivation and regulation, and their disruption, in Chapter 13. Such material is substrate for a discussion of potential causes and treatments of obesity (although not usually considered a mental disorder) and eating disorders.

Epilogue: Clinical Neuroscience: Ethical Considerations and Future Directions

The recent explosion in neuroscience data and information have presented scientists and practitioners with challenging ethical questions and moral dilemmas. For example, should aborted fetal tissue be used to repair the faulty mechanisms that regulate such neurodegenerative diseases as Parkinson's disease? Should society treat criminals differently if (or when) neuroscience finds that underlying brain mechanisms for such behavior are malfunctioning? These and other issues should be addressed as scientific questions. Therapeutic progress is being made within clinical neuroscience-related disciplines. Though some issues are controversial and presented provocatively, this chapter should stimulate necessary discussion about the future use of the data arising from the study of the brain. The field is far from definitive answers on these ethical conundrums, but we must begin to think about them: the neurobiology of human behavior is becoming clearer, with all of its implications. Students today, the professionals of tomorrow, must be equipped to make the right decisions about the issues raised here and in other contexts. We are hopeful that *Clinical Neuroscience* is one such aid.

CENTRAL THEMES IN THE TEXT

Empirical, scientific rigor. As you read this text it is apparent that only valid and empirical information is considered as conclusions about mechanisms and treatments for mental illnesses are evaluated. That is, observable, replicable data from largely well-designed experiments are described so that informed decisions can be made about the meaningfulness of such data. Although the field of mental health is rich with introspective approaches that are not amenable to scientific rigor, such approaches are not considered in this text. Throughout *Clinical Neuroscience,* the efficacy of putative and speculative treatments are critically analyzed based on the strength of their empirical evidence. In this regard, claims concerning mechanisms or treatment of certain disorders are held to the same scientific standard as any other neurobiological topic.

Multiple perspectives. Whereas the field of mental health has been dominated by the view that pharmaceutical intervention and talking therapies are the most effective modes of treatment (since the beginning of the 20th century, that is), other approaches are discussed in this text as being relevant for understanding and treating the many mental disorders that plague our society (as they both affect the brain). Psychotherapy (e.g., interpersonal therapy), behavioral therapy, brain stimulation, developmental intervention, immunomodulation, and dietary modifications are among the various treatment approaches that are considered in this text, with their plusses and minuses. Causes and treatments are also considered from an evolutionary perspective, as our present is dictated by our distant past. We believe that there are multiple inroads to understanding the brain; it is likely that these paths can be best traveled by practitioners schooled in and familiar with various treatment strategies.

A mind/brain–body balance. By including the section on maintaining homeostatic processes (Chapters 11, 12, and 13), we emphasize our observations that the boundaries between the brain and other areas of the body are becoming less distinctive. We include a chapter on psychoneuroimmunology to indicate the intimate relationship between the nervous and immune systems and how disruptions of this communication may lead to a host of illnesses ranging from the flu to depression. Our pattern of eating also influences many aspects of our mental and emotional lives and should be a variable in any mental health equation. Our reactive stress response represents extensive cross talk between the brain and the body and plays an essential role in maintaining overall homeostasis. Further, the observation that 30% of patients respond to a placebo treatment provides additional support for the importance of serious examination of the mind/brain–body relationship in mental health training.

Animal models and clinical trials. Because humans are so complex and difficult to study in some domains, animal models are a valuable tool for learning about the brain. When conducted appropriately, the use of animal models serves as a critical step to other species, including humans. These models provide insights into the human condition (and ironically, into the animals that are subjects, improving their care as well). For these reasons, appropriate animal models are discussed in *Clinical Neuroscience*. When available and well done, clinical trials with humans are certainly discussed to give students a thorough understanding of the research that has been conducted in those areas, but the foundation of clinical neuroscience, its history and future, still depends strongly on animal models.

No easy solutions. The field of clinical neuroscience is awash in data. Although it is tempting to skip through all the meaningful research so that we can present only simplistic answers to complex questions, it is a disservice to the millions of individuals who have or will suffer from some of the conditions described herein. The complexity of the issues demands complex and thoughtful answers. We have attempted to provide representative responses to the difficult questions posed throughout this text. Thus, various facets and nuances of the issues are discussed, leaving the reader with the impression that few clear answers exist concerning many aspects of mental health neuroscience (and also gives students the chance to make up their own minds about them). Unanswered and difficult questions (scientific and ethical) are characteristic of a field such as this, which is massing immense stockpiles of information but is slow to use the information to solve real-world human problems. A goal of this text is to inspire talented and curious students to go into research areas that may one day enable them to uncover and deliver some of the desperately needed mental health solutions of clinical neuroscience to the individuals so in need of them.

PEDAGOGICAL ELEMENTS

Although we both have an insatiable curiosity about the neurobiology of behavior that keeps us busy in our laboratories with our students, being professors at liberal arts institutions for the last fifteen years means also that we are passionate about teaching this exciting topic to our students.

We are, therefore, committed to providing effective pedagogical elements for this text. The narrative running throughout the text is presented in a storylike fashion, building from the classic studies marking the conception of various research areas to the latest research on each topic. Several years ago an author of an introductory psychology text wrote that he was approached by a waitress while writing his book and, on finding out that her customer was writing a book, she asked if he was writing a book with a story or the other kind. When the author indicated that he was writing the other kind, she simply said "oh" and quickly walked away, evidently not even interested enough to ask about the topic (Fernald, 1997). Presenting information in an engaging manner (including many well-developed analogy frameworks) should facilitate the learning process for clinical neuroscience students. These stories are not devoid of pertinent content, however. Each chapter is peppered with the most meaningful, relevant research that, from our perspective, represents the past and current status of the field. In sum, it is our hope that *Clinical Neuroscience* will be a solid and "other kind" of text for interested students.

Pedagogical elements include an opening vignette, called *Connections,* for each chapter that highlights connections between a clinical or applied observation and a related program of basic research. In addition to these translational vignettes, when possible, students and young investigators have been highlighted to serve as research models for student readers. It is our experience that students who observe other students conducting research are more likely to subsequently conduct research, either as students or for a career. It has been a real pleasure celebrating the accomplishments of these young and talented researchers; they are the model students at which we aimed this book.

The chapters also include case studies, titled *A Case in Point,* to help students associate human faces with the disorders covered. Students will be able to follow diagnostic and treatment paths of patients that result in varying rates of success.

Also in each chapter, a feature called *The Investigators* highlights some of the most accomplished researchers in the field, allowing students to follow academic and career journeys of these prominent scientists as they encountered some of the same challenges faced by many students, for instance, weighing uncertainties about careers and interests, overcoming personal challenges, and following childhood interests in behavior and disorders. These scientists range from Nobel Prize winners (Eric Kandel) to the recently appointed Director of the National Institute of Mental Health (Thomas Insel). They all had beginnings, like the students reading this book, and found a spark that ignited a lifelong fascination with science.

Other topics of interest are referred to as *Brain Matters.* Although we are careful not to distract the students from the text, we feel that it's important to provide related, though not integral, subjects to introduce students to the breadth of the clinical neuroscience field. Some examples include the role of religion in early mental illness perceptions; areas of the brain involved in laughter; eating and stress; the controversial research surrounding dietary treatment of autism; and the relationship between baseball rituals and obsessive-compulsive disorder.

Finally, to enhance learning of key information, important terms are presented in **bold type** and defined in the margins for the reader. A glossary of these terms appears at the end of the text. A summary of key points is included at the end of each chapter as well as a listing of the key terms and their page numbers. A section titled *For Further Consideration* is a summary of recommended readings and accompanying brief descriptions for students who wish to pursue particular topics further.

SUPPLEMENTS

As instructors, we know the importance of good supplements. We are pleased to be able to offer the following materials to assist you in your teaching of *Clinical Neuroscience.*

For Instructors

Instructor's Resources and Test Bank *by Joe Morrissey, State University of New York-Binghamton* The *Instructor's Resources* feature chapter-by-chapter topic overviews and learning objectives, thorough chapter summaries, in-class demonstrations and activities, suggested topics to launch class discussions, ideas for research and term paper projects, homework assignments and exercises, and a list of additional reading material for students looking to enhance their knowledge of the topics covered in each chapter.

The comprehensive test bank contains more than 800 multiple-choice, true/false, fill-in, and essay questions. The questions include a wide variety of applied, conceptual, and factual questions. Each question is ranked according to difficulty and keyed to the topic and page in the text where the source information appears. The test bank files are also available in Microsoft Word (on request).

Online Quizzing, Powered by Questionmark *(access via the companion Web site at www.worthpublishers.com/lambert)* With this resource, you can easily and securely quiz students online using prewritten multiple-choice questions for each chapter. Students receive instant feedback and can take the quizzes more than once. Using the online quiz gradebook, you can view results by quiz, student, or question, or you can get weekly results via email.

Presentation and Video

Chapter Art and Outline PowerPoint Slides *(available at worth-publishers.com/lambert)* These PowerPoint slides can be used directly or customized to fit your needs. There are two prebuilt, customizable slide sets for each chapter of *Clinical Neuroscience*—one featuring chapter text, the other featuring all chapter art and illustrations.

Worth Publishers' Image and Lecture Gallery *(available at www.worthpublishers.com/ilg)* The Image and Lecture Gallery is a convenient way to access electronic versions of lecture materials. Users can browse, search, and download illustrations from every Worth title as well as prebuilt PowerPoint presentations that contain all chapter art or chapter section headings in text form. Users can also create personal folders on a personalized home page for easy organization of the materials.

The Brain and Behavior *Video Segments (available on VHS)* This special collection includes targeted selections from the revised edition of the highly praised Scientific American Frontiers series. Hosted by Alan Alda, these video clips provide instructors with an excellent tool to show how neuroscience research is actually conducted. The 10- to 12-minute modules focus on the work of Steve Suomi, Renee Baillargeon, Car Rosengren, Laura Pettito, Steven Pinker, Barbara Rothbaum, Bob Stickgold, Irene Pepperberg, Marc Hauser, Linda Bartoshuk, and Michael Gazzaniga.

The Mind Video Teaching Modules, *Second Edition, edited by Frank J. Vattano, Colorado State University, with the consultation of Charles Brewer, Furman University, and David Myers in association with WNET (available on VHS and DVD)* These 35 brief, engaging video clips dramatically enhance and illustrate lecture topics. This completely revised collection of short clips contains updated segments on language processing, infant cognitive development, heredity factors in alcoholism, and living without memory (featuring a dramatic new interview with Clive Wearing). The accompanying Faculty Guide offers descriptions for each module as well as suggestions as to how they might be incorporated into class presentations.

The Brain Video Teaching Modules, *Second Edition, edited by Frank J. Vattano, Thomas L. Bennet, and Michelle Butler, all of Colorado State University (available on VHS and DVD)* A great source of classroom discussion ideas, this collection of 32 short clips provides vivid examples of brain development, function, disorders, and research. The Second Edition contains 10 new and 13 revised modules using added material, new audio, and new graphics. Individual segments range from 3 to 15 minutes in length, providing flexibility in highlighting specific topics. The accompanying Faculty Guide offers descriptions for each module as well as suggestions on how they might be incorporated into class presentations.

For Students

Clinical Neuroscience Companion Web Site *by Kelly Lambert, Randolph-Macon College, and Craig Kinsley, University of Richmond (available at www.worthpublishers.com/lambert)* The companion Web site is an online educational setting for students that provides a virtual study guide twenty-four hours a day, seven days a week. The resources are free and do not require any special access codes or passwords. Tools on the site include chapter outlines, learning objectives, annotated Web links, interactive flashcards, and online quizzes with immediate feedback and instructor notification.

Foundations of Behavioral Neuroscience CD-ROM *created by Uri Hasson, New York University, and Yehuda Shavit, Hebrew University of Jerusalem, and produced by the Open University of Israel* This innovative CD-ROM includes five modules: Neural Communication, Central Nervous System, Vision, Movement, and Research Methods. The CD-ROM features rotating three-dimensional models of the human brain and eye; more than 25 video clips; animations of key physiological mechanisms; interactive examples of new neuroimaging technologies, including MRI and CT; and a number of pedagogical features, such as a clickable glossary, search engine, and multiple-choice questions.

Making Sense of Psychology on the Web *by Connie Varnhagen, University of Alberta* Useful for the novice researcher as well as the experienced Internet user, this brief book helps students to become discriminating Web users and researchers. The guide includes a CD-ROM containing the award-winning Research Assistant HyperFolio, software that enables students to clip bits and pieces of Web sites and other electronic resources (snippets of text, illustrations, video clips, audio clips, and more) and compile them into worksheets and an electronic "filing cabinet."

Scientific American **Explores the Hidden Mind: A Collector's Edition of Readings** This reader is free on request with the purchase of *Clinical Neuroscience*. In the past decade, we have learned more about the brain and how it creates the mind than we have in the entire previous century. In a special collector's edition, *Scientific American* provides a must-have compilation of updated feature articles that explore and reveal the mysterious inner workings of our minds and brains.

Improving the Mind and Brain: A *Scientific American* Special Issue
This reader is free on request with the purchase of *Clinical Neuroscience.* This new single-topic issue from *Scientific American* magazine features the latest findings from the most distinguished researchers in the field.

ACKNOWLEDGMENTS

The content of any textbook is enhanced by the critical eyes of colleagues, who offer valuable suggestions for improvements and clarifications of material, though, in the end, any and all errors are the responsibility of the authors. We are very grateful to the following reviewers for their expertise, input, and willingness to help:

Theresa Barber,
Dickinson College

Elizabeth Byrnes,
Tufts University School of Veterinary Medicine

Bryan Castelda,
Binghamton University

Judith Horowitz,
Medaille College

Craig Johnson,
Towson University

Sabra Klein,
Johns Hopkins University

Phyllis Mann,
Tufts University School of Veterinary Medicine

William McDaniel,
Georgia College and State University

Tibor Palfai,
Syracuse University

Beth Powell,
Smith College

Lawrence Ryan,
Oregon State University

Elayne Thompson,
William Rainey Harper College

Nutan Vaidya,
The Rosalind Franklin University of Medicine and Science

Sara White,
Binghamton University

In addition, we interviewed many scientists and laypeople alike to round out our coverage of the diverse topics in *Clinical Neuroscience* and to add stories and human faces to the conditions we describe. We are grateful to the following people for taking the time to speak with us, either in person or electronically, sharing personal stories as well as professional triumphs and disappointments.

The scientists:

Robert Ader,
University of Rochester

Russell Barkley,
Medical University of South Carolina

Keith Black,
Cedars Sinai Medical Center, California

Robert Bridges,
Tufts University School of Veterinary Medicine

Kelly Brownell,
Yale University

Patrik Brundin,
Lund University

Sue Carter,
University of Illinois at Chicago

Sonia Cavigelli,
University of Chicago

Maribeth Champoux,
National Institutes of Health

Anna Rose Childress,
University of Pennsylvania

Michael Davis,
Emory University

Courtney DeVries,
Ohio State University

Mort Doran,
Canada

Casimer Fornal,
Princeton University

Eberhard Fuchs,
German Primate Center

Kim Huhman,
Georgia State University

Thomas Insel,
National Institute of Mental Health

Barry Jacobs,
Princeton University

Kay Redfield Jamison,
Washington DC

Hendree Jones,
Johns Hopkins University

Eric Kandel,
Columbia University

Sabra Klein,
Johns Hopkins University

Paul MacLean,
National Institute of Mental Health

Phyllis Mann,
Tufts University School of Veterinary Medicine

Paul McHugh,
Johns Hopkins University

Charles Nemeroff,
Emory University

Kenneth Pilgreen,
Louisiana State University

Stephen Porges,
University of Illinois at Chicago

Judith Rapoport,
National Institute of Mental Health

Paul Rozin,
University of Pennsylvania

Ronald Ruden,
Yaffe Ruden and Associates, New York

Oliver Sacks,
New York

Jeffrey Schwartz,
UCLA

Robert Sapolsky,
Stanford University

Elaine Walker,
Emory University

Daniel Weinberger,
National Institute of Mental Health

The laypeople:

Deb Bahr
Nadean Cool
Joseph Dee
Sara Hunicutt
Evan Handler

Caroline Kettlewell
Brett Nielsen
Augusto Odone
Karyn Seroussi
Katherine Sherwood

Andrew Solomon
"Andy," our interviewee with
   schizophrenia

The authors would like to thank the professionals at Worth Publishers who tended and nurtured and then brought this book to birth. We are indebted to our initial acquisitions editor, Jessica Bayne, for taking a chance on this project by supporting a book in an emerging market and then to our current acquisitions editor, Laura Pople, for continuing to be committed to producing a book that would be both informative and engaging for students. We are also grateful to Laura for identifying Katherine Sherwood and her inspiring artwork that graces the cover of the text. We truly appreciate the guidance provided by Barbara Brooks, our developmental editor, who taught two rookie textbook authors a thing or two about writing texts. Thanks is also extended to Tracey Kuehn, our associate managing editor, who worked diligently to transform the manuscript into a logical and visually appealing text format. Finally, we would like to recognize and thank the following dedicated individuals for their unflagging efforts in the face of our sometimes impenetrable language and unusual demands: Danielle Storm, Assistant Editor; Renee Altier and Carlise Stembridge, Marketing Managers; Danielle Pucci, Media and Supplements Editor; Patricia Marx, Photo Research Manager; Meg Kuhta, former Photo Editor; Nigel Assam, Photo Researcher; Babs Reingold, Design Director; Lissi Sigillo, Designer and Layout Editor; Bill Page, Senior Illustration Coordinator; Matthew Holt, Illustrator; Sarah Segal, Production Manager, and Penny Hull, Production Editor.

Of course, in no way could we have begun and completed this project without the inspiration of our colleagues, students, and especially our families. Thank you, thank you, thank you.

Kelly Lambert would like to personally thank:

My husband, Gary Lambert, and two daughters, Lara and Skylar, for their patience and loving support throughout this project.

My brother, Doug Gurley, for both support and professional biomedical advice on topics in the book.

My colleagues, Alva Hughes, Kristen Klaaren, and Robert Resnick from the Department of Psychology at Randolph-Macon College (R-MC) for their frequent discussions and feedback on the topics included in the book.

My extended R-MC family—Dean Robert Holyer for his professional support; Barbara Wirth, for administrative support; the R-MC reference librarians for their assistance accessing more research articles than one can imagine; Lily Zhang for technical support.

My impressive students who have provided encouragement for this project during challenging times, and

My many friends and family members in Virginia, Alabama, and Georgia who listened to unending conversations about clinical neuroscience.

Craig Kinsley would like to personally thank:

Nancy, my wife and best friend, and our lovely children, Devon and David. They understand and inspire.

My family in California: Parents Dorothy and Howard, and sisters Cathy and Carla

My family in Northern Virginia: Shelly and Margery Lustig

My students who have helped with many facets and details for the book, especially: Margaret Banks, Lillian Flores-Stevens, Jessica Gatewood, Abbe Hoffman-Macbeth, Kate Karelina, Rebecca Klatzkin, Lisa Madonia-Lomas, Ilan McNamara, Elizabeth Amory-Meyers, Melissa Morgan, Angela Orthmeyer, Emily Pytlik, Brandi Rima, Jennifer Wartella, Naomi Wightman

Colleagues, friends and associates who have helped along the way: the University of Richmond, for providing an atmosphere of challenge and encouragement; my colleagues in psychology, for making me think; Martha C. Beitner, for her constant assistance and hard work; Michael M. Koller, dear friend, writer, and thinker; and Fred J. Kozub, for a decade and a half of incisive comments

Last, the authors would like to thank each other. For the nearly seven years it has taken to assemble this book, there have been many challenging moments, stretches of frustration, and many highs and lows. Not once, however, did we lose sight of our goal of producing a work that was worthy of our coworkers' and students' faith in us. Throughout, a strong friendship grew even deeper. If fulfillment is to be found in the journey and not the destination, then these years have been a highlight of our professional lives.

Chapter One

Emergence of Clinical Neuroscience

Connections

Mara: Seeking Therapy

One Friday evening, Mara, Tess, Antonio, and Josh gathered at their usual table at their favorite restaurant a couple of blocks from the university. After several minutes of light-hearted banter, the conversation got serious as Mara described her recent feelings of depression. Once a confident, competent student, Mara was now experiencing self-doubt about her ability to do well on her final exams. She also said that it was an effort even to make it to class in the morning and that it had been very difficult for her to actually show up that evening—a weekly ritual that was normally the highlight of her week.

Pointing to the gyro sandwich that had just arrived, she mentioned that she didn't have a desire to eat much anymore, either. Mara had read enough about the symptoms of depression to know that she was probably suffering from this condition, but all her reading had not made it clear how to choose the best treatment. Mara was desperate for advice from her trusted friends.

Josh spoke up first, mentioning the attention antidepressants like Prozac have received, suggesting that if so many people were talking about Prozac it

must work. In fact, because he knew that his family physician had prescribed antidepressants for his aunt, he suggested that Mara simply visit her family physician so that she could start taking Prozac.

Tess, a psychology student, voiced her concern that, while general medical practitioners were certainly able to prescribe medication for mental illness, they received little training for the diagnosis, maintenance, and treatment of the vast majority of mental illnesses. She had been taught that antidepressants alter neurochemical processing in the brain and that everyone should approach these drugs with extreme caution.

As the son of a clinical psychologist, Antonio suggested that Mara talk to his dad about cognitive therapy. Antonio said that his dad tried to coach his clients into changing their cognitive perspective and to give them strategies to develop a new approach to life's challenges—such as Mara's upcoming finals.

Mara had been reading about some of the "talk" therapies used by psychiatrists. Some still used notions introduced by Freud in their therapeutic approach. Mara's buddies agreed that the psychodynamic, or Freudian, approach was probably past its prime on the treatment scene. Josh, the aspiring physician, spoke up again declaring that since depression was known as a brain disease, it would be best to go to a doctor specializing in the brain—a neurologist.

Mara said, "See what I mean? It's hard to know which treatment strategy is best." The scientific literature on depression she had perused consisted mainly of research in an entirely different discipline—behavioral neuroscience. But although the behavioral neuroscientists seemed to have a lot of ideas to offer concerning the treatment of mental illnesses, they were not practitioners, so they in fact were not even a treatment option.

Mara and her friends were struck by how difficult it was for patients experiencing depression to sift through all the information to select the most appropriate treatment.

Jasmine: Seeking a Profession

Jasmine, a senior premed student, found herself visiting the campus career center more often than any of her friends. Ever since she was 5 years old and her older brother experienced a brain injury after falling off his bicycle, she had been fascinated with the relationship among the brain, behavior, and thoughts. She wanted to spend her career pursuing this interest—but she was having difficulty identifying the most appropriate career path.

Although she had befriended the clinical psychologist who worked with her brother for so many years, she was learning that most clinical psychology curricula have few course requirements that relate behavior to the brain. After a little research she was discovering that psychiatry wasn't too different; she could conceivably complete medical school and her specialty

training with no guarantee of being a well-versed student of the brain. Thus, her desire to incorporate neuroscience principles into a psychiatric practice seemed unlikely.

Neurology was certainly an option; completing this curriculum would ensure that Jasmine would thoroughly know the brain. However, neurology seemed to focus on patients who had suffered damage to the brain. Although this aspect fascinated Jasmine, she was interested in the healthy brain as well and in preventing some of the mental disorders (for example, depression, schizophrenia, Alzheimer's disease) haunting our society today.

After taking several neuroscience courses, Jasmine considered a graduate program in neuroscience. But she had immediate doubts about this option because of the limited opportunities to actually work with patients. Jasmine persevered as she searched for an interdisciplinary graduate program that would provide training in both the basic and applied areas of neuroscience.

Alex: Seeking Support

Alex was exhausted after battling insurance agents on the phone. His 67-year-old father had been in a horrible automobile accident 9 months earlier, and now, though his wounds and broken bones had healed, his father was haunted by the memory of his accident. Alex had taken his father to his family physician and the doctor confirmed Alex's fears that his father was suffering from post-traumatic stress disorder (PTSD).

Alex immediately started gathering information about obtaining the best care for his father, who had received excellent insurance benefits for the physical injuries suffered in the accident. But to Alex's dismay, the insurance company considered PTSD a mental condition that was not covered under the medical policy.

Alex explained that his father was experiencing physical symptoms (increased heart rate and insomnia) and asked why the symptoms were not considered medical. Alex asked repeatedly why problems with the brain's functioning were not considered as "medical" as those associated with the rest of the body. Why, he asked, is there such a dichotomy between mental illness and physical illness? Bewildered, confused, and angry, Alex wondered what he could do to help his father.

We are defined by our brains more than any other organ in our body. The brain offers endless possibilities; when the brain malfunctions, however, an individual may face an unwelcome disorder, in many cases, a live-in guest for life.

The number of people suffering from mental illnesses varies; whereas schizophrenia affects about 1% of the population, depression affects about 15%, as does Alzheimer's disease in people over 65. The billions of dollars spent on mental illnesses worldwide cost our society more than any other class of disease, including cancer and cardiovascular disease (Andreasen, 2001). In fact, of the top ten causes of disability across the world, five (major depression, alcohol use, self-inflicted injuries, manic-depressive disorder, and schizophrenia) are related to mental illness (the remaining causes are tuberculosis, road traffic accidents, war, violence, and iron-deficiency anemia) (Andreasen & Black, 2001). Although exciting research is currently being conducted in neuroscience laboratories all over the world, a cure for mental illness is still elusive.

The mental health field is dominated by unanswered questions like the ones faced by the students portrayed above. Patients already in compromised health wade through a sea of disjointed recommendations from diverse fields. Students find themselves unable to distinguish among the various mental health professions. Too many patients and their caregivers experience anguish beyond that imposed by the mental illness as they struggle to identify financial support to cover treatment expenses.

How can informed research scientists and practitioners devise or acquire successful treatments for mental illness? How can they work together to promote mental health? More and more, mental health professionals are viewing the brain's functioning from as many perspectives as possible, using research methodology appropriate to each point of view. Neuroscience research is revealing multiple inroads to the brain, and it is likely that the same paths can be traveled by various treatment strategies.

Using biofeedback techniques, individuals can determine how certain thoughts influence various physiological systems. Such integration provides strong support for the intimate relationship between physiological and psychological processes.

© LEONARD LESSIN/PETER ARNOLD, INC.

The purpose of this book is to focus on perspectives that have emerged from a systematic, empirical base of knowledge. First we introduce the characters in the mental health drama—psychotherapists, neurosurgeons, neurologists, neuropsychologists, neuroscientists, behavioral scientists, and psychiatrists. These characters play various roles and contribute a diverse array of treatment strategies. Once you peel back all the layers, however, the lead actor in the mental health drama is the **empirical evidence,** scientific research that conveys objectively how specific variables influence brain function and how the brain and body interact.

Exploring how these variables—genetic, environmental, neurobiological, developmental, evolutionary, and cultural—influence our mental functioning and mental health serves as the basic approach of *Clinical Neuroscience.* It is not until we integrate these views that a true picture of mental illness, and of mental health, begins to emerge.

STATUS REPORTS ON PSYCHIATRY AND CLINICAL PSYCHOLOGY

Typically, as students consider careers in mental health, two professional paths emerge as possible choices: clinical psychology and psychiatry. Currently, the educational journeys to these career destinations diverge sharply. Psychologists, for example, receive a Ph.D. in clinical psychology and psychiatrists receive an M.D. and then specialize in psychiatry.

Until 2002, another defining difference in the practices of clinical psychology and psychiatry was the ability of psychiatrists to prescribe medication—a privilege not extended to clinical psychologists. This distinction, however, is changing. Bills were passed during New Mexico's legislative hearings in 2002 and also in Lousiana in 2004 authorizing adequately trained psychologists (the appropriate criteria for this distinction are yet to be defined) to prescribe **psychotropic (psychoactive) drugs,** medications that influence psychological processes (www.apa.org, 2002, 2004).

Psychiatrists and clinical psychologists are closely watching several other states in which bills calling for extending prescription privileges to clinical psychologists are pending, and they expect specific training standards for psychologists to be set by New Mexico and Lousiana. As the distinctive lines between these two disciplines grow increasingly fuzzy, each faces a

empirical evidence Evidence that can be confirmed by systematic observations. This evidence should play a critical role in a researcher's or practitioner's opinion of causes and treatments for certain disorders.

psychotropic (psychoactive) drug Medication that influences psychological processes.

distinct set of challenges: maintaining a separate identity and offering effective treatment options.

Psychiatrists determining treatment options for patients, for example, face increasing pressures from insurance companies (Hobson & Leonard, 2001). Some psychiatrists have adopted a **biomedical model** emphasizing medical diagnoses and drug therapy. Others focus more on a **psychosocial model,** involving such treatments as behavioral therapy, cognitive-behavioral therapy, individual psychotherapy (classical psychoanalysis, interpersonal psychotherapy), group therapy, and social skills therapy. The psychosocial therapist typically directs patients toward appropriate social services and follows up on the status of each patient (Andreasen & Black, 2000).

But researchers are discovering that the biomedical model isn't necessarily more "biological" than the psychosocial approach. Investigators are just beginning to understand how strategies used in the psychosocial model actually change the brain, enabling the patient to function more normally (Andreasen & Black, 2000). The psychosocial approach is more labor intensive, however, and HMOs no longer reimburse the cost of hour-long sessions with each patient; they rarely cover more than 20-minute appointments, and they prefer the more cost-effective treatment option of psychotropic medication. Consequently, the more time-intensive psychosocial therapies are being conducted by less expensive psychologists, counselors, and social workers. Overriding all these developments is the fact that today, most prescriptions for mental conditions are written by general practitioners, M.D.s who have little formal training in diagnosing and treating mental illness (Hobson & Leonard, 2001).

Dr. Judith Rapoport, Chief of Child Psychiatry at the National Institute of Mental Health, recently reported that she is hesitant to recommend a psychiatric residency to medical students because of this emphasis on prescription writing. In fact, American medical students are shunning psychiatry, filling fewer than one third of the 1200 positions for psychiatric residents in the United States in 2001. With restricted treatment options, it is becoming increasingly more difficult to attract talented students to the psychiatry specialty (Hobson & Leonard, 2001).

Adding to the turmoil within psychiatry is the looming prospect of clinical psychologists gaining prescription privileges. Psychiatrists may soon be faced with distinguishing themselves from clinical psychologists in ways other than prescription writing. Even if they maintain their monopoly on prescription privileges, research is already suggesting that drugs don't always offer the best relief for patients suffering from mental illness. In fact, a meta-analysis exploring the response rates of depressed patients responding to various forms of psychotherapy and drug therapy

biomedical model
Therapeutic approach using mostly medical diagnoses and drug prescriptions.

psychosocial model
Therapeutic approach emphasizing the relationship between client, or patient, and therapist while using therapies such as behavioral therapy, interpersonal therapy, classical psychoanalysis, or group therapy.

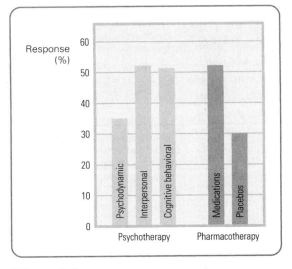

[Figure 1.1]

This figure depicts the effectiveness of several different approaches used to treat depression. As indicated, pharmacological treatments have similar outcomes to interpersonal and cognitive behavioral therapies.

FROM HOLLON, THASE, & MARKOWITZ, 2002

(Hollon, Thase, & Markowitz, 2002) suggests that interpersonal therapy can be just as effective as antidepressants in reducing typical symptoms associated with depression (Figure 1.1).

If drugs were the undisputed clear choice of treatment for mental illness, then the movement of psychiatry away from psychosocial therapies toward the prescriptive therapies would be understandable and desirable. However, the verdict is still out on many popular drugs. Even with Prozac, one of the most heavily prescribed drugs for depression, relief from depression does not come without the price of side effects, including headaches, diarrhea, nausea, constipation, and, in 40% of users, sexual dysfunction (Hobson & Leonard, 2001; Rothschild, 2000). Ironically, patients on antidepressants such as Prozac may need to take them chronically because the long list of side effects is enough to make them even more depressed.

Research–Treatment Disconnect

Whereas psychiatric services struggle to attract American medical students, clinical psychology programs reel in about 20 applicants per position, most from the best undergraduate schools in the country. Making the argument even stronger for selecting clinical psychologists as therapists is the fact that their services cost half of psychiatrists' services.

To any serious student of psychology, the thought of professional clinical and counseling psychologists applying their scientific knowledge of behavior and mental processes to mental illness sounds perfectly reasonable and desirable. Indeed, at the end of World War II, when returning soldiers were seeking treatment at VA hospitals that did not have enough psychiatrists, enlisting the help of research psychologists seemed like an ideal solution. But since that era, the emphasis on research methodology in clinical psychology has dwindled. In 1971, the American Psychological Association (APA) approved a new clinical program leading to the degree Doctor of Psychology (PsyD). As opposed to the traditional PhD received by most psychologists who conduct their own research projects, the PsyD degree's emphasis is on practical training and does not require as much research experience as the PhD because of the APA's conclusion that understanding research methodology is unrelated to the effectiveness of psychotherapy. Thus, clinical and counseling psychology has wandered far from its once strong research-based origins (Dawes, 1994).

Regardless of the graduate training (clinical psychology, PsyD, psychiatry) students who are pursuing a mental health career do both their future patients/clients and themselves a disservice if they do not take the appropriate coursework in methodology. When a new treatment is introduced, it is the responsibility of a therapist to determine the value of the treatment. This determination cannot be adequately established, however, without a requisite understanding of research design. If the therapist cannot evaluate a published manuscript on the effectiveness of a new therapy, it is impossible for him or her to make an informed decision about the effectiveness of the new treatment.

Among the intriguing therapies recently introduced are the following:

- Eye movement desensitization reprogramming (EMDR), a treatment involving the rapid movement of the eyes to relieve severe anxiety
- Use of the herb St. John's wort to treat depression
- Drilling a hole in a person's skull to achieve a psychologically healthy "blood/brain volume"
- Performing surgery on obese individuals to reduce the capacity of the stomach to the size of a human thumb
- Transcranial magnetic stimulation (TMS), the treatment of depression with very strong magnets

Some or all may be effective therapies, but each must undergo rigorous testing and evaluation before patients are subjected to them. (You'll learn which ones from the list above are effective as you progress through the text.) The best way to discern the validity of any of these proposed treatments is to carefully and critically review the research published in peer-reviewed journals. Such an inspection of the literature requires the therapist to be informed about the primary components of research design and statistics. Of course, a conspicuous absence of published studies on a particular new treatment should be a warning sign that the treatment has yet to be supported in an empirical fashion; proceeding with such a new therapy is the therapeutic equivalent of diving into unknown waters.

It can be argued that the psychosocial model does not require psychologists to be well versed in statistics and research design; they just need to be good listeners with clinical intuition to deliver adequate psychotherapy to patients and clients. An experience described by Robyn Dawes (1994) in the early days of his clinical career suggests that clinicians run the risk of making devastatingly harmful decisions when statistical methods are ignored in diagnostic decisions.

In 1960, a 16-year-old girl was presented to Dawes as a patient because she was dating a man 10 years older. He did what most therapists did at that time: he administered the Rorschach test. This test consists of a

psychometric test Paper-and-pencil test typically used by psychologists for diagnostic purposes. These tests need to pass reliability, validity and standardization assessment before use with patients and clients.

series of cards containing inkblots that are ambiguous in form (Figure 1.2). The patient is asked to describe what he or she sees in the blot. The response is used as a "window" to the patient's mind because the patient is probably projecting personal experiences onto the blot. Although this sounds like a perfectly reasonable technique to use as a **psychometric test** (or psychological measurement test), it has since been extensively reviewed and found to lack validity (Lilienfield, Wood, & Garb, 2000).

The patient, who scored at the 95th percentile on an intelligence test (126 IQ score), offered 40 reasonable responses on her Rorschach test except for card 8, which she said looked like a bear (it did not). At a subsequent staff meeting when Dawes was presenting the outcome of her tests, the head psychologist suggested that the girl must be hallucinating because card 8 did not look like a bear. When Dawes emphasized the point that the number of her good responses was higher than that of most normally functioning people, he was told that understanding statistics was not as important as understanding people and that statistics do not apply to the individual. The staff agreed that the young lady should be admitted to the mental hospital if she returned to the clinic. Dawes is not sure what happened with this client because, in frustration at the lack of methodology used in the clinical staff's decision making, he quit his career as a clinical psychologist.

[Figure 1.2]
This image is similar to that used in the Rorschach inkblot test. The ambiguity of the figures is intentional to prompt divergent responses from patients or clients.

Even today, Paul McHugh (personal communication, 2001), Chair of the Department of Psychiatry and Behavioral Sciences at Johns Hopkins University, reluctantly admits that "a professional that relies on [statistical] data to treat his patients is tarred as one who cares little about his patient." McHugh, an advocate of more empirical-based therapies, believes that the rigorous pursuit of neuroscience "will dignify the field of psychiatry."

It's difficult to predict the future of psychiatry and clinical psychology. As information about the brain's involvement in mental illness and mental health becomes more available, it is likely that stronger ties to the neurosciences will strengthen the foundation of each area, as McHugh suggests. Even though a criminal investigator might be very good at evaluating personal motives in determining the likelihood of guilt of a suspect, it would be shortsighted to ignore the availability of DNA screening in determining his or her guilt. Just as top-notch investigative reporting involves impressive deductive abilities, keen interviewing skills, cutting-edge forensic technology, and a persistence in identifying and finding the truth, the most effective mental health investigators use all available resources. They draw from the existing biomedical and psychosocial approaches to make informed decisions about the origins and treatment of the "suspects" of mental illness.

Classifying Mental Disorders

Psychiatrists and psychologists both refer to the same manual to diagnose and categorize mental illnesses, the American Psychiatric Association's *Diagnostic and Statistical Manual* (DSM). Now in its fourth edition, the DSM has been revised and is currently known as the DSM-IV-TR (the IV means it is the fourth edition; TR stands for Text Revision). The number of disorders was a modest 60 in the first edition of this manual (1952); the current DSM has ballooned to over 400 disorders. In addition to disorder inflation, McGuire and Troisi (1998) describe the "shifting sands" of purely psychological diagnostic criteria, using borderline personality disorder as an example.

The DSM-IV-TR entry for borderline personality disorder has nine criteria, with only five of the nine required for a diagnosis (Table 1.1). This summative strategy (using the number of symptoms as a diagnostic criterion) lacks precision. For instance, two individuals may each have five of the nine overall criteria but share only a single criterion. If two people in a restaurant each order the special of the day and the waitress brings one customer a chicken plate and the other a roast beef plate, each with a salad, the customers will be confused; except for the salad the entrees seem like two very different meals. Similarly, a diagnosis that is indentical for two people who differ in four of five symptoms is far from precise.

Additionally, although conditions are included in the DSM according to the four criteria of suffering, statistical variance, tissue pathology,

[Table 1.1]

DSM-IV-TR Diagnostic Criteria for Borderline Personality Disorder

A pervasive pattern of instability of interpersonal relationships, self-image, and affects, and marked impulsivity beginning by early adulthood and present in a variety of contexts, as indicated by five (or more) of the following:

(1) frantic efforts to avoid real or imagined abandonment. **Note:** Do not include suicidal or self-mutilating behavior covered in Criterion 5.

(2) a pattern of unstable and intense interpersonal relationships characterized by alternating between extremes of idealization and devaluation

(3) identity disturbance: markedly and persistently unstable self-image or sense of self

(4) impulsivity in at least two areas that are potentially self-damaging (e.g., spending, sex, substance abuse, reckless driving, binge eating). **Note:** Do not include suicidal or self-mutilating behavior covered in Criterion 5.

(5) recurrent suicidal behavior, gestures, or threats, or self-mutilating behavior

(6) affective instability due to a marked reactivity of mood (e.g., frequent displays of temper, constant anger, recurrent physical fights)

(7) chronic feelings of emptiness

(8) inappropriate, intense anger or difficulty controlling anger (e.g., frequent displays of temper, constant anger, recurrent physical fights)

(9) transient, stress-related paranoid ideation or severe dissociative symptoms

APA (2001), p. 710.

and functional impairment, the decision to include a condition as a disorder remains subjective and may, as the numbers of both clinical practitioners and disorders increase, reflect the growth of the number of therapists rather than a real need for more disorder categories. The fact that the decisions for labeling disorders in the DSM are subjective can be easily discerned from the changes in disorders from edition to edition. For example, whereas homosexuality was considered a disorder in DSM-II, published in 1968, it was removed entirely from DSM-IV (APA, 1994). These shifting diagnoses can exact a tremendous toll on people who spend years burdened by and being treated for a supposed disorder, only to be told, "Never mind; it's not a mental illness."

Paula Caplan, a clinical and research psychologist, corroborates the subjectivity of the DSM. In her book *They Say You're Crazy: How the World's Most Powerful Psychiatrists Decide Who's Normal,* Caplan (1996) writes that decisions are made about the inclusion of disorders and criteria for disorders in a subjective manner, too often lacking an adequate empirical basis. Despite the controversy, we reproduce the DSM diagnostic criteria verbatim in this text because they serve as the definitive criteria for mental disorders in practice, and they reveal the difficulty of defining mental states or traits with precision. Moreover, it is valuable to read the criteria exactly as they are presented to therapists and practitioners; therefore, no summaries or paraphrasing are used.

Lessons Learned from the Multiple Personality Disorder Diagnosis

One problematic effect of de-emphasizing empirical research in the diagnosis and treatment of mental illness is the likely occurrence of psychological fads. A tragic example of such a fad was dissociative identity disorder (DID). Table 1.2 reproduces the DSM diagnostic criteria for DID, formerly known as multiple personality disorder (MPD). The public became aware of this disorder, in which a person's personality is fragmented into several "alters," after the publication of books on two famous cases: Eve White (currently Chris Sizemore) in C. H. Thigpen's *The Three Faces of Eve* in 1957 and Sybil Dorsett in F. R. Schreiber's *Sybil* in 1973 .

Before *Sybil* was published, DID was one of the rarest mental disorders; about 76 cases were identified up until 1944. After the book was published, however, it was estimated that 40,000 cases were presented between 1985 and 1995 alone. In addition to case inflation, it has been reported that the number of "alters" or personalities has grown as well—to over a hundred in some cases (Acocella, 1998).

[Table 1.2]

DSM-IV-TR Diagnostic Criteria for Dissociative Identity Disorder

A. The presence of two or more distinct identities or personality states (each with its own relatively enduring pattern of perceiving, relating to, and thinking about the environment and self).

B. At least two of these identities or personality states recurrently take control of the person's behavior.

C. Inability to recall important personal information that is too extensive to be explained by ordinary forgetfulness.

D. The disturbance is not due to the direct physiological effects of a substance (e.g., blackouts or chaotic behavior during Alcohol Intoxication) or a general medical condition (e.g., complex partial seizures). **Note:** In children, the symptoms are not attributable to imaginary playmates or other fantasy play.

APA (2001), p. 529.

The literature contains a plethora of case studies of patients suffering from DID. Currently, case studies are invaluable methodological tools in areas of specific neuropsychological interest, such as identifying cognitive functions of specific brain areas in patients suffering from brain lesions (Banich, 1997). However, although case studies serve as valuable *starting* points for many research endeavors, they are rarely suitable *ending* points for making informed decisions about the efficacy of certain therapies (Myers & Hansen, 1997). (For a review of how Oliver Sacks cleverly uses case studies as a starting point for gathering more information about the interaction of the brain's physical and mental functioning, see Box 1.2 on page 28.) Also, because many case studies involve retrospective data, it is important to verify the accuracy of reported events. Many patients tell their therapists that they experienced some form of abuse as children, but these claims are seldom confirmed with appropriate background checks.

"Would it be possible to speak with the personality that pays the bills?"

The case study can also be problematic because the single case may not be representative of others. Stanovich (1988) writes about the case study as the "person-who" school of evidence gathering ("I knew a person who had DID and he . . ."). Person-who statistics make for interesting conversation but do not approach the scrutiny of acceptable research methodology for determining important factors and treatments related to mental health.

Aside from the anecdotal evidence, neuroscience research offers a few clues about DID. Electroencephalographs have provided limited knowledge about the activity of large populations of neurons in DID patients; scant evidence has indicated left-hemisphere dysfunction in some DID patients (Rosenstein, 1994) and visual anomalies have been reported in DID individuals (Shepard & Braun, 1995, cited in Miller et al., 1991; Miller, 1989). There is also evidence from groups of case studies that the anticonvulsant carbamazepine may be effective for DID patients (Coons, 1992). Again, the excessive use of case studies and the absence of proper controls make these conclusions highly suspect. Such methodological sloppiness can have devastating effects on the patient.

Although concerns related to the validity of certain aspects of DID have been presented, it is likely that many questions persist in your mind. If, as the empirical evidence suggests, it is uncertain that so many patients developed so many personalities, how could so many mental health professionals have found themselves both diagnosing and treating this questionable disease? And how could so many patients find themselves believing they possess dozens of personalities?

The DID patients, mostly women distraught with unmanageable anxiety, were frequently given strong medications such as Xanax, Valium, and Halcion. Many were subjected to hypnosis, during which memories related to horrifying childhoods, filled with tragedies such as sexual abuse and cult rituals, were recalled. Many psychotherapists believed that hypnosis-prompted memories were more accurate than nonhypnotic memories. Thus, the mental capacity of patients was greatly altered by heavy drug use and hypnosis, and unknowing therapists were able to plant ideas of personalities in the patients' malleable neuronal soil.

The well-known memory researcher Elizabeth Loftus points out that some therapists were unaware of the innate suggestibility of their patients and how they were reinforcing delusions and unknowingly implanting memories that corroborated the diagnosis of DID resulting from childhood sexual abuse (Loftus & Ketcham, 1994). In a sense, the patients and therapists were part of a dance—patients searching for relief from anxiety in their lives were easily influenced by the musical score introduced by the therapist.

In an alarming way, the therapist ultimately influenced the dance of the patient much as a puppeteer influences the movement of a puppet. In the background, the media (principally movies and talk shows) fueled the DID phenomenon by increasing public awareness and fascination with the topic. For example, the nature of DID began to change following the movie *Sybil* in 1977: victims were frequently found to have more "alters" and were increasingly likely to have suffered from childhood sexual abuse after the movie was released.

But what may be an interesting plot device does not make a true mental disorder. The building wave of DID started to evaporate in the early 1990s. As women began to sue therapists for the damage this diagnosis brought to their lives (for example, multiple hospitalizations, accusations of family members, time taken away from their normal family and work lives), society became less fascinated with the topic. Paul McHugh (in Acocella, 1998) stated, "Close the dissociation services and disperse the patients to general psychiatric units. Ignore the alters. Stop talking to them, taking notes on them, and discussing them in staff conferences." Around this time, the American Psychiatric Association changed the name of the disorder from MPD to DID. In 1993, *Time* magazine ran a cover story entitled "Lies of the Mind," emphasizing the danger of a diagnosis of repressed memories and MPD.

Thus, the tide has turned and there are fewer and fewer cases of women possessing dozens of personalities resulting from horrendous childhoods filled with satanic family rituals and chronic sexual abuse. Psychiatrists still discuss dissociative disorders, and certainly both women and men may suffer tremendous emotional despair following childhood abuse of any nature, but mental health professionals are more aware of the suggestibility of their patients as they attempt to discern the roots of certain emotional problems. Even though progress is being made, it is important for students of mental health to be reminded how easy it is to go down the wrong path when detours are taken from the empirical highways of mental health (see Box 1.1, on page 14 for a case study of a tragic detour). With this concern in mind, Loftus dedicated her book, which chronicles the pain suffered by patients at the hands of unskilled therapists, to "the principles of science, which demand that any claim to 'truth' be accompanied by proof" (Loftus & Ketcham, 1994).

OPENING THE WINDOWS ON MENTAL HEALTH

Exploring mental illness from multiple perspectives is like viewing a house through multiple windows. Peering through each window gives you a valuable but limited view inside. Before a house is built, only the architect with the detailed plan of the structure, akin to one's genetic blueprints, can visualize the finished building. Of course, the original blueprints can be modified as the house develops—a wall can be added between the kitchen and the family room, a deck can be added, an extra window can be placed in the kitchen. Modifications can similarly be made to someone's original genetic profile—genes can mutate or be damaged by exposure to a toxic substance or other threat.

Building a house requires planning at many levels. In addition to prescribing the construction of the overall structure and the specific rooms, architectural plans lay out house functions (electrical wiring and

Box [1.1]

A Case in Point

Diagnoses of Nadean Cool

In the early 1990s, Nadean Cool, a homemaker in Wisconsin, saw a psychiatrist for treatment of depression following an assault on her teenage daughter. Initially she was diagnosed with post-traumatic stress disorder, but following about 7 months of extensive hypnosis and use of psychotropic drugs, Cool was given the diagnosis of multiple personality disorder (MPD). She was told she was the victim of childhood abuse that included satanic rituals involving the murder and cannibalism of babies. Further, Cool's psychiatrist told her that her father was the leader of the cult and that she had repressed her memories until they were unveiled with his clinical techniques.

Near the end of her 6-year treatment, Cool was told that she was possessed by 126 personalities—including those of a heroin addict, a teenage boy, the bride of Satan, and a duck. She was placed on a variety of drugs (up to 13 at one point), including methadone (a drug used to treat heroin addiction). Her psychiatrist

prescribed the methadone because he believed, according to Cool, that since one of her personalities was a heroin addict, "the methadone would help me get in touch with additional memories" (personal communication, 2001). No mention was made of what this treatment would do to the remaining personalities (or to the duck). Further, the potential interaction of the many drugs Cool was taking was not discussed, nor were the drugs administered in any systematic way to determine if any particular drug was therapeutically beneficial for her symptoms.

During one of her repeated hospitalizations, Cool's psychiatrist performed an exorcism on her. Following protocol described in the book *Hostage to the Devil*, 1992, the psychiatrist brought along a fire extinguisher to her hospital room in case she spontaneously combusted as the demon departed from her body during her exorcism. Where were sober reflection, objectivity, and skepticism in this mix of folly and trial and error?

Conveniently, Cool's therapy persisted as long as her insurance company was willing to cover her expenses; she says that her psychiatrist repeatedly told her how fortunate she was to have such wonderful insurance coverage. However, Cool's husband, once trusting that

plumbing) and make provisions for fuel lines for cooking and heating. In the same way, genetic blueprints guide our neurobiology—*neuroanatomy*, the construction of primary brain components; *neurophysiology*, how the brain functions; and *neurochemistry*, the chemical reactions that fuel its many workings.

Should the roof supports be constructed improperly or the wiring misrouted, the house will not function in the way it was designed. Life in an otherwise wonderful home can come to a halt when the furnace breaks down. In the same way, any breakdown in neuroanatomy, neurophysiology, or neurochemistry can devastate brain development and mental capacities.

Focusing on any approach in isolation—the blueprints, the construction, or peering through a window to view a single room—provides only limited information, far less than an integrated perspective. But even the most integrative information cannot replicate the experiences of the person actually living day to day with his or her particular brain in his or her particular environment. In fact, the only true sense of the house may come from living in it day to day, experiencing its creaks, the patterns of

Nadean Cool testifies in Outagamie County Circuit Court on February 12, 1997, in Appleton, Wisconsin.

SHARON CEKADA, *THE APPLETON POST-CRESCENT*/AP PHOTO.

his wife's psychiatrist was using standard therapy that would ultimately lead to her recovery, realized that her therapy was making her worse. He finally convinced Cool that her therapy was problematic, and Cool realized that her psychiatrist had exacerbated her existing problems while creating new ones. Not only was she absent from her children during their teenage years because of 38 hospitalizations, her relationship with her father was damaged. Told that her father was the leader of the satanic cult and was responsible for making her eat dead babies, she confronted her father with these accusations. He didn't respond; a week later he died. Subsequently, Cool filed a malpractice

lawsuit against her former doctor and won a $2.4 million settlement. During her trial other women who had been patients of the same psychiatrist were shocked to learn that Cool's story was remarkably similar to their experiences.

Although Cool occasionally suffers from bouts of mild depression today, she is healthy once again and in control of her life. She is still haunted by the possibility that she contributed to her father's death, but she is learning to deal with that pain as well. In an attempt to protect others from the damage incurred by both herself and her loved ones at the hands of her psychiatrist, she has spoken out publicly about her situation, appearing on several news shows. Interestingly, her psychiatrist did not lose his medical license; he moved to a different state and continues practicing psychiatry.

Cool is currently an advocate for therapies derived from peer-reviewed empirical investigations. She made it clear during our interview that she wants to tell her story to students training to work in the mental health profession. Although MPD horror stories are on the decline, there is no guarantee that patients' lives won't be traumatized by other therapies looming in the mental health future.

light as the sun rises, and the drafts of air that flow through the halls in the cool winter evenings. These are like *environmental influences* on people during their development. The homeowner may choose hardwood floors, striped wallpaper, and antique furniture; we may furnish our mental lives with classic novels, rap music, tennis practice, the pursuit of a particular major, career, religion, or ethical cause.

For the serious observer of houses, valuable social and historical information is available. In any neighborhood a particular style of residence may predominate, and this style of house will be built more often than novel styles. Contractors like to stick with houses that have proved successful. Particularly striking or successful home designs can endure for centuries.

Similarly, through the *evolutionary window,* psychologists view humans as a species through history. How have humans adapted biologically to their environments? What are the biological effects when, for example, certain genes are selected and passed on from generation to generation? And how does geographical location influence evolution? Families in Africa prefer homes very different from homes in the American Midwest.

Thus one's *culture* also influences one's mental health—some cultures promote more social contact, others more active coping styles, and so on.

The brain, like the house, benefits from the best raw materials to build with and the best environment in which to develop. In the following sections we take a closer look at each window on mental health (Table 1.3). In the chapters that follow we consider all these perspectives as means to treat and/or to prevent mental illness.

[Table 1.3]

Perspectives Emphasized in the Field of Clinical Neuroscience

Perspective	Focus
Genetic	Role of genetics in expression of mental functioning
Neuroanatomical	Specific neuroanatomical structure(s) underlying mental functions
Neurochemical	Specific neurochemicals (e.g., neurotransmitters) underlying mental functions
Neurophysiological	Exact neural functioning accompanying mental functions (e.g., slowed action potentials in neurons)
Developmental	Specific critical windows of neuronal development and plasticity in contributing to mental functioning
Environmental	Environmental stimuli that may contribute to mental illness or mental health
Cultural	Cultural aspects that may contribute to the formation and perception of mental disorders
Evolutionary	Biological relevance of factors as they fit into the evolutionary context for particular behaviors related to mental health and mental illness

Windows on Neurobiology

Neurobiologists study brain structure and function. For example, a neurochemical profile can be created by conducting medical tests or by observing a person's response to drugs. Information about neuroanatomy can be gained by impressive neuroimaging techniques. A person's functioning capacity, or neurophysiology, can be assessed by tests ranging from brain scans that measure how cells metabolize glucose to basic neuropsychological tests such as recalling lists of items.

Neuroanatomy. Perhaps the most famous case that points up the intimate relationship between neuroanatomy and mental health is that of Phineas Gage. On September 13, 1848, while working as the foreman of a construction gang laying the bed for an Irish railroad, Gage was tamping, or packing, explosives into solid rock when a horrible accident occurred.

traumatic brain injury (TBI) Injury to a person's brain usually resulting from an accident.

neurogenesis Creation of new neurons. It was once thought that developed brains no longer produce new neurons, but research has confirmed the production of new neurons across the life span. Little is known, however, about the functional consequences of the new neurons.

His tamping rod set off an explosion, shot into the air, and passed completely through Gage's head (Figure 1.3a). The tamping rod was quite large, measuring 3 feet, 7 inches long and 1.25 inches in diameter at its widest point (Figure 1.3b). Although Gage survived, his neuroanatomy was forever altered, resulting in severe psychological disturbances and differences from his former self.

Where did the damage occur? As seen in Figure 1.3a, the tamping iron entered through Gage's cheek and exited from the top of his skull (for more precise information about the entry and exit points see Damasio et al., 1995), damaging his left frontal and temporal lobes as well as other areas. From a psychological standpoint, Gage reportedly suffered a partial impairment of his intellectual properties and a marked change in personality in the sense that he was more impulsive and irreverent than before and seemed to lack the social skills that he possessed prior to the accident (Macmillan, 2000). As you will read in the Epilogue, Antonio Damasio has used the Gage case as an impetus for a clever line of research illuminating the role of the frontal cortex in ethical and other higher-order decision making (Damasio, 1995).

The Gage case marks the beginning of the burgeoning evidence indicating how devastating the destruction of certain neuroanatomical areas is to mental health. For example, today researchers know that the mental deterioration associated with Alzheimer's disease is accompanied by damaged or tangled clusters of neurons. Further, behavioral impairments such as tremors and difficulty moving one's limbs are observed in Parkinson's disease, a disorder accompanied by the destruction of a key area of the brain that is involved in movement. Finally, as was the case with Jasmine's older brother in the chapter-opening Connections, **traumatic brain injury (TBI)** is a major threat to the developing brains of children and the number one killer and cause of disability in children and teens in the United States (Stein, Brailowsky, & Will, 1995). The knowledge researchers and practitioners have gained from the numerous cases of TBI serves as little comfort to the 80,000 Americans reportedly experiencing long-term disability each year following complications related to brain injuries (Brain Injury Association, 2002).

In addition to describing how brain damage can lead to mental deficiencies, one goal of this book is to consider how neuroanatomical modifications might be used as a form of therapy for mental illness. For example, can we induce **neurogenesis** (the birth of new neurons) by

(a)   (b)

[Figure 1.3]
Phineas Gage died in 1861, and his skull was later exhumed. (a) This computer graphic is based on measurements of Gage's skull and on brain-imaging techniques used to reconstruct the accident. Portions of both hemispheres appear to have been damaged. (b) To gain perspective on Gage's accident, the actual tamping iron that pierced his brain is displayed here alongside his skull.

LEFT: DEPARTMENT OF NEUROLOGY AND IMAGE ANALYSIS FACILITY, UNIVERSITY OF IOWA. RIGHT: COUNTWAY LIBRARY, WARREN ANATOMICAL MUSEUM, HARVARD UNIVERSITY.

(a)

[Figure 1.4]

(a) Diagram of the left hemisphere of the human brain.
(b) Magnetic resonance scans of six different people. Each brain shows variability in the cortical surface as well as in shape and size. Such individual differences present special challenges to practitioners and researchers when trying to determine specific locations in the brain.

exposure to certain enriched environments or to chemicals called **neurotrophic factors** that are related to the production and growth of neural processes?

Of course, one essential element to understanding neuroanatomy is neuroimaging. Imaging techniques enable scientists to view both postmortem and living brain tissue. Focusing on the living brain, the **computerized tomography (CT)** scanner was the first imaging instrument to enable scientists and practitioners to observe the gross structures of a person's brain (much like an X ray of the brain). Today **magnetic resonance imaging (MRI)** enables researchers to observe the three-dimensional brain in all planes, also yielding a high-resolution image.

In addition to establishing consistencies between brain areas and accompanying functions, advanced neuroimaging techniques have also revealed substantial differences among brains of individuals of the same species (Figure 1.4). These individual differences, though interesting, present special challenges for scientists and practitioners attempting to establish strong and inevitable relationships between neuroanatomical structures and functions or malfunctions.

Neurochemistry. Recall from the beginning of the chapter that as Mara searched for relief from depression, she found the reported success of drugs in treating psychological disorders hard to deny. Although researchers don't always know the exact mechanisms, they know that psychoactive drugs that modify chemical systems in the brain do influence mental health. Identifying a drug that offers relief from a certain disorder provides researchers a window of opportunity to explore exactly where and how the drug functions. This information, if discovered, leads to more insightful ways to treat disorders.

As you will learn in Chapter 5, multiple neurochemicals with multiple receptors all interact with one another in the brain. Scientists have identified functional families of neurochemicals, but the story is complex and far from complete. The well-known biopsychologist Elliot Valenstein, Professor of Psychology and Neuroscience at the University of Michigan, has spent more than 40 years investigating how neurochemicals such as hormones and drugs influence behavior.

In his latest book, *Blaming the Brain* (1998), Valenstein points out that virtually all current psychiatry department chairpersons endorse a biochemical approach to mental illness, and many physicians inform patients that they are experiencing certain psychological disturbances because of a chemical imbalance. Yet no overwhelming evidence demonstrates that a majority of mental patients actually have a chemical imbalance! This contradiction does not prove that neurochemicals are not important to mental functioning; on the contrary, from the success rates of many drugs, they most probably are involved in some way, but perhaps it is a more indirect involvement than originally envisioned. The contradictions suggest that we are far from understanding the exact consequences of the psychopharmacological treatment of mental illness.

Valenstein points out that, while he certainly believes in the importance of biological factors in mental health, he also believes that "the way all biological factors are expressed in behavior and mental states depends equally on social and psychological variables" (p. 6). Who could argue with his statement? What is troubling is that these variables are frequently dismissed in a patient's treatment regime as practitioners focus only on the type and dose of drug being administered to the patient. Valenstein wants practitioners to look through more than just the neurochemical window when assessing a person's mental capacity and functioning.

Neurophysiology. The ultimate goal of gaining information about neuroanatomy and neurochemistry is to understand exactly how the brain carries out its functions. Just knowing all the parts of an engine and the fuel it uses does not reveal how all the components interact to make the car move. Among the exciting tools that exist today to assess neurophysiology (Figure 1.5), one of the earliest to measure activity in the living

neurotrophic factors
Neurochemicals such as BDNF (brain-derived neurotrophic factor) that promote the growth and complexity of neurons.

computerized tomography (CT) Neuroimaging technique developed in the 1960s that is the equivalent of taking an X ray of the brain.

magnetic resonance imaging
Technique that provides pictures of the brain by sending a magnetic field through a person's head so that the scanners can absorb radiation from hydrogen ions so that a three-dimensional, high-resolution picture of brain tissue is generated.

[Figure 1.5]
Examples of neuroimaging techniques—computerized tomography, positron emission tomography, and magnetic resonance imaging—contrasted to a photograph of a dissected human brain. A = anterior; P = posterior.

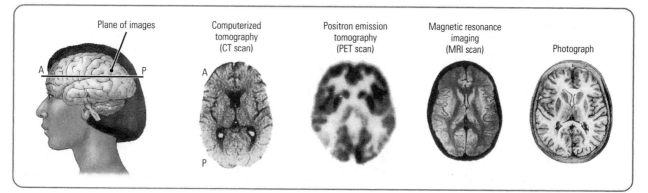

Plane of images

Computerized tomography (CT scan)

Positron emission tomography (PET scan)

Magnetic resonance imaging (MRI scan)

Photograph

electroencephalography (EEG) One of the earliest methods of recording activity of the living brain; involves placing electrodes on an individual's scalp and recording the activity of large populations of neurons. This technique has been valuable in diagnosing epilepsy and in delineating the various stages of sleep.

positron emission tomography (PET) Functional neuroimaging technique that involves injecting the patient with radioactively tagged glucose and quantifying the patient's metabolization of the radioactive glucose when the patient is presented with an experimental challenge (e.g., a cognitive task or a certain stimulus).

functional magnetic resonance imaging (fMRI) MRI that provides information about activity of the brain by quantifying cerebral blood flow during a cognitive challenge.

brain was **electroencephalography (EEG).** Electroencephalography measures and records electrical activity in large populations of neurons. More advanced imaging techniques such as **positron emission tomography (PET)** and **functional magnetic resonance imaging (fMRI)** enable scientists to assess glucose metabolism and cerebral blood flow, respectively. A plethora of more specific neuroscientific techniques to explore brain tissue functions range from single-cell recording to a neuron's production of new receptors in response to a certain stimulus.

Although the current technology enables researchers to conduct fascinating experiments related to neurophysiology, adequate interpretations lag behind the technology. It has been extremely difficult to form overarching hypotheses about neurophysiological observations. For example, does more activity in a certain area reflect the brain's enhanced ability to respond to a challenge? Or does it reflect on this particular brain area having to work harder than others (for example, employ more neurons)? An anecdote illustrates this dilemma.

Edward Peck, a neuropsychologist from Richmond, Virginia, tells the story of an experiment conducted by one of his mentors, Cesare Lombroso, a well-known pediatric neurologist at Harvard University. At the beginning of Lombroso's career, he received a grant to study EEGs of people identified as "geniuses." Lombroso had the unique opportunity to examine Albert Einstein, and he had a set of complex math problems prepared for Einstein to solve while he was hooked up to the EEG.

The story goes that Einstein was solving the problems at a rapid pace and was exhibiting a rather relaxed brain wave (alpha) when Lombroso was startled by a sudden shift in the waveform pattern to a more active wave form (beta). Excitedly, Lombroso interrupted Einstein to ask exactly what he was thinking when the shift occurred. Einstein replied, "I think I left the water on at home."

At least in some cases, more accurate thinking requires less brain activation than does uncertainty. A more recent study conducted by a team of researchers at Stanford University confirms that subjects who answered math problems correctly show significantly less brain activation than those who provided inaccurate answers (Menon et al., 2000).

Genetics Perspective

The human genome project has generated the potential for new treatments of all illnesses, even mental illness. We have certainly come a long way since the Austrian monk Gregor Mendel started crossing pea plants with different characteristics in 1860 and noted predictable patterns in the offspring. Although Mendel had no clue how peas acquire traits such as smooth or wrinkled skin, he knew that a pattern exists in the persistence of certain traits depending on the existence of these traits in the parent plants.

We now refer to the physical characteristics described by Mendel as the organism's **phenotype.** We also know that the consistencies in transmission of traits are due to the genes located in the nucleus of each of our cells. Genetic blueprints for the development of us humans are a lot more complicated than those for peas. With the exception of rare disorders such as the neurodegenerative Huntington's disease, probably very few mental illnesses are caused by one single gene. As you will learn as we focus on the description of various mental illnesses, they consist of multiple symptoms most likely caused by multiple genes.

As more is learned about genetic involvement in mental disorders, the way those disorders are viewed may change or even become confused. For example, if 30 genes are identified with schizophrenia and a person has 26 of these genes, how do we categorize this person's mental health? A popular article in *Newsweek* a few years ago suggested that most people are walking around with genes identified as contributing to mental illness. Robert Sapolsky, a neuroscientist at Stanford University, suggests the notion of a "mental health continuum: . . . a middling genetic load [of mental illness genes] gives you a personality disorder, a lighter one gives you a personality quirk and a still lighter one gives you mainstream America" (Begley, 1998, p. 53). Thus, your friend who is a very successful investment banker and spends hours cleaning her apartment each week may have a "lite" version of obsessive compulsive disorder (OCD); your uncle who is the "life of the party" each holiday may be a little manic. According to this article, as the specific genetic elements underlying mental illness are disentangled, and superimposed on a bell curve, it is likely that we will all be considered a bit crazy.

As you will learn in Chapters 7–10, although we are still far from developing cures for mental disorders from genetic information, we have learned a lot about how genes might contribute to a particular disorder. Using identical twins, who are genetic clones, as subjects, **concordance rates** are calculated to determine how likely it is for both individuals to suffer from the same mental illness. Higher concordance rates point to a stronger genetic influence.

As Table 1.4 shows, concordance rates differ for various mental disorders. What has fascinated researchers is the fact that identical twins can have exactly the same genes, yet one may develop schizophrenia

phenotype External expression of certain genetic influences. The phenotype for one genetic assortment may be long fingers; for another the phenotype may be brown hair.

concordance rate Frequency with which two individuals express the same condition. For example, the rate at which identical twins both develop schizophrenia is the concordance rate for schizophrenia.

[Table 1.4]

Concordance Rates for Mental Illness in Twins

Type of illness	Identical twins (%)	Fraternal twins (%)
Autism	60	5
Schizophrenia	40	10
Depression	50	15
Bipolar Disorder	40	10

Adapted from Andreasen (2001), p. 33.

[Figure 1.6]
The protein c-Fos produced by immediate early genes upon the presentation of a predator odor to a rat. The triangular area peppered with immunoreactive c-Fos cells (arrow) represents the paraventricular hypothalamus, an area important for sending messages to prompt the release of stress hormones.

PHOTOMICROGRAPH COURTESY TOM CAMPBELL, RMC BEHAVIORAL LABORATORY

immediate early genes Class of genes that exhibit rapid responses to certain extracellular stimuli by producing proteins that prompt the release of such neurochemicals as corticotropin releasing hormone (CRH) which is involved in the stress response

proteins Complex organic chemicals that are the essential building materials of living cells.

while the other never develops the disease. Such observations have led neuroscientists to consider genetic structure in its environmental context.

We think of our genes as unmodifiable, but neuroscientists now know, for example, that **immediate early genes** (genes that produce proteins enabling the brain to respond quickly to a changing environment) are constantly being turned on and off in our bodies in response to stimuli in the environment. This class of genes stimulates the production of particular **proteins,** the complex organic chemicals that constitute essential building materials of living cells. Using techniques to study the protein c-Fos, for example, enables neuroscientists in effect to look into an animal's brain to see which cells were active in the last hour. As shown in Figure 1.6, immediate early genes have been turned on in an area involved in the stress/fear response after the animal was exposed to predator odors. When the threat subsides, the genes turn off.

Developmental Perspective

Daylight influences the views through the windows of a house. Looking into a room when the morning sun is bright is very different from looking at the room in evening twilight. Viewing the brain and mental functions at different developmental stages of life yields different perspectives as well. For example, the brain's neurons make connections at a surprisingly fast pace from birth to 24 months of age (see Chapter 6). Depriving children of proper stimulation during this time can devastate cognitive and motor development as well as the development of neurobiological responses to stress.

Some children experience tremendous loss of brain tissue yet develop into normal adolescents and adults. In his book *Half a Brain Is Enough* (2000), Antonio Battro, a neuroscientist in Argentina, describes his introduction to 5-year-old Nico, who, because of untreatable epileptic seizures, endured a hemispherectomy (one hemisphere of his brain was surgically removed) when he was 3 years old. Following extensive rehabilitation, including sophisticated computer instruction, Nico recovered amazingly well—he learned to enjoy swimming, tennis, computers, and music and developed excellent language skills. He did not learn to draw well, however.

Extensive research has been conducted on two prominent developmental disorders, attention-deficit/hyperactivity disorder (ADHD) and autism, and brain damage has not been identified as a significant underlying cause of either condition (see Chapter 6). Rather, it is likely that altered neurochemistry affects individuals diagnosed as hyperactive or autistic. The notion that a seemingly intact brain with altered chemical functioning can lead to more severe impairment in some cases than can the removal of half the brain puzzles neuroscientists (Battro, 2000).

Another developmental interest for neuroscientists is the strong predisposition of the human brain for certain functions. For example, humans certainly seem to be "hard-wired" for language, so much so that the inability to speak fails to get in the way of language development. Laura Ann Petito at Dartmouth University has found that deaf children babble just as hearing children do. Hearing children learn to babble by listening to sounds they make, and deaf children who are being taught sign language learn to babble by watching the movements of their hands. Although the brain must relegate different parts of the body to carry out communication in deaf children, the basic language function is not impaired (Restak, 2001).

In virtually every issue central to clinical neuroscience, development is critical to forming an integrated perspective. In the chapter-opening Connections, Jasmine's brother, who experienced brain trauma at a young age, would probably recover considerably more under the supervision of a competent neuropsychologist than would an adolescent or adult with the same injury and treatment. However, the story is not grim for older adults. Research described in Chapter 6 suggests that rat brains continue to sprout new connections in old age. Being in an enriched environment is critical for this burst of neuronal connections in the twilight of life (Black, Greenough, & Anderson, 1987).

Environmental Perspective

In the early 1960s, an interdisciplinary team of researchers published arguably one of the most important papers in the field of behavioral neuroscience and the future field of clinical neuroscience. The beauty of their research is the simplicity of its design—expose rats to an enriched environment for less than 3 months and determine whether this environmental exposure alters the face of the brain in any way.

The research team, Edward Bennett, Marian Diamond, David Krech, and Mark Rosenzweig (1964), housed a group of rats in a large cage with lots of toys and activities (Figure 1.7). At the end of the exposure time, the researchers compared the rats with a control group and found the following:

- Increased levels of an enzyme that breaks down a neurotransmitter essential for learning (acetylcholine)

- Heavier cerebral cortices (a variable thought to be very stable)

simple (specific) phobia
Disorder that involves an intense fear of a particular object (e.g., heights, spiders, germs) that disrupts a person's normal functioning as he or she attempts to avoid the feared stimuli.

proximate causation
Doctrine stating that the most direct cause of an event is the most important factor. In evolutionary theory, proximate questions are most often questions of mechanism and development of certain behaviors.

[Figure 1.7]
Rats placed in an enriched environment—a large cage with other animals and toys—display enhanced brain functioning.

- Larger cell bodies in cortical neurons
- Increased neuronal connections and branching

Does an enriched environment translate to enhanced brain functioning for humans as well? As described in Chapter 6, David Snowden's work with nuns suggests that their physically and cognitively active lifestyle, coupled with low-risk behavior and considerable social support, leads to longer and healthier lives and protection against neurodegenerative diseases such as Alzheimer's (Snowden, 2001).

Experience, however, can be a blunt and indiscriminate instrument, exerting damage as readily as benefits. The brain can be molded by negative as well as positive experiences. Impoverishing experiences can lead to maldeveloped brains. Hubel and Wiesel (1965) have shown that depriving a kitten's eye of light can inhibit the number of neurons responding to visual impulses from that eye. Similarly, some forms of mental illness may be a direct result of a person's environment (social, physical, and so on). As you will read in Chapters 8 and 11, exposure to stress early on may alter the brain's response to stressful stimuli and lead to future problems with depression or anxiety (Heim & Nemeroff, 2001).

If certain environments are related to mental illness, it is only logical to conclude that therapeutic strategies that incorporate environmental variables have potential for successful treatments. One undisputable success in this area is with **simple (specific) phobias.** As you can see in Table 1.5, in some people a specific stimulus provokes extreme fear that disrupts their ability to function day to day without an ever-present anxiety about avoiding the feared stimulus.

Conservative estimates suggest that up to 11% of Americans will experience a simple phobia in their lifetimes, according to the DSM-IV-TR. This statistic may be low because so many people are hesitant to have their phobias diagnosed. Fear is a strong emotion, and phobias have among the highest prevalence rates of all mental disorders.

Think about it: virtually any stimulus may be associated with fear in some specific situation. A child shuts his hand in a car door and experiences severe pain as he watches the neighbor's dog run toward him to investigate. The association among pain and fear and dogs may be permanently etched in his emotional memory and may haunt him for the rest of his life. Most of us are familiar with acrophobia (fear of heights), agoraphobia (fear of leaving the safety of one's home), and claustrophobia (fear of enclosed spaces). The less well-known alektorophobia, a fear of chickens, and arachibutyrophobia, a fear of having peanut butter stuck to the roof of the mouth, are among the 500 phobias listed on the Web site phobialist.com (Kluger, 2001).

As detailed in Chapter 7, environmental therapies focusing on behavioral and cognitive learning approaches to overcoming anxiety have been extremely successful. As indicated by Park, Mataix-Cols, I. M. Marks, Ngamthipwatthana, M. Marks, Araya, and Al-Kubaisy (2001), both solo and clinician-accompanied exposure therapy (a prescribed strategy for systematic exposure to the feared stimulus in the context of a relaxing environment) for 14 weeks resulted in the subjects' relief from anxiety. Even more impressive, the subjects continued to be symptom free 2 years later.

Obvious benefits to such cognitive and behavioral treatments include brevity, low cost, and absence of the side effects typically observed in drug treatment regimes. Another benefit is that a person may not even need a therapist for such a treatment; a well-disciplined patient may be able to construct a self-administered therapy based on reputable literature. The use of virtual reality computer programs to simulate the stressful stimulus exposure is becoming increasingly popular.

[Table 1.5]
DSM-IV-TR Diagnostic Criteria for Specific Phobia

A. Marked and persistent fear that is excessive or unreasonable, cued by the presence or anticipation of a specific object or situation (e.g., flying, heights, animals, receiving an injection, seeing blood).

B. Exposure to the phobic stimulus almost invariably provokes an immediate anxiety response, which may take the form of a situationally bound or situationally predisposed Panic Attack. **Note:** In children, the anxiety may be expressed by crying, tantrums, freezing, or clinging.

C. The person recognizes that the fear is excessive or unreasonable. **Note:** In children, this feature may be absent.

D. The phobic situation(s) is avoided or else is endured with intense anxiety or distress.

E. The avoidance, anxious anticipation, or distress in the feared situation(s) interferes significantly with the person's normal routine, occupational (or academic) functioning, or social activities or relationships, or there is marked distress about having the phobia.

F. In individuals under age 18 years, the duration is at least 6 months.

G. The anxiety, Panic Attacks, or phobic avoidance associated with the specific object or situation are not better accounted for by another mental disorder, such as Obsessive-Compulsive Disorder (e.g., fear of dirt in someone with an obsession about contamination), Posttraumatic Stress Disorder (e.g., avoidance of stimuli associated with a severe stressor), Separation Anxiety Disorder (e.g., avoidance of school), Social Phobia (e.g., avoidance of social situations because of fear of embarrassment), Panic Disorder with Agoraphobia, or Agoraphobia Without History of Panic Disorder.

Specify type:

Animal Type

Natural Environmental Type (e.g., heights, storms, water)

Blood-Injection-Injury Type

Situational Type (e.g, airplanes, elevators, enclosed places)

Other Type (e.g., fear of choking, vomiting, or contracting an illness; in children, fear of loud sounds or costumed characters)

APA (2001), p. 450.

Evolutionary Perspective

Windows may offer the viewer a direct, realistic view. But a lens allows a more distant perspective. Grounded in the history of the human species, the evolutionary perspective is as much a lens as it is a window on mental health. Here principles of natural selection formulated by Charles Darwin and associates and followers are applied to issues such as **proximate causation,** or direct causes of behavior; **ultimate causation,** or

ultimate causation Doctrine stating that the more long-term causes of a behavior are important for a thorough understanding of the behavior. In evolutionary theory, ultimate causation questions are questions related to how and why certain behaviors evolve.

sexual selection Choosing a mate or competing for a mate.

long-term evolutionary causes of behavior; **sexual selection** (the choosing of a mate); trait variation; and environment (McGuire & Troisi, 1998).

In their book *Why We Get Sick*, Randolph Neese and George Williams (1994), discuss mental illness seen through an evolutionary lens. Neese and Williams suggest that mental illness may be an adaptation to the environment rather than a disease, a view that is very different from the traditional medical model; just as we get a fever when our immune system is working effectively to fight off infection, we may suffer from anxiety because our emotions are reacting as they should to threatening stimuli or circumstances, that is, to stress. Few of us welcome feelings of anxiety, but it may be an important emotion for evolutionary fitness.

One study categorized guppies into timid (high anxiety), normal, and bold temperament types and then placed them in a tank with a predator bass—an obvious threat to their genetic fitness (the ability to pass genes on to offspring). After 60 hours, 40% of the timid guppies remained, whereas only 15% of the "normal" guppies and 0% of the bold guppies survived (Neese and Williams, 1994). It is easy to see how an absence of anxiety may prevent us from hastily escaping from a wild animal—resulting in injury or death and decreased genetic fitness. The presence of anxiety may also keep a man from impulsively having an affair and leaving his wife and young children (possibly resulting in decreased genetic fitness because he can no longer provide for his children) or from engaging in risky behavior that may lead to death or injury.

Just as it is important to identify the source of a persistent fever, Neese and Williams argue that it is important to identify the source of persistent anxiety. If some forms of anxiety are adaptive for our species, then as more and more people attempt to reduce their anxiety with antidepressants and other antianxiety medications, we may be conducting an interesting experiment on ourselves.

Thus, aside from offering a long-term perspective about why certain "mental illnesses" persist in the human population, the evolutionary perspective explores the adaptive nature of mental phenotypes that seem far from being adaptive for our species today. The evolutionary researcher seeks to explain how the genes that contribute to a condition like schizophrenia—where multiple genes are activated by certain environmental experiences—might, in another combination of genes and experience, lead to some survival advantage.

Andreasen (2001) suggests that the genes that contribute to schizophrenia may also enable a person to see the world in unusual ways—ways not unrelated to creativity and genius. Albert Einstein was a genius, but his son suffered from schizophrenia. Isaac Newton, who first described the physical laws Einstein studied, reportedly lived an eccentric and solitary life and experienced at least one psychotic episode. Einstein and

Newton appear to have possessed or passed on some combination of genes that contribute to schizophrenialike symptoms. Could some combination of the key genes in schizophrenia be related to cognitive genius? Kay Redfield Jamison, whose book *Touched with Fire* (1993) describes large proportions of creative geniuses who suffered from bipolar episodes of mania and depression (William Blake, John Keats, Vincent van Gogh, to name a few), further corroborates this evolutionary view.

It is important to remember, however, that an adequate understanding of the adaptive benefits of our emotions requires a thorough understanding of their normal functioning, just as an understanding of internal medicine requires a fundamental knowledge of human physiology. Psychiatric training programs, however, do not systematically offer courses on topics such as evolutionary psychology or the psychology of emotions (Neese & Williams, 1994).

Window Provided by Culture

A recent *New York Times Magazine* article (Osborne, 2001) addressed the influence of culture in the etiology of mental illness. The highlight of this article is the story of a 59-year-old woman named Dibuk ak Suut who lives in the Malaysian jungle. When her husband claps his hands unexpectedly, Dibuk jumps to her feet, appears to enter a glassy-eyed trance, and starts shouting, "Grasshopper! Grasshopper!" When her husband begins a comical dance, Dibuk does the same, as if she is suddenly her husband's puppet. In the midst of her trance, she sweats and laughs excessively. Dibuk's husband breaks the trance by tapping her firmly on the shoulder. After a few moments, a cat jumps in at the window and the trance begins again.

[Figure 1.8]
Dibuk ak Suut undergoing a trancelike *latah* in her home in Malaysia. In the United States her condition is referred to as hyperstartle syndrome.
MARGARET SALMON AND DEAN WIAND.

Even with our ubiquitous media coverage in the United States of virtually every conceivable mental disorder, you probably are not familiar with Dibuk's symptoms. In Malaysia, Dibuk is thought to be *latah;* in the West, her condition is known as hyperstartle syndrome (Figure 1.8). Why is latah much more common in Malaysia than hyperstartle syndrome is in the United States? Researchers chalk it up to cultural differences.

The list of cultural influences is long. Ever wonder why anorexia is far more prevalent in the United States than in

Box [1.2]

The Investigators

Oliver Sacks

Oliver Sacks was born in London and enjoyed a childhood rich in scientific and intellectual stimulation. Both his parents were trained as neurologists but decided that more traditional medicine offered more exciting interactions with patients. Consequently, his house was full of medical stories—preparing Sacks to engage in clinical storytelling from a very young age.

At the beginning of World War II, Sacks was one of around 3 million English children sent away from the cities to families or boarding schools in the countryside for safety. The extended separation from his parents was difficult for him. As a child, Sacks endured migraines that he was assured were simply a benign dysfunction of the brain. He was fascinated, though, by the visual patterns and configurations that accompanied these headaches. His early passion was for chemistry; he did not fall in love with medicine until the advanced age of 32 years, when he obtained his medical degree at Oxford.

Sacks then moved to the United States and in 1966 he began practicing at Beth Abraham Hospital in New York, where he encountered a group of patients that would forever change his life. These patients suffered from a form of encephalitis that left them frozen like statues for decades. Sacks became obsessed with these patients and moved into an apartment close to the hospital so he could observe them up to 15 hours per day.

After learning about a new pharmacological treatment for Parkinson's disease, Sacks began to wonder if his patients' malady could be viewed as an extreme case of Parkinson's disease and that therefore they might benefit from a new drug known as L-dopa. He acquired the necessary license and arranged double-blind trials with the drug and a placebo. Sacks will never forget the excitement that permeated the summer of 1969 as he watched the encephalitis patients respond to the L-dopa. As depicted in the movie *Awakenings* (based on his book), the patients experienced a wonderful awakening from decades of being frozen. Sacks kept meticulous notes and photographs of his patients. But, devastatingly, the miracle shut down as the patients started to develop a sensitivity to the L-dopa. In most cases, the pharmacological window started to close when the patients experienced uncontrollable movements in response to the drug.

Although the world knows Sacks as a prolific and celebrated writer, he encountered rejection by the scientific community when he attempted to publish his observations of the effects of L-dopa on his encephalitis patients. At a time when there was much hope for L-dopa in reducing the symptoms of Parkinson's disease, the last news anyone wanted to hear was that it might be a false hope. This negative experience with traditional scientific writing reinforced Sacks's love for clinical storytelling. Following the path of the prominent Russian psychologist Dr. Aleksandr R. Luria [who wrote *The Mind of a Mnemonist* (1968) and *The Man with a Shattered World* (1972)], whom he admired greatly, Sacks decided that the best way to convey information about his patients was to do so by telling clinical stories, or neurographies, about his fascinating patients.

The seeds for this "romantic science" had been planted in Sacks's childhood as he listened to his parents' medical tales. Sacks observed every detail of his patients' lives in order to re-create the context of their existence. After eight books, it is an established fact that Sacks has chosen an appropriate venue to tell his stories and has consequently become the world's best-known neurologist.

Although they contain neurographies of many of his patients, Sacks's books also provide a sort of neurography of his own mental experiences. His early fascination with his migraines prompted him to write

Migraine (1999); his transformation after observing the encephalitis patients served as the impetus for *Awakenings;* his encounter with a bull and the subsequent accident that caused severe damage to his leg brought forth *A Leg to Stand On* (1984); and his early childhood fascination with chemistry served as the basis for his most recent book, *Uncle Tungsten: Memories of a Chemical Boyhood* (2001). Most prominent is his continued fascination with the resourcefulness with which his patients respond to their neurological challenges—inspiring the writing of *The Man Who Mistook His Wife for a Hat* (1985), *Seeing Voices* (1990), *The Island of the Colorblind* (1997), and *An Anthropologist on Mars* (1995).

More recently, Sacks's thoughts have been directed toward Tourette's syndrome, which he finds "endlessly fascinating." Although he is painfully aware of the challenges Tourette's patients encounter every day, he suggests that "a little holiday from our frontal lobes" may be a nice experience from time to time (personal communication, 2001).

He also muses about consciousness and the mind's refusal to present any sign of disconnection. His fascination with vision and photography prompts a visual example, that of the blind spot, to support this claim. We all have an area on the retina that, because of the exit point of our optic nerves, does not have the appropriate sensory receptors to receive light. But no one actually sees a black hole in the visual field: the mind seems to fill it in. Similarly, our memories are so intertwined with our identities that they are resistant to disruptions: young children, when asked about events that occurred when they were too young to have formed memories—or the language to describe them—typically construct elaborate stories to convey their past.

Sacks is an astute observer of both the mental and behavioral functions of his patients. His elegant accounts of how his neurologically impaired patients learn to exist in their surroundings reinforces the value of one's environment in mental health. In fact, Sacks prefers to observe his patients in their own homes to get an accurate sense of their functioning capacity.

Oliver Sacks
COURTESY OF DR. OLIVER SACKS,
PHOTO © NANCY CRAMPTON.

Sacks's writings have made the general public aware of the consequences of brain disorders and how, with compassionate respect, we can learn enough from patients with brain disorders to develop treatments or to enable the patients to live optimally with their alternative style of mental functioning. Why does Sacks write for such a broad audience? He believes that without a public awareness of the critical role of the brain in our mental functions and a general interest in trying to learn more about the brain, federal funds and public policies supporting the continuation of neuroscience research would dwindle away.

When asked about being interviewed for this book, Sacks replied that he wasn't sure whether his "idiosyncratic approach would be appropriate in a sober textbook on Clinical Neuroscience" (personal communication, December 2000). On the contrary, his approach, equally emphasizing the brain, environment, and mental functioning, could be viewed as a basis for the emerging field of clinical neuroscience. Along with other respected and accomplished investigators profiled in this book, Oliver Sacks is a true pioneer in this field, turning the general public away from an obsession with the unconscious toward an appreciation of the complexity as well as the vulnerability of our brains.

culture-bound syndrome
Condition that appears to be culture specific, for example, anorexia (United States), latah (Malaysia), koro (Malaysia), and brain fag (Nigeria). The DSM categorizes these disorders in this broad classification.

homeostasis Internal balance and regulation of physiological systems in an organism.

other industrialized countries? Or why women are more likely to suffer from anorexia than men? In Nigeria, students who are overwhelmed by fatigue are known to suffer from "brain fag," and back in Malaysia, some people suffer from "koro," a sudden fear of the genitalia receding into the body and causing death. If your own perspective prompts you to regard such conditions more as fiction than reality, you'll be surprised to learn that, since 1994, the American Psychiatric Association has included 25 such intriguing disorders in an appendix to the DSM dedicated to **culture-bound syndromes.**

The fact that the prevalence of some disorders differs among various cultures gives even more weight to the role of the environment and culture in the etiology of mental illnesses. Lynn Payer (1996) suggests that cultural norms affect how medical practitioners tend to diagnose disorders. For example, in Germany, mental illness is considered incurable. American practitioners, by contrast, emphasize treatment and prevention of mental illness.

WHAT LIES AHEAD

Understanding the neurobiological foundations of mental health provides students like you, who are interested in the interactions among mental health, the brain, and the environment, with powerful tools to investigate critical mental health issues. The empirical, multifaceted approach emphasized in this text offers hope for the emergence of promising therapies for society's mental maladies.

Multiple Perspectives

This chapter and the next lay a foundation for studying clinical neuroscience. In this chapter we've introduced the many perspectives and methods of neuroscience, and in Chapter 2 we explore how these perspectives developed and how the base of empirical evidence continues to grow and evolve. The remaining chapters approach neurobiology and clinical disorders as aspects of **homeostasis,** the internal balance and regulation of physiological systems in an organism. This approach allows a serious examination of the brain–body relationship in the quest for mental health. Although an emphasis is placed on the integration of the mind, brain, and body in upcoming chapters, we continue to use established terminology such as *psychological factors* and *physiological factors* for clarity, although in the not-so-distant-future such dichotomous terms may no longer be appropriate. The Epilogue addresses the future of clinical neuroscience, including ethical debates about the influence of brain trauma on asocial or criminal behavior, the harvesting of embryonic stem cells to treat disorders such as Parkinson's disease, and the potential effectiveness of self-directed neuroplasticity in maintaining mental health.

To bridge the gaps between common beliefs and actual research and between clinical practice and more traditional neuroscience perspectives, each chapter begins with Connections, a feature that connects two or more observations on the chapter topic. These research reviews often showcase the impressive accomplishments of undergraduate and graduate students in clinical neuroscience.

Within each chapter, *A Case in Point* boxes put a human face on research related to a special topic by describing the real-life experiences of individuals suffering from various disruptions of mental homeostasis. Brain Matters boxes provide an occasional opportunity to delve deeper into selected topics.

The Investigators boxes profile prominent researchers, recounting aspects of their academic and research journeys in clinical neuroscience. If you are currently planning your own academic and career journey, these profiles will broaden your perspective.

To assist your study, throughout each chapter, bold key terms are defined in the margins; they are also compiled in a Glossary at the end of the book. A chapter summary is presented at the end of each chapter, followed by a list of selected readings called *For Further Consideration*.

A Brain–Body Balance

More than ever before, research is revealing a seamless interaction between the nervous system and the rest of the body. For example, the biological mechanisms underlying the stress response represent extensive cross talk between body and brain. Overwhelming evidence points directly to chronic stress as a contributing factor in many mental and physical disorders. The individual's reaction to stress plays an essential role in maintaining neurobiological homeostasis and avoiding allostatic load (a new concept you will become familiar with in Chapter 11). Similarly, research on how the nervous system interacts with and is intimately related to the immune system provides compelling evidence that a healthy immune system is as critical to mental health as it is to physical health.

In the chapters at the heart of this book, we view mental functioning as it affects homeostasis in three important ways:

- *Establishing homeostasis* Chapters 3–6 link basic neural mechanisms at the anatomical, neurochemical, and developmental levels to overt conditions. For example, neurodegenerative and cognitive processing disorders such as Alzheimer's disease and attention deficit hyperactivity disorder are included in Chapter 6 on neurodevelopment. These chapters also address the role of neurobiological homeostasis in mental health, review how body and brain respond to stress, and introduce the intimate connections between the nervous and immune systems and physical and mental health.

- *Disruptions of homeostasis* As the internal milieu is disrupted by stress or illness, the nervous system attempts to compensate. These attempts sometimes lead to extreme conditions that we classify as mental disorders. Among the representative clinical disorders addressed in Chapters 7–10 are the latest findings related to anxiety disorders (specifically, obsessive compulsive disorder and Tourette's syndrome), mood disorders (major depression, bipolar disorder), schizophrenia, and addiction.

- *Maintaining homeostasis* In Chapters 11–13 we address the relationship among psychological processes, neurobiology, and immunology in maintaining mental health. For example, disruptions in communication between the nervous and immune systems may lead to a host of illnesses ranging from the flu to depression. Our patterns of eating also influence broad aspects of mental and emotional well-being. Developing an ability to cope with stress—to moderate the stress response and maintain mental and physical homeostasis—is proving vital to well-being.

Summary

Status Reports on Clinical Practitioners and Mental Illness

Although the fields of psychiatry and psychology share the common goal of treating mental illness, both face challenges to offering the most effective therapies in the most informed ways. These challenges derive in part from the diverse array of clinical practitioners (psychiatrists, psychologists, neurologists, clinical social workers), a diverse array of therapeutic perspectives, and changing insurance coverage and prescription privileges.

By focusing on the brain, empirical evidence can help to discern causal factors and effective treatment approaches for mental illness. The case of Nadean Cool, a patient diagnosed with Dissociative Identity Disorder, reveals how ineffective, and sometimes harmful, diagnoses and treatments can be when practitioners fail to rely on empirical evidence.

Opening the Windows on Mental Health

Valuable information about mental illness and mental health can be acquired using a range of approaches,

including the neurobiological (encompassing neuroanatomy, neurochemistry, and neurophysiology), genetic, evolutionary, environmental, developmental, and cultural perspectives. Focusing on only one approach harshly limits information about the mental condition.

Evolutionary and cultural perspectives are frequently left out of the causal model for mental disorders. As described throughout this text, both these approaches offer insights into the origins of mental illness.

What Lies Ahead

Understanding the neurobiological foundations of mental health yields insights about how the brain and body interact. After describing the mechanisms that establish neurobiological homeostasis in Chapters 3–6, we consider how disruptions of homeostasis lead to various mental disorders in Chapters 7–10. Ultimately, a goal of mental health is to prevent such disruptions from occurring, and maintaining homeostasis is the emphasis in Chapters 11–13.

Key Terms

empirical evidence (p. 4)

psychotropic (psychoactive) drug (p. 4)

biomedical model (p. 5)

psychosocial model (p. 5)

psychometric test (p. 8)

traumatic brain injury (TBI) (p. 17)

neurogenesis (p. 17)

neurotrophic factors (p. 18)

computerized tomography (CT) (p. 18)

magnetic resonance imaging (MRI) (p. 19)

electroencephalography (EEG) (p. 20)

positron emission tomograph (PET) (p. 20)

functional magnetic resonance imaging (fMRI) (p. 20)

phenotype (p. 21)

concordance rate (p. 21)

immediate early genes (p. 22)

proteins (p. 22)

simple (specific) phobia (p.24)

proximate causation (p. 25)

ultimate causation (p. 25)

sexual selection (p. 26)

culture-bound syndrome (p. 30)

homeostasis (p. 30)

For Further Consideration

Andreasen, A. (2001). *Brave new brain.* New York: Oxford University Press. Andreasen noted the trend of clinical practice merging with the field of neuroscience when she published *The Broken Brain* in 1988. She continues to advocate the incorporation of behavioral and neuroscientific knowledge into the fields of psychiatry and clinical psychology. Especially emphasized in this book are the burgeoning areas of neuroimaging and genetic research; she feels that these areas will soon change both our understanding of and treatment approaches for many disorders. Andreasen is able to present the need for this modified version of psychiatry so effectively that the reader is left with little doubt that a more neuroscientific version of psychiatry is going to be the only psychiatry of the future.

Dawes, R. (1994). *House of cards: Psychology and psychotherapy built on myth.* New York: Free Press. Robyn Dawes, once a practicing clinical psychologist, presents a surprising account of how far clinical psychology has wandered from its grounding in empirical evidence. He is troubled by the field's journey from objective observations to clinical observations and fears that the consequences can be devastating for clients. Dawes does a wonderful job of illustrating the importance of appropriate research methodology in clinical practice.

Hobson, J. A., & Leonard, J. A. (2001) *Out of its mind: Psychiatry in crisis.* Cambridge, MA: Perseus Publishing. In this book Hobson, a psychiatrist who has conducted a great deal of research on sleeping and dreaming, reports on the current state of psychiatry. Torn between practitioners who treat patients solely by pharmacological means and a dwindling few still endorsing psychoanalysis, the authors call for a restructuring of the field. They present the term *neurodynamic* to refer to the exciting field of brain science and the many possibilities of this new area of research to clinical practice in the field of mental health.

McGuire, M., & Troisi, A. (1998). *Darwinian psychiatry.* New York: Oxford University Press. When considering the causes of mental illness, few practitioners discuss the evolutionary relevance of a client's response profile. In this book, McGuire and Troisi make the case for the evolutionary significance of certain responses when determining both the cause and the treatment strategy for patients. As described in this book, many disorders revolve around events that have great adaptive significance (for example, romantic relationships, having children, social acceptance). This approach enables patients to understand why they are experiencing certain symptoms and offers an opportunity to address the heart of the problem in many cases. This book is highly recommended for students searching for a fresh perspective in their approach to mental illness.

Sacks, O. W. (1999). *Awakenings.* New York: Vintage Books. (Original work published 1973.) This book conveys the value of sustained, systematic observation. Sacks describes his experience working with encephalitis patients who had become frozen in time. They showed little response to their worlds, but Sacks's curiosity enabled him to unlock their neurological prison doors, if only for a brief time. His work, which later became the subject of the popular movie *Awakenings,* in which Robin Williams played Sacks, made the public painfully aware both of the vulnerability of our brains and of their key role in our conscious, awake, moments. Sacks reinforces the notion that behavioral responses in specific environmental situations should play a key role in a practitioner's assessment of a patient's functioning capacity.

Valenstein, E. S. (2000). *Blaming the brain: The truth about drugs and mental health.* New York: Free Press. Pharmacological treatments are standard fare in psychiatric treatment, yet there is no clear evidence that people suffering from disorders such as depression actually have a chemical imbalance that can be corrected with drugs. This observation reinforces the idea that factors other than neurotransmitters are involved in the expression of mental illness. Valenstein reminds us that a brain, as complex and wonderful as it is, does not exist without an environment that provides nourishment and stimulation.

Chapter Two

Research, Treatment, and Points of View: Historical Perspectives

Connections

Barbers and Neurosurgeons

The sixteenth-century physician Ambroise Paré began his career as a barber-surgeon. He didn't let the lack of a university degree or knowledge of Latin or the dictates of the Church keep him from conducting brain surgery. Without formal training, Paré nonetheless contributed valuable knowledge related to the removal of bone fragments from the brain and used elaborate drilling instruments to open the skull. In 1564, Paré was approached by a man who thought his brain was rotten. This man asked Paré to open his skull, remove his rotting brain, and replace it with another one. There is no evidence that Paré actually attempted this brain transplant, although he did write that he attempted to restore the man's brain.

Ironically, an etching of Paré portrays him standing next to a jar with a fetus in it (Finger, 1994). The irony lies in the fact that over 400 years later successful brain tissue transplants would occur with the use of fetal brain tissue. Is there a connection between Paré's thoughts about giving his patient a brain transplant and the fetus located next to him in the etching? Regardless of what Paré was thinking in the sixteenth century, the current pioneers of clinical neuroscience are conducting exciting research that has considerable therapeutic value for patients suffering from neurodegenerative disorders such as Parkinson's disease.

You may be thinking that the idea of transplanting even a small portion of the brain is the stuff of science fiction novels, not textbooks. The contemporary story of brain transplants, however, is far from fiction for Dr. Patrik Brundin, who currently directs the neuronal survival group at Lund University in Sweden. When he was just 17 years old, Brundin began doing research with experimental models of Parkinson's disease. He was passionate about learning more about Parkinson's because his father had been diagnosed with this debilitating condition.

After conducting his initial research project, Brundin started medical school at Lund. During his days as a medical student, he continued to monitor current literature on Parkinson's disease. Then one day while riding in an elevator, Brundin had a chance meeting with some special rats that had surgical clips on their heads. When he asked the technician about the clips he was told that the rats had an experimental form of Parkinson's disease and had received brain tissue transplants in an attempt to improve their condition. Brundin had to know more about this exciting research, and his questions led him to the scientist conducting the research, Dr. Anders Björklund, a leading authority in the field of brain tissue grafting.

Within a few months, Brundin was working as a junior science student in Björklund's laboratory. For the next several years, Brundin juggled his research and medical school careers so that he could get closer to his dream—replacing dead nerve cells, creating new brain circuitry, and restoring lost motor functions in human Parkinson's patients. In 1988, about the time he was finishing his doctoral thesis, he participated in the first human clinical trials in which Parkinson's patients received fetal brain tissue transplants. The results of the initial trials were disappointing, but the team persevered. In 1990, their first report documenting clear beneficial effects of nerve cell transplants in human Parkinson's patients was published in the prestigious journal *Science*. In fact, more than a decade after his surgery, one patient was doing remarkably well at 72 years of age—showing far fewer signs of the disease than would be expected without neurotransplantation. Since those early days, the team at Lund University has performed neural cell transplants on 18 patients, and about 350 transplant surgeries have been done worldwide.

The neural transplant research has successfully restored motor functions to many Parkinson's patients, but more research is needed to increase the actual number of transplanted cells that survive and grow in the host's brain. In addition to trying to increase the graft survival rate, transplant laboratories are also working to find ways to enable neural tissue from other species (like pigs) to successfully live in the human brain. They are also trying to understand more about how the patient's own stem cells taken from other parts of the body may be prompted to develop into neurons when injected into the brain.

And what about Brundin's research today? Unfortunately, his father passed away before benefiting from his work, but Brundin continues to try to improve the survival rate of transplanted tissue in Parkinson's patients and, more currently, in patients suffering from Huntington's chorea, another disabling movement disorder. He has not forgotten the professors who gave him a once-in-a-lifetime opportunity to participate in research when he was a young student. Continuing their practice, Brundin is assisted today by five graduate students—Mia Emgård, Oskar Hansson, Jenny Karlsson, Lena Larsson, and Åsa Petersén. The team's goal is to maximize the survival rate of transplanted nerve cells by identifying the perfect nurturing neurochemical environment. As graduate students, like their mentor before them, they are also participating in history-making human clinical transplant trials. You can read more on the neural tissue transplant story in the Epilogue.

Clinical neuroscience is an old idea but a young research discipline. It's impossible to know when the first human speculated on why people behave the way they do. People probably wondered about the brain's influence on our behavior, emotions, and thinking well before the advent of civilizations and written records; we take up the story with early

Greek history and end our journey in the present (see the time line depicted in Figure 2.1, pages 38–39). Because of the fast pace of events and discoveries in the last two centuries, most of the neuroscience pioneers presented in this chapter come from this period. The chapter is not exhaustive: every significant individual or event in the history of such a broad field cannot be covered here. Perhaps the most exciting aspect of clinical neuroscience is the fact that the story is not yet complete.

EMERGENCE OF THE BRAIN AS THE CONTROLLING CENTER OF BEHAVIOR, EMOTIONS, AND THOUGHT

For thousands of years of recorded human history, producing convincing theories and supporting evidence for claims about the functions of the brain proved a monumental challenge for researchers. Eventually, progress was made toward this goal and scientists began to understand the true impact of this 3-pound (1400 grams) gel-like organ on human thought and behavior. Equally fascinating as those first glimmerings of the workings of the brain are the impressive stories of how talented researchers unraveled the secrets of the once mysterious nervous system and its connections to the brain and body.

Head, Heart, and Mind–Body Problem

It's difficult to imagine a time when the brain was thought to be of no more importance than any other organ in the body. As the pioneers in this section were entering the scene, the concept that the brain plays a critical role in controlling behavior challenged the wisdom of the times.

Hippocrates: Heart of mental functions. Hippocrates (c. 460–370 B.C.) is known as the father of medicine, but he also contributed to the field of neuroscience. Most of Hippocrates' contemporaries believed that the heart controls the body's functions. Hippocrates, on the contrary, felt that the brain was the controlling center. He was not sure how the brain influenced behavior, but he was convinced that it was important:

> Men ought to know that from nothing else but the brain come joys, delights, laughter and sports, and sorrows, griefs, despondency, and lamentations. And by this, in an especial manner, we acquire wisdom and knowledge, and see and hear and know what are foul and what are fair, what are bad and what are good, mad and delirious, and fears and terrors assail us. . . . All these things we endure from the brain. . . . In these ways I am of the opinion that the brain exercises the greatest power in the man. (quoted in Finger, 2000, p. 69)

[Figure 2.1]
Pioneers and major research approaches in the evolution of clinical neuroscience. This timeline anchors the topics of the chapter's main sections at the point each of these ongoing approaches gained prominence. Selected historical events and scientific breakthroughs listed below the timeline serve as reference points. Individual research pioneers are listed at the point of their major contributions to forming and defining clinical neuroscience.

At the time, most mental illness was explained as demonic possession or a falling out of favor with the gods, but Hippocrates viewed conditions such as epilepsy to be a natural brain disease. Most of Hippocrates' treatments of the damaged or diseased brain attempted to restore order in this essential organ. In perhaps the earliest advocacy of a homeostatic theory of mental health, Hippocratic physicians promoted a **humoral theory** as an explanation of the body's functions. It was thought that four humors, or body fluids (yellow bile, black bile, phlegm, and blood), needed to be balanced for a person to be healthy.

According to the humoral theory, many illnesses could be treated simply by restoring the balance of the humors. Excessive flushing (being red in the face), for example, was a symptom of having too much blood and was treated by bloodletting (a method of draining blood from the body). The humoral theory spilled over to thoughts about the brain. A closed-head injury may have disrupted the balance of the humors as well; these injuries were often treated by performing a **craniotomy;** that is, removal of a section of the skull, exposing the brain so that excessive levels of a

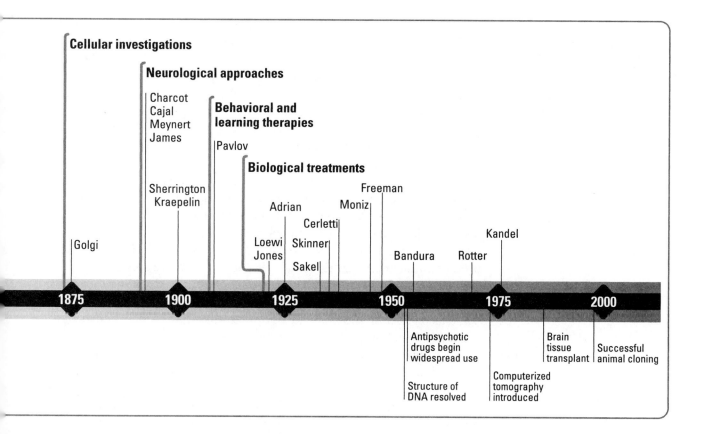

particular humor (blood, for example,) could be drained to restore the balance of humors. Obviously, the meaning of the term *brain drain* today is quite different from the one the Hippocratic physicians had in mind!

Hippocrates' accomplishments are even more impressive considering that he never performed dissections on human brains. At that time, it was thought that the human soul would be harmed if the body were manipulated before being put to rest. Additionally, there's no evidence that Hippocrates even dissected animal brains. It seems that his observations of the brain were limited to seeing patients who had brain disease or injuries—anyone whose injuries resulted in exposed brain tissue.

Galen: Spirit of mental functions. Galen (c. 129–200 A.D.) was born in Pergamon, a Roman territory. Galen's father felt that the medical god intended his son to be a physician, and he did everything possible to make sure Galen had the best possible medical training. During his training, Galen was attracted to the notion of medicine based on anatomy and physiology.

humoral theory Early physical theory of mental illness proposed by Hippocrates. Four humors, or liquids, were thought to contribute to mental illness when they became unbalanced.

craniotomy Early physical therapy in which a section of a patient's skull was removed in an attempt to restore balance to the four humors, leading to recovery from mental illness.

experiment Research technique in which variables are purposively manipulated in a systematic way to test or establish a hypothesis.

ventricles Internal capsules in the medial part of the brain that contain cerebrospinal fluid.

Unfortunately for Galen, as in Hippocrates' time, the Roman Empire did not allow human autopsies. He had an occasional encounter with a wounded gladiator, but these encounters did not satisfy Galen's desire for firsthand observations of the brain. At this point, he turned to the next best thing—animals. He did not know about the existence of the great apes of Africa, but he did focus on the Barbary ape because of its "human" qualities. Galen's curiosity did not end with these primates. He went on to conduct many dissections of a diverse array of species, including pigs, oxen, and dogs.

Galen was an advocate of Aristotle's notions of empirical observation, and in trying to understand the connections and functions of various cranial and spinal nerves, he conducted actual **experiments** on the brain to test his ideas. Galen's work extended beyond identifying the functions of nerves. He presented one of the earliest theories of brain function. Galen proposed that animal spirits inhabited the mind. These spirits were transformed from the heart's vital spirits in the brain's *rete mirabile* (miraculous net), a network of arteries surrounding the pituitary gland. The brain could also generate these animal spirits itself in the vascular linings of the **ventricles,** the fluid-filled cavities, of the brain.

Regardless of their origin, Galen theorized that these animal spirits were stored in the brain's ventricles and, when needed, could perform amazing feats, such as moving muscles or transmitting sensory information from the body to the brain. Galen also appreciated the importance of the brain tissue surrounding the ventricles: he believed that brain tissue is involved in our highest mental functions.

Galen was both a medical practitioner and a brain researcher. This may qualify him as the first clinical neuroscientist. The field, however, was off to a slow start: productive research related to the brain would not be conducted for more than a millenium. In fact, it wasn't until the European Renaissance that scientists resumed Galen's practice of dissecting and experimenting with brain tissue.

René Descartes: Body meets mind. René Descartes (1596–1650) lived in France during the post-Renaissance period. The mystique surrounding the brain at that time centered on function rather than structure. Descartes was a philosopher and did not look solely to brain dissections to understand the brain. Instead, he chose logic as the primary means to understand how the brain actually triggers behavior.

Descartes is not remembered for his neuroanatomical dissections, but he did conduct dissections as he developed his theories about brain function. Descartes, like Galen, believed that animal spirits were manufactured in the brain, and that these spirits were formed in the pineal gland instead of the *rete mirabile.* The pineal gland was thought to release animal spirits into small valves in the ventricles where they would travel through the nerves to the muscles. In fact, according to Descartes, the pineal gland gently tilted toward the directional flow of the animal spirits. This tilting increased the pressure with which the spirits traveled through the ventricles and nerves. On stimulation of these nerves, delicate filaments that attach to the valves of the ventricles were pulled open so that the animal spirits could travel to the muscle. During sleep, the tension of the nerve fibers relaxed, minimizing the likelihood of responding to external stimuli such as noise.

Descartes postulated this theory to explain basic automatic behaviors, such as **reflexes,** observed in both humans and animals. However, he felt that more advanced reasoning ability was unique to humans and required a more complex explanation. Descartes proposed that thinking is driven by a rational soul that is not necessarily restricted to the confines of flesh and blood. Descartes was faced with the delicate issue of explaining how the immaterial mind could interact with the material substance of the body or brain. This philosophical question is known as the **mind-body problem.** Descartes proposed that the immaterial soul resides in the pineal gland, where it monitors the actions of the animal spirits and consequently influences the machinery of the body.

It may seem a bit odd that, in spite of a 3-pound brain, Descartes centered his theories of both involuntary movement and reasoning ability on just one small structure—the pineal gland. Why was his focus so narrow? He wrote that the pineal gland (which is now known to be involved with physiological rhythms or biological timekeeping) is one of the few singular structures in the brain, a characteristic necessary to integrate information from the sets of sensory organs (two eyes, two ears, and so on). Also, after proposing his theory of movement, the pineal gland was familiar territory for Descartes.

You may wonder why Descartes did not choose another obvious singular structure in the brain, namely, the pituitary gland, which dangles off the base of the brain. As it happens, the pituitary gland had a bad reputation at this time. We now refer to the pituitary as the master endocrine (or hormonal) gland, but it was then thought to be the gland that drained the brain's waste (or phlegm). In fact, the well-known neuroanatomist Thomas Willis (introduced on page 42) would later refer to it as the brain's sink. Descartes probably did not want to compromise his flashy new theory with a brain structure that held such negative connotations. Because the function of the pineal gland was unknown, however, the gland was fertile ground for fresh new ideas.

reflex Most basic form of behavior that involves an automatic response to an environmental event or stimulus, for example, sucking or blinking.

mind–body problem Philosophical question posed to determine the nature, either mental or physical, of the mind.

dualism Philosophical position taken on the mind–body problem suggesting that the mind and body/brain are separate entities; Descartes proposed interactionism in which the two entities interacted in the physical brain, specifically in the pineal gland.

localization of function Notion that specific functions are localized in specific brain areas as suggested by the eighteenth-century theory of phrenology.

Descartes' theory that the mind and the brain interacted in the pineal gland became known as *interactionism* or Cartesian **dualism.** This theory, however, was not warmly welcomed by the more astute scientists and physicians of the time. Evidence of humans who seemed to have perfectly fine minds but had damaged pineal glands cast great doubt on the validity of Descartes's theory. Also, his ideas about animal spirits were hardly new and innovative. Perhaps the most valuable result of his theory were the thoughts it generated in other scientists and physicians. In addition to being skeptical about the role of the pineal gland and animal spirits, many people doubted Descartes's clear distinctions between humans and animals (or brutes, as he called them). Obviously, Descartes did not have the benefit of the writings of Charles Darwin concerning evolution and a continuum between humans and other animals.

Descartes's fascination with the separation of the mind and body was reflected even in his death. He accepted an offer from Queen Christina of Sweden to tutor her in philosophy, but his frail body was no match for the cold, drafty conditions of the queen's house. He quickly contracted pneumonia and died a few months later. Because he was too tall for his casket, his head was detached from his body so that he could be buried.

Localizing Functions in the Brain

By the seventeenth century, it was becoming well established that the brain controls the body's functions, but a compelling question remained. Does the brain work as a totality, or do certain structures within the brain have specific functions? This idea of relating structure to function in the brain is known as **localization of function.** The scientists and physicians highlighted in this section provided convincing evidence that localized areas of the brain are involved in specific functions.

Thomas Willis: Pioneer of brain functions. Thomas Willis (1621–1675) was born only 25 years after Descartes, but their ideas diverge so widely that they may as well have lived in two different eras. Willis was part of a new breed of medical physiologist that broke from the tradition of the humoral theory and other ancient philosophical notions and came to rely more heavily on clinical and scientific observations and experiments.

After receiving his medical training at Oxford, Willis immediately started building a private practice. He became interested in the brain when he met a group of natural philosophers at Oxford who were interested in neuroanatomy and neurophysiology. These men, who called themselves the Virtuosi, had a powerful impact on Willis's career. In 1660, Willis was offered a professorship at Oxford; he used this position

[Box 2.1]

Brain Matters

Mental Illness Loses Its Religion

The Dark Ages in Europe (roughly the fourth through the fourteenth centuries) were characterized by a regression in virtually every area of knowledge. Unfortunately, the field of mental illness did not escape the stagnating consequences of this unenlightened era. The Church ruled with a firm hand, and abnormal behavior became associated with the supernatural. The only cure for mental illness would not come from physicians or scientists but from God. As had been the case in ancient Greece, the Church taught that abnormal behavior was a result of the person consorting with or being possessed by the Devil. According to the Old Testament, consorting with the Devil was the worst crime a person could commit and the consequences were deadly.

The inhumanity of this demonic perspective of mental illness is epitomized in the 1484 publication *Malleus maleficarum* (*Hammer of the Witches*). Written by two Dominican monks, Heinrich Kraemer and Johann Sprenger, the goal of this document was to convince the world that people displaying abnormal behavior or thoughts were socializing with the Devil. This bizarre behavior was observed mostly in women, and these women were referred to as witches; in many cases, they were tortured and then burned to death.

In addition to being cruel and uninformed, the book is perverse in places: Kraemer and Sprenger describe in vivid detail the way witches copulate with devils. Additionally, they recommend that witches be tried in the nude, often with their pubic hair shaved because demons might hide there. Subsequently, the accused were tortured until they confessed, and with a confession, their murder was justified.

The legendary Joan of Arc, who led the French army to victory when she was only 17 years of age, was later burned as a witch after it became known that she experienced hallucinations. More than 200 years after the publication of the book, in the presumably intellectual community of Salem, Massachusetts, 19 women were hanged as witches. One brave defender of the women, Giles Corey, was put to death for supporting their innocence.

Today, it seems unimaginable that *Malleus maleficarum* went through 30 editions between 1484 and 1669. Even more unimaginable is the fact that hundreds of thousands of innocent men and women were tortured to death because of these unenlightened beliefs. As you can discern from this chapter, very little scientific knowledge was contributed to the field of clinical neuroscience during this mystical era. Ambroise Paré, introduced in Connections at the beginning of this chapter, was one of the few individuals courageous enough to challenge the deadly publication. The memory of this horrifying book should serve as a reminder that only empirically based perspectives, as opposed to mere opinions of individuals, should be accepted as actual explanations of mental illness or abnormal behavior.

---

to investigate the senses and the nervous system. Willis's collaboration with the Virtuosi was an early demonstration of the advantages of collaboration among talented scientists. In fact, working with this productive team, Willis published the impressive work known as *Cerebri anatome* (*Cerebral Anatomy*) in 1664.

Unlike Descartes, Willis saw a continuum in the mental lives of humans and animals. He observed that animals exhibit evidence of perception, memory, and cognition, as humans do; animals just experience these phenomena on a more rudimentary level. Willis thus saw value in investigating both human and animal brains. His exploration of the nervous system contributed many terms that neuroscientists still use today—*neurology, psychology, lobe, hemisphere,* and *reflexion* (reflex)—though some of these terms had slightly different meanings than they do today.

Through astute observations and dissections, Willis started to discover the true functions of some of the structures of the brain. For example, his work deemphasized the importance of the ventricles in higher functions and pointed the light toward the influence of the cerebral hemispheres. He also described the corpus striatum for the first time, correctly proposing this structure's role in movement, and suggested that the lower brain stem area is involved in the most basic functions, such as respiration.

On the clinical side, Willis described a relationship between mania and melancholia (depression), suggested that impaired intelligence may be inherited, described epilepsy as a *natural* brain disease rather than a result of demonic possession, and observed that consuming too much wine may lead to mental impairment (as observed in chronic alcoholics with *Korsakoff's syndrome,* a neurodegenerative disease caused by alcoholism-induced thiamin [vitamin B1] deficiency). Willis's impressive work elevated the brain sciences to a higher plane during the latter part of the seventeenth century. His dual interests in neuroanatomy and mental illness establish his legacy as a true pioneer in the field of clinical neuroscience.

Franz Joseph Gall: Rise and fall of phrenology. The next character in our cast of early neuroscientists interested in localization of brain function lived in Vienna. Whereas Willis identified more general functions with particular areas of the brain, Gall (1758–1828) devoted his energy to discerning where more specific functions—certain personality characteristics—are housed in the brain.

After completing his medical degree, Gall quickly built a reputation as one of the most outstanding physicians in all of Austria. A trend of the day was to associate certain physical characteristics, such as facial structure, with personality characteristics (individuals with beady little eyes, for example, were thought to be sinister—a correlation that still seems to be alive in comic strips). Gall agreed that variations in physical structures reflected variations in function, but he wasn't interested in facial or other bodily characteristics; he was solely interested in the brain.

Gall wrote that his fascination with the relationship between brain structure and personality characteristics began when he was only 9 years old. He noticed that certain boys in his class were excellent memorizers, a skill that did not come very readily to Gall. He observed that these super-memorizers had bulging eyes (he called them ox eyes) and proposed that their eyes protruded because of an overly developed cortical (or higher brain) area that controlled verbal memory. Building on these observations,

Gall later postulated that all personality characteristics (or "faculties," as he called them) were controlled by specialized organs woven into the fabric of the **cerebral cortex,** the wrinkled, outermost layer of the brain.

Gall set out to establish relationships, or **correlations,** between cortical structures and intensity of the various faculties. Since he felt that variations in the brain's cortex would be represented by variations in one's skull, he devised a protocol requiring actually feeling the skulls of many individuals to establish relationships between skull bumps and certain personality characteristics. In the end, Gall settled for 27 faculties, 19 of which were shared with animals (for example, reproductive instinct, sense of place) and 8 of which were distinctly human (for example, wisdom, poetic talent, religious sentiment, and satire). It is important to note that Gall's idea that the skull represented the delicate bumps of the cortex was not due to a lack of knowledge of the brain. On the contrary, Gall was a gifted neuroanatomist and discovered several neural pathways of the brain.

Although Gall's new theory could be easily criticized for methodological reasons (Do skulls actually have bumps?), his first obstacle was the philosophical criticism of the conservative Catholic authorities in Austria. They felt that Gall's theory reduced the intellect and soul to the materialistic brain and warned Gall that people would lose their heads over this doctrine—literally! When Gall was 47 years old, he had no choice but to leave Austria if he wanted to pursue his interest in the localization of brain function.

Subsequently, Gall started traveling around Europe giving lectures and performing dissections of the brain in the major cities and universities. Before leaving Austria, Gall made the acquaintance of Johann Spurzheim, who would become his assistant for the next 9 years. Although Gall seemed very impressed with Spurzheim early in their relationship, the two men parted ways in 1813 because Spurzheim began advocating a craniological system that differed from Gall's (Figure 2.2a, page 46).

Spurzheim introduced new faculties to Gall's list and espoused ideas that organs could be modified with training or learning, an idea with which Gall vehemently disagreed. Additionally, Spurzheim removed the more evil faculties from the list, enabling him to describe humans in a more optimistic light. Spurzheim was not the first person to use the term **phrenology** (from *phren*—"mind" and *logos*—"discourse"), but he was the person who popularized the term associated with Gall's theory of brain localization. (Actually, Gall never used the word phrenology; he felt that the term *organology* more clearly conveyed his emphasis on the brain.)

Once Spurzheim was on his own, he completed a medical degree and then became wildly popular in England, Ireland, and Scotland. In the

cerebral cortex Most recently evolved part of the brain that envelops the midbrain; also associated with complex cognitive functions.

correlation Statistical technique used to determine how strongly two variables are related; two variables may change in a similar pattern (positive correlation) or a different pattern (negative correlation).

phrenology Term popularized to describe Gall's theory of localization of function. In this theory, bumps on the surface of the skull were deemed to predict certain mental capabilities.

[Figure 2.2]
(a) Location of faculties according to Spurzheim. (b) Contemporary phrenology bust showing modified faculties that may be appropriate for the twenty-first century.

(B) BUST MADE BY ACCOUTREMENTS, SEATTLE, WASHINGTON. PHOTO COURTESY OF KELLY LAMBERT, RANDOLPH-MACON COLLEGE BEHAVIORAL NEUROSCIENCE LABORATORY

United States, the *American Journal of Phrenology* was established. By 1840, however, phrenology was no longer perceived as a science: it existed only as a source of parlor humor.

Most scientists criticized Gall for using only selective, subjective data to support his theory. One scientist, Marie-Jean-Pierre Flourens, a French experimentalist, attacked Gall's theory with a vengeance. Flourens used acceptable methodological techniques (for example, experimentation with animals) to determine the importance of various cortical areas in several different animals. He failed to find any evidence to support Gall's claims and publicly ridiculed Gall's methods and theory.

Most scientists and physicians who were contemporaries of Gall would have chosen to simply forget about him, but he is worth remembering for several reasons. In addition to his impeccable skills as a neuroanatomist, he was passionate about understanding the role of the brain in certain higher functions. In fact, in just a few decades, evidence would be presented to support the notion of localization of function within the cerebral hemispheres. Ironically, Flourens, who used solid methodology, was subsequently wrong when he concluded that cortical localization of higher functions did not exist. As you can see in Figure 2.2b, a recent phrenological bust with more contemporary faculties (playground trauma, zipper location, dot.com faculties) is evidence that the notions of phrenology remain part of our culture even today.

Paul Broca: Localization of language. Gall's organology was widely ridiculed, but not all physicians and scientists were ready to throw out the idea of cortical localization along with phrenology. Dr. Jean-Baptiste Bouillaud, a French physician interested in brain functions, and his son-in-law, Simon Alexandre Ernest Aubertin, believed that language is localized in the anterior lobes of the cerebral cortex. Their theory was based on clinical observations of people with brain damage in this area. All they lacked was a case of obvious language difficulties linked with a confirmation of cortical damage on the patient's autopsy. It happened that one person attending Aubertin's lectures about the localization of language abilities was Paul Broca (1824–1880).

Whereas Bouillaud and Aubertin had been unable to find the landmark case that would provide overwhelming evidence supporting the idea of cerebral localization of language, Broca, who practiced at the Bicêtre hospital, discovered a 51-year-old patient named Leborgne who had suffered from epilepsy since childhood and had not been able to speak for 20 years. By the time Leborgne became Broca's patient, he was suffering from severe cellulitis (an infection of the skin and subcutaneous tissue) with gangrene and was not expected to live long.

Broca immediately saw the potential in this case and invited Aubertin to witness his examination of this man who could not speak. After the patient died about a week later, an autopsy confirmed Bouillard's and Aubertin's predictions about anterior cortical areas being involved in speech, and it provided even more specificity: the damaged area was in the third convolution of the frontal cortex of the left hemisphere.

In 1861, Broca presented and published this landmark case study of the patient who would become known as Tan because this was about the only sound the man could make (Figure 2.3). Where Gall's ideas of cerebral localization were considered blasphemous half a century earlier, Broca's observations were met with enthusiasm. Finally, convincing evidence of cerebral localization had been presented. In the next several years, Broca encountered more cases that confirmed the existence of the language center. He was intrigued by the fact that the damage in all these cases was in the left hemisphere and later proposed that the language center is located there, suggesting a cerebral dominance of the left hemisphere in language abilities.

Whereas Willis had elegantly shown the existence of the localization of more general functions, Broca was the first to demonstrate the localization of higher functions—the beginning of understanding the specificity of the structures within the brain.

Broca's area

[Figure 2.3]
The brain of Tan, believed by some researchers to be the most famous brain in all of neuroscience, reveals a lesion around the third convolution of the left hemisphere. Contemporary neuroanatomists call this Broca's area.

MUSEE DUPUYTREN; COURTESY OF ASSISTANCE PUBLIQUE, HOSPITAUX DE PARIS

Pioneers of Cellular Investigations in the Brain: The Architects

In the mid-nineteenth century, when researchers were beginning to understand that various structures in the brain are related to specific functions, interest was also brewing about the makeup of these brain

[Figure 2.4]
Golgi-stained pyramidal neuron in the CA1 area of the hippocampus, an area of the brain involved in learning and memory.

histology Systematic preparation of brain or other physiological tissue for microscopic study to be used for experimental and diagnostic purposes.

nerve net theory Early theory of the nature of the nervous system implying that the nervous system is made up of continuous extensions of nervous tissue.

neuron Fundamental unit, or cell, of the nervous system.

structures. Because adequate stains for brain tissue and high-powered microscopes had not yet been invented, not much was known about the fundamental units of the nervous system. Preliminary work by Jan Evangelista Purkyne a few decades earlier had suggested that cells with branches populate the nervous system. It was also thought that these cells formed a continuous neural network so that messages, or impulses, could travel as quickly as possible. This picture of the nervous system was about to change, however.

Nerve cells couldn't be understood until advances were made in **histology,** the process of studying biological tissue. Once methods were established to visualize the cells of the nervous system, the cells had to be identified, catalogued, and documented much like new species in an exotic new land. Once stains were developed so that nerve cells could be visualized, it quickly became obvious that these tiny cells were more elaborate than anyone had ever suspected.

Camillo Golgi: Revealing neuronal structure with the perfect stain. Golgi (1843–1926) was raised in the Lombardy region of Italy and was educated at the University of Pavia. His passion for research enabled him to make a histological breakthrough. Working by candlelight in the evenings, Golgi attempted to impregnate nerve cells with a silver stain so that he could visualize their structure. He immersed the tissue in silver nitrate for a day or so, then bathed it in a series of alcohol and oil solutions. Much to Golgi's delight, this process produced a picture, or blueprint, of the neuron: beautiful black nerve cells against a yellowish background (Figure 2.4). For some unknown reason, only about 3% of the nerve cells actually stained. This partial staining is significant, because if all the nerve cells stained, the tissue would look like a black smudge under the microscope.

In 1873, Golgi published his first paper, in which he described the detailed structure of nerve cells. A few years later, he accepted a faculty position so that he could spend his time using his silver stain to understand the fine structure of the nervous system. A more accurate picture of the nerve cells was emerging, but Golgi continued to endorse the **nerve net theory** that suggested the nervous system is made up of continuous extensions of nerve cells (as opposed to individual nerve cell units). This theory, however, would soon be challenged.

Santiago Ramón y Cajal: Providing evidence for the neuron doctrine. Santiago Ramón y Cajal (1852–1934) worked a hundred years ago in Spain, and his representations of the nerve cells, or **neurons,** still appear to be accurate. His research was the first to cast significant doubt on the nerve net theory.

In Cajal's autobiography, entitled *Recollections of My Life,* (1917), he wrote that his first love was art but that his father, who was a physician, felt such a career was worthless and embarked on a campaign to persuade his son to become a physician. Ironically, Cajal's interest in anatomy was born in a graveyard. In 1868, his father took him to graveyards to examine human remains that had been exhumed because the leased burial plots had not been renewed. Once Cajal started sketching the bones from these exhumed bodies, he realized that he wanted to learn more about anatomy. His first step toward this goal was obtaining a medical degree.

While visiting Madrid to take an examination for a professorship, Cajal had the opportunity to look through a microscope. The images he saw so affected him that he decided to pursue a career in microscopy. He used his own money to purchase a microscope and started to build a modest lab. Once he was introduced to Golgi's silver stain, he modified the protocol to produce the best images of neurons.

Cajal found that neurons surrounded by fatty myelin tissue failed to produce clear staining, so he searched for less-fatty cells and discovered that birds and young animals produced high-quality stains. Armed with his passion and talent for art, Cajal then easily transferred these images to his sketchpad (Figure 2.5).

Cajal's troubles did not disappear once he perfected the Golgi staining technique. He was producing very interesting data at a rapid pace, but his isolation in Spain and in the Spanish language prohibited the dissemination of his findings. Investing his own money once again, Cajal founded a journal entitled *Trimonthly Review of Normal and Pathological Histology* so that he would have a place to rapidly publish his findings. He subsequently sent copies to leading anatomists across Europe. Unfortunately, the other anatomists did not understand Spanish.

[Figure 2.5]
Neurons from the visual cortex of a several-day-old human infant as sketched by Santiago Ramón y Cajal.

Frustrated, Cajal feared that his important findings suggesting that the nerve cells were not fused or connected, as dictated by the prevailing nerve net theory, were never going to be accepted by respected colleagues. This led Cajal to have his works translated into French. He then took his papers, slides, and microscope to the German Anatomical Society in 1889. Cajal's exhibit caught the attention of influential anatomists. During his conversations with fellow researchers, Cajal described how he had failed to find any evidence of the nerve net theory

neuron doctrine Theory that separate units, or neurons, as opposed to continuous units, made up the nervous system.

synapse Tiny gap that separates two neurons and is the location of communication between the two cells.

in his observations of the nerve cells. He went on to suggest that neurons were independent structures.

The significance of Cajal's work was recognized in 1906 when he was awarded the Nobel Prize for Physiology or Medicine, an award he shared with Camillo Golgi. The architecture of the individual neuron was established, but a lot of uncertainty remained about the interconnections among the neurons.

Charles Scott Sherrington: Describing the synapse. English scientist Sherrington (1857–1952) published his first scientific paper when he was a medical student. After graduating from medical school, he became interested in immunology, pathology, and the anatomical changes that accompany damage to the motor cortex. Sherrington became more and more enamored with the nervous system and started investigating the mechanisms of the motor reflex, specifically, the knee jerk.

Even before Cajal's work suggested the existence of individual neurons, Sherrington was already leaning in that theoretical direction. His own research suggested that cortical lesions resulted in specific, not diffuse, damage. In 1894, when Cajal was lecturing in London, he stayed in Sherrington's home and the two men discussed the likelihood of the nerve cells existing as individual units. This notion, which directly opposed the neural net theory, was later known as the **neuron doctrine.**

Sherrington went a step further a few years after his conversations with Cajal and introduced the notion of a functional junction that probably existed between neurons. Initially he used the term *synapsis* (from the Greek word meaning "to clasp") for this neuronal gap. Today it's called the **synapse.** Sherrington's hypothesis remained theoretical until more high-powered microscopes permitted researchers to detect this tiny junction.

Pioneers of Cellular Investigations in the Brain: The Chemical Engineers

The blueprints for the nervous system were becoming more and more established, but what was the microstructure of the nerve cells? If Cajal and Sherrington were correct about the neuron doctrine, how did separate neurons communicate with one another?

Toward the end of the nineteenth century, the prevailing thought was that neuronal communication was electrical in nature. Waves of electrical charges would shoot down the neurons and then jump across the tiny synaptic gaps. In 1877, Emil Du Bois-Reymond, a German physiologist, proposed that an alternate method might also be employed in neuronal communication. In addition to electrical stimulation, Du Bois-Reymond proposed that chemicals may be released from the endings of neurons. This chemical hypothesis was pretty much ignored until Otto Loewi entered the scene.

Otto Loewi: Dreaming of chemical communication. For his doctoral thesis, Loewi (1873–1963) conducted research in pharmacology, a discipline that investigates the effect of drugs on physiological systems. Scientists and the emerging pharmaceutical industry were eager to learn just how chemicals could alter physiological functioning throughout the body, such as increasing heart rate or decreasing blood pressure. Researchers were speculating that the neurons may actually work via such chemical transmission, but no convincing evidence supported such a claim.

The answer to this neuronal communication mystery turns out literally to be the stuff that dreams are made of, and indeed this was the case for Loewi. According to scientific folklore, Loewi reported that in 1921 he awoke from a dream in the middle of the night with an outline for a creative experiment that would prove that neurons communicate via chemicals.

Loewi's dream was based on the simple observation that if you expose a frog's heart and stimulate one of the major cranial nerves that is involved in basic functions such as heart rate, you can see the heart slow down. Loewi's dream suggested that a chemical was released from the nerve endings onto the muscle of the heart and, if you collected the chemical surrounding the slowed heart and simply poured it around a second frog's heart, then voilà, the second frog's heart would slow down as well. The story goes that Loewi took notes on his dream right away so that he could actually conduct the experiment the next day. Unfortunately, the next morning he could not read his scribbles and had forgotten the dream.

Frustrated, Loewi tried to remember the experiment throughout the entire next day. When he woke up after having the same dream that night, he decided not to take any chances. He quickly got up and went to the laboratory to conduct the experiment while it was fresh on his mind. In addition to slowing down the frog's heart, Loewi went a step further and stimulated the "accelerator" nerve. He saw the same general effect: The heart of the first frog accelerated, and when the fluid surrounding the heart of the stimulated frog was poured onto the second frog's heart, an increase was also observed in the heart rate of the second frog. Loewi now had convincing evidence of chemical transmission in the nervous system.

Following Loewi's significant studies, researchers speculated that the drugs, such as acetylcholine, that lower blood pressure may also work as natural substances within the nervous system. The acetylcholine used by

neurotransmitter Chemical such as dopamine and serotonin in the brain that is essential for communication between two neurons.

nerve impulse (action potential) Physiological basis of communication in the nervous system triggered by the exchange of certain ions across the nerve cell membrane.

all-or-none law Observation that, once the threshold is reached, all action potentials are the same size regardless of the intensity of the original stimulation.

the drug companies was isolated from a particular fungus, but it was thought that the body might produce this substance as well. This idea was speculative, though, until someone could actually extract the substance from animal tissue.

The respected neurophysiologist Henry Dale (1875–1968) felt up to the challenge. In 1929, he visited a slaughterhouse and harvested spleens from the horses and oxen that were just killed. He processed the tissue and was ecstatic when 70 pounds of horse spleen produced less than a gram of a neurochemical that was identical to the active substance in the drugs. Now the researchers could be sure that the drug known as acetycholine, extracted from a fungus, was exactly the same as the substance in the spleens of the horses. This was just the beginning of the identification of numerous natural chemicals, or **neurotransmitters,** in the nervous system. The significance of the contributions of both Loewi and Dale was recognized in 1936 when the two men shared the Nobel prize for their "discoveries relating to chemical transmission of nerve impulses."

Edgar D. Adrian: Amplifying the electrical language of the neuron. About the same time that scientists were trying to understand how neurons communicate, other scientists were busy trying to understand how information was coded in individual neurons: How was energy conducted within a single neuron so that it could subsequently communicate with a second neuron? Adrian (1889–1979), an English physiologist, made great strides in elucidating this process.

Adrian's first substantial discovery was that neurons react, or "fire," in an all-or-none fashion. Adrian's clever set of experiments suggested that once a neuron is stimulated, it does not matter whether the original stimulus was just minimal or was very intense: the strength of the **nerve impulse** (or **action potential,** as it was named by Du Bois-Reymond) consistently shot down the nerve at full strength. Just as a mouse trap snaps with the same intensity regardless of whether the cheese is gently or aggressively removed from the spring, the action potential, once triggered, proceeds down the neuron with amazing consistency.

Adrian's work with the **all-or-none law** was impressive, but he wanted to learn more about the intricacies of nerve cell communication. Unfortunately, the existing technology wasn't up to the task. Equipment that would amplify the electrical messages without distorting their natural characteristics had to be invented before more progress could be made. Eventually, the necessary amplifiers were introduced and Adrian went on to record from individual neurons and to conduct further research related to the coding of sensory stimulation, such as visual or auditory input. He was investigating **transduction:** how the environmental energy of light and sound are converted into neural energy used by the visual and auditory sensory neurons.

Neuroscience researchers had identified the basic structure of the individual nerve cells and discovered important information about coding and communication of information within the nervous system. The ground was now fertile for many discoveries that would shed light on the nature of how the brain is involved in mental health.

transduction Conversion of physical energy, such as light, to energy that can be used in the nervous system.

NEUROLOGICAL APPROACHES TO MENTAL ILLNESS

In this section, the focus shifts from the story of how the once mysterious nervous system came to be understood to the true nature of clinical neuroscience—how neuroscience research was applied to mental illness. Could knowledge about the structure and functioning of the nervous system translate into therapeutic benefits for the mentally ill?

Mental Illness Meets the Microscope

Looking at neurons through a microscope to gain information that could lead to therapies for mental illness was an alien notion in the mid- to late-nineteenth century. Still, a few bold scientists started to build the bridge between neuroanatomy and clinical symptoms. Theodor Meynert (1833–1892) was one of the first of the modern wave of clinical neuroscientists. After studying medicine in Vienna, he specialized in neuropathology. He also had an interest in psychiatry and subsequently acquired a faculty position in psychiatry. In this position, Meynert did what came naturally to him—he examined brain tissue under a microscope. He developed stains and spent countless hours searching for pathological lesions in the nerve tissue. (It is interesting to note that one of Meynert's students, Sigmund Freud, would later become famous for psychoanalysis, a very different approach to treating mental illness.)

Unfortunately, Meynert was unable to identify significant disease-related pathology other than lesions in advanced syphilis patients. Perhaps his greatest contribution was his vision about the relationship between the nervous system and mental illness. In 1890, he wrote: "The more that psychiatry seeks, and finds, its scientific bases in a deep and finely grained understanding of the anatomical structure [of the brain], the more it elevates itself to the status of a science that deals with causes" (quoted in Shorter, 1997, p. 77).

[Box 2.2]

The Investigators

Eric Richard Kandel: From Studying the History of Neuroscience to Becoming the History of Neuroscience

When Austrian-born Eric Kandel (1929–present) graduated from Harvard College in 1952, he knew exactly what he wanted to do: attend medical school so that he could become a Park Avenue psychoanalyst. In preparation for his dream career, Kandel received a medical degree from New York University School of Medicine so that he could follow in the footsteps of a fellow Austrian-born physician, Sigmund Freud. Following graduation, Kandel worked as a research associate in the Laboratory of Neurophysiology at the National Institute of Mental Health. This research experience convinced him that he wanted to spend his career in the laboratory, not on Park Avenue.

In the early 1960s, Kandel made the bold decision to conduct research on an unlikely animal, the large sea snail, *Aplysia californica.* Kandel found this invertebrate attractive for neuroscience research because it has fewer and larger neurons than more traditional laboratory animals. This simple neural system would subsequently serve as an invaluable model for understanding the cellular and molecular basis of learning. Armed with endless research questions about the neurobiology of simple conditioning in *Aplysia,* Kandel decided to set up his laboratory at Columbia University, where he remains to this day.

Throughout his career, Kandel has also been a student of the history of neuroscience. In 2000 he wrote (with Larry Squire) an article in *Science* entitled "Neuroscience: Breaking Down Scientific Barriers to the Study of Brain and Mind." In addition to Cajal's description of the neuron at the turn of the twentieth century (which led to the neuron doctrine), Kandel credits the work of Alan Hodgkin, Andrew Huxley, and Bernard Katz, who described the movement of ions across the neuronal membrane 40 years later, as seminal research in the history of neuroscience. According to Kandel, Cajal's cellular approach and Hodgkin and colleagues'

Eric Kandel
COURTESY OF COLUMBIA UNIVERSITY

molecular approach provided the basic floor plans of the nervous system and the basis for thousands of valuable research programs in the future (including his own work identifying cellular mechanisms accompanying events such as habituation or sensitization in *Aplysia*).

Kandel's fascination with the "giants" of neuroscience, as he calls them, became ironic when Kandel himself became a part of the history of neuroscience: He was awarded the Nobel Prize in Physiology or Medicine in 2000 (shared with Paul Greengard and Arvid Carlsson). Concerning the future of the field, Kandel reports:

> For neuroscience to address the most challenging problems confronting the behavioral and biological sciences, we will need to continue to search for new molecular and cellular approaches and use them in conjunction with systems neuroscience and psychological science. In this way, we will best be able to relate molecular events and specific changes within neuronal circuits to mental processes such as perception, memory, thought, and possibly consciousness itself. (p. 1120)

Kandel's groundbreaking research has attempted to merge basic neuroscience with the more advanced behavior of learning. Consequently, the field has already made progress toward solving the neurobiological puzzle of learning behavior.

At the same time that Meynert was making his prophetic statement about psychiatry and neuroscience, Emil Kraepelin (1886–1926) was awarded a professorship at the university psychiatric clinic in Heidelburg. Kraepelin was unable to study brain tissue through the microscope because of eye problems, but that did not stop him from contributing to the cause in an indirect way. He organized an impressive group of neuroscientists in his laboratory to help unravel the relationship between the brain and mental illness. Among his collaborators was Franz Nissl, (1860–1919) a well-known neurohistologist who described six distinct layers within the cerebral cortex. Another neuroscientist Kraepelin hired was Aloys Alzheimer (1864–1915), who in 1906 discovered the neuropathology consistent with a type of **dementia** (mental deterioration) that would later be named after him.

One barrier that existed for these early clinical neuroscientists was the absence of a systematic method of categorizing different forms of mental illness. Kraepelin made major contributions toward categorization by collecting and organizing extensive data on a wide variety of patients. His data cards on patients and their illnesses enabled him first to suggest that illnesses seemed to fall into particular categories and second to document the developmental course of the various disorders. For example, after reviewing both his data and the work of others, he wrote about patients suffering from manic-depressive illness. Also, he wrote about dementia praecox (premature mental deterioration) to describe the disorder that would later, in 1908, be referred to as **schizophrenia** by one of Kraepelin's followers, Eugen Bleuler (1887–1939).

In spite of these scientists who fought the battle against mental illness armed with microscopes, a substantial divide remained between looking at neurons and actually treating the symptoms of mental illness. Certainly, the bridge between behavioral symptoms and the structure of the nervous system needed to be more complete before real progress could be made.

Jean-Martin Charcot: Birth of Neurology

In the mid-nineteenth century, Charcot (1825–1893) was appointed to the coveted position of senior physician at the Salpetrière Hospital, a famous Parisian hospice for sick and elderly women. At the time of this appointment, the Salpetrière, however, was not in its best condition. Charcot found many buildings in ruins, and the 5000 patients seemed to be housed together at random.

Like Kraepelin, Charcot saw a great need to describe and categorize the symptoms and diseases suffered by the patients at Salpetrière. He set

dementia Progressive loss of mental functioning atypical of normal aging processes.

schizophrenia Mental illness characterized by hallucinations, delusions, social withdrawal, and cognitive deterioration. Certain brain modifications such as a smaller hippocampus and disarrayed neurons have been observed to accompany this condition.

hysteria Early characterization of mental disturbance described in women who had no known accompanying brain damage. Charcot thought that only hysterical women could be hypnotized.

psychoanalysis Therapeutic approach to mental illness developed by Freud. In this subjective theory, unconscious motives were thought to direct behavior and thoughts.

out to find some method to the madness in this asylum of misery. One strategy he employed was to meet with and examine the women, document their symptoms, and then, after they died, conduct autopsies on their brains to determine if their condition could be related to some brain pathology.

Charcot gained a reputation as an astute observer of the behavioral symptoms of his patients. It was reported that his typical session involved sitting next to the undressed patient and watching her as she made particular movements. He would also ask the patient to speak and then would test various reflexes and sensory responses. Charcot's observations, coupled with knowledge of a detailed clinical history, enabled him to determine the origin of the patient's neurological problem.

During his career, Charcot was instrumental in describing multiple sclerosis, Parkinson's disease, amyotrophic lateral sclerosis, and Tourette's syndrome. He also became interested in cerebral localization and even tried to help Broca with his research by sending him some patients with compromised speech abilities. Charcot observed that some patients had what looked like a behavioral problem but no brain pathology. For example, the patient might have been aphasic (could not speak) yet no frontal lobe lesion could be found on autopsy.

During the final stage of Charcot's career at Salpetrière, he concentrated on cases where the patients displayed significant symptoms, yet no accompanying pathology could be identified. These women were said to be suffering from **hysteria,** a Greek word meaning "uterus." Charcot studied these cases in order to differentiate them from epilepsy cases. For some reason, he began to stray from his usual employment of empirical strategies (strategies based on observable, verifiable evidence) for accurately describing the disorders of the nervous system. For example, without any known convincing reason, he endorsed the notion that only hysterical patients could be hypnotized.

In an interesting sidebar to Charcot's story, a young Sigmund Freud (1856–1939) was seated in the audience for one of Charcot's famous weekly lectures (pictured in Figure 2.6). Freud was intrigued by the notion that mental events could set off a cascade of symptoms. In fact, Charcot probably provided Freud with the foundation for what would become his theory of psychoanalysis.

Thus, Charcot, who had been so dependent on objective clinical science to categorize a host of neurological and mental diseases, gave Freud the ammunition to build his subjective theory. In many ways, **psychoanalysis,** based on speculations and theories about unconscious motives that drive behavior, was the antithesis to an empirical approach to understanding mental and nervous system diseases. Based on Charcot's introduction of hysteria as a disorder of women, Freud's psychoanalytical theories also focused on women. Because of the rise of the Nazi regime, though, psychoanalysis, which had become a mainstay of German and Austrian psychiatry, all but disappeared in Europe in the 1930s, but was resurrected in the United States, where it flourished for the next three decades. In the United States, a few adaptations were made to this form of psychiatry; mainly, the focus shifted from the more debilitating disorders (psychoses) to problems of everyday life (neuroses). Psychoanalysis was still used by some to treat psychosis but without success.

[Figure 2.6]
A century ago, Jean Martin Charcot concluded that the symptoms of "hysteria" could not be explained by what was then known about the brain. The susceptibility of his patients to hypnosis helped Charcot to convince others, including Sigmund Freud, that these states could be suggested and were therefore functional only and unrelated to neurobiology.
CORBIS-BETTMAN

Whereas Charcot studied hysterical women in the famous Salpetrière asylum, psychoanalysts in the United States migrated to private practices located in large cities. Edward Shorter, a historian of medicine, wrote that these modifications resulted in a "scientific stagnation" in the field of psychiatry during the mid-twentieth century. In fairness to the psychoanalysts of the time, there was one attempt to validate the therapeutic value of psychoanalysis. Dr. Lawrence Kubie, President of the New York Psychoanalytic Society, convened a group to collect data about the efficacy of psychoanalytic treatment. Because the statistics were questionable, the committee decided to keep the report confidential. To make matters worse, the 3000 reports sent to IBM for data analysis were lost.

Needless to say, the validation fiasco did not go very far in convincing the scientific community that the psychoanalytic strategy was an effective one. In many ways, the furor around psychoanalysis was the great distraction from a valid neuroscientific or neurological approach to treatment for mental illness. Because of Charcot's indirect influence in the development of this perspective after contributing so much valid information to the field of neurology, it is probably fair to say that, in the grand scheme of the history of clinical neuroscience, he giveth and then taketh away!

BIOLOGICAL THERAPIES FOR MENTAL ILLNESS

The therapies described in this section may seem crude, but they helped show the way to real possibilities for treating mental disorders. For example, some of the earliest biological treatments involved inducing fevers or comas to relieve psychotic symptoms. Some of the subsequently developed biological therapies (electroconvulsive shock therapy, psychopharmacology, and psychosurgery) also seem extreme but, because of their success, continue to exist in some form today.

Early Biological Treatments

The likelihood of finding effective treatments for the mentally ill was pretty dismal in the first half of the twentieth century. Even so, bright, motivated scientists and psychiatrists still kept trying to find a therapeutic path. At last, a few potential treatments were discovered. The initial treatments, though, were far from elegant and sometimes resulted in side effects that rivaled the symptoms of the original disorder. Even with these limitations, the new treatments were an incredible advance for clinical neuroscience. They provided indisputable evidence that at least some mental disorders could be treated with biological therapies.

In the later part of the nineteenth century, an Austrian psychiatrist named Julius Wagner-Jauregg (1857–1940) was working at the Vienna Asylum. There he observed a woman suffering from psychosis who experienced relief from her symptoms when she contracted an infection and accompanying fever. This prompted Wagner-Jauregg to speculate on the potential of inducing fevers to treat other forms of psychosis, such as neurosyphilis, a functional disorder that affected many of the patients who resided in asylums.

Wagner-Jauregg later infected patients with malaria so that they would develop a fever high enough to kill the heat-sensitive syphilis spirochetes that caused the neurosyphilis. (Malaria could be treated with quinine, so the risk associated with contracting this disease did not seem to him excessive.) In 1919, Wagner-Jauregg wrote a report heralding the successful treatment of this new neurosyphilis cure. This biological therapy helped treat one form of psychosis, so other clinical neuroscientists started to wonder if the so-called fever cure would help to alleviate other forms of psychosis. Unfortunately, it did not and in fact generated a set of severe side effects, leading to a dead end for the fever cure. Still, other scientists and physicians set out to find more biological therapies for mental illness, preferably without the obvious accompanying side effects. By the mid-1940s, penicillin had successfully treated neurosyphillis.

In the 1930s, Manfred Sakel (1900–1957), an Austrian physician, started to notice that some of his patients who were experiencing morphine withdrawal or agitation for other reasons enjoyed a bit of a remission following an insulin coma (hypoglycemia triggered by insulin). Consequently, he later decided to induce an insulin coma in schizophrenia patients.

Amazingly, Sakel reported full recovery in 50% of the patients. At last there seemed to be some hope for schizophrenia patients.

Although Sakel was later ridiculed for this unorthodox therapy, it began to be used by British psychiatrists as a treatment for chronic depression, and then the use of **coma therapy** spread like wildfire. In fact, in the early 1960s, there were more than a hundred insulin units in American hospitals. But the popularity of insulin therapy would soon be overshadowed.

Electroconvulsive Therapy (ECT)

During the 1930s, doctors often used some form of shock therapy (in these early cases, shock was induced by the delivery of certain drugs, such as insulin) for patients suffering from psychotic symptoms. One researcher working in Budapest, Ladislas von Meduna (1896–1964), found that the drug Metrazol produced seizures in his patients without inducing the coma produced by insulin therapy. Meduna noted significant improvements in his psychiatric patients. He later tested another drug, camphor, on schizophrenia, after noting a relationship between epilepsy and schizophrenia, and reported success. These drugs brought great hope to those suffering from psychiatric disorders, but problems such as severe anxiety and nausea led to a dead end for these shock-inducing drugs.

During this time, Ugo Cerletti (1877–1963), a psychiatry professor in Rome, was inducing epileptic seizures in dogs so that they could be used as animal models for epileptic patients. The seizures were induced by placing electrodes in an animal's mouth and anus. About this time, with all the enthusiasm surrounding then-current physical therapies in psychiatry, Cerletti decided to use the experimental approach to determine the most effective physical therapy for epilepsy.

Cerletti assigned to his laboratory assistants the investigation of insulin coma, the seizure-inducing drug Cardiazol, and the possible value of using the electrode experiment as a model for epilepsy. They quickly discovered that electrical current could be delivered by placing electrodes simply on an animal's head. With this observation, Cerletti's group went to the slaughterhouse to experiment with the proper placement of electrodes.

In 1938, Cerletti attempted to deliver electrical current to a human patient suffering from schizophrenia. Systematically increasing the amount of current, the patient finally exhibited a classic seizure. The patient's psychiatric symptoms showed significant improvement. Subsequently, **electroconvulsive therapy (ECT)** became a popular treatment for mental illness. In fact, by 1959, ECT had become the treatment of choice for depression.

coma therapy Physical therapy in which an insulin coma was induced to treat mental illness in a patient. After the 1960s the use of this therapy decreased because of rising popularity of electroconvulsive therapy and psychoactive drugs.

electroconvulsive therapy (ECT) Physical therapy used for mental illnesses such as major depression and schizophrenia; involves the delivery of electrical current to an anesthetized patient in an attempt to reconfigure neural functions for normal mental functioning.

barbiturates Group of highly addictive depressant drugs used as anticonvulsants and tranquilizers.

psychopharmacology Discipline that explores the relationship between certain psychoactive drugs and behavior and/or mental processes.

The Drug Revolution

The grueling nature of some therapies for mental illness made the thought of taking a mere drug very appealing. In the early 1800s, laxatives were considered as a cathartic, literally a release, for psychotic patients. Opium treatment also has a long history, especially for problems with anxiety and sleep; in the early 1800s, the drug morphine was isolated from opium and was taken either orally or injected into the bloodstream to calm patients. Other drugs that acted as sedatives were developed throughout the nineteenth century.

Essentially, the asylum treatment approach consisted simply of the delivery of sedatives to temporarily calm agitated patients. In 1832, chloral hydrate was manufactured by Bayer pharmaceuticals; this drug was used extensively for sedative purposes in many asylums, as well as by middle-class patients who did not want to enter the asylums.

The element bromine was isolated in 1826 from seaweed ashes and was used for a variety of illnesses, such as hysterical epilepsy. In 1897, Neil Macleod, a graduate of Edinburgh Medical School, gave a rather large dose of a bromide drug to a woman suffering from a nervous breakdown; after sleeping for several days, the woman woke up symptom free. Macleod went on to use this drug to cure other patients. Bromide-induced sleep gave scientists the idea that some psychoses may be cured with a particular drug, but it was later determined that bromine was too toxic for safe use with patients.

At the turn of the twentieth century, a new class of sedatives, **barbiturates** (named after the inventor's girlfriend, Barbara) hit the therapeutic scene. The barbiturates had the added benefit of enabling patients to wake up feeling refreshed after 8 hours of sleep, so it had wide appeal. Deep-sleep therapy was used with various combinations of barbiturates and seemed to offer modest benefits for patients suffering from mood disorders. The fate of sleep therapy acquired an interesting twist in mid-century when a Canadian psychiatrist named Ewen Cameron started exposing his patients to taped messages (he referred to it as brainwashing) during the prolonged sleep. To make matters worse, he exposed patients without their consent to electroconvulsive shock therapy to "depattern" previous brain circuits that might have led to the psychotic behavior. By 1960, sleep therapy was tainted and, with the rise of other more promising therapies on the horizon, it fell by the wayside.

The 1950s marked a veritable explosion in the field of **psychopharmacology**, a discipline that explores the relationship between certain psychoactive drugs and behavior and/or mental processes. Neuroscientists were beginning to understand the nature and functions of various neurotransmitters, and specific drug treatments were developed for specific disorders. Later chapters discuss the development of chlorpromazine for schizophrenia, lithium for bipolar disorder, and the various tricyclics for depression and anxiety.

Psychosurgery

Around the middle of the sixteenth century, some elaborate instruments were constructed to facilitate the craniotomy procedure initiated in ancient Greece. John Verano, a biological anthropologist at Tulane University, suggests that the first cases of **trepanning** (from the Greek word *trepanon,* "borer") were found along the south coast of Peru and date back to about 400 B.C. But discoveries of trepanned skulls that date back to prehistoric times show that the practice of intervening with the brain in order to relieve symptoms has been around even longer (Figure 2.7).

The modern story of removing frontal lobe and/or surrounding tissue to restore peace and sanity to those suffering from various forms of mental illness begins with a Lisbon neurologist, Egas Moniz (1875–1955). After being nominated for the Nobel prize twice but not winning it, Moniz seemed to be looking for a discovery that would seal his chances for the elusive prize. In 1935, he attended the Second International Congress of Neurology, held in London. At this conference, Moniz attended a full-day symposium on the frontal lobes of the brain that was headed by Carlyle Jacobsen and John Fulton, both from Yale University. In the talks, these researchers described the emotional changes that were observed in a chimp after the frontal lobes were damaged. Moniz was particularly interested in a case in which the chimp went from being prone to tantrums to being downright cheery.

After hearing these preliminary reports, Moniz stood and asked if such effects might also be observed in humans. Obviously, no one had the answer to this question. The data presented at this conference, however, became the inspiration for a new endeavor, namely, removing parts of the frontal lobes in psychotic patients to release them from their agitated symptoms. Moniz recruited a neurosurgeon, Almeida Lima, to actually perform the neurosurgery. The technique, which Moniz called *prefrontal leucotomy,* consisted of boring two holes in the top of the cranium and inserting a whisklike instrument called a leukotome through the holes to cut the white matter in the center of the brain's frontal lobes. Moniz did not divulge a lot of details to support his claims of success, but his initial reports indicated successful outcomes.

Back in the United States, the neurologist Walter Freeman (1895–1972) and the neurosurgeon James Watts (1904–1994) became interested in the procedure, which they referred to as **lobotomy.** In 1946, they modified Moniz's technique to that of a *transorbital lobotomy* (Figure 2.8), in which they entered the brain via the orbital cavity (eye socket). In his *History of*

trepanning Medical process of drilling a hole in the skull in an attempt to correct a problem associated with the brain (for example, a buildup of pressure on the brain).

[Figure 2.7]
This trepanned skull, found in Europe by archaeologists, dates to Neolithic times.
KEITH AND BETTY COLLINS/VISUALS UNLIMITED, INC.

lobotomy Faddish operation to treat mental illness used in the 1930s and 1940s. The procedure involved separating sections of the frontal lobe from the rest of the brain.

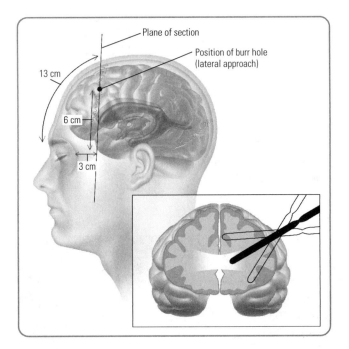

Plane of section

Position of burr hole
(lateral approach)

13 cm

6 cm

3 cm

[Figure 2.8]
A schematic of the lobotomy procedure in which a leucotome is inserted into a 6 millimeter burr hole and whisked back and forth. Watts later changed his technique to a procedure in which he entered the brain through the eye socket.

ADAPTED FROM FULTON, 1951, P. 107.

Psychiatry (1997), Shorter recounts a conversation between two doctors at the Georgia State Sanatorium. The conversation captures the casual brutality of this technique.

Dr. Hatcher: *Peter, I'm doing transorbital lobotomies this morning. Come watch me.*

Dr. Cranford: *If I saw one, you'd have to do the next one on me.*

Dr. Hatcher: *Nothing to it. I take a sort of medical icepick, hold it like this, bop it through the bones just above the eyeball, push it up into the brain, swiggle it around, cut the brain fibers like this, and that's it. The patient doesn't feel a thing.*

Dr. Cranford: *And neither do you. I was going to breakfast but I've changed my mind.*

Dr. Hatcher: *You can change your mind, but not like I can change it.*

(quoted in Shorter, 1997, p. 228)

After Freeman started conducting the procedures outside of his office, Watts started to feel uncomfortable with the relaxed nature of the surgery and ceased working with Freeman in 1947. Freeman proceeded to travel around administering transorbital lobotomies. Because he carried all his equipment in his car, some people referred to his automobile as the lobotomobile.

In his 1951 book entitled *Frontal Lobotomy and Affective Behavior,* John Fulton estimated that about 20,000 human patients had been subjected to some form of lobotomy. He also recounts an interesting observation by the well-known physiologist David Ferrier of King's College Hospital in London. Ferrier made significant contributions in the field of cortical localization by finding areas involved with voluntary control as well as different sensory systems. More relevant to the discussion at hand, he ablated, or lesioned, part of the frontal lobe in monkeys and made the following statement in a public lecture:

> The experiments show conclusively that an animal deprived of its frontal lobes retains all its powers of voluntary motion unimpaired, and that it continues to see, hear, smell and taste, and to perceive and localize tactile impressions as before . . . and yet the facts seem to warrant the conclusion that a decided change is produced in the animal's character and disposition. For this operation I selected the most active, lively, and intelligent animals which I could obtain. . . . They seemed to me, after

having studied their character carefully before and after the operation, to have undergone a great change . . . instead of being actively interested in their surroundings, they ceased to exhibit any interest in their environment beyond their own immediate sensations, paid no attention to, or looked vacantly and indifferently at, what formerly would have excited intense curiosity, sat stupidly quiet or went to sleep . . . and generally appeared to have lost the faculty of intelligent and attentive observation. (Quoted in Fulton, 1951, p. 21)

You may be thinking how wonderful it would have been if these observations had been made prior to subjecting humans to a similar procedure. Well, Ferrier's observations were made in 1875! The dangers of lobotomy were later reported by the famous experimental psychologist Harry Harlow in 1948. Essentially, Harlow exposed lobotomized monkeys to a battery of different learning tasks and concluded his study by suggesting that the animals showed deficits in several of the learning tasks.

Apparently, studies that cast doubt on the value of the lobotomy did not compromise Moniz's chances for winning the Nobel prize that had escaped him before. In 1949, one year after the publication of Harlow's findings, Moniz was awarded the coveted honor because the technique seemed to be more effective than sedatives when used on schizophrenia patients. Shortly after this time, however, frontal lobotomies stopped being so freely used. As you will read in Chapter 7, a more refined lobotomy (a smaller lesion in an anesthetized patient in the context of a fully operational surgical facility) is currently used as a last resort for treating obsessive-compulsive disorder.

IMPORTANCE OF A THERAPEUTIC ENVIRONMENT

A great deal of interesting research linked the brain with mental illness. The observation that biological therapies could be used to treat patients suffering from various forms of mental illness validated the use of biological therapy. Still, the field of clinical neuroscience is an interdisciplinary endeavor. This section addresses the role of the environment in therapy for mental illness.

Phillipe Pinel and the Fall of the Asylum

One of the first physicians to write about the importance of environment to mentally ill patients was the French psychiatrist Philippe Pinel (1745–1826). In 1793, this young doctor was asked to direct the operations of the Bicêtre hospice. He became famous the same year when he asked to have the chains removed from the patients. Two years later Pinel became the director of the Salpetrière (hospital where Charcot studied

[Box 2.3]

A Case in Point

The Couple Who Needed Each Other Like a Hole in the Head

In 1965, Joe Mellen, a London publisher and art dealer, had a life-changing conversation with Bart Huges, a research librarian who lived in Amsterdam. The topic of this conversation was Huges's idea that there is an intimate relationship between consciousness and the volume of blood in the brain, or "blood-brain volume," as he called it. Similar to the trepanning described on page 61 of this chapter, Huges actually drilled a hole in his own skull. He felt more relaxed after the trepanation, which led him to write a book entitled *Trepanation: The Cure for Psychosis*. As discussed in his book, trepanations enable us to go back to the time of infancy when the soft spot, or fontanel, in the skull led to a greater blood-brain volume. Once the skull hardens, according to this book, the pulsation decreases, robbing the brain of the appropriate amount of blood.

Because he felt that "life as an adult was rather flat, dull, and uphill," Huges's friend Joe Mellon was also eager to expand his mind by trepanning. As recounted in his book *Bore Hole*, Mellon's trepanation experience was nothing short of a fiasco. After consuming a dose of LSD and making the incision in his scalp, he could not cut through his skull. Following several subsequent botched attempts, Mellon finally tried an electric surgical drill and was at long last able to drill a hole through his skull. He reported feeling more energy and less self-consciousness just a few hours after his trepanation.

After seeing the benefits in Mellon, Mellon's companion, Amanda Fielding, decided that she wanted the procedure as well. Because she was unable to find a doctor to perform a trepanation, she decided to do it

herself. Mellon was at her side during the procedure, filming every gory detail of her experience for a video documentary that would later be entitled *Heartbeat in the Brain* (definitely not a film for the faint of heart).

Wearing a white robe, Amanda drills a hole in her skull and then wraps her head with a bandage, eerily smiling at the camera through the whole experience. She also reported psychological benefits shortly after the trepanation; she went out to eat and then to a party that very evening. Giving new meaning to the notion of holy matrimony, Mellon and Fielding stayed together for several years. They ran an art gallery in London and had two sons (neither of whom wants a trepanation). Several years later the couple split up, and Fielding married Lord James Neidpath, a former professor at Oxford. After their marriage, Neidpath traveled to Cairo where they found a surgeon willing to cut open his head for $2000. He, too, reports that the effects of the trepanation have been beneficial.

Just in case you are thinking that there may be something to this hole story, it is important to look at the procedure from another perspective. Although trepanning has been around for thousands of years, the artifacts suggest that, like now, this procedure was typically done to relieve pressure in a swelling or injured brain. Neurosurgeons agree that this process could result in blood clots, injuries, and infections that could easily lead to death. Scientists tell us that blood flow, not volume, is critical for the brain's functioning, and that trepanation in a normal brain would fail to affect blood flow.

But what about the positive effects reported? Any student who has had a course in research methodology would recognize that Mellon and friends were most likely experiencing a **placebo effect.** They believed that the procedure would work, and consequently, they experienced some benefit.

---

hysterical women) and ordered the removal of the chains from those patients as well. He went on to publish a textbook in 1801 in which he advocated the asylum as a place where a therapeutic environment could be used to strengthen patients' faculties so that they could be returned to society. Pinel was observed to put his words into practice; he is said to have been endearing with his patients—calming them with warm baths and organizing interesting activities to fill the many idle hours of the day. Because of his practices, Pinel is considered the father of modern psychiatry by many in the field.

Pinel and others envisioned the asylum as a place that would offer a healing environment for patients suffering from mental illness, but this goal was not met. Asylums became larger and larger. By the time of World War I, asylums had become vast warehouses for patients suffering from mental illness. Back in 1800, the number of beds in the more well-known asylums, such as Bedlam in England, was limited to hundreds. A hundred years later, there were 150,000 patients in mental hospitals in the United States alone. In a mere century's time, the confinement of psychiatric patients to an asylum or mental hospital went from being an unusual tactic done as a last resort to society's initial response when confronted with the slightest hint of psychotic illness. This problem is epitomized by the Georgia State Sanatorium in Milledgeville, Georgia. Its 10,000 beds made it the largest mental hospital in existence in 1950. As charted in Figure 2.9, the number of patients in mental hospitals in the United States has drastically decreased since the mid-1950s.

placebo effect Term used to describe a therapeutic effect resulting from the consumption of a physiologically inactive substance (for example, a sugar pill or some other unrelated treatment); used as evidence for mind–body communications.

classical conditioning Basic form of associative learning originally studied by Ivan Pavlov; involves pairing a neutral stimulus with an unconditioned stimulus known to automatically evoke a response so that, eventually, the neutral stimulus will lead to the behavior originally produced by the unconditioned stimulus.

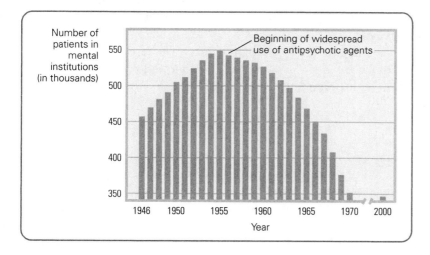

[Figure 2.9]
At its peak, the resident population in U.S. public mental hospitals exceeded half a million patients. The steep decline in patient populations since the mid-1950s is attributed to a growing reliance on the use of antipsychotic medications.

Behaviorism: A Different Type of Therapeutic Environment

The notion of providing a therapeutic environment in mental hospitals did not survive through the twentieth century. A different twist on environmental manipulation began to emerge as the asylums were becoming a hopeless dead end. The landmark **classical conditioning** studies of

[Figure 2.10]
The interlocking arms of physiologist Ivan Pavlov, who created classical conditioning, and Harvard medical researcher Walter Cannon, who coined the term *fight or flight* for the body's response to stress, preview interactions to come. Today, clinical neuroscience embraces brain–body interrelationships. Hobson (1999) recounts the scientists' meeting, pictured here, as Pavlov arrived in Boston after a harrowing journey from New York.
COLLECTION OF J. A. HOBSON

behaviorism Theory advocated by J. B. Watson calling for a shift of emphasis in the field of psychology from unconscious processes to the empirical manipulation of environmental stimuli and observable responses.

the Russian physiologist Ivan Pavlov (1849–1936) in the early twentieth century marked the beginning of this new therapeutic approach (Figure 2.10).

Everyone knows that a dog will salivate in response to food being placed in its mouth. Pavlov took this very simple observation and designed an elegant study that would literally change the face of psychology. He simply presented the dogs with a neutral stimulus, such as a tone or the proverbial bell, before presenting the food to the dogs. His dogs formed an association between the tone (the conditioned stimulus) and the food (the unconditioned stimulus), so eventually the dogs would salivate on hearing the tone.

Pavlov's work gave the field of experimental psychology, which was desperately looking for an empirical approach to understanding mental events, new hope for becoming a respectable science of the mind. Following the establishment of one of the first psychological laboratories in Leipzig, Germany, around 1879 by Wilhelm Wundt, another psychology pioneer, the Harvard professor William James wrote a textbook of psychology, published in 1890. The work of Wundt and James played a significant role in the establishment of experimental psychology in the United States.

The field of psychology, though, quickly wandered from its intended experimental roots and Pavlov's work was viewed as a means to return to the desired experimental rigor. J. B. Watson (1878–1958), a southern-educated, charismatic, emerging leader in the discipline of psychology took special interest in Pavlov's work. In a famous speech entitled "Psychology as the Behaviorist Views It" in 1913, Watson suggested that the entire field of psychology needed to focus on the empirical manipulation of environmental stimuli and observable responses, or **behaviorism,** as modeled by the great Dr. Pavlov.

What does this trip down the memory lane of behaviorism have to do with mental illness? Toward the end of Pavlov's career, he experimented with presenting his dogs with ambiguous stimuli. Animals that had been trained to associate a circle with a food reward and an ellipse with a mild shock, for example, became extremely agitated (a condition Pavlov called *experimental neurosis*) when presented with an ambiguous oval stimulus, intermediate between the circle and the ellipse.

Pavlov's classical conditioning procedure is adaptive for animals and humans in that different conditioned stimuli enable us to predict the occurrence of other stimuli in our environments (for example, lightning usually presages thunder). Emotional problems can arise when an animal or person loses the sense of control over environmental stimuli, as was the case with the dogs and the ambiguous stimuli. In another application of classical conditioning to mental illness, Watson conducted a study in which he prompted a toddler (the famous Little Albert) to associate a harmless white rat with a loud noise, creating an intense fear, or phobia, of white rats in the little boy. In this study, which is considered unethical today, Watson provided evidence that emotions such as anxiety can be learned through the environment.

Perhaps the most relevant of the observations that environmental changes may have some therapeutic value for the mentally ill were contributed by Mary Cover Jones (1896–1987) in 1920. Jones had worked with Watson and became interested in developing a strategy to use the environment to treat fears and phobias instead of creating them. In her most famous case, a little boy, Peter, came to her with an intense fear of rabbits. She reduced this fear by encouraging him to engage in relaxing, enjoyable activities, while she slowly introduced a rabbit into the environmental setting. Jones was desensitizing little Peter to the presence of the rabbit: his fear in the presence of rabbits was slowly being replaced with feelings of relaxation and pleasure in the presence of rabbits. This early application of behavior modification would become a powerful tool in treating various symptoms in patients suffering from mental illnesses such as phobias (Schultz & Schultz, 2000).

Beyond Behaviorism: Rethinking the Role of Mental Processes in Mental Health

With behaviorism, the face of psychology changed from its original emphasis on conscious processes to an emphasis on observable events in the environment. In 1963, 50 years after the publication of the landmark article by J. B. Watson calling for a change toward behaviorism, Harvard behaviorist B. F. Skinner, a pioneer in operant conditioning, wrote an article describing how behaviorism had contributed to tremendous progress in the field of psychology (Skinner, 1963). In a sense, psychology had lost its mind in this transformation, a change many psychologists considered good. As you may suspect, though, not all psychologists were willing to completely dismiss the importance of mental functions.

Albert Bandura (1925–present) was one disgruntled psychologist who was not willing to throw out the pursuit of mental abilities. Although he valued the inclusion of observable behavioral and environmental events, he was not comfortable ignoring the influence these events had on thought processes such as beliefs and expectations. After conducting a classic series of studies showing that young children learn to be

social learning theory Theory proposed by Albert Bandura emphasizing the importance of observations of models in social situations and how observations can lead to learning without direct exposure to a reinforcer.

self-efficacy Term proposed by Albert Bandura to describe a person's assessment of his or her competence in dealing with life's problems.

internal/external locus of control Components of a theory proposed by Julian Rotter that emphasized the importance of one's perception of his or her source of control in life—either within the individual or in the environment.

aggressive simply by observing an aggressive model, Bandura had empirical support for his theory that learning could occur without an individual receiving direct reinforcement from the environment. Bandura later introduced the term **social learning theory** to emphasize how learning occurs following the observation of models in social situations. Consequently, models have become a component of behavior modification therapy: individuals are exposed to models demonstrating desired behavioral responses to certain stimuli (snake, bully, or dog).

Later, Bandura continued his emphasis on more cognitive factors and introduced the term **self-efficacy**—one's sense of self-worth and efficiency or competence in dealing with life's problems—into the psychology literature. Extensive work has been conducted on the self-efficacy measure; relevant to this text, individuals high in self-efficacy measures have better physical and mental health than their lower self-efficacy counterparts (Bandura, 1997).

Another psychologist who was not comfortable with radical behaviorism was Julian Rotter (1916–present). Rotter's world changed drastically in his early teens when his well-to-do father lost his business at the beginning of the 1929 depression. He later wrote that this environmental event "began in me a lifelong concern with social injustice and provided me with a powerful lesson on how personality and behavior were affected by situational conditions" (Rotter, 1993, p. 274).

Rotter went on to become an accomplished psychologist. Like Bandura, he accepted certain aspects of behaviorism but disagreed with the total exclusion of mental, or cognitive, processes. Like the radical behaviorists, he believed that behavior was determined by external stimuli and by reinforcement. But Rotter maintained that the ultimate influence these factors have on behavior is actually determined by a person's cognitive processes. For example, we place different values on reinforcers—you may place considerable value on a chocolate reinforcer, but this form of reward is not powerful for your friend who is allergic to chocolate or who just doesn't like sweets.

Rotter also emphasized that our beliefs about the source of reinforcers play a powerful role in our behavior. People who believe that reinforcement depends on their own behavior are described as having an **internal locus of control** whereas those who believe that reinforcement depends on environmental, or outside, forces such as fate or other people, are described as having an **external locus of control.** Accordingly, a student who responds to a bad grade on an exam by modifying his or her study strategy has an internal locus of control. A student who responds to the bad grade by claiming that his or her performance on the next test depends on whether the professor gives a "fair" test is operating with an external locus of control. Subsequent research has shown that individuals with an internal locus of control are at less risk for heart attacks and have less anxiety and depression than their external locus of control counterparts (Schultz & Schultz, 2000).

Self-efficacy and locus of control are unexpected topics in a neuroscience text, but they illustrate beautifully the need for integrated approaches to mental health. Rotter's and Bandura's work helps us understand how mental functions influence the brain's functions and alter our homeostasis to either reduce or increase toxic symptoms that may lead to illnesses, such as cardiovascular disease or depression. Obviously, identifying mental strategies that alter neurobiological functioning and subsequently mental and physiological health further supports the integrated brain–body approach to mental health.

PROFILING THE PIONEERS OF CLINICAL NEUROSCIENCE

Let's take a step back and look at the personal characteristics of the impressive scientists and physicians we've discussed. Are there any common denominators among the complex lives of the great contributors to this field? In his book entitled *Minds Behind the Brain* (2000), Stanley Finger, a historian of neuroscience, asks that very question. He conducted an informal analysis of some of the historical figures (including Galen, Santiago Ramón y Cajal, Camillo Golgi, Paul Broca, Charles Scott Sherrington, and Otto Loewi) and found some interesting similarities.

Educationally, the giants of clinical neuroscience had cultured parents who sought the best educational opportunities for their children. The neuroscientists did not conclude their education on graduation; in fact, the end of formal education marked the true beginning of their learning. They settled in cities that provided environments full of cultural and educational opportunities and embarked on lifelong journeys of discovery. Perhaps this lifelong love of discovery was the most important characteristic the scientists shared.

As you think about the lives of these individuals you may envision the stereotypical "nerdy" scientist who shows little interest in anything outside the laboratory, but the scientists Finger describes are far from stereotypical. They were likely to be married and have children and were even actively engaged in the fine arts. For example, Sherrington loved the poetry of Keats, Ramón y Cajal was an artist, Loewi wanted to study art history. Charcot, who was a painter himself, was a fan of the French Impressionists and loved to listen to the music of Mozart and Beethoven.

He even looked to Shakespeare as the unrivaled master of understanding the complex mental lives of humans. More recently, Eric Kandel, the featured investigator in this chapter, started his academic career in the humanities—far from the scientific laboratories that would lead him to the Nobel prize.

Perhaps the most obvious similarity among the individuals included in this chapter is their gender. Aside from the behaviorist Mary Cover Jones, the researchers introduced here all were men. Admittedly, male bias has influenced past scientific and medical research. Women are better represented in clinical neuroscience today, poised to contribute to research advances in a new century.

Summary

Emergence of the Brain as the Controlling Center of Behavior, Emotion, and Thought

The ancient Greeks had long believed that the heart was the controlling center of the body when Hippocrates introduced the notion that the brain controls behavior. His theory that mental illness could be treated by restoring balance to the four humors of the body constituted one of the earliest biological theories of mental functioning.

Galen dissected numerous animal brains and proposed that animal spirits in the brain enable the body to transmit sensations and to move. Descartes went on to suggest that these animal spirits are housed in the pineal gland, traveling through ventricles and nerves to initiate movement in the muscles.

Once it was established that the brain plays a role in orchestrating the functions of the body and mind, researchers tried to find out whether specific areas of the brain have specific functions (localization of function). Willis's initial work with animal brains suggested that the cerebral hemispheres are involved in higher functions, the corpus striatum is involved in movement, and the lower brain stem is involved in basic physiological functions such as respiration. Gall's phrenology stimulated further interest in the localization of function.

Paul Broca, for example, discovered that an area in the left frontal lobe was involved in the production of speech.

Before the nervous system could be fully understood, the nature of the individual units, or neurons, had to be identified and described. Golgi's discovery of a silver stain for the neuron enabled researchers such as Cajal to describe the structure of different types of neurons. Cajal's work also provided evidence that each neuron is an individual unit, thus casting doubt on the existing nerve net theory. Sherrington's description of the junction between neurons, the synapse, also supported the neuronal doctrine.

Using frogs, Loewi discovered that the neurons communicate with one another via the release and reception of specific chemicals. Research conducted by investigators like Dale subsequently showed that certain drugs that influence the nervous system do so by acting similar to the nervous system's natural chemicals, or neurotransmitters. This research set the stage for the field of psychopharmacology.

Finally, Adrian's all-or-none law provided information about how neurochemicals stimulate the neurons and how neurons, once stimulated, transmit information to the next neuron.

Neurological Approaches to Mental Illness

In an attempt to integrate neuroscience and psychiatry, Kraepelin organized an impressive group of neuroscientists, including Alzheimer, who discovered the neuropathology of the dementia that bears his name, and Nissl, a histologist who described the six layers of the cortex. Kraepelin went on to categorize mental illnesses so that they could be studied more efficiently.

Charcot also attempted to describe the various neurological conditions by observing patients and conducting autopsies of brains. His work led to findings that contributed to understanding mental disorders such as Parkinson's disease and Tourette's syndrome. In the later part of his career, Charcot focused on patients exhibiting "hysterical" symptoms that had no obvious physical cause.

Biological Therapies for Mental Illness

In the later part of the nineteenth century, findings suggested that biological therapies might have significant value in treating mental illness. Encouraging results from induced fevers and insulin coma fueled research to identify less dangerous biological interventions. Ultimately, electroconvulsive shock therapy, psychosurgery (especially lobotomies), and certain drugs showed promise as biological therapies.

Importance of a Therapeutic Environment

Pinel emphasized the importance of a therapeutic environment for the treatment of patients suffering from mental illness. Attempts to humanize the conditions in asylums as well as to incorporate classical conditioning techniques have led to the development of treatments such as behavioral modification. More recently, cognitive approaches (for example, determination of locus of control and self-efficacy) have been incorporated into behavioral therapies.

Profiling the Pioneers of Clinical Neuroscience

Focusing on the lives of the significant figures featured in this chapter, a few common denominators can be found among their professional and personal lives. Many loved the arts and humanities as well as being passionate about neuroscience.

Key Terms

humoral theory (p. 38)
craniotomy (p. 38)
experiment (p. 40)
ventricles (p. 40)
reflex (p. 41)
mind–body problem (p. 41)
dualism (p. 42)
localization of function (p. 42)
cerebral cortex (p. 45)
correlation (p. 45)
phrenology (p. 45)
histology (p. 48)
nerve net theory (p. 48)

neuron (p. 49)
neuron doctrine (p. 50)
synapse (p. 50)
neurotransmitter (p. 52)
nerve impulse (action potential) (p. 52)
all-or-none law (p. 52)
transduction (p. 53)
dementia (p. 55)
schizophrenia (p. 55)
hysteria (p. 56)
psychoanalysis (p. 56)
coma therapy (p. 59)

electroconvulsive therapy (ECT) (p. 59)
barbiturates (p. 60)
psychopharmacology (p. 60)
trepanning (p. 61)
lobotomy (p. 61)
placebo effect (p. 65)
classical conditioning (p. 65)
behaviorism (p. 66)
social learning theory (p. 68)
self-efficacy (p. 68)
internal locus of control (p. 68)
external locus of control (p. 68)

For Further Consideration

Unlike research included in other chapters in this text, many original historical sources are unavailable or difficult to obtain; for this reason, we were fortunate to have access to many wonderful contemporary accounts of the intriguing stories that are included in this chapter such as the ones recommended below.

Finger, S. (2000). *Minds behind the brain*. New York: Oxford University Press. Finger tells the life stories of 19 key figures in the history of neuroscience. The idea for this book came from the interest that Dr. Finger's students had in the behind-the-scenes details surrounding the landmark discoveries in neuroscience. Finger tells us that Descartes, who spoke of animals as beast machines, actually had a dog named Monsieur Grat (Mr. Scratch), and that David Ferrier, a groundbreaking neuroscientist who located certain motor and sensory functions in the cerebral cortex during the 1870s, was arrested after being accused of animal abuse by militant animal rights activists. Additionally, Finger describes the personal characteristics of the pioneers of neuroscience that helped them to persevere with their new theories at a time when other leading authorities in the field were advocating opposing theories.

Finger, S. (1994). *Origins of neuroscience: A history of explorations into brain function*. New York: Oxford University Press. Finger documents the history of neuroscience from the ancient Egyptians, Greeks, and Romans to the twentieth century. Covering topics such as sensory systems, motor systems, intellect and memory, cerebral dominance, and treatments and therapies, Finger reports the details of the discoveries of the brain. More than 350 illustrations help to bring the history of neuroscience to life.

Kandel, E. R., & Squire, L. R. (2000). *Neuroscience: Breaking down scientific barriers to the study of brain and mind. Science, 290*, 1113–1120. This is a wonderful brief overview of the history of brain science. It does an especially good job of placing the cellular and molecular discoveries into the context of the broader brain sciences. A timeline with pictures of the history-making scientists is a valuable tool for students of the history of neuroscience.

Shorter, E. (1997). *A History of Psychiatry*. New York: Wiley. Shorter is a historian, and he covers the changing perspectives in the field of psychiatry from a sociological and historical point of view. Shorter's thorough coverage of the influential figures in the field of brain science, psychiatry, and psychology paints a vivid picture of the many views and explanations of mental illness that have been introduced over the past three centuries.

Chapter Three

Macroanatomy and the Dynamic Brain

Connections

Brain Plasticity in *Evolutionary* and in *Real* Time

A major theme throughout this text is the dynamic, adaptive nature, or **plasticity,** of the brain. In Chapter One you learned that enriched environments lead to a thicker cortex and increased neural connections. Research currently being conducted by Leah Krubitzer at the University of California at Davis shows clearly that the functional areas of the cortex have assumed many different shapes, sizes, and positions throughout their evolution.

Committed to unlocking nature's grand design for cortical development, Krubitzer and her students are using histological analyses and neurophysiological recording to map the functional and neuroanatomical cortical areas of a vast array of mammals including hedgehogs, mice, squirrels, flying foxes, sheep, rhesus monkeys, marmosets, and yes, even humans. It seems a daunting task to try to understand how the cortex changed from such a small size in the earliest mammals to its generous size in humans. But Krubitzer is taking creative approaches to manipulate cortical development in mammals to try to under-

stand the different developmental paths taken as successive species climbed the phylogenetic tree.

One current project in the Krubitzer laboratory is investigating the evolution of our ability to explore and manipulate the world around us with our hands. In addition to the involvement of the motor cortex in the fine control of hand movement, other specialized areas of the cortex must contribute sensory information about tactile, positional, and visual information to gain such impressive control over an individual's hands.

It probably comes as no surprise that the cortex has the ability to change over millions, thousands, even hundreds of years. But from a therapeutic point of view, you may be thinking that it's more important to know how plastic the brain is in "real" time, or over the course of an individual's life.

The case of 40-year-old Australian Brett Neilsen suggests considerable cortical reorganization is possible within an individual's lifetime. During an interview with Brett, his behaviors—smoking a cigarette, drinking coffee, playing with his hair, and patting his dog Tara—are by no means atypical; however, considering that he does all this with his toes suggests considerable

Brett Neilsen at work in his studio.
(BRETT NEILSEN)

restructuring of his motor cortex. Brett was the first Australian baby born with the effects of Thalidomide, a drug withdrawn from use 40 years ago due to its role in causing several birth defects—in Brett's case, being born with no arms. Due to his persistence to engage in "normal" behaviors, Brett can carry out an impressive array of tasks. He taught himself to play the piano with his feet at age 12. Currently, he is a successful composer, recording artist, and filmmaker and has his own music production company named Big Toe Productions. And when he's out of the studio, he's busy being a parent to two children, mentor for children with no arms, a backhoe operator, and a motivational speaker (James, 2003; Ostrow, 2003; Wyllie, 2002).

Brett's apparent cortical reorganization during prenatal development is impressive, but what about the brain's ability to reorganize itself following maturation? The case of 24-year-old Barbara Guerra provides evidence that this is possible as well. When Barbara was 2 years old, she grabbed an electrical transformer while playing in the yard, and several thousand volts of electricity surged through her arms, eventually exiting from her thighs. She lost both arms and had to face the rest of her childhood learning how to manage without the arms and hands to which so much cortical tissue in her brain was already devoted.

Barbara's mother avoided doing everything for her and pushed her to learn to manipulate her environment with her feet. (Brett's parents acted similarly.) Today Barbara is the single mom of two young boys and is able to bathe her sons, change diapers, and dress and feed them—all with her feet. She plays the piano, swims, drives, eats with a fork, cooks, answers her cell phone, and even brushes her hair—again, using her feet (Thorpe, 2002).

Where is the empirical evidence for real-time cortical reorganization observed in cases such as Brett's and Barbara's? Currently we don't have neuroimaging data to support observations of reorganized cortices. However, it happens that Krubitzer's former mentor at Vanderbilt University, John Kaas, has investigated this very question in the squirrel monkey. Following therapeutic amputation of the forearm, the deprived cortex is subsequently stimulated to determine the surgery's effects. Interestingly, areas of the body adjacent to the amputated limb (e.g., shoulder, stump, trunk) all move, providing evidence of neuroanatomical reorganization. Thus, the area of the cortex once assigned to the movement of the arm is capable of moving other body parts following forearm removal (Wu & Kass, 1999, 2002).

Thus, there is overwhelming evidence that the cortex is a dynamic brain structure that doesn't get too comfortable in any evolutionary position, always leaving the door open for adaptations to changing circumstances. Ongoing research illuminating more secrets about cortical reorganization offers hope for the many individuals suffering from impaired nervous systems and/or bodies. If science can facilitate this reorganization, the possibilities for recovery of function are staggering.

The brain is a benevolent tyrant. Its subjects are the entire extent and breadth of the body, virtually every cell. Still, the brain itself is an amalgam of interacting structures that regulate behavior. This neural concert has served us well, sweeping up in its breadth both the minutiae and magnitude of our existence. There is control of internal activities together with simultaneous observance of external sensory stimuli. There is coordination of maintenance activities necessary for existence and the rapid response to an ever-changing world. And there is recognition of the role of the past in shaping behaviors yet to be performed. From millisecond to millisecond, hour to hour, day to day, the brain processes its sensory input and makes decisions that become its motor output, that is, behavior.

How does the brain maintain its own level of activity and that of the body? How does it monitor and regulate internal processes while simultaneously tracking the external environment? By understanding the architecture of the nervous system, we can begin to address a full range of behavior and how disruptions in the nervous system lead to clinical disorders. Whether the information in this chapter is new to you or just a refresher on the brain's macroanatomy, it will serve as a reference later, as you explore the clinical disorders presented throughout the book.

GROSS STRUCTURE AND FUNCTION OF THE NERVOUS SYSTEM

The two primary divisions of the nervous system in the mammal are the **central nervous system (CNS),** comprising the brain and the spinal cord, and the **peripheral nervous system (PNS)**—all the nervous tissue outside the CNS. The CNS largely regulates the PNS. The PNS does not per se regulate CNS activity; rather, it transmits sensorimotor information (Figure 3.1). Information about sensory stimuli moving from the periphery toward the brain is called **afferent** (to carry toward) **information;** motor information moving from the CNS to the periphery is referred to as **efferent** (to carry away from) **information.**

Neurons are the building blocks of the nervous system. Clusters of neurons, observed through a variety of staining techniques, form functional units within the brain called **nuclei.** As detailed in Chapters Four and Five, projecting fibers (*axons*) link neurons into communications networks. Bundles of these fibers, called **tracts** or **fiber pathways,** run like the cables from your stereo to your loudspeakers within the CNS. Tracts outside the CNS are termed **nerves.** As you are reading this text, your optic nerve, for instance, is carrying information about changes in light patterns to the back of your brain where the information is de-coded into meaningful images.

plasticity Inherent flexibility of the brain in responding to environmental changes; for example, by learning or to compensate for loss of function to damaged areas.

central nervous system (CNS) One of the two main divisions of the human nervous system, consisting of the brain and spinal cord; the main coordinating and controlling center of the body that processes information to and from the peripheral nervous system.

peripheral nervous system (PNS) One of the two divisions of the human nervous system, consisting of the sensory and motor nerves outside of the brain and spinal cord (12 pairs of cranial nerves and 31 pairs of spinal nerves).

afferent information Information carried inward toward the brain.

efferent information Information carried outward from the CNS to the periphery.

nuclei Functional collections of neurons in specific brain regions; can be identified by histological techniques.

tract (also called **fiber pathway**) Bundle of axons within the CNS that traverses long distances and connects different parts of the brain (distal) or is relatively short (local) and connects close-in nuclei and groups of neurons.

nerve Cordlike collection of nerve fibers outside the brain and spinal cord; conveys information to and from the CNS and the periphery.

[Figure 3.1]
The human nervous system is organized and subdivided into efficient modules that can respond and attend to the flow of external and internal information.

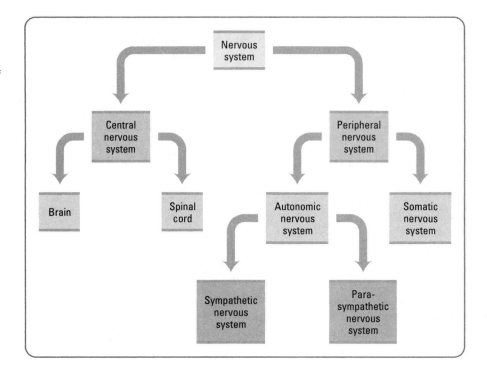

Organization of the Peripheral Nervous System

Anatomists subdivide the PNS into a voluntary component, the **somatic nervous system (SNS),** and an involuntary component, the **autonomic nervous system (ANS),** as shown in Figure 3.1. The somatic component includes sensory nerve projections that transmit information from the skin to the CNS (the skin is the largest human information sensor, covering, as it does, the entire body) and motor nerves that control the movement of the skeletal muscles. The ANS is involuntary because it largely regulates and maintains internal activities and organs beyond the ken or control of the person (Figure 3.2). Its innervation of the endocrine glands, gastrointestinal and vascular organs, and their accompanying sensations make the ANS integral to activities that are considered vegetative, or necessary to the organism's survival.

Just imagine how overwhelming it would be to have to monitor your heart rate, blood pressure, immune function, or digestive processes. It is not important to "know" and monitor each item, but their control is critical to your survival. Hence, the ANS, which typically operates without overt control but is sensitive to the demands of facing and overcoming a challenge, is capable of rapid sensitivity and on-the-fly responsiveness.

somatic nervous system (SNS) Voluntary part of the peripheral nervous system that controls the movement of skeletal muscles or transmits somatosensory information to the central nervous system.

autonomic nervous system (ANS) Maintenance component of the nervous system, composed of sympathetic and parasympathetic divisions.

ANS and Homeostasis

The ANS epitomizes the principle of homeostasis, or physiological balance, within our bodies. This balance must be struck between the perpetual demand for reparative and restorative activities that maintain the body and the ability to effectively manage an immediate threat to survival. The balance is struck between the two subdivisions of the ANS shown in Figure 3.2, the **sympathetic nervous system** that regulates arousal and the **parasympathetic nervous system** that maintains internal homeostasis via feedback and control processes within the nervous and endocrine systems. Following is an illustration of how these complementary systems work.

sympathetic nervous system Arousing component of the autonomic nervous system.

parasympathetic nervous system Maintenance component of the autonomic nervous system.

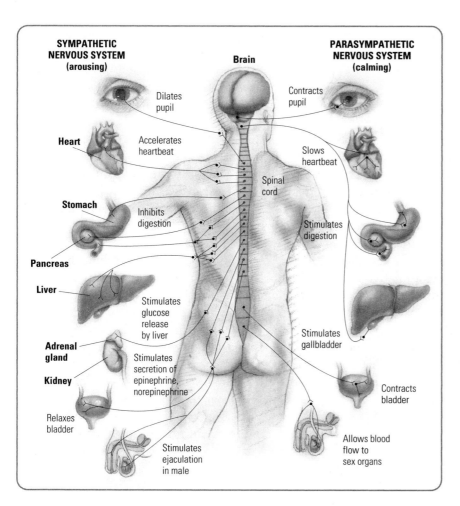

[Figure 3.2]
The sympathetic and parasympathetic divisions of the Autonomic nervous system largely innervate the same structures and organs, though they control very different forms of activity. The sympathetic system arouses the body to defend itself against a threat; the parasympathetic system calms the body post-threat and maintains homeostatic functioning during nonthreatening times.

Imagine that you are driving down the road one afternoon, relaxed, enjoying the scenery and the CD you just slipped into your stereo. Under these conditions you are utilizing the somatic nervous system to take in the sensory world and control the steering wheel, the stereo, and the gas and brake pedals. Because of your relaxed demeanor, the parasympathetic nervous system is regulating your visceral functions—maintaining your heart rate, glandular secretions, and even the digestion of the bagel you ate for breakfast.

You decide to change the CD, and as you look up you realize that the car in front of you has slammed on its brakes. For a fearful moment, you are sure you will crash. Within milliseconds, your sympathetic nervous system is activated—increasing your cardiovascular output, converting stored energy into a usable form, and inhibiting the diversion of energy toward long-term investments such as digestion, growth, or reproduction (Habib et al., 2001). You sharply and reflexively turn the steering wheel, thereby avoiding the slowing car. And, although it takes a while to wear off, a period of time that is different for every individual, eventually you start to calm down and focus once again on driving. At this point, the parasympathetic nervous system reestablishes physiological homeostasis. The transition occurs smoothly, like a car downshifting, and the system resets.

The stress response described in this example comes closest to being a common denominator or at least a shared, contributing circumstance in virtually every disorder in this text. For example, stressful stimuli are associated with a neural fear circuit in anxiety disorders (Chapter Seven). Mood disorders are characterized by an altered stress response, and environmental stressors may modulate these disorders (Chapter Eight). Stressful situations may trigger schizophrenia (Chapter Nine). And stress can exacerbate the onset and reinstatement of a brain circuit that influences addictive behaviors (Chapter Ten).

Strategies for maintaining homeostasis in the face of stress, which are critical to physical and psychological well-being, are discussed in Chapters Eleven through Thirteen. It is a knife's edge on which the organism is perched, for falling too far to the sympathetic nervous system side depletes necessary energy stores, whereas remaining in parasympathetic nervous system stasis in the face of a threat tempts disaster. Each side needs the other, as teeter needs totter. Among the topics in Part Four are the role of the sympathetic nervous system in stress responsivity and in coping styles and strategies, the intimate relationship between stress and the immune and digestive systems, and how the stress response is linked to one's susceptibility to disease.

Development of the Central Nervous System

The brain and spinal cord are striking in their complexity and elegance, as are the care and protection afforded them by the skull and backbone. The skull is light yet durable, inert but alive. Under microscopic examination the bone appears as a series of spidery arches, interwoven with geometrically intricate openings that provide enhanced structural support and protection.

The skull and backbone absorb a lifetime of insults directed at the soft masses that lie beneath them, blows that would otherwise exact a steep price in mental and physical function. However, despite its sturdy protection, the CNS today is at the mercy of our technology, which threatens to outstrip our evolutionary progress. The brain and spinal cord and their protective and recuperative systems evolved over millions of years and have yet to—and probably never will—catch up to our ability to damage them.

Consider the limitless ways propulsive or accelerative damage can be inflicted. Bullets, explosives, fast cars, and contact sports are examples of the dangers posed by modern society. Just as our progenitors could never have envisioned today's technological innovations, so evolution could not prepare the CNS and its associated protective devices for the dangers introduced by technology. We must rely on the awareness and avoidance of such potential damage rather than on recovery from it.

Layers of protection. The skull and backbone, formidable barriers to injury and infection, are but the first line of defense for the CNS. A triple layer of connective tissue, the **meninges,** further protects and encloses the brain and spinal cord (Figure 3.3).

meninges Three connective tissue membranes (arachnoid, dura, pia mater) that protect and enclose the brain and spinal cord.

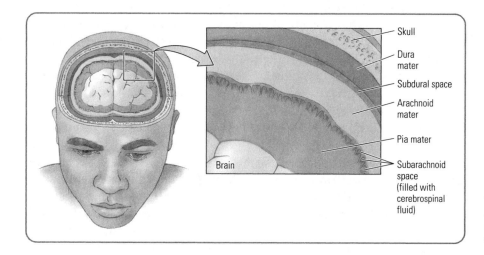

Skull

Dura mater

Subdural space

Arachnoid mater

Pia mater

Subarachnoid space (filled with cerebrospinal fluid)

Brain

[Figure 3.3]
The meninges are literally a skull-cap: shielding, protecting, and infusing with blood the fragile tissue underneath.

cerebrospinal fluid (CSF)
Normally clear, salty liquid produced in the ventricles, filling them and circulating around the brain in the subarachnoid layer of the meninges and central canal to nourish and protect the brain and spinal cord.

cerebral aqueduct Narrow tube interconnecting the third and fourth ventricles of the brain, located in the center of the mesencephalon.

central canal (also **spinal canal**) Pathway through the vertebral column for cerebral spinal fluid and the vertebral arteries.

The tough, light gray outer layer of the meninges, the *dura mater* ("hard mother"), resembles a vein-covered shower cap. It covers the brain and spinal cord and provides a spongy, cushioning protection. The middle layer of the meninges, the *arachnoid mater* ("spider "), is a thin sheet of tissue that adheres to the bottom of the dura mater. The space between them is called the *subdural space*. The inner layer, called the *pia mater* ("gentle mother"), is a relatively thin, nearly clear membrane that covers the surface of the brain and spinal cord and insinuates itself into every cerebral crevice.

The subarachnoid space between the arachnoid mater and the pia mater is filled with a salty, seawaterlike concoction called **cerebrospinal fluid (CSF)**. CSF is produced in the ventricles (described below) and circulates around the brain and spinal cord, bathing them and buffering them from external concussion. CSF simultaneously floats the brain and reduces its weight.

CSF resembles blood plasma in its salinity (~0.9%) and mineral make-up, and it is a source of information about the brain's metabolic and infection status. Close to 130 milliliters of CSF circulates in the closed system of the CNS each day. Should fluid pressure build within the brain, the CSF can depress its soft surface, damaging the delicate cortical tissues. In this scenario, the developing brain is at risk and a condition known as *hydrocephalus* ensues. An artificial opening or shunt must be made to remove the built-up pressure, or damage follows. Having too little CSF can be harmful as well, as anyone who has ever undergone a spinal tap can attest. Its removal can leave a fluid void that produces a spectacular headache in the patient.

Ventricular system. Literally "holes" in your head, the four ventricles in the brain are as integral to its activities as the aqueducts were to Roman society. Without them embryonic and fetal brain development would not occur, and adult activity would be severely curtailed. Further, the ventricles are an internal irrigation system capable of venting wastes and metabolic by-products.

The human body is essentially a long tube surrounded by tissues of varying complexities. The developing nervous system follows similar engineering principles. Early in our development the cells that go on to become the different parts of the nervous system proliferate, cell after cell. They fold over and around each other using the basic fluid-filled neural tube as a guide, utilizing the outward negative pressure. The cells grow around the ventricles, following a preprogrammed set of genetic instructions. Like a spelunker's dream, the ventricles eventually become enclosed and differentiate into separate, moderately sized caverns, connected to one another by a series of small-diameter channels (Figure 3.4).

The two lateral ventricles near the top of the brain spread into each of its two roughly symmetrical cerebral hemispheres. Beneath the lateral ventricles and connected by two thin, open rivulets is the third ventricle, which divides the brain into roughly symmetrical right and left halves. The third ventricle is continuous with the fourth by means of a thin conduit called the **cerebral aqueduct.**

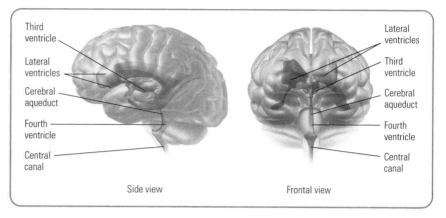

Third ventricle
Lateral ventricles
Cerebral aqueduct
Fourth ventricle
Central canal

Side view

Lateral ventricles
Third ventricle
Cerebral aqueduct
Fourth ventricle
Central canal

Frontal view

[Figure 3.4]
The ventricular system is like the brain's irrigation system, both providing the organ with nutrients and removing waste products.

The fourth ventricle shunts the CSF along in its circulation down through the spinal or **central canal** to the spinal cord, where it reenters the circulation. In fact, the ventricles operate like an astronaut's spacesuit, another closed, liquid-circulating system in which all wastes are excreted and subsequently recycled. From the ventricles, CSF is eventually absorbed by the bloodstream, filtered, recycled, and returned as metabolic constituents to the brain by means of its blood supply.

Geography of the developing brain. Just three to four weeks into its development (detailed in Chapter Six), the embryonic brain can be anatomically subdivided into the three main sectors shown in Figure 3.5a (page 82): the **prosencephalon** (forebrain), the **mesencephalon** (midbrain) and the **rhombencephalon** (hindbrain). Each division is defined by its order of embryonic development in relation to the ventricles.

As shown in Figure 3.5b, by seven weeks the forebrain has begun to differentiate into the **telencephalon** (endbrain) and the **diencephalon** (between brain). The diencephalon develops around the third ventricle into the structures that synthesize sensory information and regulate motivated behaviors, including the thalamus and hypothalamus. But what the average person conceives of as the human brain, the general image that comes to mind when the phrase "gray matter" is uttered, is what neuroanatomists call the telencephalon. It is also the organizing term for the subcortical structures that surround the lateral ventricles, and it is the most recent evolutionary addition to our brains. The telencephalic regions regulate such higher-order responses as cognition and forethought.

As the forebrain differentiates, the hindbrain also develops further into the *metencephalon* (across brain) and the *myelencephalon* (spinal brain), as shown in Figure 3.5b. The hindbrain, or brainstem, controls overall

prosencephalon Forebrain controlling sensation, perception, emotion, learning, thinking, and other intellectual functions; includes the olfactory bulb and tracts, cerebral hemispheres, nasal ganglia, thalamus, optic tracts, and hypothalamus.

mesencephalon Midbrain joining the brainstem and forebrain and serving as a passageway for impulses to higher brain centers.

rhombencephalon Hindbrain, or brainstem, that surrounds the fourth ventricle.

telencephalon "Endbrain" portion of the forebrain that includes the cerebral hemispheres, basal ganglia, olfactory bulb, and olfactory tracts.

diencephalon "Between" area of the forebrain that surrounds the third ventricle; includes the thalamus, hypothalamus, and pineal gland, structures that synthesize sensory information and regulate motivated behaviors.

movement, balance, and some vegetative functions. The midbrain (mesencephalon) is a small area separating the endbrain from the brainstem. Functionally, this middle brain area is involved in some sensory processing and basic attention and arousal processes. As we explore brain structure and function in the next section, we move from the evolutionarily older structures and more basic functions of the brainstem and midbrain to the newer components and higher-order activities of the human forebrain as diagrammed in Figure 3.5c.

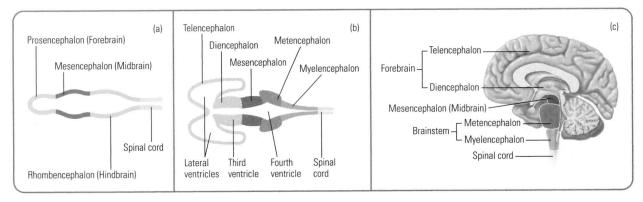

[Figure 3.5]
The brain's growth functions by incorporating early structures into the more complex organ it becomes.

CENTRAL NERVOUS SYSTEM STRUCTURE AND FUNCTION

To navigate around the brain, our first task is to orient ourselves (Figure 3.6). When locating structures in the nervous system, the term *neuraxis* (neural axis) describes a line from the spinal cord to the front of the brain. The orientation of the neuraxis depends on whether the animal in question walks upright on two legs, as do humans, or on all fours, like the rat. In the human, the brain and spinal cord are at right angles, as is the neuraxis. The rat's neuraxis is straight.

The top of the neuraxis is the *rostral* or *anterior* end. The bottom of this imaginary line is *caudal* or *posterior* end. The front of the human body, the face, stomach, knees and chin, is *ventral* to the neuraxis. The back is the *dorsal* region. Compare these orientations in humans and rats in Figure 3.6. Areas close to the middle of the body are *medial*, whereas those toward the periphery are *lateral*. Your nose and belly button are medial, your ears and love handles lateral, as are the rat's.

These anatomical terms orient an observer toward the body or brain structure of interest by its location on these three planes of reference. The names of numerous brain structures specify their location relative to the

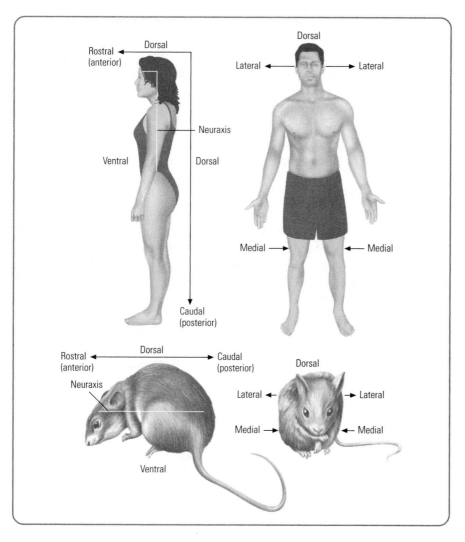

[Figure 3.6]
The terms for the anatomical and neuroanatomical orientation in humans (four-legged mammals) and rats (two-legged mammals) are dependent on the normal orientations of the body to the ground.

neuraxis (e.g., ventromedial hypothalamus, anterior pituitary). Bear in mind, though, that neuroscientists differ on how they organize the brain and may fail to agree on which structures are part of which subdivision. Further, new staining and imaging techniques are developed all the time. The information they reveal can actually shift structures into different regions. Thus, the brain's nomenclature is nearly as dynamic as its functions.

Brainstem

On September 10, 1945, Lloyd Olsen of Fruita, Colorado, went out to kill a chicken for dinner. He strategically positioned the ax at the back of the chicken's skull to please his visiting mother-in-law, who savored eating

Mike, the headless chicken. Most of the regulatory functions and basic behaviors of chickens are controlled by the brainstem.

BOB LANDRY/TIME LIFE PICTURES/
GETTY IMAGES

the neck. Once the ax fell and the five-month-old Wyandotte chicken lost its head, it scampered around awhile, typical of freshly beheaded chickens. Eerily though, the chicken kept on walking around long after it should have expired. Hours later, Mr. Olsen observed it sleeping with its now phantom head tucked under its wing, like a fowl demon of Ichabod Crane. Olsen decided that if the chicken had such a will to live, he would face down his disappointed mother-in-law and help it along.

He discovered that he could feed the bird with an eyedropper—placing feed and water in its esophagus—and took it to the University of Utah to be examined. Scientists determined that, because of the placement of the ax's blow, most of the brainstem remained intact. The cut missed the jugular vein, and a fortuitous blood clot had formed at just the right moment to keep the chicken from bleeding to death. Now known as "Mike, the Headless Chicken," the pullet went from rotisserie to notoriety. The Olsens soon realized that many people wanted to see this headless wonder, so they took the chicken on (and, presumably, across) the road. Mike traveled to New York, Atlantic City, Los Angeles, and San Diego, where people paid 25 cents apiece to see it. Mike was valued at $10,000 and highlighted in *Life* magazine ("Headless Chicken," 1945; "Quirk Fowl Play," 1999).

By all accounts, he seemed to thrive after losing his head—he gained 2.5 more pounds and lived 18 more months. He died while traveling in Arizona, choking on a kernel of corn. But Mike is not forgotten. Over half a century later, people gather in his hometown every third weekend of May for Mike the Headless Chicken Day. They celebrate Mike's will to live by eating chicken salad, playing pin-the-head-on-the-chicken, and participating in a clucking contest.

Mike's story celebrates the power of the brainstem (Figure 3.7). At the base of the head, the brainstem begins where the spinal cord enters the skull and extends into the mesencephalon. The brains of fish, frogs, and lizards are the basic equivalent of the brainstem and midbrain in mammals.

Medulla and basic survival. The **medulla oblongata** is a major regulatory site for basic vegetative or maintenance activities and the primary component of the myencephalon. Nuclei in the medulla regulate respiration and cardiovascular functions (e.g., heartbeat and blood pressure) and control muscle tone. Whereas damage to other brainstem structures is serious and of grave concern for the regulation of various behaviors, damage to the medulla is nearly always fatal.

The medulla sits at the lowest, or most caudal, portion of the brainstem and appears as a tiny bulge at the upper end of the spinal cord. It is a rich neural structure with multiple types of neurons and neurochemicals. Via its multiple fiber pathways for nerve impulses entering

medulla oblongata Lowest part of the brain stem;, an extension into the skull of the upper end of the spinal cord; regulates basic vegetative functioning.

and leaving the brain, the medulla directly controls signals to and from more rostral brain areas and the periphery of the body.

Cerebellum and motor control. The **cerebellum** (little brain) is among the most compact and complex brain structures. The cerebellum does for movement what the rest of the brain does for other behaviors: it monitors and controls and creates a variety of gross and fine movements. With the exception of olfactory impulses, the cerebellum must regulate a steady stream of cacophonous sensory information and respond with less-than-split-second motor commands.

Coordination among the fine and gross muscles must be tightly regulated. Imagine the sensorimotor requirements that underscore a violinist's solo. The proper placement of the fingers on the strings, the tension on the bow, the immediate reactivity to the notes being played, the feedback to the cerebellum, and the proper integration of all the stimuli must be processed rapidly. Further, the integration of the information must be fluid when combined with internal stimuli about memory of the movements and the sounds desired and in anticipation of the next flood of ever-changing information.

Consider the requirements of even simple movement—touching your right index finger to your left ear, for instance. The finger, hand, arm and shoulder motions must all be integrated and coordinated, distances calculated, and speeds maintained before digit and ear meet, whereupon the sensory inputs from both finger and ear are fed to cerebellum prompting the cessation of the movement. Minimission accomplished.

The cerebellum does all this and more from its perch at the base of the brain (see Figure 3.7). When damaged, whether through trauma, stroke, or alcohol abuse, movement ceases to be the well-regulated phenomenon we have come to expect. Depending on the damage, movement reverts to the infantile, the dyscoordinated, where eye and hand are just beginning to work together haltingly. In fact, police commonly use simple motor coordination tasks, such as asking suspects to close their eyes and touch their noses, to determine whether a driver is intoxicated.

Pons and information transfer. The **pons** is a large bulge in the hindbrain immediately ventral to the cerebellum that relays information

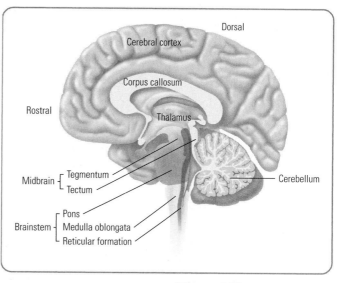

[Figure 3.7]
Structures of the brainstem and midbrain, relative to other "higher" structures in humans. The brainstem and midbrain play pivotal roles in vital biological functions.

cerebellum Hindbrain structure concerned with the coordination and control of voluntary muscular activity and movement.

pons Large bulge in the brainstem immediately ventral to the cerebellum; relays information from the cerebral cortex to the cerebellum and contains a portion of the reticular formation, nuclei that appear to be important for sleep and arousal.

reticular formation Collection of nuclei and fiber pathways traversing the brainstem from midbrain to medulla; play a primary role in arousal, attention, and sleep and wakefulness.

tectum Dorsal part of the midbrain; made up of the inferior and superior colliculi, control centers for auditory and visual stimuli.

tegmentum Ventral part of the midbrain, composed of various nuclei related to movement and to species-typical behaviors.

superior colliculi Nuclei in the mesencephalon that takes part in controlling the body's reflexes to visual stimuli.

inferior colliculi Nuclei in the mesencephalon that take part in localizing sounds, integrating hearing reflexes, and orienting the body toward auditory stimuli.

substantia nigra Nucleus of the tegmentum; communicates with the caudate nucleus and putamen in the basal ganglia to initiate movement.

periaqueductal gray (PAG) Region of the midbrain surrounding the cerebral aqueduct; contains neural circuits involved in species-typical behaviors and pain perception.

from the cerebellum to the cerebral cortex and regulates arousal. The pons contains a portion of the **reticular formation,** a staggering variety of nuclei and fiber pathways that play a primary role in arousal, attention, and sleep and wakefulness. The reticular formation extends from the medulla into the forebrain and coordinates information regarding the organism's baseline responses to the environment.

The spinal motor inhibition that occurs during REM sleep does not prevent the brain from moving in its reverie: the pons is active, guiding the dreamer through these hallucinatory movements. Though the body is slumbering, the brain works away as if waking and sleeping were but a matter of semantics (Hobson, 2003).

Together the cerebellum and the pons make up the metencephalon. The name *pons* derives from the Latin word for bridge, and unlike many other structures identified by literal-minded anatomists, it is named for its function rather than its appearance. A major site for the crossing of fibers from the right side of the body up to the left side of the brain and vice versa, the pons bridges the divide between the cerebral hemispheres. This crossing (the *pyramidal decussation*) contributes to the characteristic right-hemisphere regulation of the left side of the body and left-hemisphere regulation of right side of the body.

The number of neural connections between and within the pons and other structures in the brain suggests that the pons is a very important regulator of sensorimotor activities and a hub of information transfer. In fact, it is because of the enormous number of entering and crossing tracts that, like stitches in a thick rug, the pons bulges as it does.

Midbrain

Shown in Figure 3.7 at the tip of the brainstem, the midbrain is among the least well-defined brain areas in terms of boundaries and nuclei, but its importance in mediating autonomic and orienting behaviors is unquestionable. The two main subcomponents of the midbrain are the **tectum,** the "roof" of the third ventricle, and the **tegmentum,** its "floor," an agglomeration of nuclei that surround the cerebral aqueduct (Figure 3.8).

The tectum in the dorsal midbrain is a control center for visual and auditory stimuli primarily comprising two sets of nuclei. The **superior colliculi** take part in controlling bodily reflexes to visual stimuli, and the **inferior colliculi** take part in localizing sounds, integrating hearing reflexes, and orienting the body toward auditory stimuli. The tectum is at work when you turn your head to see where a sound is coming from as, for example, the whisper of your name draws your attention to its source.

The reticular formation passes from the brainstem through the tegmentum, which is itself composed of various nuclei related to eye movement, limb movement (red nuclei), and to initiating movement (substantia nigra). The **substantia nigra** (black substance), the largest neuronal collection in the midbrain, is rife with neurotransmitters that play major regulatory roles in initiating and inhibiting movement. For example, the loss or degeneration of the dopamine-generating neurons of the substantia nigra produces the symptoms of Parkinson's disease, the terrible lack of well-articulated movement. Its projections to distant brain sites that are involved in movement underscores the pervasive role that the substantia nigra plays in motor events.

The agglomeration of nuclei in the tegmentum gives rise to the **periaqueductal gray (PAG)** region, which separates the tegmentum from the tectum. The PAG is involved in the perception of pain. Its nuclei are sensitive to opioidlike neurochemicals, and a fiber pathway descending from the PAG into the spinal cord appears to be capable of terminating pain sensations.

Forebrain

The anatomical divisions of the forebrain (prosencephalon) are the telencephalon and the diencephalon (see Figure 3.5c). Streams of sensory input travel to specific sites within the forebrain for simple, early deconstruction and processing and subsequently to other sites for richer evaluation and resolution. When subsequently reassembled, the information has much more meaning attached to it because it has been connected to and associated with other information.

For example, the letters *D, O,* and *G* are merely combinations of lines and curves when first scanned by the visual system. These stimuli give way to recognition as symbols, or letters, and we see the word *DOG*. As this perception reverberates around the brain, utilizing ever more circuits and building layer upon layer of connections, the simple is transformed into the complex. Thus, a single word can conjure up images of thousands of kinds of dogs, their sounds and smells and other characteristics, together with particular and emotional memories one may have for a dog—all accomplished in a moment.

Owing to the rich associations spun off from the original perception, we build on layer after layer of personally compelling information. In fact, our

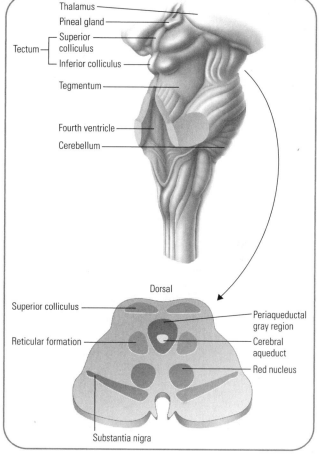

[Figure 3.8]
Midbrain structures are involved in very important motor activities, the loss or compromise of which can be devastating.

thalamus Structure of the forebrain; main source of input to the cerebral cortex.

realities are a construct of the brain; what we perceive as the external world is in actuality the disassembly and reassembly of the sensory stimulation being fed to our brains. Every thought and every memory is a reconstruction, association, and recombination of its neuronal elements. In the sections that follow we review the workings of the evolutionarily newer brain structures that enable such sophisticated information processing to occur.

Diencephalon: Regulating social and survival behaviors.
Sitting like an overlord, rostral to the brainstem, the diencephalon is a major nuclear complex whose small size belies the necessary and varied activities it regulates. We will focus on the thalamus and hypothalamus, its two major components, and the pituitary gland (Figure 3.9).

The diencephalon represents only ~2% of the CNS, but its contacts with other regions of the brain, not its absolute size, imbue it with its unique characteristics. Because the diencephalon regulates a host of similar social behaviors (aggression, sexual behavior, maternal behavior, and the like) in a variety of diverse species, it has been a focal point of much behavioral research.

Sensory information exists in the world in the form of physical stimuli: sights, smells, sounds, tastes, and touch and balance information. Photoreceptors in the eyes transduce light into visual sensations. The nose has olfactory receptors that bind odor molecules, causing neural impulses to course back to the brain. The tongue has taste buds that transform food-embedded chemicals into taste sensations. The skin possesses a variety of sensory receptors that respond to touch or pressure and heat or cold with unique patterns of firing. Nerve cells in the joints and muscles and the inner ear fire a constant stream of information back to the brain, informing it about its location and any imbalance.

This perpetual flow of sensory information must be regulated, synthesized, and evaluated before proper action can be taken. Imagine a major hub airport with hundreds of incoming and connecting flights. Traffic flow must be effectively and efficiently regulated and directed to its destination site. Once there, each "package" (mail, passengers, or information) affects the site in a unique way.

The **thalamus** is the main hub for sensory input to the cerebral cortex (see Figure 3.9). It operates like an airport hub: incoming sensory information is routed to the thalamus (with the exception of smells, which are carried directly into the olfactory bulbs at the base of the frontal cortex and sent to the amygdala for processing). Once sensory stimuli arrive in the thalamus, the afferent, sensory projections move along to local routing via visual, auditory, somatosensory, and so on, nuclei. These local sites then project to specified regions of the cortex, thereby allowing information to be processed quickly and specifically.

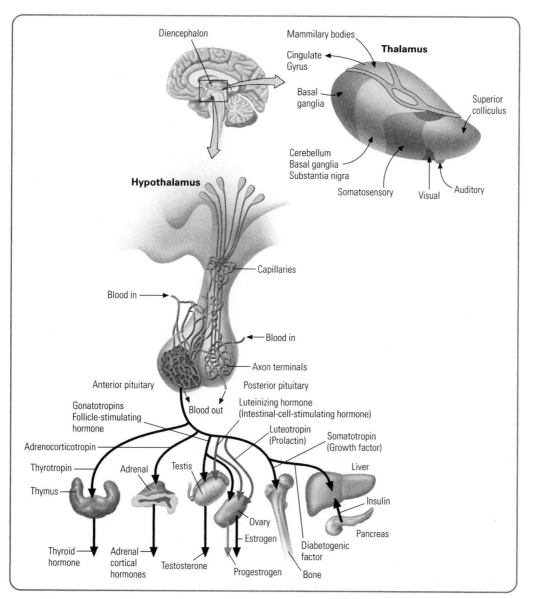

Diencephalon

Mammilary bodies

Thalamus

Cingulate Gyrus

Basal ganglia

Superior colliculus

Cerebellum
Basal ganglia
Substantia nigra

Somatosensory   Visual   Auditory

Hypothalamus

Capillaries

Blood in

Blood in

Axon terminals

Anterior pituitary   Posterior pituitary

Gonatotropins
Follicle-stimulating hormone

Blood out

Luteinizing hormone
(Intestinal-cell-stimulating hormone)

Luteotropin
(Prolactin)

Somatotropin
(Growth factor)

Adrenocorticotropin

Thyrotropin

Thymus

Adrenal   Testis

Liver

Insulin

Pancreas

Ovary

Estrogen

Diabetogenic factor

Thyroid hormone

Adrenal cortical hormones

Testosterone

Progestrogen

Bone

[Figure 3.9]
Shown here are the diencephalon, the pituitary gland, and the hormones released from the anterior portion of the pituitary. Note the rich supply of blood vessels in and around the pituitary, which allows for rapid and complete conveyance of allied chemical and hormonal signals from the diencephalon.

AFTER FRANK NETTER.

hypothalamus Brain nuclei that control the endocrine system and regulate motivated behavior.

pituitary gland Master endocrine gland at the base of the hypothalamus; releases a variety of hormones that influence the activity of other glands throughout the body.

Subsequently, the sensory information is summed and collated along with cognitive information from other sites.

The complexity of the thalamic nuclei is a wonder to behold (Carpenter and Sutin, 1983). But, like a successful business, one of its defining features is the efficient division of labor and the delegation of responsibilities. What the thalamus does is vitally important to the survival of the organism. The information that the thalamus processes is coin of the realm for the brain: sensory inputs that allow for contact with, evaluation of, and action about the external world.

The **hypothalamus,** located directly under (*hypo*) the thalamus, is about the size of a teaspoon. It regulates motivated behaviors that maintain the individual both proximally and ultimately: minute by minute, day by day, and year by year. It motivates the organism to obtain food and water, to rest, and to find, defend, and mate with partners. Like the thalamus, the hypothalamus is a masterwork of overlapping and related subnuclei, neural catacombs that can be collected functionally under the umbrella of motivated behaviors. For instance, as detailed in Chapter Thirteen, two subnuclei in the hypothalamus play at least an indirect role in regulating feeding (in concert with other CNS and PNS structures) and may also govern bodily growth (Nakazato et al., 2001).

In addition to its other activities, the hypothalamus regulates the **pituitary gland,** the body's so-called master endocrine gland (see Figure 3.9). The anterior pituitary receives information about hormone release from chemical messages that travel from the hypothalamus through the hypothalamic-pituitary circulatory system (connecting the pituitary to the hypothalamus). Additionally, neurons in the hypothalamus have processes that extend to the posterior pituitary which, when activated, release two neuropeptides (discussed in Chapter 5). Though the hypothalamus regulates their release, pituitary hormones exert themselves at very distant sites in the body.

The tiny pituitary, under hypothalamic control (another small structure), regulates the body's most important and fundamental physiological processes, including the autonomic response to stress. When a stimulus is perceived as threatening, the hypothalamus responds by sending hormones through the hypothalamic-pituitary circulatory system. As we will see in Chapter Five, the CNS has engineered two regulatory processes: fast-acting, fast-duration chemical events via neurotransmitters and slow-acting, long-duration effects via hormones. The hypothalamus controls both processes.

Telencephalon and higher-order behaviors. *Telencephalon* is the organizing term for the cerebral cortex and subcortical structures that surround the lateral ventricles (see Figure 3.4). Relative to the deeper structures we have considered so far, these are the brain's most recent evolutionary additions. When viewed in the context of behavioral complexity, the telencephalic regions regulate mental processes such as cognition (thinking about dogs, for example) and forethought (planning to adopt a particular breed of dog).

The anatomical term *cortex* (from the Latin word for the bark of a tree) refers to any outer layer of cells. The kidneys, adrenal glands, even your hair all have a cortex. But to neuroscientists, **cortex** (also *neocortex*) refers to the outermost layer of the brain. This thin, layered sheet of neurons, about the size and thickness of a fine linen napkin, ranges in thickness from about 1 millimeter to 5 millimeters, both among individuals and in different brain regions (Fischl & Dale, 2000). The cortex contains the majority of the brain's neurons. A piece the size of a large match head contains tens of thousands of neurons and millions of their connections (Crick, 1994).

Different mammals have cortices of varying complexities and sizes, but the human has one of the most wrinkly, or convoluted (Figure 3.10). As the anthropologist Helen Fisher (1982) and others have speculated, these convolutions may be anatomical evidence of our evolution from small-brained mammals to large-brained social beings. Imagine that you want to put that linen napkin into your pocket, an enclosure that will not accommodate the cloth in its original shape. What do you do? You might lightly compress the napkin and crumple it, maintaining its surface area while reducing its overall size. It now fits into a more compact area, but you have lost none of its mass. More important, you have lost none of its function. Some researchers speculate that the folding is due to a specific gene protein and may allow for more surface area in a constrained space (Chenn & Walsh, 2002).

The brain, especially the cortex, grew bigger as it evolved, and as complex social interaction became the norm, this larger brain both created and was capable of responding to ever-new social and environmental challenges. Some authors, among them Wyles et al. (1983), believe that natural selection operated on these social innovations and produced more rapid change. The acceleration of anatomical evolution, fueled by social interactions, therefore might have enhanced forebrain size relative to other neural structures. To fit the newly super-sized cortex into the regular-sized skull, folding and crimping were required.

Eventually, there was a constraint on the rapid evolution of the brain: the size of the skull and, more important, the uterus and birth canal in and through which the skull must develop and pass (Montagu, 1965). A large brain contained in a bulky skull would be more likely to lodge itself in the birth canal during birth. A birth canal wide enough to accommodate such a skull would be anatomically difficult to develop in the human female. Absolute brain size, therefore, is limited by the vessel designed to

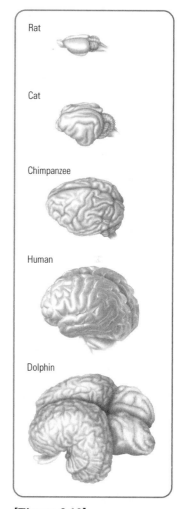

Rat

Cat

Chimpanzee

Human

Dolphin

[Figure 3.10]
Should humans be considered atop the phylogenetic scale? Based on the complexity and size of the brain, maybe not. A glance at the dolphin brain portrayed here should make us wonder.

cortex (neocortex) Phylogenetically the newest cortex, the outermost layer of cerebral gray matter, including the sensorimotor and association cortices.

frontal lobe Part of the cerebral cortex in either hemisphere of the brain found directly behind the forehead; helps to control voluntary movement and is associated with the higher mental activities and with personality.

temporal lobe Division of the cerebral cortex lying at each side within the temple of the skull that responds to auditory inputs and contains areas related to language production and recognition; underlying areas regulate and maintain memory and emotional processes.

carry it. The evolutionary end run around this problem was a brain that was folded in on itself, a larger gift stuffed into a smaller package.

Structures and functions of the cortex. The structure of the cortex is bilaterally symmetrical—two hemispheres of roughly the same size. Structures and functions are not exactly mirrored in the right and left hemispheres. Functionally, for most of us, the left hemisphere is more involved in logical reasoning and language, whereas the right hemisphere is more involved in spatial manipulation, musical ability, emotional processing, and facial recognition. Anatomically, for example, the area of the temporal lobe that is involved in language comprehension is considerably larger in the left hemisphere than the right, whereas the area located just above it is considerably smaller in the left hemisphere than the right (Kandel et al., 2003).

Each hemisphere is divided functionally into four lobes (Figure 3.11). Moving ventral to dorsal:

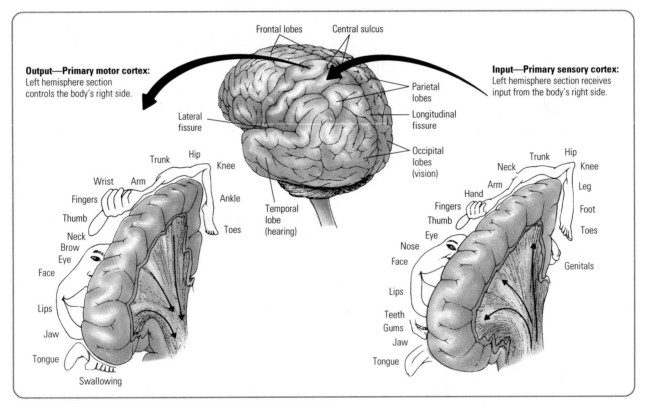

[Figure 3.11]
Interestingly, the external world is represented topographically on the surface of the brain. Note how more sensitive areas of the body (lips, tongue, and fingertips, for instance) occupy more neural "real estate."

- **Frontal lobe** regions, which are detailed throughout the text, regulate movement of the skeletal muscles, integrate memory and emotional activities with real-time events, and control planning and executable (realistic) strategies. The frontal cortex also imbues the human with personality, including such characteristics as sympathy, judgment, and empathy. (Recall from Chapter One the story of Phineas Gage.)

- The **temporal lobe** responds to auditory inputs and contains areas related to language production and recognition. Its underlying areas regulate and maintain memory and emotional processes.

- The **parietal lobe** interprets somatosensory information and spatial relationships.

- The **occipital lobe** is primarily responsive to visual sensory inputs and associations.

This functional arrangement creates significant processing abilities and attaches a richness of detail to even the simplest sensation. It is not surprising that the brain became too big for its skull as more and more cognitive abilities developed. Two main divisions of labor in the cortex reflect the sensory and motor information the brain regulates. Recall too from the chapter-opening cases of Barbara Guerra and Brett Neilsen that these motor and sensory areas can be quite plastic. Cortical functions are by no means carved in stone or flesh.

A third activity, information integration, is performed by the ubiquitous **association cortex** that functions to integrate multiple aspects of information leading to enhanced cognition. A seemingly uncomplicated external event becomes subtly involving and full because of its associations. First, the sensory information is processed ("What is this?"). Next, association areas compare the sensory input to stored information and evaluate it for a response ("What does it mean and how should I respond?"). Finally, the information flow moves to motor areas for a reaction and response ("This is what will happen."). Depending on the initial sensory inputs, this simple example could involve a large proportion of neural tissue throughout the cortex, which should dispel the myth that we use but 10% of our brains.

The wrinkled surface of the cortex, the result of all that brain compaction, forms peaks and valleys, or mounds and grooves, which are called, respectively, **gyri** (gyrus, singular) and **sulci** (sulcus). Sulci that extend deep into the brain and actually indent the ventricles are called **fissures.** The **longitudinal fissure,** for example, separates the left and right cerebral hemispheres, and the **lateral fissure** separates the temporal lobe from the frontal and parietal lobes. At the top of the brain, the

parietal lobe Main division of each hemisphere of the cerebral cortex, located beneath the crown of the skull; interprets somatosensory information and spatial relationships.

occipital lobe Region of the cerebral cortex lying at the very back of the brain, caudal to the parietal and temporal lobes; site of the primary visual cortex.

association cortex Areas of the cortex that integrate information to produce cognition.

gyri (sing. **gyrus**) Convolutions of the surface of the brain, caused by the infolding of the cerebral cortex.

sulci (sing. **sulcus**) Small grooves or mounds on the surface of an organ.

fissures Deep grooves covering the outer surface of the brain.

longitudinal fissure Deep groove that separates the left and right cerebral hemispheres of the brain.

lateral fissure Prominent groove that separates the temporal lobe from the frontal and parietal lobes.

central sulcus Deep sulcus that separates the frontal lobe (motor cortex) from the parietal lobe (sensory cortex).

basal ganglia Subcortical cluster of nuclei in the telencephalon that forms a circuit with the cortex, thalamus, and midbrain to coordinate body movements and links to the limbic system via the amygdala.

limbic system Collection of brain regions (amygdala, mammilary bodies, hippocampus, fornix and cingulated gyrus) that collectively produce, respond to and regulate emotional responses.

amygdala Almond-shaped structure at the tail end of the basal ganglia within the temporal lobe; functions as part of the limbic system involved in regulation of emotion and sexual urges.

striatum Terminal for all afferent fiber pathways forming the basal ganglia; dysfunction in this motor system is believed to be involved in OCD and Tourette's.

central sulcus divides the parietal and frontal lobes and primary sensory and motor functions (see Figure 3.11).

Subcortical circuits: Limbic system and basal ganglia. Deep within the forebrain lie two interconnected complexes that link forebrain and brainstem functions. The structures of the **basal ganglia** that are located beneath the rostral extent of the lateral ventricles coordinate body movements. The basal ganglia link to a functional grouping, the **limbic system,** which controls emotional (affective) behaviors and certain forms of memory infused with emotion by a grouping of basal nuclei called the **amygdala** (almond). Anatomically the amygdala forms the tail end of the basal ganglia within the rostral temporal lobe; functionally it classifies as a limbic structure because the amygdala regulates both the perception and production of emotions, especially fear.

The basal ganglia form a circuit with the cortex and also connect to the thalamus and midbrain (Figure 3.12). Together, the *caudate nucleus,* the input nuclei involved with control of voluntary movement, and the *putamen,* a nucleus that also controls body movement, comprise the **striatum,** the terminal for all afferent fiber pathways forming the basal ganglia. One of the ways this important anatomical alliance regulates is by inhibition; that is, the striatum limits the activity of downstream, or efferent, structures. This inhibition of movement, however, is just as important as the initiation of movement. Dysfunction in the striatum, along with other regions that may also be involved, contributes to the uncontrollable movements and tics observed in obsessive-compulsive disorders and Tourette's syndrome, as detailed in Chapter Seven.

[Figure 3.12]
The basal ganglia comprise a group of structures that regulate movement and that have closely allied projections to inhibitory activities.

The striatum is especially affected in the debilitating, hereditary condition of **Huntington's chorea,** in which patients endure slow, inexorable degeneration of motor control, which eventually slides into constant, uncontrollable movements (choreas) and the herky-jerky shakes of a marionette. People with Huntington's have some hope, though: a transplant of fetal brain tissue or stem cells (Bachoud-Lévi, 2000). If the transplant takes, partial or even full reversal may occur. (The Epilogue details how research into this vitally important area and others of similar value may be compromised by societal and political influences.)

Complementary to the striatum's inhibitory control, the *globus pallidus* initiates voluntary movement through regulation of its inhibitory output. Diseases of this segment of the basal ganglia usually involve abnormal involuntary motor movements called **dyskinesias** and an overall loss of muscle tone. Typical of the movement disorders are ballism (a sudden forceful movement involving the shoulder), tremor (shaking involving primarily limbs, digits, and the lips), tics such as the head twitches one sees in Tourette's syndrome, and the choreas. Treatment of the diseases of the motor components of the basal ganglia have met with little success to date, but the search for effective treatments and cures continues.

The limbic system encircles the brainstem, lining the inner border (limbus) of the cortex at an area called the *cingulate cortex,* a structure that serves as a conduit between the frontal cortex and the limbic circuit (Figure 3.13). Limbic structures are both primitive—from an evolutionary standpoint, they have been around in one form or another for a long time—and primal in service of the organism's survival. In Box 3.1, you will discover how Paul MacLean played an instrumental role in naming and emphasizing the importance of this emotional circuit.

Collectively, limbic structures regulate appropriate physiological and behavioral responses to social and environmental stimuli, such as stress and fear. For example, the **nucleus accumbens** is a limbic component involved in motivation and in translating environmental stimuli into the appropriate behavioral response, which is convenient because anatomically the nucleus accumbens is also part of the striatum. Neurons in the tegmentum project into the nucleus accumbens—sometimes referred to as the pleasure center of the brain—reinforcing behaviors critical for sur-

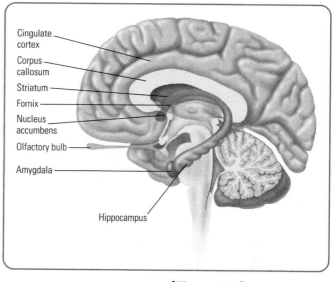

Cingulate cortex
Corpus callosum
Striatum
Fornix
Nucleus accumbens
Olfactory bulb
Amygdala
Hippocampus

[Figure 3.13]
The limbic system, shown here, is believed to be an evolutionarily ancient collection of structures that cohere to regulate rapid responses to environmental events, and the recollections of their past dangers.

Huntington's chorea
Hereditary neurodegenerative disorder of motor control characterized by ongoing involuntary jerky movements and progressive dementia; associated with hyperactivity of the dopaminergic system.

dyskenesias Abnormal involuntary motor movements and difficulty in carrying out voluntary movements.

nucleus accumbens Limbic component of the striatum sometimes referred to as the "pleasure center" of the brain; involved in motivating behavior and reinforcing survival responses; linked to disorders ranging from anxiety and depression to addiction.

[Box 3.1]

The Investigators

Paul MacLean

Paul MacLean, the third son of a Presbyterian minister, was born in Phipps, New York, in 1913. His first thoughts about the power of impulsive, emotional behavior—thoughts that would become the crux of his fascinating research—occurred when young MacLean was about 4 years old. He was seated in his father's congregation when he became captivated by a young girl who was looking at the ceiling and giggling uncontrollably.

Impulsively, MacLean climbed over the partition in the pew, a behavior that prompted his father to yell "PAUL!" from the pulpit. Before the service was over, the guilt-ridden young boy had jumped on his tricycle and run away from home. He was later located by his older brothers and delivered into the welcoming arms of his parents. During this episode, MacLean recalls thinking about why people do things that can get them into trouble even when they know better.

Toward the end of his undergraduate education in English literature at Yale University, MacLean found himself increasingly interested in philosophy. His interest turned to medicine, however, after observing a local physician diagnosing and successfully treating MacLean's ailing mother and realizing how rewarding it would be to help people in this manner. MacLean later attended Yale Medical School, completed an internship at prestigious Johns Hopkins University,

and served in the Medical Corps in World War II. He had the opportunity to learn more about the brain during his military service when he was placed in charge of the psychiatric ward.

Because he was fascinated by the brain, MacLean accepted a U.S. Public Health Fellowship in 1947 working under Stanley Cobb, founder of the Department of Psychiatry at Massachusetts General Hospital. MacLean soon became intrigued by psychomotor epilepsy, seizures that were not accompanied by convulsions. Additionally, these seizures produced a modified sense of self—a kind of exaggerated feeling of what is real and important.

Upon investigation, MacLean learned that the epileptic focus of these seizures occurred in the anterior temporal region. At the heart of this region was the hippocampus, a brain area known at the time to be involved with olfaction; in other words, it was a rhinencephalic, or olfactory brain, structure. Puzzled by the question of why a brain area supposedly involved in smell might be involved in these pure emotional experiences in epileptic patients, MacLean turned to the literature for answers. He stumbled across an article written by James Papez in 1937, entitled "A Proposed Mechanism of Emotion." In this article, Papez pointed out that the hippocampus is connected to the hypothalamus, a structure thought at the time to be involved with emotional expression. Knowing that he was onto something meaningful, MacLean traveled to Cornell to meet with Papez, whom he referred to as "the Odyssean navigator of the brain" (MacLean, 1996, p. 258).

---

hippocampus Arching limbic structure within the temporal lobe important in learning, memory, and navigating the environment.

vival, such as hunger and sex, as well as another pleasurable activity, laughter (Box 3.2). Chapters Seven, Eight and Ten detail how the functioning of the nucleus accumbens, cingulate cortex, and other limbic areas have been implicated in disorders such as anxiety, depression, and addiction.

Lying beneath the medial temporal cortex and merging into the cingulate, the **hippocampus** plays a role in memory formation and spatial navigation. The hippocampus is a large, arching limbic structure that has a prominent anterior-posterior extension, as well as a medial-lateral extension (see Figure 3.13). It plays a prominent role in spatial maneu-

Dr. Paul MacLean in his sunroom.
KELLY LAMBERT, RANDOLPH-MACON COLLEGE
BEHAVIORIAL NEUROSCIENCE LABORATORY

In 1949, MacLean published his landmark article entitled "Psychosomatic disease and the 'visceral' brain," in which he emphasized that, although we have a highly developed cortex, our emotional behavior continues to be influenced by more primitive parts of the brain. In his later writings, MacLean changed the term *visceral,* which was confused with internal organs, to *limbic,* a term used earlier by Paul Broca to describe the circular structure of the cingulate cortex.

In essence, MacLean wrote that we have an ancient reptilian brain component that contains hard-wired neurological programs for very basic, specific behaviors, such as those involved in aggression and sexual displays. The limbic lobe, or the paleomammalian system, is involved with play behavior, parental behavior, and the separation cry of infants. Finally, the neomammalian brain, or the neocortex, has evolved to integrate the more basic functions with the environment. In an attempt to convey how all three components interact in the human to produce behavior, MacLean introduced the term *triune* (from the Greek word meaning "three in one") brain. In 1990, MacLean published *The Triune Brain in Evolution: Role in Paleocerebral Functions,* a book that captures his life's work in this area.

In this day of reductionistic neuroanatomy, MacLean's more global view of the brain as a collection of circuits is refreshing. It has enabled him to consider some very "big" issues, such as "Why, in a time when there is so much suffering, do humans continue to have children?" The answer, he feels, lies in the limbic structures and their relationship with the newly evolved neocortex. That is, the parental and social bonds that form because of the activity of the limbic lobe influence the neocortex. Consequently, the neocortex is involved in anticipation, planning, empathy, and altruism, and it probably promotes an awareness of the well-being of family members and other acquaintances. In a sense, the neocortex might play a crucial role in promoting the welfare and proliferation of the species.

Today, in his nineties, MacLean continues to be a brain investigator, traveling weekly to the National Institute of Mental Health to work on a project that he jokingly refers to as the "5000-year project." Keenly aware of his race against time, he continues to pursue his interest in learning more about the circuits of the brain. Always a student of neuroanatomy, MacLean likens his continued adventures in the microscopic world of brain anatomy to "walking into a cathedral." He warns young investigators not to let a day go by without communing with neuroanatomical nature—"if you don't observe the brain on a daily basis, you won't hear the music." Indeed, the intricate and delicate connections of the circuits of the brain are like a symphony to his temporal, or emotional, cortex.

vering, attending to environmental cues and place signals that can aid in movement from one point to another and back again. Neurons in the hippocampus called *place cells* respond to specific locations in space (Wilson & McNaughton, 1993). Place cells provide rapid feedback about the location of the organism in its environment (the original backseat drivers), and they appear to be reactivated during dreaming, or REM sleep, a sleep stage characterized by rapid eye movements (Wilson & McNaughton, 1994).

The hippocampus plays a primary role in the formation of temporal as well as spatial memories, particularly those involving autobiographic

[Box 3.2]

Brain Matters

Joking Around in the Laboratory

Question: What do engineers use for birth control?
Answer: Their personalities!

Did you laugh at this joke? If you did, why did you laugh? Was your laughter voluntary, or did it seem out of your control? Although you're probably thinking that these questions take the fun out of a joke, they are the questions researchers ask in the attempt to understand the neuroanatomical underpinnings of laughter.

A few researchers suggest an evolutionary role. Ramachandran (1998) suggests that laughter is the result of being led down one cognitive path, expecting an answer of a particular nature, and then having the old cognitive expectation switcheroo pulled on you. Because there's a deflation of expectation for the initial cognitive journey, a loud explosive sound is employed to warn others that the expectation is a false alarm.

This theory is supported by several studies reporting more laughter occurring in social groups than in isolated individuals. In his book *Laughter* (2000), Provine reports several interesting social twists on laughter. Women laugh more at men than men do at women (sorry, guys), speakers laugh more than listeners, and, believe it or not, laughter is more rarely a response to jokes than it is to "It was nice to meet you" social interactions. Indeed, laughter seems to be an attempt by humans to ingratiate themselves with others. Next time you're observing people introduce themselves observe how often they start moving their shoulders up and down in laughter—even though you're certain no jokes are being told.

What about the brain structures involved in this mysterious behavior? Working in London's Institute of Neurology in Queens Square, Vinod Goel and Raymond Dolan (2001) collected fMRI scans of individuals listening to two types of jokes: semantic jokes (*Why don't sharks bite lawyers? It's a matter of professional courtesy*) and phonological jokes or puns (*Why did the golfer wear two pants? He had a hole in one*). Believe it or not, they found separate neural circuitries for these two types of jokes. The semantic joke route includes bilateral temporal lobe activity, and the pun activates Broca's area in the temporal lobe, where language is processed, and the floor area of the cortex known as the insula. When jokes were funny, the medial ventral prefrontal cortex around the area of the pleasure center, or the nucleus accumbens, was activated (Dunn, 2001).

In another clever study, researchers separated the time in which subjects were "getting" the joke from the time they were "laughing" at the jokes. The subjects viewed a *Seinfeld* episode. For the duration of the episode, experimenters collected fMRI scans time-locked with the laugh track (mirthful experience—laughter) and for the moment directly preceding the laugh track (getting the joke experience). As subjects were just getting the joke, their scans showed activation of the left dorsal and inferior frontal cortex and bilateral activation of the temporal lobes. During the laughter moments, the insula of the cortex was activated, as was the amygdala (Kelley et al., 2002).

Interestingly, the insula controls autonomic functions such as breathing, and most people display altered breathing patterns as they verbalize their mirthful feelings (laugh). By exposing their subjects to visual comics during PET scans, Iwase et al. (2002) found

---

episodic memory Autobiographic memory for personal experiences (episodes) pinpointed to specific place and time contexts.

events, or **episodic memory.** Many studies demonstrate that when the hippocampus is damaged, a person will suffer from a condition known as **anterograde amnesia,** in which no memories from the time of the damage to the present can be remembered easily, if at all. Older memories are spared, however (Kandel et al., 2000).

These data suggest that the hippocampus regulates new learning and the forming of new memories. Memory researcher Daniel Schacter bilateral activation (increased blood flow) of the supplementary motor area of the cortex and left putamen, as well as visual association areas, left temporal, orbitofrontal, and medial prefrontal cortices. Alternatively, when subjects were asked to force a smile, the only areas activated were in the primary and supplementary motor cortices. Fried et al. (1998) reported producing laughter through electrical stimulation of a small, 2-square-centimeter area of the motor cortex during surgery to treat a 16-year-old girl's epilepsy. This supplementary motor area may be part of a larger circuit that regulates emotional output.

We can understand more about laughter through the use of animal models. Panksepp (2000) reported a type of laughter in his laboratory rats. When the rats were tickled, they emitted a high-frequency chirping response. In natural social interactions, the animals emitted similar responses during social play. The tickling seems to be rewarding—as is the case in humans—because the rats would seek out the hand that previously tickled it.

Panksepp contends that this animal model may be valuable in learning more about positive emotional responses such as joy. Regardless of the philosophical question of whether you can actually tickle a rat—as a comedian might ask—*what is this behavior all about?* How can it be that if you run your fingers up your own rib cage you have no response but if someone else does it you withdraw, assume a fetal position, and begin a series of hearty belly laughs?

Scientists think the cerebellum may play a role in this mysterious dichotomy of responses to tactile stimulation. If you are tickling yourself, the cerebellum, involved in motor coordination, seems to predict the tactile stimulation and promptly sends a message to

Laughter incorporates several areas of the brain including the supplementary motor area, frontal cortices, and nucleus accumbens.
LYDIA KIBIUK

disregard the meaningless sensation. But the cerebellum cannot predict the exact movement of an external "tickling" stimulus and send the appropriate messages to ignore the sensation; laughter results when the stimulus is determined to be nonthreatening (Blakemore, Wolpert, & Frith, 1998).

Did you ever imagine that having the giggles could evoke so many scientific questions? Brain researchers continue to ponder whether laughter serves some specific evolutionary function or is just a *cognitive juxtaposition* (Goel & Dolan, 2001) and what areas of the brain are activated in different types of humor. But as you'll read in Chapter Twelve, health researchers have already discovered that laughter appears to be good medicine.

(1996) and others suggest that the hippocampus, which merges into the cingulate cortex, assembles memories from constituent associations, like a puzzle with interchangeable pieces. Each time a memory is recalled, then, there are slight differences from the previous recollection. Memory is fluid, not static, and can be influenced, subtly or otherwise. For example, excessive levels of stress hormones can compromise hippocampal structure and functioning (see Chapters Eight and

anterograde amnesia Ability to recall long-ago events but not recent events, and a general inability to incorporate recent events into memory.

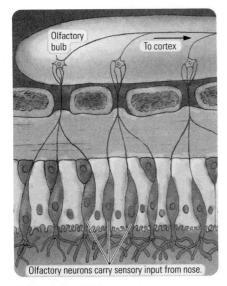

[Figure 3.14]
The nose and olfactory system have an anatomically intimate relationship with the brain.

spinal cord Tube of central nervous system tissue extending from the base of the brain through the central canal to the upper part of the lumbar spine; conducts sensorimotor impulses between the brain and the body and is a site of reflex activity.

vertebral column Firm, flexible bony column extending from the base of the skull to the coccyx; longitudinal axis and chief supporting structure of the human body.

Eleven). The hippocampus may play a role even in false memories (Schacter, 1996, 1997). You might remember that the case of Nadean Cool in Chapter One demonstrates how memories can be prejudiced and even planted by a well-meaning but misguided clinician.

Located at the tip of the basal ganglia, just rostral to the hippocampus, the amygdala, noted earlier, is another main functional component of the limbic system. Damage to the amygdala renders an individual incapable either of registering or expressing the appropriate emotion, and also interferes with the perception and regulation of fear. Disruption of social interaction is one consequence of damage to this site, as the amygdala-damaged person meets the relating of a sad story with amusement or other inappropriate responses (Adolphs, Baron-Cohen, & Tranel, 2002; Adolphs, Tranel, & Damasio, 1998; Adolphs, Tranel, Damasio, & Damasio, 1994). Further, subtle modifications in its activity through hormonal exposure or developmental insults may subtly alter the person's expressed emotions.

Rhinencephalon: Smell and the brain. The olfactory system in humans is an ancient, active, and influential sense. In many species, smell has primacy in governing behavior. In humans, olfactory afferents project to the amygdala for immediate processing of odors. The anatomical arrangement of the olfactory system makes it the part of brain that is closest to the outside world. In fact, the sensory receptors of olfactory neurons that are embedded in the nasal mucosa are separated by mere millimeters of bone and a single short synapse from the olfactory bulb itself (Figure 3.14).

The olfactory bulb in the human mammal is small (microsmatic) relative to the rest of the brain (see Figure 3.13). A macrosmatic animal like the rat has a highly evolved sense of smell. The rat's olfactory bulb is large relative to the rest of its brain, whereas the human has a pair of olfactory bulbs the size and shape of shoelaces. Still, size does not matter. The intimacy of smell harks back to a time when olfaction was explicitly important in human social interactions and in navigating the environment. But even today smell has a most powerful effect upon the human, subtly altering perceptions of the world—and the people who inhabit it—and influencing our behavior.

Research has demonstrated the existence of receptors for pheromones in the human and their subtle effects on behavior (Whitten, 2000). *Pheromones* act as chemical signals among animals of the same species. When a pheromone is released by one individual, it creates a specific behavioral response in the individuals who perceive it. Likewise, very subtle odors outside our awareness can guide human behavior. There is a tendency for us to think that we are so far evolved and so far different and removed from the forces that shaped us that we are impervious to such base biological influences. Research suggests, however, that the role olfaction played millions of years ago is still being played out today, dictating how we act and react (Doty, Ford, Preti, & Huggins, 1975; Jacobs, McClintock, Zelano, & Ober, 2002; McClintock, 1998).

Spinal Cord

The nervous system enables split-second decisions that ensure the organism's survival. The field mouse that takes a few extra seconds to detect an approaching cat becomes a feline delicacy instead of a surviving animal. Recall that the nervous system is made up of tracts designated as efferent (outgoing) or afferent (incoming) transports for neural messages. Afferent information is sensory as it goes from the body to the brain for processing. Once the information is processed, it goes from brain to periphery in efferent motor impulses. Orderly regulation of this sensorimotor information is vitally important for the control of behavior.

The CNS structure that facilitates brain–body communication is the **spinal cord**, a delicate, cylindrical tube of nervous tissue about the diameter and consistency of a large stalk of tender asparagus. It is encased within the **vertebral column** (backbone), which is composed of individual bony vertebrae separated by cartilaginous, cushiony disks running the length of the neck and back. From the base of the brainstem, from which it is pinched off and continuous, the spinal cord runs down to the small of the back, just above the buttocks.

The vertebral column provides flexibility and mobile protection for the spinal cord during the range of movements and contortions required of or inflicted on the individual. The spinal cord, as protected as it is, is still fragile tissue. It traverses the spinal column's bony vertebrae, neck to tail, in three main segments, *cervical, thoracic,* and *lumbar,* and two minor, fused segments, *sacrum* and *coccyx,* or tailbone (Figure 3.15).

Ascending sensory impulses move up the spinal cord toward the brain via the vertebrae's dorsal columns or

[Figure 3.15]

The spinal cord is a delicate collection of long axons, conveying afferent (sensory) information to the brain, and efferent (motor) impulses away from it.

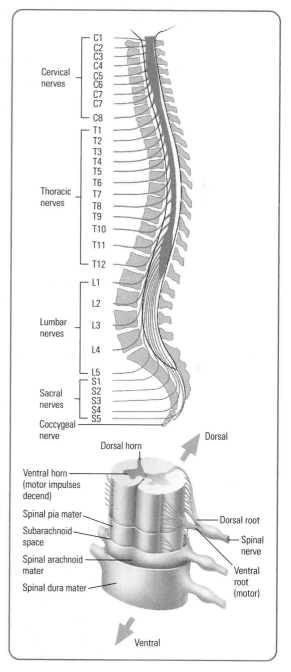

interneurons Nerve cells that associate sensory and motor activity in the central nervous system.

cranial nerves Twelve pairs of nerves, each pair having sensory and/or motor functions, extending to and from the brain without passing through the spinal cord.

horns. Descending, efferent motor impulses are transmitted via the ventral columns/horns. The sensory and motor pathways are joined together in 31 pairs of ascending (sensory) and descending (motor nerve) bundles called the *dorsal* and *ventral roots,* respectively, which innervate the periphery of the body with the means of commerce with the brain (Figure 3.15 inset).

The dorsal and ventral roots are joined by a mass of nerve tissue, the intermediate zone, where association cells called **interneurons** project to the motor neurons that in turn project to the muscles. Here we see some similarity in the activity of the spinal cord and the brain, with input, processing and output of information best exemplified by the simplest of behaviors, the *spinal reflex.*

When a shard of glass, a tack, a hot surface, or some other potential threat is sensed, say, by foot or finger, the afferent sensory information en route to the brain also undergoes some initial processing in the intermediate zone that results in the limb being pulled away. That is, rather than traversing the distance between the spinal cord and the brain's sensory regions and then descending before any action or motor response, the spinal cord initiates the reflex. Having "local" say over the withdrawal of the damaged appendage is much more efficient. Spinal reflexes protect sensitive tissues from additional damage by automatically and rapidly pulling away from a threat.

Should the spinal cord be damaged or, worse, severed, motor paralysis and lack of sensation ensue. The route of entrance to the brain is near the rostral end of the spinal cord, so the higher the damage occurs, the more functions are impaired. As you'll read in the Epilogue, much ongoing research is aimed at treating spinal cord injuries. The hope is that basic research can develop a treatment for reassembling the neurons and the axons that have been sundered. Promising treatments include the use of stem cells and attempts to differentiate these cells into spinal neurons or axons. To date, however, the preliminary successes that have been optimistically reported in various animal models have yet to be applied to humans.

CRANIAL NERVES AND BLOOD SUPPLY

The spinal cord is the main conduit for information transfer between the brain and the periphery of the body. In addition, a specialized set of **cranial nerves** emanate from nuclei in the brainstem and cortical areas to regulate information flowing to and from the internal organs and the specialized sensory systems and muscles in the head and neck. Twelve pairs of cranial nerves transmit sensory and motor impulses to and from the face, neck, and head and to the gut (Figure 3.16). Each pair has a different function.

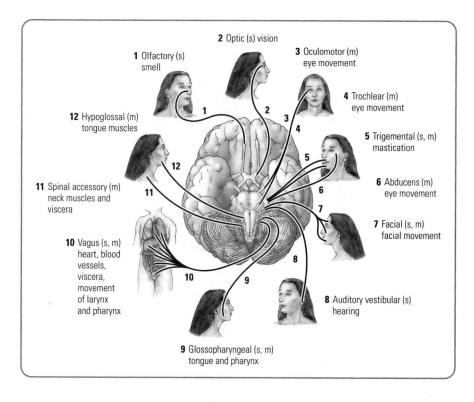

2 Optic (s) vision
1 Olfactory (s) smell
3 Oculomotor (m) eye movement
4 Trochlear (m) eye movement
12 Hypoglossal (m) tongue muscles
5 Trigemental (s, m) mastication
6 Abducens (m) eye movement
11 Spinal accessory (m) neck muscles and viscera
7 Facial (s, m) facial movement
10 Vagus (s, m) heart, blood vessels, viscera, movement of larynx and pharynx
8 Auditory vestibular (s) hearing
9 Glossopharyngeal (s, m) tongue and pharynx

[Figure 3.16]
Functional anatomy of the cranial nerves. The letters *s* and *m* refer to sensory and motor function, respectively, of the nerve.

Some cranial nerves are sensory, some are motor, and some are mixed nerve pairs that convey both afferent and efferent information. The **vagus nerve,** for example, is a mixed nerve that regulates activities further afield than the other cranial pairs. The sensory portion of the vagus transmits sensations of pain and nausea from the viscera, whereas the motor component exerts parasympathetic control of cardiovascular and abdominal function, as well as controlling the muscles of the throat.

It is imperative for an animal to respond to the changing features of the environment, and humans are no exception. Stephen Porges (2002), Director of the Brain-Body Center at the University of Illinois at Chicago, argues that certain components of the vagal-peripheral nervous circuit enable the animal to maintain homeostasis during these changes. Porges's work is forcing neuroscientists to redefine exactly which nervous system is running the behavioral show. After all, the ANS includes brainstem structures that monitor the physiological state of the internal organs, so technically it isn't completely separated from the CNS. Although their research is still in an early stage, the Porges team is providing further evidence that the boundaries between the brain and the body are even less distinct than once thought.

vagus nerve (cranial nerve 10) Mixed cranial nerve pair; sensory portion transmits sensations of pain and nausea from the viscera, motor component exerts parasympathetic control of cardiovascular and abdominal function, as well as controlling the muscles of the throat.

[Figure 3.17]
Arteries in the brain supply necessary fuels and nutrients; veins remove the wastes that result from the brain's many activities.

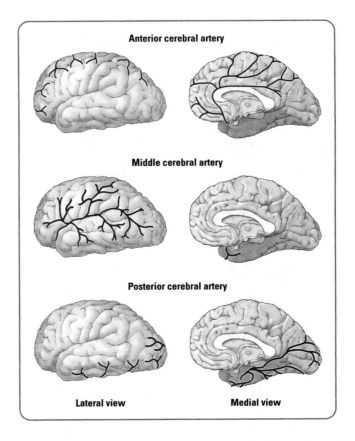

Anterior cerebral artery

Middle cerebral artery

Posterior cerebral artery

Lateral view   Medial view

The brain is occupied every second of our lives. Brain activity consumes approximately 20 percent of the oxygen available in the body at any time (Vogel, 1992). To maintain this level of activity requires a large and steady supply of blood (Figure 3.17).

The brain requires about the same amount of blood that a large, hardworking muscle receives and produces an equivalent amount of heat. The blood circulation also regulates brain temperature within critical limits. A temperature just a few degrees above normal (hyperthermia), poses a dangerous risk of damage or death, and if the temperature drops too low (hypothermia), brain activity will begin to slow and shut down.

A disruption of blood flow in any portion of a cerebral artery, such as a rupture or clot, poses equally serious consequences. One is **stroke,** a loss of brain tissue caused by blockage of a blood vessel and resultant loss of blood and hence oxygen to that region. Stroke can result in a sudden loss of consciousness, sensation, and voluntary movement. Deprived of oxygen, nerve cells in the affected part of the brain begin to die. Box 3.3 describes how the road to recovery is often difficult, but in some cases patients are able to make remarkable advances from the stroke-induced injury.

stroke Loss of brain tissue caused by blockade of a blood vessel and resultant loss of blood and hence oxygen; can result in sudden loss of consciousness, sensation, and voluntary movement.

[Box 3.3]

A Case in Point

Katherine Sherwood

At the age of 44, Katherine Sherwood had everything going for her. She enjoyed a successful career as an artist on the faculty of the University of California at Berkeley. On the personal side, she was married to an artist and had a 5-year-old daughter. One afternoon in May 1997, however, within a matter of 2 minutes, her world changed forever.

After experiencing a severe headache, Sherwood collapsed. When she awoke in the hospital, the right side of her body was paralyzed. She could no longer speak or read or paint. Sherwood had experienced a stroke in the left cerebral hemisphere. Doctors told her that the hemorrhage had realigned her brain's circuitry, probably impairing the ability of the left hemisphere to seek explanations, order, and reason. For a lawyer, this realignment could result in the end of a career, but for an artist, it might enhance creativity.

After about four months, Sherwood was able to speak once again, and she gained enough motility in her right leg to be able to walk. She hoped that she would regain movement in her right arm and hand, but that never happened. Understandably, Sherwood became depressed. She experienced an epiphany, however, when she was in her radiologist's office having a carotid angiogram to determine whether any further bleeding was occurring in her brain.

Although she was still groggy from the anesthetics, she caught a glimpse of the blood vessels in her brain on the computer screen. The image of the wandering vessels reminded her of a favorite 1000-year-old painting of a Chinese landscape. Suddenly she felt that she had to have these images and asked the technician for them. Although confused, her neurologist obliged, and Sherwood went home with the X-ray images of her brain's vascular landscape.

Inspired by the pictures of her own brain, Sherwood wanted to incorporate the images into her art. She also felt compelled to incorporate into her work seventeenth-century symbols of healing purportedly created originally by King Solomon. From a symbolic point of view, she knew that the contrast between the clinical, scientific images of her brain and the ancient emblems from a sorcery handbook would be compelling. Artistically, the angiograms and mystical symbols share a curving linearity. The juxtaposition of these disparate images reminds the viewer of the multiple dimensions of our identity.

Although inspired to commence her painting once again, Sherwood still faced the challenge of learning to use her left arm, controlled primarily by her right cerebral hemisphere, to paint. Slowly she found that she could paint with her left hand. Although fine movements were limited, she discovered that her left hand painted with a more creative flow, allowing her to work with less of the creative angst that frequently had accompanied her right-handed painting.

Today Sherwood's work is better than ever. She has received more awards and recognition following the stroke than she received prior to it. She is also teaching a course focusing on healing and art, a natural endeavor considering how her art transformed her from a depressed stroke patient to a thriving artist.

We are honored that one of Sherwood's paintings graces the cover of this text. When our editor found these paintings—capturing brain anatomy, symbols of wellness, and an overriding story of recovery of function—she knew we couldn't find a better representation and interpretation of the exciting new discipline of clinical neuroscience.

Katherine Sherwood in her studio.
LANCE IVERSON/SAN FRANCISCO CHRONICLE

Chapter Summary

Gross Structure and Function of the Nervous System

The central and peripheral nervous systems and the activities they regulate bring sensory/afferent information to the brain and take motor/efferent information away from it. This efficient arrangement regulates rapid and appropriate responses to internal and external events.

The skull is a light and tough encasement that provides excellent protection from physical insult. The three layers of the meninges also provide cushioning and support to the brain.

The ventricular system manufactures and circulates cerebrospinal fluid throughout the brain. This system provides a mechanism for the circulation of the major extracellular fluid involved in the movement of metabolites and nutrients to and through the brain.

The brain is divided into three main sections, owing to anatomical and developmental relationships. These are the prosencephalon (or forebrain), the mesencephalon (the midbrain), and the rhombencephalon (the hindbrain).

CNS Structure and Function

Brainstem structures are associated with vegetative and basic physiological regulatory processes.

The midbrain structures such as the tectum and tegmentum control eye, auditory, and attentional activities.

The forebrain has as its main structures the cortex, which is responsible for the majority of an organism's higher cognitive activities, and the thalamus and hypothalamus. Respectively, they regulate motivated responses and sensory routing.

The spinal cord is the major contact between brain and peripheral nervous system.

Cranial Nerves and Blood Supply

The cranial nerves are a set of 12 pairs of contacts conveying sensory and motor information to and from the brain.

The blood supply to the brain is rich and complex and enables this most demanding of organs to have an adequate amount of oxygen, nutrients and waste removal to accommodate the second-to-second activities it controls for a lifetime.

Key Terms

plasticity (p. 73)

central nervous system (CNS) (p. 75)

peripheral nervous system (PNS) (p. 75)

afferent information (p. 75)

efferent information (p. 75)

nuclei (p. 75)

tract (p. 75)

nerve (p. 75)

somatic nervous system (SNS) (p. 76)

autonomic nervous system (ANS) (p. 76)

sympathetic nervous system (p. 77)

parasympathetic nervous system (p. 77)

meninges (p. 79)

cerebrospinal fluid (CSF) (p. 80)

cerebral aqueduct (p. 81)

central canal (p. 81)

prosencephalon (p. 81)

mesencephalon (p. 81)

rhombencephalon (p. 81)

telencephalon (p. 81)

diencephalon (p. 81)

medulla oblongata (p. 84)

cerebellum (p. 85)

pons (p. 85)

reticular formation (p. 86)

tectum (p. 86)

tegmentum (p. 86)

superior colliculi (p. 86)

inferior colliculi (p. 86)

substantia nigra (p. 87)

periaqueductal gray (PAG) (p. 87)

thalamus (p. 88)

hypothalamus (p. 90)

pituitary gland (p. 90)

cortex (neocortex) (p. 91)

frontal lobe (p. 93)

temporal lobe (p. 93)

parietal lobe (p. 93)

occipital lobe (p. 93)

association cortex (p. 93)

For Further Consideration

Cajal, S., Swanson, N., & Swanson, L. W. (1995). *Histology of the nervous system of man and vertebrates.* New York: Oxford University Press. Santiago Ramon y Cajal was a man ahead of his time. It makes one wonder what Cajal could have accomplished had he had access to the tools available to the average neuroscientist today. His intricate and highly accurate drawings, made from detailed and painstaking observations of the nervous system of a variety of species, are absolutely beautiful. And they are as valuable today as they were when he first penned them. The Swansons have done a wonderful job of translating the text. Cajal's descriptions are as fresh as ever. This two-volume set is a must-have for the artwork alone—over a thousand meticulous images grace the pages of this magnum opus. Cajal's love for his work, and it is prodigious, comes through in his writings as well. This book represents the pinnacle of a man's life's work. It is a love story disguised as a scientific treatise.

Freedman, D. J., Riesenhuber, M., Poggio, T., & Miller, E. K. (2001). Categorical representation of visual stimuli in the primate prefrontal cortex. *Science, 291,* 312–315. The flood of information with which the brain is inundated minute by minute is determined by the sensory system. In the brain, the information is disseminated and categorized. The latter operation is critical to the efficient processing of information by the brain. In this paper, the authors examine the neural correlates of categorization in the nonhuman primate. The paper demonstrates how the process occurs. The authors trained monkeys to group animals such as cats and dogs in categories that reflected the "catness" versus the "dogness" of the forms they learned. By recording activity of specific neurons in the prefrontal cortex (PFC) and presenting the monkeys with ambiguous forms (a morphing combination of a dog and cat), they demonstrated activation of a specific set of PFC neurons in response to the category, either dog or cat, to which the stimulus belonged. The data show that the brain has robust categories into which the world is distributed and from which the brain can draw conclusions about its sensory world.

Gray, P. M., Krause, B., Atema, J., Payne, R., Krumhansl, C. & Baptista, L. (2001). The music of nature and the nature of music. *Science, 291,* 52–54. **Tramo, M. J.** (2001). Music of the hemispheres. *Science, 291,* 54–56. The adage that music is the universal language may be truer than ever before. Recent research is showing that music, in a variety of forms, is practiced and perceived by animals and humans. Gray and colleagues discuss the use of music by a variety of species, humans included, and conclude, that "the roots of music lie closer to our ancient lizard brain than to our more recent reasoning cortex" (p. 54). Therefore, music, perhaps by the rhythms inherent to its production, unite animal and human with a beat whose reverberations can be traced to our very origins.

Tramo's piece focuses on the human (brain's) capacity for and fascination with music. According to this analysis, our brains are wired up to respond to music, with specific sites (e.g., auditory cortex [superior temporal lobe], thalamus, hypothalamus, cerebellum, and so on) showing some form of activation. The article suggests that a single piece of music has the ability to involve in unison many disparate brain regions. Therefore, perhaps music brings us closer to other animals as well as closer to ourselves.

Keenan, J. P., Nelson, A., O'Connor, M. & Pascual-Leone, A. (2001). Self-recognition and the right hemisphere. *Nature, 409,* 305. Have you ever wondered how you recognize your face when you see it as a reflection in a mirror or a pool of water? That is, by what processes are you able to perform self-recognition? Keenan and colleagues examined that question in a sample of human patients in which one or the other cerebral hemisphere was inactivated by means of intracarotid anesthesia administration (the so-called Wada test). With the right hemisphere deadened by the anesthesia, the patients were unable to recognize their own faces shown to them in photographs. In another set of patients, photographs of their own faces or those of celebrities were shown. There was greater activity in the right hemisphere when viewing pictures of their own faces. The interesting speculation is raised that self-awareness, a hallmark of consciousness and hence being human, derives from such right-hemisphere activity.

Masino, A. A., & Frostig, R. D. (1996). Quantitative long-term imaging of the functional representation of a whisker in rat barrel cortex. *Proceedings of the National Academy of Sciences, 93,* 4942–4947. The brain receives sensory stimulation from the entire body, within and without. The cortex receives and coordinates this information. The barrel cortex of the rat, which is the somatosensory region that regulates responses to whisker stimulation, is a very interesting model system of input and output. Using intrinsic signal optical imaging (ISI), which collects video images of functional activity from the cortex, the authors examined the activity produced by a single whisker following rostro-caudal deflection. The results suggest that the cortex is dynamic and more integrative than previously thought, and that cortical processing of sensory information is both stable and plastic throughout the life span. Such flexibility defines the brain.

McEwen, B. S. (1998). *The hostage brain.* New York: Rockefeller University Press. This under-promoted book is an excellent general text on neuroscience and neurobiology. It is particularly notable for its illustrations. Clear, colorful, detailed, and complementing the text extremely well, the drawings are as valuable as the text in providing the reader with insight into the neuron's and the brain's functions. McEwen, who is past president of the Society for Neuroscience, is a concise writer with a lot to say. The information is presented clearly and accurately, and his passion for the field shines throughout. This fine book requires more attention from both lay and academic audiences.

Panksepp, J. (1998). *Affective neuroscience: The foundations of human and animal emotions.* New York: Oxford University Press. This volume describes the complex and difficult-to-define field of affective research—studies of emotion. If one thing is clear after reading this book, it is that what we call emotion in the human and in other animals is clearly a brain-derived phenomenon. When the brain works properly, emotion is regulated normally; when something goes awry, look out. With a particular focus on the neurochemistry of emotion, Panksepp makes the brain skeptic a fundamental believer in the biochemistry of affective responses.

Chapter Four

Microanatomy and Neurotransmission

Connections

Human and Mouse Genius

Do you remember the classmate who never studied but always got the best grades? Why do some people seem to learn so easily whereas others have to sweat for every grade? What causes such variability in learning ability?

Philosophers and psychologists have contemplated the constituents of genius for centuries. James Mill, a nineteenth-century Scottish philosopher, decided to sculpt the intellectual capacities of his son, John Stuart Mill, to make sure that John developed into a genius. To test his particular theory of mind, the elder Mill provided an enriched environment and proceeded to make his son into a regular reasoning machine.

By age 3, the younger Mill was studying Greek, and by age 8, he was studying Latin. By the time he was 10 years old he had read many classic works in these languages, and by age 12 he had written a book-length manuscript on the history of the Roman government. He later became a well-known British philosopher and eventually played a critical role in shaping the history of psychology. In his 1843 book, *A System of Logic,* Mill argued for a "science of human nature" at a time when many thought that a science of the mind was a preposterous idea (Benjamin, 1993).

The enriched environment probably contributed greatly to the development of John Stuart Mill's genius, but environment alone does not explain why one individual learns better or more quickly than another. Meet Greg Smith, a latter-day J. S. Mill and a college senior at Randolph Macon College at age 12. Although Greg was born to two intelligent, nurturing parents, it was not their intent to provide an environment fit for a genius. No Mozart sonatas played softly while Greg was in the womb, nor were flashcards introduced in the crib. Nevertheless, young Greg started flexing his cognitive muscles in infancy. He said his first words when he was 3 months old, and he was speaking in complete sentences and reciting entire books from memory before his first birthday. (In the average child, these events do not occur until the second or third year.) He was solving math problems by 14 months of age and was reading about dinosaurs by his second birthday.

Greg's parents fostered his intellectual development by always encouraging him to ask questions and to seek the most informed answers. This precocious child began school by spending two weeks in the second grade, then skipping to the fourth, and, by the spring of the same year, he was flourishing in a sixth-grade honors course. At the age of 8, Greg commenced high school and went to college just two years later. With an undergraduate degree in math, Greg plans to obtain four Ph.D.s by his eighteenth birthday.

How might neurobiology contribute to the genius Greg Smith displays? Dr. Joseph Tsien's work at Princeton University may point to an answer. Tsien became interested in a classic theory proposed by the Canadian psychologist Donald O. Hebb that is believed to be the cellular basis for learning and eventually memory. As we will see in this chapter and the next, the basis for genius may involve changes in the very basic interactions between and among neurons.

More than half a century after Hebb proposed his theory, Tsien and his group are focusing on the relationship between a chemical the brain produces and the sites that the chemical targets. This neurotransmitter-receptor coupling (involving *glutamate,* the major CNS excitatory neurotransmitter, and its specific receptor, *NMDA,* both described in Chapter Five) seems to follow Hebb's proposed learning rule that requires simultaneous neuron activation and a consequent change in the interaction between two or more neurons in a circuit. Essentially, there is a difference between the biochemical activity of "learned" versus "ignorant" neurons.

Tsien and his associates genetically engineered some mice that were able to make increased amounts of certain types of NMDA receptors and then tested them in a variety of learning situations (Tsien, 2002). Interestingly, the mice with enhanced NMDA receptors, dubbed *Doogie* mice after the child doctor on a TV show in the 1980s, outperformed the control animals. Tsien's work became quite popular; Doogie mice even became the topic of one of David Letterman's top ten lists!

Doogie mouse. BILL BALLENBERG.

Despite Tsien's efforts, neuroscientists still do not know how generalizable his findings are to human memory. Even so, it is instructive to think about possible neuronal mechanisms of enhanced and impaired learning abilities.

To look into the brain is to see living tissue and wonder. Francis Crick, a microbiologist and Nobel Prize winner, has noted that everything we do and everything we think is regulated by the complex actions and interactions of wet tissue, of neurons and glia (Crick, 1994). Joseph LeDoux (2002), a well-known neuroscientist interested in the fear response and other emotions, maintains that the synapse, the point of communication between two neurons, is the defining element of the human being. There is nothing mystical here, nothing cosmic, just basic biochemistry available for study and explication. The phenomenon of thought begins and ends with essential, basic biological processes.

Neurotransmission is accomplished by elegant, understandable, and very describable electrochemical events open to study by neuroscientists. Keep in mind (that is, in your own firing neurons) that what we are describing may be infinitely complex, but it is subject to exploration and study—unlike subjective models of mind that are incapable of defining the variables they purport to study (see Chapter One). Understanding how neurons maintain and generate their activities forms the foundation for understanding how neurons communicate. This is the objective of this chapter. Knowing this basis of neuronal communication prepares you to understand its disruption in the mental disorders discussed throughout the text.

MICROANATOMY OF THE NEURON

In many respects, the neuron is similar to every other cell in the body. For example, neurons react to a variety of chemical and physical agents with some internal and, subsequently, some external modification. Whereas skin cells respond to continuous rubbing by forming a blister and then a callus, a neuron, according to the electrical and chemical inputs it receives, modifies its activity, accelerating or decelerating its interaction with other cells. This ebb and flow of neuronal activity governs and defines nervous system activity.

Two major features separate neurons from other cells and represent major evolutionary adaptations. First and most important, neurons can transmit the information they receive to other neurons and to tissues, including muscles and blood vessels. This feature enables rapid signaling and communication throughout the body. Second, neurons function collectively as circuits—the nuclei, fiber pathways, and nerves described in Chapter Three—moving information quickly and efficiently from inception to conclusion, adding to its richness en route to consciousness and behavior. We describe neural circuitry, including the neuroanatomy of stress, in Chapter Five.

Another functional peculiarity of neurons that adds somewhat to their uniqueness is their collective inability to recover naturally from damage. Although there is evidence that neurons are produced throughout the lifetime of an individual, the cells do not regenerate and regain function as simply as other cells in the body. If you fall down and scrape the skin off your knee, those cells grow back. That may not happen with

sensory neurons Refers to the specialized cells that transmit, input, and interpret physical stimuli (light, sound, touch, etc.) from the external world and translate it into neuronal impulses.

motor neurons Broad phrase referring either to the output neurons carrying-out the commands from sensory and interneurons, or to neurons at the interface of glands, muscles and blood vessels.

cell membrane Membrane that retains the cell's shape and contains the cytoplasm, nucleus, and assorted organelles. The membrane is a bimolecular leaflet with semi-permeable properties.

a damaged nerve fiber or cell body. Neurons contain biological information: when they die, they take that information with them.

Information begins its journey from neuron to brain in the form of sensory stimulation, signals that are unreadable by the CNS in their raw, physical state. Their capture involves **sensory neurons,** specialized cellular receptors that reside at the beginning of the chain of peripheral nervous system transmission. Sensory neurons transduce physical energy into neural impulses (propagated action potentials). That is, they convert stimuli—sound waves (hearing), photons (light/dark and color), chemicals (taste and olfactory), pressure (touch), and gravity/spatial stimuli (proprioceptive)—into electrochemical signals recognizable by the CNS. The simplest spinal reflexes, discussed in Chapter Three, are accomplished by the coordination of sensory neurons (information getting into the nervous system), interneuron activity (association, processing, and decision making); and **motor neurons** (output or action). What we call behavior is the net result of electrochemical neurotransmission; consciousness, our awareness of some of the brain's activity, is merely one point along this continuous loop of neural transmission.

External Structure and Function of the Neuron

How does all this highly complex activity come about? The answer, not so simply, is through the activity of the neuron, the basic unit of the nervous system. Sophisticated imaging and neurophysiological techniques utilizing single active neurons have provided a wealth of new data about the neuron, its structure and function, its chemistry and electrical activity. These data demonstrate how groups of neurons dictate brain function and flexibility. Plasticity is inherent to the brain; the brain can respond to nearly every exigency for which evolution has prepared it.

Neurons take on a nearly infinite number of shapes, lengths, branching patterns, activity levels, and interactions with other neurons and CNS structures (Figure 4.1). Neurons of all types, however, share similar characteristics and functions. For example during neurotransmission information travels from an input signal delivered through the cell membrane to a trigger zone near the cell body and is conducted via the axon to output through the terminal buttons (Figure 4.2). Like links in a highly specialized and dynamic chain, each neuron has the capacity to receive, process, and transmit information. But because neurons are forceful and fluid structures, defining their beginning and end is subjective. Like stepping into a rapidly flowing river, we arbitrarily define upstream and downstream.

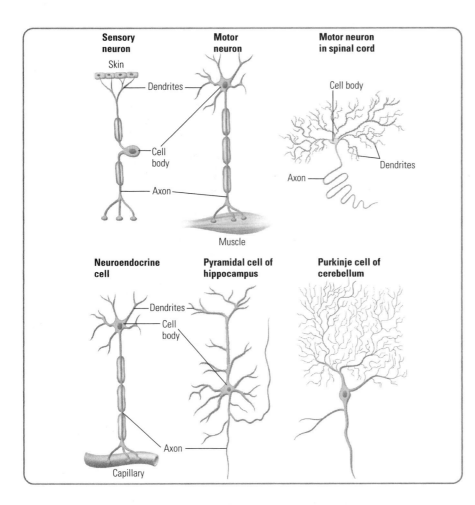

Sensory neuron
Skin
Dendrites
Cell body
Axon

Motor neuron
Muscle

Motor neuron in spinal cord
Cell body
Dendrites
Axon

Neuroendocrine cell
Dendrites
Cell body
Axon
Capillary

Pyramidal cell of hippocampus

Purkinje cell of cerebellum

[Figure 4.1]
Types of neurons. The nervous system is rife with variety in shape, activity, and function in its basic unit, the neuron. Though the three general components—dendrites, cell body or soma, and axon—are present in each neuron, neurons can take on a spectacular array of shapes, sizes, and lengths, any of which may be plastic and responsive to the surrounding environment throughout the course of the organism's life.
ADAPTED FROM KANDEL, SCHWARTZ, & JESSEL, 1995, FIGURE 2.8.

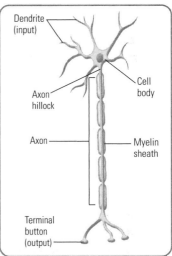

Dendrite (input)
Axon hillock
Axon
Cell body
Myelin sheath
Terminal button (output)

[Figure 4.2]
Functional areas of the neuron. The neuron's functional areas operate together to generate an action potential or to remain at rest. The action potential travels from an input zone on the cell membrane (the dendrites are a major input zone) to a trigger component near the cell body where information is integrated and a biochemical decision is made to fire or not, a conductile zone (the axon) that carries the action potential down the length of axon, and an output of neurotransmitter at the axon terminal.
ADAPTED FROM KANDEL, SCHWARTZ, & JESSEL, 1995, FIGURE 2.8.

Cell membrane and its gateways. The neuron's three-dimensional structure is maintained and defined by the **cell membrane,** the enclosure that surrounds the neuron and all other animal cells. The double-layered cell membrane acts as a flexible boundary between the intracellular and extracellular environments and encloses the internal structures that regulate cellular function. The cell membrane is semipermeable, functioning simultaneously as barrier and gateway to regulate the flow of chemicals (mostly water and dissolved salts) into and out of the neuron according to its activity state.

If too much water enters a cell, for example, it will burst; with too little water it will shrivel. Likewise the chemical balance between the inside and the outside of the cell must be regulated for the neuron to function properly. Water and dissolved salts play prominent roles in cellular function. Like the seawater that surrounded the earliest living cells billions of

[Figure 4.3]
Structure of the cell membrane. The primary feature of the cell membrane is its semipermeable nature. When the neuron is at rest, the ionic balance between intracellular and extracellular space is tilted slightly toward negative inside the neuron. When an action potential is signaled, the membrane selectively allows ions to enter or leave the neuron through the pores or channels that permeate its surface, thereby briefly modifying the electrical properties of the membrane.

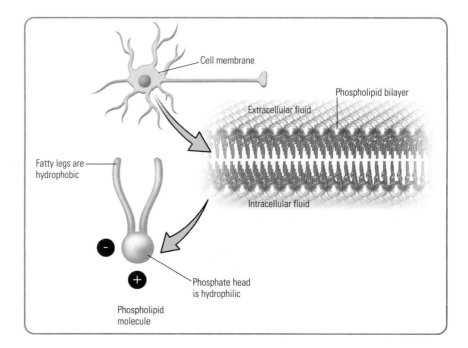

Cell membrane

Phospholipid bilayer

Extracellular fluid

Intracellular fluid

Fatty legs are hydrophobic

Phosphate head is hydrophilic

Phospholipid molecule

phospholipid bilayer Basis of neuron cell membranes. Each molecule has a water-soluble head (a protein compatible with water) and a water-rejecting tail (consisting of a lipid). The head faces a watery solution (cytoplasm or extracellular fluid between cells) while the lipid tail faces another lipid tail in the interior of the cell membrane.

ion channels Membrane-spanning proteins that form a pore allowing passage of ions from one side of the membrane to the other. The process results in either depolarization or hyperpolarization of the cell.

years ago, the fluid outside our cells is in the main a solution of dissolved sodium chloride (that's right: table salt). The extracellular fluid is relatively more positive in electrical charge and the intracellular space slightly negative in charge due to the differing concentration of dissolved ions (charged atoms) inside and outside the cell. Sodium (Na^+) and chloride (Cl^-) ions are prominent, along with many other dissolved salts, including potassium chloride (KCl) and calcium chloride ($CaCl_2$).

The barrier portion of the cell membrane is made up of a dual, complementary set of phosphate and fat (lipid) molecules, arranged head to leg to form a **phospholipid bilayer** (Figure 4.3). The phosphate-containing head of the molecule is permeable to water (hydrophilic), and the fatty hydrocarbon leg portion is repellent to water (hydrophobic).

Whereas the fatty legs are electrically neutral, the phosphate heads are polar. That is, like water, phosphate carries a slight positive charge in one area and a slight negative charge in another. As shown in Figure 4.3, the heads are in contact with water inside and outside the cell while the legs form the sheltered inner layer of the membrane. This "oil and water" arrangement acts as an effective barrier to the free passage of materials into and out of the neuron.

Charged atoms, particularly Na^+ and K^+, do leach through the cell membrane via embedded proteins that form its permeable portions. In fact, the membrane is peppered with proteins that act as **ion channels** for substances entering and leaving the cell and as **receptors,** or binding locations, for neurochemicals. These protein mechanisms selectively allow substances to cross the cell membrane to accommodate neural activity and intercourse with the extracellular space—in short, to enable neural communication.

Proteins can do all this because they have the ability to change shape when chemicals bind to them or when triggered by other chemical or electrical changes. Channels of differing sizes and shapes allow the passage or block the passage of specific substances; for example, channels allow potassium ions free entry and exit into and out of the cell (Figure 4.4a). Gated channels allow the passage of substances when open but block passage when closed (Figure 4.4b). Protein pumps change shape to ferry materials across the cell membrane (Figure 4.4c).

The cell membrane thus constitutes a mosaic of structures that defines the activity of dendrite, cell body, and axon. It becomes very apparent that the life and activity of the neuron depends in large part on the cell membrane, without whose constraints neural activity would not occur.

Dendrites: Extending the neuron's reach. The **dendrites,** pinched and elongated sections of the cell body, gather information for the neuron by extending the cell membrane's surface area. Imagine a surgical glove filled with water, where the palm and back of the hand is the cell body and the fingers are the dendrites. The word dendrite is derived from the Greek *dendron,* meaning "tree." A glance at a leafless tree in wintertime is nothing so much as the image of a neuron.

Indeed, the diverse patterns of branching that dendrites display (*dendritic arborization*) are the major contributor to the anatomical complexity of neurons and can take many shapes, numbers, and ramifying directions (see Figure 4.1). The dendrite allows a neuron to probe well beyond its geographical location (defined as where the cell body sits) to establish synapses with more distant neurons and body tissues. This probing extends the reach of the neuron, the informational net that any one neuron casts. For

receptors Areas on a neuron specialized to be highly sensitive to a specific type of stimulation or chemical.

dendrites Thin, widely branching fibers that emanate from the cell body of a neuron and "collect" information from adjacent neurons and other cells.

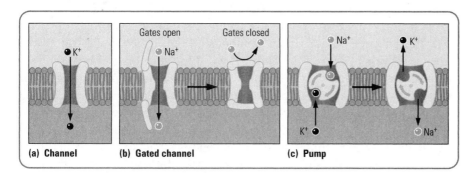

[Figure 4.4]
Types of ion channels in the cell membrane. (a) Ions can pass through appropriately shaped channels in the cell membrane. (b) When a gated channel is open, substances can pass through, but when the gates are closed, the substances are prevented from crossing the membrane. (c) Pumps change shape to ferry material across the cell membrane and are active most of the time, using a tremendous amount of cellular fuels.
ADAPTED FROM KOLB & WHISHAW, 2004.

(a) Channel **(b) Gated channel** **(c) Pump**

Purkinje neurons Neurons in the cerebellum that are responsible for all the output from the cerebellar cortex to cerebellar nuclei.

dendritic spines Short, plastic outgrowths along the dendrites that increase surface area and where the majority of synapses are found.

cell body (*or* soma) Structure of the cell that contains the nucleus, cytoplasm, and various organelles used in cell metabolism.

organelles "Organlike" structures in the cytoplasm of the cell membrane that help in the maintenance and metabolism of the cell.

example, as shown in Figure 4.1, dendrites from **Purkinje neurons** (neurons found only in the cerebellum) have an elaborate branching network, with trails going in every direction. Next to a neuron from the hippocampus, whose dendritic branching is sedate by comparison, the cerebellar neuron is notable for the amount of information processing of which it and its associated cells are capable. Thus, we have an example of a unifying principle that is repeated throughout the brain: Form follows function.

Dendrites extend the surface area of the neuron well beyond its otherwise limited radius, and tiny, thornlike projections called **dendritic spines** extend the surface area of some neurons even farther. Increased surface area enables dendrites to establish more connections with ever more neurons. Dendritic spines can number in the thousands per neuron, depending on the brain region. Each spine affords the neuron an additional site for communicating with additional neurons, thereby enabling the neuron to increase its information inputs.

More or longer spines give this structural latticework the capability of actively responding to stimuli and actively seeking out new connections, and this neuronal plasticity can substantially alter the information processing capabilities of any one neuron (Engert & Bonhoeffer, 1999; Maletic-Savatic, Malinow, & Svoboda, 1999). Indeed, changes in dendritic spines, in addition to other manipulations that modify neuronal transmission (such as the altered glutamate receptors observed in the Doogie mice discussed in the chapter opening Connections), may contribute significantly to the brain's capacity to learn throughout life. The numbers of dendritic spines can fluctuate, depending on data load (the activity levels of the neuron) and the type of neuron, and form distinct neuronal networks, as first suggested by Hebb. That such anatomical features wax and wane in the face of alterations in stimulation suggests an efficient adaptation to the demands of input, processing, and output of information.

Cell Body and Organelles: A Cellular Factory

The **cell body,** or **soma,** is the site where the neuron assembles proteins, generates energy and maintains metabolism (Figure 4.5). *Soma* is both the Greek word for body and the Sanskrit word for an intoxicating Vedic religious ceremonial drink. In Aldous Huxley's *Brave New World,* a tale that presaged the current search for wonder neurochemicals (it was published in 1932), a substance called "soma" was ingested for correcting one's brain.

The shape of the soma can range from a tiny round body in, for example, the anterior hypothalamus to an enormous ovoid shape in spinal neurons and to the striking triangular shape characteristic of pyramidal neu-

Dendrite: Cell extension that collects information from other cells

Dendritic spines: Small protrusions on dendrites that increase surface area

Nucleus: Central structure containing the chromosomes and genes

Nuclear membrane: Membrane surrounding the nucleus

Endoplasmic reticulum: Folded layers of membrane where proteins are assembled

Mitochondrion: Structure that gathers, stores, and releases energy

Intracellular fluid: Fluid in which the cell's internal structures are suspended

Microtubules: Tiny tubes that transport molecules and help give the cell its shape

Cell membrane: Membrane surrounding the cell

Golgi body: Membranous structure that packages protein molecules for transport

Microfilaments: Threadlike fibers making up much of the cell's "skeleton"

Lysosomes: Sacs containing enzymes that break down wastes

Axon: Extension that transmits information from cell body to other cells

rons in the hippocampus. Within the cell, individual subcomponents, the **organelles,** carry out the protein production and metabolic regulation functions. Like a thriving factory, neuron function depends on the coordination of specialized organelles under the control of the genetic instructions that are encoded and transmitted to them.

Collectively, the organelles interact within the cell, but each is a discrete unit defined and enclosed by its own semipermeable membrane. The differences that abound among organelles have led many scientists to conclude that during the early stages of evolution formerly independent subcellular components banded together because it was advantageous to do so. The resulting give and take of exchanging functions ensured survival of the cell and eventually the neuron (Edelman, 1993; Woese, 2002). It is an interesting scenario to ponder—and one whose likelihood increases with better understanding of the various activities of the different organelles.

[Figure 4.5]
Cell body and organelles.
Many of the neuron's internal structures and organelles reside in the dendrites and axon as well as in the cell body, which is illustrated in detail here. These organelles and features collaborate to render the neuron capable of plasticity and rapid and longlasting responsiveness to its environment.
ADAPTED FROM KOLB & WHISHAW, 2004.

nucleus Structure within the cell that contains the chromosomes.

deoxyribonucleic acid (DNA) Molecule that composes the chromosomes.

messenger RNA (mRNA) RNA molecule transcribed from DNA and translated into amino acid sequence of a polypeptide.

amino acids The so-called building blocks of proteins, composed of an amino group (NH2) and a carboxylic acid (COOH). These are essential components of proteins and the basis for organic life.

transcription The process by which DNA is "copied" and transferred to mRNA for subsequent protein synthesis.

endoplasmic reticulum Network of thin tubes within a cell that transport newly synthesized proteins to other locations.

ribosomes Bulbous structures in the nucleus that are the primary destination for mRNA and the location of translation and assembly of proteins.

translation The process by which messenger ribonucleic acid (mRNA) is "read" by ribosomes in the neuron and protein synthesis is initiated.

Nucleus and executive function. Nucleus is from the Latin word for nut. Like many anatomical descriptions that are based on what the object resembles in the namer's experience, the image of the "nut" or nucleus located roughly centrally within the "shell" or soma probably explains its moniker.

The nucleus has as its main occupants delicately beautiful molecules of double-stranded **deoxyribonucleic acid (DNA)**. Each strand of DNA is composed of chromosomes, long strands of genes, that are the repository of the organism's heredity. Each gene carries a set of instructions for synthesizing a specific protein necessary to the neuron's structure or function.

Protein synthesis begins with the formation of a complex of molecules called **messenger ribonucleic acid (mRNA)**. The "message" is composed of a string of nucleotides that give rise to **amino acids**, organic molecules that are the constituents of proteins derived from a specific gene on the DNA and, metaphorically, is like copying a note and giving it to a person to deliver to someone else. The process of copying the DNA onto a quantity of mRNA is called **transcription**. The transcript, the bit of extruded mRNA, leaves the nucleus by means of pores in the nuclear membrane.

Endoplasmic reticulum, ribosomes, and protein synthesis. The **endoplasmic reticulum (ER)** resembles stacks of folded sheets, one on top of the other, and forms a continuous membrane with the nucleus. Such continuity and contiguity enable efficient transfer of instructions from the genome for the synthesis of proteins.

Structurally, the rough ER looks like its name: the membrane possesses groups of associated bulbous structures that resemble irregularly shaped BBs or pellets. These structures, called **ribosomes,** are the primary destination for mRNA and the location of translation and assembly of proteins in the neuron. The ribosomes come in several varieties, each of which performs some specific form of protein synthesis within the neuron. In clusters, as viewed in electron photomicrographs, they resemble tiny, round footprints, like those of a cat.

Ribosomes can be attached to the rough ER; they can be floating free in the cytoplasm; and several free ribosomes can be attached to each other by means of a thin strand of mRNA (see Figure 4.5). The mRNA transcripts arrive at these sites, amino acids are recruited in a set sequence for each protein, and synthesis ensues as determined by the codons. The messenger has taken the message, and it has arrived at its destination; it is ready to be "read." The means whereby an mRNA transcript is read and directs the formation of proteins is called **translation.**

The smooth ER lacks the number of ribosomes observed on the rough ER and, though continuous with the rough ER, synthesizes different proteins. The major difference between smooth ER and rough ER is the eventual destination for the proteins that each produces. The smooth ER produces proteins destined for use inside the cell. **Enzymes,** for example, are proteins that facilitate chemical reactions and are intimately involved in the regulation of activity inside the neuron. The rough ER produces proteins that migrate to the cell membrane to act as channels, gates, or pumps or outside the neuron for extracellular purposes. Neurotransmitters, for example, are produced for use outside the neuron.

Mitochondria and metabolism. As the neuron's energy center, the **mitochondria** are the site of cellular metabolism. Here the **precursors** (foundational ingredients) of cellular fuels (fats, sugars, and proteins from food) react with oxygen to produce **adenosine triphosphate (ATP).** This cycle, first proposed by the German-British chemist Hans Krebs, now bears his name.

ATP is the essential metabolic fuel used by the neuron to power its myriad activities. Chief among these metabolically expensive activities is maintaining the neuron's resting internal electrical charge as negative relative to the slightly more positive extracellular fluid. This fundamental charge, found in the simplest battery, underlies neurotransmission, the basis of thought and consciousness.

Golgi apparatus and lysosomes: Packaging and recycling centers. The **Golgi apparatus** resembles and is actually a variation of the ER. Lying farther away from the nucleus than the ER, the Golgi apparatus is involved in the post-translational sorting and packaging of proteins for transport. Many proteins are enveloped in a thin sac or membrane called a **vesicle** before they are routed to other specific regions within the neuron.

Contrasting with these constructive activities are the activities of the **lysosomes,** mild acid-containing vesicles that permit cells literally to digest and assimilate targeted material. These organelles are very effective at clearing the neuron of the residue of neuronal activity. And since neurons are incapable of replication and substantial self-repair, the lysosomes provide the neuron with an efficient system for recovering and reusing proteins and amino acids that are the byproducts of cellular activity, and for removing troublesome proteins that may enter the neuron.

Neuronal Cytoskeleton: Structure and Transport

The neuron is a three-dimensional structure that requires support so that the three dimensions do not sag and collapse into two. The neuron also

enzymes Proteins that facilitate chemical reactions and are intimately involved in the regulation of activity inside the neuron.

mitochondria (sing. **mitochondrion**) Structures in the cell that perform the metabolic activities that provide energy.

precursors Constituent and elemental substances that serve as the initial components in a chain of chemicals. For instance, fats and sugars combine with oxygen to form cellular fuels.

adenosine triphosphate (ATP) Chemical the body uses as its primary way of delivering energy where it is needed; also used as a neurotransmitter.

Golgi apparatus Set of membranes in the cytoplasm that wraps around chemicals released by secretory cells. In neurons this structure manufactures the synaptic vesicles.

vesicle Tiny, nearly spherical packet at the axon terminal filled with the neurotransmitter.

lysosomes Neuronal organelles that engage in cellular cleansing and similar "house-cleaning" activities to maintain neuronal function.

[Figure 4.6]
Cytoskeleton. The cytoskeleton is the scaffold on which the neuron "hangs." It is composed of different forms of fibril structures that provide the neuron with shape, support, and a variety of trafficking functions. (a) The neurofilaments (also neurofibrils) are rope-like or cablelike strands of proteins wound together in a sinewy length of filament that extends throughout the axon. (b) The microfilaments are extremely thin strands of actin that provide structural support for the neuron. (c) As the name implies, the microtubules are tiny tubular structures.

(a) Neurofilaments   (b) Microtubules   (c) Microfilaments

25 nm   25 nm   25 nm

is capable of subtle movements, shifting back into place as the brain is propelled through space. The neuron's significant internal distances pose a delivery problem for the proteins and nutrients it synthesizes, stores, and releases. The cytoskeleton is an ingenious evolutionary solution to these problems. Made up of three different systems, the cytoskeleton functions as both flexible scaffold and transport system, bending to the waves that buffet the neuron but allowing for uninterrupted commerce from site to site inside the cell. The three components of the cytoskeleton we will discuss here are the neurofilaments, the microfilaments, and the mictotubules (Figure 4.6).

Resembling a chain of squat, fingerlike appendages stacked one on top of another, the **neurofilaments** are similar to structural proteins found in other cells in the body and are involved in the control and transport of membrane proteins (Kandel, Schwartz, & Jessell, 2000). Recent data using live cell imaging (Wang, Ho, Sun, Liem, & Brown, 2000) suggest that proteins move along the neurofilaments by means of "sprints, not a marathon" (Brady, 2000, p. E-43). What this means is that in addition to structural support, the neurofilamants participate in the transfer of neuronal products within the cytoplasm through an intermittent process of stop/start down their lengths. What happens when these fibrillary elements age is another matter. The data suggest that damage to or breakdowns in the neurofilaments contribute to the neurofibrillary tangles characteristic of Alzheimer's disease and described in Chapter Six (Arendt, 2001; Ashford & Jarvik, 1985; Ashford, Mattson, & Kumar, 1998; Ashford & Schmitt, 2001; Ashford, Soultanian, Zhang, & Geddes, 1998; Mesulam, 2000).

The second cytoskeletal component is the **microfilaments,** found in abundance in dendrites and axons and believed to provide structural support for them (Kandel et al., 2000). They are membrane-associated proteins attached by means of fibrous connections to the intracellular portion of the cell membrane. Numerous microscopic examinations have demonstrated that microfilaments are a rather dynamic set of cytoskeletal elements because they provide scaffoldlike support for the neuron's movement, including the changing structure of its neurites (dendrites and axon) in response to a host of external stimuli (Peters, Palay, & Webster,

neurofilaments Neuronal structural proteins involved in membrane protein transport.

microfilaments Intraneuronal flexible supporting elements associated with membranes.

1991). They also act like micromuscles, flexing and bowing and allowing contractions within the neuron to compensate for the external movements of head and body.

Microtubules are twice the size of neurofilaments and, as their name implies, are very small tubes. They run down the length of the dendrites and axon. Microtubules play a role in the transfer and movement of various substances and organelles throughout the cytoplasm to intracellular locations. In particular, together with the neurofilaments, the microtubules make possible the processes of fast and slow axoplasmic transport.

Fast axoplasmic (anterograde) transport, which moves in the same direction as the action potential, refers to the movement of proteins, primarily synaptic vesicles and their internal products and precursor proteins (that may require integration into existing complexes). These materials move from the soma down the length of the axon to the terminal buttons at a rate of up to 400 millimeters per day—an enormous distance in cellular terms. The movement of substances is probably accomplished by means of the transport molecule, kinesin, which resembles cilia or molecular feet on the body of the microtubules. The kinesin literally walks the proteins to and fro along the microtubule.

Slow axoplasmic (retrograde) transport, on the other hand, shuffles proteins around the soma, usually from axon to soma (perhaps to alert

microtubules Proteins in the cell bodies and axons of neurons that transport nutrients within the cell, especially from the cell nucleus out to the axon and down to the terminal buttons.

[Table 4.1]

Inner Transport System of the Neuron

	Speed	Rate of flow	Function	Motor protein used	Enzyme used	Type of cytoskeletal component involved
Anterograde transport (carried away from cell body)	Fast	Up to 400 mm/day	Carries synaptic vesicles to and throughout axon	Kinesin	ATPase	Microtubules
	Slow (slow axonal or axoplasmic flow)	0.2–2.5 (slow) and 0.4–5.0 (less slow) mm/day	Carries cytosolic proteins as well as intraneuronal "housekeeping" enzymes to and throughout cytoskeleton	Not currently known	Not currently known	Microtubules and neurofilaments
Retrograde transport (carried toward the cell body)	Fast	Up to 300 mm/day	Recycles used synaptic vesicles; works in conjunction with lysosomes	Dynein	ATPase	Microtubules

axon Fiberlike outgrowth from the cell body of a neuron that is cylindrical until the very end, when it breaks into numerous small branches; the "sending" fiber of the neuron, it carries the nerve impulse.

axon hillock Swelling of the soma of the neuron, the point where the axon begins and an action potential "firing decision" is made.

terminal buttons At the tip of an axon, the points from which the axon releases chemicals (neurotransmitters).

glia (or glial cells) Nonneuronal cells in the nervous system that provide, among other things, support for neuronal structures and insulation of neuronal messages.

the soma to alterations in metabolic requirements). Whereas kinesin is the legs for fast axonal transport, for slow axonal transport the transport molecule is dynein (which acts similarly to kinesin). Overall, the movement of proteins and organelles and substances around the neuron, including those to be used inside the neuron for cellular maintenance and structural integrity, and those to be released for neuronal communication, is accomplished efficiently by means of these transport assemblies.

Dynamic Elements of the Neuronal Communication and Connection and the Synapse

Axon: Information conductor. The neural membrane is drawn out into radiating processes, like a piece of taffy stretched in different directions. These processes encompass the neuron's information-gathering apparatus—the dendrites and branches—and the **axon,** the information-conducting apparatus that transmits the action potential.

The axon is a long, threadlike structure with smooth contours and a cylindrical shape that resembles a thin peninsula off the soma and ramifies by branching at obtuse angles. Its initial segment, as it leaves the soma and begins its meandering, is the **axon hillock,** the trigger zone where the action potential is initiated (see Figure 4.2). Where the axon branches, the divisions are generally the same diameter, demonstrating the principle of neuronal segregation of function (e.g., segregation of the actions of the axons and the actions of the dendrite). The diameter of the axon ranges in size, depending on species and type of neuron, from less than 1 μm (micron; 0.000001 meter) to 25 μm (in the human) to over 1 mm in the giant squid. The axon may also extend at great distances from the soma, traveling for meters in some individuals (e.g., into the peripheral nervous system). Basketball players Shaquille O'Neal and Yao Ming have very long axons.

In fact, neurons can be classified by the length of their axons. A projection neuron is one in which the axon is long, extending from one part of the brain to another, for example. A neuron with a short axon has mainly local effects within a local circuit. The filamentous nature of the axon belies its ruggedness as an amazing regenerating station for the conduction of the action potential and the propagation of a nerve impulse from one neuron to the next. The axon transmits the nervous signals around the brain and from the brain to distant sites in the body.

Terminal buttons: Getting the message across. As the axon snakes its way to the neurons on which it synapses, it reaches its terminus, which may involve many smaller branches from a single axon, looking like Medusa standing on her head. At the end of these multiple axonal endpoints are the **terminal buttons,** or *boutons. (Bouton* is the French word for "button." *Bouton* also bears some relation to the French term *boutade,* a sudden fit of temper, which conjures up an interesting metaphor. When one imagines the events taking place at the synapse, it is not difficult to envision a tiny explosion as neurotransmitter is propelled across the synapse.) The terminal button takes many shapes, but generally it is a bulbous outgrowth from the axon tip that increases the surface area for the release of neurotransmitter to the postsynaptic neuron or organ (Figure 4.7).

The synapse is a general term referring to the way in which one neuron connects to another or to a target organ, depending on the system with which it is associated. In general, there are only two types of synapses, excitatory and inhibitory; both involve the release, action, reuptake, and degradation of the released substances. But the way in which the regulation of pre- and post-synaptic events occurs and the multiplicity of targets on which neurons synapse is testament to the variety of nervous regulation. But all is maintained by this simple on-off system. Add to this the self-regulation that some neurons have by means of recurrent axonal collaterals (self-synapsing connections that are largely inhibitory), and it is apparent that a neuron is an impressive complex of activity.

NEUROGLIA

Neurons are wondrous structures. (Ironically, it is our neurons telling us this.) Perhaps less amazing but more mysterious are the **glia** (or *neuroglia,* literally, "nerve glue"), or glial cells, cells in the nervous system that insulate neurons, provide support and nutrition, and remove waste products. Glia are a class of brain cell whose contributions to brain function and maintenance are just beginning to be understood, and whose potentially novel role in brain activities, formerly attributed to neurons alone, is coming to light.

[Figure 4.7] Synapses. The neuron is like the movie star at a Hollywood premier. All manner of external activity impinges on it to attract its attention. The neuron, however, is contacted by synapses that are laid on it at every level. Axodendritic (axon to dendrite) synapses, the prototypical neuronal connection, involve dendritic spines. The majority of such synapses are excitatory in nature. Axosomatic (axon to cell body) synapses are largely inhibitory. Axoaxonic (axon to axon) synapses are also largely inhibitory. Axon collaterals are synapses that arise from the neuron's own axon; they, too, are primarily inhibitory.
ADAPTED FROM THOMPSON, 2000.

Astrocyte
Star-shaped, symmetrical; nutritive and support function

Microglial cell
Small, mesodermally derived; defensive function

Oligodendroglial cell
Asymmetrical; forms myelin around axons in brain and spinal cord

Schwann cell
Asymmetrical; wraps around peripheral nerves to form myelin

[Figure 4.8]

Types of neuroglia. The ubiquitous glial cell is shedding its image as a caretaker of neurons; its role as a mediator of neurotransmission is broadening and deepening as new techniques demonstrate the glial cell's importance to nervous function. The glial cell takes on many forms throughout the CNS.

ADAPTED FROM KOLB & WHISHAW, 2004.

blood-brain barrier Protective environment formed by tightly packed capillaries and neutroglia that prevents passage into the brain of most substances circulating in the blood.

astrocyte Relatively large, star-shaped glial cell found in the CNS.

myelin sheath Insulating material that covers many vertebrate axons.

Neuroglia outnumber neurons by a ratio of 50:1 (Kandel et al., 2000). Figure 4.8 illustrates classes of neuroglia.

In the mid-nineteenth century, Rudolf Virchow examined neuroglia in the spinal cord and the ventricle walls of the brain. He named the cells "nerve glue" because they surround the neurons and bind them in place in the three-dimensional space of the brain. Virchow reported that the neuroglia are situated between neurons and blood supply and appear to act as a barrier between the two—a **blood-brain barrier** that prevents unwanted substances in the blood supply from entering the brain (Figure 4.9).

Virchow's observation presaged the role ascribed to the glia thereafter, that of neuronal support and maintenance. Peters, Palay, and Webster (1991) classify neuroglia as *macroglia* (including astrocytes and oligodendrocytes, on which we will focus) and *microglia,* macrophagelike scavenger cells in the CNS. Their classification system—one of many for glia—uses data largely derived from electron microscopy studies, which may differ in many ways from what is observed using other techniques and stains.

The **astrocyte,** which has a star or stellate shape, is the most numerous cell type in the brain. The astrocytes are interposed between the neuron and the blood vessels, where they act as a metabolic intermediary transferring nourishing glucose to the neuron from the blood supply and regulating glutamate production and neurotransmission, thereby maintaining a balance between intracellular and extracellular stores of neuronal synaptic resources. Further, the astrocyes' endfeet, the terminal portions of the glial cell that resemble the neurites of neurons, function as a capillary boundary that contributes to the functional blood brain barrier that protects the brain from blood-borne pathogens and chemicals.

Astrocytes "harvest" excess ions from the extracellular fluid, thereby maintaining the delicate balance of chemical concentrations necessary to neurotransmission and nervous activity. Also, should a neuron die or become morbid, the astrocytes and microphages function as scavengers, moving quickly to eliminate (by ingesting the remains) and in some cases kill off damaged neurons in a process referred to as phagocytosis, described in Chapter Twelve (Kandel et al., 2000). Further, at these times, the astrocytes can also reorganize some of the synaptic relationships, playing a role in the plasticity of the neuronal substrate. Therefore, the astrocytes, together with the microglia, perform a valuable set of services to ensure that necrosis and neuronal littering, which could interfere with the efficient processing of electrochemical signals, are minimized and compensated for.

The *oligodendrocyte* complements the astrocyte. Whereas astrocytes nurture and police the neurons, the oligodendrocytes add support, particularly during development, and an engineering adaptation to neurons in the form of a lipid : protein (~80 : 20) axonal wrapping called the **myelin sheath.** The myelin sheath increases the efficiency of the neural impulses in the CNS as they fire along axons (Figure 4.10). The oligodendrocytes produce segments of myelin during early brain development. The featured Investigator in this chapter, Keith Black (Box 4.1, page 129), has made contributions to understanding the workings of myelin and the blood-brain barrier through his work with chemotherapy agents and brain tumors.

The PNS counterpart to the oligodendrocyte is the Schwann cell. Both gently embrace naked axons, whereupon layer after layer of the myelin is deposited from inside out. The result is an axon wrapped in a lipid-protein covering that serves as both a protective coating and a functional enhancement for the electrochemical activities of the neuron.

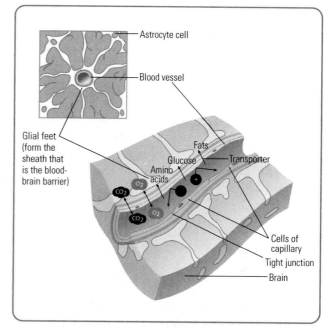

[Figure 4.9]
Blood-brain barrier. Cells that form capillaries in the brain have tight junctions and are blanketed by the glial feet of astrocytes, properties that prevent substances from moving in and out easily. Oxygen and carbon dioxide can flow freely across this blood-brain barrier. Substances such as fats, glucose, and amino acids can be transported across it, but most large, ionic molecules cannot cross.

[Figure 4.10]
Myelination. (a) Oligodendrocytes myelinate axons in the CNS. (b) Schwann cells myelinate axons in the PNS. Unmyelinated gaps between the glial cells are called nodes of Ranvier. These nodes play an important role in the propagation of the action potential, as they allow the electrical signal to "jump" across the gap where the signal strength of the action potential is revivified.

ADAPTED FROM KOLB & WHISHAW, 2000.

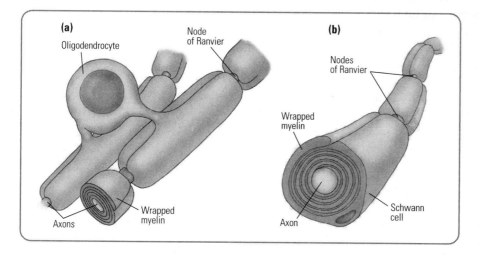

depolarization The actual change in the resting charge of the neuron, from slightly negative (polarized) to less negative/more positive (i.e., less polarized).

resting (or membrane) potential Electrical potential across a membrane when a neuron is at rest.

GENERATING AN ACTION POTENTIAL

Ultimately, what we do, who we are, and what we aspire to are no more than the sum of the parts of neurotransmission. Action potentials are the foot soldiers of neurotransmission, marching along an individual neuron to the incipient roar of **depolarization** (reduction in electrical charge across a membrane) to presynaptic electrochemical volleys and the firing of postsynaptic impulses that follow. Thought arises from this electrochemical activity (Figure 4.11).

Electrochemical Activity at the Cell Membrane

The fluids on either side of the cell membrane differ in charge because of their basic ionic compositions. Recall from your grade school science classes that like electrical charges repel, whereas opposite charges attract. Thus, a natural affinity exists between *anions* (negatively charged ions) and *cations* (positively charged ions), whereas like charges (+/+, cation/cation, and –/–, anion/anion) repel one another. Na^+ attracts Cl^-, whereas Na^+ and K^+ repel each other.

The predominant ions inside and outside the neuron are potassium (K^+), sodium (Na^+), and chloride (Cl^-), but their concentrations on either side of the cell membrane differ. Na^+ and Cl^- are in high concentration outside; K^+ and negatively charged (anionic) protein molecules (A^-) are highly concentrated inside the cell (Figure 4.12a). The semipermeable cell membrane must consume energy to maintain the separation and largely prevent the intracellular and extracellular components from coming into contact.

The difference in electrical charge between the intracellular state of the neuron (relatively more negative) and the extracellular surround (relatively more positive) creates a charge, the **resting (or membrane) potential,** across the cell membrane of an unstimulated neuron. The difference between the two sides is approximately 65 to 70 mV (millivolt = 0.001 volt; a single double-A battery, by comparison, holds a charge equivalent to 1.5 volts or 1500 mV). In other words, the interior fluid of the cell is –70 mV *relative* to the fluid outside (Figure 4.12b).

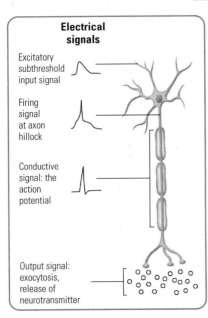

Electrical signals

Excitatory subthreshold input signal

Firing signal at axon hillock

Conductive signal: the action potential

Output signal: exocytosis, release of neurotransmitter

[Figure 4.11]
Path of neurotransmission. Stimulation from excitatory and inhibitory synaptic activity generates electrical signals within the neuron. As a result of integrating these signals, the neuron may maintain its slightly negative (resting) charge, or it may fire a signal that generates an action potential. Each functional area introduced in Figure 4.2 produces a characteristic electrical signal. At the cell membrane input zone, the neuron remains at rest, stimulated by excitatory and inhibitory (subthreshold) signals. Above-threshold stimulation at the cell membrane results in a firing signal at the trigger zone, that is, the axon hillock. The action potential signal is conducted down the axon, resulting in an output signal, represented in the release of neurotransmitter.
ADAPTED FROM KANDEL, SCHWARTZ, & JESSEL, 1995, FIGURE 2.8.

(a) Ion concentrations inside and outside the neuron

Low concentration

High concentration

Extracellular fluid

K⁺   Force of diffusion   Cl⁻   Electrostatic pressure   Force of diffusion   Na⁺   Electrostatic pressure

Intracellular fluid

Cannot leave cell   A⁻   Force of diffusion   K⁺   Electrostatic pressure   Cl⁻   Na⁺

Low concentration

High concentration

(b) Resting potential

Voltage (mV)   0   -70

Time   0 1 2 3 4

(c) Action potential

Na⁺   K⁺   Na⁺   K⁺

Voltage (mV)   20 0 -20 -40 -60 -80   Na⁺+ K⁺

Time   0 1 2 3 4

[Figure 4.12]
Electrochemical activity at the cell membrane. (a) At rest, the neuron is an electrical spring waiting to be sprung. The ion concentrations are a balance between positive ions (cations) and negative ions (anions), with the balance tipped slightly in the direction of anions because of the intracellular charge. (b) The resting membrane potential (RMP) is depicted here as a relative difference in intracellular and extracellular ionic charge. The cell membrane acts as a barrier to the two forces (electrostatic and diffusion pressure), attempting to bring the internal and external environments into equilibrium. (c) As the action potential is conveyed along the axon, voltage-gated channels open, allowing cations and anions to briefly exchange position, thereby changing the electrical properties of the membrane. As the channels reset, sodium-potassium pumps circulate the ions to exchange cations for anions. The neuron then readies itself for the subsequent action potential and the infinite number of ones to follow. The entire process occurs in milliseconds.
ADAPTED FROM CARLSON, 1999

Thus, the cell membrane at rest is polarized and holds the *potential* to change. The most extreme change from its resting state is the **action potential,** a lightning quick combination of chemical and electrical activity inside and outside the neuron that actually reverses the polarity of the axon's cell membrane. For about 1 msec (millisecond = 0.001 sec), the intracellular fluid acquires a positive charge relative to the extracellular fluid (Figure 4.12c).

Two processes basic to physics operate to maintain the resting potential and to set the stage for the action potential. The first is **electrostatic pressure,** the force exerted by the attraction or repulsion of electrical charges. The complementary force is **diffusion:** if no barrier were to separate them, cations and anions would diffuse and spread evenly within a given space. Eventually the positive and negative charges would be evenly distributed. For example, when regular table salt (NaCl) is dissolved in

action potential Physical basis of the nerve impulse; the depolarization of an axon produced by a stimulation beyond threshold potential.

electrostatic pressure Electrical attraction and repulsion (+/– and +/+, –/–, respectively); complement to diffusion.

diffusion Tendency for dissolved ions or molecules to move from areas of high concentration to areas of low concentration.

concentration gradient In diffusion, the attraction of a region of high concentration for one of low concentration.

threshold potential The electrochemical point at which a neuron will respond to incoming stimulation with an action potential.

graded potential Series of incoming electrical signals that have little or no effect on the neuron depolarizing or firing.

a glassful of room-temperature water (H_2O), its chemical bond is broken, and the Na^+ and Cl^- ions diffuse into the surrounding fluid.

The force governing the breakup and movement of salt ions is a **concentration gradient,** the attraction of a region of high concentration for one of low concentration. Imagine a chain link fence with thousands of music fans milling around on one side and their favorite band on the other side. If that fence, the barrier, were not there, the fans in high concentration on the outside would move to the area where their concentration is low on the other side of the fence. This same irresistible force drives ions to equilibrate within a space unimpeded by barriers such as a cell membrane. For example, as the concentration of Na^+ ions increases, it moves toward the region in which sodium concentration (and positive charge) is lowest, thereby establishing equilibrium, or homeostasis, of both sodium and the positive charges within that medium. (Because ions carry an electrical charge, the equivalent term *voltage gradient* is also used.)

The neuron has a **threshold potential** below which any stimulation results in little or no change in the membrane potential. A subthreshold voltage change, or **graded potential,** is a passive signal that degrades over time and distance, like waves on the shore (Figure 4.13). As a way to

[Figure 4.13]
Subthreshold potentials.
Graded potentials are ultralocalized voltage changes that increase or decrease membrane voltage. (a) Hyperpolarization results when the extracellular fluid becomes more positive because of either an efflux of potassium ions or an influx of chloride ions. Hyperpolarization increases membrane voltage, making the membrane more negatively charged. (b) Depolarization results from an influx of sodium ions, decreasing membrane voltage and making the membrane more positively charged.
ADAPTED FROM KOLB & WHISHAW, 2004.

(a) **Hyperpolarization**

(b) **Depolarization**

[Box 4.1]

The Investigators

Keith Black, M. D.

World-renowned neurosurgeon Keith Black was born in 1957 in Tuskegee, Alabama. His father, Robert Black, was principal of an elementary school in Auburn, Alabama, and Keith Black grew up during the racially tense George Wallace era. When asked about significant influences on his life, Keith Black quickly points to the stimulating environment his father provided during his childhood. When the boy expressed an interest in dissection, his father brought him frog and cow hearts to explore, and when he expressed a desire to swim in the all-white community pool, his father encouraged him to swim there, defying the ban against it.

When Black was 13 years old, his family moved to Cleveland, Ohio, where he spent many hours in the science laboratories of Case Western Reserve University learning various surgical techniques on animals. While in high school, Black published his first scientific study investigating red blood cell damage in patients who had experienced heart valve replacement surgery. He won the prestigious Westinghouse Science Award in 1975. Not surprisingly, Black was accepted into the University of Michigan's accelerated program that enabled students to earn degrees in both biomedical science and medicine in just six years.

From his first days at the University of Michigan, Black was drawn to the brain. "If you want to understand the artist, you study his art," he quips. "If you want to understand God, you study the brain." To develop his knowledge of the brain, Black took every class he could find in neuroanatomy and physiology. It didn't take long for him to discover that he wanted to specialize in neurosurgery.

While completing his medical degree, Keith couldn't dismiss his desire to conduct research. He typically burned the midnight oil in the lab between about 11:00 P.M. and 3:00 or 4:00 A.M. His future wife, also a medical doctor, frequently visited during these late-night sessions. Black went on to complete residencies in general surgery and then neurosurgery.

Keith Black

COURTESY OF KEITH L. BLACK, M.D., CEDARS-SINAI MEDICAL CENTER.

In 1987, the rising young neurosurgeon accepted an assistant professorship at the University of California at Los Angeles. By the young age of 37, he was promoted to full professor. His position at UCLA required Dr. Black to conduct research in addition to managing a heavy patient load—he published well over 100 articles, evidence of his expertise in both the clinical and neuroscience research demands of his position.

From the beginning of his career, Black was committed to unlocking the mysteries of brain cancer treatment. Although some successful chemotherapies are used to diminish malignant tumors throughout the body, the brain presents a different set of challenges. Most of the time, the blood-brain barrier is a highly valuable feature of our brains, protecting against the many foreign agents that can harm its vulnerable cells. In the case of brain cancer, though, the blood-brain barrier keeps the important chemotherapy agents from entering the area containing the tumors.

One of Black's early findings was that the body's own immune system may be the key to cracking the security system provided by the blood-brain barrier. After reading about certain compounds that make blood vessels become leaky (the initial phase of the process of inflammation, described in Chapter Twelve), Black realized that a leaky blood-brain barrier could be the "break" he was looking for.

As he continued his research, he came across the natural peptide bradykinin, a plasma protein that exerts a strong influence on smooth muscle contraction, blood flow, and the permeability of capillaries. Bradykinin was especially interesting because it induces a leaky blood-brain barrier only in the area of a tumor. Eventually, under Black's supervision, chemotherapy agents were delivered to the specific site of the tumor with the assistance of bradykinin.

More recently, Black has become interested in another treatment strategy for using the body's own immune system to fight invasive malignant brain tumors. This treatment involves extracting the tumor cells during the surgery to remove the tumor and genetically altering the cells so that they can be injected back into the patient, much like a "tumor vaccine." The goal is to induce the patient to produce a store of antibodies for particular tumor cells should they surface again.

In 1997, Black became Director of the Cedars-Sinai Neurological Institute in Los Angeles because of the abundance of resources and the opportunity to create a team of the most talented scientists and clinicians in the United States. These days, when Black isn't removing brain tumors, conducting research, or rallying for more federal funds for the National Cancer Institute, he's with his wife and two children. Black's play time is just as adventurous as his work time—scuba diving, flying planes, sailing, sky diving, even climbing to the highest point in Africa.

When asked about what he would like to be doing 20 years from now, Black replies that he would like his research to be so successful that it puts him out of business as a neurosurgeon. If this dream becomes a reality, Black would happily expose his brain to an entirely different career, perhaps in marine biology or astronomy. Black is already reaching for the stars in his research. He has maintained the insatiable curiosity of childhood throughout his career. Black reinforces the value of this passion in another saying: "Art is a discipline that is practiced with passion and science is a passion that is practiced with discipline." It is easy to understand why this accomplished neurosurgeon was recognized in *Time* magazine's "Heroes of Medicine" special issue in 1997 (Lemonick, 1997).

visualize the neuron under different polarization events (polarized, depolarized, or hyperpolarized), imagine a couple on a dance floor. Before the music begins, they are standing apart, separated from each other by an arm's length (I   I): they are polarized. As the music begins, they move toward each other, thereby decreasing the distance (I I) and becoming, if you will, depolarized. As the music rises in pitch, leading to a crescendo, the couple detaches and spins in the throes of a dancing fury, ending up farther apart than when they began (I   I): they are now hyperpolarized. The electromolecular dance within neurons that is occurring second by second is not unlike the dancing couple.

Membrane Activity as Trigger of the Action Potential

Think of the action potential as the pulling of a trigger. If the neuron receives a series of subthreshold graded potentials, they degrade easily, like a gentle, but only partial, pulling back on a pistol's trigger, causing slight movement but no overt event. The subthreshold stimuli are accompanied by the opening of some ion channels but not enough to reach the threshold of excitation, and they quietly dissipate. If, however, the signal received exceeds the threshold for excitation, it is like the trigger being pulled all the way back, past the point of no return: the neuron fires (Figure 4.14).

Embedded in the phospholipid bilayer of the cell membrane is a collection of proteins, a mosaic of channels and gates that both maintains the resting membrane potential and facilitates the action potential. Ion channels selectively permit Na^+, K^+, Cl^- and other ions to travel between the intracellular and extracellular spaces. These ion channels, however, are closed to Na^+ when the neuron is at rest. In combination with channels selective for K^+ and Cl^-, they maintain the difference between intracellular and extracellular electrical charge. They are capable of being opened or closed by variations present in the local environment of the membrane. Hence, they are referred to as "gated."

The relative concentration of extracellular Na^+ is very high. Na^+ is a cation, and is attracted to the slightly more negative intracellular space; further, it is attracted to the lower intracellular concentration of Na^+. The pressure to bring Na^+ into the neuron, therefore, is very high. Potassium ions (K^+) are present in higher concentration in the intracellular space than in the relatively positive extracellular space. This difference sets up a concentration gradient. So the neuron at rest strains to correct these natural imbalances.

The electrical charge of the action potential changes the shape and size of the **voltage-gated channels,** opening the "gates" and allowing the specific ions to move freely across the barrier. When the action potential finally happens and the membrane is depolarized beyond threshold, momentary equilibrium is reached inside and outside the neuron, and polarity is eventually reversed.

The voltage-gated Na^+ channels open quickly, allowing the Na^+ ions to rush in. As Na^+ streams into the neuron through the opened channels, the voltage of the membrane, the membrane potential, rises to $^+40$ mV or more. This is known as sodium influx, and it is rapid. The neuron

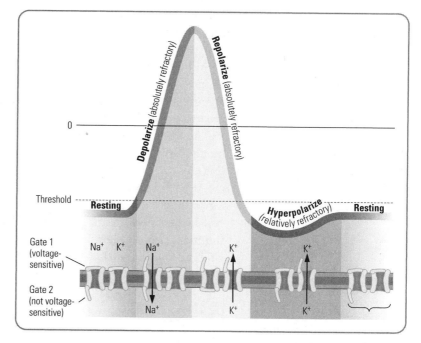

[Figure 4.14]
Phases of an action potential.
The depolarizing neuron resembles a roller coaster. It has a resting, a rising, and a falling phase. The process begins (1) with the opening of sodium channels, which allow for the rapid influx of sodium, propelled by the forces of diffusion and electrostatic pressure. These are then followed by the closing of the sodium channels (2) and the opening of the potassium channels (3). Finally, the neuron overshoots its resting potential (so-called hyperpolarization), and, with the activity of the sodium-potassium pumps in full force, restores the neuron back to its resting state (4).

ADAPTED FROM KOLB & WHISHAW, 2004.

voltage-gated channels
Passageways for ions through a neuron's cell membrane that are opened or closed in response to changes of the membrane potential.

responds with everything it has, holds nothing back, and cannot quickly return to its former state until all internal mechanisms have been reset.

The membrane charge changes rapidly, and the conductance of the signal moving from negative to positive causes a second set of voltage-gated channels, the K^+ channels to open. The K^+ channels lag behind the Na^+ channels; they are less sensitive to the fluctuating charge and require a greater level of depolarization.

The potassium channels allow K^+ to leave the intracellular space (potassium efflux), propelled by the force of electrostatic pressure (Figures 4.14 and 4.15). The movement of K^+ ions through the voltage-gated K^+ channels begins to change the membrane potential back to its more negative resting state, following the influx of Na^+. After about 1 msec, the opening of the K^+ channels initiates the resetting of (rectifies) the membrane potential and begins to shut down the Na^+ channels, preventing any more Na^+ channels from opening.

[Figure 4.15]
Saltatory conduction. Normal gaps in the myelin sheath, called nodes of Ranvier, are important for the repropagation of the voltage that propels the action potential. At these nodes is an increased concentration of voltage-gated sodium channels. As the action potential fires along the axonal segment, it loses its voltage slightly because of the cable properties and associated resistance in the axon. At the nodes, the sodium channels open and cause a rush of sodium into the neuron and an invigoration of the voltage. Hence, the action potential moves onto the next axonal segment, having lost none of its vigor.

ADAPTED FROM KOLB & WHISHAW, 2004.

saltatory conduction The electrical movement or jumping of the action potential across gaps (called nodes of Ranvier) in the myelin sheath.

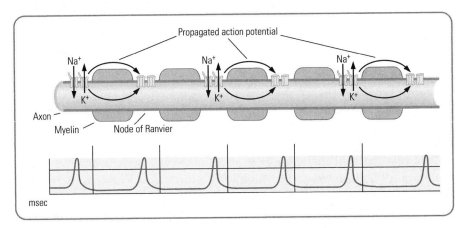

Propagating the action potential. Recall that myelin is an important player in the movement of the action potential down the axon. Intermittent gaps in the segments of myelin (nodes of Ranvier) are packed with sodium channels, significantly more concentrated there than anywhere else on the axon. Something interesting happens to the action potential at these nude spots: the propagated action potential, or neural impulse, skips and leaps over the gaps, like the sparks of static electricity you unwittingly receive on cold, dry days (see Figure 4.15). In this **saltatory conduction** (a nod to the Latin word for "dance" or "jump": *saltare*) the impulse is regenerated at the node and facilitates the movement of same-voltage signals down the length of the axon. Myelin facilitates the impulse flow from node to node and refers the signal to the next segment in the chain much faster than it could traverse a naked axon. The myelin and its associated nodes are intimately involved in the propagation of the action potential.

Any variation in the many mechanisms of neural transmission, from modulation in receptors in Doogie mice to altered nerve impulse speed and blocked transport of ions such as sodium and potassium, may result in significant psychological and physical change. Some changes, enhanced intelligence, for instance, are for the better; some are for the worse, as discussed in Box 4.2.

Refractory periods: The neuron recharges. The neuron is returning to its resting membrane potential, but it still has a way to go. The K^+ channels are open and functioning, letting K^+ efflux persist. As more K^+ leaves the intracellular space, the neuron approaches its resting membrane potential. Driven by both electrostatic and diffusion pressure (at this time the intracellular space is more positive, and there is less extracellular K^+), heavy forces are operating on K^+. Following the movement back to the resting state, the K^+ channels start to close.

But an interesting phenomenon occurs. The neuron becomes **hyperpolarized:** it achieves an even greater negative charge relative to the extracellular space. As the K^+ is forced out of the neuron, it accumulates around the cell membrane, making the membrane more positive. Until the K^+ diffuses away, which it does slowly through diffusion and electrostatic pressure and K^+ harvesting (to which the neuroglia, especially astrocytes, contribute), the neuron cannot respond to another normal action potential: The ionic "dancers" are separated by a greater expanse of dance floor.

This total inability to respond is the **absolute refractory period.** (The neuron may, however, respond to a series of rapid, staccato impulses or ones with a greater depolarizing charge, a *relative refractory period.*) The neuron must in principle return to its resting potential, resetting like the cocking of the pistol's trigger, before it can fire again. In general, a neuron can fire at a rate of 500 Hz, or 500 times per second. Thus, each action potential takes about 2 msec.

Another important event involved in restoring the neuron to its resting state concerns active membrane-embedded protein mechanisms called **sodium-potassium pumps,** which work—very hard and continuously—to ensure that Na^+ remains in high concentration extracellularly and that K^+ remains in high concentration intracellularly. The pumps are metabolically expensive, using the majority of the ATP the neuron produces (and up to 40 percent of the neuron's overall energy production). As the action potential dissipates, these pumps, densely packed along the cell membrane, are integral to the removal of the Na^+

hyperpolarization A shift in the membrane potential to more negative (i.e., more polarized and farther apart). Neuron is inhibited from firing and must receive more insistent electrochemical signals to be undone.

absolute refractory period A point during the action potential, while the cell is returning to its resting potential, when the neuron cannot respond to another action potential.

sodium-potassium pumps Mechanisms that actively transport sodium ions out of the cell while simultaneously drawing potassium ions in.

[Box 4.2]

A Case in Point

Lorenzo Odone's Battle with Adrenoleukodystrophy

Until he was 4 years old, Lorenzo Odone's brain seemed to be working beautifully. The son of Augusto, an economist, and Michaela, a linguist, Lorenzo already spoke three languages and enjoyed listening to opera. The family had just returned home from a posting with Augusto's employer, World Bank, in the Comoro Islands off the southeastern coast of Africa when Augusto and Michaela noticed changes in young Lorenzo's behavior.

His speech became slurred, he frequently lost his balance, he initiated behavioral outbursts at school, and one evening when his mother was reading to him, he asked if she could talk louder because he couldn't hear her. After visiting many doctors, the Odones received the devastating news that Lorenzo was suffering from a rare genetic neurological disorder known as adrenoleukodystrophy (ALD).

What exactly happens to the brain in ALD patients? The disease is the result of an X-linked male-predominant metabolic disruption that leads to the loss of the myelin sheath that insulates nerve fibers and to the progressive degeneration of the adrenal glands. Because females have the protection of two X chromosomes, males (with one X chromosome) are more severely affected. ALD affects one in 45,000 births and in the classic childhood form leads to the disruption of an individual's ability to metabolize long chains of fatty acids. The fatty deposits eventually build up in

Lorenzo Odone (left), age 4, in Comorro with Oumouri Hassane before ALD.
AUGUSTO ODONE/THE MYELIN PROJECT (WWW.MYELIN.ORG).

the myelin and in the adrenal gland, rendering both ineffectual. As the destruction of myelin progresses throughout the nervous system, the patient is incapacitated and inevitably dies.

ALD is the nervous system's equivalent of having the power lines cut. The horror of ALD is that the power cannot be reconnected. The elegant process of neurotransmission works only when the myelin insulation so important to neurotransmission is intact and functioning. Once the myelin becomes compromised, the neural circuitry grinds to a halt. Young patients, typically between 4 and 10 years of age, diagnosed with the early-onset variety of ALD usually die within two years.

The Odones were devastated. They quickly became very knowledgeable in the science of ALD, devouring the literature, convening the world's leading scientists to share ideas, considering every possible treatment. After learning of a connection between certain oils in food and the fatty acid chains, Michaela tracked down a supply of pure oleic oil, which began to decrease Lorenzo's fatty acid levels but failed to bring them to baseline levels. Augusto focused on animal experiments and discerned that a second ingredient, erucic

and the influx of the K^+ required to restore the resting potential and ready the neuron for the next action potential. When examined in its totality, the enormous resources devoted to maintaining the resting membrane potential make perfect sense: How else could the neuron ready itself for an immediate response?

Understanding the mechanisms that maintain neural transmission is no easy feat—if you have come this far, you have realized it. But painful as it is to attempt to understand these complex physiological systems and relaacid, a substance toxic to animals but tolerated in humans, should be added to the oleic oil. The result, called "Lorenzo's oil," was successful.

Lorenzo, however, was not out of the woods. By the time he started showing symptoms of ALD, the therapeutic window was already closing. Lorenzo's oil halted the degeneration, but now the challenge was finding a way to rebuild Lorenzo's deteriorated myelin so that he could regain function. The Odones founded the Myelin Project, a foundation that funds promising research that may lead to a way to promote myelin regrowth. The Odones' story may be familiar to you: it's recounted in the award-winning 1993 movie *Lorenzo's Oil.*

At this writing, Lorenzo is 24 years old and lives with his father outside Washington, D.C. After years by her son's bedside, Michaela passed away in 2000. It's amazing that Lorenzo is still alive, but he is severely limited—he cannot move or see or speak. Augusto reports that his mind is functioning as he responds to being read to, listening to music, or being placed in a swimming pool.

And how has the scientific community responded to Lorenzo's oil? With a healthy or, according to Augusto, an unhealthy dose of skepticism. Augusto remains troubled by the resistance of scientists to accept the effectiveness of Lorenzo's oil as an ALD treatment (see van Geel et al., 1999, for a skeptical scientific report). In 2002, Dr. Hugo Moser, a leading ALD scientist at Johns Hopkins, however, released the results of a 10-year study suggesting that Lorenzo's oil decreases the onset of ALD by approximately 70 percent—a finding prompting Augusto to say "I told you so" to many doubting scientists. Moser admits that his study lacked

strenuous controls, so the results remain controversial.

Even with the skepticism surrounding the efficacy of Lorenzo's oil, many parents of sons with ALD report that taking this oil every day (at a cost of about $440 for a two-week treatment) has kept their sons from losing their nervous tissue to this crippling disease. The Myelin Project is still in full force, and parents of ALD sons all over the world hold high hopes that current investigations will provide efficacious treatments for ALD. For example, Schwann cells, which make up the myelin sheath in the peripheral nervous system of multiple sclerosis (MS) patients, are currently being harvested from the ankle region of MS patients and transplanted into their brains. MS is also the result of the deterioration of myelin sheath, and although the causes of these two diseases are different, the treatments for MS may be applicable to ALD.

Lorenzo's case provides a powerful lesson about the importance of mastering basic neuroscience information before progress can be made in the treatment of clinical conditions such as ALD—a perfect example of the bridges that are necessary for successful clinical neuroscience.

Lorenzo Odone at 20 in the pool with Oumouri Hassane.
AUGUSTO ODONE/THE MYELIN PROJECT (WWW.MYELIN.ORG).

tionships, it is important to remember how very important every element is to human survival. In subsequent chapters, you will see how certain drugs and other chemicals modify components of neural transmission; they have strong influences on psychological functions. And speaking of pain, those of you familiar with dentists and the inherent pain of dental procedures know that Novocain reduces the pain. You can thank your sodium and potassium channels for the relief. Specifically, one way that Novocain exerts its anesthetic effects is by altering the lipid layers of the

exocytosis The fusion of vesicles with the plasma membrane, thereby opening the contents of the vesicles to the synaptic space, leading to the forcible release of neurotransmitter into the synapse.

affected cell membrane and blocking the Na^+ and K^+ channels. The pain messages, therefore, cannot be transmitted (Feldman & Quenzer, 1984).

Integrating Information at the Cell Membrane

The nerve impulse races down the axon to the terminal buttons all the while rapidly opening and closing ion channels like a flautist's fingers on a flute. As we discussed, the neuron is continually engaged in the synthesis and distribution of various proteins. Included among these proteins are neurotransmitters that are packaged and stored by Golgi bodies in a collection of vesicles moved by microtubules to congregate at the terminal ends of the axon. The vesicles cluster near the presynaptic membrane, awaiting an action potential.

Activity at the Synapse

Some of the vesicles "dock" with the terminal membrane and attach to it. The docking is accomplished by aligning proteins embedded in the membrane of the vesicle with proteins in the cell membrane. Docked and undocked vesicles both are present. The undocked vesicles will soon attach themselves to the membrane.

Once the action potential reaches the terminal buttons, it stimulates voltage-gated calcium (Ca^{++}) channels, causing them to open. The open Ca^{++} channels trigger a rapid influx of Ca^{++}, which is found in high concentration in the extracellular spaces around the axon terminals and is attracted by the relatively negative charge inside the neuron. As with sodium ions, electrostatic pressure and diffusion force in Ca^{++} through specific Ca^{++} channels. Once Ca^{++} arrives, it stimulates the fusion of the docked vesicles with the membrane, producing a structure that momentarily resembles the Greek letter omega, Ω. As its shape demonstrates, the formerly enclosed vesicle is now open to the extracellular space. It releases the molecules of neurotransmitter into the synapse.

This release, called **exocytosis,** is the process by which the membrane of a fused vesicle releases its contents (Figure 4.16). This release may be of a quantal nature (i.e., each vesicle contains roughly the same amount of neurotransmitter), so a single vesicle can release enough neurotransmitter to effect some graded postsynaptic potential. The number of vesicles involved and the number of times fusion and release occur represent another expensive metabolic proposition for the neuron. A form of recycling (endocytosis) goes on in the neuron. Used membrane is brought back to the soma and transferred to the Golgi apparatus, where it is incorporated into it and becomes membrane for the later generations of vesicles that will work their way down to the terminal buttons for fusion and release. This ballet of movement, release, and recycling occurs countless times per second in the tens of millions of neurons required for a specific behavior.

There are, however, some data that may modify the thinking about the traditional exocytosis model. Gaining acceptance is a new phenomenon referred to as "kiss and run" (Aravanis, Pyle, & Tsien, 2003; Ghandi & Stevens, 2003). In this model, the vesicle only transiently binds to the membrane (creating a small fusion pore) and is open only long enough to release its contents. It then closes and thereafter binds transiently with another portion of the membrane, again loosing into the synapse molecules of neurotransmitter. The process is repeated until the vesicle's contents are exhausted. With less turnover of the vesicle and its membrane, the process would represent an obvious economical advantage to the neurons that employ it. Both vesicular fusing and "kiss and run" exocytosis may occur, depending on brain site.

The descriptions provided here are of the chemical synapse, the predominant type to be found in the mammalian nervous system. In the invertebrate nervous system (e.g., insects), *electrical synapses* are much more common. Electrical synapses involve a gap that is only 2 to 4 nm (nanometer: 1 billionth of a meter) compared with the 20–30 nm of a typical chemical synapse. Further, these electrical synapses possess the *gap junction,* a point where the membranes of the pre- and postsynaptic neuron are continuous, allowing for very rapid signaling between pre- and postsynaptic neurons. The main functional feature of such synapses is their rapid rate of firing, an advantage for the sites where they are frequently found: regions associated with escape behaviors in invertebrates, and in vertebrates (including mammals), the control of eye movements.

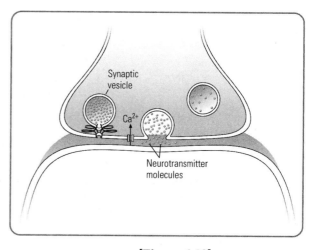

[Figure 4.16]
Exocytosis. The process by which neurotransmitter release is realized is called exocytosis. It involves the fusion of a synaptic vesicle, a membranous container filled with molecules of neurotransmitter. As calcium rushes into the neuron's terminal buttons, these vesicles fuse with the cell membrane to create a fusion pore and an egress to the synapse. The vesicle membrane then is recycled—or, in a new model of exocytosis, the vesicle only "flickers" open momentarily, releasing neurotransmitter before closing up and moving to another portion of the terminal button.

Postsynaptic Potentials

Now that the neurotransmitter has been released into the synapse, it binds to specialized receptors on the postsynaptic membrane. Like a coin in a slot, the neurotransmitter binds with the receptor and produces one of three effects:

1. **Excitatory postsynaptic potential (EPSP):** Excitation of the postsynaptic neuron, causing a depolarization and subsequent propagation of the action potential in the postsynaptic membrane

excitatory postsynaptic potential (EPSP) Graded depolarization of a neuron.

inhibitory postsynaptic potential (IPSP) Temporary hyperpolarization of a membrane.

temporal summation
Additive effects of a single neuron firing in rapid succession onto a postsynaptic membrane. Each new depolarization builds on the dissipating graded postsynaptic potential to eventually result in the appropriate hyperpolarization or hypopolarization threshold.

spatial summation
Summation of excitatory or inhibitory synaptic effects on a postsynaptic membrane resulting from the simultaneous action of several synapses at one time on one local area of the cell.

2. **Inhibitory postsynaptic potential (IPSP):** Inhibition of the postsynaptic membrane by hyperpolarization

3. No effect

Effects 1 and 2 each depend on the ion channels to which the respective neurotransmitter binds.

Whether an EPSP or IPSP occurs depends on the relative strength and type of the postsynaptic stimulation. An influx of Na^+ will probably trigger an EPSP, whereas an influx of Cl^- or an efflux of K^+ will result in an IPSP. Subthreshold stimulation (graded potentials) brought about by inadequate amounts of neurotransmitter result in postsynaptic indifference to the presynaptic neurons' signals that is neither strongly excitatory nor inhibitory.

Because most postsynaptic membranes require a change of about 15 mV to achieve threshold changes in membrane potential and most single postsynaptic potentials results in only a 1 mV change in membrane potential, the neuron needs a specific strategy to assure that threshold is actually reached. Two types of neuronal signal summation take into account the quanta released by the presynaptic neuron and the graded or other potentials they subsequently produce: temporal summation and spatial summation. **Temporal summation** takes advantage of the graded potentials that dissipate back to resting membrane potential following hyperpolarization or hypopolarization. As the membrane potential is moving toward resting membrane potential, quick successions of nerve impulses in the postsynaptic axon result in the accumulation of membrane changes that eventually reach suprathreshold or subthreshold levels. Eventually, this additivity of a series of postsynaptic potentials results in a stairstep type of change in membrane potential comparable to the threshold for an action potential. Therefore, the number of synapses received per unit of time can affect the neuron's decision to fire or not.

Spatial summation refers to the accumulation of excitatory or inhibitory postsynaptic potentials simultaneously activating the postsynaptic membrane in a particular local area. For example, 15 excitatory postsynaptic potentials coming from 15 different neurons may sum to the 15 mV change in threshold necessary to trigger an action potential.

Together, the signals received and the graded membrane potentials they produce via the two media, one next to the other on top of the other, are figuratively weighed, and a decision to fire or not or to be inhibited or not is made. Thus, the two major forces of the outer universe, space and time, are brought to bear on the most elegant of biological interactions of the inner universe, the relationship between two neurons.

A postsynaptic neuron is peppered with excitatory and inhibitory synapses. It often receives conflicting chemical information and must determine a course of action or inaction. Being presented with information about the timing (temporal) and location (spatial) of the various synaptic signals and their consequences (supra- or subthreshold) regulates the action. (See Box 4.3 on page 140 for a description of action potentials that are uncontrolled. The normal synchrony inherent to neuron-to-neuron communication degenerates in epileptic seizures to become the neural equivalent of a wildfire, with devastating consequences.)

Activity at the Receptor

When a molecule of neurotransmitter binds to a receptor, ion channels are set in motion; this may initiate an action potential. Two effects, direct or indirect, can be initiated, depending on the transmitter, the neuron, and the receptor to which the neuron is binding. As we show in more detail in Chapter Five, on neurochemistry, whatever chemical is used and whatever effect is observed will involve some combination of ionotropic and metabotropic receptors.

Ionotropic receptors produce direct effects, as the direct binding of neurotransmitter to ion channels governs them (Figure 4.17). They are the much simpler type of receptor, require less energy from the neuron, occur more quickly, and last for a shorter period. The ionotropic receptor binding results in a direct opening of a specific ion channel. It happens like this: the molecule of neurotransmitter moves across the synapse and binds directly to receptors on the ion channel on the postsynaptic membrane, causing that channel to open and begin the influx of ions that initiate the action potential. The ionotropic receptor is not unlike a mousetrap, simply and swiftly springing open at the touch of the switch.

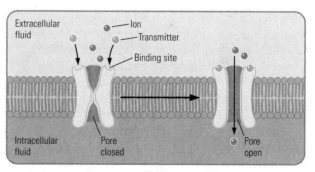

The effects produced by **metabotropic receptors,** as the name suggests (*metabolic* and *tropic,* for change-promoting), require an expenditure of energy by the neuron and may bring about long-lasting alterations in its metabolism. These receptors utilize the cellular fuel ATP. Metabotropic receptors produce indirect effects because they take longer to happen and involve a complex series of postsynaptic intracellular activities.

The receptor-mediated effects involve intracellular events that engage a substance called **G protein** (guanosine nucleotide-binding protein), a class of intraneuronal coupling proteins that can modify the neuron's internal state and hence its activities. A model of metabotropic receptors

[Figure 4.17]
Ionotropic receptor. Ionotropic receptors have direct effects: the ion channels, like a mousetrap, open when a molecule of neurotransmitter binds to the receptor. These effects are generally rapid and short-acting.
ADAPTED FROM KOLB & WHISHAW, 2004.

[Box 4.3]

Brain Matters

Epilepsy: Continued Intrigue and Lessons Learned

In Robin Cook's recent medical thriller *Seizure*, a zealous southern senator convinces a cutting-edge neuroscientist to implant stem cells (prompted to become dopaminergic cells) into his substantia nigra to cure his Parkinson's disease. Following a minor accident resulting in movement of the surgical apparatus (necessary to guide the cannula placement to the exact area in the substantia nigra), the cells intended to go toward the dopamine-producing substantia nigra went to the temporal cortex—the seat of the limbic system. Within a short period, the politician was experiencing an interesting smell, that of pig feces. Subsequently, an intense seizure occurred, accompanied by the immediate contraction of many muscles, as well as bizarre behavior ranging from identifying with Jesus Christ (here the fictitious stem cells were derived from blood samples obtained from the Shroud of Turin) to rude outbursts. It turned out that the stem cells were growing and activating the temporal lobe—leading to increasingly intense emotional outbursts that eventually led to the senator's demise. The fact that this contemporary medical thriller is about temporal lobe epilepsy confirms the intrigue that this condition has held for neuroscientists and medical practitioners for the past several centuries.

The famed neurologist Wilder Penfield writes that epilepsy is older than humans, evidenced by its appearance in other mammals. Further, trephined skulls (i.e., those with holes drilled in them) excavated from the caves of the Neolithic period are probable evidence of early humans' attempt to release the demons thought to be responsible for epilepsy (Penfield, 1941). Neurologist John Hughlings Jackson formally defined the condition of epilepsy about 150 years ago. He stated that epilepsy was a condition characterized by sudden, excessive local discharges within the brain's gray matter. The actual term *epilepsy* was derived from the Greek word *epilesia,* which means to seize as grabbing with one's hand (Beatty, 2001).

Without initiation and propagation of the action potential, there would be no communication in the nervous system—in other words, there would be no functional nervous system. In the case of epilepsy, these well-timed action potentials get out of control, leading to a storm of discordant activity in the brain. Because of this salient feature, the EEG examination is the most important laboratory test for the diagnosis of epilepsy (Avoli & Gloor, 1987). Epileptic seizures are either categorized as more *diffuse generalized seizures* or more localized *partial seizures*. Given that *auras,* a preview or transient sensory event typically preceding seizures, include certain movements or sensations, the pig feces olfactory aura experienced by the fictional senator is certainly plausible. But what about the senator's religious experience during the temporal lobe, or complex partial, seizure? Research conducted by Vilayanur Ramachandran and his colleagues at University of California at San Diego reported at the Society for Neuroscience annual meeting in 1997 suggested that patients suffering from a specific form of temporal lobe epilepsy prompted those patients to experience more intense religious beliefs. In response to Ramachandran's research, the media dubbed this area of the temporal lobe that triggered these religious beliefs the *God Module* (Holtz, 1997).

Whether the topic of epilepsy is the focus of fact or fiction, it remains a topic of immense interest among the medical and research communities. This condition, which affects between 0.5–2.0% of the general population, is not considered a disease because it has no single cause. A host of causes including genetic factors, environmental conditions, CNS infections, CNS tumors, and metabolic disorders have been known to cause seizures (Avoli & Gloor, 1978). As researchers have tried to identify mitigating factors for epileptic patients, much has been learned about seizure-inducing factors. Among the more interesting seizure-inducing factors have been the reports that certain video games and their accompanying flashing lights and visual patterns can be epileptogenic. A study in the Netherlands reported that the video game *Mario World* played on a 50 Hz television was more provocative than playing the game on a 100 Hz television. Thus, patients with photosensitive epilepsy should be careful about spending extended time in front of certain TV or computer visual presentations (Fylan, Harding, Edson, & Webb, 1999; Kasteleiun-Nolst et al., 2002). This line of research supports the notion that epilepsy can be triggered solely by environmental stimuli; thus, *reflexive epilepsy* is the most common form of epilepsy (Singh, Bhalla, Lehl, & Sachdev, 2001).

Because of the variety of causes of epilepsy, it's no surprise that there is no single treatment for this condition. The initial treatment regime involves antiseizure medication. In the past decade, ten new anticonvulsant drugs have been introduced as researchers and clinicians search for more efficacious drugs with fewer negative side effects (Bazil, 2002). Many of the current anti-epileptic drugs enhance GABA-facilitated inhibition (e.g., benzodiazepines, barbiturates). Other mechanisms of antiseizure medications include increasing the speed of repolarizing K^+ currents and reducing depolarizing currents (Avoli & Gloor, 1987). Another approach to altering the neuron's biochemistry is through one's diet; consequently, the ketogenic diet, a high-fat, adequate protein, low-carbohydrate diet, has been a treatment option for the past eighty years (Stafstrom, & Bough, 2003). It is thought that this diet, which alters glucose and ketone metabolites, may re-establish brain energy homeostasis (Greene, Todorova, & Seyfried, 2003).

For patients who find themselves unresponsive to pharmacotherapy and dietary restriction, surgery is a viable option. Beginning in the nineteenth century, surgeons tried to remove the specific focal area of seizure activity in epileptic patients. Surgical techniques have ranged from the removal of specific brain areas, disconnection by commissurotomy (transecting the corpus callosum), and, as you will read in Chapter Six, removal of the entire or partial hemisphere in which the seizure activity originates (Kolb & Whishaw, 1996). Some clinicians argue that surgery should be used more often in drug-resistant patients due to the high success rates, up to seventy percent, for all surgical treatments (Ryvlin, 2003). Vagal nerve stimulation is an alternative surgical procedure that has recently been developed. This technique involves implanting electrodes to produce afferent stimulation of the vagus nerve and shows promise for temporal lobe epilepsy (Andrews, 2003; Kuba, Brazdil, Novak, Chrastina, & Rektor, 2003).

Although epilepsy has been an unfortunate clinical condition for the patients suffering from seizures, this condition has presented a valuable window into the workings of the brain. As described in Chapter Three, temporal lobe epilepsy prompted Paul MacLean to begin thinking about the role of the temporal lobe in emotional processing. Canadian neurologist Penfield investigated cortical specificity while conducting surgeries on his epileptic patients, determining that specific areas provoked specific sensations, movements, and cognitions. Roger Sperry won the Nobel prize for his work investigating the functions of right and left hemispheres in patients receiving commissurotomies to relieve seizures (Pinel, 2000). More recently, forensic psychologist Anneliese Pontius has proposed that certain random violent acts committed by otherwise mild-mannered individuals could be the result of limbic seizures (LoPiccolo, 1996). Thus, although a priority in epilepsy research is the identification of mechanisms and successful treatment strategies, a host of researchers ranging from philosophers to neuroscientists continue to learn from these epileptic patients as their brain activity provides glimpses into such profound questions as the origin and characteristics of thought.

[Figure 4.18]
Metabotropic receptors.
Metabotropic receptors activate G proteins to produce effects indirectly on the opening of ion channels and to exert influences on other parts of the neuron, especially the nucleus. These effects are generally slow to start and long-lasting. (a) A receptor is bound by a molecule of neurotransmitter and begins a cascade that results in a signal to the α-subunit, binding intracellularly to ion channels to open them.
(b) The α-subunit activates an enzyme that produces a second messenger that both binds to and opens an ion channel and may have effects in other regions of the neuron, prolonging the effect of the neurotransmitter's or neuromodulator's effects on the neuron.
AFTER CARLSON, 1994

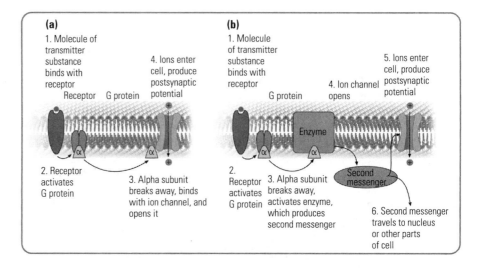

second messenger systems
A multiple-step and complex signal amplification process that occurs in the neuron that translates, for example, hormonal signals into long-lasting cellular events.

hypothesizes that, as the neurotransmitter binds to the receptor, the G protein that is associated with the receptor is activated. A portion of the G protein called the α subunit peels off and is transported through the intracellular space to the ion channel, where it binds to an intracellular portion of the receptor (Figure 4.18a). The binding of the α subunit then opens the ion channel. This is a more complex and energy-utilizing act that takes longer to bring about, and the effects are more extensive than the ionotropic transmitter-gated reception.

A second form of metabotropic response also involves the binding of neurotransmitter to the postsynaptic receptor, activation of the G protein, and the split-off of the α-subunit. It is called the **second messenger system,** and it shares similarities with the just-described version. In the second messenger system, however, the α subunit activates an effector enzyme, typically adenyl cyclase, in a common form of reaction (Figure 4.18b). In addition to binding to intracellular ion channels and causing them to open, it also initiates changes in proteins inside the neuron. Hence, the effects of this type of reaction (e.g., hormonal effects on neurons) last longer.

Summary

Microanatomy of the Neuron

The neuron is described in terms of its external characteristics and internal characteristics. External characteristics include the shape of the neuron and the major structures that produce its characteristic activities, including the cell membrane (or plasma membrane), the dendrites, the cell body or soma, the axon, and the presynaptic terminal buttons. Internal characteristics of the neuron include the nucleus, the mitochondria, the endoplasmic reticulum (ER), the ribosomes, lysomes, the Golgi apparatus, and the cytoskeleton.

The functions of the many intracellular components of the neuron demonstrate that the neuron is in actuality a complex of interacting and inter-dependent structures each operating on its own; the sum of the activities produce overall neuronal function. The shape and function of the neuroglia, the ubiquitous and essential partners to the neurons, complement the activities of the neurons and may perform some functions formerly assigned exclusively to neurons.

Generating an Action Potential

The action potential is the behavior of neurons that best exemplifies neural activity. It is the commerce of the brain, moving from individual neuron to individual neuron, and thence, from region to region, culminating in thought and action. It is a biochemical event with fundamental chemical processes that define it and make it available for study. The neuron at rest is called the resting potential. When the neuron fires, the resting potential changes, and the cell becomes depolarized, moving down the axon to the terminal buttons, where neurotransmitter is released.

The release of neurotransmitter across the synapse has effects only when it binds to receptors on the postsynaptic neuron. These digital or on/off events, called excitatory postsynaptic potentials (EPSPs) and inhibitory postsynaptic potentials (IPSPs), are the result of the action potential. Their action is spread to the postsynaptic neuron with an effect that is repeated billions of times per second across the brain.

Key Terms

sensory neurons (p. 112)

motor neurons (p. 112)

cell membrane (p. 113)

phospholipid bilayer (p. 114)

ion channels (p. 114)

receptors (p. 115)

dendrites (p. 115)

Purkinje neurons (p. 116)

dendritic spines (p. 116)

cell body (p. 116)

organelles (p. 117)

nucleus (p. 118)

deoxyribonucleic acid (DNA) (p. 118)

messenger RNA (mRNA) (p. 118)

amino acids (p. 118)

transcription (p. 118)

endoplasmic reticulum (p. 118)

ribosomes (p. 118)

translation (p. 118)

enzymes (p. 119)

mitochondria (p. 119)

precursors (p. 119)

adenosine triphosphate (ATP) (p. 119)

Golgi apparatus (p. 119)

vesicle (p. 119)

lysosomes (p. 118)

neurofilaments (p. 120)

microfilaments (p. 120)

microtubules (p. 121)

axon (p. 122)

axon hillock (p. 122)

terminal buttons (p. 123)

glia (p. 123)

blood-brain barrier (p. 124)

astrocyte (p. 124)

myelin sheath (p. 125)

depolarization (p. 126)

resting potential (p. 126)

action potential (p. 127)

electrostatic pressure (p. 127)

diffusion (p. 127)

concentration gradient (p. 128)

threshold potential (p. 128)

graded potential (p. 128)

voltage-gated channels (p. 131)

saltatory conduction (p. 132)

hyperpolarization (p. 133)

absolute refractory period (p. 133)

sodium-potassium pumps (p. 133)

exocytosis (p. 136)

excitatory postsynaptic potential (EPSP) (p. 137)

inhibitory postsynaptic potential (IPSP) (p. 138)

temporal summation (p. 138)

spatial summation (p. 138)

ionotropic receptors (p. 139)

metabotropic receptors (p. 139)

G protein (p. 139)

second messenger systems (p. 142)

For Further Consideration

Cowan, W. M., Sudhof, T. C., & Stevens, C. F. (Eds.) (2000). *Synapses.* Baltimore: Johns Hopkins University Press. This book, in a sense, combines the information contained in the two books on dendrites and the axon listed next. In *Synapses,* the editors draw together a wealth of information from some of the major names in the area (themselves included). A crystal-clear picture emerges of brain activity and regulation from the standpoint of the interaction between one neuron and another. The book is of great value because of the synthesized nature of the material the authors and editors provide and the fact that brain activity is the product of the firing of countless synapses and their coordination. *Synapses* is thorough, detailed, and readable.

Engert, F., & Bonhoeffer, T. (1999). Dendritic spine changes associated with hippocampal long-term synaptic plasticity. *Nature, 399,* 66–70. How is a known thing represented in the brain? How does the brain respond physically to the bombardment of sensory stimuli to which it is exposed every second of every day? It apparently creates new surface area in the form of dendritic spines, particularly in the hippocampus. These spines, in turn, may regulate the learning and memory that takes place in the hippocampus.

Gross, C. (2000). Neurogenesis in the adult brain: Death of a dogma. *Nature Reviews Neuroscience, 1,* 67–73. For most of the last century, dogma dictated that the brain was born with its allotment of neurons, that organisms lost them through means both natural and unnatural but no longer had the capacity to generate new ones. This view held sway in laboratories and in theories until the last couple of years. Now the dogma is slowly being revised, overturned, and revisited. Gross reviews the data for the last century, focusing on the most recent work and all its implications. It now appears that the production of new neurons, called neurogenesis goes on throughout life. This process has implications for a host of behaviors, ranging from learning and memory to depression. These data point out again the seemingly limitless capacity for the characteristic plasticity of the brain.

Kandel, E. R., Schwartz, J. H., & Jessell, T. M. (2000). *Principles of neural science* (4th ed.), New York: McGraw-Hill. The bible of neuroscience and the singular source for all things brain. It is 1500 pages of facts, information, data, theory, and on a level of scholarship that is unparalleled. Ever since its first edition came out in the early 1980s, this book has set the standard for erudition in the sciences and is probably on the bookshelf of almost every neuroscientist in the world—right alongside Cajal (1989). It is not for the faint of heart, however, and it can be dense, like the field it covers. But as a reference it cannot be equaled. (Kandel, by the way, won the 2002 Nobel Prize in Physiology or Medicine for his path-breaking studies on the molecular neurobiology of learning and memory. See Chapter Two's Investigator box.)

Maletic-Savatic, M., Malinow, R., & Svoboda, K. (1999). Rapid dendritic morphogenesis in CA1 hippocampal dendrites induced by synaptic activity. *Science, 28,* 1860–1861. Neural development is thought to be confined to the time period when the brain and CNS are forming. At the critical time, neurons must establish synaptic relationships with each other in ways that will be efficient and mark the proper pathways by which information will flow freely. In adulthood, however, new pathways must be established or reinforced to accommodate learning throughout the life span. Maletic-Savetic and colleagues demonstrate how one neuron may respond to stimulation by extending filopodia, footlike extensions of particular dendritic spines, which snake their way through the neuropil in search of new synapses to establish. The brain is dynamic and never stops in its quest for the efficient processing of information. Nor does it ever cease to amaze those who study it.

Peters, A., Palay, S. L., & Webster, H. D. (1991). *The fine structure of the nervous system: Neurons and their supporting cells.* New York: Oxford University Press. As the name suggests, this outstanding contribution to neuroscience devoted almost exclusively to the fine structure of the brain. With page after page of photomicrographs, mainly electron microscopic images, this volume takes the reader through the details of the neuron, neuroglia, and spinal cord. Furthermore, the accompanying text provides a complete description of the images. A solid historical approach permeates the book. Though new data about the brain and neurons have come to light since this book was first published, the images and the authors' descriptions are timeless.

Stuart, G., Spruston, N., & Hausser, M. (Eds.) (1999). *Dendrites.* New York: Oxford University Press. *Dendrites* compiles much of the information on the subject and presents it in a logical fashion, from structural to functional phenomena. The book contains and presents exhaustive detail on the dendrite, but at the end, the reader is not inundated so much as fascinated by these members of the neuron's anatomy. The dendrite is a much richer and more complex entity than one could ever imagine. Given the number of dendrites and their extent throughout the brain, the information-processing capacity of these delicate anatomical features staggers the imagination.

Waxman, S. G., Kocsis, J. D., & Stys, P. K. (Eds.) (1995). *The axon: Structure, function and pathophsiology.* New York: Oxford University Press. This volume could be subtitled "Everything you always wanted to know about the axon but were (a) unaware existed, (b) afraid to ask, (c) sure no one knew anything about." This is a wonderfully deep book that covers virtually everything about the conductile component of the neuron. The editors have gathered a collection of authors and chapters that present the most esoteric and most interesting information about the axon. The writing is sometimes turgid (as is so much standard scientific writing) and the depth uneven, but overall this volume is a state-of-the-art reference volume that will be authoritative for years to come.

Young, D., Lawlor, P., Leone, P., Dragunow, M., & During, M. (1999). Environmental enrichment inhibits spontaneous apoptosis, prevents seizures and is neuroprotective. *Nature Medicine, 5,* 448–453. Your parents always told you that they knew what was best for you. "Read; don't watch TV," they exhorted you. "Go outside and play," they cajoled. Had you listened, you might feel better about their advice as you mature. It turns out, according to Young and colleagues, that an enriching environment—an environment that stimulates the brain by providing it with an assortment of new challenges in context-appropriate and evolutionarily appropriate ways—has an effect on the brain not unlike the way exercise affects a muscle. Apoptosis, or programmed cell death, in which neurons commit a form of cellular suicide, also appears to be reduced. Overall, the effects on the brain are cumulative and beneficial. Now, go call your mother and apologize.

[Chapter Five]

Neurochemistry and Psychopharmacology

Coffee: Changing Our Culture and Our Nervous Systems

According to Ethiopian legend, the discovery of coffee can be traced to a goatherd named Kaldi, who enjoyed playing his pipe as he followed the goats across the mountainside. One afternoon, the goats didn't respond to their usual musical cue to return home, and a puzzled Kaldi eventually found them bleating with excitement, dancing on their hind legs, running around and butting one another. Kaldi thought his goats were bewitched, until he observed them eating red berries from an unfamiliar tree. As if lingering at the first forest coffeehouse, they remained for hours before returning home.

Intrigued, the next day Kaldi joined the goats in consuming the leaves and berries from this mystery tree. Feeling a tingle moving from his tongue to his stomach and a subsequent newfound energy, he spread the word of his "coffee experience" and coffee became part of the Ethiopian culture. This event, or one like it, probably preceded the first printed description of coffee by an Arabian physician in the tenth century (Pendergrast, 1999).

We have come a long way from chewing leaves and coffee beans to achieve our morning jolt; the preparation of coffee has evolved into a ritualistic roasting and grinding of choice coffee beans and the careful addition of nearly boiling water to create a wonderful, aromatic brew. As observed by author Mark Pendergrast in his book *Uncommon Grounds* (1999), caffeine has become the world's most popular psychoactive drug. In coffee and other food and drink including chocolate and soft drinks, an estimated 120,000 tons of caffeine are consumed across the world each year. In the United States, about 90% of the population regularly indulges in some form of caffeine consumption.

Of particular interest to clinical neuroscience is the actual neurobiological effect of caffeine. At various times throughout history, coffee has been touted as a nerve tonic, aphrodisiac, enema, and extender of life. In 1679, French doctors, afraid that coffee consumption was threatening the rate of wine consumption, claimed that coffee dried up the brain's cerebrospinal fluid leaving the person suffering from paralysis, exhaustion, and impotence. Just

30 years later, however, a Paris physician recommended coffee to his patients to freshen their complexion and improve lower bowel function.

Aside from these diverse medical claims, coffee's incorporation into the social lives of various cultures was affected by the impression that it served as an intellectual stimulant. Coffeehouses emerged across the world where people gathered for lively conversation, poetry readings, and entertainment. Today, Starbucks and similar coffee establishments are immensely popular; indeed, in the once popular TV comedy *Frasier*, the psychoanalyst brothers Frasier and Niles Crane frequented a coffeehouse in Seattle, Washington, for their daily brew and intellectual conversations—a coffeehouse appropriately named Café Nervosa.

Research has shown caffeine to affect synaptic sites of the neurotransmitter adenosine (a CNS neuromodulator at inhibitory synapses) throughout the brain, especially in the reticular formation area of the brainstem. Caffeine's effects throughout the body include increased heart rate, enhanced breathing, constricted blood vessels, and more efficient muscle contraction. In 1911, when Coca-Cola was being pushed to remove caffeine from their sodas, they hired two psychologists, Harry and Leta Hollingworth, to conduct the first laboratory tests of caffeine's influences on humans. The reason there is still caffeine in that Coca-Cola you may be drinking is because, in general, the Hollingworths found caffeine to produce mild improvement in motor skills and reaction times with no other serious effects (Pendergrast, 1999).

Habitual caffeine consumption has been associated with enhanced long-term memory, faster locomotor speed, and, in rats, reduced neurochemical response to stress (Hameleers et al., 2000; Yamato, Yamasaki, Misumi, Kino, Obata, & Aomine, 2002). Research focusing on neurons indicates that caffeine administration leads to increased growth of dendritic spines, an effect that could be an important mechanism of enhanced memory (Korkotian & Segal, 1999). In a recent study conducted on Navy SEALS, caffeine mitigated many of the adverse effects of 72 hours of sleep deprivation and repeated stress exposure. The caffeine subjects were observed to have improved choice reaction time, alertness, and visual vigilance and less fatigue and sleepiness, especially one hour after administration (Lieberman, Tharion, Shukitt-Hale, Speckman, & Tulley, 2002). On the other hand, Keith Corodimas and his students at Lynchburg College (2000) found evidence that acute caffeine exposure may interfere with certain forms of hippocampal-dependent learning in rats (Cordimas, Pruitt, & Steig, 2000).

Research reports also suggest that caffeine may provide neuroprotective effects against certain neurodegenerative diseases. In a study following the health of 8000 Japanese-American men for 30 years in Hawaii, higher coffee intake was associated with significantly lower rates of Parkinson's disease (Ross et al., 2000). Looking more closely at the mechanism of such neuroprotection, caffeine was admininstered at doses comparable with human consumption levels in a mouse model of Parkinson's disease. Caffeine, along with other specific adenosine antagonists, served a protective role against the development of Parkinsonlike symptoms in these mice (Chen et al., 2001). Accordingly, adenosine antagonists are entering clinical trials to determine their therapeutic potential in Parkinson's disease (Ross & Petrovitch, 2001; Schwarzschild, Chen, & Ascherio, 2002).

After standing in line with dozens of other folks at the local Starbucks to get your morning "hit," you might guess that caffeine has addictive qualities; the empirical evidence does not clearly suggest that caffeine is addictive. Whereas Solinas and his colleagues (2002) found increased levels of DA in the nucleus accumbens shell (known to be involved in addictive behaviors) in free-moving rats following behaviorally relevant doses of caffeine, Acquas, Tanda, and DiChiara (2002) found no increase in DA in the nucleus accumbens of rats following caffeine administration. Accordingly, evidence of physical addiction is variable across individuals but is apparent when people take themselves off caffeine. Withdrawal effects of headaches, fatigue, and muscle pain typically result. Thus, concerning the question of addiction, the jury is still out, making it a prime topic to discuss, that's right, over coffee.

The evidence provided by legendary goats and contemporary rats, mice, Navy SEALS, and faithful customers of coffeehouses across the world suggests that there's no denying that caffeine has some effect on our brains. Future research may uncover additional medicinal uses of this pervasive psychoactive drug.

At each moment of each day we are perched on the brink of a chemical precipice. On one side are the depths that characterize the relative lack of essential neurotransmission; on the other are the effects that occur when too much of a natural chemical is present. Both states disrupt neurochemical homeostasis and may lead to mental illness, transient or chronic. The natural balance of neurochemistry maintains this knife's edge. It can be disrupted through diet, substance abuse, damage, or stress. When the tilt happens, we see the emergence of depression, violence, irritability, improper responses to stimuli, lethargy—the whole gamut of behavior disorders.

In this chapter we consider neurochemistry, the currency, or means of exchange, between and among neurons. As you learned in Chapter Two, Otto Loewi's 1921 insightful dreams led to the realization that neurons spoke to one another via chemical means. As discussed in Chapter Four, we now know that neurotransmitters are released by activated neurons, travel across the synapse, and activate specific receptors on the receiving neuron.

Here, we discuss selected neurotransmitters that have received considerable attention from researchers. Each is involved in diverse behavioral and mental functions and has profound effects. Then we explain the neurochemistry of the stress response and how prolonged stress can influence the brain. We conclude with an introduction to fundamental information characterizing the important field of psychopharmacology.

NEUROCHEMICALS

Currently, a few dozen neurotransmitters have been formally identified. But more and more neurochemicals are being identified all the time, leading neuroscientists to believe that the actual number may exceed 100.

The more recently discovered neurotransmitters are actually peptides, or small proteins, and are known as **neuropeptides** (for example, endogenous opioids are neuropeptides). **Neurohormones** are yet another form of neurochemical that falls in an intermediate position between neurotransmitters and the hormones of the endocrine systems that are discussed in Chapter Six. Neurohormones (for example, oxytocin and vasopressin) are released by neurons, but instead of traveling across a synapse to receptors on the receiving neuron, they travel through the blood to a target organ where they have an effect.

Another descriptive label that is frequently used for certain neurochemicals is **neuromodulator.** Neuromodulators are chemicals that influence ongoing synaptic activity—either enhancing or impeding neuronal transmission as seen in the effects of caffeine on neurotransmission (see Connections; Cooper, Bloom, & Roth, 1996; Julien, 2004). Much like a brain, a radio detects certain wavelength frequencies and transmits that information in the form of, say, music or news. But many factors may modulate (modify) the intensity of the transmitted message. You may change the tuning so that the reception is clearer or turn down the volume so that the message is not as loud; a thunderstorm may interfere with the signal. Although none of these factors is critical for the radio to be able to actually function, they all have the ability to modulate the newscast or music that you actually hear. This analogy characterizes the function of chemical neuromodulators; they don't activate or deactivate an existing neurochemical system—they use a variety of strategies to enhance or diminish the existing neurochemical actions and relationships.

Although these neurochemical categories exist to simplify our understanding about how the chemicals of the nervous system function, their boundaries are sometimes fuzzier than one might desire. Further, as seen in Table 5.1 on page 150, the categories are not mutually exclusive.

All these chemical substances are united in a delicate balance that regulates responses to the environment. Brain-derived compounds have evolved to undertake specific behavioral and physiological activities by joining the electrochemistry we discussed in Chapter Four. We cannot hope to cover the vast array of neurochemicals that the brain synthesizes, so we will focus on a set of substances that are both ubiquitous and exemplary of the other substances and their principles.

neuropeptides Proteins that are released by neurons and act as intercellular messengers

neurohormones Brain substances that act like hormones and are released by neurons into the circulatory system

neuromodulator A substance that modifies or regulates the effect of a neurotransmitter

[Table 5.1]

Neurochemical Categorizations

Neurochemical categorization	General description	Examples*
Neurotransmitter	Synthesized in neurons, released across synaptic cleft, received by specific receptors in receiving neuron	ACh, NE, DA, 5-HT, GABA, Glu
Neuropeptide	Similar properties as small-molecule neurotransmitter	Endorphins, oxytocin, AVP
Hormone	Released by endocrine gland, travels through circulation to target organ where it has an effect	Estrogen, testosterone, cortisol, insulin, thyroxin
Neurohormone	Released by neuron into circulation and travels to target organ where it is received by specific receptors	Oxytocin, AVP
Neuromodulator	Neurochemical that modifies an existing synaptic circuit in some way	DA and 5-HT serve as modulators for the obsessive-compulsive disorder neural circuit (Chapter Seven)

*Note: Some neurochemicals fall into more than one category.

The neurochemistry of the brain is in exquisite balance. Timed, synchronous, and multilayered, neurochemicals flow in infinite whorls and eddies, controlled by the neurons that regulate their release.

Thought arises from the brain and the brain arises from the conjoint activities of its many neurochemicals. As we gain understanding concerning the brain's infinite chemical interactions, we come closer to treating the many disruptions of neurochemical homeostasis that haunt so many individuals.

Before exploring the neurochemicals of the nervous system, it is important to be familiar with some of the staple terms of the neurochemical language. Now that you have mastered the concept of synaptic transmission covered in the last chapter, your own neurochemical landscapes are seeded and ready to understand these related terms, summarized in Table 5.2. Table 5.3 at the end of this section about neurochemicals (see page 174) streamlines the essential information contained in the section, summarizing the receptor types and functions of each of the neurochemicals discussed.

Small-Molecule Neurotransmitters

The earliest neurotransmitters that were identified were small-molecule transmitters. These neurotransmitters are abundant in the brain and are involved in many behavioral, emotional, and cognitive functions. In the current chapter we introduce the neurotransmitters in a broad sense. In the rest of this text, you will learn how specific neurotransmitters are involved in specific mental illnesses.

Acetylcholine. Relative to some of the other substances in this section, **acetylcholine (ACh)** has roles both within the CNS and in the periphery: in short, it gets around. First identified as a substance with central and peripheral activity in the early twentieth century and as a neurotransmitter in the early 1920s, ACh has been shown to play many roles in the regulation of physiology and behavior. In fact, ACh is thought of as an exemplary neurotransmitter, in the sense that it serves as a model of classical neurotransmitter activity. The interaction of the ACh ligand with its receptor—the key and the lock, respectively—and the ease with which this interaction can be observed and measured, enabled the early neurophysiologists you read

acetylcholine (ACh)
Neurotransmitter in the somatic and parasympathetic nervous systems involved in cognition and at the neuromuscular junction

[Table 5.2]

Terms Associated with the Neurochemical Nature of the Brain and Psychological Processes

Term	Defin
Drug	Chemical compound that affects living organisms in some way and is usually intended for the diagnosis, cure, or prevention of a disease; psychoactive drugs influence behavioral, emotional, or cognitive processes
Agonist	Drug that attaches to a certain neurochemical receptor and mimics or modulates the activity of the endogenous neurochemical
Antagonist	Drug that attaches to a certain neurochemical receptor and blocks or hinders the action of the endogenous neurochemical
Autoreceptor	Receptor located in the membrane of the presynaptic neuron that is sensitive to the neurochemical being released by the neuron so that it can monitor the neurochemical activity of the neuron
Synthesis	Formation of a particular neurochemical—typically occurs after the introduction of several enzymatic steps
Ligand	Substance that binds to a postsynaptic receptor or an ion channel (e.g., transmitter, hormone, drug)
Receptor	Binding location for neurochemicals so that they can exert their effect on specific neurons; most are specific, genetically encoded, specialized proteins
Precursor	Substance that, on entering the CNS, serves as a foundational ingredient for the subsequent formation of a neurochemical. Tryptophan, found in bananas, turkey, and milk, crosses the blood-brain barrier, interacts with certain enzymes, and results in the formation of the neurotransmitter serotonin.
Deactivating enzyme	Enzyme that alters the formation of a certain neurochemical that is activating a receptor so that the activation is terminated and the cell can regain homeostatic levels of activity to respond to the next important ligand
Metabotropic receptor	When a neurochemical binds to this type of receptor, a conformational change occurs in the receptor that binds to and activates G proteins that ultimately trigger a series of enzymatic steps necessary to produce the desired response of the neurochemical. These effects typically have a slower onset and longer duration than ionotropic processes (described below).
Ionotropic receptor	When a neurochemical binds to this type of receptor, this large multi-subunit complex undergoes a series of conformational changes that trigger the opening of the ion channel so that the desired result of the neurochemical can be obtained. These effects are typically very rapid and short-lived.
Reuptake	Reabsorption of a neurochemical that is activating a receptor into the cell that secreted it, usually so that it can be repackaged and used again

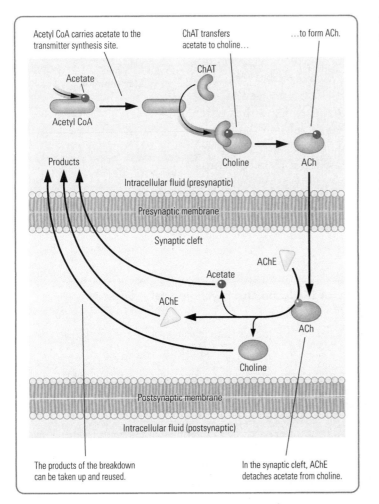

Acetyl CoA carries acetate to the transmitter synthesis site.

ChAT transfers acetate to choline...

...to form ACh.

ChAT

Acetate

Acetyl CoA

Products

Choline   ACh

Intracellular fluid (presynaptic)

Presynaptic membrane

Synaptic cleft

AChE

Acetate

AChE

ACh

Choline

Postsynaptic membrane

Intracellular fluid (postsynaptic)

The products of the breakdown can be taken up and reused.

In the synaptic cleft, AChE detaches acetate from choline.

[Figure 5.1]

Synthesis of ACh Acetylcholine was among the earliest neurotransmitters to be examined and to have its metabolic pathways elucidated. It is considered a "classical" neurotransmitter because its synthesis, release, and reuptake properties demonstrated the principles for other neurotransmitters to follow.

AFTER ZIGMOND, BLOOM LANDIS ET AL., 1999, P. 217

about in Chapter Two to conduct the necessary research and to confirm one another's observations.

The neuronal synthesis of ACh is straightforward when compared with that of the other neurochemicals (Figure 5.1). Generally, the chemical precursor *choline*, found in high amounts in lipids (fatlike substances) and compiled by a choline transporter, and the cation (positive ion) *acetate*, which is bonded to the molecule acetyl coenzyme A (acetyl CoA), are combined. Specifically, when the enzyme choline acetyltransferase (ChAT), which is synthesized in the cell body and then is translocated to the terminal end of the axon, catalyzes the reaction by transferring a molecule of acetate from CoA to the choline molecule, a molecule of ACh is produced.

The cytosolic ACh product is then stored in vesicles until its docking and release into the synapse. Once in the synapse, ACh binds to specialized receptors, referred to as *nicotinic* or *muscarinic receptors*, located on the pre- and postsynaptic membrane, and more important for this discussion, on the postsynaptic neuron. Although both types of receptors are responsive to ACh they are differentially responsive to specific drugs. As indicated by their names, the nicotinic receptors are activated by nicotine and the muscarinic receptors are activated by muscarine, a chemical found in the mushroom *Amanita muscaria* (Feldman & Quenzer, 1984).

Following release, the ACh molecules still occupying the synapse are brought back into the presynaptic neuron by specific choline transporters for recycling and repackaging (also known as reuptake). Any ACh that is left over from the act of neurotransmission is then scavenged by the deactivating enzyme *acetylcholine esterase* (AChE) which fractures the ACh molecule and returns it to its constituent materials, acetyl and choline. The process is repeated thousands of times per second.

ACh binds to its specialized receptors, either muscarinic (which are metabotropic receptors) or nicotinic (which are ionotropic). From there it exerts its peripheral effects on diverse neuromuscular junctions such as heart, lungs, and muscles and its central effects on cognition and sleeping/dreaming. ACh is the neurotransmitter released at every neuromuscular junction affecting the skeletal musculature throughout the body.

The biosynthesis, storage, and release of any neurotransmitter involves a multiplicity of steps. At any point along that long metabolic pathway, an **agonist** (which mimics or facilitates the action of the endogenous neurotransmitter it targets) can act to promote the natural neurotransmitters actions, or an **antagonist** (which blocks or interferes with its neurotransmitter) can act to block the actions. For example, ACh antagonist compounds such as the botulinum toxin, which inhibits the release of ACh from axon terminals, and curare, which occupies postsynaptic receptors, both block the action of ACh, thereby causing peripheral muscle paralysis. An agonist drug such as physostigmine, which inactivates the synaptic cleft enzyme AChE, therefore accumulates ACh in the synapse. Depending on dosage, it can be toxic, causing choking and blurred vision, or clinically useful, causing EEG desynchronization (a characteristic brain wave pattern observed in both wakefulness and REM sleep).

ACh is also widely distributed throughout the brain (Figure 5.2). The cholinergic cell bodies located in the basal forebrain (septal nuclei and nucleus basalis) and the projections are directed to the forebrain (hippocampus and cortex). The cholinergic cell bodies located in the midbrain project to the basal ganglia, thalamus, diencephalon, pons, cerebellum, cranial nerve nuclei, and reticular formation. It should come as no surprise, given the diverse ACh projections throughout the brain, that ACh is involved in many brain activities that require adaptability and flexibility.

The most agreed-on cognitive function of ACh involves learning and memory; this neurotransmitter, however, has also been implicated in attention, mood, and sleep's REM cycle. Research focusing on learning and memory has shown that drugs that increase the activity of ACh enhance memory, whereas any disruptions of CNS ACh neurotransmission disrupt memory (Gold, 2003). (A painful example of the devastating effects of ACh disruption occurs in the neurodegenerative disease known as Alzheimer's disease.)

Cells in the basal forebrain are among the first ones to perish as Alzheimer's disease begins its early progression. As discussed in Chapter Six, in the race to minimize age-related cognitive deficits in our aging society, many researchers are exploring neurochemicals and drugs that may slow down the memory decline often observed in aging brains. Estrogen, the female gonadal steroid hormone responsible for maintaining reproduction-related structures, behavior, and activity, reduces the

agonist A drug that mimics the endogenous actions of the targeted neurotransmitter

antagonist A drug that blocks the actions of an endogenous neurotransmitter

[Figure 5.2]
Distribution of ACh neurons Acetylcholine is found throughout the brain, but it is localized primarily in cognitively important sites such as the basal forebrain and cortex.
AFTER BEAR, CONNORS, & PARADISO, 1996, P. 518.)

Acetylcholine system
Neocortex
Thalamus
Hippocampus

catecholamines A group of three different amine neurotransmitters that contain catechol. These three neurotransmitters are dopamine, norepinephrine, and epinephrine (also called adrenaline).

dopamine (DA) The resulting neurotransmitter when dopa reacts with the enzyme dopa decarboxylase. This is an important neurotransmitter involved in movement and brain reward systems.

norepinephrine An amine neurotransmitter that contains tyrosine hydroxylase, dopa decarboxylase, and the enzyme dopamine B-hydroxylase (DBH). DBH is responsible for converting dopamine into norepinephrine.

epinephrine One of the three catecholamine neurotransmitters that is also called adrenaline, epinephrine neurons contain phentolamine N-methyltransferase (PNMT). PNMT is the enzyme that converts norepinephrine to epinephrine.

production of AChE, which would be expected to increase ACh-related activities, such as cognition (Daniel & Dohanich, 2001; Kadish & Van Groen, 2002).

Recently, it has been reported that estrogen, similar to other drugs that enhance ACh functioning, can provide some benefit to sufferers of Alzheimer's disease (Cholerton, Gleason, Baker, & Asthana, 2002; Hosoda, Nakajima, & Honjo, 2001; Schonknecht et al., 2001; Silva, Mor, & Naftolin, 2001; Zec & Travedi, 2002). Perhaps there is an estrogen–ACh link worth investigating. Another neurosteriod, *pregnenolone,* a substance that enhances ACh release in the amygdala, hippocampus, and cortex, is related to enhanced cognitive performance in aging rats (Mayo et al., 2003).

You may be thinking that another way to increase ACh in the brain might be through the simple act of eating choline in anticipation of it being synthesized into more ACh in the cholinergic cell bodies. This idea, though theoretically sound, has not been met with empirical success. Enhanced choline consumption has not been found to increase brain ACh levels under normal conditions. Past research, however, suggests that choline supplements protect against various drug-induced cholinergic challenges, serving a neuroprotective role. Perhaps such a dietary manipulation might protect against the ACh deficits associated with the late stages of Alzheimer's (Wecker, 1986).

It is also of some interest that the ACh system and the activities it regulates appear to be similar across a large number of species. This preservation of function in so many different animals suggests an evolutionarily conserved ligand-receptor relationship with broad value (Aldrich, Dionne, Hawrot, & Stevens, 1985). For example, Wright and Huddart (2002), at Lancaster University in the United Kingdom, are exploring ACh receptors in the pest slug *Deroceras reticulatum.* In other words, that ACh exists and works in such phylogenetically diverse species shows that it is an effective and efficient neurotransmitter that has been extant for a very long time. In fact, its existence in very simple organisms is evidence that it may have evolved very early in this planet's life. Evolution, therefore, has been working on refining its activities for many millennia.

Catecholamines. The **catecholamines** include **dopamine (DA), norepinephrine (NE)**—also known as noradrenaline—and **epinephrine (Epi)**—also known as adrenaline. (Given Epi's limited distribution in the brain—mainly it is a peripheral nervous system constituent involved in sympathetic responses—its discussion here will be limited.) The catecholamines are very closely related, sharing a catechol nucleus (the omnipresent benzene ring, together with its adjacent hydroxyl substituents). They also share a common biosynthetic pathway that involves many different enzymes acting on each step of the process to convert the previous molecule into the next transmitter product. That is, depending on the neuronal type (DA, NE, or Epi), additional enzymes further refine and shape the raw materials to produce the required neurotransmitter.

The study of DA has a history that goes back only to the middle part of the twentieth century, but the discoveries associated with it touch many aspects of our lives. Originally believed to be an antecedent to the catecholamine NE, experimental verification revealed that there were distinct populations of DA and NE throughout the brain, with the amount of DA constituting the vast majority of the catecholamine content of the brain. Much of what we now know of the distribution of DA was discovered by the Swedish groups including Hokfelt, Fuxe, and Dahlstrom, whose pioneering methodologies, which included fluorescence and immunocytochemical visualization of the catecholamines, demonstrated the distribution and localization of DA systems (Cooper, Roth, & Bloom, 1996).

The metabolic assembly is a multilayered process that, like an assembly line, involves the movement of a precursor chemical through a series of steps that modifies the molecule until the proper neurochemical is formed (Figure 5.3). Beginning with intraneuronal stores of the precursor amino acid tyrosine, the enzyme **tyrosine hydroxylase (TH)** converts the amino acid into L-dihydroxyphenylalanine, which is subsequently modified by dopa decarboxylase into DA. The production of DA is part of the overall synthesis of the catecholamines. In the neurons in which DA is the final neurotransmitter product, once the DA is formed the synthesis is complete. In other catecholamine-containing neurons such as NE and Epi, DA is transformed into NE by the enzyme DA hydroxylase and further transformed into Epi by phenylethanolamine N-methyltransferase (PNMT).

Therefore, as seen in Figure 5.3, an Epi-containing neuron would use four enzymes to produce its store of transmitter substance. In an NE-containing neuron, the process would involve only three, and two enzymes are required to produce DA from tyrosine (Bear, Conners, & Paradiso, 1996). Obviously, many potential targets exist for the pharmaceutical companies; interrupting any of these enzymatic steps in the synthesis of these neurotransmitters would drastically alter catecholaminergic functioning.

Following the synthesis of DA, the transmitter substances are stored in vesicles in the terminal buttons, waiting to be released into the synaptic

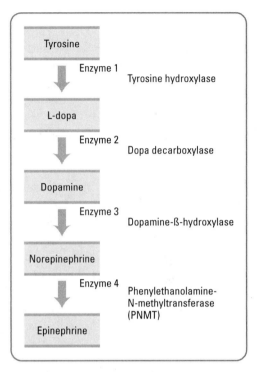

[Figure 5.3]
Cathecholamine synthesis
There is an economy to the production of the catecholamines, with intermediate enzymatic steps converting a previous neurotransmitter into another neuroactive substance.
AFTER ZIGMOND ET AL., 1999, P. 199

tyrosine hydroxylase (TH) An enzyme found in all catecholaminergic neurons. TH is a catalyst in the conversion of tyrosine to dopa, which is the first step in catecholamine synthesis.

reuptake The return of spent neurotransmitter from the synapse to the presynaptic neuron by means of specialized receptors

cleft. For NE, there is an additional twist to its synthesis and storage. The enzyme dopamine-beta-hydroxylase (DBH), which converts DA to NE, is found mainly in the vesicles in the neuron terminals. Therefore, DA must be driven into vesicles and into contact with DBH for the enzyme to be effective. There is a transport mechanism, akin to a molecular border collie, called vesicular monoamine transporter (VMAT) that herds cytosolic DA into the vesicles, where it then is converted by DBH into NE. You'll learn more about how VMAT may be manipulated to treat addiction in Chapter Ten.

In general, neurotransmission of catecholaminergic neurons is virtually identical to the processes described for other transmitter systems: receipt of the depolarizing signal, the influx of Ca^{2+}, the docking of vesicles, and *exocytosis,* or release of transmitter molecules into the synapse. There are, however, some notable additions. Catecholamine release also can be evoked through a reversal of the VMAT, in which case the movement of the transmitter into the vesicle is outward instead of inward. Another intriguing avenue does not even involve the axon. Data show that DA can be released from the dendrite in a nonexocytotic pattern. These examples further complicate our understanding of the catecholamine system (and explain why thousands of papers that relate to this system are presented at the Society for Neuroscience annual meetings) while simultaneously increasing our respect for the complexity of the brain and its regulation (Deutch & Ross, 1999).

Once the transmitter is released, it can produce either the excitatory postsynaptic potentials (EPSPs) or inhibitory postsynaptic potentials (IPSPs) discussed in Chapter Four, depending on the form of the receptor to which it binds. The regulation of DA and NE activity is rich and diverse, with the presence of the presynaptic receptors, or autoreceptors, playing a major role in the control of their release. These autoreceptors control the catecholamine chain from synthesis through release. By modulating molecular feedback to the neuron regarding the levels of the neurotransmitter, there is an effective governor at work to modulate all levels of neurotransmitter activity (Feldman & Quenzer, 1984; Julien, 2004).

Once the catecholamine is released and has acted on the postsynaptic neuron, its rapid removal and deactivation is critical. Overstimulation of the postsynaptic neuron is undesirable, since the signal would cause deleterious downstream behavioral events (some of which are described later). Thus, there are several mechanisms by which the transmitter is rendered inactive.

The process of **reuptake** is foremost among the strategies employed. In the catecholamine neuron, reuptake—the process by which the cell that secretes a neurotransmitter reabsorbs it—is an efficient means of removing the spent neurotransmitter. This process allows the intracellular enzymatic processes to break down the neurochemical and the extracellular processes to focus on a smaller concentration of neurochemical. Two transporters utilized in the reuptake process for catecholamine neurons are the DA transporter and the NE transporter. These proteins are efficient at removing the catecholamines from the synapse.

The reuptake transporters are complemented by other mechanisms that also are effective at removing the synaptic catecholamine from the cleft, among them the simplest of all, diffusion. Diffusion would allow the excess transmitter to move to extracellular areas of lower concentration, thereby diluting it to noneffective levels. In other cases, deactivation of the excess catecholamine is accomplished by enzymes such as monoamine oxidase (MAO) and catecholomethyltransferase (COMT). MAO inhibitors have been used successfully in the treatment of depression; however, their clinical value has been limited due to potential toxicity when consumed along with ingestion of foods containing tyramine (found in foods such as aged cheese) and serious side effects including high blood pressure, insomnia, dizziness, sexual dysfunction, and weight gain. A newer MAOI, Moclobemide, does not interact with tyramine but may interact with certain medications. Thus, MAOIs still have clinical value but are best used only after other front-line treatments have been explored (see Chapter Eight for a full discussion on antidepressants) (Berman, Belanoff, Charney, & Schatzberg, 1999).

The distribution of catecholamine neurons is widespread. As seen in Figure 5.4, the DA neurons project from two sources (ventral tegmental and substantia nigra) to many forebrain areas, for example the striatum (including the nucleus accumbens and the caudate), as well as cortical regions such as the prefrontal cortex. Moreover, the limbic system also receives substantial DA inputs to amygdala, hippocampus, and septum. There are also DA cell bodies in the hypothalamus, with projections from that site moving outward as far afield as the spinal cord, and in the olfactory bulb and retina.

In the case of NE, cell bodies have been found in the brainstem, mainly the medulla and the pons. The influence of these cells, belying their small number, goes well beyond the brainstem. Projections ascend to thalamus, hypothalamus, limbic system, and cortex.

The main agonists for DA—and those with which too many individuals are familiar, at a staggering cost to society—are cocaine or its derivatives, crack, and amphetamines. As discussed

[Figure 5.4]
NE projections The preponderance of NE and DA projections suggests tight regulation of both behavior and thought (cognition).
AFTER ZIGMOND ET AL., 1999, P. 208

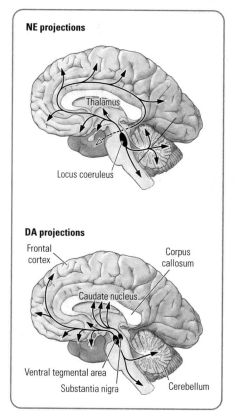

NE projections

Thalamus

Locus coeruleus

DA projections

Frontal cortex

Corpus callosum

Caudate nucleus

Ventral tegmental area

Substantia nigra

Cerebellum

serotonin (5-HT) A major neurotransmitter involved in mood, aggression, and appetite regulation

tryptophan The amino acid from which the neurotransmitter serotonin is derived. The availability of tryptophan in the extracellular fluid of neurons regulates the synthesis of serotonin.

in Chapter Ten, cocaine hydrochloride/crack and amphetamines are considered to be CNS stimulants or psychostimulants. They act on the DA system as agonists by promoting and exacerbating the normal effects of DA or DA receptor binding. In Chapter Nine you will learn about the value of DA antagonists in the treatment of schizophrenia.

Now that we've covered the characterization and pharmacology of the catecholamines, let's consider the functions associated with these transmitter substances. As just mentioned, DA appears to be involved with the psychological symptoms associated with schizophrenia (Chapter Nine), and DA transporters have been implicated in attention deficit hyperactivity disorder (Chapter Six). Dopaminergic cell bodies in the substantia nigra, however, are involved in movement, with their disruption leading to Parkinson's disease and related symptoms (discussed further in Chapter Six). Finally, DA pathways involving the nucleus accumbens and related areas are associated with the brain's reward circuit (Chapter Ten).

Functions of the NE system include attention, orienting, reward, analgesia, hunger, thirst, and other motivations (Julien, 2004). In subsequent chapters you'll learn that disruptions of this system may be involved in stress-related disorders such as post-traumatic stress disorder, as well as other disorders such as depression (Cooper, Bloom, & Roth, 1986; Feldman & Quenzer, 1984; Julien, 2004).

Serotonin. The study of **serotonin (5-HT)** stretches back farther than the study of some of the other substances discussed. In the 1950s, serotonin was synthesized from the stomach and identified as 5-hydroxytryptamine (5-HT). Preparations made from the gut yielded a concoction that had the ability to stimulate gastric secretions such as mucus while suppressing gastric acids, complementing observations of similar nervous effects of endogenous release of serotonin from the duodenum.

At first, the peripheral substance was given the name of "enteramine," and the substance derived from blood platelets (the original source of this mysterious substance for experimentation) was called serotonin. As analysis apparatus improved, the scientists realized that both enteramine and serotonin were one and the same, 5-HT. Adding to the data from the gut were observations wherein metabolism of serotonin was identified in the rat brain. Thus, serotonin was recognized as a potential neurotransmitter substance with diverse functions.

Serotonin shares with the catecholamines a relatively simple series of metabolic steps that leads to its synthesis. Because serotonin cannot cross the blood-brain barrier, CNS neurons possess the capacity to manufacture it readily, depending on the adequate and timely supply of its basic amino acid, **tryptophan.** The process begins with the entry of diet-derived tryptophan into the neuron. (Because the system is very sensitive to the levels of tryptophan, diet—especially foods rich in tryptophan such as milk, bananas and turkey—can have significant effects on the production of serotonin. You think what you eat.)

In the process of manufacturing serotonin, after the serotonergic cells collect tryptophan from the CNS circulatory system, it is transformed by the enzyme *tryptophan hydroxylase* into *5-hydroxytryptophan* (5-HTP). A second enzyme, *aromatic amino acid decarboxylase* (AADC), metabolizes 5-HTP into the final product, serotonin. Again, any interruption of these enzymatic reactions alters the brain's serotonin levels.

Once synthesized, serotonin resembles the ideal or classical neurotransmitter: it follows many of the same rules and steps for neurotransmitters in general. It is moved about and stored in the vesicles by means of a serotonin transporter that is similar to the one utilized in the catecholamine neuron. The vesicles reside in the terminal portion of the axon near their docking and release sites on the inner perimeter of the presynaptic membrane. There they await the depolarizing signal and the consequent docking and exocytosis of the stored serotonin. The release of serotonin is also under the marked control of autoreceptors that, being intimately responsive to feedback, modulate its production and release. Such regulation produces a delicately balanced system that is extremely sensitive to changes and that may contribute to the labile nature of some serotonin-regulated responses.

To date, at least 18 serotonin receptors have been identified in eight subtype families designated as 5-HT_1–5-HT_8 and with further subtypes A–D. One receptor subtype, the 5-HT_{1A} receptor, acts as both postsynaptic receptor and as presynaptic autoreceptor, governing serotonin release. The 5-HT_3 receptor subtype is ionotropic, whereas the remaining ones are metabotropic, utilizing G proteins to effect their postsynaptic potentials. Serotonin's effects on postsynaptic neurons are mainly inhibitory, as are the accumulated effects of serotoninlike drugs. The differentiation of receptor subtypes and their stimulation have ramifications for the therapeutic value of any serotonin analog.

Following its discharge and receptor binding, two primary mechanisms, reuptake and enzymatic degradation, inactivate any excess serotonin. Again, these events are similar to those for the catecholamines. The surplus serotonin is removed from the synapse by a specific transporter located on the presynaptic neuronal membrane called the serotonin transporter (SERT). This molecular 18-wheeler conveys the serotonin back into the presynaptic neuron. Once there, the serotonin undergoes enzymatic degradation by means of the enzyme MAO. The catabolic reaction eventually produces **5-hydroxyindole acetic acid (5-HIAA)**, which is often

5-hydroxyindole acetic acid (5-HIAA) A metabolic breakdown product of serotonin (5-HT). Found in the cerebrospinal fluid, 5-HIAA is the main metabolite of serotonin.

used as an after-the-fact marker for serotonin activity in neuroscience studies.

Focusing on 5-HT distribution in the brain, there is a great concentration of serotonin-containing cell bodies in the brainstem area known as the raphe nuclei. These neurons send extensive projections to many other parts of the brain, including the forebrain, hippocampus, thalamus, hypothalamus, cerebellum, and midbrain (substantia nigra and ventral tegmental area). There are large concentrations of cell bodies in the pons and medulla that send long axons to the dorsal horn of the spinal cord. The brain receives multiple serotonin inputs, mediating CNS activities and outputs (Figure 5.5).

Serotonin influences many different behaviors. In general, serotonin has been reported to mediate the following activities: body temperature, respiration, blood pressure, hormone release (growth hormone, adrenocorticotropic hormone—ACTH—prolactin, luteinizing hormone), uterine activities, attention and arousal, food intake, mood, aggression, nociception, and sleep and dreaming (Cooper, Bloom, & Roth, 1996; Hardman, Limbird, & Gilman, 2001; Julien, 2004). Several physiological effects of serotonin alterations can be seen in the sometimes fatal MDMA (Ecstasy)-induced serotonin syndrome described in Box 5.1 on page 162.

The wide number of serotonin agonists and antagonists is impressive and growing all the time as new receptor subtypes are uncovered. We will discuss only a few of each. One of the most popular agonists is the antidepressant fluoxetine, also known as Prozac. It is a selective serotonin reuptake inhibitor (SSRI). As the name describes, it disables the reuptake mechanisms, thereby allowing serotonin to remain in the synapse for longer (similar to what cocaine does to the DA transporter; Figure 5.6). As you'll learn in Chapter Eight, it has revolutionized the treatment of conditions such as depression. Also, because serotonin is a monoamine along with norepinephrine and dopamine, MAOIs affect this neurotransmitter as well. As previously mentioned, MAO degrades serotonin, dopamine, and norepinephrine and its effect is reversed by MAOIs.

The number of antagonists available for serotonin is equally impressive. The main ones are exemplified by lysergic acid diethylamide (LSD). Evidence exists that LSD blocks specific serotonin receptors (5-HT_1 and 5-HT_2), preventing serotonin from binding. (There is also evidence that LSD is a serotonin agonist, so the serotonin road must be traveled with great caution.) The vivid hallucinations LSD produces have been suggested to mimic the hallucinations we have all experienced under more licit conditions: the dreams of the average sleeper (though differences

Serotonergic system

Raphé nuclei

[Figure 5.5]
Serotonergic projections With cell bodies embedded in deep neural structures, and long axonal projections emanating outward, serotonin exerts strong regulation over the brain's activities.
AFTER ZIGMOND ET AL., 1999, P. 211

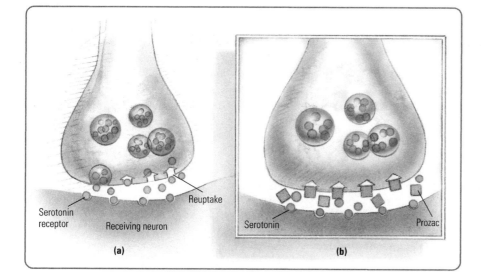

(a)   (b)

Serotonin receptor   Receiving neuron   Reuptake   Serotonin   Prozac

[Figure 5.6]
SSRI mechanism Certain antidepressants operate through a selective serotonin reuptake inhibition (SSRI) mechanism. In this example showing fluoxetine (Prozac), serotonin is being released into the synapse and its reuptake slowed by the drug having blocked sites into the presynaptic neuron, thereby prolonging the effects of the synapse-bound neurotransmitter.

abound). The hallucinations that occur with LSD overlap with those experienced by the schizophrenia patient. Hence, serotonin involvement in that disease has been intensively studied.

Amino Acid Transmitters

Although the "traditional" neurotransmitters (ACh, DA, NE, 5-HT, and so on) are very important in regulating behavior and understanding the mechanisms of psychoactive drugs, these substances are not as prevalent in the brain as the amino acid transmitters. Small amino acid molecules serve as neurotransmitters for all the other neuron populations in the brain.

Excitatory amino acid. Although aspartate and **glutamate (Glu)** are the principal excitatory neurotransmitters in the brain, most of the research has been directed toward Glu. For that reason, we focus on Glu in this discussion. Receptors for Glu can be found on most neurons, suggesting an important regulatory role for this excitatory substance. The Glu neurons are represented by and have been mainly studied in cortical pyramidal neurons, where they reside in complementary GABAergic company (the inhibitor neurotransmitter described shortly). These neurons, as well as the majority found throughout the brain, are projection neurons with long and proliferated axons, which suggests diverse regulation by the cortex. The study of Glu has been intense recently, and it has been implicated in a variety of conditions.

The neurotransmitter Glu is derived from a nonessential amino acid,

glutamate (Glu) A principle excitatory neurotransmitter that regulates cortical and subcortical functions

[Box 5.1]

Brain Matters

MDMA: Ecstasy or Agony for the Brain?

Beginning in the 1970s, some psychiatrists used MDMA (3,4-methylenedioxymethamphetamine) as a legal adjunctive, or supplemental, therapy for psychoanalysis because it induces an altered state of consciousness accompanied by enhanced sensual overtones. Eventually, MDMA became available as a recreational drug known as Ecstasy. Although this substance later became a controlled substance (illegal for recreational purposes), in 1988 Ecstasy continued to be used as a recreational substance (Valentine, 2002). In 2001, 9.2% of high school seniors reported using Ecstasy, and over 4000 Ecstasy-related emergency room visits were reported in 2000 (National Institute of Drug Abuse, 2001).

What is the appeal of Ecstasy? An oral dose of about 100 milligrams of MDMA is known to produce heightened pleasure and a boost in self-confidence that may lead to extroversion and a feeling of excitement. These effects typically peak about 15 to 30 minutes following administration of the dose with a duration of about 3 to 4 hours (Valentine, 2002).

But the effects are not all pleasurable. Ecstasy also causes hyperactivity and hyperthermia in some users and, in extreme cases, death (Gore, 1999). The increased use of this drug at warm, overcrowded parties and dance clubs can lead to an exacerbation of the drug-related effects sometimes known as the *serotonin syndrome* (characterized by restlessness, tremors, and altered mental status). Other side effects include confusion, depression, anxiety, paranoia, sleep disruptions, muscle tension, nausea, involuntary teeth clenching, rapid eye movement, chills, and sweating.

Known as a hallucinogenic amphetamine, MDMA doesn't regularly induce hallucinations and it is not a strong psychostimulant as are other amphetamine drugs. Psychopharmacologically, the direct effect of MDMA is difficult to pinpoint because of its lack of neurochemical specificity. For example, Ecstasy increases synaptic serotonin levels and then leads to prolonged serotonin depletion due to the blocking of serotonin reuptake. To a lesser extent, MDMA also promotes dopamine release and subsequent

---

gamma-aminobutyric acid (GABA) An amino acid that acts as an inhibitory neurotransmitter in the central nervous system

N-methyl-D aspartate (NMDA) receptors A subtype of glutamate receptor that uses both Na+ and Ca2+ influx to mediate its effects

kainite receptor A subgroup of glutamate receptors whose functional role is not clearly understood but has been related to hippocampal plasticity

alpha-amino hydroxy-methyl-isoxazolepropionate (AMPA) receptor A subtype of glutamate receptor in which Na+ influx causes an excitatory postsynaptic potential (EPSP)

and it is synthesized during the body's normal utilization of the sugar glucose, adding to both the ease of the reactions involved and their ubiquity. Also, glutamate serves as the precursor for **gamma-aminobutyric acid (GABA)**; specifically, the enzyme glutamic acid decarboxylase (GAD) acts on glutamate to form GABA (Julien, 2001). The role of glial cells (astrocytes) in the synthesis and control of Glu is very strong and intertwined (literally) with the neuronal synthesis. One precursor for Glu is *glutamine,* which is produced in large pools in the glia. The glutamine leaves the glia and travels to the terminal boutons, where it is converted by means of the enzyme *glutaminase* into Glu. From there it is stored in vesicles that, when depolarized, react to the influx of calcium with release of their contents.

Once released, Glu activates one of a number of receptors that are either ionotropic or metabotropic. Each of the two types of receptors (there are subtypes, as well) regulates different postsynaptic events. For example, there are three ionotropic subtypes: **N-methyl-D-aspartate (NMDA)**, **kainate**, and **alpha-amino hydroxy-methyl-isoxazolepropionate (AMPA)**. For the metabotropic receptors, there are two forms of receptor, decreases in reuptake. And making the picture even more complicated, MDMA has a high affinity for certain noradrenergic transporters. Knowing the involvement of these three different neurotransmitters, it is likely that serotonergic alterations lead to symptoms related to altered anxiety, sleep, and temperature modifications; dopamine influences may lead to increased confidence, pleasure, and excitement, and noradrenergic alterations may lead to the symptoms seen in sympathetic arousal (Hatzidmitriou, McCann, & Ricaurte, 1999; Valentine, 2002).

Scientists have debated whether acute or chronic use of MDMA leads to long-term brain effects. MDMA use has been associated with serotonergic neurotoxicity, shown by shorter processes in animals receiving ecstasy. Amazingly, even seven years after being given a four-day dosing regimen of MDMA, primates continued to show serotonergic neuronal deficits (Hatzidimitriou, McCann, & Ricaurte, 1999).

In human Ecstasy users, memory deficit is a common effect (Parrott, Lees, 1998). Additionally, using fMRI scans, MDMA users had smaller parietal and striatal cortices (Daumann et al., 2003). In a study focusing on adolescent use of MDMA, Ecstasy users had impaired attention and altered functioning in the left hippocampus (Jacobsen, Mencl, Pugh, Skudlarski, & Krystal, 2003).

In sum, although "ecstasy" is defined as intense joy, a convergence of evidence suggests that the effects of the drug on the user's brain fail to live up to its name. The rash of negative psychological and physiological side-effects, accompanied by research suggesting neurotoxicity, add up to agony instead of ecstasy for the consumer's brain. There is some controversy, however, about the validity of the aforementioned results, especially those suggesting that Ecstasy leads to neurotoxicity. The techniques used to assess neurotoxicity are somewhat questionable because they measure neurochemical content as opposed to neuroanatomical damage. Additionally, human studies are always problematic because of the polydrug use histories of many subjects. Nevertheless, the continued high number of MDMA users (an estimated 750,000 tablets consumed in New York and New Jersey each weekend) are engaging in a very risky neuroscientific experiment until there is further clarification of the effects of this drug on brain functioning (Valentine, 2002).

cleverly named metabotropic-1 and metabotropic-2. It is of some interest that in many sites in the brain, AMPA and NMDA receptors are co-localized (Figure 5.7). Further, NMDA receptors are distributed throughout many areas of the brain and spinal cord, especially in the cerebral cortex and hippocampus.

One of the major roles for Glu in the CNS is in the regulation of cortical and subcortical functions, particularly those associated with cognitive activities. There is significant Glu regulation in the hippocampus, with the aforementioned AMPA and NMDA receptors implicated in brain plasticity and learning and memory processes (as discussed in Connections). Accordingly, Cortex Pharmaceuticals has developed Ampakine to improve cognitive impairment seen in conditions such as Alzheimer's disease. As the name implies, this drug enhances AMPA receptor activity.

Overexcitation of NMDA receptors is thought to lead to **neurotoxicity,** especially following brain injury such as ischemia (decreased oxygen). It is the constellation of effects regulated by Glu that has convinced neuroscientists that schizophrenia, especially the cognitive complica-

neurotoxicity Neural damage due to some threat presented to the nervous tissue such as toxins, low oxygen, decreased glucose etc.

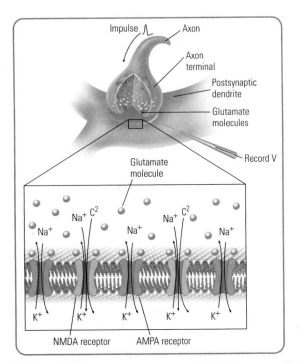

Impulse · Axon
Axon terminal
Postsynaptic dendrite
Glutamate molecules
Record V
Glutamate molecule
Na^+ C^2 Na^+ C^2
Na^+ Na^+ Na^+
K^+ K^+ K^+ K^+ K^+
NMDA receptor · AMPA receptor

[Figure 5.7]
NMDA/AMPA receptors As the excitatory neurotransmitter glutamate (Glu) is released into the synapse, it binds to so-called NMDA (Na+ and Ca2+ ionic influx) and AMPA (Na+ ionic influx)-gated channels, both of which produce EPSPs.

AFTER BEAR, CONNORS, & PARADISO, 1996, FIGURE 6.8

tions of the disorder, may involve a glutamatergic facet. Of the agonistic drugs known to affect Glu regulation, the barbiturates bind to AMPA-type receptors, whereas the volatile gas nitrous oxide and the drug phencyclidine (PCP) have antagonist effects at the NMDA receptor. Other effects mediated by the Glu system include those associated with food allergies. For instance, some individuals with a taste for Chinese or other Asian foods find themselves in gustatory heaven (as a result of the actions on the taste buds of foods laced with monosodium glutamate—MSG), only to experience the aftereffects of dizziness and swelling, also due to the (allergic) effects of the MSG (Julien, 2004).

Inhibitory amino acids. Whereas Glu is the principal excitatory neurotransmitter, GABA is considered the principal inhibitory CNS transmitter. However, although opposite in function, as mentioned, their production is similar: GABA is actually formed from Glu. Initially, one of the features that intrigued scientists working with GABA was its wide and apparently diverse distribution across regions and sites in the mammalian brain. This widespread scattering of GABA neurons and regulation is due, in part, to its intraneuronal and extraneuronal synthesis, which involves glucose metabolism.

Like other neurotransmitters, GABA is stored in vesicles at the terminal end of the axon, awaiting docking and release following the receipt of the action potential. Once it is released into the synapse, it binds to several different postsynaptic receptors. The primary GABA receptor is the GABA$_A$ receptor, which is associated with the chloride (Cl$^-$) ion channels. When a molecule of GABA binds to this receptor, the Cl$^-$ channels open and there is an influx of chloride into the intracellular space. The rapid influx of this negative ion causes hyperpolarization of the postsynaptic neuron (the poles, negative and positive, get farther apart), and the neuron is made much more negative. It is consequently harder to get it to fire. Hence, GABA is inhibitory. Autoreception and regulation of neuronal activity are accomplished by means of the GABA$_B$ receptor, found on axon terminals. The presence of autoreceptors for GABA ensures the rapid regulation of GABA release from the presynaptic neuron; that is, a reduction in the amount of GABA that is released.

The exocytosed (released into the synapse) GABA bound neither to postsynaptic receptors nor to the autoreceptors on the presynaptic neuron undergoes removal from the synaptic cleft by an interesting mechanism. It has been documented that the released GABA is taken up by contiguous neurons and glia, mainly astrocytes. Further, the recycling and utilization of the expended GABA (given its glucose antecedents) provide raw materials for the manufacture of additional glial and neuronal products. As glucose usage is the foundation on which neuronal activity is based, glia that harvest glucose from expended transmitters seem to be engaged in an efficient and necessary strategy.

Following the release of GABA, the main mechanism by which the neurotransmitter is inactivated is through reuptake back to the presynaptic neuron. The reentry is accomplished through multiple *GABA transporters (GAT)*, the different versions of which may be due to their distribution on various neurites and on glia. There is also enzymatic degradation of GABA accomplished by means of the enzyme *GABA-oxoglutarate transaminase (GABA-T)*.

GABA is inhibitory in many preparations and under a variety of experimental conditions. The concentration of GABAergic neurons is very high in the cortex, the most recently evolved area of the brain, which reinforces the persistence of inhibitory functions throughout the evolution of the brain. Recent work has demonstrated the presence of long-axonal GABAergic projections from the cortex to other, distant regions of the brain such as the striatum and thalamus.

Another arena in which the GABA system and its regulation have been implicated is in seizure and epileptic activity. As this activity represents misfiring of the electrical activity of the brain, with outwardly spreading neural waves, the seizure moves rapidly from its initial localized site to incorporate other areas of the brain. It is usually a chronic and maddeningly intermittent condition that occurs with a rapid commencement and from which the sufferer has little respite. GABA has been shown to regulate some seizure activity, and its augmentation in regions such as the amygdala and the hippocampus can ameliorate seizure activity.

Drugs that affect GABA are also those that have myriad significant effects in humans, causing well-known and well-described behavioral events. For instance, **benzodiazepines** and **barbiturates** are significant GABA agonists, leading to relaxation and sedation (Cooper, Roth, & Bloom, 1996).

Perhaps the most popular drug that interacts with GABA is alcohol. This drug, as ubiquitous as it is abused, has an affinity for both GABA and glutamate receptors. Focusing on the former for now, alcohol augments the inhibitory effects of GABA by increasing the influx of Cl^- ions in neurons. In essence, alcohol adds more inhibition to an inhibitory system. Hence, the characteristic effects of alcohol consumption include dampening of cognitive and motor skills, sedation, and motor relaxation. And following excessive consumption, there is a failure to recognize that these

benzodiazepines A class of drugs (usually of the tranquilizer variety) that increases the frequency of chloride channel openings in the presence of GABA

barbiturates Psychoactive drugs that act as CNS depressants, producing a wide array of effects ranging from relaxation to coma

glycine (Gly) An excitatory amino acid that mediates most CNS synapses along with glutamate and GABA

impairments exist because the intoxicated individual's judgment is significantly impaired (evidenced by the overwhelming number of alcohol-related car accidents in the United States).

Whereas GABA is the primary inhibitory neurotransmitter for the brain (cortex and subcortical structures), **glycine (Gly)** is the major inhibitory neurotransmitter for the brainstem and spinal cord and retina. Of interest because of its wide distribution in bodily fluids, Gly plays a vital but circumscribed role in CNS activity compared with GABA. Because of its limited CNS activity and the fact that it is found exclusively in vertebrates, Gly has been difficult to characterize experimentally.

A clear role for Gly in neurotransmission was slow in coming, and information is still being marshaled about the activities of this substance. Werman, Davidoff, and Aprison (1968) demonstrated a strong inhibitory effect of Gly in cat spinal neurons (in particular, interneurons and the regulation of their associated motor neurons). Radioactive localization studies have placed Gly in the terminal boutons of spinal interneurons, where it exerts its downstream hyperpolarization effects. These effects, like those for GABA, involve the rapid influx of Cl^- into the intracellular space through activation of the Cl^- channel. The fate of Gly once released into the synapse—whether set on by enzymes or drawn back into the presynaptic neuron by means of specific channels or whatever—is not clear. Therefore, even though not much is known about Gly relative to the other neurotransmitters, its inhibitory actions and regions/site of action are clear. The poison strychnine, a culprit in many a murder mystery novel, is a potent Gly antagonist. So is the tetanus bacteria, which works by long-term blockade of the receptors for Gly. Anyone acquainted with this affliction, known as *lockjaw*, will attest to the graphic appropriateness of the term: blockade of the actions of Gly results in hyperstimulation of the motor neuron junction and a tetanic effect, that is, the inability of the muscles to relax. The muscles of the face, especially of the mouth, lock in a closed grimace. Still, the grotesque and deadly ramifications of infection of the Gly system, ironically, shed some light on the function of this amino acid neurotransmitter.

Neuropeptides and Neurohormones

As mentioned earlier, new neuropeptides are being identified each year, and it is becoming increasingly difficult to keep up with their names and functions. Obviously, we can't cover them all in this chapter, but we want to introduce a few key neuropeptides that have functional significance for mental health: endogenous opioids, oxytocin, and vasopressin. As you read through this section, you'll notice that each chemical is also considered a neurohormone since they are secreted by neuronal tissue into the circulatory system. Corticotropin-releasing hormone, a neuropeptide that is also categorized as a neurohormone, is described in the neurochemical stress response section.

Endogenous opioids. Whereas opiate products (opium, morphine, codeine, heroin, and so on) have caused misery to many who have abused them, opium was used for centuries as a treatment for dysentery and other maladies, and the development of the morphine derivatives has proved to be a boon to the patient or soldier suffering intractable pain. Ironically, the opiates and their effects have been around for thousands of years, yet the research to understand and control them is a relatively new venture.

Collectively referred to as the **endogenous opioids,** the term merits some discussion. Given the long history of human familiarity with opiate drugs and the many effects attributed to them, it was clear that they worked on the brain—but how? The drugs had very powerful properties, suggesting that the brain had some receptors for these plant alkaloids (derived from the poppy). It was not clear, however, that the brain manufactured an endogenous substance that matched the receptors for the exogenous variety of opiate drugs. It was like having a big key ring with many keys on it but not knowing what locks they fit into or how. There was an effect and a cause, but everything in between was a mystery. Not until the early 1970s were the receptors and their brain-manufactured ligand elucidated, a set of discoveries that revolutionized the neurosciences and the pharmacological industry. Actually solving this mystery took the work and dedication of many talented scientists, including Solomon Snyder and Candace Pert. Within a pretty short time frame in the early 1970s, natural opiate receptors were identified and characterized. This discovery led to the identification of a natural endorphin substance that is involved in pain and emotional processing (Bear, Conners, & Paradiso, 1996).

There are three families of opioid peptides, the **endorphins** (endogenous morphines), the *enkephalins,* and the *dynorphins.* All are derived from a different long-chain amino acid precursor, *pro-opiomelanocortin (POMC), proenkephalin,* and *prodynorphin,* respectively. Unlike the situation for classical neurotransmitters, the neuropeptides are neither synthesized using direct enzymatic oversight nor are they synthesized locally, at the terminal ends of the axon. Instead, the gene product, the prohormone, is the precursor to the individual neuropeptide that is being manufactured, and the final product is moved by slow axonal transport

endogenous opioids
Naturally occurring neurotransmitter-like substances found in the brain that produce analgesic and euphoric effects similar to heroin and morphine

endorphin An opioid-like substance produced in the hypothalamus and elsewhere that is related to pain reduction and reward, but also facilitates the release of epinephrine from the adrenal medulla during the stress response

oxytocin A posterior pituitary neuropeptide involved in complementary activities such as bonding, sexual behavior, and childbirth

down to the bouton. As discussed earlier, neurotransmitters act quickly, and their effects dissipate quickly. For neuropeptides, the effects take longer to occur, and they last longer. For the neurons that contain and release neuropeptides, the process to increase production of the substance requires genomic involvement (increase in expression) and the slow transport outlined earlier. Again, this requires time.

A variety of receptors and receptor subtypes have been identified for the opioids, each regulating slightly different responses. The various opioids may bind to different receptors with different affinities, bringing about different effects and behaviors. For instance, the opiate agonist morphine binds to mu receptors with very high affinity and to kappa receptors with less affinity, but not to delta receptors or sigma receptors. The opioid antagonist naloxone, a highly effective treatment for opiate (heroin and others) overdose, for example, has a high affinity for the mu receptor, where it not only blocks an opiate's effects but actively displaces the opiate from the receptor.

Once the opioid has been released and recovery from the synaptic event is under way, there is little evidence that traditional reuptake mechanisms are in place to inactivate the opioids. The major sources of inactivation of levels of synaptic opioids include enzymatic degradation and the passive process of diffusion.

There are numerous agonists for the opioids. For instance, morphine, codeine, heroin, and Demerol are strong agonists for the various receptors, especially mu and kappa. The effects generated by these agonists are many. At the mu receptor, the effects brought about include analgesia, euphoria, and respiratory depression (a common cause of death in cases of overdose). At the kappa receptor, the effects are analgesia, *dysphoria* (emotional lows), and respiratory depression. Recent work has established that more complex behaviors may be under the regulation of endogenous opioid systems. Research conducted by Robert Bridges and his colleagues (Byrnes & Bridges, 2000; Byrnes, Rigero, & Bridges, 2000; Gulledge, Mann, Bridges, Bialos, & Hammer, 2000; Mann, Foltz, Rigero, & Bridges, 1999) has revealed that the display of maternal behavior is under regulation by the endogenous opioid system. As you'll read in Box 5.2, opioid-like substances have been found in the urine of children suffering from autism and may play a causal role in some of the autistic symptoms.

Oxytocin. The famous British physician Sir Henry Dale spearheaded the study of **oxytocin** in the modern era (the last 100 years or so). His studies on posterior pituitary lobe function were difficult to perform. Because of its physical location—tucked away in a small bony enclave at the base of the brain—the pituitary gland is hard to get to for experimental purposes. In the process of studying feline uterine contractions, however, Dale chanced on the observation that posterior pituitary extracts could cause striking contractions of the uterus. He reasoned that the posterior pituitary manufactured/released some substance involved in uterine contractions and expulsion of the fetus. Thus he discovered one of oxytocin's major peripheral effects.

The fact that oxytocin is released by hypothalamic neurons that extend to the posterior pituitary makes this substance a neurohormone. Specifically, exocytosis of oxytocin into the capillaries of the posterior pituitary occurs when an action potential arrives at the terminal bouton of the oxytocin neuron. The expressed oxytocin then travels from the posterior pituitary area (Figure 5.8) into the extensive vascular and blood supply that surrounds the pituitary. From there it traverses the entire body, binding to receptors on the membranes of target organs or sites, for example, the uterus, mammary glands, and some selective brain regions. Once oxytocin is released, something akin to a refractory period occurs, during which replenishment of oxytocin stores happens as the system resets itself. The postrelease consequences of oxytocin as it diffuses through the body serve to terminate its actions.

Oxytocin targets a fascinating array of regions, ranging from basic motivations to more complex behaviors and systems. It affects the reproductive organs, like uterus and mammary glands, where contraction leads, respectively, to expulsion of the term infant (on average) and milk ejection. Oxytocin also stimulates orgasm in the female (by effecting vaginal contractions) and orgasm and ejaculation in the male, again through its effects on contracting muscles. Other research has implicated oxytocin in social bonding. Oxytocin receptors are more numerous in species that demonstrate pair bonds—such as the prairie vole—than in those that do not. Recent work on this theory (Bales & Carter, 2003; Ferguson, Aldag, Insel, & Young, 2001; Francis, Young, Meaney, & Insel, 2002; Insel, Gingrich, & Young, 2001) has yielded some fascinating data suggesting that oxytocin may underlie the familial and warm feelings that we all have toward our loved ones. For this reason, oxytocin has been dubbed by some as the *cuddle chemical*.

[Figure 5.8]
Pituitary releasing oxytocin and vasopressin The posterior pituitary is a repository for neuropeptides, such as oxytocin and vasopressin, that are produced in the hypothalamus. The posterior pituitary then regulates the release of these substances following receipt of releasing signals from the hypothalamus.
AFTER ROSENZWEIG, BREEDLOVE & LEIMAN, 2002

[Box 5.2]

A Case in Point

Controversial Dietary Intervention for Autism: Karyn Seroussi's Struggle to Help Her Son

Karyn Seroussi's son, Miles, seemed perfectly normal for the first 15 months of his life. Then all of a sudden he stopped using the words he had recently acquired, started engaging in repetitive behaviors (such as filling up a cup with sand) stopped interacting with others, which included pointing and maintaining eye contact, began dragging his head across the floor, and developed a chronic case of diarrhea. Karyn Seroussi, a business owner, and her husband, a Ph.D. chemist, were heartbroken when they were told that their son suffered from autism. Although Seroussi didn't know much about this condition at the time, she was told that her son would probably never be able to make friends, engage in social conversations, participate in a normal classroom environment, or live independently.

After the shock wore off, Seroussi started reading voraciously and became intrigued by a theory suggesting that milk consumption might be related to autism. She recalled that Miles was developing perfectly normally while he was drinking soy milk (he didn't seem to tolerate her breast milk well) but started developing autistic symptoms shortly after being switched to cow's milk. Also intriguing was the fact that he seemed to crave milk, often drinking a half gallon per day. Seroussi soon learned of a possible theoretical connection between dairy products and autism. Jaak Panksepp, a behavioral neuroscientist at Bowling

Green State University, had previously written about how young rats chronically treated with opiates exhibited symptoms similar to those observed in autism. For example, pain insensitivity, communication deficits, and little evidence of curiosity were observed in the rats—all symptoms similar to those observed in autism (Panksepp, 1998).

After reading Panksepp's work, Seroussi learned that the urine of some children with autism contained metabolic products of the milk protein (casein) that had opioid characteristics. Could Miles's consumption of dairy products be the cause of his autistic symptoms? Could his craving for milk actually be a craving for opioids? Could milk, the substance advertised as doing "a body good," actually be causing brain damage in her son? After all, autistic children's brains had been observed to have abnormalities such as a smaller cerebellum and brainstem, a larger than normal cerebrum, and excessive small neurons in the hippocampus, perhaps due to low levels of apoptosis (Panksepp, 1998). Ever the skeptic, Seroussi decided to test this hypothesis by taking Miles off dairy products. The results were dramatic. Soon after this diet commenced, he stopped dragging his head on the floor, started interacting with the outside world by pointing and establishing eye contact, and began the long process of reacquiring language. After learning that the protein gluten, found in wheat, rye, oats, and many packaged foods, also broke down into a harmful substance, she removed it as well from Miles's diet and found that her son's motor coordination improved and his language development continued to improve. At this point, although most of the pediatricians Seroussi visited

---

In Box 5.3, you will read about Thomas Insel's interest in oxytocin. His lab has begun to consider the role of oxytocin in social dysfunction, as observed in autism. Further, recent work by Tomizawa and colleagues (2003) demonstrates that the learning and memory improvements that have been reported as a function of maternal experience and parity may be attributable to oxytocin's reorganization of the neuronal structure and relationships within the hippocampus. The neurobiology of maternal affiliation, therefore, is certainly regulated by neurochemistry, and these refused to acknowledge the role of diet in Miles's improvement, she persisted with the diet, becoming a self-motivated expert in the area of diet and autism.

To Seroussi's delight, Miles continued to improve, eventually to the point that the doctor removed the autism diagnosis. Subsequently, Seroussi started a newsletter and a support organization called Autism Network for Dietary Intervention (ANDI) to help other parents looking for alternative treatments for their children's autistic symptoms. In 2000 she wrote a book, *Unraveling the Mystery of Autism and Pervasive Developmental Disorder* (updated in 2002). In her book, she discusses potential roles of immune functions, gastrointestinal health, and the value of behavioral therapies in the development and treatment of autism. At the time she wrote the book, Miles was continuing to progress normally—at age 6 he was in a normal first-grade class, was reading at a fourth-grade level, had many friends, frequently engaged in imaginative play with his older sister, and had just successfully played a part in his school play. More recently, at age 9, Miles tested in the intellectually gifted range. Seroussi told us that she was reminded of how far Miles had come one day when this once socially impaired, nonexpressive child told her, "Mom, I love you more than I can express; in fact I love you even more than even a very expressive person could express."

As fascinating as Karyn Seroussi's story is, her results are of course based on a single case—that of her son—hardly an acceptable objective amount of data for a scientific conclusion. But case studies are valuable starting points in the development of hypotheses. Interest in the role of dietary and neurochemical imbal-ances on the brains of children suffering from autism has sparked more traditional empirical investigations. Karl Reichelt and his colleagues at Stavanger University College in Norway have found opioid peptides (exorphins) in the urine of autistic patients (Reichelt & Knivsberg, 2003) and have found both decreased autistic symptoms in patients on gluten-free and casein-free diets and a reappearance of autistic traits on resuming consumption of these proteins (Knivsberg, Reichelt, & Nodland, 2001; Knivsberg, Reichelt, Hoien, & Nodland, 2002). Further, scientists at the University of Rome La Sapienza also reported worsened neurological symptoms in autistic patients following the consumption of wheat and milk and decreased symptoms after the commencement of a restricted diet. Additionally, increased antibodies for casein were observed in the autistic patients compared with a control group (Lucarelli et al., 1995). The research is not clear-cut, though. A recent study reported increased essential amino acid deficiencies and lower levels of dietary neurotransmitter precursors such as tyrosine and tryptophan in children placed on the restricted diets (Arnold, Hyman, Mooney, & Kirby, 2003). When discussing the efficacy of dietary interventions for autism, the National Institute of Mental Health reminds parents that treatments need to be subjected to randomized, double-blind trials before they are accepted as proven treatments (National Institute of Mental Health, 2004). Regardless of what the future research tells us about the efficacy of this treatment for autism, it is important to consider dietary manipulations as another therapeutic window with the potential to alter neurochemicals and mental health.

studies are the first steps toward elucidating the neurochemical path. More about the role of oxytocin in stress reduction is discussed in Chapter Eleven.

Vasopressin. **Arginine vasopressin** (AVP; also known as antidiuretic hormone or ADH) is another interesting neurohormone released by the posterior pituitary. Not only is this substance released in close proximity to oxytocin, it is also very close phylogenetically to oxytocin. AVP shares

arginine vasopressin A neuropeptide that is secreted by the posterior pituitary gland and also by nerve endings in the hypothalamus. It affects learning functions and water resorption in mammals.

[Box 5.3]

The Investigators

Thomas Insel

Thomas Insel began his formal education at Boston University where he completed a six-year undergraduate premed program. During the first two years of this program, Insel focused on English and writing. He is very grateful for this emphasis because he feels that an inability to write is the biggest stumbling block many of today's most talented scientists face. Shortly after graduation, Insel traveled to South Asia where he had a short career as a "jungle doctor," completed a psychiatric internship at Berkshire Medical Center in Massachusetts, completed graduate courses in psychophysiology at Stanford University, and completed his residency in neuropsychiatry in San Francisco. Although diverse, Insel's interests were certainly narrowing toward the brain, sparked by attending lectures by two gifted neuroscientists—Wally Nauta, a well-known neuroanatomist, and Norman Geschwind, well known for his neuropsychological research. As a student, Insel felt that these two men were "spectacular" professors and gives them credit for his decision to become a psychiatrist and eventually a neuroscientist.

After completing his residency in psychiatry and picking up a mild case of the research bug along the

Thomas Insel
COURTESY OF THOMAS INSEL

way, Insel and his wife decided to build a solar house—a family project—in the Washington, D.C., area, near their families. A job offer in the Clinical Neuropharmacology Branch of the National Institute of Mental Health (NIMH) made the move to Washington professionally legitimate, and family and construction tools in tow, the Insels moved to the East Coast. Things went well following this move—the Insels finished the house, and in 1983, Insel was appointed chief of the Unit on Brain and Behavior at NIMH. In 1991 he was then promoted to chief of the Unit on Developmental Biopsychiatry, Laboratory of Neurophysiology.

Insel's specific research interests have always revolved around neurochemistry and behavior. Early on, his interests were in the area of obsessive-compulsive disorder, and he conducted pioneering studies in the psychopharmacological treatment of this disorder. From there, his interests turned to developmental neuroscience, conducting research in maternal behavior. Insel is best known, however, for his more recent work in the neurobiology of social behavior, a change of interest

seven of nine amino acids with oxytocin, and both neuropeptides are synthesized by the hypothalamus and the products are carried to the posterior pituitary via axonal transport, where they are stored and released into circulation by means of the intimate vascularization that surrounds the so-called master gland (see Figure 5.8). An interesting feature of the two neuropeptides is their exclusive localization in mammals. It has been suggested that both play a role in the social aspects of mammalian behavior (Albers & Bamshad, 1998; Insel, Gingrich, & Young, 2001; Insel & Shapiro, 1992; Winslow, Hashing, Carter, Harbaugh, & Insel 1993) and hence are necessary for the unique properties that make mammals mammals.

AVP plays multiple roles. Peripherally, it regulates the resorption of water by the distal tubules of the kidneys and controls the osmotic content (thickness) of blood. AVP acts by increasing the physiological per-that occurred after hearing Sue Carter (see Chapter Eleven) give a research talk about monogamous prairie voles. These small rodents are serious about commitment—they remain monogamous throughout their entire lives. Consequently, in the early 1990s, Insel focused on the neurochemistry of affiliation, using the prairie voles as a natural animal model.

A few years later, Emory University attracted Insel away from NIMH and his solar house, appointing him director of Yerkes Regional Primate Center and professor in the Departments of Psychiatry and Psychology. In 1999, Insel became the director of the newly created Center for Behavioral Neuroscience, a multi-institute, interdisciplinary program composed of 80 scientists and 8 institutions in the Atlanta area—all committed to investigating the neural basis of complex behaviors.

After taking a sabbatical to learn advanced molecular techniques, Insel's research skills repertoire became increasingly molecular, allowing him to introduce more behavioral genetic techniques into his research. Throughout the mid-90s at Emory, Insel and his colleagues researched the "love potion" of prairie voles. This potion, consisting of a dash of the neurohormones, oxytocin and vasopressin, may also provide interesting information about other mammals, even humans. In fact, by knocking out the gene involved in the production of the affiliative hormone, oxytocin, the animals' ability to form social relationships is compro-mised, creating a possible animal model of autism, a recent research interest for Insel.

So now that Insel has mastered the most cutting-edge research in social neurochemistry, what's next? As we spoke for this interview, Insel was gearing up for yet another career move. After a couple of decades in neuroscience research, he felt drawn back to his roots as a physician. He wanted to play a bigger role in translating the exciting research occurring in neuroscience labs across the world into treating mental illness. What's the best job to accomplish such a goal? Most would argue that becoming the director of the NIMH is not a bad start. In this position, Insel is eager to utilize 3 billion U.S. "taxpayer" dollars each year to generate significant therapeutic advances for mental illnesses. Ironically, although we showcase Insel as an icon for neurochemistry research, as he puts on his new NIMH hat, he told us that he thinks there is too much emphasis on neurochemistry and pharmacology: all major mental disorders have treatments, but no mental disorders have explanations concerning causes, and even more distressing, none of these illnesses currently have cures. Being a clinical neuroscientist in every sense of the word, Insel's broad range of expertise and interests within the field of mental health should enable him in his new position to make important strides toward obtaining his goal of identifying actual cures for the various mental illnesses that exist today.

meability of the distal tubules to fluids. When released in greater amounts, AVP contracts arterioles and capillaries, thereby increasing blood pressure. Obviously the peripheral functions of AVP are critical to maintaining homeostasis (of body fluids) within the body, but it is the central features of AVP that concern us here. When administered to the CNS, AVP has been shown to modulate various types of learning. Avoidance learning—mainly passive avoidance—is facilitated by AVP, and AVP also interferes with the extinction of avoidance learning (Kovacs, 1987). AVP infusions into the lateral septum of rats improves the memory for the cues of a conspecific, whereas an AVP antagonist into the same region interferes with such recall (Dantzer, Koob, Bluthe, & Le Moal, 1987, 1988). AVP has evolved to provide mammals with the ability to recognize members of the same species, same social group, and perhaps same family (Landgraf et al., 2003). Recently, AVP has also been linked to autism and psychiatric conditions

fight-or-flight response The sympathetic branch of the autonomic nervous system triggers this response that prepares the animal to either fight the stressor, or flee from the stressor.

such as depression and schizophrenia (Insel, O'Brien, & Leckman, 1999). Its roles as we ascend the phylogenetic scale are yet to be elucidated and may prove to be important and vital to our understanding of brain interactions and human social behavior.

Thus, both oxytocin and AVP have strong influences in the development of the social behaviors that characterize mammalian behavior. Larry Young at Emory University's Department of Psychiatry has explored the effects of genetic manipulations of these systems in animal models and has proposed that the genes underlying these neuropeptides and their respective receptors may have potential for a genetic model of treatment for disorders characterized by social deficits such as autism and social phobias (Young, 2001).

NEUROCHEMISTRY OF THE STRESS RESPONSE

On your way to your front door late one night, as you fumble with your keys, you hear footsteps coming toward you, then silence. Out of the corner of your eye, you catch the bushes moving. You freeze in place, focused on the bushes. In an instant your autonomic nervous system has shifted from parasympathetic homeostasis to sympathetic arousal.

[Table 5.3]

Summary of Neurochemicals, Receptors, and Associated Functions

Neurochemical	Receptors	Function
Acetylcholine (ACh)	Muscarinic (M_1–M_5); nicotinic (N_N and N_M)	Sensory functions, memory, motor coordination, neurotransmission at neuromuscular junction, ANS and PNS function
Norepinephrine (NE)	Alpha$_1$ and alpha$_2$; beta$_1$, beta$_2$, and beta$_3$	CNS sensory processing, sleep, mood, memory, learning, anxiety, SANS, cerebellar function
Dopamine (DA)	D_1–D_5 in both D_1 family and D_2 family	Movement, olfaction, reinforcement, mood, concentration, hormone control
Serotonin (5-HT)	18 receptors identified existing as part of 8 families designated $5HT_1$–$5HT_8$	Mood, appetite, sleep, emotional processing, pain processing, hallucinations, reflex regulation
Glutamate (Glu)	NMDA, AMPA, quisqualate, and kainate	Major excitatory function in the CNS and PN, long-term potentiation, memory
Gamma-aminobutyric acid (GABA)	$GABA_A$, $GABA_B$	Major inhibitory neurotransmitter in the CNS
Glycine (Gly)		Major inhibitory function in the spinal cord
Oxytocin		Uterine contractions during childbirth, milk letdown, stress reduction, learning, social facilitation
Vasopressin (AVP, or antidiuretic hormone [ADH])		Fluid conservation, social recognition, aversive learning

Adapted from Julien, 2004, p. 67.

Heart pounding, respiration peaking, attention focused, you must decide: Will you stay and face your fear or run away?

Autonomic Stress Response

Physiologist Walter Cannon first described the neuroanatomical circuit underlying the stress response in 1914. He noted that the secretion of epinephrine and norepinephrine from the adrenal medulla and sympathetic nerves, respectively, enables an animal to mobilize its forces to survive a threat. He called this response, mediated by the sympathetic arm of the autonomic nervous system, the **fight-or-flight response.**

At this time, Cannon viewed the autonomic nervous system as controlling the various components of the body that maintain homeostasis, including body temperature and the body's pH and oxygen levels. These pertinent critical systems are maintained within a narrow range (Cannon, 1935; Lovallo, 1997; McEwen, 2000). Viewing stress from a homeostatic perspective is especially important in the forthcoming discussions of stress disorders and coping with stress.

You'll recall from Chapter Three that after being activated by the hypothalamus, sympathetic nerves exit from the spinal column and project to virtually every organ, blood vessel, and sweat gland in the body (see Figure 3.2). We have even conserved an evolutionary sympathetic memory from our ancestors that leads to the development of goose bumps during sympathetic arousal. Animals that have fur on their bodies benefit from having their hair follicles stimulated because the fur standing on end leaves them looking larger and more intimidating should they choose the fight option of the sympathetic menu.

For us humans the effect is a little less dramatic—the almost invisible hair on our bodies serves as little protection against a potential assailant. Other effects of the sympathetic nervous system, however, including increased heart rate, blood pressure, metabolism, and respiration and decreased digestive and reproductive activity, facilitate our ability to survive a threat. All these physiological effects are designed to help an animal mobilize its internal forces within seconds to successfully fight or flee and survive (Habib, Gold, & Chrousos, 2001).

"Oh, that's Edward and his fight or flight mechanism."

The sympathetic-induced piloerection displayed in this frightened cat (in this case, the true "scaredy cat") results in the appearance of a larger body, making the animal more intimidating to an approaching threatening opponent.

FRANK SITEMAN/STOCK, BOSTON

Hypothalamic-Pituitary-Adrenal Axis Response

When a stimulus is perceived as threatening, the hypothalamus responds by releasing hormones through the hypothalamic-pituitary circulatory system. As seen in Figure 5.9, the major releasing hormone, actually a neurohormone, **corticotropin-releasing hormone** (CRH) is primarily manufactured in the paraventricular nucleus (PVN) of the hypothalamus and subsequently triggers the release of **adrenocorticotropin hormone (ACTH)** from the anterior portion of the pituitary gland.

CRH also inhibits the neurons involved in the secretion of reproductive hormones, leading to an inhibition of reproductive processes. The pituitary, the principal endocrine gland in the body, releases ACTH, which flows through the bloodstream and triggers the release of the stress hormones **glucocorticoids** such as the stress hormone **cortisol** from the adrenal cortex. Additionally, the levels of glucocorticoids are monitored at each step of this **hypothalamic-pituitary-adrenal (HPA) axis** (Figure 5.9). Whereas the sympathetic response occurs within seconds, the HPA axis requires minutes to be fully activated.

In addition to CRH, the hypothalamus releases beta endorphin, which plays a role in pain reduction but also stimulates the release of epinephrine from the adrenal medulla. Finally, AVP is also released from the PVN of the hypothalamus and seems to facilitate the release of ACTH from the anterior pituitary. As you learned in the previous section, in times of severe stress, AVP plays an important role in regulating blood pressure (for example, by conserving body fluids) (Habib, Gold, & Chrousos, 2001).

Other Brain Areas Involved in the Stress Response

In addition to the two neurochemical stress circuits in the brain, the hippocampus, amygdala, locus coeruleus, and neocortex also appear to play an integral role in stress responsivity.

The hippocampus. The hippocampus, a component of the limbic system noted for its involvement in emotional expression and memory formation, is a central brain structure for the stress response. The

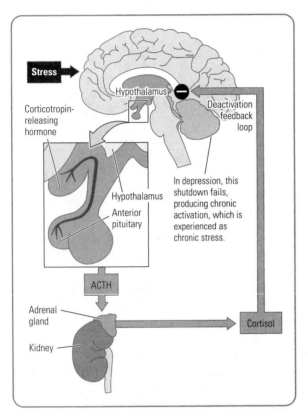

[Figure 5.9]
HPA axis Everyone responds to stress differently. Once a stressful stimulus is perceived, however, the steps leading to the initiation of its response are similar for each individual because of the mechanism of the HPA axis. Through a series of releasing hormones (CRF and ACTH) and eventual release of glucocorticoids from the adrenal cortex, there is a feedback loop onto the brain that enables regulation of (and sensitivity to) the response.

hippocampus has two types of adrenal steroid receptors—*Type I* (mineralocorticoid) and *Type II* (glucocorticoid) receptors. Together, when these receptors are activated, an abundance of neurophysiological events (for example, excitability and plasticity) take place in hippocampal neurons. In fact, Woolley, Gould, and McEwen (1990) found that three weeks of glucocorticoid injections led to less elaborate neuronal branching in the hippocampus.

A few years earlier, Uno and his colleagues (1989) found hippocampal damage in vervet monkeys that had died from prolonged exposure to severe social stress. The aforementioned finding that just three weeks of chronic stress leads to neurological impairment is important as many of our human stressors exceed this duration. In reality, however, the data may be even more frightening—it may take even less time to start seeing the negative impact in the hippocampal neurons. It is important to note that not all restructuring is permanent; researchers are currently investigating the nature of damage that is reversible (McEwen & Magarinos, 2001). Lambert and her colleagues (1998) observed hippocampal neural restructuring after just six days of chronic exposure to the activity–stress paradigm (consisting of increased activity and decreased availability of food).

Considerable research has been conducted to identify key neurochemicals involved in stress-induced hippocampal damage. The excitatory amino acid Glu plays a role, given the fact that an antiepileptic drug, phenytoin, which blocks Glu release, prevents the stress- and corticosterone-induced neuronal changes (Moghaddam, Boliano, Stein-Behrens, & Sapolsky, 1994). Additionally, drugs that block the Glu NMDA receptors also protect against hippocampal damage (McEwen et al., 1995).

Because cellular damage and death have been linked to excessive levels of Glu and activation of associated NMDA receptors, this process is sometimes known as **excitotoxicity.** The inhibitory neurotransmitter GABA also seems to play a role in stress-induced hippocampal damage. Benzodiazepine, a GABA agonist, blocks dendritic restructuring (Magarinos, Deslandes & McEwen, 1999). Additionally, serotonin plays a role in the demise of the hippocampal neurons during stress. An atypical antidepressant drug, tianeptine, which enhances serotonin uptake resulting in decreased extracellular levels of serotonin, has been found to reduce stress-induced dendritic shrinkage in tree shrews undergoing severe chronic stress (Czeh et al., 2001).

To date, no single mechanism has been identified as being the critical factor that leads to the damaged CA3 pyramdial cells. Robert Sapolsky has written extensively about how possible actions initiated by gluco-

corticotropin-releasing hormone (CRH) A releasing hormone produced in the hypothalamus that travels to the anterior pituitary where it triggers the release of ACTH from the anterior pituitary.

adrenocorticotropic hormone (ACTH) A hormone released by the anterior pituitary which stimulates the adrenal gland to release glucocorticoids from the adrenal cortex. ACTH is a critical component of the hypothalamic-pituitary-adrenal-(HPA)-axis stress response.

glucocorticoids Compounds that belong to the family of substances called corticosteroids. They affect metabolism and have anti-inflammatory and immunosuppressive effects.

cortisol The stress hormone secreted by the adrenal cortex in primates

hypothalamic-pituitary-adrenal axis (HPA axis) The stress response originally described by Hans Selye, in which the hypothalamus secretes a releasing factor (CRH) which travels to the anterior pituitary and triggers the release of ACTH. ACTH then travels to the adrenal cortex where it stimulates the release of glucocorticoids. Generally an adaptive response (in short bursts), this sequence and its aftermath help the animal produce enough energy to survive the impending stressor.

excitotoxicity An effect on cells (usually neurons) that results in damage or death due to overexcitation of the cell

Robert Sapolsky
LINDA A. CICERO/STANFORD NEWS SERVICE

corticoids might lead to neuronal damage. He has suggested that gluco-corticoid exposure leads to a metabolic vulnerability in the neurons, probably the result of an inhibition of glucose uptake. Further, it has been proposed that glucocorticoids exacerbate the damaging effects of excessive levels of Glu, oxygen radicals, and calcium mobilization. Glucocortoids can lead to electrophysiological alterations that damage and disrupt the functions of neurotrophic (growth) factors in the hippocampus (Sapolsky, 1996; Yusim, Ajilore, Bliss, & Sapolsky, 2000). Although it is not clear if a reduction in neurogenesis might be related to hippocampal restructuring, psychosocial stress has been reported to reduce the production of new neurons in the tree shrew hippocampus (Gould, McEwen, Tanapat, Galea, & Fuchs, 1997).

Amygdala. Just as with the hippocampus, the amygdala, a second structure in the limbic system, also plays a significant role in an organism's response to stress (see Figure 3.13). Joseph LeDoux, working in the Center for Neural Science at New York University, has used a simple fear-conditioning model to identify the neural circuit underlying defensive behavior displayed by animals. As described in Chapter Seven, the defensive behaviors that interest LeDoux are innate and relatively hard-wired responses to danger stimuli. These innate responses, however, involve the activation of several physiological systems including autonomic (for example, heart rate), endocrine (glucocorticoid release), and skeletal (freezing) systems.

According to LeDoux, the lateral amygdala is the reception area for sensory information related to fear, such as a tone consistently presented prior to a shock (LeDoux, Cicchetti, Xagoraris, & Romanski, 1990). If the lateral amygdala is temporarily inactivated, fear conditioning is disrupted. The fear-related information is subsequently routed to the central nucleus of the amygdala, which functions as the principal output station of the amygdala. Output from the amygdala will eventually activate the HPA and sympathetic neurochemical systems (Labar & LeDoux, 2000).

Locus coeruleus. The locus coeruleus is the home of the noradrenergic neurons that have been implicated in the stress response and stress-related illnesses such as post-traumatic stress disorder. As seen in Figure 5.9, an immense projection system leaves the locus coeruleus and innervates all levels of the neuroaxis. Specifically, the locus coeruleus is responsible for the norepinephrine in the forebrain and hippocampus. Additionally, CRH has been identified as an influential neurotransmitter in the locus coeruleus, contributing to the nonendocrine components of the stress response. The hippocampal and forebrain activation heightens arousal and sharpens cognitive functions in the initial phase of stress—probably leading to enhanced problem-solving ability and survival (Van Bockstaele, Bajic, Proudfit, & Valentino, 2001).

FOUNDATIONS OF PSYCHOPHARMACOLOGY

Now that you're aware of some of the fundamental neurochemical processes in the brain, it is easy to discern that there are limitless opportunities to develop drugs that intervene with the many neurochemical metabolic pathways. Modifications of dietary precursors, critical enzymes, or transport molecules can have dramatic effects on human behavior, emotions, or thoughts. Like an undercover agent, **psychoactive drugs** act as antagonists or agonists and actually use the brain's own neurochemical processes to do their work to influence these systems. As a drug's **affinity** for the natural receptor approaches that of the actual neurotransmitter it is mimicking, it becomes stronger as the **efficacy** of the drug, or its chance of activating the receptor, becomes more likely.

The development of psychoactive drugs for a treatment of a particular mental illness is no easy process. During the early stages of research, investigators must establish an understanding of the drug's **pharmacokinetics,** or movement throughout the body. In accomplishing this understanding, researchers focus on the four basic processes (Julien, 2004):

1. *Absorption* refers to the journey of the drug as it passes from the external world to the bloodstream. The administration route (oral, intravenous, or intranasal) has a significant impact on the absorption of a drug.

2. Once absorption is understood, researchers must track the drug's *distribution* throughout the brain and body. This is especially important for pregnant women because a drug distributed to the developing fetus could be harmful or detrimental to the new life. Many times the drug is distributed to destinations that are not the primary target—this is the root of many of the unwanted side effects of many drugs.

3. It is also important to understand how the body *metabolizes* or breaks down the drug so that the effect can be terminated.

4. Once metabolized, the *elimination* route is identified. Typically, metabolites are excreted in the urine, which provides an ideal "test" to determine if a person has recently consumed a particular drug.

As seen in Table 5.4, getting a drug from the idea stage to FDA approval is a long and tedious process. Additionally, getting a drug from the initial

psychoactive drugs Drugs that produce a noticeable change in mood or perception

affinity The strength of attraction that a neurotransmitter has for a particular type of receptor

efficacy The capacity to produce a desired effect with a drug or treatment

pharmacokinetics The study of the action and reaction of and to drugs in the body.

[Table 5.4]
Phases of Drug Development

Appx. 5 years:	Discovery of the drug, development of efficient methods of synthesis, and testing with animal models
Appx. 1 year:	Application to begin clinical trials and the review of basic research by government agency
Appx 1.5 years:	Phase I of Human Clinical Trials: Screening for safety and finding the maximum safe dose
Appx. 2 years	Phase II of Human Clinical Trials: Establishing most effective doses and schedules of treatment
Appx. 3.5 years	Phase III of Human Clinical Trials: Clear demonstrations that the drug is therapeutic
Appx. 1.5 years:	Application to begin marketing and reviews of results to clinical trials by government agency
Ongoing:	Recovering development costs and continuing to monitor the safety of the drug

Adapted from Pinel, 2003, and Zivin, 2000.

laboratory investigations to the drugstore is an expensive endeavor. According to a 1993 report published by the Congressional Office of Technology Assessment, a pharmaceutical company spends over $350 million to develop a new drug. Consequently, a company such as Hoffmann-LaRoche, spends about one-third of its 3 billion dollar budget on research (Cohn, 1995). Further, marketing and sales costs for 12 months increase the price tag to 1.7 billion for the total drug development package (Mullin, 2003). The pharmaceutical companies often invest this significant amount of money with no guarantee that the drug will ever make it to paying consumers.

Of course, some drug consumption is not as dependent on the research, development, and marketing of pharmaceutical companies. For drugs that have desirable psychological effects, humans have been impressively creative about obtaining sufficient quantities to achieve the desired effect. These drugs have been obtained mostly from plants over the years, but individuals with a little chemistry knowledge and home-based labs have also become significant sources of "recreational" psychoactive drugs. The various effects of these substances include relaxation, increased concentration, hallucinations, and extreme excitement; some are illegal and others are sold legally every day (see Connections for information on the culturally accepted psychoactive substance caffeine). Many of these potentially addictive drugs are discussed in detail in Chapter Ten; see Table 10.3 for a summary of the neurochemical actions of representative drugs of abuse.

Summary

Neurochemicals

The brain is fueled by many types of neurochemicals including neurotransmitters, neurohormones, hormones, and neuromodulators. Now that more and more neuropeptide transmitters are being identified, it is clear that there are literally hundreds of functionally significant neurochemicals in our brains. If an imbalance occurs in any of these systems, it is likely that an individual may experience a significant cognitive, behavioral, or emotional effect.

Acetylcholine is derived from the dietary precursor choline, binds to muscarinic and nicotinic receptors, and is deactivated by acetylcholine esterase. ACh neurons project from the basal forebrain to the hippocampus and cortex; other ACh neurons project to the basal ganglia, thalamus, pons, and cerebellum. ACh is involved in learning and memory; Alzheimer's patients have decreased cholinergic levels. ACh is also present at all neuromuscular junctions; consequently, interruptions lead to paralysis.

Dopamine and norepinephrine are catecholamines synthesized from the dietary protein tyrosine. DA pathways project to forebrain and limbic areas. DA cell bodies in the substantia nigra control movement; damage to this area results in Parkinson's disease. Other DA functions include pleasure and cognitive processing. Norepinephrine cell bodies are located in the brainstem and project to the thalamus, hypothalamus, limbic system, and cortex. NE is involved in attention, reward, and other motivational systems.

Serotonin is synthesized from dietary tryptophan and is received by at least 18 receptor types. 5-HT cell bodies are located in the medulla and their projections extend to the forebrain, hippocampus, thalamus, hypothalamus, cerebellum, and midbrain. Drugs such as fluoxetine increase synaptic 5-HT levels by inhibiting reuptake. 5-HT is involved in several functions, such as temperature control, mood, aggression, sleep, and hunger. The deactivating enzyme monoamine oxidase degrades both the catecholamine and 5-HT synaptic molecules.

Glutamate and gamma-aminobutyric acid are two amino acid neurotransmitters. Glu is the principal excitatory neurotransmitter in the CNS and its receptors are found on most neurons. The N-methyl-D-aspartate Glu receptor has been implicated in cognitive functions; disruptions lead to neurotoxicity and schizophrenia symptoms. GABA is the principal inhibitory neurotransmitter, and most of its cell bodies are located in the cortex. GABA agonists such as benzodiazepines lead to hallucinations, amnesia, insomnia, and anesthesia; alcohol is perhaps the most popular GABA-affecting drug.

We now know that the brain has receptors for exogenous opioids because it produces its own form of endogenous opioids. Three families of opioid peptides exist, as do three main receptor classes. Generally, the endogenous opioids produce effects such as analgesia, euphoria, and respiratory depression; recent research implicates opioid involvement in more complex systems such as maternal behavior and social communication.

Oxytocin and vasopressin are neurohormones released by the posterior pituitary. Oxytocin is involved in orgasm, ejaculation, uterine contractions, lactation, and social bonding. AVP influences the osmotic content of the blood and blood pressure, as well as social recognition. Both neuropeptides have been implicated in learning and may play a role in mental illnesses characterized by disrupted social behavior.

Neurochemistry of the Stress Response

A stressful event triggers the sympathetic nervous system to secrete NE to recruit immediate energy necessary to survive the threat; additionally, the hypothalamic-pituitary-adrenal axis is activated to provide subsequent energy to maintain the battle against the stressor. When the HPA axis is stimulated, corticotropin-releasing hormone is released into the pituitary portal system leading to the release of adrenocorticotropin hormone from the anterior pituitary, which travels to the adrenal cortex and triggers the release of glucocorticoids.

In the face of chronic stress, long-term health projects are sometimes compromised; additionally, brain areas full of glucocorticoid receptors, such as the hippocampus, become compromised after days to weeks of elevated stress hormone levels. Other brain areas involved in maintaining stress hormone release include the amygdala and locus coeruleus.

Foundations of Psychopharmacology

An exogenous substance that activates a receptor in the brain is said to have an affinity for the receptor. The closer the match, the stronger the efficacy of the sub-stance. As a drug is being evaluated for efficacy and safety, considerable time and money are required to conduct the necessary research. Among other things, researchers are interested in the pharmacokinetics of a drug: its absorption, distribution, metabolic, and elimination characteristics.

Key Terms

neuropeptides, p. 149

neurohormones, p. 149

neuromodulator, p. 149

acetylcholine (ACh), p. 151

agonist, p. 153

antagonist, p. 153

catecholamines, p. 154

dopamine, p. 154

norepinephrine (NE), p. 154

epinephrine, p. 154

tyrosine hydroxylase (TH), p. 155

reuptake, p. 156

serotonin (5-HT), p. 158

tryptophan, p. 158

5-hydroxyindole acetic acid (5-HIAA), p. 159

glutamate (Glu), p. 161

gamma-aminobutyric acid (GABA), p. 162

N-methyl-D-aspartate (NMDA), p. 162

kainite receptor, p. 162

alpha-amino hydroxy-methyl-isoxazolepropionate (AMPA), p. 162

neurotoxicity, p. 163

benzodiazepines, p. 165

barbiturates, p. 165

glycine (Gly), p. 166

endogenous opioids, p. 167

endorphins, p. 167

oxytocin, p. 168

arginine vasopressin (AVP), p. 171

fight-or-flight response, p. 175

corticotropin-releasing factor, p. 176

adrenocorticotropin hormone (ACTH), p. 176

glucocorticoids, p. 176

cortisol, p. 176

hypothalamic-pituitary-adrenal (HPA) axis, p. 176

excitotoxicity, p. 177

psychoactive drugs, p. 179

affinity, p. 179

efficacy, p. 179

pharmacokinetics, p. 179

For Further Consideration

Cooper, J. R., Roth, R., & Bloom, F. E. (1996). *Biochemical Basis of Neuropharmacology,* 6th ed. New York: Oxford University Press. This book is a must-have for anyone who wants to know about the brain and its chemistry without overwhelming details. A fair amount of swagger and a little personal infor-mation enlivens the dense collection of neurochemi-cal data that is packed into this fine book. It should be on every curious brain student's shelf.

Goodman, L. S., Limbird, L., & Hardman, J. G. (2001). *Goodman and Gilman's The Pharmacological Basis of Therapeutics,* 10th ed. New York: McGraw-Hill. This is one of the authoritative volumes in pharmacology. If this book does not have it, it has not been invented or developed or discovered yet. *Goodman and Gilman* (as it is called) has the best descriptions of the body's chemistry and a wealth of information on the brain, as well. From the stand-point of finding a quick and detailed description of an agonist or an antagonist or understanding possi-ble interactions and their medical relevance, *Goodman and Gilman* has been a reliable resource for decades.

Julien, R. M. (2001). *A Primer of Drug Action: A Concise, Nontechnical Guide to the Actions, Uses, and Side Effects of Psychoactive Drugs,* 10th ed. New York:

Freeman. This is a fine introduction to the area of drugs and the brain. Its coverage of neurotransmitters, interactions among neurons, and the sledgehammerlike effect that drugs have when they slam into the brain are all well documented and discussed. How the brain responds to the smallest drink of beer or the biggest line of cocaine (and the ensuing seizure and death) is described for the reader to consider. The brain is like the wilds of Alaska, pure, pristine and unsullied; a drug introduced into that kind of an environment, like an oil spill, can have untold and untoward consequences.

Medvei, V. C. (1984). *A History of Endocrinology.* Boston: Kluwer. In a history that goes back thousands of years, this book gives myriad accounts of drugs, chemicals, and hormones that course and have coursed through the body over the ages—providing accounts of how the drugs were discovered, by whom, and how the discoveries then led to new ones.

[Chapter Six]
Neurodevelopment over the Life Span

Connections

Fate of the Aging Brain: Popular and Scientific Perspectives

Have you ever heard someone forget something and declare that they are experiencing a *senior moment?* That statement conveys how our society feels about an aging brain—that it is compromised, past its prime, and on a steady decline to dementia. Movies portray the elderly as vulnerable, confused, and in need of constant supervision. But does cognitive decline automatically occur in the aged? We all know that a child's brain is fertile territory for neuronal growth, but what about the aging brain? Can new connections form into old age?

A scientific exploration of these questions provides data that challenge the stereotypes of the aging brain. We now know that Alzheimer's or some other form of dementia is not a natural, automatic progression of the aging process; many people live full, long lives with very little cognitive decline in their final years. And research suggests that individuals can do more than merely maintain their level of cognitive functioning into old age; on the contrary, evidence suggests that the brain has the ability to make new connections throughout our lives.

Working at the University of Illinois, William Greenough and his colleagues (1985) have found that adult rats have the ability to form new neuronal connections, not unlike their preadolescent counterparts. Similar to the traditional enriched environment work conducted in the 1960s by Mark Rosenzweig and colleagues (1999), Greenough exposes his adult rats to a form of rat Disneyland, with lots of toys and ladders and tubes to explore. Middle-aged adult rats develop about five times more neuronal branching in the occipital cortex following a 45-day Disney excursion than do rats that don't experience the enriched environment (Green, Greenough, & Schlumpf, 1983). Additionally, exposing the rats to the rodent equivalent of a jungle gym produces increased cerebellar synapses in the acrobatic rats compared with voluntary exercise animals (Kleim, Swain, Armstrong, Napper, Jones, & Greenough, 1998). Certainly Greenough's lab has found that the adult brain is anything but static if it is placed in the appropriately stimulating environment.

David Snowden, working at the University of Kentucky Medical Center, has investigated this question using a unique subject population (Snowden,

2001). As an epidemiologist, he is interested in the factors related to the mystery of aging, and on hearing a graduate student recount her experiences living as a nun, he decided that nuns might provide some clues to the mystery of aging. As opposed to other human populations, nuns live healthy lives filled with cognitive and physical activities, healthy diets, social support, and a sense of control in stressful or trying times. The icing on the empirical cake for epidemiologists is the meticulous records kept of every member of the community throughout their lives. Snowden nervously asked Minnesota's School Sisters of Notre Dame to allow him to study them, and they agreed, welcoming him into their convent. Later, when Snowden decided that the nuns might provide meaningful information about the aging brain's biggest threat—Alzheimer's disease—a group of 678 nuns agreed to donate their brains following their death. Snowden has collected several hundred brains, and he and neuropathologist William Markesbery have uncovered several interesting bits of information about the susceptibility and progression of Alzheimer's disease. Living a healthy, stimulating life is related not only to longevity but to a delay in age-related cognitive decline and accompanying signs of an Alzheimer's brain (which occurs in 45% of people 85 years and older).

Interestingly, factors such as idea density and the expression of positive emotions in essays written when the nuns were in their early twenties are related to reduced risk for Alzheimer's in their eighties, nineties, and hundreds. One of the nuns, Sister Esther, is 106 years old at the time of this writing and, even at her advanced age, continues to live an independent, healthy life, riding an exercycle for 10 minutes each day and frequently completing various crafts.

Although life-style doesn't always protect against the development of Alzheimer's disease, it seems to buffer against its effects. Snowden and Markesbery have found a few brains of perfectly cognitively competent sisters to be riddled with the plaques and tangles characteristic of Alzheimer's. In other cases, brains of nuns with no visible cognitive impairment were found to be considerably smaller than their sister counterparts' brains, suggesting that their enriched cognitive and physical lives created a buffer against the neurodegeneration of their brains, allowing them to live several years before showing evidence of the disease. The Nun Study is far from over, and it is certain that other valuable variables contributing to a slowing of the aging process will be identified as the brains of more nuns are added to the study.

E pluribus unum, the dictum on our coins, is Latin for "From many, one." It is an apt statement when referring to the brain, as well, for from the enormous number of neurons and their connections in a single brain come the raw materials from which the unique characteristics of the human mind emerge. How you got to the point in your life at which you are sitting where you are, reading these words, and interpreting them in your own unique fashion owes more to the movement and interaction of countless developing neural cells and their eventual destinations than anything else. Without active guidance of the mass of new cells being born at an alarming rate during nervous system development, the democracy of the brain would end up as neural anarchy.

PRENATAL BRAIN DEVELOPMENT

Many authors divide development of the brain and nervous system into a chronology of six to eight overlapping stages (Bloom, Nelson, & Lazerson, 2001; Rosenzweig, Leiman, & Breedlove, 1999): induction, proliferation, migration, aggregation, differentiation, circuit formation, programmed cell death or apoptosis, and synapse rearrangement. During *induction,* a portion of the *ectoderm,* one of three layers of the developing embryo, becomes the nervous system, whereas other cells become hair and fingernails. As seen in Figure 6.1, the *proliferative* stage is, as the name implies, a time of immense cellular division, also known as neurogenesis. *Migration* involves the movement of newly minted cells to various places in the forming brain. *Aggregation* is the process whereby similar neurons associate to become specific neuronal populations. *Differentiation* involves finer delineation of cells into specific neurotransmitter types and the like and occurs early as well as later on in development. *Synaptogenesis* leads

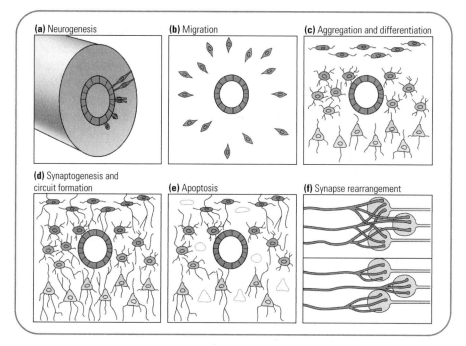

[Figure 6.1]
Building a brain. The nervous system requires many interrelated steps (parts of which are ill defined and overlap) in order to develop. Essentially, neurons and glial cells must be born (neurogenesis); move to their sites of eventual activity (migration); associate with similar cells (aggregation); have their activity and function become more finely tuned (differentiation); establish connections and circuits with complementary neurons (synaptogenesis and circuit formation); have excess neurons and circuits pruned away (apoptosis); and have the final pathways refined and established (synapse rearrangement).

AFTER ROSENZWEIG, LEIMAN, & BREEDLOVE, 1999, P. 160

apoptosis Programmed cell death initiated by nuclear signals associated with age or other health related variables of the cell; serves as a form of neuronal sculpting in the developing brain.

pluripotent The potential of a single stem cell to develop into many types of cells in the body.

stem cells Cells that, when nurtured in the appropriate chemical culture, have the ability to divide and develop into specialized cells for an indefinite time period.

ectoderm The outer layer of the fertilized egg, or zygote, that eventually gives rise to the skin, nerve cells, and most of the neuroglia.

mesoderm The middle layer of the fertilized egg, or zygote, that eventually gives rise to many muscles, the skin, skeleton, and connective tissue.

endoderm The innermost layer of the fertilized egg, or zygote, that eventually gives rise to the developing fetus's internal organs.

neural plate A group of cells derived from the embryonic ectoderm that subsequently develop into the neural groove and neural tube, the origins of the mature nervous system.

neural groove The groove found between the neural folds in the developing embryo; once the neural folds join, the neural groove becomes the neural tube.

neural folds A portion of the ectoderm of the embryo develops into folds that form around the neural tube; eventually, these folds will give rise to the entire nervous system.

to *circuit formation,* which comprises two elements, axonal and synaptic growth and regulation, concerns the segregation of groups of neurons into discrete pathways and connections with logical precision. **Apoptosis,** or programmed cell death, renders the tremendous overproduction of neurons into a cleanly operating collection by selectively pruning synapses and eliminating inefficient or redundant pathways. Finally, following the death of certain neurons, *synapse rearrangement* occurs as neural connections reestablish synaptic arrangements with neurons that did not fall victim to apoptosis.

Emergence and Journey of the Brain's Neurons

In the human, late in the first month of life, the developing nervous system begins to take shape and the process of induction and differentiation are initiated. As we describe this process, keep in mind that the genes are the primary influence guiding development: they dictate the number, size, and rate of cell division as well as the qualities of the cells being born and their potentials, at this time and later on during brain formation. Aside from the obvious complexity inherent in building a human being (or other organism) from scratch, the principles are rather straightforward. As one layer of cells is created, using signals that are thus far indistinct, it makes way for another and another and so on. Layer is placed on layer, as with bricks or phyllo dough, until later on when differentiation of cell types occurs. Until then, cells are **pluripotent,** able to become many different things, from skin to neurons. These are the so-called **stem cells** that, as discussed later in the chapter, have evoked such excitement and passion from scientists and such fear from the moralists and ethicists, who envision their misuse or the lengths to which some will go to obtain them.

Working backward from the adult peripheral and central nervous systems, how does all this organized chaos happen? Late in the third week of the human's life, following fertilization and implantation of the egg, a thickened layer of cells forms from the ventral surface of the dividing egg (it is derived from the former initial group of cells called the inner cell mass). This cellular carpet is called the **ectoderm.** It is accompanied by the **mesoderm** and then the **endoderm,** and together they form the three layers on which the human is built. These plates of cells, formed very early in the development of the nervous system with the most dorsal, the ectoderm, giving rise to the **neural plate,** are very active and programmed to proliferate at varying rates (Figure 6.2). For example, the rate of cell division at the ends of the neural plate exceeds the rate in the medial section, which leads to a thickening at the ends and a thinning in

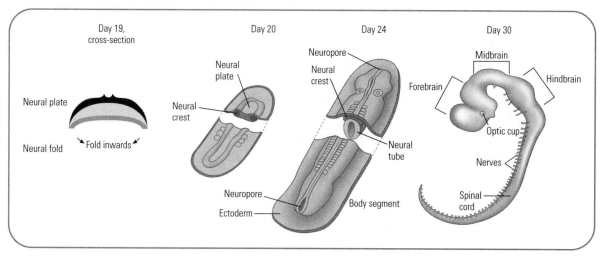

Day 19, cross-section

Neural plate

Neural fold

Fold inwards

Day 20

Neural plate

Neural crest

Neuropore

Ectoderm

Day 24

Neuropore

Neural crest

Neural tube

Body segment

Day 30

Midbrain

Forebrain

Hindbrain

Optic cup

Nerves

Spinal cord

[Figure 6.2]
The embryonic nervous system
The head versus body orientation is represented here by the neuropore, openings at either end, rostral and caudal, of the embryonic neural canal.
AFTER BLOOM, NELSON, LAZERSON, 2001, P. 62

the middle, called the **neural groove.** As the neural groove deepens, the continued thickening creates the **neural fold.** When viewed from the side, the neural fold appears like two waves approaching and then enveloping each other. The resulting space in the middle, formed when the two sides of the neural fold meet, results in a fluid-filled cavity called the **neural tube.** The neural tube is bounded on its dorsal surface by a layer of cells resembling a cape about the shoulders of the neural tube. This is called the **neural crest,** and eventually it splits, both halves moving to the dorsomedial region of the neural tube. There they become incorporated into the yet-to-be-formed spinal cord, forming the portion of the cord that relays sensory information to the brain.

At either end of the neural tube, prior to closure of the margins of the neural plate, lie two openings that are conduits to the amniotic fluid that swirls around the developing embryo. These openings are called the anterior and posterior **neuropores.** As further development commences, the anterior neuropore undergoes specific and increased cell division, which begins to create the premature brain. It is from these three main vesicles or enlargements that the developing brain begins to elaborate and form. Cellular division at this time (proliferation) occurs at a rate that staggers the imagination. At its peak, given the enormous capacity of the geometric progression of cell division, tens of thousands of neurons can be produced per minute. These neurons go on to become organized and integrated into an organ capable of pondering the intricacy of its own genesis.

Cell division continues apace. By the fourth week of life the embryonic nervous system, including the nascent brain, begins to resemble its

neural tube An early form of the nervous system observed during prenatal development: The rostral section develops into the brain and the caudal section eventually develops into the spinal cord.

neural crest The tissue that starts to develop on each side of the neural tube that later becomes the peripheral nervous system.

neuropore An opening at each end of the neural canal that eventually give rise to the brain and spinal cord.

neuropil The intricate network of interwoven glial and neuronal processes that lie between axons.

mature version, cells have begun moving from sites of creation to sites of eventual integration (migration), and the neural tube nears closure. Spatial arrangement of the structures is in place, but the size, density, and activity are all vastly different from what they are in the fully formed nervous system. The three vesicles that are being formed prior to closure of the neural tube are the basis for the three main divisions of the brain that are discussed in Chapter Three: the forebrain, the midbrain, and the hindbrain. These structures elaborate to assume the characteristic shape of the mature brain, and the more caudal elements of the now-closed neural tube thin, elongate, and branch out to become the spinal cord (see Figure 6.2).

Following closure of the anterior neuropore and the beginnings of the three main divisions/vesicles, the aggregation stage commences, in which cells with similar structure and function accumulate geographically. The three vesicles at this stage are fluid-filled, the precursors to the eventual ventricular system. The pressure exerted by these fluid-filled cavities contributes to maintaining the shape of the developing brain and the compartmentalization into specific brain regions, but there is much cell proliferation and the formation of connections and **neuropil** that ultimately dictate the final shape of the structure under construction. The form and function, too, are regulated in large measure by the external events that swirl around the developing nervous system. Though much more prevalent after birth, these external events contribute to the formation of the connections that arise during this time.

By 12 weeks or so, the brain becomes brainlike: it begins to assume the shape it will have in the mature person (Figure 6.3a). The fundamental pattern of the ventricles and their distinctive shape are apparent in the 8-week-old embryo, already assuming the characteristics of its adult counterpart. The ventricles become integrated into the adult form not by any kind of migration or movement but rather by their function as hydraulic casts around which the proliferating brain is forming. By 12 weeks of age, the embryonic brain has the appearance of all five subdivisions discussed in Chapter Three: the telencephalon, the diencephalon, the mesencephalon, the metencephalon, and the myelencephalon (Figure 6.3b). An interesting feature of the newly formed brain is the exclusive but interrelated forms it assumes. Though the regions are separate, each establishes discrete connections with the other regions, connections that are formed early and under a variety of conditions but that remain with the organism for the rest of its life.

If one stops to consider the fate of the newborn nervous system, it is apparent that cells that are born are at but the beginning of a figurative

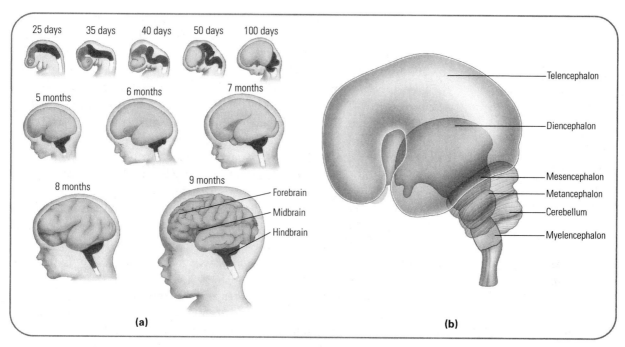

25 days 35 days 40 days 50 days 100 days

5 months 6 months 7 months

8 months 9 months

Forebrain
Midbrain
Hindbrain

(a)

Telencephalon
Diencephalon
Mesencephalon
Metancephalon
Cerebellum
Myelencephalon

(b)

[Figure 6.3]
Embryonic and fetal brain development. (a) Spreading upward and outward, the developing human brain demonstrates the ever-increasing facets that accompany maturation of the nervous system and, early on, resembles its adult counterpart. (b) In more detail, it is apparent that the brain regions that are present early as the nervous system develops remain and grow ever more convoluted and larger as the nervous system continues to develop.

A: AFTER COWAN, 1979, P. 116; B: AFTER BLOOM, NELSON, LAZERSON, 2001, P. 63

and literal lifelong journey. There is much left to do to sculpt the mature brain out of the new and raw materials of neurons, glia, neurotransmitters, neuropeptides, and so on. As wondrous as it sounds, each neuron can establish tens of thousands of connections with other neurons, and the proper establishment of these connections is essential for proper functioning. The process whereby this assembly occurs is multifaceted and intricate. Further, it is susceptible to the many internal and external forces that roil the waters of development, from the initial directives of the genes through diet, hormones, environmental toxins, trauma, and the mass of sensory stimuli that flood the new brain with novel and compelling information about its unfamiliar world.

Establishing and Fine-Tuning the Brain's Circuits

The process of circuit formation forges the ultimate relationships among neurons, stamping them with the markers of chemistry and function. Together with the local connections, or intra-nuclear associations, there are distant, region-to-region connections that are established, fostering the eventual transfer of more and more involved information for additional processing (Restak, 2003).

filopodia An extremely fine tubular shaped extension that emerges from the neuron's growth cone.

neurotrophins Neurochemicals secreted in an activity-dependent fashion that are thought to be involved in the restructuring of synaptic connections

brain derived neurotrophic factor (BDNF) A stimulating factor localized in the CNS that promotes the growth and survival of neurons.

nerve growth factor A neurochemical secreted by the postsynaptic neuron during the formation of synaptic connections between neurons; it is considered a trophic factor because it stimulates the growth of the presynaptic neuron's axon.

cell adhesion molecules (CAM) Glycoproteins located on the cell surface that play a role in guiding growing axons as they move toward their final destinations in the brain.

The processes involved in forming the circuits of the brain bear some further discussion. The neurons that have moved into position following their migratory travels are in the process of establishing final synapses with the adjoining cells in the vicinity. They send out probes that snake toward their neighbors, searching out connections, like travelers on a defined but circuitous path. There is a scene in the final moments of the movie *Field of Dreams* in which the camera pulls away from a nighttime view to reveal what looks like thousands of cars moving toward the farm where much of the film takes place. It is an apt visual metaphor for the way in which neuronal circuits are being established in the early brain. A catch phrase from that movie is similarly apropos of brain development: "If you build it, they will come." In essence, the circuits that arise at this time are constructed and constricted by active processes such as internal neurochemistry and commands, and as much by external stimulation as by the sensory load being processed by these new cells and circuits. Sensory stimulation can direct connections.

Circuits are formed in the new brain by a combination of seeker neurons and target neurons and their interaction. As the new neurons are born, they move through the three-dimensional space literally by feel, using the end plate of the axon called the growth cone. At the extreme ends of the growth cone are delicate digitlike projections called **filopodia** (Figure 6.4). Like toes tentatively dropped into a hot bath to test the water, the filopodia inch along the forming neuropil in search of connections. They follow a chemical gradient that is a further example of the digital nature of the nervous system. The filopodia depend just as much on chemical signals (chemosignals) that repel them as on signals that attract. Some examples of these signals are the **neurotrophins** or neurotrophic factors, chemicals such as **brain-derived neurotrophic factor (BDNF), nerve growth factor (NGF), cell adhesion molecules (CAMs);** other signals are present in various amounts and locations at these critical stages of development. Together, there are four possible ways in which synapses are formed by axons—*chemoattraction* and *chemorepulsion* (whereby the filopodia are affected distantly by the chemicals) and *contact attraction* and *contact repulsion* (in which the axon literally bounces off a neuron on which a connection was sought but is chemically inappropriate). These chemoattractants and chemorepellants (one neuron's attractant may be another's repellant) work in tandem, like molecular tugboats, to navigate an axon into place or push it away from its docking site, establishing pre- and post-synaptic connections that may last a lifetime. Once the synapse is complete, there is a burst of activity that follows, reinforcing the fresh connection.

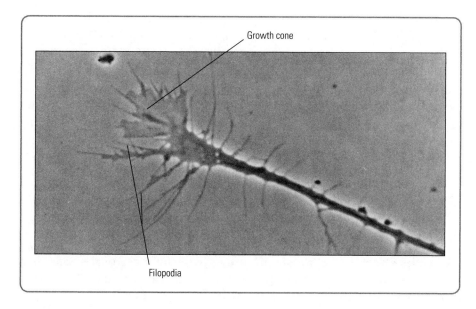

Growth cone

Filopodia

[Figure 6.4]
Filopodia. The developing brain is represented by millions of migrating neurons, moving great distances to establish contact with complementary cells by means of chemical attractants and repellants. Filopodia, the vital tips of migrating neurons, are like a hand reaching up to feel around an unknown surface, searching for an object or direction in the dark.
COURTESY DENNIS BRAY

With this process writ large—billions of times once the brain has nearly reached the end of its early development (with its approximately 100 billion neurons)—the connections that are in place are difficult but not impossible to dislodge. In fact, the brain has a built-in process akin to natural selection that ensures that only the best and most efficient connections remain. It can be thought of as *neural Darwinism* (the title of a book by Gerald Edelman). That is, there is a dramatic cellular struggle that takes place once the brain has begun to slow down its production of new cells and connections. It is synaptic competition of the most severe sort, with the victorious neurons and connections remaining to exert influences on virtually every facet of brain activity thereafter and the losers consigned to reabsorption.

The loss of existing neurons and connections is regulated by multiple factors, among them the access to neurotrophic factors, the interaction with the postsynaptic elements (target organ, neuron), and interestingly, the sensory information that floods into the new nervous system. All these sources represent feedback to the neurons that the connection is a working one. Like the atrophy that occurs when a muscle is not worked, neurons cease to be connected if the connection is shown to be unnecessary. One reason that physical rehabilitation is attempted so soon after an injury is that the feedback provided to the brain by means of the muscle helps to maintain the neural regulation of the muscle. It prevents having to rehabilitate both ends of the connection.

Among the neurons and their synapses that are lost in development are the ones that are lost through apoptosis, or programmed cell death. This phenomenon was first reported by Dale Purves and Jeff W. Lichtman (in 1980), causing much interest in the reasons for the event. This process, designed to naturally rid the newly formed brain of redundant, unnecessary, or inefficient synapses, produces a lean and functional organ with inherent speed and capabilities. When a gardener prunes trees in the spring, he is guiding development of the branches and promoting efficient growth. Subsequently, the pruned tree is usually healthier and better functioning. Like the pruned tree, the shape that the brain takes is intended to produce an efficient final product. As discussed, though, getting to that point may be accomplished in basic, brutal, Darwinian fashion, as neurons and their synapses compete.

The brain manufactures neurons at an astonishing rate. At that pace, it begins its existence with a significantly greater number of neurons than it will end up with; estimates place the excess at more than 50% and in some regions at more than 80% (Gilbert, 2000; Kandel, Schwartz, & Jessell, 2000). That is, the brain is overproducing neurons in massive amounts, resulting in a shapeless blob of vital cells with little functionality that must be reduced in size and density—it must be brought under control. Apoptosis, then, can be likened to a sculptor who starts out with a mass of marble or other material and slowly and meticulously shapes it into a final object, a vision realized. But in the case of a brain, the process begins with a large number of functioning neurons.

The production of too many neurons and their connections, however, creates a situation that is both advantageous and maladaptive. If too many neurons are produced and kept, the speed and efficiency of neural transfer of information is imperiled; furthermore, dependence on faulty connections increases the likelihood of loss of function in a "weak link" scenario. The large number produced, however, sets the stage for tremendous competition among the neurons, ensuring that only the best will survive to establish themselves in neural circuits. It is a process that is designed to winnow the wheat from the chaff, producing a neural substrate that will work well for a long time.

Recently much attention has been focused on apoptosis. There may be a genetic cue to onset of apoptosis that is linked to the number of cell divisions that the neurons undergo. With accumulated activity associated with each cell division, programmed cell death may be set into motion by genes that lead to overexpression of various proteins so that subsequently divided neurons are marked for death. Other cellular dynamics, such as the removal of neurotrophic factors, may contribute to apoptosis.

Neurotrophins are like rainwater for neurons; they contribute to their growth and elaboration and maintenance—their survival. Removing their influence would have the effect that a drought would have on a garden. For instance, one mechanism that NGF may mediate is suppression of an apoptotic program that is set to operate in neurons. The presence of NGF may keep the program from turning on in the neuron, keeping that neuron in the circuit.

Last, another mechanism that ensures survival of neurons and their connections and circuits is the feedback provided by the target to the neuron. The reciprocal signaling is prima facie evidence that the connection is a fully functioning one. Thus, maintaining a feedback loop between pre- and post-synaptic neurons holds the apoptotic processes at bay. This signaling process may operate through stimulation of neurotrophic factors or suppression of internal apoptotic programs, but it exemplifies the importance of maintaining and exercising the existing links between neurons. There are a couple of adages that apply to brain and circuit formation, and they apply here in relation to apoptosis: (1) Neurons that fire together, wire together; and (2) Use it or lose it. Like the pioneering work by Hubel and Weisel (e.g., 1970) that demonstrates loss of innervation and complexity of visual cortex if that portion of brain is deprived of sensory (visual) stimulation, circuits and connections depend on regular activity and the traffic moving through them.

The cells that survive the apoptosis phase of development must adapt yet again by establishing connections with the surviving neurons. Connections formed with previously existing neurons are rerouted to existing neurons so that an optimal synaptic web forms for each neuron to maximize potential for adaptive functioning.

We have focused on neuron-to-neuron and neuron-to-target interactions, but keep in mind that there are other cells in the brain that also establish connections and are involved in the facilitation of neuronal organization. As discussed in Chapter Four, these cells, the glia, play an integral role in the formation of the brain, in its maintenance and protection, and also in the arrangement of the neurons. During the process of migration, for instance, **radial glia,** formed prior to the migration of newly minted neurons, extend long fibers that can reach for many millimeters. New neurons attach themselves by means of their growth cone and move up the radial glial fiber as if they were climbing a rope, using the fiber as a kind of scaffold on which to achieve purchase, orientation, and direction (Figure 6.5). Thus, glia are integral to the migration of new neurons and in the development of distant brain sites (distant, that is, from the area where the population of neurons is born).

radial glia Neuroglial cells characterized by very long branches that serve as a physical guide or road map for developing neuroblast cells as they migrate toward their final destinations; following the development of the brain, it is thought that these cells are develop into astrocytes.

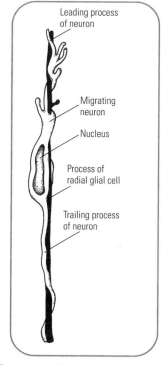

Leading process of neuron

Migrating neuron

Nucleus

Process of radial glial cell

Trailing process of neuron

[Figure 6.5]
Radial glia and development.
The most abundant cells in the brain, the glia, play a major role in the assignment of neurons to brain regions. Here, we see a radial glial cell being used as a scaffold over which a migrating neuron is moving en route to its destination.
FROM BLOOM & LAZERSON, 1988, P. 62

POSTNATAL BRAIN DEVELOPMENT

The neonatal brain resembles the adult brain in the same way that a stripped-down Mini Cooper resembles a fully loaded Mercedes 500 SEL: all the basic parts are there, and you can do some of things with the Mini that you can do with the Mercedes, but the Mercedes is much more massive and complex than the Mini. Unlike the Mini, however, the neonatal brain will grow to become the equivalent of the Mercedes with all its bells and whistles. The process by which this development occurs relies heavily on the external world and its many sensory and experiential forces. The brain at birth is a cavernous labyrinth that swallows up whatever sensory information is near its entrance. One consequence of this unyielding stream of sensory information is a dramatic alteration in the neuronal relationships within the brain. The brain changes to accommodate this information flood, much as a library adds folders, then binders, then, shelves then stacks, then rooms, and then new wings and buildings to hold the information that comes into it. The brain changes, adding new storage space to the various regions charged with recording, or memorizing, the new information. The exact manner in which the information storage is accomplished remains a mystery.

[Figure 6.6]
Early brain development and stimulation. It is apparent that the brain grows dramatically between conception and birth. It grows even larger and more complex during the extended and critical postnatal period, during which the infant is fast soaking up the information that stimulates new neurons and, mainly, the new connections among those and existing neurons.

AFTER CONEL, 1939-1967

Neonatal infant   6-year-old-child

Infancy and Childhood

Figure 6.6 shows the dramatic growth and development of the brain between birth and 6 years of age. What is apparent is that the brain is becoming more detailed with age, a reflection of the never-ending stream of new information it must process to stay alive and adapt. Adaptation, or learning, is the response to the world that the brain makes in the face of change. Learning is the brain's hedge against extinction, and the brain accommodates learning by making more and more space for it. Moreover, in addition to the space that is created, new connections are established between disparate bits of neuronal information, formerly disconnected pieces of data that, when combined, represent a wholly novel way of looking at the information—in other words, new connections, new ways of making sense of or *thinking about* information.

The brain accomplishes these amazing cognitive processing feats by changing physically. At birth, the brain has capacity, awaiting information to stimulate it. But it is shrunken, emaciated compared with what it looks like about age 6. The greatest difference does not appear to be in the number of neurons; rather, it is the myriad connections among the neurons. And no wonder! A child masters hand-eye coordination, walking, social recognition and communication, love, laughter, and a sense of self-awareness (virtually everything defining the human) during this important developmental window, so it is obvious that dramatic increases in neuronal elaboration are necessary. The area that has experienced the most growth in the human 6-year-old is the cortex; in fact, the cortex, containing approximately 70% of the brain's neurons, is the area of the brain that truly differentiates us from other animals. Although the macaque monkey is a fellow primate, its cortex is only 10% the size of the human cortex. And although most of the neuroscience research is conducted on rats, the human cortex is 1000 times larger than the modest rodent cortex (Restak, 2003).

A body of elegant work has shown experimentally the effects of experience on the brain. As mentioned in Chapter One and in the Connections of this chapter, Greenough and his colleagues have demonstrated how the neurons respond to stimulation. For instance, Greenough, Larson, and Withers (1985) investigated the effects of experience on the sensorimotor forelimb cortex of rats. Rats were trained to reach into a tube to retrieve a food reward with their preferred paw (rats, like humans, are right- or left-handed). The rats were then trained to use their nonpreferred paw to grasp the food. After training to use the nonpreferred paw, the rats' cortices were examined for changes in the neuronal structure—in particular, changes in oblique branches from pyramidal neurons. The training caused increased branching of the dendrites with accompanying (but implied) increases in synapses, and overall it magnified the dimensions of the neurons' dendritic fields. Other examples of neural responsiveness to behavioral demands are discussed in the Epilogue; these behavior-induced brain changes are akin to going from a whisper to a shout as the range of neuronal influence spreads outward farther and wider.

The postnatal production of new neurons, or **neurogenesis,** accompanies the increasing brain volume in the developing child. The brain needs to add neurons to the more developed infrastructure in order to add new computing power to the brain as a whole. Fred Gage and his colleagues at the Salk Institute in La Jolla, California, have shown that rich environments can stimulate neurogenesis much as the novel environment of the neonate probably stimulates similar processes (everything is novel to a baby) (Kempermann, Kuhn, & Gaye, 1997). There are more neurons in the

neurogenesis Mitotic division of cells to produce new neuronal cells neuropil of an older child, but the biggest differences are in the branching patterns of the existing neurons. Therefore, the tremendous growth that is apparent in brain size between the two ages is attributable primarily to expansion of existing neurons. By making them more elaborate, adding to their structure the equivalent of more library space, the vast amount of information with which the child must contend is seamlessly integrated into what was integrated before and is ready to accommodate new information that awaits the child. The plasticity of the nervous system into childhood is seen in children from whom, because of persistent epilepsy, an entire hemisphere has been removed. As discussed in Chapter One and in Box 6.1 on page 200, children have an astonishing capacity to recover lost function by increasing the structure and functions of the remaining hemisphere.

Adolescence and Attention Deficit Hyperactivity Disorder

It is interesting how the development of the brain occurs in repetitive motions, much like waves washing on the shore—slowly building up momentum and then washing away the excess as the wave reaches its destination on the shore. After experiencing massive proliferation followed by apoptosis during neonatal and infant development, it was once thought that the brain was fully developed by the end of childhood, needing only fine-tuning in the upcoming adolescent and adult years. But once again, the rhythm of proliferating and pruning must occur to produce the optimally functioning adult brain. This second wave of apoptotic pruning occurs during adolescence.

Jay Giedd, a neuroscientist at the National Institute of Mental Health in Bethesda, Maryland, subjected normal children and adolescents to MRI scans to investigate brain changes that might underlie behavioral changes during adolescence. His findings suggest that, although the brain size stays roughly the same, specific areas undergo dynamic changes (Giedd et al., 1999). For example, the gray matter increases in preadolescence and decreases prior to adulthood, whereas the white matter increases with age without the downward spiral (Durston et al., 2001). The heightened flexibility of the brain during adolescence reinforces the importance of this developmental stage in the formation of the brain's hoped-for final product—a massive yet efficient processing machine.

The final area of the brain to mature is the executive portion, or the frontal lobes. Considering that the development of this rational component of the brain lags behind the maturation of limbic areas involved in sexual and aggressive behaviors, it becomes easy to see why adolescence is such a turbulent time in development—the brain is literally trying to keep up with the emerging emotional and motivational behavior. Just as

attention deficit hyperactivity disorder (ADHD) A condition observed in children and adults characterized by inattention, hyperactivity, and impulsivity.

the mice will play while the cat's away, the mature limbic lobes will play while the frontal lobes are delayed.

An increasingly common developmental disorder, **attention deficit hyperactivity disorder (ADHD)**, is characterized by an inability to sustain one's attention for an appropriate amount of time, accompanied by frequent inappropriate impulsive behavior (Table 6.1 gives diagnostic criteria).

[Table 6.1]

Diagnostic Criteria for Attention Deficit Hyperactivity Disorder

A. Either (1) or (2):

    (1) six (or more) of the following symptoms of **inattention** have persisted for at least 6 months to a degree that is maladaptive and inconsistent with developmental level:

    Inattention

        (a) often fails to give close attention to details or makes careless mistakes in schoolwork, work, or other activities

        (b) often has difficulty sustaining attention in tasks or play activities

        (c) often does not seem to listen when spoken to directly

        (d) often does not follow through on instructions and fails to finish school work, chores, or duties in the workplace (not due to oppositional behavior or failure to understand instructions)

        (e) often has difficulty organizing tasks and activities

        (f) often avoids, dislikes, or is reluctant to engage in tasks that require sustained mental effort (such as schoolwork or homework)

        (g) often loses things necessary for tasks or activities (e.g., toys, school assignments, pencils, books, or tools)

        (h) is often easily distracted by extraneous stimuli

        (i) is often forgetful in daily activities

    (2) six or more of the following symptoms of **hyperactivity-impulsivity** have persisted for at least 6 months to a degree that is maladaptive and inconsistent with developmental level:

    Hyperactivity

        (a) often fidgets with hands or feet or squirms in seat

        (b) often leaves seat in classroom or in other situations in which remaining seated is expected

        (c) often runs about or climbs excessively in situations in which it is inappropriate (in adolescents or adults, may be limited to subjective feelings of restlessness)

        (d) often has difficulty playing or engaging in leisure activities quietly

        (e) is often "on the go" or often acts as if "driven by a motor"

        (f) often talks excessively

    Impulsivity

        (g) often blurts out answers before questions have been completed

        (h) often has difficulty awaiting turn

        (i) often interrupts or intrudes on others (e.g., butts into conversations or games)

B. Some hyperactive-impulsive or inattentive symptoms that caused impairment were present before age 7 years

C. Some impairment from the symptoms is present in two or more settings (e.g., at school [or work] and at home)

D. There must be clear evidence of clinically significant impairment in social, academic, or occupational functioning

E. The symptoms do not occur exclusively during the course of a Pervasive Developmental Disorder, Schizophrenia, or other Psychotic Disorder and are not better accounted for by another mental disorder (e.g., Mood Disorder, Anxiety Disorder, Dissociative Disorder, or a Personality Disorder).

APA, 2000, pp. 92–93

[Box 6.1]

A Case in Point

Relieving Ashlee's Seizure-Induced Wiggles

March 23, 1993, is a date forever etched in Deb Bahr's mind. On this day, Terry and Deb's 1-year-old daughter, Ashlee, experienced her first seizure and was rushed to the hospital. After having another seizure the next morning, Ashlee was placed on anticonvulsant medication. Unfortunately, the seizures continued; at one point, when she was experiencing 30 to 50 seizures per day, Ashlee's parents and doctors became desperate to find a way to decrease their frequency. They decided to place Ashlee in a coma to slow down the seizures while possible treatment solutions were considered. Unfortunately an effective treatment was not identified and, for the next three years, Deb Bahr took little Ashlee to occupational and physical therapy each week. During this time, a neurologist at UCLA offered a diagnosis of *cortical dysplasia*, a condition in which disorganized gray matter induces seizures.

By November 1995, it was becoming obvious that Ashlee was not responding to anticonvulsant medications. Consequently, Ashlee visited neurologists at UCLA and was evaluated for an alternative treatment strategy. However, it was determined that Ashlee was not a good candidate for surgical therapy at this point. Four years and nine anticonvulsant medications later, Ashlee's parents took her once again to UCLA for another round of evaluations. Deb and Terry had been reading about treatment options especially for medically intractable seizure patients such as Ashlee. Their reading led them to the conclusion that surgery—a form of hemispherectomy (removal of the hemisphere in which the seizures originate)—was probably the best option for Ashlee.

A critical step in determining whether surgery was the best option was capturing a seizure with EEG telemetry. So, at 8 years of age, Ashlee entered UCLA once again and was fitted with an electrode cap with leads to a computerized video camera so that her next seizure would be recorded for a more detailed analysis. Much to everyone's dismay, Ashlee, who had been experiencing frequent seizures, went an astounding 30 days with no seizures—a record for any epileptic patient being tracked with EEG telemetry. Convinced that her head needed a rest, the doctors sent Ashlee home, where, after a few days, she had a seizure. After another failed attempt to record a seizure in the hospital, Ashlee was sent home with a portable telemetry unit and once again defied the odds by going seven weeks without a seizure. And just two days after removing her electrode cap, Ashlee experienced a seizure. It is interesting to speculate why Ashlee didn't experience seizures while she had her electrode cap on—perhaps the electrodes altered the electrical fields or activity of the neurons involved in the genesis of the seizures.

Desperate to take action, Terry Bahr convinced the neurosurgeons that they knew enough about the origin of the seizures to go forward with the surgery. They observed Ashlee time and time again as she experienced seizures and knew that the left side of the body was the first to be affected during seizures, indicating that the right hemisphere was damaged. Additionally, Ashlee was experiencing physical disabilities with her left hand and foot, indicating that the repeated seizures had further damaged the right hemisphere. The panel of surgeons at UCLA were convinced by Terry's astute observations and agreed to perform surgery to fix Ashlee's seizure-induced "wiggles" on August 17, 2000. Because complications, namely leakage of blood into the resection cavity, had been observed in some patients with a complete hemisphere removed, a *functional hemispherectomy* was performed, in which tissue from the frontal and occipital poles was left in the cavity with the existing blood supplies intact, but all nerve connections were severed.

Although approval for the surgery was the answer to the Bahr's prayers, the hemispherectomy was still a very scary endeavor. Following a hat's off party at which

Ashlee's friends and family gave her 53 hats and 14 scarves for her soon-to-be shaved head, Ashlee was admitted to the hospital for surgery. Fearful but hopeful, Terry and Deb waited patiently during the 12-hour procedure and were elated when they were told that everything had gone smoothly and that their daughter was expected to be fine. During this stressful day, the Bahrs agreed to allow the Discovery Channel to follow Ashlee's progress throughout the day in an attempt to share Ashlee's story with the public. Even with successful surgery, recovery was a challenge. First came a 10-day bout of depression and frequent headaches. However, after about 12 days, Ashlee was walking, and after nearly three weeks, she was given a day pass to go to Disneyland. She was released from the hospital just a few days later.

Six months after Ashlee's surgery, the whole family traveled to Disneyworld in Orlando, Florida, a trip given to the Bahr family from the Starlight Wish Foundation. Today, nearly four years after her surgery, 12-year-old Ashlee is thriving—and has not had a single seizure since the removal of her right hemisphere. Her language improved immediately following surgery: the frequent seizures had interrupted processing prior to the hemispherectomy. Because the motor cortex that controlled her left body was removed, Ashlee is still striving to gain control of the left side of her body. She wears a brace on her left leg but is able to walk with a slight limp, she can move her left shoulder and arm but is still working to gain control over her left fingers, and she has an impaired visual field. Ashlee and her family agree that, although challenging, these surgery-related effects are small costs to pay for the removal of the frequent seizures that were interrupting her life every day. Following her surgery, Ashlee was placed in a special school class with fewer students to facilitate her recovery as she works to make up lost school time and catch up with her age-matched peers. As a preventative measure, Ashlee still takes a mild dose of an antiseizure medication to ensure that seizures will not begin in her left, seizure-free, hemisphere.

Ashlee today
COURTESY OF DEB AND TERRY BAHR

From a psychological perspective, we were interested in Ashlee's personality—did the removal of nearly half her brain interrupt the essence of her personality—her sense of humor, interactive style, optimism, and so on? Deb told us that prior to Ashlee's surgery, she was a bit demanding, asking for a drink of orange juice, something she could not have as she was about to undergo anesthesia and prolonged surgery. When Ashlee returned to the intensive care unit and finally woke up—after 12 hours of anesthesia and having nearly half her brain removed, her parents were relieved at the first words out of her mouth: "Mom, I want that orange juice NOW." From not knowing if Ashlee would be able to speak, it turned out that her language was fine, her memory was perfect (even ECT disrupts immediate memories), and, to her parents' delight, their little girl was just as determined as ever—her personality was definitely intact. It is reasonable to assume that Ashlee's strong sense of determination has facilitated her recovery and will continue to enable her to live a seizure-free life. Her case is a testament to the plasticity of the human brain (personal communication, 2003).

This condition, observed in 3% to 5% of children (and perhaps more in some studies), is the most prevalent neurobiological condition treated in children and adolescents and presents special challenges for preadolescents and adolescents as they encounter the whirlwind of neuroanatomical changes that accompany these developmental periods (Wilens, Biederman & Spencer, 2002). Of considerable concern for adolescents with ADHD is the observation that they are about twice as likely to abuse drugs during this volatile phase of development. Some turn to drugs as an attempt to calm the feelings of restlessness and anxiety produced by the disorder; others seek stimulants to enhance their ability to focus (such as the psychostimulant Ritalin) (Restak, 2003).

Although there are no obvious brain deficits in ADHD individuals, subtle yet significant changes have been observed. A study conducted at the National Institute of Mental Health found that ADHD children had significantly smaller brain volumes (approximately 3%), specifically around the cerebrum and cerebellum (Castellanos et al., 2002). Other brain areas such as the caudate nucleus also appear to be involved with ADHD symptoms. PET scans reveal lower metabolic rates in the basal ganglia and frontal cortex (Pary, Lewis, Matuschka, & Lippmann, 2002). Focusing on neurochemical factors, researchers have found that the dopamine transporter (DAT) may be altered in ADHD patients (Krause, Dresel, Krause, la Fougere, & Ackenheil, 2003). Consequently, the most popular treatment for ADHD is the use of psychostimulants (e.g., Ritalin), drugs that activate the dopaminergic system. Although most physicians feel that psychostimulants are effective in reducing ADHD symptoms, many are concerned about side effects, including loss of appetite, sleeping problems, and more rarely, movement tics and flat affect.

In a chapter titled "Attention Deficit: The Brain Syndrome of Our Era," the neuropsychiatrist and author Richard Restak (2002) implicates our contemporary fast-paced environment in changing attention spans. He suggests that our society may be selecting brains that can process several pieces of information at one time as opposed to being able to sustain uninterrupted focus on a single problem. Thus, some researchers view attention deficits as a cognitive style that is actually an adaptive response to our fast-paced world filled with instant messages, cell phones that never stop ringing, and split-screen TVs so that we don't have to choose to devote our attention to just one source of information. (Still other clinicians are concerned about possible overdiagnosis of ADHD.)

The role of the environment in ADHD, however, is controversial. Many researchers, such as Russell Barkley (Box 6.2 on page 204), a clinical psychologist at the Medical University of South Carolina, emphasize the important roles of genetics and neurology in the genesis of ADHD. Barkley argues that ADHD is not a problem related to input; rather, it is a problem with the organization of the output of the brain. In support of this hypothesis, he has found that children diagnosed with ADHD pay attention appropriately in the immediate context but have difficulties *responding* in an effective manner, suggesting that ADHD may be more aptly described as a problem of *intention*—the ability to plan the most appropriate response to incoming stimuli. For example, in a simulated driving study, when subjects with ADHD encountered an invasive approaching stimulus, such as an oncoming car, they would steer toward the sidewalk and pedestrians and accelerate, whereas the control subjects would hit the brakes or steer away from the impending danger on both sides (the oncoming car and the pedestrians) (personal communication, April 2001).

THE AGING BRAIN

As discussed in Connections, it is obvious that brain and cognitive decline need not be the defining events of the last decades of life. Understanding the neurobiology of the aging brain is vital to knowing what events lie behind normal brain maturation. Further, comparing normal with abnormal aging of the brain and pathological with nonpathological conditions provides insights into what goes wrong and how to treat the conditions.

Normal Aging Processes

Though flexible, adaptable, and plastic, the brain is still subject to the wear and tear of a lifetime of use. Like other organs, the brain endures the cumulative effects of major and minor insults that take a toll on structure and function, inexorably wearing it down. Ironically, although the brain knows a lot and possesses an overwhelming store of information (the neural components of *wisdom*), the aging brain becomes less and less effective at retrieving and processing it all. Cognitive activity in the older brain is more susceptible to disruption and damage from a host of small and large threats, any one of which can dramatically and permanently reduce the utility of the brain.

Early histological analyses suggested that aging was accompanied by significant neuronal loss; however, more recent accurate **stereological analyses** have not supported the earlier claims (Long, Mouton, Jucker, & Ingram, 1999). When researchers compared cortical areas of 20-year-olds

stereological analysis
Unbiased optical method of counting cells by randomly sampling various areas and depths within neural tissue.

[Box 6.2]

The Investigators

Russell Barkley

Russell Barkley, a professor in the College of Health Professions at the Medical University of South Carolina, has spent his entire career attempting to understand attention deficit hyperactivity disorder (ADHD) and disseminate his findings worldwide to peers and the lay public. He has published more than 170 scientific articles and book chapters related to the nature, assessment, and treatment of ADHD and related disorders. He has shared his knowledge with the general public in books such as *Taking Charge of ADHD: The Complete Authoritative Guide for Parents* (2000) and by appearing on various news shows such as *Good Morning America, Today Show,* and *60 Minutes,* and through interviews in magazines such as *Time* and *Newsweek.* Obviously, ADHD is a topic that interests many mental health professionals, parents, and teachers.

In one interview, Barkley recalled his introduction and entrée into the field of neuropsychology. As a child, he was curious about the natural world, and in high school he founded and was the first president of his school's psychology club. After graduation, he served in the Air Force from 1968 to 1972, during the Vietnam War, a time that shaped Barkley's commitment to understanding human behavior.

Later, as an undergraduate at the University of North Carolina–Chapel Hill, two seminal events captured his attention and set in motion his career path. First, he came under the influence of an attentive and forward-looking mentor. At UNC–Chapel Hill, Don Ruth took

Russell Barkley
COURTESY OF RUSSELL BARKLEY

Barkley under his wing, solidifying his interest in psychology and fomenting a deep fascination with the brain and behavior. At this time, Barkley also was enrolled in courses in biology and psychology, including a class exploring the effects of medication on hyperactive children. It was a potent blend, the effects of which Barkley feels to this day.

Barkley went on to Bowling Green State University, where he conducted research on hyperactive children and earned his Ph.D. in 1977 in clinical psychology. He studied clinical psychology for very practical and opportunistic reasons, he said, because "that was where the jobs were then." But his focus was on the science end, not the clinical end, of the work he was doing. Continuing in the field of neuropsychology with a focus on ADHD solidified Barkley's career direction: he embarked on an attempt to elucidate the effects and causes of ADHD.

Following his graduate studies, Barkley interned at the Oregon Health Sciences University, working with the developmental, learning, and behavioral disorders of children. Subsequent to his internship, he joined the Department of Neurology at the Medical College of Wisconsin and Milwaukee Children's Hospital. While

with 90-year-olds, the number of neurons was fewer by only 10% in the older subjects; significant reductions were not observed in cortical glial cells, either. There were some significant changes, however. The length of myelinated axons and number of synapses decrease (Pakkenberg et al., 2003), and in rodents, neurogenesis declines in the hippocampus (Bizon &

there, he founded the Neuropsychology Service, and served as its chief until 1985. Then he moved to the University of Massachusetts Medical School, there serving as the director of psychology and establishing research clinics for both child and adult ADHD until his recent move to the Medical University of South Carolina.

Because of his expertise and passion about this area of research, Barkley has thought long and hard about the many controversies that characterize the ADHD diagnosis—even the validity of the condition as a disorder resulting from more than environmental influences. He defends the ADHD diagnosis as valid, stating that the scientific community doesn't question the validity of the disorder (recently questioned in an NIH consensus report); however, with our society's entrenched ideas about the strong influence of parenting and educational instruction, many individuals still perceive these variables as the strongest influences in a child's behavior. Barkley focuses on the role of neurology and genetics in the etiology of ADHD, stating that it is the most inherited of all psychiatric disorders. Responding to statements that children are overmedicated, he conveys that most surveys report the number of children diagnosed with ADHD to be about twice the number on psychostimulant medication (for example, Ritalin), suggesting that this statement is false. Although he agrees that the use of labels can be dangerous, he reports that it is necessary to categorize the ADHD symptoms as a disorder to generate further research and protection of the rights and privileges for individuals possessing this disorder.

In his laboratory work, Barkley's research is literally the driving force in the formation of his ideas about ADHD. He has focused on driving skill to investigate perception, self-control, and intentions in ADHD subjects. Currently, his research suggests that the disorder is not as much about attention deficit as it is about persistence of task-oriented behavior. Barkley investigates these variables in his simulated driving lab consisting of the front end of a Ford Crown Victoria situated in the midst of computer screens and auditory simulators to make the experience of driving appear more realistic. This experimental setup has certainly put him on the road to discovering more about the characteristic responses in ADHD subjects responding in real time.

When asked to speak about the more general topic of clinical neuroscience, Barkley believes that the future of this science will feature ever increasing cross talk between geneticists and behaviorists. The Human Genome Project, he believes, will revolutionize the way in which psychology is utilized, and the mental health profession must adapt to this bright and different future or go the way of the dinosaur. He stated that the way in which behavioral science is heading, the "linking up with genes for disorders with phenotypic events in individuals," will focus research and treatment—effective treatment—as never before. The pace of the growth in knowledge will be exceeded only by the applications produced. According to Barkley, we must be ready.

If Barkley was starting his career over, he said he would go into some combination of evolutionary psychology or an amalgam of neuropsychology and evolutionary biology, what he calls "evolutionary neuropsychology." As he looks to the future, with its promise of human genome-derived treatments, stem-cell-grown tissues, and science-driven clinical neuroscience therapies, he conveys that this bright future will require mental health disciplines to embrace more rigor and self-correction.

Gallagher, 2003). Also seen in the aging brain is a reduction in dendritic expansion. Although the healthy 70-year-old brain is able to compensate for subtle cellular loss by developing more enhanced dendritic connections, this ability declines in the normal 90-year-old brain—and much earlier in those with Alzheimer's (Restak, 2003).

neurodegenerative diseases
Conditions that are sometimes inherited or acquired due to some sporadic condition that result in the progressive deterioration of some portion of the nervous system.

Complicating the picture is a disconnect often found between brain condition and cognitive function. Some research, such as Snowden's nun aging project and certain hemispherectomy case studies, suggests that it is difficult to make direct connections between function and neuronal density. Supporting this notion in research on aging, researchers have found that old tree shrews (squirrel-like primates) demonstrated impairment in a working memory task; there was, however, no discernible differences in the young and aged hippocampal areas (Keuker et al., 2004).

As described in Connections, the studies indicating continued brain growth into old age are perhaps the most encouraging of all research on aging. In one study, BDNF increased in elderly rats (22 months) following the simple regime of daily swimming exercise; increased BDNF was also observed following antidepressant administration (Garza, Ha, Garcia, Chen, & Russo-Neustadt, 2004). Thus, not only are some aging brains able to hold their own until an advanced age, many are able to continue to grow until the final days.

Neurodegenerative Decline: Alzheimer's Disease and Parkinson's Disease

Unfortunately, many neurobiological conditions accelerate the normal pace of the aging brain. Any form of brain damage caused by stroke, tumors, or traumatic brain injury will lead to compromised functioning, and that will lead to signs of cognitive aging. Other conditions, known as **neurodegenerative diseases,** have a slower onset but ultimately lead to severe behavioral and cognitive impairment. Although several neurodegenerative diseases threaten the mental health of aging adults, we'll discuss only two: Alzheimer's disease and Parkinson's disease.

The main features of Alzheimer's disease seem to be plaques and neurofibrillary tangles that are present in the brain. These neuronal features are anything but normal and are reminiscent of the underbrush that clutters an otherwise clear forest. Like neural kudzu, the plaques (deposits of an otherwise necessary neuronal protein called beta-amyloid) and tangles clog up and interfere with the normal processing of action potentials. Further, these deposits hamper interneuronal associations, packing the adjacent neuropil with clutter. As neurons become more and more encumbered and choked off, they begin to die; formerly useful pathways, some in use since infancy, lose efficacy. Dendritic arbors, the span of a neuron and its range of influence, also show changes, though these are region-specific and may reflect compensatory mechanisms on the part of affected neurons or nuclei. Although much research is currently being conducted on this debilitating disease, especially research related to declining levels of ACh observed in Alzheimer's patients, a cure still eludes the medical community.

Another condition that compromises the functioning of the brain is Parkinson's disease, characterized by a slow deterioration of motor (mainly voluntary) movements. This disorder has recently received a renewed focus because some high-profile individuals have been diagnosed with the disease or have announced their battle with it. Former Attorney General of the United States Janet Reno, the boxer Muhammad Ali, and actor Michael J. Fox are affected by this disease that targets the neural processing that is the response to sensory input—namely, movement.

As you read this text or get up to walk across the room, you are engaging in voluntary movements, small and numerous, that combine to provide you with the smooth movement to which you have become accustomed. Again, movement demonstrates the translation of the digital/robotic actions of the go/no-go firing patterns of neurons into the analog/even motions of muscular episodes. In the Parkinson's patient, movement is made staccato, or stuttered, and the patient is unable to move or does so with only the greatest of effort. Involuntary movement or reflexive movements are less affected by the Parkinson's disease state, highlighting the dual regulation of movement by the basal ganglia.

In the United States, the incidence of Parkinson's disease is around 1% for people over the age of 50, and there are some cases of *primary Parkinsonism,* in which individuals are struck with the disease in their forties. Though it is a rare condition, neuroscientists are working to identify the etiology of this variable and early-onset version of the disease. There is also some variability displayed in the severity of the symptoms of the disease. In most cases, the disease displays a slow and steady progression, lasting decades until the patient's death, usually from secondary infections that are associated with the Parkinson's-induced chronic immobility. In some, the progression of the disease is marked by a rapid and spiraling deterioration, whereas in others there is little noticeable impairment.

The cause of Parkinson's remains unknown, although links to viruses, environmental toxins, and repeated head trauma have been proposed. The underlying pathology of the disease is characterized by the relentless destruction of dopamine-containing cell bodies in the substantia nigra (a part of the midbrain; refer to Chapter Three). For reasons that are little known, the neurons begin to undergo a steady loss of activity and eventually die, taking their neurochemical regulatory responsibilities with them. The subsequent relay of neural impulses from the substantia nigra to one of its targets, the striatum, becomes disrupted. Rigidity, tremor, and many other movement disruptions result.

MPTP A neurotoxin that causes a neural disorder resembling Parkinson's disorder in primates

An unintended animal model has provided important information related to the mechanisms underlying Parkinson's disease. In the early 1980s, doctors in northern California saw something they had never seen before: a young man with the symptoms of Parkinson's disease. This one anomalous patient was followed by several others in rapid succession, and the cluster raised the possibility of some type of new and powerful infection or poison. Several related items were of interest in the group. First, the patients were displaying symptoms of Parkinson's. Second, they were all young, much younger than the age at which the symptoms would be expected to manifest themselves. Third, the patients all had a history of drug abuse with a homemade potion that was marketed to them as a heroin facsimile. This drug, with the composition of 1-methyl-4-phenyl-1,2,3,6-tetrahydrapyridine and the name of **MPTP,** eventually attracted the attention of affiliated scientists. Animal studies confirmed what the doctors originally had surmised, that the drug somehow targeted the substantia nigra with devastating precision. Ironically, after causing so much misery, studying the drug has helped many people by encouraging research into the mechanics of Parkinson's disease (Brownell et al., 2003).

Treatment with the dopamine precursor L-DOPA has had success, but it is transitory. The brain shows remarkable ability to adapt, even to a treatment designed to fix a problem. Compensatory mechanisms at the neuronal level preclude the drug having a permanent effect, in a process similar to the neural rebound from addictive levels of a neurotransmitter mimic such as heroin or cocaine. Further, because the brain continues to lose dopamine-containing neurons, it is a losing battle for the Parkinsonian brain to continue to secrete necessary levels of dopamine. Eventually, ever greater amounts of L-DOPA become necessary to have the same effect as a previously lower dose. And ultimately, they have no effect.

At present, some promise has been shown with the use of fetal tissue transplants of brain precursors to substantia nigra neurons, which contain dopamine-secreting tissues (as described in Chapter One). In human trials, the results using these approaches are mixed, though success rates may improve as more and more research is accomplished. The use of stem cells (discussed later in this chapter) may have therapeutic value with less ethical controversy than the use of fetal tissue transplants. Additionally, increased focus is currently being directed toward the microglial cells because they have been observed to secrete neurotoxins that may play a role in both Alzheimer's and Parkinson's (Liu & Hong, 2003).

DEVELOPMENT OF KEY NEUROHORMONAL CIRCUITS

Once the brain is formed, it continues to influence the many neurobiological systems that shape the organism's future. Because it is rare for just one brain area to be involved in certain behavioral responses, we speak of neurobiological circuits to describe a collection of areas that communicate with one another to assure the most effective responses. As you learned in Chapter Five, neurochemicals such as neurotransmitters and hormones greatly facilitate the communication among various brain and body structures. In this section we discuss two *neurohormonal circuits*—these pathways integrate appropriate brain and body areas through specific hormonal signals that significantly influence important response systems, namely sexual differentiation and the development of the stress response. As we discuss these systems, two among many such circuits, the importance of hormones in maintaining appropriate functions becomes apparent. Although the sexual and stress hormones are emphasized here, most of the influential hormones, all important in the orchestration of development and maintenance of important physiological functions, are presented in Table 6.2 (on page 210) and the structures that release these hormones are shown in Figure 6.7.

Sexual Differentiation and Brain Development

In mammals, the developing organism receives an X-chromosome-bearing gamete (the egg) from the mother and a Y-chromosome-bearing or an X-chromosome-bearing gamete (the sperm) from the father. If the offspring receives two X chromosomes, the child will be a genetic female; if the child receives both an X and a Y chromosome, the child will be a genetic male. At the foundation of the respective sexes lies a brain that is shaped by these genetic forces to become male or to become female—an effect that will color virtually everything the individual person is capable of doing.

From the standpoint of the brain, what does it mean to be male or female? How is the dichotomy accomplished? The genes set into motion a cascade of events that culminates in the differential exposure of the developing brain to gonadal steroid hormones. The hormones direct the development of brain regions (and gross body

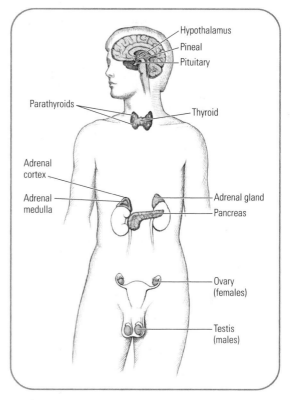

[Figure 6.7]
Endocrine system. Shown here are the major endocrine glands that release hormones throughout the body
AFTER STRAUB, 2001, P. 94

[Table 6.2]
_____

Major Hormones Influencing Development in the Body

Source	Hormone	Primary Function(s)
Hypothalamus	Hypothalamic releasing hormones (e.g., CRH, GNRH)	Stimulates or inhibits the release of pituitary hormones
Anterior pituitary	Luteinizing hormone (LH)	Stimulates the production of testosterone (in men) and progesterone (in women); promotes ovulation
	Follicle stimulating hormone (FSH)	Promotes spermatogenesis in men; stimulates estrogen secretion and maturation of the ovum (female)
	Growth hormone (GH) (also known as somatotropin)	Promotes protein synthesis and body growth
	Adrenocorticotropic hormone (ACTH)	Promotes glucocorticoid secretion
	Thyrotropin/Thyroid stimulating hormone (TSH)	Promotes thyroxin secretion and increases metabolic rate and growth
Posterior pituitary	Vasopressin/Antidiuretic hormone (ADH; AVP)	Promotes water re-absorption in kidneys; involved with social interactions
	Oxytocin (OT)	Promotes milk letdown and uterine contractions during the birth process; involved in social interactions such as maternal and sexual behavior
Pineal gland	Melatonin	Influences biological rhythms (e.g., sleep/wake cycles) and reproductive functions
Parathyroid Gland	Parathyroid hormone (PTH)	Increases calcium levels in the blood
Thyroid gland	Thyroxine	Increases metabolic rate and growth
Adrenal cortex	Glucocorticoids (cortisol; corticosterone)	Elevates blood sugar levels in liver; increases protein and fat metabolism (typically during stress)
Adrenal medulla	Epinephrine; norepinephrine	Promotes increased blood pressure and other responses characteristic of sympathetic arousal
Pancreas	Insulin	Facilitates storage of glucose in cells; promotes storage of fats
Ovary	Estrogens	Promotes female sexual maturation; regulates sexual behavior
	Progesterone	Promotes uterine and mammary gland development; maintains pregnancy
Testis	Testosterone	Promotes male sexual maturation; spermatogenesis

Adapted from Kalat, 2001; Nelson, 1995.

anatomy) that eventually respond to the activating actions of male versus female hormones during puberty and thereafter. For the female, additional hormonal fluctuations that are attributable to the menstrual cycle, pregnancy, and lactation contribute to a brain that is vastly different from the male's brain (Box 6.3). In general, nature produces male and female brains that are similar, but hormones push the brains into different ends of a continuum that produces nearly as many differences as similarities.

[Box 6.3]

Brain Matters

The Maternal Brain

"'M' is for the many things she does," is a variation of the venerable old paean to mother. Have you ever stopped to notice the behavior of a typical mom? Carrying a child on one hip while preparing dinner with the other hand and holding the phone under her chin, at the same time calling spelling words out to an older child at the kitchen table. Every mother, whether human or rat, does a vast number of things for her offspring to ensure their survival, growth, and development. In the process and underlying her motivations, she protects her own priceless genetic investment. Of the systems that are affected as a result of pregnancy and that regulate the many behavioral changes characteristic of the maternal female, the brain experiences striking modifications.

We (the authors) have been examining the changes in the mother rat that mark her transition from virgin to pregnant to postpartum female. The experiences combine to fundamentally change structural, neural, glial, and behavioral facets of the female's pup-related repertoire—all designed to protect the female's large genetic and metabolic investment in her offspring. Interestingly, we are finding a kind of symbiosis in the postpartum period: the mother helps her offspring, but the offspring seem to help their mother, as well. We have observed improvements in learning and memory and, more recently, reductions in neural and behavioral indices of anxiety, stress responsiveness, and propensity to addiction in maternal rats. Further, we have found that the offspring themselves may directly—through sensory stimulation of their mothers—contribute to both their and their mother's development.

In short, pregnancy and the resulting offspring stimulation characteristic of the postpartum period may represent a type of enriching environment to the mothers, which may produce ancillary effects that extend far beyond the maternal-infant interaction.

Among the brain changes we have observed in the maternal rat are increased cell size in the hypothalamus (mPOA), more dendritic spines in the hippocampus, and less stress-induced c-fos activation in the amygdala and hippocampus. Additionally, these effects appear to be long-lasting or permanent. Senescent females who have had one or two litters maintain learning and memory performance on some tasks that far exceeds that of their age-matched nulliparous counterparts when tested at 6, 12, 18, and 24 months of age. Further, the levels of a protein that presages neurodegeneration (for example, Alzheimer's disease)—amyloid precursor protein (APP)—is significantly higher in the brains of the old (24 months) rats that have had no maternal experience.

Together, these data paint an interesting picture of offspring-induced changes in the female that supports the hypothesis that the effects on the mother may extend far beyond the postpartum period and into neurobiology and behavior associated with, but not directly controlling, infant care and protection. Furthermore, the offspring may play a much more active role in their own survival and care through sensory cue-induced modifications of their mother's (or caregiver's) neurobiology. The mother and pup relationship may be much more of a symbiosis than the current, generally held unidirectional (mother → young) model. The reproductive changes we and others are observing may represent a wholesale alteration of brain and behavior that reaches into many more facets of the female's life, and for significantly longer, than currently realized (Kinsley et al., 1999; Wartella et al., 2003).

During prenatal development, once the respective gonads are established, the stage is set for sexual differentiation, the process whereby males become male and females become female. The ovaries of the female and the testes of the male come into play as the embryo becomes the fetus. From the standpoint of the male's tissues, including the brain,

testosterone A steroid hormone produced by the testes that is important in the differentiation of the male brain and body

sexually dimorphic nucleus of the preoptic area (SDN-POA) Region of the anterior hypothalamic preoptic area that has a larger volume in male rats than in female rats.

it is the presence of **testosterone** that marks him as a male. Possessing the XY genotype is no guarantee that the fetus will be male in the ways in which it is idiomatically understood: phenotypically, a male acts malelike, engaging in sex-specific/stereotypical aggressive, parental, and sexual behaviors. Only through the stimulation of the brain by male hormones does the male become male. For the female, exposure to malelike levels of testosterone would masculinize her and render her sterile.

Males and females are born and shaped into their respective neurobiological roles through a succession of hormone-neuron interactions. Males have two complementary processes that male hormones initiate. One is called *defeminization,* the process by which inherent female characteristics and behaviors are suppressed by exposure to male hormones. The complementary process to defeminization is *masculinization,* in which malelike behaviors and characters are promoted. The effects of both processes are played out in the standard repertoire of male behaviors. For the female, the processes required for development include behavioral mechanisms that ensure femalelike behavior and physiological systems. The female therefore undergoes a process of *feminization,* in which female-characteristic behaviors are developed, and *demasculinization,* in which any malelike tendencies are suppressed. Together, male and female development depends on the proper timing and levels of exposure to the requisite hormonal states. For males, testosterone is required; for females, the lack of testosterone is important and necessary. Deviations from these basic structures may result in alterations, or variation, in sexual differentiation.

The steroid hormones released by the testes, primarily testosterone, interact with the brain to guide development similar to the way in which neurotransmitters interact with neurons to influence action potentials. The hormones circulating in the bloodstream (or hormones produced directly by the brain, called *neurohormones*) are lipophilic substances, able to gain easy access to and through fatty membranes like the cell membrane. Some hormones, like testosterone, bind to specific receptors either on the membrane of neurons or, once inside the neuron, to receptors in the cytosol or on the nuclear membrane. Once bound to the receptor, the hormone is actively transported to the nucleus via intracellular proteins (in the case of cell membrane or cytosolic receptors). Once the hormone molecules gain access to the nucleus, they have the capacity to alter the genomic modulation of intraneuronal activities. They can speed up or slow down or otherwise change what the neuron is designed to do. In essence, hormones are modulators, prodding the activity of neurons in specific directions (Figure 6.8).

Testosterone makes changes in the brain that have to do with alterations of structure and function. Its presence increases the size of various nuclei in the male's brain, for instance in a well-described structure called the **sexually dimorphic nucleus of the prepotic area (SDN-POA).** The male nucleus is significantly larger than the female's, an effect that disappears if the newborn male is deprived of testosterone (i.e., demasculinized). Conversely, a female treated with testosterone displays a male-like SDN-POA. At puberty, the ebbs and flows of hormones cascade and wash over the *organizational* infrastructure of the brain to enact so-called *activational* effects (e.g., body hair growth, sexual behavior). That is, the hormones characteristic of puberty— testosterone in the male, estrogen and progesterone in the female—feed back to the brain, again binding to and occupying receptors on the neurons and contributing to further development of the brain.

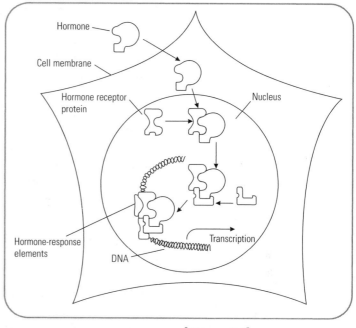

[Figure 6.8]
Hormone-neuron interactions
The hormones that exert such striking effects on brain and behavior begin by exerting their effects on the neuron. By binding to receptors on the surface of the neuronal membrane, or by being absorbed into the neuron, the hormone travels to the nucleus. There it interacts with the DNA to modify its inherent program of neuronal regulation.
AFTER MCEWEN, P. 69.

Sex hormones produce brain differences beyond the SDN-POA. Generally, male brains are larger and more asymmetrical than female brains (Kovalev, Kruggel, & von Cramon, 2003). A plethora of more microanatomical sex differences persist as well, but they are too numerous to discuss in the constraints of this chapter. It is important to know, however, that such brain sex differences exist. Sex differences in the brain, referred to as *organizational* because of their apparent permanent effects, dictate the ways in which neurons act individually or in combination and the many ways in which the neurons establish synapses with each other. Certainly, hormonal and neuroanatomical differences contribute to sex differences in mental health.

Development of the Stress Response

Although Hans Selye advocated the generalized adaptation syndrome in which different stressors led to standard stress responses, the research shows more and more that significant individual differences exist in responding to stress (see Chapter Eleven for more on Selye's research). For example, a student in one of our labs undertook the simple task of exposing young adult laboratory rats to fox urine, a predator odor. The student reported that the rats had very different responses to the urine-saturated cotton ball. Some fled to the opposite sides of the cages and remained frozen for several minutes. Some approached the cotton balls, picked them up, stuffed them in the cage tops above, and proceeded to move around the cages, digging and moving the bedding. Still others approached the cotton balls and proceeded to shred them to pieces.

Keep in mind that these rats are practically genetic clones of one another and had been exposed to very similar environments up to this point. What could account for such differing behavioral responses to this stressful stimulus? Research on parental involvement, aging, and sex differences suggests reasons for these differing responses.

Mom's impact on the developing stress response. Those of you who embrace Freud's ideas will be interested to discover that an animal's infancy and relationship with its mother play a critical role in the subsequent development of the stress response. Seymour Levine, now at the University of California-Davis, has conducted extensive research on a period during postnatal days 4 to 14 known as the *stress hyporesponsive period,* in which young rats do not show the normal stress response that you learned about in Chapter Five. Specifically, Levine and others have shown that maternal factors play an integral role in suppressing the ACh and glucocorticoid responses to most stressful stimuli. He reports that tactile stimulation (for example, grooming), feeding, and passive contact all contribute to the suppressed HPA activation (Levine, 2001).

Although there is no specific evidence of such a rigid time of hyporesponsiveness in human infants, research by Megan Gunnar and her colleagues at the University of Minnesota's Institute of Child Development suggests that striking parallels exist in human children. She has observed a suppressed HPA response in infants with healthy relationships with their caregivers. These infants mature into children who respond to novel situations with lower cortisol responses than their counterparts who experienced weaker attachments with their caregivers during this critical time (Gunnar, 1998).

Michael Meaney and colleagues at McGill University have also shown that maternal contact has a prominent impact on the development of a rat's stress response (Meaney, Aitken, & Sapolsky, 1991). In this line of research, Meaney briefly separates the rat pups from their mothers for about 15 minutes each day for the first two weeks of postnatal life—a process known as *handling,* or *maternal separation.* Considering Levine's research, it seems likely that the separation would impair the healthy development of the stress response.

On the contrary, this experimental manipulation results in a *more* efficient stress response when the rat reaches adulthood, protecting it from the damaging effects of a hyperresponsive HPA axis. When the handled offspring are tested in adulthood, they show increased binding capacity at the glucocorticoid receptors but not the mineralcorticoid receptors in the hippocampus. More glucocorticoid receptor sites lead to a more efficient negative feedback system in the hippocampus, resulting in lower levels of glucocorticoids than in nonhandled controls (Meaney et al., 1985).

Specifically, handling increases glucocorticoid-receptor binding capacity in the frontal cortex and hippocampus but interestingly not in the amygdala, septum, hypothalamus, or pituitary. The net effect of the handling seems to be an enhanced negative feedback system that results in approximately a 50% reduction in stress hormone production for the entire life of the rat (Caldji et al., 2001; Meaney, Aitken, & Sapolsky, 1991).

Meaney's investigations into the mechanisms involved in this effect have revealed that it is the mother's *increased* attention, not *lack* of attention, that is critical. When Meaney and his colleagues observed the mother-pup interactions in handled animals, they found that the mothers of handled pups spent significantly more time manipulating (for example, licking, as seen in Figure 6.9) their offspring than did mothers of nonhandled pups (Francis & Meaney, 1997).

In an article titled "Like mother, like daughter . . . ," Champagne and Meaney (2001) describe how the maternal strategy, defined by variations in licking, grooming, and arched back nursing, is passed on to the next generation—or from mothers to daughters. This intergenerational transmission, however, is not based on genetics. When rat pups from a low-contact mother were raised by a high-contact foster mother, the grown rat exhibited maternal behavior similar to the high-contact mother, suggesting a behavioral, or nongenomic, transmission of maternal behavior (Francis, Diorio, Liu, & Meaney, 1999).

Stress and aging. Life is stressful. This observation is discouraging, considering the detrimental role the stress hormone, cortisol or corticosterone, has on the hippocampus (described in Chapter Five). As we age, the *stress time* of the hippocampus accumulates, resulting in increased vulnerability to upcoming challenges. According to Sapolsky, in addition to reduced dendritic processes, hippocampal cells exposed to excessive levels

[Figure 6.9]
Maternal-offspring interaction is the foundation of the development of the social life of the mammal. The subtle interactions that occur between mother and young set the stage for the offspring's reaction to, and survival in, the world to come. Here a mother rat is shown licking one of her pups, an intimate and reciprocal behavior that can modify the pup's responsiveness, and can contribute to the mother's enhanced maternal behavior.
COURTESY OF DOUG BUERLEIN, R-MC BEHAVIORAL NEUROSCIENCE LABORATORY

of glucocorticoids are also likely to undergo reduced synaptic plasticity, inhibited neurogenesis, and finally, when the neurons cannot respond to the usual neuronal insults, cell death (Sapolsky, 1996).

Any method of reducing glucocorticoid levels, such as Meaney's handling technique, leads to increased survival of these important neurons. In a more drastic attempt to remove glucocorticoids in rats, adrenalectomies (the removal of the glucocorticoid-secreting adrenal gland) have been conducted. Six to nine months after removing the primary source of glucocorticoids, the animals had fewer signs of hippocampal aging (measured by assessing pyramidal neuronal density and astrocyte reactivity) than their same-age adrenal-intact counterparts (Landfield, 1987; Landfield, Baskin, & Pitler, 1981).

A dramatic demonstration of the importance of glucocorticoid levels in successful aging was reported by Sonia Cavigelli and Martha McClintock at the University of Chicago (2003). Juvenile male rats were divided into either exploratory (neophilic) or inhibited (neophobic) behavioral dispositions according to their exploration of a novel environment. When tested in novel environments across the life span, the shy rats remain shy—they show hesitancy to explore the environment accompanied by a long-lasting elevation of stress hormones (40 minutes)—whereas the bolder animals continue to be exploratory in the novel environment across their lifetime and show a more transient rise in glucocorticoid levels and a faster return to baseline. Additionally, the shy rats' total life span was reduced by 20%. The two brothers in Figure 6.10 are the same elderly age of 27 months but, because of differential stress responses, vary greatly in health status. It was hypothesized that a lifetime of more efficient stress responses and uninhibited responses led to a healthier brain (especially hippocampus) and body in the bolder rat (personal communication, December 2003).

[Figure 6.10]
Coping These two brothers are 27 months of age, although the one on the left looks considerably older than his sibling. They were both raised in identical environments, but they each displayed different coping strategies from their juvenile days. The rat on the right was bolder and exhibited lower corticosteroid levels than its shy brother.
COURTESY OF SONIA A. CAVIGELLI

Sex differences in the stress response. As discussed earlier in this chapter, different reproductive hormonal landscapes characterize males and females. It should come as no surprise, then, that there are sex differences in the stress response. When male and female rats are observed in different stressful tests, sex differences are often observed in both physiological and behavioral responses. For example, in the exploratory open field test, females are more active, suggesting that they are less emotional than males (Heinsbroek, van Haaren, & van de Poll, 1988). On the physiological side, however, females typically show higher baseline and stress-induced levels of glucocorticoids, suggesting that they may be more emotionally reactive in stressful situations (Michaelis et al., 2001). Thus, it appears that levels of glucocorticoids are not always a reflection of the degree of "emotionality" observed in the animal's behavior. This should not be surprising given the multifaceted stress response.

Turning to research on humans, some findings suggest that, whereas women may be more susceptible to stress-related mental illness, men may be more susceptible to stress-related cardiovascular illness. In one study, men and women were asked to perform stressful mental arithmetic and public speaking and were monitored throughout the stress and recovery period. Compared with the women, men had higher blood pressure measures during this task (Matthews, Gump, & Owens, 2001).

In another interesting study, married couples were brought in to the laboratory and asked to discuss a topic on which they disagreed. Generally, men were more likely to demonstrate increased blood pressure and anger, accompanied with a more hostile interpersonal style (Matthews, Gump, & Owens, 2001). Such stress-related effects in men might explain their increased vulnerability to cardiovascular disease in midlife (McEwen, 1998). On the other hand, most epidemiological studies suggest that women are more likely to develop psychiatric disorders, such as depression, as a byproduct of stress. In Chapter Eleven we discuss more research related to the development of the stress response and, more important, effective coping strategies for stress-induced illness.

SCIENTIFIC INTERVENTIONS WITH DEVELOPMENTAL NEUROBIOLOGY

Thus far, we have discussed nature's developmental path toward the final destination of brain development. Scientists have learned much about CNS development; in fact, so much has been learned that researchers now have the ability to intervene at certain developmental

embryonic stem cells
Undifferentiated cells derived from the embryo that have the potential to develop into a wide variety of cell types

blastocyst The 150 cell preimplantation embryo comprising an outer layer, a fluid-filled cavity, and a cluster of interior cells

stages in an attempt to aid a disabled brain. Following we discuss two examples of advanced technologies and their implications for psychobiological disorders.

Stem Cells

The developing brain is a fount of potential. Among the sources of this enormous potential are so-called **embryonic stem (ES) cells** (Figure 6.11). These cells are referred to as pluripotent: they can differentiate into virtually any type of cell in the body, from fingernail to neuron. They are derived from the inner cell mass of the **blastocyst,** the early ball of pre-embryonic tissue, where they can be harvested as undifferentiated cells and maintained as such theoretically forever. The strength of these cells lies in their pluripotency: they can be chemically coaxed into becoming whatever type of cell is needed. Thus, they represent a singular opportunity for repair of the human body.

The promise of ES cells is vast, but thus far it is just that: promise. There is a tremendous amount of research devoted to their study, but practical uses for the cells remain years away. The cells generate such high hopes because of their two major properties. First, they are virtually immortal. That is, in the proper media and with adequate stimulation, they can generate copies of themselves indefinitely. Among the questions about stem cells is the one of chromosomal integrity: Is the millionth copy of the ES cell identical to the original?

Further, the cells are undifferentiated, unassigned, as it were, and require a signal or series of subtle signals that sets them on their path to a lifetime of function. The chemosignals, derived nominally from adjacent tissues, regulate the cells and direct their genomes to alter the production of specific proteins. The shape and activity—indeed, the cell itself—are altered. The cell becomes what it is instructed to become. Thus, an unlimited supply of stem cells can be produced and maintained following their harvest. This supply of ES cells can then be made to augment or replace the dead and dying or absent cells that are the result of disease or damage.

Recent work has suggested that ES cells are capable of treating Parkinson's disease (Kim et al., 2002). In a mouse model of the disease, the authors were able to produce ES cells by expressing a protein that is a transcription factor that regulates the differentiation of ES cells into neurons that express dopamine (DA). As previously mentioned, the loss of DA from midbrain neurons is the cause of Parkinson's disease. Hence, the cells that Kim and colleagues (2002) produced and subsequently transplanted in the 6-hydroxy-DA- (6-OH-DA-) lesioned midbrains of rats

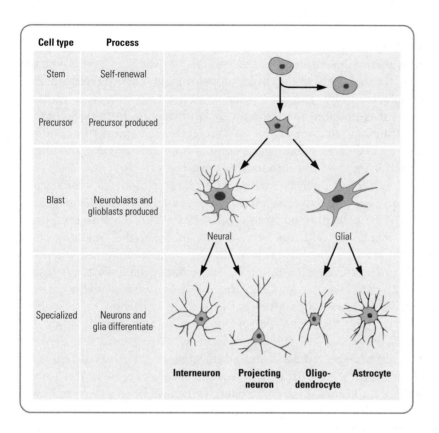

Cell type	Process	
Stem	Self-renewal	
Precursor	Precursor produced	
Blast	Neuroblasts and glioblasts produced	Neural / Glial
Specialized	Neurons and glia differentiate	**Interneuron** **Projecting neuron** **Oligo-dendrocyte** **Astrocyte**

[Figure 6.11]
Stem cell differentiation. The promise and peril of renewing the nervous system are exemplified by the use of embryonic stem cells. Such cells are theoretically infinitely adaptable, possessing the capacity to become or replace any cell in the body. Here, embryonic stem cells are depicted as differentiating into neurons and glia. Other tissues and organs, too, may be the beneficiaries of the embryonic stem cell's chameleonic properties. As much more basic research is required before the applications and limits of stem cells are known, political and moral obstacles must be addressed. The accompanying dilemmas must be adjudicated; otherwise progress or alternatives—and the human lives involved—will be hindered.

led to both electrophysiological and behavioral recovery. That is, these cells behaved just like the animals' own normal cells. Extending this promising work to humans will mean an effective treatment for a debilitating neurological disease caused, usually, by aging.

Parkinson's disease has several characteristics that make it a primary target for ES cells. First, the site of the damage that underlies Parkinson's symptoms is very constrained. Unlike other conditions, the neural damage that produces Parkinson's is localized to the substantia nigra in the midbrain of the patient, making it a discrete lesion whose regional inputs and outputs have been well characterized. Second, Parkinson's has been shown to be the result of a loss of specific neurotransmitter activity. The damage that produces Parkinson's is limited to a set of cells that produces the neurotransmitter DA. Augmenting DA levels or replacing the malfunctioning or absent DA-neurons restores DA levels to normal and halts the neurodegenerative decline.

Researchers at Johns Hopkins University explored the therapeutic value of ES cells in an animal model of paralysis. Rats were injected with

adult stem cells
Undifferentiated cells located in a currently differentiated tissue; these cells have the ability to renew themselves and differeniate, within certain limits, to various specialized cell types characteristic of the tissue from which it was derived.

a virus that targeted the motor neurons in the spinal cord resulting in paralysis of their hindquarters. ES cells derived from human embryonic germ cells were administered to the animals via the CSF and navigated their way through the spinal fluid, appearing to have developed into mature motor neurons. The final outcome of the cells, however, remains a question. It is possible that trophic (growth) factors in the ES cocktail stimulated the new growth of the virus-infected cells (Kerr et al., 2003). It is easy to see how such results would provide hope for the many humans suffering from neuromuscular impairment.

Other conditions, such as Alzheimer's disease, diabetes, spinal cord injuries, and arthritis, may also one day be treatable by means of ES cell therapy. The ES cells derived from human embryos have, however, been embroiled in controversy almost from the moment that scientists first identified them (see the Connections in the Epilogue). Another type of stem cell, **adult stem cells,** might be less controversial. These cells are undifferentiated cells that are taken from differentiated cells in a developed organism. These cells give rise to mature cells that have specific characteristics and functions. For example, stem cells that develop into blood cells are found in the bone marrow. The primary difference between embryonic stem cells and adult stem cells is their origin. It is thought that adult stem cells exist in several types of tissue in the human body and are quite rare. Embyronic stem cells have been shown to develop in tissue culture following their derivation from the inner cell mass of the developing embryo. Further, adult stem cells do not seem to have the pluripotency of ES cells that allows for differentiation into a vast number of cell lineages; this threshold limits their use. Overall, their flexibility and promise are not as great as those of ES cells, but they evoke fewer moral dilemmas than their contentious ES counterparts (NIH, 2004).

Mammalian Cloning

In a famous scene in the 1946 Disney movie *Fantasia,* Mickey Mouse, as the Sorcerer's Apprentice, is confronted by the scores of brooms he has inadvertently created. Starting with one, he ends up with rooms full of brooms full of swishing activity but none behaving as he had anticipated. The image that ensues is a disastrous slapstick of chaos and confusion. Today, it symbolizes the average person's fears about the idea of cloning, the marriage of technology and the immaturity of the forces that would control it, like a child waving a gun. Could Mickey's tribulations be a metaphor for the perception of chaos that may result from cloning technology?

The promise and specter of artificially creating identical copies of an organism has been around for decades. Though nature performs cloning in a variety of ways, many of which we have come to take for granted, having the means and motive to do it ourselves raises the process to another level. Inbreeding does (more or less) naturally what cloning does but with a large difference: the descendents are nearly genetically identical (sharing more than 99% of genes), but they are not copies of one another. A parthenogenetic (asexual) organism such as the diploid Colorado checkered whiptail (*Cnemidophorus tesselatus*), in which nearly all the offspring are female and reproduction takes place in the male's absence, is closer to the idea of a clone. But this organism has a different chromosomal set and a vastly different natural history than a mammal has.

In the cloned sheep Dolly, researchers removed the DNA of an adult sheep from well-defined somatic cells and injected it into an egg whose genome had been removed, thereby replacing the resident DNA with the adult's version. The resulting "offspring," born on July 5, 1996, was the first true clone. What made Dolly different was that she contained the DNA from just a single parent, the donor, following a process referred to as "somatic cell nuclear transfer." In essence, she was a deferred twin of the donor animal (Wilmut et al., 1997).

It had been theoretically possible to take an adult organism, remove a portion of the DNA—its genetic "blueprint"—and then "grow" the DNA as an identical copy of the organism. In fact, research into this very technique had been going on since the 1960s. The creation of Dolly confirmed the theories, but the work by Ian Wilmut's group added features to the theory. For instance, removing the genome of an established adult cell, then finding that its function could be reestablished in a blastocyst, had not been known. Further, the work demonstrated that the implanted DNA was capable of full activity, though the host was a mature cell. The steps leading to Dolly's creation, a delayed copy of an existing adult, were almost as significant as the act itself.

The notion of the word "copy," however, causes the rub. A clone will be a genetic replica, sharing the superficial and silent characteristics of the donor, but the resemblance is, nearly literally, only skin deep. And, it has been demonstrated, not even that: Dolly, who died sooner than expected, evinces some marked phenotypical differences from her parent. In Figure 6.12 on page 222 you'll see a kitten (named CC for copy cat) cloned from the cat beside it (Rainbow)—their fur patterns are not even similar. Because of different environmental pressures, not only is their appearance very different but also the researchers at Texas A&M report that CC is much more playful than the reserved Rainbow. Thus,

[Figure 6.12]

Cloning The kitten is a clone of the cat but, as evident in the picture, genetic clones do not always develop identical phenotypes.

COURTESY OF TEXAS A&M UNIVERSITY, COLLEGE OF VETERINARY MEDICINE

this clone is far from a phenotypical copy cat. That is, the donor and the clone share the nature portion of the nature-nurture equation, but a shared or even a remotely similar environment is impossible to duplicate. We have to remember that clones have been among us for as long as women have been having children. The "natural" clones are identical twins. Even when two individuals who are genetic clones are raised in the same home by the same parents at the same time, many individual differences can exist between the twins.

In the case of cloning an organism from an adult, the unique experiences that shaped the brain of the organism cannot be recreated in its clone. They are lost. Consequently, those who promote cloning of mammals—themselves, their friends and loved ones, and their pets as a way of preserving the loved qualities of the donors—fundamentally miss the point: How does one re-create in the clone those personal memories that make up the personality of the donor individual, when the memories are exclusive and irreproducible?

On hearing the word "clone," the average person conjures up a science fiction image of cell scrapings morphing into identical copies of the original—the Sorcerer's Apprentice's brooms. This type of cloning is referred to as *reproductive cloning*, and it bears the brunt of the ethical criticisms related to cloning. Another type of cloning, *therapeutic cloning*, is less likely to evoke the stiff resistance that has met the announcement of cloning technology. Similar to reproductive cloning, therapeutic, or research, cloning also includes the replacement of the donor egg nucleus with DNA from an adult cell. But unlike reproductive cloning, the cell is not transplanted to a uterus so that it can develop into an organism. In therapeutic cloning protocols, after a few days of dividing, embryonic stem cells are harvested. It is thought that these cells may be prodded into the development of specific cells to replace degenerating cells, such as the degenerating substantia nigra cells in patients with Parkinson's disease, discussed earlier. Thus, therapeutic cloning offers hope for those suffering from neurodegenerative disease.

Summary

Prenatal Brain Development

Following fertilization, the emerging nervous system goes through a whirlwind of changes on its journey to becoming the organ we recognize as a brain. Following the pattern of induction, proliferation, migration, aggregation, differentiation, circuit formation, apoptosis, and synapse rearrangement, a brain is born. Prior to differentiation these pluripotent cells have the potential to become various types of cells, ranging from skin to neurons. During the developmental process, the layer of cells known as the ectoderm gives rise to the neural plate, leading to the eventual emergence of the neural tube from which the rostral opening becomes the premature brain. During this intense time of development, tens of thousands of neurons can be produced per minute. By just 12 weeks of prenatal age, the human brain assumes the shape it will have in the mature individual. At this point, neurotrophins and radial glia play an important role in establishing the many important connections among the immature neurons. Unnecessary neurons are pruned away to make room for the essential neurons necessary to form the brain's many circuits.

Postnatal Brain Development

The postnatal brain is further influenced by the many sensory and experiential forces that the newborn encounters throughout its development. Research suggests that exposure to more enriching environments leads to enhanced complexity of cortical neurons. During this continued development, neurogenesis, or the production of new neurons, continues to accommodate increasing brain volume. The final areas of the brain to mature are the executive frontal lobes, which typically mature during adolescence. Altered brain development may result in conditions such as attention deficit hyperactivity disorder.

The Aging Brain

As the brain ages, about 10% of its neurons are lost; however, the brain maintains its capacity for neural plasticity. In some cases, neurodegenerative diseases such as Parkinson's disease and Alzheimer's disease result in accelerated loss of brain tissue and accompanying function.

Development of Key Neurohormonal Circuits

Differentiated neural areas that communicate with one another comprise the neurobiological circuits essential for efficient brain processing. Further, neurohormonal circuits exist to integrate appropriate brain areas with important hormonal signals. One such circuit oversees sexual differentiation. In the genetic male, testosterone plays a critical role in leading to masculinization of the animal. One well-known sexually dimorphic brain structure is the preoptic area of the hypothalamus, which is larger in males than in females. After influencing the organizational infrastructure of the brain, neurohormonal circuits continue to play critical developmental roles by triggering activational effects, such as body hair growth, as the animal matures. Another critical neurohormonal circuit is the stress response. There is evidence that some animals undergo a stress hyporesponsive period early in postnatal development that may play a critical role in CNS maturation. Alterations of stress hormones early in an animal's life have been shown to influence stress responsiveness across the animals' lifespan. Animals experiencing elevated stress hormone secretion across their lifetimes are susceptible to hippocampal damage and other health risks later in life.

Scientific Interventions with Developmental Neurobiology

As scientists have learned more about how the CNS develops and technological breakthroughs have been made, practitioners and researchers have been able to intervene with the developing brain. Stem cells are the topic of intense discussion as scientists consider ways to guide their development into cells that may be damaged in an individual's brain, such as the substantia nigra in a patient suffering from Parkinson's disease. Therapeutic cloning is also being considered as a possible mechanism to replace failing nervous system structures. These techniques, however, are controversial and must satisfy both scientific and public concerns before being used for therapeutic purposes.

Key Terms

apoptosis (p. 188)

pluripotent (p. 188)

stem cells (p. 188)

ectoderm (p. 188)

mesoderm (p. 188)

endoderm, (p. 188)

neural plate (p. 188)

neural groove (p. 188)

neural fold (p. 188)

neural tube (p. 189)

neural crest (p. 189)

neuropores (p. 189)

neuropil (p. 190)

filopodia (p. 192)

neurotrophins (p. 192)

brain-derived neurotrophic factor (BDNF) (p. 192)

nerve growth factor (p. 192)

cell adhesion molecules (CAMs) (p. 192)

radial glia (p. 195)

neurogenesis (p. 197)

attention deficit hyperactivity disorder (p. 199)

stereological analysis (p. 203)

neurodegenerative diseases (p. 206)

MPTP (p. 208)

testosterone (p. 212)

sexually dimorphic nucleus of the preoptic area (SDN-POA) (p. 213)

embryonic stem (ES) cells (p. 218)

blastocyst (p. 218)

adult stem cells (p. 220)

For Further Consideration

Bainbridge, D., (2001). *Making babies: The science of pregnancy.* Cambridge, MA: Harvard University Press. This book could be subtitled "Everything you always wanted to know about pregnancy but didn't know how to ask." The author explains a multidetermined process in a very entertaining fashion. A good writer, Bainbridge is able to convey the wonder he feels about the entire process together with the science that is at the heart of his descriptions.

Colapinto, J. (2001). *As nature made him: The boy who was raised as a girl.* New York: Harper Perennial. Twin infant boys are taken to a hospital to be circumcised. In one circumcision, the cauterizing device goes awry, reducing the infant's penis to an ashen stalk. The parents, faced with an awful decision, and getting the then "best guess" medical advice, choose to raise their son as their daughter. The decision in this case would prove to be a bad one. Although the parents made every attempt to turn the boy into a girl, his life was rife with self-doubt and confusion, and he never felt comfortable with the fiction surrounding him. When, in his middle teens, he decided to abandon the charade and came to grips with the fact that he was a male, the process was wrenching and eventually fatal. The book emphasizes the important influences of pre-natal and early postnatal gonadal hormone exposure.

Gilbert, S. (2000). *Developmental biology.* Sunderland, MA: Sinauer Associates. Understanding neural development is aided by an appreciation of the basic processes of developmental biology. Gilbert does a fine job discussing such diverse but necessary topics as life cycles and patterns, cell partitioning, transcriptional regulation, cell-cell communication and interaction, and other topics, some with historical perspectives. This text is a good reference for the basics of development, and it draws on a long and colorful history of techniques, theories, and experimentation. The book would help the nonspecialist to acquire some of the language of development.

Langston, J. W., Ballard, P., Tetrud, J., & Irwin, I. (1983). Chronic Parkinsonism in humans due to a product of meperidine-analog synthesis. *Science, 219,* 979–980. For the addict on a perpetually quixotic quest for the perfect high, the hazards are magnified. What makes the person feel good may also irrecoverably damage the delicate brain. This article describes the case in the early 1980s when a number of young patients began showing up in emergency rooms in California with a peculiar set of symptoms. They were in various stages of paralysis, shuffling, uncoordinated, generally incapacitated. They appeared to be significantly younger than usual sufferers of Parkinson's disease. It turned out that this cluster of young people had ingested an artificial heroinlike drug concocted in a makeshift illicit drug laboratory. The drug had targeted the victims' substantia nigra, killing neurons there that help to regulate voluntary movement. The damage to the brain and loss of movement were permanent. The inadvertent benefit to these unfortunate cases was the creation of an animal model that will aid future sufferers of Parkinson's disease.

LeVay, S. (1991). A difference in hypothalamic structure between heterosexual and homosexual men. *Science, 253,* 1034–1037. How does sexuality develop? It is apparent that the forces of sexual differentiation that dictate maleness and femaleness must also direct sexual preference. Homosexuality is atypical but, like heterosexuality, must be regulated by the brain. LeVay examined the brains of postmortem homosexual males and heterosexual males and females. In a region of the hypothalamus, a cell group or nucleus, the third interstitial nucleus of the anterior hypothalamus (INAH-3), was found to be significantly smaller in volume in homosexual males than in heterosexual males. The structure was intermediate in size between heterosexual males and females. The data suggest that the brains of homosexual males are different from those of heterosexual males.

Purves, D. (1994). *Neural activity and the growth of the brain.* Cambridge, UK: Cambridge University Press. This small volume is packed with very interesting information on the formation of the brain, embryo to adult. The book begins with an examination of the steps involved in nervous system development and follows with the layer-upon-layer maturation that gives rise to the mature brain. The images in the text, drawings and photomicrographs, also capture the diverse and rich steps involved in the formation of the brain and nervous system. Purves, a stalwart in the field of developmental neuroscience, has managed to produce a book that is free of unnecessary clutter, focused like a lens on the myriad biochemical interactions that define the developing brain.

Raisman, G., & Field, P. M. (1971). Sexual dimorphism in the preoptic area of the rat. *Science, 173,* 731–733. Before this pioneering study was undertaken and reported, the question of physical differences between the sexes—that males and females look different—was little contested. Behavioral sex differences, the subtle and not so subtle palette of activities undertaken by males and females and usually viewed in terms of deficiencies on the part of one sex or the other, were more grudgingly accepted. The possibility that the brains of males and females were different, though obvious now, was viewed with tremendous skepticism 30 years ago. Using electron microscopy, Raisman and Field examined the hypothalami of males and females. They studied the synaptic input to neurons from that region, reporting that females had a greater number of synapses than did males on a comparable set of hypothalamic neurons. These data were provocative because they were among the first set to document with great clarity what many scientists and the general public already believed: that the brains of males and females were different, leading to behavioral differences. These data set into a motion a field that today is finding remarkable effects of hormones on a variety of neural systems.

Zhou J. N., Hofman, M. A., Gooren, L. J., & Swaab, D. F. (1995). A sex difference in the human brain and its relation to transsexuality. *Nature, 378,* 68–70. Sexual preference is only one aspect of a person's sexuality. Gender identity, the feeling that one is male or female, may be regulated by brain structures and influenced by developmental forces such as hormones. For instance, homosexual males are male, they "think" of themselves as male, but they are attracted to males. Male-to-female transsexuals, on the other hand, feel that they are *females* and are attracted to males—an important distinction. Zhou and colleagues examine the volume of a structure called the bed nucleus of the stria terminalis, central subdivision (BNSTc) in postmortem heterosexual males and females, homosexual males, and male-to-female transsexuals. The BNSTc was shown to be virtually identical in heterosexual and homosexual males and significantly larger than those of the heterosexual females. In the male-to-female transsexuals, however, the BNSTc was very similar to those of the heterosexual females. These data suggest strongly that this brain region may play a role in self-identification with the gender to which one is fated.

Chapter Seven

Disorders of Anxiety: Obsessive-Compulsive Disorder and Tourette's Syndrome

Connections

Common Denominators in Real-Life and Laboratory-Induced Compulsions?

Caroline Kettlewell is a woman with a secret: She compulsively cut herself for two decades to relieve anxiety. Caroline grew up at a boy's boarding school where her parents were on the faculty. As she entered puberty in this environment, Caroline experienced insurmountable anxiety: She felt that she was "on display" for all the older male students. Finding no refuge in family and friends at the time, she searched for alternative ways to calm herself. Her cutting compulsion started when she was 12 years old.

Intrigued with dissections and the symbolism of blood, Caroline found solace in cutting herself, in controlling the most important substrate of her existence. After being caught in the seventh grade trying to carve her arm with a Swiss army knife, she subsequently perfected her technique with razor blades. Caroline kept her self-mutilating obsession a secret as she continued to carve her hips and shoulders through middle school, high school, college, and into adulthood. Although her skin still bears witness to her emotional scars, Caroline eventually settled into a successful marriage, gave birth to a son, and learned to cope with her anxiety in constructive ways. In an attempt to provide encouragement for the estimated 2 to 3 million Americans who compulsively hurt themselves, she also wrote the book *Skin Game: A Cutter's Memoir,* a book she describes as a "coming of age memoir with an edge".

Just north of the city where Caroline Kettlewell lives, a team of undergraduate student researchers at Randolph-Macon College—Cathy Aurentz, Erica Glasper, and Stacie Lin—have investigated why rats, when housed in activity wheels and fed for only 1 hour per day, voluntarily increase their running levels to about 7 miles per day. Similar to compulsive cutting, this compulsive running seems to represent a maladaptive response strategy. Why would an animal with restricted food resources expend so much energy running? What brain mechanisms accompany this compulsive behavior?

The student researchers' data suggest that increased activity in a brain area involved in reward, the nucleus accumbens, accompanies the rats' increased running. Closing the access door to the wheel creates something akin to withdrawal (see photo on page 228). The animals experience changes

After being exposed to the activity-stress paradigm, the rat is actively trying to open the access door to the wheel—demonstrating a strong motivation to run.

COURTESY OF KELLY LAMBERT, RANDOLPH-MACON COLLEGE BEHAVIORAL NEUROSCIENCE LABORATORY

in two components of the brain reward circuit—a drop in nucleus accumbens activity and reduced levels of dopaminergic immunoreactivity (Aurentz et al., 1999; Glasper et al., 2000; Lin et al., 2001).

Compulsions, like personalities, take different forms. In both cases described here, the subjects were faced with anxiety—for Caroline, produced by excessive self-consciousness brought on by entering puberty on an all-male campus; for the rats, brought on by restriction of valuable resources. Caroline's cutting compulsion was very different from the rats' running compulsion, but it is possible that both relieved anxiety—at least momentarily—and both were reinforcing, probably incorporating the brain's reward mechanisms. Thus, learning the common denominators of the diverse compulsions observed across individuals and species will help us understand their genesis and discover the most effective modes of treatment.

comorbidity Presence of two or more health problems in the same individual.

The range of topics covered in this chapter on anxiety disorders strays a bit from the traditional categorization used in the DSM. We limit our discussion to generalized anxiety disorder and panic disorder in the overview section and then focus the bulk of the chapter on roots and remedies for obsessive-compulsive disorder (OCD) and Tourette's syndrome. Recall that phobias, also classified as anxiety disorders, were presented in Chapter One in the context of behavioral interventions in mental disorders. Post-traumatic stress disorder (PTSD), which is triggered by an actual stressful event or the memory of an experienced stressful event, appears in Chapter Eleven.

The onset of Tourette's typically occurs during childhood, and the syndrome is presented within the category of childhood disorders in the DSM. But the building evidence of **comorbidity** (the presence of two or more health problems in the same individual) of OCD and Tourette's and of shared familial risk and brain mechanisms suggest an alternative categorization. Tourette's has an affinity with other anxiety disorders, especially OCD (Johannes et al., 2003; Leckman et al., 2003; Muller et al., 2003). The characteristic responses vary in OCD and Tourette's, but anxiety appears to be the genesis of both disorders. Both involve excessive responding.

OCD may defend against the anxiety provoked by perceived threats; the involuntary, repetitive movements and verbal responding observed in Tourettic **tics** are highly sensitive to the person's anxiety levels.

ANXIETY DISORDERS: AN OVERVIEW

Our highly adaptive stress response has evolved to help us deal with challenges we encounter throughout our lives. Approached by someone with a weapon, for example, our sympathetic nervous system is activated so that we will engage in the "fight or flight" necessary to survive the situation (see Figure 3.2). There is no denying that sympathetic activation and subsequent HPA axis activity (see Figure 5.9) enable organisms to mobilize their physiological forces and survive threatening situations.

A problem emerges, however, if aspects of emotional and physiological arousal creep into our lives when immediate doom is not obvious. Harboring feelings of intense fear when viewing the latest horror film is perfectly normal even though our cognitions tell us the movie is not real, but actually experiencing these symptoms when no threat stimulus is present can become problematic and is the crux of anxiety disorders.

The first diagnostic category of anxiety disorders was identifed in 1871 when DaCosta published an article describing a condition he referred to as *irritable heart* in the *American Journal of Medical Sciences*. DaCosta attributed the primary symptoms of this disorder (dizziness, chest pain, and palpitations) to an overactive nervous system. Freud later emphasized the psychological rather than physiological aspects of anxiety as he introduced the term *anxiety neurosis* (Andreasen & Black, 2001). Today, if you look at the DSM, several conditions are categorized as anxiety disorders, including (but not limited to) generalized anxiety disorder, panic disorder, OCD, post-traumatic stress disorder, and certain phobias.

In a sense, our "anxiety response" exists on a continuum ranging from fear of a very specific event in our environment (for example, exposure to spiders) to a nonspecific sense that something is just not right in our lives (for example, chronic worrying). When the response becomes less specific and more and more ubiquitous, the typical diagnosis is **generalized anxiety disorder (GAD)**, a vague sense of anxiety that isn't directly related to an anxiety-provoking event. Individuals suffering from chronic generalized anxiety (about 4% to 7% incidence rate in the general population) worry excessively about single or multiple aspects of their lives— finances, romantic relationships, health—without tangible reasons for worrying.

Although an actual threat does not exist, the body responds as it does in other threatening situations, and the person experiences restlessness,

tics Rapid, repetitive, stereotyped movements or vocalizations; characteristic symptom of Tourette's syndrome.

generalized anxiety disorder (GAD) Vague sense of anxiety not directly related to an anxiety-provoking event.

panic disorder Intense anxiety-stress response, typically without an actual fear stimulus present. Physical components, including chest pain, shortness of breath, and nausea, resemble the symptoms of a heart attack.

obsessive-compulsive disorder (OCD) Chronic condition characterized by recurring upsetting thoughts (obsessions) and subsequent ritualistic acts (compulsions).

obsessions Recurring, upsetting thoughts typically observed in OCD patients; typically related to contamination, doubts, order, aggression, and sexual imagery.

compulsions Ritualistic acts that accompany obsessions in OCD patients; typically include hand washing, checking, repeating actions, ordering, praying, and counting.

sleep complications, and impaired concentration. As detailed in the Box 7.1, acute episodes of anxiety are observed in **panic disorder,** an intense anxiety-stress response typically without an actual fear stimulus present. Physical components include chest pain, shortness of breath, and nausea. Observed in about 3% of women and half as frequently in men, the panic response is so severe that early attacks frequently lead people to the emergency room fearing they are suffering from a heart attack (Andreasen & Black, 2001).

OBSESSIVE-COMPULSIVE DISORDER

Obsessive-compulsive disorder (OCD) is a chronic condition characterized by **obsessions** (recurring upsetting thoughts) and **compulsions** (subsequent ritualistic acts). The most prevalent obsessions include repeated thoughts about contamination, doubts, order, aggression, and sexual imagery (American Psychiatric Association, 1994). Frequently observed compulsions include excessive hand washing and repeated checking, ordering, praying, and counting.

Patients report that they feel driven to perform these ritualistic behaviors in an attempt to mitigate the anxiety produced by unsettling obsessive thoughts. For example, patients experiencing contamination obsessions may try to reduce their anxiety by repeatedly washing their hands until the skin is actually raw. For the most part, OCD involves thoughts and behaviors that are appropriate for normal functioning—who doesn't wash their hands, make sure they turned off the oven before leaving on a trip, or check a few times to confirm that an essential step in a recipe was not omitted? The problem is that these appropriate responses are taken to an extreme level—a level that is not a logical means to protect the person against the invading obsession (Table 7.1 on page 232).

OCD affects about 2% to 3% of the population. It is the fourth most common psychiatric disorder after phobias, substance abuse, and major depression (Jenike, Rauch, Cummings, Savage, & Goodman, 1996). The typical age of onset is late adolescence or early twenties; men typically develop the disease at 17.5 years of age, whereas the average age of onset in women is a bit older—19.8 years (Rasmussen & Eisen, 1990). Box 7.2 (page 234) describes a man who developed the disorder in childhood. Overall, OCD is found in equal numbers of men and women. Early-onset cases, however, are most frequently observed in males and are accompanied by motor tics such as head twitches and shrugging shoulders (Miguel, Rauch, & Jenike, 1997). Researchers have not yet discovered the reasons for these sex differences.

[Box 7.1]

Brain Matters

Panic Disorder: A Faulty Brainstem Surveillance System?

We usually take it for granted, but a breath of fresh air is the most critical fuel for our existence. Perhaps you have had a nightmare about the walls closing in, being trapped in a car submerged in water, or being buried under dirt or debris. If ever our bodies needed an alarm system, it is in a situation like this, because death will inevitably follow the depletion or restriction of life-giving air.

As discussed in Chapter Three, the brainstem controls the basic autonomic response of breathing. We currently don't know exactly how the neurons can detect vital signs such as blood levels of carbon dioxide and oxygen (Feldman, Mitchell, & Nattie, 2003), but these mechanisms may operate in panic disorder. The symptoms—increased heart rate, shortness of breath, chest pain, dizziness, fear of dying, chills—are similar to the symptoms experienced by someone suffering a heart attack or suffocation.

If we use the U.S. Homeland Security alert system as an analogy, a person's normal stress response—for example, to giving an impromptu talk to a group of strangers (a common stressor used in experiments)—may fall in the middle yellow category or even register in the orange category. Orange alert represents a significant event that requires the body's undivided attention, but a panic attack represents the most severe category of threat—the red alert. When the brain interprets the situation as leading to suffocation and death, a full-blown stress response is the body's best chance at mobilizing the person to find air.

But panic disorder rarely involves an actual incident of restricted air. On the contrary, a person may simply be sitting in class and suddenly experience a panic attack for no apparent reason. In fact, some researchers propose that this kind of panic attack may be the product of a false alarm emitted by the brainstem.

Researchers have investigated the sensitivity of patients suffering from panic disorder to levels of carbon dioxide and oxygen. A popular model is the infusion of sodium lactate, a natural salt and metabolic byproduct of lactic acid that the brain interprets as indicating low oxygen levels (hypoxia). Patients suffering from panic disorder exhibit more pronounced cardiovagal responses to the lactate infusion than do control subjects (Yeragani, Srinivasan, Balon, Ramesh, & Berchou, 1994). And when subjects are exposed to hyperventilation challenge tests (taking about 30 breaths per minute for 4 minutes), patients with a panic disorder diagnosis are more responsive (for example, have higher heart rates) than normal subjects (Nardi, Valenca, Nascimento, & Zin, 2001).

Because the brain's reaction to hypoxia is an exaggeration of the stress response, factors that exacerbate or mitigate this response can be influential in the development and maintenance of panic disorder. Early life events such as childhood physical and sexual abuse have been linked with panic attacks (Friedman et al., 2002), and various therapies aimed at reducing anxiety or stress have been beneficial in the treatment of panic attacks.

Antidepressant medication (which also influences levels of anxiety, a telltale sign of depression), antianxiety drugs such as the benzodiazepines, and drugs such as beta-adrenergic blockers that interfere with autonomic arousal have all been used with success. Behavioral strategies that encourage avoiding stimulants such as caffeine are also recommended. And any cognitive-behavioral therapy that may either distract a patient during an attack or help the patient make a more accurate cognitive appraisal of the actual trigger (autonomic response, not real restriction of oxygen) may be helpful (Andreasen & Black, 1991). In sum, evidence is building that taking mom's advice to sit down and take deep breaths may actually reestablish homeostatic processing in the brainstem's cells that survey levels of carbon dioxide, oxygen, and lactate and prevent the onset of an approaching panic attack.

[Table 7.1]

Diagnostic Criteria for Obsessive-Compulsive Disorder

A. Either obsessions or compulsions:

Obsessions as defined by (1), (2), (3), and (4):

(1) recurrent and persistent thoughts, impulses, or images that are experienced, at some time during the disturbance, as intrusive and inappropriate and that cause marked anxiety or distress

(2) the thoughts, impulses, or images are not simply excessive worries about real-life problems

(3) the person attempts to ignore or suppress such thoughts, impulses, or images, or to neutralize them with some other thought or action

(4) the person recognizes that the obsessional thoughts, impulses, or images are a product of his or her own mind (not imposed from without as in thought insertion)

Compulsions as defined by (1) and (2):

(1) repetitive behaviors (for example, hand washing, ordering, checking) or mental acts (for example, praying, counting, repeating words silently) that the person feels driven to perform in response to an obsession, or according to rules that must be applied rigidly

(2) the behaviors or mental acts are aimed at prevention or reducing distress or preventing some dreaded event or situation: however, these behaviors or mental acts either are not connected in a realistic way with what they are designed to neutralize or prevent or are clearly excessive

B. At some point during the course of the disorder, the person has recognized that the obsessions or compulsions are excessive or unreasonable. Note: This does not apply to children.

C. The obsessions or compulsions cause marked distress, are time consuming (take more than 1 hour a day), or significantly interfere with the person's normal routine, occupational (or academic) functioning, or usual social activities or relationships.

D. If another Axis I disorder is present, the content of the obsessions or compulsions is not restricted to it (for example, preoccupation with food in the presence of an Eating Disorder; hair pulling in the presence of Trichotillomania; concern with appearance in the presence of Body Dysmorphic Disorder; preoccupation with drugs in the presence of a Substance Use Disorder; preoccupation with having a serious illness in the presence of Hypochondriasis; preoccupation with sexual urges or fantasies in the presence of a Paraphilia; or guilty ruminations in the presence of Major Depressive Disorder).

The disturbance is not due to the direct physiological effects of a substance (e.g., a drug of abuse, a medication) or a general medical condition.

APA, 2000, pp. 462–463.

There is evidence of a genetic basis for OCD. Studies conducted on twins report concordance rates in monozygotic (identical) twins that range from 53% to 87%. Concordance rates observed in dizygotic (fraternal) twins range from 22% to 47% (Miguel et al., 1997; Rasmussen, 1993). Statistics also suggest that if a person in your nuclear family suffers from OCD, then there is a 23% chance (nearly 1 in 4) that you will develop the disorder (Rasmussen & Eisen, 1990). But a person's genetic profile is not the sole contributing factor to OCD susceptibility. Because the concordance rate for monozygotic twins is less than 100%, environmental factors also influence the development of this disease (see Chapter One).

Research suggests remarkably consistent prevalence rates for OCD across the world. OCD is found in both developed and developing countries, which suggests little or no influence of culture. In fact, even the types of obsessions are strikingly consistent across countries. The most common obsessions appear to be related to contamination, followed by obsessions related to aggression, body issues, religion, and sex (Table 7.2).

Tracing the Neurobiological Roots of OCD

As neuroscience technology advances, it is becoming increasingly evident that specific brain structures contribute to OCD and certain neurochemicals modulate the responses observed in OCD patients. In this section, we discuss the involvement of neurotransmitters such as serotonin, dopamine, glutamate, and gamma-aminobutyric acid (GABA) in OCD symptoms. Finally, the involvement of the neuropeptide oxytocin will be discussed. Generally, the brain systems involved with threat assessment, anxiety, movement, and reward have been implicated.

OCD neuroanatomical circuit. On February 3, 1967, Jean Talairach and his colleagues at a Parisian hospital accidentally identified one of the components of the OCD circuit (Talairach et al., 1973). In an attempt to localize the foci, or origins, of seizures in epileptic patients, these doctors stimulated various areas of the patients' brains. When the cingulum of one of the patients was stimulated, this patient could not suppress the urge to engage in repetitive behaviors. The **cingulum** (Latin for belt) is a principal association tract located directly above the corpus collosum in the cingulate gyrus. The cingulum projects to the **entorhinal cortex,** a cortical area proximal to the amygdala that is rich in interconnections with the hippocampus and other limbic structures (Carpenter & Sutin, 1983).

cingulum An association tract located in the cingulate gyrus that projects to the entorhinal cortex; stimulation of this area results in a desire to engage in repetitive behaviors.

entorhinal cortex Cortical structure on the medial surface of the temporal lobe that surrounds limbic structures such as the amygdala and has rich interconnections with the hippocampal formation.

[Table 7.2]

Percent of Sample (N) Reporting Obsessions in Six Countries

Country (N)	Obsession				
	Dirt/ Contamination	Harm/ Aggression	Somatic	Religious	Sexual
United States (425)	38%	24%	7%	6%	6%
India (410)	32%	20%	14%	5%	6%
United Kingdom (86)	47%	27%	N/A	5%	10%
Japan (61)	39%	12%	13%	N/A	5%
Denmark (61)	34%	23%	18%	8%	6%
Israel (34)	50%	20%	3%	9%	6%

N/A Not available
Adapted from Sasson et al. (1997).

[Box 7.2]

A Case in Point

Joseph Dee's Life with OCD

Joseph Dee cannot remember a time in his life that didn't include OCD symptoms. As a young boy, meals with his family became a source of anxiety invaded by one of his earliest obsessions—making the sign of the cross in a perfect motion during grace—and then repeating the motion until, as he described it, his head told him he had done it right. If he failed this task, he was certain he would go to hell. So he kept making the sign, sometimes having to go to the restroom to complete the ritual.

The number 8 had a special significance because there were eight people in Dee's family. Failure to engage in his rituals eight times would, according to his obsessive thoughts, result in the death of a family member. When he watched TV and happened to look over his shoulder, another obsession compelled Joseph to look over each shoulder eight times. At school, when a friend brushed up against him he was compelled to lick his finger and touch the "offended" area eight times.

Even as a young child, Dee had an eerie feeling that he was not sane. When he was 10 years old, he watched an afternoon television special about an insane person being thrown into a mental institution and decided that he had to hide his condition—even from his parents—to avoid a similar fate. It's difficult to imagine having such overwhelming anxiety as a child—fears of being responsible for a family member's death, fears that his own soul might burn in hell, and fear that he must keep his rituals a secret to avoid being committed to a mental institution. Although it may seem obvious to you that Dee was suffering from OCD during his childhood, he didn't know about such a condition, nor did anyone close to him. Thus, on top of all his anxiety, he lived with the fear that he was different from everyone else in the world.

Dee's problems continued in adolescence. Driving brought about a whole new set of obsessions and compulsions. Every bump evoked obsessions about running over someone—requiring Joseph to engage in the compulsion of looking excessively in the rearview mirror, stopping the car, and looking around for bodies. The anxiety got so unbearable he turned to alcohol and drugs for relief. Alcohol calmed his OCD, but the other drugs usually exacerbated the symptoms.

One day Dee decided to quit his chemical habits, including smoking. He succeeded, but this new goal became prime territory for a new set of obsessions and compulsions. He feared that everything

---

OCD loop Brain structures thought to be involved in the maintenance of OCD; loop includes the orbitofrontal cortex, cingulate gyrus and embedded cingulum, caudate, thalamus, and amygdala.

A subsequent study of 52 epileptic patients confirmed the suggestion of the initial findings that the cingulum is involved with complex repetitive movements such as rubbing fingers and pinching skin. Subsequently, neuroanatomical investigations of OCD provided evidence that the cingulum is interconnected with other brain areas implicated in OCD, specifically, the limbic system and the striatum (Marino & Cosgrove, 1997). Recall from Chapter Three that limbic structures regulate emotional responses and that the striatum, a motor structure comprising the caudate nucleus, putamen, and globus pallidus is the terminal for all afferent pathways that form the basal ganglia.

In a more elaborate neural-circuit model, Jack Modell and his colleagues (1989) at the University of Michigan Medical Center proposed the existence of an **OCD loop** comprising specific components of he touched might contain alcohol that would be absorbed into his body and lead to a relapse—he could never be sure that the pizza or the chicken or the salad served him wasn't contaminated with alcohol or other drugs. The new obsessions led to more anxiety, but the OCD enabled him to be extremely vigilant about avoiding drugs.

After being sober for a year and a half, Dee started seeing a psychiatrist who, after hearing about his life, recommended a book entitled *The Boy Who Couldn't Stop Washing,* (1990) written by the Investigator for this chapter, Judith Rapoport (Box 7.3). This book provided Joseph, at age 24, the first evidence that he wasn't completely alone with his bizarre behavior; other children had lived similar lives. This revelation was so powerful that just reading the book—and his subsequent cognitive reappraisal of his symptoms as a brain disorder experienced by other people—resulted in significant improvement.

The next year Dee moved from New York City to Los Angeles, where he eventually ended up in the care of Jeffrey Schwartz at UCLA (see Box E.2). Schwartz's cognitive-behavioral program, which we discuss in the "Therapies for OCD" section of this chapter, proved priceless in helping Dee live a successful life with OCD. When Dee felt an obsession coming on, he pulled a sheet of paper from his pocket with the words

Joseph Dee
COURTESY OF ANDREA ALBERTS

caudate nucleus written on it to remind him that his obsessions were the result of the misfiring of his brain, not a real threat. He subsequently refocused his attention to another task.

Because of the severity of his symptoms, Dee has opted for a multifaceted approach to treatment. Ten years later, he continues to participate in Schwartz's group sessions and has made prayer and meditation priorities in his life. He has struggled to identify the best pharmaceutical treatment, taking various doses of many antidepressants, but he has suffered seizures and unwelcome side effects.

Dee's cognitive therapy has taught him to avoid giving in to the obsessions in his head—fearing a downward OCD spiral much as an alcoholic fears falling off the wagon as a result of one drink. On all counts, Dee has learned to live a functional life with his OCD, feeling that he has "rewired" his OCD brain. He has written two screenplays and a novel and is currently writing a thriller in which the main character suffers from—you guessed it—OCD.

the orbitofrontal cortex, striatum, and thalamus (Figure 7.1, page 236). The **orbitofrontal cortex (OFC)** is an anterior area of the frontal cortex, the cortical area involved in advanced cognition and associations. In support of this neuroanatomical circuit, neurosurgical interruption of the OFC area or the thalamus is associated with improvement of OCD symptoms. More recently, research has suggested that the frontal lobes and cingulate cortex project, or send neural messages, to the caudate component of the striatum, which in turn projects inhibitory impulses to the thalamus. The thalamus completes the circuit by feeding back into the cortex.

Adequate functioning of this neuroanatomical circuit depends on appropriate information being transmitted from the thalamus to the frontal cortex. Just like an air-conditioning system with a faulty thermostat (that, for example, registers that the air is warmer than it really is),

orbitofrontal cortex (OFC)
Anterior area of the prefrontal cortex, involved in more advanced cognitions and associations.

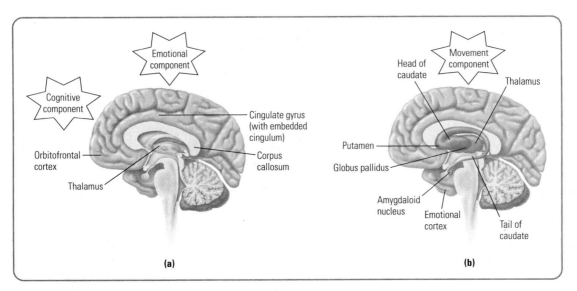

[Figure 7.1]

OCD loop. The vast interconnections among the components of the proposed neuroanatomical circuitry of OCD enable the circuit to engage at multiple sites to activate OCD responses. **(a)** Thoughts generated in the orbitofrontal cortex (cognitive/obsessive component) may send neural messages to the cingulate gyrus and embedded cingulum (emotional/integrative component) that activate the caudate nucleus (movement/compulsion component) shown in (b). Likewise, a movement that activates the caudate may activate the cingulum and then the orbitofrontal cortex. **(b)** Projecting laterally from thalamus to temporal cortex, the amygdala, located in close proximity to the entorhinal cortex, also contributes to the emotional component of OCD, for example, as it relays information about fear stimuli.

the OCD system may continue to run excessively. A person whose neural circuit is not responding to feedback from the thalamus may engage excessively in a particular behavior.

Why might the striatum and related limbic structures be involved in the excessive responding observed in OCD? After all, the striatum is known for its involvement in movement, not emotional processing. Some researchers suggest that the striatum is involved with very basic learning processes—and it enables us to carry out automatic behaviors (grooming, for example) without having to consciously focus on every step (Rauch & Savage, 1997). For example, many people find it difficult to avoid self-grooming (playing with hair, pulling on beards, picking dried, peeling skin) although they try to suppress it in public. Recall that when the anterior cingulate gyrus, with its projections to the striatum, was stimulated in the studies on epileptic patients, they exhibited simple, repetitive, automatic behaviors such as rubbing and touching.

Further evidence of the "automatic" nature of striatum-induced behavior is our ability to perform simple movements while concentrating on something more complex—doodling while concentrating on a challenging lecture, typing while carrying on a deep discussion with a friend, or tapping your pencil to the beat of your favorite CD while you read this text. Thinking in terms of computers, the striatal area allows us to multitask; that is, to run one program (carrying on a telephone conversation with a friend) while another (folding clothes) runs in the background. It seems adaptive for us, as it is efficient for a computer, to carry out these simple behaviors without devoting all our attention to them.

Our preparedness to engage in automatic behaviors may be easily nudged to excessive responding because these movements, which often are related to survival, are reinforcing—and rightly so, to assure that animals will perform them. In fact, rather than being classified as an anxiety disorder, OCD may be may more accurately classified as a point on a continuum of movement disorders that results from altered striatal activity (Chiocca & Martuza, 1990).

If OCD is characterized by disruptions of movement, why is it typically classified as an anxiety disorder? Recall that a major component of the proposed OCD loop, the cingulate gyrus, is part of the limbic system. Another component of the OCD circuit, the orbitofrontal cortex, is activated during threatening situations, suggesting that this area is also involved in processing anxiety-related information. Convincing research also suggests the involvement of another limbic structure, the *amygdala*.

Joseph LeDoux at the Center for Neural Sciences at New York University examined the role of the amygdala in the threat response. As illustrated in Figure 7.2a, on page 238, his research shows that information about a threatening stimulus (for example, an overflowing garbage can and its associated germs) is processed visually, then sent to the visual component of the thalamus where it is projected to the visual cortex. In some situations, very preliminary information about the stimulus is sent directly from the thalamus to the amygdala to prime the amygdala for interpreting the impending threat.

Once the visual stimulus is actually decoded as a garbage can, projections quickly activate the amygdala, which is intimately involved in evaluating the *emotional significance* of certain stimuli (for example, should you be fearful of the germs?). The OFC receives information from the amygdala and projects it back to the lateral amygdala. The fact that the amygdala is activated by a lower brain area (the thalamus) ultimately saves time in dangerous situations, because if you had to wait to receive a message from the frontal cortex about your cognitive assessment of the situation, it might be too late!

Of course, with our advanced cortex, we humans need not actually encounter a stressful or fearful stimulus; we can simply remember or imagine such stimuli (Figure 7.2b). David Zald and SuckWon Kim (1996a, 1996b) at the University of Minnesota have proposed that the ability of the OFC to maintain mental images of fear-related stimuli in our working memory (for example, remembering that you just played with the dog, so you need to wash your hands before eating) may simply go into overdrive in OCD patients (Goldman-Rakic, 1987). This excessive responding of the orbitofrontal cortex results in the patients' failure to inhibit thoughts about the anxiety-provoking stimuli (dog slobber and accompanying germs in this case).

[Figure 7.2]
Threat response. Real and imaginary fears can activate the same neural circuits. **(a)** The *actual threat* scenario depicts the activation of the emotional circuit described by LeDoux (1994). The visual stimulus (germs associated with the garbage can) is processed through the visual component of the thalamus and then projected to visual cortex, where the information is decoded and subsequently activates the amygdala. Occasionally, preliminary information about the threatening stimulus (dashed line) is sent directly from thalamus to amygdala for quicker evaluation. **(b)** In the *imagined threat* scenario, the mere thought of garbage and germs activates the cingulate cortex, thalamus, and amygdala (as described by Zald & Kim, 1996). Consequently, equivalent emotional responses are experienced following exposure to both real and imagined threat stimuli.

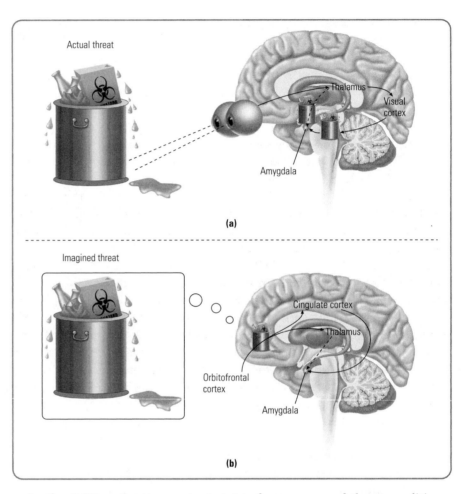

In the OCD patient's constant state of awareness of these conditions, the information becomes *locked online.* Accordingly, the desire to wash one's hands to avoid being contaminated by dog germs takes primary importance over other cognitive or behavioral events. In support of this interesting theory, when OCD patients were exposed to contaminants, activity in the OFC was positively correlated with the intensity of the patients' desire to start cleaning (McGuire, Bench, & Frith, 1994). Perhaps the increased orbitofrontal activity observed in these OCD patients increased the chances of developing a hand-washing obsession.

Evidence from neuroimaging studies. Using magnetic resonance imaging (MRI), Michael Jenike, Hans Breiter, and their colleagues at Massachusetts General Hospital and Harvard Medical School (1996) found that female OCD patients had less white matter volume than control subjects. Additionally, these patients had significantly greater *opercu-*

lar cortex volumes. (This area in the frontal cortex lies adjacent to the banks of the lateral sulcus and covers the internal area of the insula.) Severity of OCD symptoms positively correlates with opercular volume. Therefore, patients with heavier opercular cortex volumes were more likely to experience OCD symptoms than patients with lighter volumes. Focusing on caudate morphology, at least two studies report reduced *caudate* volumes in OCD patients (Luxenberg et al., 1988; Robinson et al., 1995).

These observed differences in the volume of certain brain structures prompt some researchers to hypothesize that OCD may be due to delayed maturation of the frontostriatal circuitry, or components comprising the frontal cortex, striatum, or integrating circuits. Further evidence of the *delayed maturation theory* of OCD is found in a study in which the cingulate volume was measured in pediatric OCD patients and control subjects. Whereas a significant correlation between age and cingulate volume was found in the control subjects, no such relationship was found in the OCD children. Thus, this study suggests that the maturation of the cingulate may be delayed or even arrested in OCD patients (Rosenberg & Keshavan, 1998).

Neuroimaging provides the most influential data supporting the proposed OCD circuit. In addition to suggesting that the structures in the circuit have different shapes and volumes in OCD than they have in non-OCD patients, neuroimaging studies enable researchers to look at the level of activity (using a PET scan) in each critical area while the patients engage in various activities or thought processes. For example, when OCD patients are asked to engage in the simple activity of resting quietly, researchers observe more neural activity in the orbitofrontal cortex, anterior cingulate cortex, and striatum than they do in the same structures of non-OCD subjects at rest.

Thus, the baseline neuronal activation levels in the various structures of the OCD loop are higher in OCD patients than in control subjects. Following therapy, the baseline hyperactivity subsides. These areas are still quite functional, however, because once the patient is actually shown the object of his or her prior obsessions (germs, for example), activity in the OCD circuit increases once again (Miguel et al., 1997).

Some studies even suggest **lateralization** (hemisphere dominance) of neural activation in OCD. In one PET study, OCD symptoms were provoked by exposing patients to either a dirty glove or a sterile glove. In the dirty glove trials, activation was observed in the OFC in *both* hemispheres, whereas activation of the anterior cingulate cortex and caudate nucleus was observed only in the *right* hemisphere of OCD patients (Rauch et al., 1994).

lateralization The observation that different functions have been assigned, or lateralized, to each hemishpere of the brain.

behavioral addiction Notion that an animal or human may develop a physiological addiction (similar to drug addiction) to engaging in certain behaviors such as compulsions.

activity-stress paradigm Animal model of chronic stress and compulsive behavior in which rats are housed in activity wheels and exposed to restricted food resources. Rats typically increase running and exhibit multiple signs of stress-induced illness when faced with these conditions.

(a)

(b)

[Figure 7.3]
Activity-stress pathways. The stained processes in each photomicrograph depict pathways that are actively utilizing the neurotransmitter dopamine in the area of the amygdala in **(a)** an activity-stressed rat and **(b)** a pair-fed control rat.

COURTESY OF KELLY LAMBERT, RANDOLPH-MACON COLLEGE BEHAVIORAL NEUROSCIENCE LABORATORY

When interpreting these neuroimaging studies, however, it's best to be mindful of the many characteristics of the subject population, which complicate any conclusions. For example, one study failed to find structural abnormalities or altered metabolic rates in the caudate of OCD patients. The authors subsequently suggested that the heterogenous nature of this disorder (OCD with and without tics) might contribute to some of the inconsistencies found in the literature, a problem typical of research in the field of mental illness (Aylward et al., 1996; Trivedi, 1996).

Neurochemistry of OCD. If you envision OCD as an addiction to specific cognitive-behavioral rituals, then the addiction literature might be useful in understanding this disorder (see also Chapter Ten). Recall that the nucleus accumbens is the limbic component of the striatum sometimes referred to as the "pleasure center" of the brain (see Figure 3.13). Substantial research suggests that *dopaminergic activity* in the nucleus accumbens plays an integral role in the rewarding properties of psychotropic drugs such as cocaine and amphetamine (Koob & Nestler, 1997). One distinctive difference, however, between substance abuse and OCD is that an exogenous substance (one originating outside the body) is continuously introduced into the central nervous system in substance abuse, an event that does not occur in OCD.

Could the nucleus accumbens be involved in a **behavioral addiction?** This is the idea that an animal or human can develop a physiological addiction to engaging in certain behaviors. Looking back at the model of rat behavior described in the chapter-opening Connections might provide a clue. Recall that the rats are fed for 1 hour per day and housed with activity wheels. The rats increase their running to such excessive levels that they die of stress-related symptoms if the experimenter does not intervene (Lambert, 1993; Lambert et al., 1998).

These animals have increased cellular activity in the nucleus accumbens, as well as increased dopaminergic activity (the neurotransmitter involved in addiction) throughout the extended amygdala, as shown in Figure 7.3 (Aurentz et al., 1998). The effect is so pronounced that researchers have suggested this **activity-stress paradigm** as a valid model of OCD. In fact, one study found that antidepressants, a sometimes successful treatment for OCD, are also effective for the compulsive running observed in this paradigm (Altemus, Glowa, & Murphy, 1993). Thus, it appears that rats that engage in such a severe behavioral compulsion fit the same neurobiological profile of animals addicted to cocaine. These findings begin to convey just how intense the desire to engage in certain behaviors is in OCD patients (Figure 7.4).

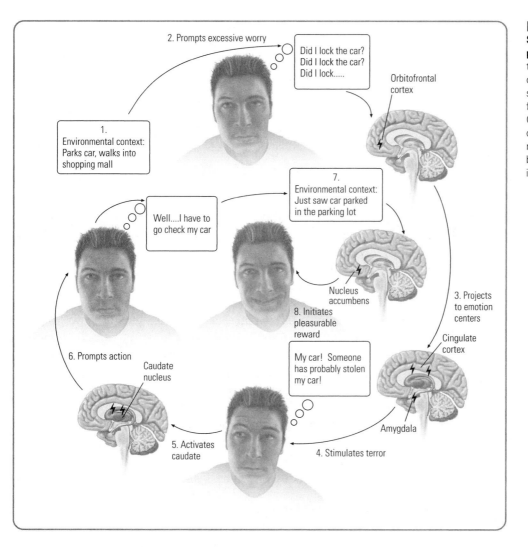

[Figure 7.4]
Spiraling behavior pattern. A simple trip to the shopping mall can trigger a complex series of responses for a person with OCD. Environmental context, cognition, neural activity, and behavior all intersect in a spiraling pattern.

Drugs that enhance serotonergic (5-HT) activity, namely the selective serotonin reuptake inhibitors (SSRIs) discussed in Chapter Five, are somewhat effective in treating OCD. It is therefore easy to conclude that OCD is caused by lowered or modified serotonergic levels. Research, however, does not support this conclusion.

Isolated findings of 5-HT abnormalities have been reported (Insel, Mueller, Alterman, Linnoila, & Murphy, 1985), but no consistent serotonin abnormalities have been identified (Rapoport & Fiske, 1998). In fact, among the transmitters associated with the proposed OCD loop, two additional transmitters stand out: glutamate activity between the

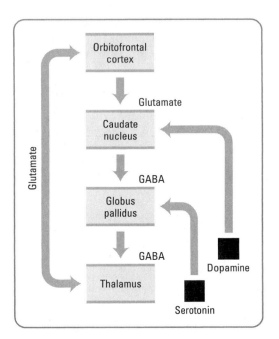

[Figure 7.5]
Neurochemistry of the OCD loop. Glutamate pathways are necessary for communication between the OFC and caudate nucleus and between the thalamus and OFC. GABA pathways are found between the caudate and globus pallidus and the globus pallidus and thalamus. Although not specifically part of the transmitter communication among the circuit structures, dopamine acts as a neuromodulator in the caudate and serotonin in the globus pallidus.

ADAPTED FROM JENIKE, RAUCH, ET AL., 1996.

orbitofrontal cortex and the caudate nucleus (part of the striatum) and GABA, the principal transmitter among the components of the striatum. So where does serotonin come into play? It has been suggested that serotonin, in addition to dopamine, serves as a neuromodulator, a neurotransmitter that increases or decreases the activity of other neurotransmitters (see Chapter Five).

As depicted in Figure 7.5, dopamine may modulate a specific aspect of the OCD circuitry (the caudate nucleus), whereas serotonin modulates another component (the globus pallidus). The brain needs glutamate and GABA to receive and transmit messages in the OCD circuitry, yet the volume and clarity of reception may be adjusted in the presence of neuromodulators such as dopamine and serotonin.

The indirect involvement of serotonin in the OCD circuitry may account for the variability observed in studies in which OCD patients are given serotonergic reuptake inhibitors (SRIs). About 40% to 60% of OCD patients improve when placed on SRI therapy, whereas others only partially respond (Jenike, Rauche, et al., 1996). Focusing on a potential indirect role of dopamine, dopaminergic receptor subtype-2 (D_2) antagonists are effective for motor tics, providing more evidence that dopamine may be a modulator involved in the behavioral compulsions observed in OCD.

Pregnant animals, including humans, change their behavior around the time of giving birth—building a nest or nursery, checking the surroundings, cleaning up. At least in humans, this behavior often is exacerbated by obsessional thoughts about the delivery or being a competent parent. Neill Epperson and his colleagues at Yale University had the fertile idea that the compulsions and obsessions observed in these "glowing" women might offer a clue to what may be going on in OCD.

The researchers focused their attention on oxytocin, a neuropeptide released by the posterior pituitary and involved in uterine contractions and milk ejection, as well as in social bonding (see Chapter Five). From a behavioral perspective, oxytocin seems to enhance the expression of grooming, reproductive, and affiliative behaviors in animals (Epperson, McDougle, & Price, 1996). Interestingly, some women with preexisting OCD report worsening of symptoms during pregnancy (Epperson, McDougle, Brown, & Price, 1995). Although this oxytocin hypothesis is extremely interesting, the jury is still out about its actual role in OCD or OCD-like behavior (Epperson et al., 1996; Leckman et al., 1994).

Evolutionary Perspectives: Fixed Action Patterns and Ritualistic Behavior

Evolutionary biologists and psychologists refer to behavioral responses that are rigid, consistent, and predictable as **fixed action patterns (FAPs).** In most cases, these seemingly inherent behaviors serve some function related to survival. A young bird opens and closes its mouth to initiate feeding from its parent. A frog flicks its tongue to catch flies.

Because FAPs are important to survival, animals are biologically prepared to make the patterned response. From an evolutionary viewpoint, then, people with OCD clean to avoid contamination and sickness. They check and count to confirm the safety of family and friends. They repeatedly order items in their environment in an attempt to protect their resources.

It is easy to conceive many of these rituals as closely related to FAPs (Turbott, 1997). Most of the ritualistic behaviors associated with OCD—avoiding contamination, purifying the body, vigilance for environmental threats, observing social rules or religious rituals, checking to make sure an important task has been completed—are related to survival in some manner (Rapoport & Fiske, 1998). Recall also that the ritualistic behaviors of OCD are consistent across cultures. Given this cross-cultural consistency, OCD rituals can be likened to more elaborate FAPs observed in nonhuman animals.

A personal experience illustrates how behaviors critical for survival can escalate into compulsions. A few years ago I was dropping my then 14-month-old daughter off at her babysitter's one rainy morning. When I got out of the van I accidentally hit the lock button, leaving my keys inside; by the time I ran around to get my daughter from her car seat I realized that I couldn't get to her. I stood next to her window for 30 minutes in the pouring rain trying to make reassuring faces as she was reaching out for me and screaming in fear.

This experience created a heavy dose of maternal anxiety. Almost four years later, I continue to check to make sure I have my keys at least twice every time I get out of my vehicle—regardless of whether my children (now old enough to unlock the doors) are in the car. This compulsive checking behavior began with the need to protect my daughter—who, in evolutionary terms, represents a significant genetic investment.

Animal models. FAPs also seem to be ballistic in the sense that once they are triggered by the appropriate stimulus they are difficult to suppress. If you've ever been around cats, you are familiar with the stereotypical behavior they demonstrate after they use the litter box—digging

fixed action pattern (FAP)
Motor program that seems to develop automatically in particular species of animals (e.g, the courting displays of many birds); once triggered, these rigid, consistent, and predictable responses are continued to completion.

and covering, digging and covering. In the cat's natural environment this behavior is perfectly reasonable to keep unwanted visitors from knowing that the cat had eliminated in the area.

Have you also observed a cat's behavior when it defecates on a bare floor? The cat still goes through all the motions of burying even though the burying response makes no sense when there is nothing to move over its feces. In this situation, the cat seems unable to respond to the environment and spends the same amount of time moving air over the soiled area.

This behavior may be similar to that of humans who wash their hands to remove dirt that is not there or check locks they have checked dozens of times. Seksel and Lindeman (1998) investigated the effectiveness of the antidepressant clomipramine on compulsive behaviors of the cat, such as urine spraying, overgrooming, and excessive vocalization. The drug was well tolerated in the feline patients and, when combined with behavior modification, was effective in ameliorating the annoying behaviors in 100% of the cases!

Further evidence that OCD may be related to FAPs can be seen in raccoons. In its natural habitat, the raccoon spends lots of time along the riverbank running its sensitive fingers through the shallow water looking for food. In captivity, these animals are known for compulsivelike food washing—dropping the food in the water, losing it, picking it up, dropping it again. It is likely that the raccoon is interested not in cleaning its food but in hunting for it; it is more plausible that these behaviors are caused by their inability to hunt for their food in captivity. FAPs are difficult to suppress even when they are not necessary for a specific animal's survival. Our featured Investigator, Judith Rapoport (Box 7.3), currently works with human OCD patients, but the ritualistic behaviors of animals initially sparked her interest as an undergraduate student.

Human models: Baseball rituals. Watching a baseball game after studying this chapter may inspire armchair diagnostics of some players. For example, you may observe a pitcher who always adjusts his hat, hits his glove, twists his ankle counterclockwise, and spits over his left arm before delivering a pitch. Like an FAP, once initiated, the pitcher always goes through the entire sequence before ending the behavior. Similar to behaviors observed in OCD, the pitcher engages in the behavior excessively and if asked why says he feels—irrationally—that something bad will happen if the compulsion is not expressed to completion.

Could it be that these talented, disciplined, physically fit men all have a specific form of baseball-induced OCD? Although these behaviors meet

[Box 7.3]

The Investigators

Judith L. Rapoport

Judith Rapoport, currently chief of the Child Psychiatric Branch of the National Institute of Mental Health (NIMH), began her training at Swarthmore College where she studied with primatologist Wolfgang Kohler. Kohler taught her to view the brain's functions as complex, integrative processes, not simple sensory and motor events. She received her medical degree from Harvard Medical School with an emphasis on neurology and psychiatry.

During medical school and her subsequent psychiatric residency, Rapoport became fascinated with the new drug treatments that were beginning to offer psychiatric patients considerably more relief than the existing psychological treatments. In 1972 she visited Stockholm's Karolinska Hospital where she learned about a new drug, clomipramine (Anafranil), that successfully reduced OCD-related symptoms in adults. This visit marked the beginning of her fascination with this disease—a fascination that continues to this day.

During Rapoport's Stockholm visit, many of the patients on the ward told her that they began to show symptoms as children—an observation that she would take back with her to the NIMH. Subsequently, she began to investigate the effectiveness of clomipramine on children expressing OCD symptoms. Her research team found that the drug brought an end to the OCD nightmare of many of the children.

Although OCD was thought to be rare at that time, Rapoport found many cases in the Washington, D.C., area. Because it became painfully clear that this disorder affected so many people, especially so many children, she wrote the book *The Boy Who Couldn't Stop Washing* in 1991 so that the general public could understand the symptoms and treatments associated with OCD.

Judith Rapoport
COURTESY OF JUDITH RAPOPORT, M.D.

Today Rapoport is considering the question of why OCD might have evolved in our species. Interestingly, her ideas on this topic originate with her undergraduate studies in animal behavior at Swarthmore in which she learned how parrots build their nests, how cranes dance, and so on. It doesn't appear that these animals were taught their species-specific behaviors, yet each performs them with remarkable similarity.

Perhaps some OCD behaviors, such as repeated checking, are human species-specific behaviors, or fixed action patterns. After all, aren't we all checkers to some extent? Rapoport told us, "Humans are social animals. Rituals concerned with acceptance to others may be an exaggeration of highly adaptive 'checking' behaviors to make sure one's behaviors are appropriate." When asked about the future of therapies for OCD, Rapoport reported that several groups are looking at candidate genes for OCD, but this is a long-shot approach with no guaranteed payoff. She feels that although there are currently no treatment breakthroughs, perhaps some of the brain imaging studies will shed light on new pathophysiology.

superstitious behavior
Response resulting from random reinforcement; thought to explain some ritualistic behavior.

some of the criteria for OCD, it is important to note that players don't typically engage in these rituals off the field, they don't perceive their compulsions as excessive, and they don't feel that the compulsions interfere with success on the field. On the contrary, many players feel that their specific rituals are necessary for their success. And who could argue that someone who has a career playing their favorite game and is receiving a seven-digit salary is not successful?

In most cases, the ritualistic behavior observed in athletes is considered **superstitious behavior,** that is, responses that result from random reinforcement. For example, if a pigeon receives a pellet of food every minute regardless of whether or not it engages in a specific behavior, many times the pigeon will form an association between its last behavior and the food reward. Before long, the animal is repeatedly engaging in the random behavior (for example, turning in a semicircle) to prompt the delivery of the food. After a baseball player wears a red undershirt and eats pineapple-flavored jelly beans before a game in which he goes four for four and hits a home run, the distinctive cues of the T-shirt and jelly beans become linked in his mind to his success in the game. From that point on the player is likely to engage in these behaviors repeatedly in an attempt to repeat the initial success.

The next time you wear your lucky socks to an exam, you may want to analyze your reasons. Is the behavior truly related to the consequences? Well, if it makes you feel more confident, it probably won't do any harm as long as you continue to realize that studying is the most important behavior for producing the consequences of the good grade you desire. Although superstitious behaviors can lead to dysfunctional responding, they may serve as confidence boosters in certain situations, leading to reduced anxiety and more successful responding.

Therapies for OCD

Three treatments benefit OCD patients: pharmaceutical therapy, neurosurgical treatment, and cognitive-behavioral therapy. Pharmaceutical therapy attempts to reestablish more normal baseline neurochemistry in the brain. Five drugs currently have FDA approval for the treatment of OCD. Unfortunately, pharmaceutical therapy does not suppress symptoms in all OCD patients. Some experience improvement with certain behavioral and/or cognitive therapy; others, out of desperation, turn to neurosurgery.

Psychopharmacological therapy. Recall that, although no prevailing serotonergic abnormalities have been observed in OCD patients, drugs that alter 5-HT functioning (SRIs and SSRIs) improve the symptoms of many OCD patients. These observations suggest that serotonin may have an indirect effect on OCD. However, with the more sophisticated assays of the serotonergic system currently available, differences in 5-HT systems may become apparent in the near future. For example, decreased platelet 5-HT levels in adolescent OCD patients have been correlated with clinical improvement (Flament, Rapoport, Murphy, Lake, & Berg, 1987). Further, focusing on 5-HT metabolites might yield interesting information; for example, increased levels of 5-HIAA (a 5-HT metabolite more easily detected in CSF than 5-HT) have been observed in OCD patients (Insel et al., 1985).

Although the specific explanation for the success of SRIs is yet to be uncovered, it hasn't prevented the prescription of such drugs for OCD. After all, OCD patients are more interested in the successful outcome of a treatment than a scientific explanation for the treatment's effectiveness. Let's look at some of the drugs that successfully treat OCD symptoms.

Clomipramine (Anafranil), originally introduced as an antidepressant in Europe in 1966, was the first serotonergic treatment that proved effective for some cases of OCD (Kobak, Greist, Jefferson, Katzelnick, & Henk, 1998). Clomipramine blocks 5-HT and norepinephrine (as well as having some dopamine receptor-blocking properties) and is considered a more global SRI than the contemporary SSRIs (McDougle, 1999). Although effective in treating OCD symptoms, clomipramine induces side effects such as sedation, constipation, insomnia, nervousness, and male impotence (Ackerman, Greenland, Bystritsky, & Datz, 1996) and can be lethal in overdoses (Kobak et al., 1998).

Fewer side effects attend the prescribed SSRIs, which include *fluoxetine* (Prozac), *sertraline* (Zoloft), *paroxetine* (Paxil), and *fluvoxamine* (Luvox). The SSRIs, however, are not free from side effects; some produce nausea, headaches, and sleep disturbances. In many cases, however, SSRI side effects wane after several months. Generally, OCD patients require higher doses than the doses given to depressed patients. In the case of all pharmacological treatments, it seems to take as long as 3 months before OCD patients notice an initial response and up to 6 months for a maximum effect (Dolberg, Iancu, Sasson, & Zohar, 1996). (See Chapter 8 for more information on SSRIs.)

How effective are these pharmacologial therapies? This is a difficult question to answer because much of the data do not come from controlled studies and many patients are placed on more than one treatment protocol. Treatment "packages" for OCD patients might consist of multiple pharmacological interventions along with behavioral and/or cognitive therapy. There also appears to be a considerable placebo response when treating OCD pharmacologically—as high as 50%, although up to 20% report getting worse (Zohar, Judge et. al., 1996).

clomipramine SRI that prevents the reuptake of serotonin and norepinephrine from the synapse, ultimately increasing the availability of serotonin; similar in structure to imipramine, a tricyclic antidepressant; used as therapy for OCD.

anxiolytics Drugs such as the benzodiazepines that work to reduce anxiety.

stereotaxic apparatus Scientific device that enables the experimenter or surgeon to access any three-dimensional point in the brain; used for placement of electrodes and various forms of neurosurgery.

Despite these complications, it is reported that drug therapies have a success rate that ranges from 50% to 70% (Dolberg et al., 1996). This recovery rate is impressive, but relapse rates are high when patients cease taking their medication (Dolberg et al., 1996). Additionally, other drugs may be prescribed to augment recovery. For example, D_2 antagonists may be used for prevalent tics (Jenike, Rauch, et al., 1996) and **anxiolytics,** or anxiety-reducing agents (for example, benzodiazepines), may help to reduce anxiety associated with OCD (Miguel et al., 1997).

Neurosurgical treatment. Neurosurgery is sometimes used in the most extreme OCD cases, when patients treated with drugs fail to improve or, once improved, find themselves relapsing (Mindus & Jenike, 1992). In this case, *neurosurgical treatment,* a more contemporary term than *psychosurgery,* introduced in Chapter Two, may be defined as "a destruction of histologically normal brain tissue with the objective of alleviating severe symptoms of chronic psychiatric disorders" (p. 922). Why perform the extreme act of cutting into an OCD patient's brain? Is there sufficient evidence that neurosurgical treatment works? Let us start with a little history.

In the 1930s, accumulating evidence suggested that the frontal lobe and connections might be involved in anxiety-related disorders (Fulton & Jacobsen, 1935; MacLean, 1954; Papez, 1937). Following the introduction of the **stereotaxic apparatus** in 1947, surgeons could enter the brain and manipulate structures with great precision (Figure 7.6). In 1947, Talairach and other surgeons attempted to treat patients suffering from anxiety neurosis by interrupting the frontal-thalamic connections. Because the side effects on personality were not as severe as those observed in the more traditional frontal lobotomies, an increase in stereotaxic surgeries occurred for a variety of psychiatric illnesses

[Figure 7.6]
Stereotaxic apparatus. A fearful patient is fitted into a stereotaxic apparatus, or calibrated frame, so that the neurosurgeon can maneuver through the brain with great precision (accurate to the millimeter) to cut particular nerve fibers. In the case of intractable OCD, the lesions, or cuts, generally separate some of the pathways of the frontal cortex from the emotional circuit of the limbic system. JOE MCNALLY

(Bingley, Lekskell, & Meyerson, 1977; Chiocca & Martuza, 1990). The most successful results, however, were observed in OCD patients (Fodstad, Strandman, Karlsson, & West, 1982).

Currently, four surgical protocols show the greatest potential as effective treatments for OCD patients: anterior capsulotomy; anterior cingulotomy; subcaudate tractotomy; and limbic leukotomy (Chiocca & Martuza, 1990). Most of these procedures require local anesthesia accompanied by mild sedation or light general anesthesia. The surgery itself has been described as painless, inducing little stress in the patient, although individual cases vary (Marino & Cosgrove, 1997). Generally, improvement takes anywhere from weeks to months after the surgery (Mindus & Jenike, 1992).

[Table 7.3]

Summary of Neurosurgical Procedures for Severe OCD

Type of surgery	Manipulation	Success rate	Side effects
Anterior capsulotomy	Bilateral lesions of anterior internal capsule	Approx. 70%	Impulse control problems and personality changes
Anterior cingulotomy	Excision of the anterior cingulate gyrus	Approx. 30–50%	Hemiplegia and medication-controlled epilepsy in less than 1% of patients
Subcaudate tractotomy	Lesions of the rostral orbital cortex (ventral to head of caudate)	Approx. 50% (minimal research)	Minor personality alterations such as overeating and extravagance in some patients
Limbic leukotomy	Bilateral lesions of lower medial quadrant of the orbitofrontal areas and anterior cingulate bundle	Approx. 84%	No long-term side effects observed

As you read the descriptions and accompanying success rates for each surgery, keep in mind that these observations are far from scientific perfection. Obviously, no control groups are included—it would not be ethical to conduct a sham surgery on OCD patients. Additionally, the follow-ups are generally only for the first couple of years, so long-term data are not available for most of the studies. For these reasons, countries such as the Russian Republic and Japan prohibit neurosurgical intervention to treat intractable or persistent OCD (Mindus & Jenike, 1992). The following neurosurgical procedures are summarized in Table 7.3:

- *Anterior capsulotomy* Introduced by Leksell in the 1950s (Herner, 1961), this procedure involves placing bilateral lesions in the anterior part of the *internal capsule*. This band of nerve fibers projects from the brainstem to the frontal lobe; the anterior portion separates the caudate from the putamen (see Figure 7.1 and Figure 3.6 to review anatomical directions). This procedure successfully suppressed symptoms in up to 70% of the patients, but disturbing side effects related to impulse control and other personality changes were observed in some patients.

- *Anterior cingulotomy* Originally performed by Whitty in 1952, the anterior portion of the cingulate gyrus is exised (Whitty, Duffield, & Tow, 1952). Overall, this surgery has a success rate of about 50% and a very low complication rate. A long-term follow-up has reported a more conservative success rate of 30% (Jenike et al., 1991). Interestingly, the anterior cingulotomy appears to have no effect on the patient's intellectual, behavioral, or emotional capacities, making it the most prevalent among the neurosurgical protocols for OCD (Marino & Cosgrove, 1997). It has been speculated that this surgery improves symptoms by diminishing the anxiety component rather than the compulsion component of the disease. For example, if an individual consistently engaged in compulsive hand washing when she felt anxious, the compulsions would decrease if, following this surgery, she were less likely to feel anxious. Nonetheless, when faced with final exams or another significant stressful event, compulsive rituals would probably reemerge for the duration of the anxiety.

■ *Subcaudate tractotomy* This procedure, in which lesions are made in the orbital cortex (positioned ventral to the head of the caudate nucleus), was introduced by Knight in 1969. Although research on this procedure is minimal, researchers suggest that clinical improvement was also seen in about 50% of the patients with minor rates of adverse personality traits—an outcome not observed with anterior cingulotomy (Goktepe, Young, & Bridges, 1975).

■ *Limbic leukotomy* Introduced in 1973 by Kelly, Richardson, and Mitchell-Heggs, this procedure consists of bilateral lesions of the lower medial portion of the orbitofrontal areas plus bilateral lesions of the anterior cingulate bundle area. The disruption of both areas influences connections among the thalamic and the limbic pathways. Not surprisingly, this more extensive surgery seems to be more successful than the aforementioned procedures, with success rates as high as 84% with no long-term side effects. Consequently, there is considerable enthusiasm for the limbic technique (Perse, 1988).

Given this information, how should an intractable OCD patient who has not responded to pharmacological or cognitive-behavioral therapies be treated? Because of the low side effect rate and modest tissue damage, it is often recommended that the surgeon start with cingulotomy. If this surgery fails to lead to a satisfactory recovery, then the surgeon can reenter the brain and create a lesion in the orbitomedial frontal areas, making the procedure a limbic leukotomy or anterior capsulotomy (Chiocca & Martuza, 1990).

Even with all the information on these techniques, it is important to remember that surgical therapy is still in its infancy. It is hoped that more sophisticated neuroimaging techniques will help identify more specific areas critical for understanding OCD. The identification of such areas will lead to interventions requiring the least possible neurological damage (Mindus & Jenike, 1992).

Cognitive-behavioral therapy. Behavioral therapy was used to treat OCD as early as 1900. Unfortunately, behaviorism was suppressed by Freud's psychoanalytic movement, which explored the *meaning* of obsessions and compulsions rather than treatment for them (Miguel et al., 1997). A second wave of behavior therapy, **exposure and response prevention**

(ERP), surfaced in the early 1970s and proved to be the first empirically validated successful treatment for OCD (Kobak et al., 1998). Research suggests that about 50% to 70% of patients improve as a result of ERP, an improvement rate similar to pharmacological therapies (Dolberg et al., 1996). In fact, a few studies have indicated that behavioral therapy is slightly more effective than individual medications for OCD (Marks, 1997).

Patients undergoing ERP are instructed to expose themselves to feared stimuli and encouraged to stay in contact with the stimuli through the subsequent anxiety. During this *exposure,* patients are instructed to actively suppress the usual rituals (*response*) used to minimize anxiety. For example, a patient with a germ obsession might have to come into contact with the most feared germs and refrain from cleaning or avoiding the germs. Patients are assigned these tasks as *homework,* to be carried out on the patient's own for 1 hour daily.

The average therapy time is 10 hours for outpatients and 20 hours for more difficult cases (typically inpatients). ERP was initially thought to be most useful for treating ritual behaviors but is now used for obsessions as well. The patient is instructed to think anxiogenic (anxiety-producing) thoughts and then suppress the mental rituals or neutralizing thoughts that usually accompany the anxiety (Marks, 1997).

Because ERP involves contact with the OCD patient's most feared situations, it comes close to the patient's worst nightmare. The anticipated fear and anxiety make some patients reluctant to proceed, and some drop out of therapy early (Marks, 1997). One recent innovation, *virtual reality ERP,* in which a person interacts with a fearful stimulus through interactive video, may reduce their trepidation (Clark, Kirdby, Daniels, & Marks, 1998). For the more cautious patient, vicarious computer-aided techniques in which a patient merely watches another patient encounter fearful stimuli on a computer screen leads to significant improvement in OCD patients, although not as much as *actual* ERP (see Epilogue for more about virtual reality treatment). ERP can be uncomfortable for patients, but it can eliminate fear and anxiety, often without pharmacological aids. As described in Chapter One, this behavioral therapy is also used successfully to treat phobias.

Perhaps the most promising form of behavioral therapy is ERP used in combination with cognitive therapy. In an innovative study, Jeffrey Schwartz and his colleagues at the University of California in Los Angeles (Schwartz, Stoessel, Baxter, Martin, & Phelps, 1996) demonstrated the

THE FAR SIDE®   By GARY LARSON

Professor Gallagher and his controversial technique of simultaneously confronting the fear of heights, snakes, and the dark.

exposure and response prevention (ERP) Behavioral therapy for OCD; patients are encouraged to remain in contact with a feared stimulus while simultaneously suppressing the rituals they typically use to decrease anxiety.

interactions among behavioral therapy, cognitive therapy, and neuro-science. (Schwartz was discussed earlier in Box 7.2 and later in Box E.2.) Schwartz's team had patients meet once or twice a week with a therapist to review individualized ERP assignments. Patients were further instructed to keep diaries to help them self-monitor their progress.

The cognitive component consisted of the *four R's* (Schwartz, Stoessel, Baxter, Martin, & Phelps, 1996):

- *Relabeling* the unwanted thoughts as mere obsessions and compulsions

- *Reattributing* the origin of the thoughts to a physiochemical disorder of the brain and not a danger that exists in reality

- *Refocusing* during the unwanted thoughts so that the patient can quickly substitute more comfortable thoughts for the anxiety-provoking thoughts

- *Revaluing* so that the patient realizes that the unwanted thoughts are merely worthless distractions and should be ignored

The PET scan in Figure 7.7a compares the energy being used in the brains of a control subject and a person with OCD. PET scans of patients who responded to the treatment show significant decreases in caudate glucose metabolic rates, an effect that was not observed in the poor responders (Figure 7.7b). Prior to treatment, high activation of the orbital gyri, the head of the caudate nucleus, and the thalamus (especially in the right hemisphere) was observed. After treatment, this activity was minimized in both hemispheres. These data demonstrate that an effective cognitive therapy changes the patient's neurobiology. These findings provide further support of the existence of the OCD loop consisting of the orbitofrontal cortex, striatum, and thalamic components (see Figure 7.1). According to Schwartz (1996), this circuit "locks" the brain in gear inducing the repetitive obsessions and compulsions.

[Figure 7.7]
PET scans of relative energy use in OCD. (a) The level of cellular activation (denoted by lighter-colored areas) is higher in the OCD patient on the right compared with the control subject on the left. **(b)** Right caudate (rCd) activity in the patient's brain post-self-treatment is less than it was pretreatment.

SCHWARTZ & BEYETTE, 1996. COURTESY OF JEFFERY SCHWARTZ, M.D., AND LEWIS R. BAXTER, JR., M.D.

Normal control   Obsessive-compulsive   Pretreatment   Posttreatment

These data confirm what cognitive-behavioral therapists have thought for some time—that this form of ERP therapy can modify the brain in ways similar to pharmacological or surgical therapies. The idea of brain changes being self-generated and not dependent on pharmacological intervention makes ERP very attractive. It should be noted, however, that medication is used at times during the cognitive-behavioral therapy. The use of drugs early in the treatment, as patients begin to expose themselves to their worst fears, has been likened to children's use of water wings to reduce the anxiety that accompanies many early encounters to water (Schwartz, 1996). Just as most children grow out of that anxiety and learn to float or swim without aids, patients are removed from pharmacological interventions following the early stages of treatment (Schwartz, 1996). The bottom line is that any clinical improvement must be accompanied by neurobiological alterations in the brain.

Tourette's syndrome A neurological condition characterized by involuntary "tic" movements and vocalizations.

TOURETTE'S SYNDROME

Have you ever developed a hacking cough that persisted through an important lecture? Been at an interview when your stomach started growling voraciously? Gotten the hiccups while trying to give an oral presentation in class? The fact that your body is making disruptive noises is very distracting as you muster all your energy to try to suppress the coughing, growling, or hiccuping. These experiences offer only a partial insight to the constant dread many Tourette's patients experience as they try to suppress their vocal and motor tics in public. For deeper insight, read Box 7.4. on page 254.

Similar to other clinical disorders addressed in this text, **Tourette's syndrome** is multifaceted. Like OCD, Tourette's involves excessive responding, in this case, involuntary movement along with vocal outbursts of sounds such as barking or words, often scatological. Similar to the obsessions we discussed in the OCD section, many Tourette's patients report that their symptoms become more intense in times of anxiety, emotional stress, or excitement.

Tracing the Neurobiological Roots of Tourette's Syndrome

In 1825, it was reported that a French noblewoman, the Marquise de Damplerre, developed body tics, made barking sounds, and frequently uttered obscenities. Much to her dismay, all these responses were involuntary. In 1885, Georges Gilles de la Tourette, a French physician, became interested in patients such as the marquise. Eventually this collection of symptoms became known as Tourette's syndrome (Singer & Walkup, 1991).

[Box 7.4]

A Case in Point

Living with Tourette's Syndrome

Growing up in Galashiels, Scotland, John Davidson faced the typical challenges encountered by other teenagers and more. At an age when most people were trying to fit in, John really stood out in the crowd. Even today, his thoughts are constantly focused on suppressing embarrassing language, movement, and gestures. "It's hard to explain—when I feel like I'm going to say something I feel like I *have* to say it." His involuntary vocal tics, the result of Tourette's syndrome, make Davidson feel as if the words are being forced out of him.

As a documentary film crew follows Davidson and his mother through the grocery store, he holds his lip in an attempt to keep the words from erupting from his mouth. Even so, he repeatedly chirps, "F— off." At times, the vocal tics seem to be related to the environment; for example, Davidson is more likely to emit tics of a sexual nature when he is in the presence of young females. At times, they are directed to individuals; "Slut, Mom, you're a slut," he says as he shops with his mother. Displaying admirable tolerance and understanding of her son's condition, Davidson's mother is not distracted by such outbursts and continues her shopping journey through the grocery store.

As you might imagine, Tourette's syndrome is especially difficult to tolerate in the quietness of the classroom. Some of Davidson's teachers were impatient with his tics, making it difficult to continue his education in mainstream classrooms. He ultimately focused on more specific vocational training and settled on hor-

ticulture. In another arena the simple task of having dinner was incredibly stressful for Davidson and his family because of his most invasive tic, spitting. His father chose not to eat with the family because of this behavior. The rest of the family joined Davidson at mealtimes, but dishes were strategically covered to protect the food from his saliva.

It is interesting that Davidson's facial tics, barks, spitting, head jerks, and obscenities seem prompted by anxiety associated with being in the presence of others. As he fishes along a tranquil river in solitude, there is no evidence of his disorder. He also feels more relaxed when he plays basketball. His motor and vocal tics are less conspicuous in the midst of all the loud sounds and movements inherent to the game. In agreement with anecdotal evidence that Tourette's patients are skilled musicians and athletes, Davidson is an impressive basketball player.

Davidson's situation has improved in the years following the BBC documentary on his condition, filmed when he was 15 years old. "The reaction was tremendous. When I went into town the day after the programme was broadcast, people weren't walking across the street to avoid me. For the first time in my life I felt people now understood that I wasn't a freak" [Tourette Syndrome Association (UK), 2002].

Unfortunately, aside from fishing and sports, John is one of those patients who does not find relief from this disorder through drug or behavioral therapy. Although he still lives with the fear of approaching an attractive woman and then spitting on her or offending her with vile language, he has found some peace by learning to live with his mental illness and organizing an annual summer camp for children living with Tourette's.

Today, multiple motor tics and one or more vocal tics are considered the essential diagnostic features of Tourette's syndrome (Table 7.4). Tourettic tics may be simple or complex. Eye blinks and head twitches are considered simple motor tics; touching patterns, facial movements, and obscene gestures are considered complex motor tics. Clearing one's throat or making barking noises are simple vocal tics; multiple syllables or words are more complex vocal tics (for example, saying *no, no* or *oh, boy*).

[Table 7.4]

Diagnostic Criteria for Tourette's Disorder

A. Both multiple motor and one or more vocal tics have been present at some time during the illness although not necessarily concurrently. (A *tic* is a sudden, rapid, recurrent, nonrhythmic, stereotyped motor movement or vocalization.)

B. The tics occur many times a day (usually in bouts) nearly every day or intermittently throughout a period of more than 1 year, and during this period there was never a tic-free period of more that 3 consecutive months.

C. The disturbance causes marked distress or significant impairment in social, occupational, or other important areas of functioning.

D. The onset is before age 18 years.

E. The disturbance is not due to the direct physiological effects of a substance (e.g., stimulants) or a general medical condition (e.g., Huntington's disease or postviral encephalitis).

APA (2000), p. 114.

In addition to tics, many patients suffering from Tourette's frequently express symptoms indicative of attention deficit hyperactivity disorder (see Chapter Six) and/or OCD (Singer & Walkup, 1991).

Boys are more likely to be diagnosed with Tourette's syndrome than girls; prevalence rates are approximately 1:2,000 for boys and 1:10,000 for girls (Barr & Sandor, 1998). The onset of Tourette's may occur as early as 2 years of age, but the typical age of onset is 7 years. The duration of the disorder is typically lifelong; some patients, however, may experience remission periods lasting from weeks to years (APA, 1994).

Research suggests a genetic basis for Tourette's syndrome. Focusing on evidence provided by twin studies, concordance rates range from about 50% to 90% for monozygotic twins compared with 8% to 25% for dizygotic pairs (Price, Kidd, Cohen, Pauls, & Leckman, 1985; Walkup et al., 1988). Although strong, the concordance rates of less than 100% for Tourette's in monozygotic twins opens the door for environmental factors that may influence the development of this disorder. Interestingly, in monozygotic twins who are not concordant for Tourette's, the twin with the lower birth weight is more likely to be the Tourette's twin (Leckman et al., 1987).

Role of the basal ganglia and associated neurochemistry. The bizarre behavior and sounds prompted early therapists to think that Tourette's had emotional or psychiatric roots. Today, these psychogenic theories have been replaced with theories related to neurotransmission within certain neuroanatomical areas (Singer & Walkup, 1991).

The basal ganglia seem to be intimately involved. One neuroimaging study reported a reduction in the size of certain areas of the basal ganglia

PANDAS Pediatric autoimmune neuropsychiatric disorders associated with streptococcal infection; thought to be the cause of Tourette's syndrome in some children.

in the left hemisphere (Peterson et al., 1993). Confirming its involvement, one study investigated five sets of monozygotic twins who both had Tourette's but differed in the severity of symptoms (Wolf et al., 1996). These researchers delivered a potent dopamine receptor antagonist (D_2 subtype) in different regions of the striatum. Binding of this antagonist was greatest in the caudate nucleus, a specific area within the basal ganglia, in each of the more severely affected twins (Robertson, 1996). These findings suggest that the more severely affected twins had more D_2 receptors in the striatum—possibly leading to more activation of this motor area, that is, frequent tics.

The observation that dopamine receptor antagonists decrease motor and vocal tics in Tourette's patients provides additional evidence that some dysfunction of the dopaminergic system, either directly or indirectly, is central to the disorder (Singer & Walkup, 1991). Endogenous opiates have also been implicated. Decreased responses of *dynorphin A* (a specific endogenous opioid) were observed in the fibers projecting to the globus pallidus in one Tourette's patient. And increased levels of this opiate have been observed in the cerebral spinal fluid of Tourette's patients (Haber, Kowall, Vonsattel, Bird, & Richardson, 1986; Leckman et al., 1988). Other neurotransmitter systems have been implicated, including GABA, serotonin, and noradrenaline, but more research is necessary to fully illuminate the role these substances play in the disorder.

Possible environmental factors. Some researchers maintain that infectious processes may play an integral role, at least in some Tourette's cases. The observation of a few children who developed Tourette's following streptococcal infection was the initial evidence that an infection may be involved. These children did not respond to the standard dopaminergic treatment but did respond to prednisone, a drug that suppresses immune reactivity.

These observations suggest that, in some cases, Tourette's syndrome is an autoimmune disorder that manifests itself in the basal ganglia (Kurlan, 1998). The research prompted the American Psychiatric Association to create a new category of Tourette's called **PANDAS** (pediatric autoimmune neuropsychiatric disorders associated with streptococcal infection). See Chapter Twelve for a full discussion of the role of the immune system in mental health.

Treatment for Tourette's Syndrome

Tourette's syndrome presents a fascinating combination of symptoms. The sudden movements have no meaning in some contexts but are directly related to the surrounding environment in others. Vocal tics range from meaningless jibberish to verbal tirades of the most bizarre, obscene nature. The repertoire of exhaustive tics may disappear in a calming or engaging environment only to reappear when the environmental context becomes more stressful.

Psychopharmacological therapy. Drugs that interrupt dopaminergic transmission are the most effective pharmacological defense against Tourette's symptoms. **Haloperidol** (Haldol), a dopamine blocker widely used to treat schizophrenia, is effective in suppressing tics in about 80% of Tourette's cases, but it leaves the patient with debilitating side effects such as sedation, depression, phobias, and even more movement abnormalities. Fewer side effects are seen with other dopamine-interfering drugs such as pimozide (Orap) and fluphenazine (Prolixin) (Singer & Walkup, 1991).

Clonidine (Catapres), a drug that interferes with presynaptic norepinephrine release, may prove helpful in patients with milder symptoms (Singer & Walkup, 1991). The original success rate of about 70%, however, has not been confirmed by other researchers (Goetz et al., 1987). Even so, the side effects are modest, consisting mostly of transient sedation.

Paul Sanberg and his colleagues at the University of South Florida are conducting research that may lead to a new therapeutic approach to Tourette's. In the late 1980s Sanberg conducted research in rats suggesting that nicotine enhances the effects of neuroleptic drugs such as haloperidol that alleviate psychotic symptoms, especially psychomotor activity, whereas nicotine delivered by itself had no effect on movement in the study. When Tourette's children were given nicotine gum as an adjunctive treatment, about 80% showed improvement. Unpleasant side effects (such as bitter taste and nausea), however, prompted most of the children to discontinue the gum (Sanberg et al., 1989).

In another study, these researchers showed that the gum even had some therapeutic value by itself, but only while it was actually being chewed (McConville et al., 1991). Using a nicotine patch instead of gum, they found a reduction in Tourette's symptoms in patients ranging from 9 to 15 years old who were not on other neuroleptic therapy (Silver, Shytle, Philipp, & Sanberg, 1996). The researchers initially thought that the nicotine enhanced the effects of haloperidol because it acted as a nicotine acetylcholine receptor agonist—as it does in smoking. They now believe, however, that the low doses of nicotine actually desensitize the receptor, acting more like a cholinergic antagonist instead of an agonist, that is, blocking instead of facilitating cholinergic activity.

With that in mind, Sanberg and colleagues tested the cholinergic receptor antagonist **mecamylamine** (Inversene) and found that in initial trials this medication reduces symptoms in Tourette's patients. The drug offers most benefit, however, when used as an adjunctive therapy with

haloperidol Neuroleptic drug that blocks dopaminergic activity; used in the treatment of schizophrenia and Tourette's syndrome.

mecamylamine Drug that acts as a chonlinergic receptor antagonist; currently being tested for use with Tourette's symptoms.

Mort Doran   COURTESY OF ELAINE DORAN

haloperidol (Silver, Shytle, Sheehan et al., 2001; Shytle, Silver, & Sanberg, 2000). If this drug becomes an accepted adjunctive therapy for Tourette's syndrome, it is likely to have far-reaching effects for other disorders influenced by the dopaminergic system, including OCD, attention deficit hyperactivity disorder, and schizophrenia.

Behavioral and cognitive strategies. A case presented by the Chapter One Investigator, Oliver Sacks (Box 1.2), is perhaps most representative of the contrasts that exist in this disorder. In *An Anthropologist on Mars*, (1995) Sacks describes a Tourette's patient, Mort Doran (in the book, the pseudonym Carl Bennett is used), who is a surgeon—and a pilot!

Doran is certainly a study in contrasts. At one point during the day he may be having a conversation with his colleagues during which he is in distorted positions and repeatedly tapping them on the shoulders with his toes as he discusses a relevant surgical case. The following hour, he strides confidently into the operating room and performs highly skilled, life-saving, two-hour surgery exhibiting no evidence of tics. The minute the operation is over, Doran returns to his ritualistic touching (tapping various objects and people), coupled with his obsession with symmetry (touching things in a particular symmetrical pattern).

Doran is now semiretired from his career in surgery. Each winter he enjoys teaching classes in anatomy and surgery at the University of Arizona Medical School. Although the pace of his career has slowed down, Doran reports that his tics are as active as ever; the distracting thoughts, however, have decreased.

Doran calms himself each morning by pedaling furiously on a stationary bike while smoking a pipe and reading a pathology book. He displays no tics and no compulsions during this time. It is easy to look at this calming behavior and apply some of the knowledge presented in this chapter and other areas of this book to hypothesize why this seemingly bizarre coping response may be effective.

Exercise is related to endogenous opioid release; the rhythmic circular motion and repeated pedaling may be related to increased serotonergic release and a subsequent reduction in anxiety (more on this in Chapter Eight). Nicotine in the pipe tobacco may potentiate the effect of other medication or at least alter the cholinergic receptors in a way that calms the tics, and the pathology text provides a cognitive activity that directs Doran's thoughts away from the impending tics. We cannot prove that any of these proposed therapeutic mechanisms work, but theoretically this surgeon's self-prescribed treatment may be just what the doctor ordered!

Summary

Anxiety Disorders: An Overview

Although most of us try to avoid it, anxiety plays an important role in our lives: it directs our attention toward potentially harmful stimuli. Some of us direct our attention toward stimuli that do not pose a reasonable threat, and the anxiety response becomes more of a danger to mental health than the initial perceived threat. At times this kind of anxiety is directed toward a specific threatening stimulus, as in phobias, and at times it is difficult for individuals to pinpoint the source of their debilitating anxiety, as in generalized anxiety disorder. Severe acute attacks of anxiety are observed in individuals experiencing panic attacks, as they fear they are suffocating and frantically attempt to reestablish physiological homeostasis.

Obsessive-Compulsive Disorder

OCD is multifaceted, consisting of recurring, upsetting thoughts (obsessions) and ritualistic behaviors (compulsions). Areas of the brain involved in anxiety, movement, and reward are probably involved in OCD. The proposed OCD neuroanatomical loop is composed of primarily the orbitofrontal cortex, the cingulate cortex, the thalamus, and the caudate nucleus. Other areas such as the amygdala and nucleus accumbens may also play a role. Glutamate and GABA are the principle neurotransmitters that directly communicate among the components of the OCD circuit. Dopamine and serotonin act as neuromodulators for the synaptic activity within the OCD loop.

The consistency of many compulsions observed in OCD patients (for example, checking, cleaning, grooming) and in animal models, coupled with the relationship of these rituals to survival or fitness, suggest that animals are biologically predisposed toward OCD-like responding. Adaptive responding transforms into excessive responding when humans or other animals find themselves experiencing threatening or disrupting stimuli and/or environments. Some of the compulsions observed in OCD have been compared with species-specific behaviors in animals known as fixed action patterns. The involvement of the striatum in both FAPs and compulsions provides further evidence that compulsions may be remnants of species-specific behaviors that at one time had significant relevance for our survival.

Therapies aimed at modifying neurochemicals, neuroanatomy, and behavior and/or cognitions have all been moderately successful for OCD patients. Antidepressant drugs that enhance the activation of the serotonergic synapse (SRIs, for example) are effective in suppressing OCD symptoms in some patients. In severe cases, neurosurgical techniques that disrupt various components of the OCD loop have proved effective. Cognitive-behavioral therapies such as exposure and response prevention (ERP) yield success rates that rival pharmacological rates—with fewer side effects. Clinicians must consider all relevant components of OCD to create an optimal treatment regime for each patient.

Tourette's Syndrome

Patients suffering from Tourette's syndrome exhibit both motor and vocal tics. The basal ganglia constitute the most likely neuroanatomical area involved in the activation of the tic response. Excessive dopaminergic activity seems to be a causal agent in Tourette's; dopamine antagonists provide relief of tics in some patients. In addition, mecamylamine, a cholinergic receptor antagonist, is currently being investigated for efficacy as an adjunctive treatment for Tourette's. Environmental factors such as streptococcal infection may also cause some cases of Tourette's. It is possible that several cognitive-behavioral strategies may also benefit an individual, for example, by altering neurochemicals through exercise, diverted attention, and relaxation techniques.

Key Terms

comorbidity (p. 228)

tics (p. 229)

generalized anxiety disorder (GAD) (p. 229)

panic disorder (p. 230)

obsessive-compulsive disorder (OCD) (p. 230)

obsessions (p. 230)

compulsions (p. 230)

cingulum (p. 233)

entorhinal cortex (p. 233)

OCD loop (p. 234)

orbitofrontal cortex (OFC) (p. 235)

lateralization (p. 239)

behavioral addiction (p. 240)

activity-stress paradigm (p. 240)

fixed action pattern (FAP) (p. 243)

superstitious behavior (p. 246)

clomipramine (p. 247)

anxiolytics (p. 248)

stereotaxic instrument (p. 248)

exposure and response prevention (ERP) (p. 250)

Tourette's syndrome (p. 253)

PANDAS (p. 256)

haloperidol (p. 257)

mecamylamine (p. 257)

For Further Consideration

Dolberg, O. T., Iancu, I., Sasson, Y., & Zohar, J. (1996). The pathogenesis and treatment of obsessive-compulsive disorder. *Clinical Neuropharmacology, 19*(2), 129–147. Although this article describes several treatment strategies, it focuses on pharmacologic treatments, including a crtitical analysis of several popular drugs used in the treatment of OCD.

Jenike, M. A., Rauch, S. L., Cummings, J. L., Savage, C. R., & Goodman, W. K. (1996). Recent developments in neurobiology of obsessive-compulsive disorder. *Journal of Clinical Psychiatry, 57*(10), 492–503. This article highlights a symposium held by the American Psychiatric Association at which some of the most respected OCD researchers presented their latest findings. Topics include neuroimaging, neuropharmacology, and the neuropsychology of OCD.

LeDoux, Joseph. (1996). *The emotional brain: The mysterious underpinnings of emotional life.* New York: Simon & Schuster. Emotions are an important factor in many psychological disorders, especially in OCD and Tourette's. In this book, LeDoux explores the origins of human emotions. He also describes the neural network systems that underlie the emotional response.

Marks, I. (1997). Behaviour therapy for obsessive-compulsive disorder: A decade of progress. *Canadian Journal of Psychiatry, 42,* 1021–1027. This article is a wonderful review of the studies that have tested the effectiveness of exposure and ritual prevention (ERP). Many issues are reviewed, including the long-term effects, value as an adjunctive therapy with antidepressant medication, and cost-effectiveness of behavioral therapy.

Rapaport, J. L. (1991). *The boy who couldn't stop washing: The experience and treatment of obsessive-compulsive disorder.* New York: Signet. This book, written for a popular audience, is a comprehensive introduction to the world of OCD. Dr. Rapaport's descriptions of her fascinating patients give this disorder a human face.

Sacks, O. (1995). *An anthropologist on Mars.* New York: Knopf. Dr. Sacks is unmatched in his ability to describe the adventures of the human mind and its underlying neural mechanisms. In the chapter "A Surgeon's Life," you are exposed to the daily activities and challenges faced by someone with Tourette's. The fact that this Tourette's patient is a surgeon makes the chapter unforgettable.

Schwartz, J. M. (with Beyette, B.) (1996). *Brain lock: Free yourself from obsessive-compulsive behavior.* New York: HarperCollins. After convincing his readers that OCD is a brain disorder, Schwartz presents persuasive cases and evidence that cognition and behavior can influence the OCD neurocircuitry. His step-by-step cognitive-behavioral therapy has proven to be quite successful for some patients.

Chapter Eight

Mood Disorders

Connections

Foods and Moods

After a particularly bad day, do you turn to food to help relieve your anxiety and make you feel better? Growing up, grandmother's homemade vegetable soup, chicken and dumplings, and peach cobbler were dietary artillery against the blues. You'll probably agree that going home after a stressful exam and eating your favorite food does wonders for your mood.

The relationship between food and mood is a popular notion in today's society. After collecting uplifting life stories of dozens of people, Jack Canfield and Mark Hansen, both motivational speakers, thought long and hard about the best title for their optimistic anthology. It is no great surprise that they likened the ability of their heartwarming stories to . . . what else . . . the most famous "comfort" food—chicken soup. The *Chicken Soup for the Soul* series has sold over 50 million copies and won numerous awards. It seems that the connection between food and an elevated mood is a natural association easily understood by the book-consuming public. Speaking more directly to the effectiveness of food as regulators of our mood, books such as Amanda Geary's *The Food and Mood Handbook* are popular sellers these days.

The notion that a favorite, familiar food warms the soul and heals emotional pain sounds reasonable, but is there empirical evidence to support such a claim? In the 1950s, it was discovered that drugs leading to depleted levels of monoamines (serotonin, norepinephrine, and dopamine) caused depressionlike symptoms, whereas drugs leading to increases in these neurotransmitters produced antidepressant effects in patients. In 1974, Fernstrom and Wurtman demonstrated that the consumption of foods rich in tryptophan (a dietary amino acid that is a precursor to serotonin in the brain), such as bananas, milk, and turkey, increase levels of serotonin in the brain. Because carbohydrate consumption is necessary for the brain's utilization of serotonin, it is troubling to consider the effect the low-carbohydrate Atkins diet is having on millions of dieters in the United States and Europe. According to Judith Wurtman, Director of the Program in Women's Health at the MIT clinical Research center, "Carbohydrates are essential for effective dieting and good mood, and filling up on fatty foods like bacon and cheese makes you tired, lethargic, and apathetic—an emotional zombie" (MIT News Office, 2004).

If you have ever fallen asleep after a hefty turkey dinner at Thanksgiving you can attest to tryptophan's effect. Further, this finding gave credence to the old saying that drinking milk before going to bed facilitates relaxation and sleep. Since Fernstrom and Wurtman's seminal findings, some doctors are recommending that their patients take a nutritional supplement, 5-hydroxytryptophan (5-HTP), a compound naturally produced by tryptophan in the body, because it has a significant boosting effect on serotonergic levels in the central nervous system (Murray, 1998).

In an interesting line of research at the National Institutes of Health, Joseph Hibbeln and Maribeth Champoux are investigating a different type of connection between foods and moods. They are interested in the impact of removing docosahexaenoic acid (DHA), an omega-3 fatty acid that is highly concentrated in the central nervous system, from the diets of infants. DHA is present in all mammalian (including human) breast milk but, because of negative marketing factors such as a short shelf-life, DHA has only recently been included in commercially available infant formulas in the United States (Austad et al., 2003). The removal of such a product from the diet may have had a significant impact on mental health: research has suggested that rates of depression are higher in populations that consume low levels of omega-3 fatty acids.

Are individuals who received a diet devoid of DHA susceptible to depression later on? Hibbeln and Champoux examined this question by manipulating

Working at the National Institutes of Mental Health, scientist Maribeth Champoux feeds a young rhesus monkey a special diet to determine the importance of docosahexaenoic (DHA) acid on development.

She gently assesses the infant for motor capabilities and emotional responsiveness.
COURTESY OF MARTIN F. KRIETE

the formula fed to infant rhesus monkeys. Most recently, they found greater motor deficits in the DHA-deprived animals than in the supplemented-formula group. Anxiety and temperment scores, however, were not affected by the diet. Further research will verify the influence of DHA consumption in human infants by determining any long-lasting effects of DHA deprivation in bottle-fed babies (Champoux et al., 2002).

Many connections exist between food and moods (see Chapter Thirteen for more on this topic). Neurochemistry is altered by our diets, and we certainly learn to associate certain feelings with the consumption of certain foods. Thus, through cognitive expectations and neurochemistry, we may be able to temporarily curb the blues with a generous helping of our favorite comfort food.

We begin this chapter by discussing the diverse variables that may contribute to a person's susceptibility to mood disorders. No single, logical, neat, or simplistic explanation exists, but it is this very fact that makes the quest for understanding the mood disorders so compelling. Because humans evolved in an ever-changing environment, it seems adaptive that our moods (temporary emotional states) evolved to help us interact effectively with the environment's changing demands. For example, the pleasureable moods associated with food consumption lead to foraging and the anxiety produced by being in proximity to a larger more aggressive animal may lead to avoidance of aggression and physical harm. To be effective, this must be a plastic system influenced by multiple internal and external factors—neurobiological, social, and environmental.

Problems arise when mood does not fluctuate in synchrony with environmental demands. Symptoms associated with mood disorders involve neuroanatomical areas from the brainstem to the prefrontal cortex. Although serotonin has been considered the primary contributing neurochemical in producing depressive symptoms, several leading researchers suggest that this system may be secondary to dopaminergic modulation or to other neurophysiological events, such as neurogenesis.

With so many contributing paths leading to depression, it is not surprising that multiple roads to treatment exist. Although a single drug therapy that is equally efficacious for everyone suffering from depression would be more than welcome, current research suggests that finding such a single treatment is as unlikely as finding one size of shoe that fits everyone. Cognitive-behavioral therapy or conjunctive therapies that involve more than one approach may offer more long-term potential, as they probably modulate the global neurobiological system underlying mood expression as opposed to selected neurochemicals.

MOOD DISORDERS: AN OVERVIEW

Most of the time we are able to shift moods effortlessly, and our oscillating moods contribute to the rich tapestry of our emotional lives. We laugh when our friends tell us jokes, we cry when we lose a loved one. In fact, we would be considered abnormal if we failed to respond to these situations with the appropriate emotions. We sometimes engage in behaviors for the sole purpose of temporarily changing our moods: We may pay money to sit through a sad movie or attend a comedian's performance. Although these temporary shifts in mood probably have little meaning for the ongoing reality of our lives, it may be reinforcing just to experience a shift in mood.

mood (affective) disorders
Disturbances of mood typically accompanied by inappropriate expression of pleasure or misery; some people experience vigorous swings between the two extremes.

major depressive disorder
One of the most common psychiatric illnesses, occurring in about 17% of the population, with females suffering at about twice the rate of males and characterized by one or more major depressive episodes of at least two weeks and at least four additional symptoms of depression (for example, sleep disturbances, loss of concentration, decreased energy, guilt).

Mood, or **affective, disorders** emerge when one experiences difficulty in changing or controlling mood states. In some ways, mood disorders are like a car transmission that is stuck in one gear. Different moods help us respond and evaluate our lives at any given moment. These moods, however, lose their value if they do not correspond appropriately to the demands of life. If our mood gets stuck in one position, we are unable to function effectively.

Although we are focusing in this chapter only on **major depressive disorder** (characterized by more than one episode of severe depression) and **bipolar disorder** (characterized by mood swings from mania, or euphoric states, to depression), they are but two variations on the diverse menu of mood diagnoses. Table 8.1 lists brief descriptions of the range of mood disorders included in DSM-IV-TR. This range, however, has not always been recognized. According to the early work of Emil Kraepelin (the pioneer clinical neuroscientist introduced in Chapter Two), a century ago, any disruption of mood states was diagnosed as manic-depressive insanity (Healy, 1997).

[Table 8.1]
DSM-IV-TR Range of Mood Disorder Diagnoses

Major Depressive Disorder is characterized by one or more Major Depressive Episodes (i.e., at least 2 weeks of depressed mood or loss of interest accompanied by at least four additional symptoms of depression).

Dysthymic Disorder is characterized by at least 2 years of depressed mood for more days than not, accompanied by additional depressive symptoms that do not meet criteria for a Major Depressive Episode.

Depressive Disorder Not Otherwise Specified is included for coding disorders with depressive features that do not meet criteria for Major Depressive Disorder, Dysthymic Disorder, Adjustment Disorder with Depressed Mood, or Adjustment Disorder with Mixed Anxiety and Depressed Mood (or depressive symptoms about which there is inadequate or contradictory information.)

Bipolar I Disorder is characterized by one or more Manic or Mixed Episodes, usually accompanied by Major Depressive Episodes.

Bipolar II Disorder is characterized by one or more Major Depressive Episodes accompanied by at least one Hypomanic Episode.

Cyclothymic Disorder is characterized by at least 2 years of numerous periods of hypomanic symptoms that do not

meet criteria for a Manic Episode and numerous periods of depressive symptoms that do not meet criteria for a Major Depressive Episode.

Bipolar Disorder Not Otherwise Specified is included for coding disorders with bipolar features that do not meet criteria for any of the specific Bipolar Disorders defined in this section (or bipolar symptoms about which there is inadequate or contradictory information).

Mood Disorder Due to a General Medical Condition is characterized by a prominent and persistent disturbance in mood that is judged to be a direct physiological consequence of a general medical condition.

Substance-Induced Mood Disorder is characterized by a prominent and persistent disturbance in mood that is judged to be a direct physiological consequence of a drug of abuse, a medication, another somatic treatment for depression, or toxin exposure.

Mood Disorder Not Otherwise Specified is included for coding disorders with mood symptoms that do not meet the criteria for any specific Mood Disorder and in which it is difficult to choose between **Depressive Disorder Not Otherwise Specified** and **Bipolar Disorder Not Otherwise Specified** (e.g., acute agitation).

APA, 2000, pp. 345–346.

[Table 8.2]

DSM-IV-TR Criteria for Major Depressive Episode

A. Five (or more) of the following symptoms have been present during the same 2-week period and represent a change from previous functioning; at least one of the symptoms is either (1) depressed mood or (2) loss of interest or pleasure

Note: Do not include symptoms that are clearly due to a general medical condition, or mood-incongruent delusions or hallucinations.

(1) Depressed mood most of the day, nearly every day, as indicated by either subjective report (e.g., feels sad or empty) or observation made by others (e.g., appears tearful). Note: In children and adolescents, can be irritable mood.

(2) Markedly diminished interest or pleasure in all, or almost all, activities most of the day, nearly every day (as indicated by either subjective account or observation made by others)

(3) Significant weight loss when not dieting or weight gain (e.g., a change of more than 5% of body weight in a month), or decrease or increase in appetite nearly every day. Note: In children, consider failure to make expected weight gains.

(4) Insomnia or hypersomnia nearly every day

(5) Psychomotor agitation or retardation nearly every day (observable by others, not merely subjective feelings of restlessness or being slowed down)

(6) Fatigue or loss of energy nearly every day

(7) Feelings of worthlessness or excessive or inappropriate guilt (which may be delusional) nearly every day (not merely self-reproach or guilt about being sick)

(8) Diminished ability to think or concentrate, or indecisiveness, nearly every day (either by subjective account or as observed by others)

(9) Recurrent thoughts of death (not just fear of dying), recurrent suicidal ideation without a specific plan, or a suicide attempt or a specific plan for committing suicide

B. The symptoms do not meet criteria for a Mixed Episode.

C. The symptoms cause clinically significant distress or impairment in social, occupational, or other important areas of functioning.

D. The symptoms are not due to the direct physiological effects of a substance (e.g., a drug of abuse, a medication) or a general medical condition (e.g., hypothyroidism).

E. The symptoms are not better accounted for by Bereavement, i.e., after the loss of a loved one, the symptoms persist for longer than 2 months or are characterized by marked functional impairment, morbid preoccupation with worthlessness, suicidal ideation, psychotic symptoms, or psychomotor retardation.

APA, 2000, p. 356.

bipolar disorder Mood disorder characterized by episodes of mania interspersed with episodes of depression. This disorder occurs in about 1% to 1.6% of the population and is sometimes referred to as manic depression.

depression Mood disorder characterized by feelings of sadness, diminished pleasure, alterations in sleep, fatigue, difficulty concentrating, and feelings of worthlessness; several variations exist (for example, major depression, dysthymic disorder).

The most prominent signs of **depression** are a profound sadness and a drastic reduction in one's activity levels. As originally described by Kraepelin in 1921, mood disorders differ from disorders such as schizophrenia because, rather than taking a continuous, progressively worsening course, they follow an intermittent pattern, fluctuating, for example, between bouts of mania and bouts of depression (Post & Weiss, 1999). Even without treatment, a person suffering from depression usually enters a recovery phase after about four months (APA, 2000). (See Table 8.2 for dignostic material on major depression.)

MAJOR DEPRESSION IN CONTEXT

Research has uncovered interesting individual differences, from population and cultural factors to genetics and environmental exposures, related to susceptibility to mood disorders. Examining possible evolutionary explanations for changes in moods and how they might relate to evolved survival strategies has helped researchers understand individual differences.

Sex Differences and Sociocultural Influences

Major depressive disorder is perhaps the most common mental illness, with a lifetime prevalence of about 17% in the U.S. population (Fava & Kendler, 2000). One interesting feature of depressive illnesses is the disproportionate rate of this disorder in women. Specifically, it has been estimated that 21% of women will experience an episode of depression in their lifetimes compared to a lifetime incidence of 13% in men (Yonkers, Kando, Hamilton, & Halbreich, 2000). Further, women experience depressive episodes about twice as frequently as men (American Psychiatric Association [APA], 2000).

The underlying causes for this discrepancy between the sexes remains unclear, but likely involve mechanisms described in Chapter Six. Current research on the potential mechanisms underlying this gender variation emphasizes differences in stress responsivity, and it may offer some answers in the near future (Cousino-Klein & Corwin, 2002). Further, now that researchers know that sex differences exist in the brain's metabolic rates of utilizing some antidepressant drugs—in addition to differential rates of the disorder in males and females—all new drugs are tested on both sexes. Originally, only males were examined to sidestep testing women whose fluctuations in reproductive hormones during their childbearing years complicate research.

Although depression can be observed in virtually every culture, Joseph Hibbeln and Norman Salem of the National Institute of Alcohol Abuse and Alcoholism (1995) have presented a fascinating hypothesis that attempts to explain some differences in the rates of depression across cultures. Their theory centers on the dietary consumption of fish. Obviously, it is not likely that a condition as complex as depression is regulated solely by the amount of fish we eat, but this intriguing hypothesis has value in explaining some of the cultural differences that exist in rates of depression, so let's explore it a bit further.

Hibbeln and Salem (1995) argue that humans evolved on a diet that consisted of fewer saturated fats (fats that are solid at room temperature, like butter) and more polyunsaturated fats (liquid at room temperature, like olive oil) than Americans currently consume. Of the polyunsaturated fats we do consume, we eat more n-6 polyunsaturates than n-3 polyunsaturates; n-3 polyunsaturates, which are found in the meat of wild and free-ranging animals, were also a bigger part of our ancestors' diets than they are of ours. In fact, Hibbeln and Salem argue that societies that consume more fish, which have high levels of n-3 polyunsaturates, are less likely to experience depression than nonfish-consuming societies.

In one study, rates of depression for North Americans and Europeans were ten times higher than for a Taiwanese population that consumed more fish. Rates in the United States were about five times higher than rates in Hong Kong where fish is consumed more than in the United States. In Japan, where fish consumption is high, low rates of depression have been observed; among the elderly in one Japanese fishing village, the depression rate was observed to be 0% (Hibbeln, Umhau, George, & Salem, 1997). In a related study, a community in Finland was surveyed for depression and consumption of fish (Tanskanen & Hibbeln, 2001). The researchers found that the residents of the community who consumed more fish were less likely to experience depression and were also less likely to have suicidal thoughts.

Another factor influencing the occurrence of depression in a particular population is related to the level of anxiety its members experience. For example, the literature suggests that the sick and the aged are at higher risk for depression (Schwartz, Gunzelmann, Hinz, & Brahler, 2001). Theo Sandfort and his colleagues at Utrecht University in the Netherlands have been investigating rates of depression in homosexual populations, who are likely to experience high levels of anxiety resulting from increased social isolation (Sandfort, de Graaf, Bijl, & Schnabel, 2001). In a study of more than 7000 subjects, these researchers reported that homosexual men are more likely to experience depression than heterosexual men, and homosexual women are more likely to develop addiction disorders than heterosexual women. In a recent interview conducted by Andrew Solomon (2001), Sandfort described additional research suggesting that rates of depression are higher for closeted homosexuals than for those who are more open about their orientation.

Genetic Influences and Evolutionary Factors

Studies conducted with identical and fraternal twins certainly indicate a strong genetic contribution in mood disorders. Concordance rates for mood disorders in identical twins has been reported as high as 60% to 70% compared with rates of 20% for fraternal twins (Sanders, Detera-Wadleigh, & Gershon, 1999).

The search for a single depression gene is an ongoing endeavor. It is looking more and more likely that a whole set of "blue" genes contributes to depression (Stahl, 2000). Although there is convincing evidence that individuals inherit a susceptibility for mood disorders, the concordance rate is well under 100%, so the environment appears to be a significant contributor—even the ultimate trigger—for the manifestation of depressive disorders.

Evolutionary explanations for moods offer clues about how environmental factors contribute to mood disorders. Is it adaptive that so many people suffer from depression? Or is depression a pathological condition not related to a specific adaptive function? It appears that Charles Darwin struggled with these questions well over a century ago: "Pain or suffering of any kind, if long continued, causes depression and lessens the power of action; yet it is well adapted to make a creature guard itself against any great or sudden evil" (*The Life and Letters of Charles Darwin,* 1887).

Evolutionary theories are intriguing and offer possible explanations of depressive-like behaviors, but they must be approached with caution. Obviously, once an evolutionary change has occurred, it is extremely challenging to secure empirical evidence to support such proposed evolutionary theories. Randolph Neese of the Institute for Social Research at the University of Michigan has long pondered the evolutionary adaptiveness of many conditions, including depression (Neese, 2000). He is intrigued by the observation that depressive-like behaviors, or low moods, may have evolved in social animals as a means to obtain help from others—such as a baby crying to get the attention of the mother to provide nourishment and protection. But it is not clear that the passive withdrawal that so often characterizes severe adult depression consistently results in help being offered.

Thinking more about the adaptiveness of low mood, Neese contends that they probably evolved to steer animals away from sources of threat that might result in bodily harm and thus compromise their viability and subsequent reproductive fitness. For example, though a deer may be starving, in conditions of extremely low temperatures and deep snow it is adaptive to depress the urge to forage because the deer will save vital energy by sitting motionless until the conditions for foraging become more favorable. In Chapter Twelve, we offer evidence indicating that low moods might be adaptive to the extent that they keep sick people at rest when their bodies are extremely vulnerable because of a challenged immune system.

Thus, moods may serve to upregulate our motivation when a payoff is predicted and downregulate our motivation when the behavior will likely lead to a greater cost than gain. Neese is quick to point out that, although low moods and a degree of depression may be adaptive in some contexts, we should not let this distract us from the reality that major depression is one of the most serious medical problems facing Americans today.

In a book edited by Leon Sloman and Paul Gilbert (2000), the role of subordination and defeat in the evolution of depressive disorders is considered. As complex social behaviors evolved hundreds of millions of years ago, submissive behaviors such as defeat, flight, infantile appeals, and submissive displays coevolved to facilitate the social dynamics of aggression and affiliation. Although animals or people exhibiting submissive behavior are often viewed as weak and extremely vulnerable, expressing submissive behavior may also be viewed as a strategic defense that will prolong the animal's life. According to Paul MacLean (1990), the featured Investigator in Chapter Three, "a passive response (a submissive display) to an aggressive display may make it possible under most circumstances to avoid unnecessary, and sometimes mortal, conflict. Hence it could be argued that the submissive display is the most important of all displays because without it numerous individuals might not survive" (p. 235).

If you were a late bloomer (physically speaking), frequently bullied by more aggressive students in your school, you might have prolonged your life (or at least maintained the composition of your facial features) by demonstrating submissive rather than aggressive behavior. The submissive episodes might not have contributed to high self-esteem, but, in keeping with Neese's and MacLean's aforementioned views, as a strategy they probably kept you from bodily harm. Gilbert argues, however, that once individuals pass adolescence and enter adulthood, where it is more difficult to either fight or flee in complex social relationships, they sometimes switch from active submission to depressive demobilization, a condition characterized by a feeling of being trapped, spiraling into more depressive symptoms.

TRACING THE NEUROBIOLOGICAL ROOTS OF DEPRESSION

Once mental health researchers established that drugs effectively treat some forms of depression, they placed emphasis on the neurochemistry of the disorder. Now that neuroimaging technology allows researchers to glimpse the depressed brain, the neuroanatomical circuits involved are also being identified and mapped out. It is becoming increasingly apparent that the brain's plasticity—its ability to restructure itself—may also underlie a person's susceptibility to depression. Finally, an individual's cognitive responses to environmental changes may also contribute to the onset of a depressed mental state.

prefrontal cortex (PFC) Area of the frontal cortex involved in many higher functions. Evidence suggests that atrophy of neurons or compromised activity in this area may lead to symptoms of depression.

Depression's Neuroanatomical Circuit

Before the introduction of neuroimaging technology, neuroanatomical research was restricted to postmortem analysis of volumetric measures of specific brain structures or numbers of neurons, glial cells, or specific receptors in an area of interest. Although these studies are still valuable, we can now use neuroimaging to observe the activity of the brain in real time and *in vivo* and suggests a depression circuit in the brain (Figure 8.1).

[Figure 8.1]
Neuroanatomical circuit of depression. NEMEROFF, 1998; ADAPTED FROM RESSLER & NEMEROFF, 2000.

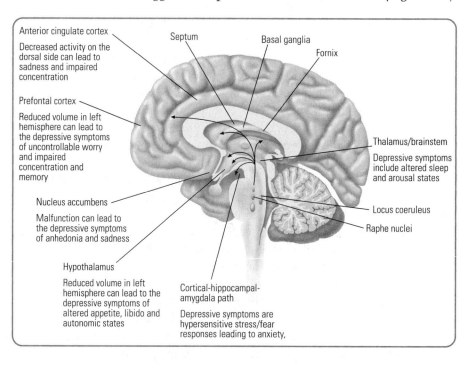

Anterior cingulate cortex
Decreased activity on the dorsal side can lead to sadness and impaired concentration

Septum

Basal ganglia

Fornix

Prefrontal cortex
Reduced volume in left hemisphere can lead to the depressive symptoms of uncontrollable worry and impaired concentration and memory

Thalamus/brainstem
Depressive symptoms include altered sleep and arousal states

Nucleus accumbens
Malfunction can lead to the depressive symptoms of anhedonia and sadness

Locus coeruleus

Raphe nuclei

Hypothalamus
Reduced volume in left hemisphere can lead to the depressive symptoms of altered appetite, libido and autonomic states

Cortical-hippocampal-amygdala path
Depressive symptoms are hypersensitive stress/fear responses leading to anxiety,

Prefrontal cortex (PFC). Both postmortem and neuroimaging data support the involvement of the **prefrontal cortex** in major depression. Postmortem studies indicate both cellular atrophy and cellular loss in this area of the frontal cortex that is involved in higher cognitive functions (Rajkowska, 2000). Focusing on the living brain, some studies indicate that the PFC in depressed patients has decreased blood flow and metabolism when compared with healthy controls. This decrease in activity and resources is probably related to a reduced PFC volume in the left hemisphere.

The PFC and its surround are a prime association area of the cortex, meaning that it receives information from a number of brain areas, enabling this advanced brain structure to associate many different types of information in arriving at a solution or conclusion to some query. In fact, the PFC has been described as the *crucial convergence zone* because of its two very important roles: sustaining attention to the animal's external world and receiving important information from the limbic cortical pathways that convey information about internal states such as mood and immune functioning (Liotti & Mayberg, 2001). Rajkowska (2000) describes the PFC as the common site of neuropathology in major and bipolar depression.

Just to give you a taste of how complicated nueroimaging data can be, when scientists control for the reduced PFC size in the left hemisphere, PET data show that metabolic rates are actually increased (Drevets, 2000). This finding makes sense when we consider that some antidepressants ultimately result in decreased PFC metabolic activity (Drevets, 1999). In fact, one study looked at the effects of five different antidepressant medications on PFC activity and observed decreases in just 48 hours. Interestingly, no decrease in PFC activity was observed in patients who failed to experience therapeutic recovery from using the antidepressants (Cook & Leuchter, 2001). More recently, however, it was reported that cognitive-behavioral therapy leading to clinical improvement was accompanied by decreased PFC activity. The authors noted the contrast between this outcome and the effect of the antidepressant paroxitine (Paxil), another clinically effective treatment, on depression. In this case, the antidepressant increased PFC activity. Thus, the PFC seems to play a critical role in depression, although the specific nature of this role has yet to be clearly defined (Goldapple et al., 2004).

Hippocampus and amygdala. The PFC has well-established reciprocal connections with the hippocampus, as well as other areas in the limbic system. Recall from Chapter Five that chronic stress leads to decreased hippocampal volume, suggesting its integral role in the stress response. Accordingly, MRI studies of depressed patients who have been in remission for at least four months have shown reductions in hippocampal volume—with the larger reduction consistently occurring in the left hemisphere (Bremner et al., 2000; Sheline, Wang, Gado, Csernansky, & Vannier, 1996).

A multitude of theories has been proposed to explain both stress- and depression-induced atrophy including neurotoxicity, glial cell loss, and inhibited neurogenesis (Sheline, 2000). The hippocampal volume reduction observed in depression, however, does not seem to be an immediate effect. Younger depressed patients in their thirties and forties do not show the atrophy that their depressed counterparts in their late sixties show in MRI scans (Vakili et al., 2000). Thus, if the hippocampus is indeed grossly altered following chronic depression, it is very likely that communication with the PFC is also disrupted—leading to altered neuronal functioning in this circuit.

[Box 8.1]

A Case in Point

Andrew Solomon's Noonday Demon

An observer of Andrew Solomon's childhood in the 1960s probably would not predict that life-threatening depressive breakdowns lay ahead. Although Solomon received support from his parents and brother at home, he endured bantering from other kids in elementary and middle school because he had no real athletic ability. However, he managed to graduate from high school with many friends and an increased sense of self-confidence. He attended Yale University, where he studied hard and played hard and made many lifelong friends. Following graduation, he went to London to acquire a master's degree and then, uneventfully, commenced a career as a writer.

You may wish your life had been so "all-American" in young adulthood. Solomon's life, unfortunately, subsequently took a turn for the worse as he experienced the torturous symptoms of major depression. Although looking back Solomon vividly remembers several times during his childhood and adolescence in which he experienced acute anxiety, at the time of his first depressive breakdown he was totally unprepared for a battle with depression for the rest of his life. In fact, the depression didn't invade Solomon's emotional life until after he had experienced several emotional challenges. The most traumatic challenge occurred with the death of his mother, who suffered from ovarian cancer. He appeared to work through this tremendous loss, bought a new house, and was writing for *The New Yorker*.

In 1994, Solomon published his first novel, entitled *A Stone Boat*. Although the book received praise and was a runner-up for the LA Times First Fiction Prize, Solomon was unaffected by these exciting events. He kept going through the motions of life but was undoubtedly heading for what would be the first of three depression-related breakdowns. Already emotionally vulnerable since the death of his mother, the physical event of kidney stones, which led to severe pain, might have been a triggering event for his subsequent descent into emotional turmoil. He wrote of this time, "It is not pleasant to experience decay, to find yourself exposed to the rav-

Andrew Solomon
TIMOTHY GREENFIELD-SANDERS

ages of an almost daily rain, and to know that you are turning into something feeble, that more and more of you will blow off with the first strong wind, making you less and less" (2001, p. 17).

After establishing an emotional balance with antidepressant medication and psychotherapy, Solomon regretfully decided to cease his medication—cold turkey. The sudden disruption of neurochemicals precipitated a second breakdown, which was so severe that he decided to try to acquire AIDS by having unprotected sex with strangers so that his body would be as sick as he felt his mind was at the time. Fortunately, Solomon's strategic attempt at prolonged suicide failed. His third breakdown occurred in 1999 following the breakup of a relationship and, once again, acute pain related to a dislocated shoulder. With the proper mix of medication, rest, social support, and psychotherapy, he was able to bounce back from this breakdown sooner than from the earlier ones.

Solomon's depression left such a mark on his emotional life that he decided to write a comprehensive book chronicling his experience and those of other individuals suffering from depression. *The Noonday Demon: An Atlas of Depression* has been described as a "definitive" work on depression. Solomon spent five years writing the book, and now he is trying to make a difference in the lives of those suffering from this disease by increasing awareness in other ways.

Solomon strongly believes that more financial assistance and/or insurance coverage should be provided for the treatment of mental illness, reporting that his first breakdown cost him five months of work, $4000 worth of visits to the psychopharmacologist, $10,000 for psychotherapy, and $3500 for medication. It currently costs him about $20,000 a year to maintain his mental health with an antidepressant cocktail consisting of Effexor, Wellbutrin, BuSpar, and Zyprexa, as well as other prophylactics such as talk therapy and exercise. As he pointed out in his book, only a limited segment of the population can afford to defend themselves against depression.

The hippocampus and amygdala are actually continuous structures, so it is difficult to imagine that a significant disruption in hippocampal functioning (as observed in chronic stress and depression) would not affect the amygdala or vice versa. Indeed, a few studies also show an effect of major depression on the amygdala: not a decrease, but an increase in volume (Bremner et al., 2000). A modest relationship was found in these patients: the smaller the hippocampal volume, the larger the amygdala (in the right hemisphere, in this case).

It is not clear how depression leads to a larger amygdala. Bremner suggests that, because of the amygdala's role in emotional processing, the demands on its cells may be increased, thereby leading to an increased volume. PET scans of depressed patients have shown increased activity in both the prefrontal cortex and the amygdala (Nemeroff, 1998). The increased activity in both areas is not surprising since the amygdala communicates directly with the PFC. Whereas investigating the neural inputs and outputs of the amygdala is important, it is also worthwhile to document information transfer with another limbic structure, the hypothalamus. The hypothalamus plays a role in triggering the release of stress hormones that contribute to the damage to the hippocampus just described.

The PFC and amygdala areas share extensive connections with the mediodorsal nucleus of the thalamus and ventral striatum (the ventromedial caudate and the nucleus accumbens). Neuroimaging and postmortem studies show that thalamic and ventral striatum volumes are significantly decreased in patients suffering from major depression (Baumann et al., 1999; Krishnan et al., 1992). Further, metabolic rates are reduced in the caudate of depressed patients, and blood flow is decreased in depressive relapse when patients are subjected to tryptophan depletion (Drevets, 2000).

Cingulate cortex. One brain area that relays information from the limbic areas to the PFC is the **anterior cingulate cortex,** the front portion of the older lobe of the cerebral cortex that surrounds the corpus callosum, introduced in Chapter 7. The anterior cingulate cortex is involved in attentional processing in healthy individuals (Liotti & Mayberg, 2001). But research focusing on the involvement of this area in depression has pointed to decreased activity in the dorsal anterior cingulate.

Mario Liotti at the University of Texas in San Antonio and Helen Mayberg at the University of Toronto describe some interesting methodologies for further exploring the role of the cingulate cortex in depression. Because a hallmark symptom of depression is profound sadness, one way to focus on the brain areas involved is to simply induce sadness by having subjects read rehearsed autobiographical scripts intended to elicit either a sad or neutral mood.

anterior cingulate cortex
Front portion of the older lobe of the cerebral cortex that surrounds the corpus callosum. Decreased activity in this area has been found to accompany profound sadness; thus, this area has been implicated in the symptoms of depression.

In accordance with neuroimaging studies with depressed patients, a decrease in activity was observed in both the dorsal anterior cingulate and the PFC. If these researchers focused on the ventral anterior cingulate, however, a different response was observed: induced sadness activates this area. Thus, extreme sadness induces a reciprocal pattern of responses—deactivation of the PFC and dorsal anterior cingulate and activation in the ventral anterior cingulate and related limbic structures.

In a second exploration, these researchers attempted to tease apart sadness from anxiety by using autobiographical scripts to induce sadness, anxiety, or a neutral mood. Whereas sadness was accompanied by deactivation of the right PFC and parietal cortex, anxiety was accompanied by activation in areas of the PFC such as the orbitofrontal cortex and deactivation of the parahippocampal gyri and inferior temporal cortex (cortical areas surrounding the hippocampus area).

Hence, sadness seems to be characterized by selective dorsal cortical deactivations, whereas ventral cortical deactivations are observed in anxiety (Liotti, Mayberg, et al., 2000). Providing further evidence of the functional differences of the dorsal and ventral corticolimbic streams, Pizzagalli and colleagues (2001) have found that patients who respond to antidepressants with more activation in the ventral area of the anterior cingulate demonstrate a better response to drug treatment several months later. Confirming this finding, more recent research shows that patients who respond to negative stimuli with greater anterior cingulate activity demonstrate the most robust improvement with antidepressant therapy (venlafaxine) (Davidson, Irwin, Anderle, & Kalin, 2003).

These findings help explain why depressed patients experiencing profound sadness may have difficulty focusing their attention and concentrating on tasks. If structures in the brain—for example, the PFC and associated areas—that are typically involved in sustaining attention are deactivated, it is easy to see that the person is going to experience difficulties focusing attention. In a clever series of studies, Liotti, Woldorff, Perez, and Mayberg (2000), explored further this notion of deactivation of attentional circuits during depression or induced sadness. In the Stroop test of perception, the name of a color, such as green, is typed in a different color, for example, purple. Subjects are instructed to report the color, not the word. In this challenging task the brain has to suppress information—the actual word—so that it can report another bit of information—the actual color. Research on humans who have experienced damage to the anterior cingulate cortex suggests that this area is important in monitoring the competing pieces of information and inhibiting the inappropriate response. Interestingly, Stroop performance is impaired in depressed individuals (Liotti, Woldorff et al., 2000; Pardo, Pardo, Janer, & Raichle, 1990).

Nucleus accumbens. Essentially the relay between limbic and basal ganglia structures, the nucleus accumbens, which is involved in reinforcement and pleasure, mediates the interface of emotional and motor responses (see Chapter Seven). Naranjo, Trembley, and Busto (2001) reasoned that, because depression is characterized by **anhedonia** (loss of pleasure) and deeply entrenched feelings of sadness, it makes sense to focus research on the nucleus accumbens. In fact, if the nucleus accumbens processes information about our environment so that we may respond in an appropriate, adaptive manner, then this structure can be viewed as regulating an animal's learning to adapt to a changing environment. Depression has been equated to the experimental model known as **learned helplessness.** In this paradigm, an animal or person fails to respond appropriately to his or her environment and that condition might result from a malfunctioning nucleus accumbens (Naranjo et al., 2001).

To test the involvement of the brain's reward system in depression, depressed subjects were given an injection of d-amphetamine to stimulate the brain's reward system. This drug, which works via the dopaminergic system, has a powerful ability to promote feelings of reward and pleasure. Naranjo and colleagues call this administration of d-amphetamine a *probe test;* it activates the reward center in the subjects' brains. Once subjects receive the pharmacological probe, their feelings of depression are measured using the Hamilton Depression Scale, a paper-and-pencil test of depression. Compared to nondepressed subjects, depressed subjects have greater drug-induced rewarding effects.

You may be thinking that this is just the opposite of Naranjo's hypothesis, but let's thoroughly consider these results. If a person was experiencing less dopaminergic activity in the nucleus accumbens, it is very likely that the brain would produce more sensitive dopaminergic receptors in an attempt to compensate for the reduction so that the person could maximize the response to existing low levels of dopamine. When, with more sensitive receptors (for example, upregulation or higher affinity for ligand) this person receives a dose of d-amphetamine, a dopaminergic agonist, the receptors will probably respond in a wildly active manner due to their increased sensitivity to dopamine.

Even if this explanation is not correct, the fact that differences are observed between depressed and nondepressed subjects provides substantial evidence that the brain's reward system is somehow affected in depression. For that reason, this sensitivity may be used as a biological marker for depression and may give some insight about the patient's response to treatment. If this is the case, then the dopaminergic–nucleus accumbens area may have potential as a therapeutic target area for pharmaceutical development.

anhedonia Lack of desire or pleasure. Drugs that interfere with the mesolimbic dopaminergic system produce this state.

learned helplessness Usually resulting from several bouts with failure, the acquired belief that no effort can remove an individual from a stressful environment. Seligman suggests that this phenomenon may be a basis for clinical depression.

Brainstem tracts. The brainstem is another critical brain area that communicates with the PFC. Two neurochemical circuits critical to depression and anxiety, serotonin and noradrenaline—are produced by nuclei in the brainstem. The dorsal raphe nucleus is the brainstem area that houses the serotonergic (5-HT) neurons that project to the PFC (as well as to a host of other areas in the brain; see Figure 5.5).

Bligh-Glover and colleagues (2000) reported that suicide victims with major depression have significantly increased serotonin transporters throughout the dorsal raphe nucleus. Additionally, an increase in the number and density of 5-HT neurons in the dorsal raphe nucleus of depressed suicide victims has been reported (Underwood et al., 1999). Generally, it is thought that these effects are due to a suppression of the serotonergic system in the brainstem.

The second brainstem area contributing to the massive cellular communications with the cortex is the locus coeruleus (LC), which contributes to over 70% of the forebrain's norepinephrine (NE) innervation by projecting to the cortex and the subcortical and limbic structures (Ressler & Nemeroff, 2000) see Figure 5.4). Utilizing a variety of measures, norepinephrine activity is enhanced or increased in depression (Ressler & Nemeroff, 2000).

The locus coeruleus fires fastest when an animal is alert and responding to its environment. For example, when a rat is grooming, a behavior in which there is low NE activation, the LC neurons suddenly become active if a loud noise occurs, prompting the rat to cease grooming and orient toward the sound. In fact, while the animal is grooming, which is a more internal, homeostatic behavior, serotonin firing increases. Hence, according to Ressler and Nemeroff of Emory University, the serotonergic activity in the dorsal raphe nucleus maintains more homeostatic behavior whereas the LC noradrenergic system maintains the animals' vigilant responses to the environment.

White matter. Now that we have established the brain circuits involved in depression, it is also relevant to explore the integrity of its communication pathways. Would disrupted communication among all these sites lead to negative effects? Working at the Erasmus University Medical School in the Netherlands, Jan de Groot worked with a team of researchers to explore this question (2000). They conducted MRIs on a sample of over 1000 nondepressed elderly subjects to assess the number of lesions in the subcortical white matter.

The white matter is also known as the communication matter because it comprises primarily the myelinated axons of neurons (see Chapter Four). Subjects with severe white matter lesions were more likely to experience symptoms of depression than subjects who did not display lesions. These authors propose that white matter lesions, often due to cerebrovascular events such as stroke, may be a factor in late-onset depression (occurring after the age of 40 years).

Neurochemistry of Depression

Finding a single brain area or a single type of damage that leads to a depression syndrome seems less and less likely as neuroscientists uncover new and complex information related to the disorder. As suggested by Ressler and Nemeroff (2000), depression may be thought of more accurately in terms of balances between internal homeostatic processes and vigilant processing of our external worlds. See Box 8.2 (on page 278) for more about Nemeroff's career and research.

If monitoring systems get out of balance, too great a focus may fall on internal processes monitored by the serotonergic system or on external processes monitored by the norepinephrine system. This homeostatic imbalance is then reflected in an unbalanced expression of moods. Beginning in the 1950s, a whirlwind of research activity took aim at identifying the role of specific neurotransmitters in depression. (See Table 8.3 for a description of these neurotransmitters.)

Serotonin (5-HT). Since the 1950s, substantial evidence has supported the hypothesis that a dysfunctional serotonergic system may play a role in depression. If drugs that increase levels of serotonin help treat the

[Table 8.3]

Summary of Evidence Supporting Neurochemical Involvement in Depression

Neurotransmitter	Supporting evidence
Norepinephrine	Norepinephrine-deficient diet promotes symptoms of depression in patients on norepinephrine uptake blockers; efficacy of norepinephrine uptake blockers
Serotonin	Low levels of 5-HIAA in CSF of depressed patients; reduced platelet serotonin transport sites in depressed patients; serotonin depletion diets promote depressive symptoms in patients currently taking SSRIs; efficacy of SSRIs; SSRI-induced alterations in specific serotonergic receptor sensitivity
Corticosteroids	Increased levels of corticosteroids in depressed patients; reduced CRH-binding sites in suicidal victims; insensitivity of depressed patients to dexamethasome test; preliminary efficacy of anti-CRH antidepressants
Combination of monoamines	Efficacy rates of tricyclic antidepressants; current preliminary efficacy rates of SNUBs.

[Box 8.2]

The Investigators

Charles B. Nemeroff

In his freshman year at City College of New York, Charles Nemeroff's general psychology class visited Manhattan State Hospital. Nemeroff was intrigued by how debilitated the chronically ill patients were, and he decided to pursue a career that would enable him to learn more about mental illness. According to Nemeroff, an exciting event that fueled his enthusiasm for research was the opportunity to participate in an undergraduate research program sponsored by the National Science Foundation. At the Museum of Natural History, he undertook a project classifying fish according to their caudal skeletons. Although his first research project was not related to mental illness, he was exposed to a wonderful series of research seminars during this time that sparked his interest in evolutionary biology.

With both clinical and basic science interests, Nemeroff was prepared for a successful career in clinical neuroscience. Interestingly, Nemeroff did not go directly to graduate or medical school after completing his undergraduate work. He worked as a technician in a neuropathology laboratory in Boston. The director of the lab, Alfred Pope, who was impressed with Nemeroff's interest and pertinent questions related to neurobiology, simply asked him why he was a technician and not a graduate student. At that point he considered seriously the option of graduate school.

Nemeroff subsequently earned a masters degree in biology at Northeastern University in Boston. He then went on to the University of North Carolina in Chapel Hill to obtain a Ph.D. in neurobiology. Not content with a Ph.D., Nemeroff decided to attend medical school while managing a research laboratory at UNC; he subsequently completed two residencies in psychiatry—one at North Carolina Memorial Hospital and one at Duke University Medical Center. After completing his residency, he became an assistant professor in pharmacology at Duke and eventually became chief of the Division of Biological Psychiatry; in 1991 he joined Emory University, where he is currently professor and chairman of the Department of Psychiatry and Behavioral Neurosciences.

Having both research and clinical degrees, Nemeroff epitomizes the clinical neuroscientist: he is able to transfer observations from clinic to the laboratory and

symptoms of depression, it seems obvious that depression must be caused by low levels of serotonin. We have to proceed with caution, however, with this line of reasoning. It is a bit like assuming that because a rash on your foot improves after placing steroid cream on it, the rash is caused by a steroid deficiency (Delgado & Moreno, 2000).

Nonetheless, evidence does support the serotonin depletion hypothesis. For example, lower levels of one breakdown, or metabolic, product of serotonin, known as 5-hydroxyindoleacetic acid (5-HIAA), have been found in the cerebrospinal fluid of depressed patients (Cheetham, Katona, & Horton, 1991). Further, fewer serotonin transporter sites are found on the platelets of depressed patients before they are placed on antidepressants (Healy & Leonard, 1987).

The serotonin depletion theory is not clearcut, however, because several studies have failed to find evidence of reduced serotonergic functioning in depressed patients (Gjerris, 1988). In a fascinating study, Pedro Delgado (2000) at the University of Arizona's Department of vice versa. At the time he commenced his neuro-science career, Nemeroff was uncomfortable with the current dichotomy between mental health professionals who favored "psychological" causes and those who emphasized "biological" causes. Didn't one's psychological world interact with one's neurobiological world?

Nemeroff is uniquely positioned for an integrative viewpoint, and he has had a fascinating research career. While he was training at UNC, he became interested in the role of the hypothalamic-pituitary-adrenal axis in depression and conducted critical research demonstrating hyperactivity of this axis in depressed individuals. While at Duke, Nemeroff and his colleagues were struck by how many of their patients with mood disorders reported horrendous personal histories of child abuse and/or severe emotional neglect. Another finding that has contributed greatly to the depression literature was the discovery that the peptide corticotropin-releasing hormone (CRH) was also higher in the cerebrospinal fluid of depressed patients than in the fluid of patients with other disorders or healthy controls. Currently, Nemeroff is excited about the potential of anti-CRH drugs as antidepressants.

Nemeroff's research investigating the influence of both psychological and neurobiological factors in the de-

Charles Nemeroff
COURTESY OF DR. CHARLES B. NEMEROFF

velopment of depression has contributed greatly to the field of clinical neuroscience. His research continues to thin the walls between old views emphasizing purely psychological or purely neurobiological causes of mental illness. Being able to go from patients to the laboratory is a very rewarding experience for Nemeroff—enabling him to engage in what he calls *translational* research.

Nemeroff has certainly come a long way from the curious laboratory technician who was told he had graduate school potential. A Ph.D., an M.D, two residencies, several career appointments, and over 600 publications later, Nemeroff still has the passion for neurobiological research that was so obvious to his mentor. His work has contributed to a greater understanding of the delicate neurobiological interactions that underlie the chronic mental illnesses he observed on his class field trip to the mental institution over three decades ago (personal communication, 2003).

Psychiatry hypothesized that, if a depletion of serotonin leads to depression, then a diet low in tryptophan, the precursor of serotonin, would lead to a return to symptoms of depression in patients being treated with antidepressants. Indeed, two-thirds of the subjects experienced a relapse of depressive symptoms within a mere 5 to 7 hours of dietary tryptophan depletion.

But when Delgado placed depressed patients who were not on antidepressant medication on the tryptophan-free diet, he saw a minimal change on the first day, and only a few patients got worse on the second day (see this chapter's Connections for more about dietary tryptophan). These patients did not seem to be as sensitive to fluctuations in serotonin as the patients on antidepressant medication. Even more interesting, when healthy subjects were placed on the tryptophan-free diet, minimal evidence of depression emerged in those with no family history of depression, whereas symptoms occurred in about a third of the subjects with a family history of affective disorders.

[Figure 8.2]
The serotonergic synapse.
Serotonin is released from the presynaptic cell and travels across the synaptic cleft to the postsynaptic cell where it attaches to specialized receptors. Auto receptors on the presynaptic cell help to regulate the amount of serotonin released, and reuptake transporters facilitate the reuptake of released serotonin into the presynaptic cell.

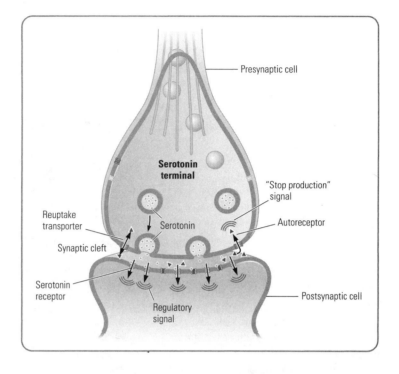

This research suggests that the onset of depressive symptoms may depend less on actual levels of circulating serotonin and more on the sensitivity of the postsynaptic neurons that respond to this neurotransmitter (Figure 8.2). This probably explains the observations in the depressed patients on antidepressants. These subjects had been on their medications long enough for the receptors to change in sensitivity to the newly increased levels of serotonin. As a result, they responded immediately (or within hours, in this case) to a diet devoid of the essential elements for the production of serotonin.

These findings also address one of the most puzzling questions concerning the serotonin depletion hypothesis of depression. Antidepressant drugs increase serotonergic activity within a matter of days, but their therapeutic action depends on chronic administration for several weeks. One explanation for this delay is that the autoreceptors on the serotonergic neurons that monitor the amount of serotonin released by its own cell quickly adapt to the increased levels of serotonin induced by the antidepressant medication (see Figure 8.2). The activation of these autoreceptors results in a decreased firing rate for the monoaminergic neurons to compensate for the increased levels of circulating monoamines.

But remember, to see therapeutic improvement, increased levels of serotonin, or monoamines, are desirable. Using animal models, researchers have observed that this compensatory increase in the autorecep-tor activation and subsequent inhibition of the firing of the 5-HT neuron diminishes over time—interestingly, about the time of the observed clini-cal improvement (Blier & Montigny, 1994; Duman, 1999). In fact, most of the current research focusing on the serotonergic system is providing evi-dence that the activity of the serotonergic receptors that detect the pres-ence of serotonin in the synapse, rather than absolute levels of circulating serotonin, are an integral piece of the serotonin hypothesis of depression.

In addition to the autoreceptor, other receptors on the presynaptic and postsynaptic surfaces have also been investigated. Research suggests that chronic administration of some antidepressant medications leads to an in-crease in sensitivity to the 5-HT$_{1A}$ receptors located on the post-synaptic surface (Duman, 1999) (see Chapter Five). Research on the 5-HT$_{1A}$ recep-tor is far from conclusive, however, and depends on the type of antide-pressant and the area of the brain being investigated. For example, Fujita and his colleagues have found decreased receptor sensitivity in presynap-tic 5-HT$_{1A}$ receptors in depressed subjects (Fujita, Charney, & Innis, 2000). (See Figure 8.3 for illustration of 5-HT$_{1A}$ and 5-HT$_{1B}$ receptors on the serotonin neurons.)

A group of researchers in the Department of Psychiatry at Oxford University explored the role of a different serotonergic receptor, the 5-HT$_{1D}$ receptor found on both the presynaptic and postsynaptic surfaces of the serotonergic neurons. After recruiting men and women suffering from major depression, the Oxford researchers gave the patients a drug known as zolmitriptan, a 5-HT$_{1D}$ receptor agonist. After manipulating this receptor system, they went on to assess the patients' responses to an-tidepressant treatment—which increases levels of serotonin. The Oxford

[Figure 8.3]
Drug mechanisms that influ-ence serotonergic functioning.
5-HT$_{1A}$ and 5-HT$_{1B}$ autoreceptors inhibit 5-HT neuronal firing and re-lease of transmitter. Plus signs in-dicate activation whereas minus signs indicate antagonism of a particular function. Circles on the 5-HT neuron represent the reup-take transporters; if they contain an X, they are inhibited. Small dots represent the concentration of the 5-HT transmitter, which is twice as dense around the 5-HT cell bodies compared with post-synaptic structures.
BLIER & ABBOTT, 2001, P. 39.

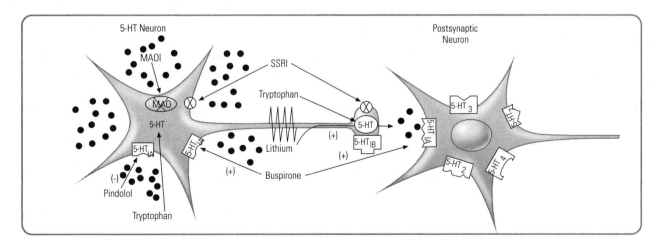

researchers found that, prior to treatment with the agonist, patients had an impaired sensitivity of the postsynaptic 5-HT_{1D} receptor. Following antidepressant treatment, a further reduction in 5-HT_{1D} sensitivity was observed, probably resulting from a compensatory response to increased levels of synaptic 5-HT (Whale, Clifford, Bhagwagar, & Cowen, 2001).

As the name *receptor* implies, these structures receive and respond to the presence of serotonin in the synapse; ultimately, receptors pass on their information to intracellular structures for further processing. Accordingly, researchers are currently focusing on the effects of antidepressants on cellular processes such as the second-messenger signal transduction pathways discussed in Chapter Four (Duman & Nestler, 1995).

A behavioral study conducted by Patrick Ronan and his colleagues at the Department of Veterans Affairs Medical Center in Dallas, Texas, also demonstrates that the absolute levels of serotonin are less critical than the nature of the activity induced by serotonin (Ronan, Steciuk, Kramer, Kram, & Petty, 2000). These researchers exposed rats to shock while they were in restraint tubes and unable to escape the aversive stimulus. On the second day the animals were shocked and given an opportunity to escape the shock by running across the shuttlebox. Subsequently, the rats were required to run across twice to terminate the shock. Interestingly, about half the animals worked to turn off the aversive stimulus of shock while the other half did not attempt to escape it. Box 8.3 describes the previously mentioned phenomenon known as learned helplessness as well as other paradigms used to study depression.

Following this behavioral testing, microdialysis probes were placed in the animals' lateral septum (a limbic structure) so that levels of serotonin and its breakdown product 5-HIAA, as well as other monoamines, could be assessed. The only neurochemical difference detected between the helpless and nonhelpless rats was an increase in 5-HIAA in the nonhelpless rats. These results suggest that increased metabolism of serotonin might play a role in protecting the organism against stress, a condition that often precipitates depression.

Norepinephrine (NE). In 1965, Joseph Schildkraut of Harvard University introduced the catecholamine hypothesis in which he stated that depression results from a deficiency of norepinephrine whereas mania results from an abundance of NE (Schildkraut, 1965). Although the discovery in the 1980s of the clinical effectiveness of selective serotonin reuptake inhibitors (SSRIs) elevated serotonin as the preeminent neurotransmitter influencing depression, other research has supported the theory that norepinephrine is influential (Nemeroff, 1998).

As reviewed by Delgado and Moreno (2000), norepinephrine depletion studies initially brought researchers back to the norepinephrine hypothesis of depression. In these depletion studies, alpha-methyl-para-tyrosine (AMPT—an inhibitor of tyrosine hydroxylase, an enzyme that is important in the production of catecholamine transmitters) was used to decrease the amount of norepinephrine in subjects. Researchers found that depressed patients given an antidepressant medication (desipramine) that selectively increases norepinephrine instead of serotonin, suffered a relapse when given AMPT to reduce norepinephrine. AMPT had no effect on the continued effectiveness of antidepressant drugs that manipulate the serotonergic system.

As mentioned in the serotonin section, similar depletion studies suggest that subjects who respond positively to drugs that increase serotonin suffer relapses when placed on a serotonin-deficient diet but fail to be affected by a norepinephrine-deficient diet. This dichotomy of responses to specific neurotransmitter depletion diets provides evidence that norepinephrine is probably a legitimate player in the depression game.

Working in the clinical physiology and neuroscience departments at Sahlgrenska University in Sweden, Gavin Lambert and his colleagues conducted an interesting study providing evidence of the involvement of norepinephrine in depression (Lambert, Hohansson, Agren, & Friberg, 2000). They brought patients into the lab who either were suffering from depression or were healthy. Internal jugular venous catheters were placed in the subjects so that blood from the brain could be collected for the subsequent analysis for the presence of the monoaminergic transmitters.

Blood samples indicated that depressed patients had significantly lower plasma concentrations of norepinephrine and other principal CNS metabolites (Figure 8.4). Administration of the NE transporter blocker desipramine resulted in a significant reduction in norepinephrine turnover, or use, in depressed patients. Interestingly, these researchers found that turnover rates in dopamine, not in norepinephrine, seemed to be a stronger predictor of the patients' severity of depression.

The results obtained by Lambert and his colleagues provide strong support for the role of norepinephrine in depression but do not rule

[Figure 8.4]
Norepinephrine levels and depression. Levels of norepinephrine (NE) and metabolites (DHPG, MHPG, and HVA) were significantly reduced in depressed patients. No statistical difference was found between sertonergic levels (5-HIAA) in healthy and depressed patients.
LAMBERT ET AL., 2000, P. 791.

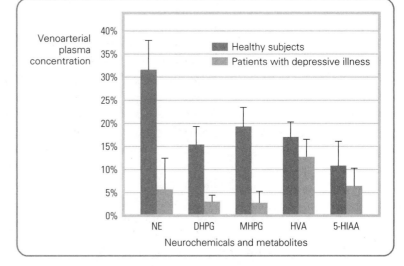

corticosteroids Hormones secreted by the adrenal cortex during stress. These neurochemicals influence the brain and are thought to be a trigger for depressive symptoms. Some drugs targeted at reducing corticosteroids reduce symptoms of depression.

out the involvement of other monoamines (dopamine and serotonin). In support of the ubiquitous involvement of the monoamines in depression, Ressler and Nemeroff (2000) suggest that depression is probably due not to specific malfunctions in the norepinephrine or serotonergic systems but to the role of the systems in modulating other neurobiologic systems that mediate the symptoms of depression.

Corticosteroids. In a research review, Glorian Holsboer (2000) of the Max Planck Institute of Psychiatry in Munich, Germany, proposed that four convincing lines of evidence support the involvement of **corticosteroids,** the stress hormones, in depression:

1. Secretory impulses of adrenocorticotropic hormone (ACTH), which stimulate the release of corticosteriods from the adrenal cortex, and cortisol are increased in depressed patients. These increased impulses are reflected in increased cortisol levels in the depressed patients' urine (Rubin, Poland, Lesser, Winston, & Blodgett, 1987).

2. Levels of corticotropin-releasing hormone (CRH), the neurochemical that stimulates the release of ACTH from the pituitary, are elevated in depressed patients (Nemeroff et al., 1984).

3. The number of neurons that secrete CRH are increased in limbic regions of the brain such as the hypothalamus (Raadsheer, Hoogendijk, Stam, Tilders, & Swaab, 1994).

4. When looking at the brains of depressed patients who committed suicide, reduced CRH-binding sites were observed in the frontal cortex, a likely compensatory reaction to the increased CRH found in depressed patients (Nemeroff, Owens, Bissette, Andorn, & Stanley, 1988).

Also implicating the hypothalamic pituitary adrenal (HPA) axis in depression is the administration of the synthetic glucocorticoid, dexamethasome, in the dexamethasone suppression test (DST). In healthy patients, natural levels of cortisol should decrease in response to the administration of a cortisol-like substance. Depressed patients, however, fail to experience the suppression of cortisol after receiving the DST (Carroll, 1982). Researchers are focusing on mouse breeds in which pertinent genes necessary for the regulation of the HPA axis are inactivated (making it difficult for the animals to maintain HPA homeostasis) so that a clearer picture of the role of HPA functioning in anxiety and depressive-like behavior can be investigated (Holsboer, 2000).

As discussed in Chapter Five, there are dozens and dozens of neurotransmitters, and it is likely that many play either direct or indirect roles in major depression. In addition to the monoamines and corticosteroids, researchers have investigated the role of vasopressin, glutamate, substance P, thyroid hormones, and growth factors in depressive disorders. In the next section, we will discuss how altered neurochemistry within the neuranatomical circuit of depression (and elsewhere) may converge to produce mutations in the brain. When neuroplasticity is interrupted, the brain may become vulnerable to depression.

Brain Plasticity

Recent research on the role of brain plasticity in the etiology of depression proves how quickly the field of clinical neuroscience changes. Less than a decade ago we were just learning that neurons continue to be generated throughout a human's life; now we're finding out that the production of new neurons, as well as the expansion of existing neurons, may contribute to depression (Eriksson et al., 1998). In a short time, some convincing evidence of the involvement of brain plasticity in depression has been published, making this field one of the most exciting new research areas in depression. As stated by Fred Gage (2000), former president of the Society for Neuroscience and a researcher at the Salk Institute, "Clearly, this is an exciting field of study, and the evidence supporting structural changes in major depression is likely to have significant impact on diagnosis, treatment, and therapy" (p. 714).

Brain structure and neurogenesis. As discussed in Chapter Three, the hippocampus is involved in learning and memory, a most important function as animals constantly process new information about their environments. Focusing on the rat and mouse hippocampus, the granule cell layer of the hippocampus contains about 1 to 2 million cells. Every day, however, 1000 to 3000 new cells are produced. These new cells may play an important role in processing current information (Jacobs, van Praag, & Gage, 2000).

It is likely that these baseline neurogenesis rates are influenced by external factors such as stressful stimuli in the environment. Indeed, studies suggest that exposure to a stressor such as fox odor suppresses neurogenesis in the dentate gyrus of the rat (Galea, Tanapat, & Gould, 1996). Chronic psychosocial stress has led to reduced neurogenesis in tree shrews (Gould, McEwen, Tanapat, Galea, & Fuchs, 1997).

What about humans? As we've discussed, the hippocampus can shrink in chronically stressed and/or depressed subjects. Temporal lobe epilepsy affects the brain area containing the hippocampus and is associated with extensive cell loss in various structures surrounding the hippocampus. People with temporal lobe epilepsy are more likely to experience depression than patients suffering from any other form of epilepsy (Perini et al., 1996).

[Box 8.3]

Brain Matters

Animal Models of Depression

Presented here are a few of the more popular animal models used to investigate depressivelike behavior. Brief summaries are provided for each model, but it is important to note that each paradigm has strengths and weaknesses; a thorough investigation should always be performed prior to making a decision about the appropriateness of a particular model. Information about these models was taken from several sources (Holsboer, 1999; Redei et al., 2001; Seligman & Beagley, 1975; Suomi, 1983; Weiss & Kilts, 1995; Willner et al., 1992).

Learned helplessness. In this paradigm, animals are presented with a stressor such as a shock and not allowed to escape. Researchers subsequently test for deficits in escaping from this task; when animals exhibit behavioral deficits they are thought to demonstrate learned helplessness. Animals that are allowed to turn off the shocks are less likely to exhibit behavioral deficits. Hence, perception of control seems to be pertinent in this paradigm. In the diagram, the avoidance rats are able to turn off the stressor whereas the yoked animal has no escape from the stressor. Antidepressants reduce behavioral deficits in some cases.

Social defeat. When an intruder animal is placed in the home cage of another animal, the resident is likely to aggressively attack the intruder animal (some animals need to be trained to reliably defeat intruders).

Learned helplessness

This single episode appears to trigger a cascade of effects leading to defeated animals exhibiting depressivelike behavior for around a week. Because of their aggressive tendencies, hamsters are a popular animal used in this paradigm.

Forced swim test. In this paradigm, rats or mice are placed in a cylinder or tank that is half-filled with water, as shown in the figure. Variables such as latency to swim, latency to float, number of dives, and number of attempts to escape up the wall are recorded. Some researchers view floating in this paradigm as "behavioral despair." This paradigm has been used as a test for antidepressants with the notion that effective antidepressants should prolong the latency to float. It may be adaptive, however, for rodents that have had previous

We also discussed the role of the prefrontal cortex in depression. Recent postmortem studies suggest significant reduction in the number of glial cells in the PFC of depressed patients. Additionally, the size of the neuronal cell bodies are smaller than nondepressed counterparts (Rajkowska, 2000).

It is difficult to assess the parameters and existence of new cells in living depressed patients. One way to determine whether alterations of brain plasticity play a role in human depression is to verify whether therapies that are successful for depressed humans also influence plasticity in the animal models. When electroconvulsive therapy (ECT) is administered to rats repeatedly—that is, five times over ten days—the number of 5-hydrox-

Forced swim test

range from very mild stressors, such as tilted cages, to more intense stressors, such as exposure to predator odors. After about two weeks in such a paradigm, some animals develop anhedonia, or a reduction in their motivation to obtain rewards such as sucrose solution or to carry out such maintenance behaviors such as nest building (see photo). This model is useful because its unpredictable nature closely simulates chronic human stress.

Stress-sensitive rats. Selective breeding for particular traits related to depression (e.g., anxiety, lack of activity) have also been used to produce an animal model of depression. The Maudsley reactive rats have been selected for their emotionality (e.g., freezing in place) in the open field test; these rats also show depressivelike behaviors in other paradigms. Additionally, the Wistar Kyoto (WKY) rat is thought to be a valuable animal model for endogenous (internally driven) depression. These animals show increased anxious and depressive behavior in several behavioral tests and respond to antidepressants.

experience with this inescapable task to float sooner to conserve energy.

Early life stressors. Recall from Chapter Six that when infant monkeys are separated from their mothers they respond with agitation, vocalizations, and sleep disturbances. Interesting individual differences, however, contribute to the severity of this response. Steve Suomi, who is currently at the National Institutes of Mental Health, is interested in why some primates are more vulnerable to the effects of separation stress and respond with "despair," whereas others seem to take it in stride.

Chronic unpredictable stress. This model includes the exposure of animals to various stressors in an unpredictable pattern. The paradigm includes stimuli that

Nest building
California deer mouse building a nest.
COURTESY OF KELLY LAMBERT

ytryptamine fibers sprouting off the axon doubles. Additionally, increased levels of 5-HIAA have been observed (Madhav, Pei, Grahame-Smith, & Zetterstrom, 2000).

One study investigated the effect of either single or multiple ECT seizures on neurogenesis in the dentate gyrus of the rat hippocampus (Madsen et al., 2000). Just one ECT seizure significantly increased newborn cells and a series of seizures increased neurogenesis in a dose-dependent fashion. The authors concluded that ECT may be an effective therapy for depression because of the generation of new neurons, an effect we discuss in the section "Treatment for Depression."

Role of BDNF in depression. Antidepressant drugs have been shown to influence brain plasticity via increased production of a major growth factor in the brain, brain-derived neurotrophic factor, or BDNF. As you learned in Chapter Six, BDNF contributes to the maintenance and growth of neuronal systems. When rats are given antidepressant medications, an upregulation of BDNF mRNA is found in the hippocampus and cortex (Nibuya, Morinobu, & Duman, 1995).

Depressed patients also report relief from depression following exercise, and physical activity is known to upregulate BDNF mRNA (Hill, Storandt, & Malley, 1993). In an interesting extension of the antidepressant and exercise studies, Russo-Neustadt, Beard, Huang, and Cotman (2000), working at the University of California, Santa Barbara, investigated the combined effects of exercise and antidepressant medication. They found that this combination increased levels of BDNF mRNA more than the treatments used in isolation. In fact, this laboratory has confirmed that BDNF mRNA expression is related to an animal model of depression. When rats were placed in an unescapable water tank, increased swimming, which is interpreted by many as the more adaptive, nondepressed response, was correlated with increased BDNF mRNA levels (Russo-Neustadt, Ha, Ramirez, & Kesslak, 2001).

A certain strain of rats known as the Flinders sensitive line (FLS) expresses several depressive symptoms such as reduced activity, learning disturbances, anhedonia, and abnormal circadian rhythms, all of which are diminished by antidepressants. To assess baseline levels of growth factors including BDNF in these depressed rats, researchers working at the Karolinska Institute in Stockholm, Sweden, and the Institute of Neurobiology in Rome, Italy, focused on the hypothalamus, hippocampus, striatum, and frontal cortex. Expecting to find that the rats had lower baseline growth factor levels, they were surprised that the FLS rats had higher BDNF and NGF (nerve growth factor) levels in some brain regions than the nondepressed strain of rats. Additionally, the females had significantly less NGF than males. These findings are important because they show that there are indeed altered levels of neurotrophins in an animal model of depression. Because antidepressants are known to increase neurotrophins, the unexpected increase in BDNF and NGF levels might reflect the brain's attempt to reverse the altered cellular or glial alterations. If so, it's likely that BDNF and NGF changes are not the fundamental causes of depression but rather a compensatory mechanism used by the brain to bring structural and functional processing back to an acceptable baseline level (Angelucci, Aloe, Vasquez, & Mathe, 2000).

In accordance with the Roman study, Vollmayr, Faust, Lewicka, and Henn (2001), working at the University of Heidelberg, assessed BDNF in the hippocampus of another strain of rat, a congenital helpless strain, bred for its intensity of depressive symptoms. This strain has lost behavioral plasticity in response to antidepressants. As found by Angelucci and colleagues (2000), the hippocampus of the congenital helpless strain had higher levels of BDNF in response to shock stress (in the learned helplessness paradigm) than did the control animals. These findings reinforce the fact that more research is needed to clarify the exact nature of BDNF in depression. Currently, it is not clear whether compromised neuronal growth is the cause of depression or if the depressed brain, which has compromised structural complexity, compensates by producing higher levels of some of the growth factors.

STRESS AND DEPRESSION

No one can deny that internal events vary in response to environmental conditions. Anyone who has experienced a tragic loss can verify that a single external event can instantaneously throw a healthy, optimistic person into a prolonged state of severe depression. Prolonged stress can also trigger depression, as can the changing of the seasons.

Life's Losses

Episodes of depression due to a profound life loss constitute an expected reaction that subsides with time. But there is evidence that losses encountered early in life may alter a person's susceptibility to depression later in life. Rat pups that are separated from their mothers for up to 6 hours per day for the first 3 weeks of their lives have increased levels of stress hormones when subjected to stress as adults (Ladd, Owens, & Nemeroff, 1996). On the contrary, as previously mentioned, rat pups that are stimulated by being handled by humans for 15 minutes per day for the first 3 weeks of life develop a reduced stress reaction as adults (Plotsky & Meaney, 1993). Rhesus monkeys that are raised individually in isolated nurseries from the time they are 8 weeks old exhibit increased symptoms of anxiety and depression such as reduced social interaction and impaired cognitive function as adults (Sanchez, Hearn, Do, Rilling, Herndon, 1998). Thus, animal models suggest that early stress conditions, such as the loss of essential early contact, can alter the stress response of the adult, leading to an increased susceptibility to depression (Kauffman, Plotsky, Nemeroff, & Charney, 2000).

seasonal affective disorder (SAD) Form of depression that occurs in winter months when the duration of natural light decreases.

Sexual Abuse in Childhood

Childhood sexual abuse makes humans more susceptible to adult-onset depression. This finding might shed light on the gender difference in depression. As stated earlier, women are much more likely to suffer from depression than men. Likewise, childhood sexual abuse of girls is much more common than of boys (Weiss, Longhurst, & Mazure, 1999).

Christine Heim, working with colleagues at Emory University, conducted a study with three groups of women: women with a history of early childhood abuse with no current symptoms of depression, women with a history of childhood abuse with current depression, and women with depression who suffered no childhood abuse (Heim, Newport, Bonsall, Miller, & Nemeroff, 2001). The researchers measured the responses of each group to the administration of the various stress hormones, CRH and ACTH.

The women suffering depression with no history of sexual abuse exhibited a blunted response to the CRH and the abused women with no signs of depression exhibited an exaggerated response to the CRH compared with the control group. These findings suggest that women who had suffered childhood abuse but were currently experiencing no depression had an altered pituitary and adrenal response to the administration of stress hormones. Because of continuous homeostatic processes in the brain, these alterations could lead to a downregulation of CRH receptors and the future expression of anxiety and depression. That the brain continued to be modified 20 years after a stressful event is testament to both the impact of the abuse and the brain's resilience.

Seasonal Changes in Light

Seasonal changes influence moods in some of us. People who experience depressive symptoms during the winter in high latitudes, when the days are short, suffer from **seasonal affective disorder (SAD).** A common therapy for this "winter depression" is mere exposure to bright light.

Locations with extended darkness are especially likely to induce SAD in vulnerable people. For example, in the northern Russian village of Lovozero, at 10:00 A.M. in the winter it looks more like midnight. Actually, if artificial light was no longer available, it might be adaptive to experience lower activity levels at a time when it would be difficult to maneuver around a dark environment. In fact, although disturbed sleep is one of the most prominent symptoms of depression, evidenced by longer sleep latencies, more nighttime wakefulness, and earlier awakenings in the morning, SAD patients are more likely to sleep longer than their control counterparts (Soldatos & Bergiannaki, 1999).

In places such as Lovozero, light therapy begins early to reestablish hormonal balances; in young children, the light seems to be necessary for bone growth; as they grow older, light therapy may be used to alter moods (Achenbach, 2001). Interestingly, a SAD patient who responds successfully to just an hour of light therapy is likely to respond successfully with pharmacological therapy as well (Sher et al., 2001).

TREATMENT FOR DEPRESSION

With so much information relating to causes of depression, you might think that researchers are close to finding an effective treatment for this condition. Although impressive research is being conducted, a miracle cure is certainly not within our grasp. Given the multifaceted nature of depression, it is no surprise that treatment strategies are diverse. Pharmacotherapy, electroconvulsive shock therapy, transcranial magnetic stimulation, and cognitive-behavioral therapies all are enlisted in the fight against depression, as is the herbal remedy St. John's wort, described in Box 8.4 on page 292.

Pharmocotherapy

In the 1950s, **iproniazid,** a compound developed as an antibacterial agent, was serendipitously found to improve the moods of patients taking the drug to treat tuberculosis. This prompted the American psychiatrist Nathan Kline to carry out clinical trials of ipronizid's behavioral effects, which showed that it was an effective antidepressant. Although it was widely used at the end of the 1950s, the mechanism of action of this drug was not known.

In the next few years, it became apparent that iproniazid inhibited monoamine oxidase (MAO), an enzyme described in Chapter Five that participates in inactivating the monoamine transmitters: serotonin, norepinephrine, and dopamine. Thus, iproniazid seemed to work because it increases the duration of synaptic activation of some combination of the three monoamines. This drug was the first of the **monoamine oxidase inhibitors (MAOIs).**

Another drug, **imipramine,** was originally synthesized by the Swiss pharmaceutical company Geigy as a potential antipsychotic drug to be used with schizophrenia patients. After finding that it was not an effective antipsychotic, Roland Kuhn, a Swiss psychiatrist, observed that it had antidepressant properties. The acceptance of imipramine as an antidepressant quickly spread, and it became the first in a long series of drugs known as **tricyclic antidepressants,** drugs that increase the activity of

iproniazid Drug developed in the 1950s as an antibacterial agent but later found to have antidepressant effects in patients. Researchers later showed that this drug was a monoamine oxidase inhibitor, which prolonged the presence of monoamines in the synapse.

monoamine oxidase inhibitors (MAOIs) Class of drugs that deactivate monoamine oxidase in the synaptic area so that the monoamines have a prolonged period of activity.

imipramine Synthesized originally for treatment of schizophrenic patients, this drug was observed to have antidepressant qualities. Researchers found that it influenced the synapse by blocking the reuptake of monoamine transmitters back into the terminal.

tricyclic antidepressants Drugs such as imipramine that increase the activity of serotonin (along with other monoamines) in the synapse by blocking its reuptake into the presynaptic neuronal terminal.

[Box 8.4]

Brain Matters

St. John's Wort

St. John's wort (*Hypericum perforatum*) is a small shrub with bright yellow flowers that appear in midsummer. It is thought that the shrub received its name because the flowers bloom about the time of St. John the Baptist's birthday. In the seventh century, this wild flower was found to be a useful treatment against worms, madness, and melancholy (Field, Monti, Greeson, & Kunkel, 2000). Today worms are less a threat to our health, and interest in the plant's ability to treat depression is at an all-time high. In 1998, sales of this herbal remedy approached $400 million in the United States, which was modest compared with the $6 billion spent on St. John's wort in Europe. In Germany, St. John's wort is the leading treatment for depression—it is prescribed twenty times more often than fluoxetine (Prozac) (DiCarlo, Borrelli, Ernst, & Izzo, 2001; Greeson, Sanford, & Monti, 2001).

Because St. John's wort is considered a natural remedy for depression, it might be more attractive than other antidepressants prescribed by a physician. It is difficult, however, to differentiate between natural remedies and synthesized drugs concerning actions in the brain; it's not always the case that a "natural" remedy is milder or less harmful than a prescribed medication. Even if a product can be easily bought in any health food store, it is always important to check the empirical literature to investigate clinical efficacy, toxicity, and side effects of any product before using it. Although a few European studies suggest that St. John's wort is more effective for the treatment of mild to moderate than severe depression, a recent multisite, randomized, double-blind, placebo-controlled study found no significant improvement compared with placebo in patients diagnosed with major depression. It is interesting to note that the approved antidepressant sertraline (Zoloft) also failed to differentiate itself from placebo in the two primary outcome measures (Kupfer & Frank, 2002).

Fewer adverse side effects have been noted with St. John's wort than with synthetic antidepressants, but some users report tiredness, dizziness, dry mouth, gastrointestinal irritation, headaches, and restlessness. High doses might lead to photosensitization (resulting in skin irritations on exposure to ultraviolet light) in fair-skinned people (DiCarlo et al., 2001). The mode of action of St. John's wort is still a bit of a mystery. A considerable amount of research suggests a complex array of effects. Primarily, like other antidepressants, it inhibits reuptake of monoamines—noradrenaline, dopamine, and serotonin—with equal efficacy. Unlike other antidepressants, St. John's wort also inhibits the reuptake of GABA and glutamate.

Because of the number of transmitters affected by this medicinal herb, it is considered a nonselective reuptake blocker. St. John's wort achieves its reuptake ability by elevating sodium ion concentrations. This treatment has similar effects on the regulation of certain receptor types of the monoamine transmitters as do antidepressants (Nathan, 2001). In a more "radical" line of research, St. John's wort has been observed to be a potent inhibitor of oxygen-free radicals (at low doses) that inhabit the nervous system causing damage with their high reactivity levels. If this finding holds true, this herb might also have therapeutic potential in protecting against neurodegenerative diseases in the elderly (Hunt, Lester, Lester, & Tackett, 2001). Obviously, more scientific digging is required to determine the efficacy of this flowering weed.

---

serotonin in the synapse by blocking its reuptake back into the presynaptic neuron.

Once again, clinical efficacy was determined before any idea of the mechanism of the drug was known. In a few years, however, researchers discovered that, like iproniazid, imipramine alters the amine transmitters.

Julius Axelrod, a biochemist, found that imipramine worked by blocking reuptake of the monoamine transmitters. In 1970, he won the Nobel prize for this important work elucidating the biosynthesis and subsequent degradation of the monoamine transmitters.

Are you surprised at the lack of insight that attended the discovery of the early antidepressant drugs? Clearly it would have been preferable to have had a plan and then conduct studies to confirm the hypotheses, but like so many important events in science, the discoveries happened quite by accident. The important aspect of this story is that the scientists were clever enough to identify something important and further develop that line of research.

The process became a little more organized at the point when Axelrod went on to establish that specific proteins could be used to selectively transport norepinephrine, dopamine, or serotonin. Although attention was first directed toward the selective reuptake of norepinephrine and dopamine, research eventually shifted toward the selective reuptake of serotonin—the selective serotonin reuptake inhibitors (SSRIs) discussed in Chapter Seven as a treatment for OCD. As you are probably aware, the SSRI fluoxetine (Prozac) has enjoyed enormous popularity. It is interesting to note that it is not more effective than its antecedent imipramine; it just has fewer side effects (Barondes, 1993).

Although we will now discuss the antidepressant drugs in terms of the relevant neurotransmitters, some general aspects of the antidepressants need to be clarified. As previously discussed, antidepressants alter the synapse of a particular neurotransmitter system in a number of hours or days. Their clinical effects, however, are not experienced for weeks.

Although more questions than answers remain concerning the mechanisms of antidepressants, their administration is the front line of defense for most practitioners. In many cases, antidepressants are prescribed in combination with some form of supportive psychotherapy (Richelson, 2001). The following discussion considers antidepressant drugs in the following five categories: MAOIs, SSRIs, NE transport blockers, dopamine transport blockers, 5-HT2$_A$ receptor blockers, and CRH blockers (Table 8.4).

[Table 8.4]

Various Antidepressants and Their Associated Functions

Function	Antidepressant
Monoamine oxidase inhibitor	Isocarboxazid Phenelzine Tranylcypromine
Norepinephrine transport blocker	Amoxapine Desipramine Doxepin Maprotiline Nortriptyline Protriptyline Reboxetine
Serotonin transport blocker	Amitriptyline Citalopram Clomipramine Fluoxetine Fluvoxamine Imipramine Paroxetine Sertraline Trimipramine Venlafaxine
Dopamine transport blocker	Bupropion
Serotonin 5-HT$_{2A}$ receptor blocker	Mirtazapine Nefazodone Trazodone
Corticotropin-releasing hormone blocker	Antalarmin

Adapted from Richelson, 2001, p. 513.

fluoxetine Selective serotonin reuptake inhibitor (SSRI) produced by Eli Lilly pharmaceutical company in 1985; this drug had the specific effect of blocking the reuptake of serotonin.

Serotonergic manipulation. As described in Chapter Seven, the earlier MAOIs are unpopular in practice today because of side effects including elevations in blood pressure (if the patient ingests food containing tyramine, such as cheese and beer), headaches, nausea, and sweating. A newer MAOI, moclobemide, does not interact with diet, but it is currently not available in the United States (Tiller, 1993).

In the midst of a flurry of activity springing from scientists in various labs working on versions of more general and specific reuptake inhibitors, on May 8, 1972, David Wong and his colleagues at the Eli Lilly pharmaceutical company produced **fluoxetine.** Eventually research started to suggest that the SSRIs might have an antidepressant effect and, in 1985, clinical trial evidence suggested that the drug might be helpful in humans. Fluoxetine was licensed in the United States in 1987 (Richelson, 2001).

Although researchers knew they had produced an SSRI, they were not clear about how the drug might be useful. Because serotonin was known to be so widely and diffusely dispersed across the brain, it was doubtful that a drug that increased the synaptic availability of 5-HT would have the specific effect of treating depression. Long-term administration of SSRIs to animals results in desensitization and down regulation of serotonergic autoreceptors. These effects result in increased firing rates in the raphe neurons, increased manufacturing of serotonin, and an enhanced release of serotonin (Richelson, 2001).

These specific effects in animals, however, have not been confirmed in humans. In addition to the research on $5HT_{1A}$, $5HT_{1B}$, and $5HT_{1D}$ receptors, there is conflicting evidence of both down regulations in $5\text{-}HT_{2A}$ receptors in depressed patients and antidepressant-induced up-regulation of these receptors (Massou et al., 1997; Yatham et al., 1999). Even more confusing, in the studies that reported the down regulation due to antidepressant treatment, the down regulation of the $5\text{-}HT_{2A}$ receptors was not due to a clinical effect of the drug; both responders (who were experiencing less depression) and nonresponders (whose condition had not changed) demonstrated reduced receptor numbers.

Nevertheless, certain antidepressants specifically antagonize the $5\text{-}HT_{2A}$ receptors (examples are amoxapine, nefazodone, and mirtazapine). Research suggests that these antidepressants might be superior to SSRIs since they are less likely to induce sexual side effects. In fact, these drugs may be used in combination with SSRIs in patients who have intolerable sexual side effects due to SSRI administration (for example, lack of arousal and difficulty achieving orgasm) (Richelson, 2001).

Helen Mayberg and her colleagues at the University of Texas Health Science Center at San Antonio found a metabolic effect in the brain specific to an SSRI-induced clinical effect (Mayberg et al., 2000). Using PET scans, these researchers looked at the changes in brain glucose metabolism in depressed men being treated with fluoxetine. The patients were tested following both one week and six weeks of pharmacological treatment.

Whereas the glucose metabolic patterns were similar for the nonresponders and responders at the one-week examination, differences were observed after six weeks. Specifically, clinical improvement was associated with decreases in glucose metabolism in the limbic and striatal areas (for example, the cingulate and hippocampal areas) and increases in the brainstem and dorsal cortical areas (for example, the prefrontal, parietal, and cingulate cortices). Similar findings were reported when depressed patients were given a different SSRI, paroxetine. Following successful therapy, increased metabolic rates were observed in the prefrontal areas and decreased rates in the hippocampal area (Kennedy et al., 2001). Thus, according to these studies, it seems that a reciprocal as opposed to a unidirectional pattern of glucose metabolism is important for treatment success.

Another recent study suggests that the effects of SSRIs are quite complicated. In this investigation, Eberhart Fuchs and his colleagues at the German Primate Center in Göttingen gave the European drug tianeptine to tree shrews (small primates) undergoing social stress (Czeh et al., 2001). Whereas animals typically respond to this paradigm with a shrinkage in the hippocampal area (also observed in chronic depression), this drug blocked the effect. The interesting and counterintuitive part of this study is that tianeptine is not an SSRI but an *SSRE,* specific serotonin reuptake enhancer; instead of inhibiting reuptake, it enhances reuptake. Certainly, more research needs to be done on this drug before we understand its effect and potential therapeutic value.

In sum, although the SSRIs are the most popular pharmacological treatment for depression, we are just beginning to determine the complexity of their effects in the brain. Recall that SSRIs have been implicated in neurogenesis, suggesting that these drugs mitigate depressive symptoms because of this effect. A major concern surrounding SSRIs is their side effects. Up to 75% of patients experience sexual disturbances; other side effects include gastrointestinal problems and motor effects (Richelson, 2001). Finally, some have proposed that the evidence supporting SSRI's clear superiority over placebos in clinical trials is not sufficient.

Using a meta-analysis to investigate the influence of SSRIs over a placebo, Kirsch and Sapirstein (1998) conclude that inactive placebos contribute to 75% of the effect of this class of drug. As you might guess, this article is controversial, as shown in the editor's explanatory disclaimer

reboxetine Relatively new drug that selectively inhibits the reuptake of noradrenaline in the synapse. Used as an antidepressant, this drug is thought to be more effective than other antidepressants in restoring social functioning in depressed patients.

antalarmin New drug that inhibits the release of corticotropin-releasing hormone and has been found in animal models to reduce anxietylike behaviors in animals. Researchers are hopeful that this drug may be used as an antidepressant in humans in the future.

SNUBs (super neurotransmitter uptake blockers) New drugs that are designed to block the reuptake of more than one monoamine transmitter. These drugs differ from the original tricyclics in their weaker nature and consequently fewer side effects.

which appears at the bottom of the title page. Such a disclaimer is rarely included in research articles, suggesting that, for better or for worse, this research question about the clinical efficacy of Prozac has become much more than a simple research question but rather a question complicated by ethics, politics, and profits.

Noradrenergic manipulation. In an attempt to identify an antidepressant that is superior to the older tricyclics, drugs are also targeted toward the noradrenergic system. Recall that the noradrenergic system is involved in vigilance and drive—two factors involved in depression—and that the effects of all three monoamines involve mood, emotion, and cognition (see Figure 5.9). Serotonin and dopamine also influence appetite and sex, which might be related to some side effects of the SSRIs.

Noradrenaline, however, influences social functioning but has no effect on sex and appetite. Perhaps a drug that influenced only the noradrenergic system would have fewer side effects and an added benefit of restoring social function (a symptom listed in the DSM diagnostic criteria for major depression). That is exactly what is observed with the new selective noradrenergic reuptake inhibitor **reboxetine.** In addition to restoring social functioning, this drug increases the latency for patients to enter REM sleep. Additionally, when patients who are not responding to fluoxetine are switched to reboxetine, positive results have been observed with manageable side effects (Fava, McGrath, & Sheu, 2003). Although reboxetine is not currently approved for use in the United States, it has been approved in 21 countries, including the United Kingdom, Italy, and Germany. It will be interesting to follow its effects and success if and when it is introduced in the United States (Dencker, 2000).

Inhibiting corticotropin-releasing hormone. As you know, the stress response is an integral component of the symptoms of depression. Consequently, researchers are beginning to think about drugs that might influence the HPA axis. One such anti-CRH drug, **antalarmin,** was recently tested with rhesus macaques. Monkeys were exposed to intense social stress consisting of placing two unfamiliar males in cages adjacent to their home cage. Antalarmin reduced anxietylike or stress responses such as grimacing, body tremors, teeth gnashing, urination, and defecation while increasing exploratory and sexual behaviors. Further tests confirmed that this drug diminished the increases in CRH in the cerebrospinal fluid (Habib et al., 2000). Based on such results, it is likely that we will hear more about anti-CRH drugs in the near future.

In sum, whereas SSRIs still enjoy successful sales, many new types of drugs have been introduced. New attention is being focused on noradrenaline manipulation, specific serotonergic receptors, and anti-CRH drugs. Whereas dopaminergic reuptake blockers such as Zyban have been used, it is suspected that this drug (also marketed as Wellbutrin) also influences noradrenergic systems (Ascher et al., 1995).

Additionally, pharmaceutical companies are seeking drugs that block both norepinephrine and serotonergic transporters (double-action drugs such as venlafaxine and milnacipran) or that block the transport of norepinephrine, serotonin, and dopamine. These drugs are known as **SNUBs** (super neurotransmitter uptake blockers) (Montgomery, 2000; Richelson, 2001).

You may be thinking that the new drugs are simply new versions of the original tricyclics that blocked the reuptake of all of the monoamines. In a sense that is correct, but the new generation of antidepressants is weaker than the original tricyclic compounds. This weaker inhibition of reuptake should minimize the adverse side effects that plagued the originial tricyclics (Richelson, 2001).

Electroconvulsive Therapy (ECT)

ECT involves using electrical stimulation in anesthetized patients to induce a series of seizures to help patients combat the symptoms of depression (Krystal et al., 2000). As mentioned in Chapter Two, ECT is one of the oldest neurobiological treatments for mental illness. As psychopharmacology became a more appealing method of treatment in the 1960s, the use of ECT decreased dramatically. During the past 20 years, however, its popularity has once again increased.

It is no surprise that ECT is back in favor: it is one of the most effective treatments for depression. The efficacy rate falls between 60% and 80%, a higher success rate than that of any other somatic treatment (Abrams, 1992). Because of the intensity of this treatment strategy and its fairly characteristic side effects (including transient disorientation and memory impairment), ECT is not a front-line therapy. Generally, ECT is offered as a second- and third-line defense against depression following unsuccessful attempts with antidepressants and cognitive-behavioral therapies.

Since the resurrection of ECT, research has been conducted on parameters such as optimal electrical dose, electrode placement, and treatment schedules. Optimal electrical doses are determined by the degree to which the dose exceeds the individual's seizure threshold. Bilateral electrode placement therapies are more effective than unilateral placements. And although a schedule of three sessions per week is associated with the most rapid recovery from depression, it carries the cost of significant side effects such as memory loss. Consequently, this treatment schedule is used only in drastic cases such as when patients are refusing to eat; in most cases, two treatments per week are administered (Nobler, Sackheim, & Devanand, 2000).

Although ECT sounds draconian, it is effective in reducing depression symptoms. Research suggests that ECT does not create any new brain damage in the patient. For example, Zachrisson and colleagues at Goteborg University investigated the effect of ECT on cerebral structure and function by measuring markers of degeneration in neurons and glial cells found in the cerebrospinal fluid. Following six ECT treatments over a two-week period, all nine patients were significantly improved (less depressed), demonstrating the clinical efficacy of this treatment. Interestingly, ECT did not significantly alter levels of the markers; further, the integrity of the blood brain barrier was found to be unaltered by the treatment (Zachrisson et al., 2000).

Perhaps the most curious aspect is the fact that, after all these years of using ECT, researchers are still unsure about exactly how it works to reduce depression. Recently, however, several studies have identified ECT effects that provide clues concerning its clinical efficacy. In one study, patients who responded successfully to ECT demonstrated increases in regional cerebral blood flow (rCBF) that approached the rCBF of nondepressed patients (Milo et al., 2001). Additionally, as previously mentioned, ECT leads to enhanced neurogenesis in rats. Another study conducted on rats found that ECT, along with antidepressants, decreases spontaneous firing in the locus coeruleus, which reacts to environmental events (Grant & Weiss, 2001). Yet another study reported that ECT results in lower glucose metabolism in the areas of the frontal and parietal cortex, left temporal cortex, and cingulate gyrus (Nobler et al., 2001). Perhaps, in some cases, part of the recovery mechanism of ECT involves decreased activity around certain perseverating cognitive/emotional brain circuits.

In sum, although ECT is controversial, recent research has provided guidelines for its administration that result in fewer cognitive side effects and increased clinical efficacy. The acceptance of this treatment, however, remains highly variable across the spectrum of mental health practitioners.

Repetitive Transcranial Magnetic Stimulation (rTMS)

Although the overwhelming treatment emphasis for depression has been on antidepressant drugs since the 1950s and 1960s, a different somatic treatment strategy introduced in 1985 involves the use of powerful electromagnets (Barker, Jalinous, & Freeston, 1985; George, Nahas et al., 1999).

Because electricity and magnetism are interdependent, **repetitive transcranial magnetic stimulation (rTMS)** works by placing a powerful electromagnet on the scalp (Figure 8.5). The magnet emits high-intensity currents in a rapid on/off succession that depolarize the underlying neurons. The rTMS magnetic field is about 1000 times the strength of a refrigerator magnet (enough to wrench a paper clip from grasp) and lasts from about 100 to 200 microseconds.

Conveniently, rTMS treatments can be administered in outpatient settings. Unlike ECT, this treatment neither causes seizures nor requires anesthesia (George et al., 2000). Although rTMS is a new technique that requires further research, the side effects currently seem to be fewer and less severe than those related to ECT. Typically, patients report mild to severe headaches and discomfort at the stimulation sites; these effects usually respond to acetaminophen.

It is important to distinguish rTMS from the questionable new age technique of placing low-intensity magnets on the body. These magnets are weaker, are not necessarily placed on the brain, are constantly on—and there is no empirical evidence concerning their effectiveness. rTMS treatments, on the other hand, have been subjected to clinical trials. George et al. (2000) delivered daily rTMS to the left prefrontal cortical area for 2 weeks and found this treatment to reduce the depression symptoms in significantly more depressed patients than the sham treatment (50% of patients in the treatment group improved whereas 0% in the sham group improved). In this study, about 6% of the sessions resulted in mild headaches, and no seizures or memory deficits were observed.

As is the case with ECT, researchers are still not certain how rTMS works, but a few studies suggest some possible mechanisms. Functional neuroimaging studies of healthy, nondepressed adults indicate that prefrontal rTMS results in subsequent activation in the cingulate gyrus, amygdala, and other areas that have been implicated in the maintenance of mood (George, Stallings et al., 1999). In another study, conducted on rats bred for either high or low anxiety-related behavior, rTMS had an effect on coping behavior in the high anxiety animals. When placed in the forced swimming test, the high-anxiety animals actively struggled more to escape the tank and floated less. The high-anxiety rats receiving rTMS had lower corticosterone levels than the nontreated high-anxiety animals (Keck et al., 2000).

Similar to the effects observed with antidepressants, rTMS exerts an effect on depressed human patients while having no effect on the nondepressed individuals (Keck et al., 2001). Another rat study found that,

[Figure 8.5]
Transcranial magnetic stimulation. Transcranial magnetic stimulation (TMS) involves situating a strong magnet on the scalp. Changes in the magnetic field influences action potentials in neural tissue and has been found to have clinical efficacy in depression patients.

GEORGE RUHE/THE NEW YORK TIMES

repetitive transcranial magnetic stimulation (rTMS)
Relatively new antidepressant treatment that involves placing a powerful electromagnet or coil on the scalp. The magnet produces depolarization in the underlying neurons in the brain.

cognitive-behavioral therapy (CBT) Therapy developed in the 1960s that involves the therapist working with the depressed patient to educate him or her about the disorder so that they can eventually alter behaviors and cognitions to reduce the symptoms of depression.

manic episodes Hyperactivity characterized by euphoria and impaired judgment; exists with depression in bipolar disorder.

similar to antidepressants, rTMS results in decreased sensitivity of the 5-HT_{1A} and 5-HT_{1B} autoreceptors. Thus, it is possible that rTMS and antidepressant drugs may share some common mechanisms of action (Gur, Lerer, Dremencov, & Newman, 2000).

rTMS is still in its preliminary stages of testing, but the current research suggests that it exerts at least short-term effects on depression symptoms. Although we don't know the true duration of the benefits of rTMS, this strategy may be used as an alternative to ECT in treatment-resistant patients. Additionally, rTMS could potentially be used to relieve the symptoms of depression until the clinical effects of the drugs are apparent (George, Nahas et al., 1999).

Cognitive-Behavioral Therapy

The most popular form of **cognitive-behavioral therapy (CBT)** was established by Aaron Beck and his team in the 1960s and was tested for clinical efficacy in 1977. Since that time, Beck's CBT has received extensive support in both group and individual formats and in both inpatient and outpatient settings. Generally, CBT involves (1) educating the patient about how cognitions influence emotions, (2) discussing how patients can serve as their own cotherapists and change their behavior and cognitions to alter depression, and (3) treatment sessions in which the patient and therapist construct and work through an agenda in which role playing and imaging serve as tools for restructuring the patients' cognitions and behaviors (Deckersbach, Gershuny, & Otto, 2000).

When compared to antidepressants, CBT offers approximately equal clinical efficacy. In one study, treatment outcomes for a 12-week session of either CBT or imipramine were compared. Following treatment, 62% of the patients receiving CBT demonstrated significant improvement whereas 56% of the imipramine patients responded favorably (Hollon et al., 1992). Consistent with this finding, a review of 58 studies conducted between 1976 and 1986 investigating the effectiveness of CBT found that, generally, CBT was equally as effective as antidepressants (Robinson, Berman, & Neimeyer, 1990).

Some researchers have attempted to combine pharmacotherapy and CBT to augment the success rate. Although response rates are a bit higher than either treatment in isolation, the differences have failed to reach statistical significance (Deckersbach et al., 2000). In T. M. Luhrmann's book *Of Two Minds: The Growing Disorder in American Psychiatry* (2000), a case is made for the combination of talk therapy and pharmacotherapy, citing evidence of a compromised psychological treatment system resulting from drastic financial cuts for talk therapy with patients. Based on the effectiveness of both pharmacotherapy and CBT, Deckersbach and colleagues have proposed that pharmacotherapy be used for severe cases and CBT for low to moderate depression.

One advantage CBT appears to have over pharmacotherapy is its long-term protection against the hauntingly high relapse rate of 80% observed following pharmacotherapeutic approaches (Jarrett et al., 2001). Relapse rates are lower following CBT than following antidepressant therapy. For example, in one interesting study, 121 depressed patients were assigned to groups receiving CBT, relaxation therapy, nondirective psychotherapy, or pharmacotherapy. Two years following treatment, 64% of the CBT patients remained significantly improved compared with 28% of the pharmacotherapy patients (psychotherapy and relaxation treatments resulted in 36% and 26% sustained recovery rates, respectively) (MacLean & Hakstian, 1990).

Because of the long-term effects of cognitive therapy, Martin Seligman and his colleagues at the University of Pennsylvania investigated the effectiveness of exposing at-risk individuals to an 8-week prevention workshop (Seligman, Schulman, & DeRubeis, 1999). This workshop decreased the number of subsequent moderate depressive episodes but had no effect on severe depressive episodes. Certainly, the establishment of therapies that might prevent subsequent depression in vulnerable individuals deserves further study.

Of course, other behavioral and cognitive therapies have been effective. Physical exercise relieves depression symptoms in humans (Hill, Storandt, & Malley, 1993). In a rat model, exercise, used in combination with antidepressants, was found to increase BDNF, a neurotrophic factor discussed earlier that has been implicated in depression (Russo-Neustadt et al., 2001).

BIPOLAR DISORDER

As observed in Table 8.1, mood disorders consist of more than one variation of mood extremes. In addition to experiencing depressed emotions and activity, some people experience abnormally elevated moods. These elevated moods are typically described as **manic episodes.** About 1% to 1.5% of the population experience symptoms of both depression and mania and are diagnosed with bipolar disorder (National Institute of Mental Health, 2001; Strakowski, DelBello, Adler, Cecil, & Sax, 2000). See Table 8.5 on page 302 for diagnostic criteria.

Typically, the onset of mania occurs abruptly and lasts from a few days to a few weeks. The manic episodes are usually briefer than the depressive episodes. Unfortunately, manic episodes often are followed by depressive episodes—placing the patient on an emotional roller coaster.

[Table 8.5]

Diagnostic Criteria for Manic Episode

A. A distinct period of persistently elevated, expansive, or irritable mood, lasting at least 1 week (or any duration if hospitalization is necessary).

B. During the period of mood disturbance, three (or more) of the following symptoms have persisted (four if the mood is only irritable) and have been present to a significant degree:

   (1) inflated self-esteem or grandiosity

   (2) decreased need for sleep (e.g., feels rested after only 3 hours of sleep)

   (3) more talkative than usual or pressure to keep talking

   (4) flight of ideas or subjective experience that thoughts are racing

   (5) distractibility (i.e., attention too easily drawn to unimportant or irrelevant external stimuli)

   (6) increase in goal-directed activity (either socially, at work or school, or sexually) or psychomotor agitation

   (7) excessive involvement in pleasurable activities that have a high potential for painful consequences (e.g., engaging in unrestrained buying sprees, sexual indiscretions, or foolish business investments)

C. The symptoms do not meet criteria for a Mixed Episode.

D. The mood disturbance is sufficiently severe to cause marked impairment in occupational functioning or in usual social activities or relationships with others or to necessitate hospitalization to prevent harm to self or others, or there are psychotic features. The symptoms are not due to the direct physiological effects of a substance (e.g., a drug of abuse, a medication, or other treatment) or a general medical condition (e.g., hyperthyroidism).

Note: Maniclike episodes that are clearly caused by somatic antidepressant treatment (e.g., medication, electroconvulsive therapy, light therapy) should not count toward a diagnosis of Bipolar I Disorder.

APA, 2000, p. 368.

Although some patients report that the exhilaration experienced when manic can be rewarding and pleasurable at times, these episodes typically come with great personal cost. They affect patients' marriages, businesses, finances, and health, and they lead to exhaustion, occasional drug use, and other risk-taking behaviors that place the patient in frequent danger. At the extreme, the manic patient is at an increased risk for death due to cardiac complications and has an increased tendency toward suicide in the transition from mania to depression, when patients realize the inappropriateness of their behavior (Andreasen & Black, 2000). Box 8.5 focuses on Kay Redfield Jamison's bout with bipolar disorder.

Tracing the Neurobiological Roots of Bipolar Disorder

A review of the literature by Baumann and Bogerts (2001) suggests that the brains of patients suffering from bipolar disorder differ significantly from those of patients who are not suffering from mood disorders. Specifically, the basal ganglia are somewhat smaller in both bipolar and depressive patients; the most drastic reductions are found in the nucleus accumbens, that key structure in the translation from environmental stimuli to motivation of response. Structural deficits are also found in the dorsal raphe nucleus, a site for serotonin production.

In another review of the neuroimaging literature, abnormalities were observed in the striatum, amygdala, and the prefrontal cortex. This review supports the notion of frontal–subcortical circuits being involved in bipolar disorder (Strakowski, DelBello, Adler, Cecil, & Sax, 2000). Additionally, decreased cerebellar size has been observed (Stoll, Renshaw, Yurgelun-Todd, & Cohen, 2000).

The most common finding of MRI studies is the presence of white matter hyperintensities at higher rates than expected. *White matter hyperintensities* are small areas characterized by a higher signal intensity than that of the surrounding tissue. These hyperintensities are most commonly found in aging patients and patients suffering from cardiovascular events. Also, processes such as demyelination, astrogliosis (formation of new or growth of existing astrocytes), or axonal loss may lead to the formation of white matter hyperintensities.

Although these anomalies are observed in bipolar patients at a higher rate than expected, the observation that most bipolar patients do not have the hyperintensities suggests that they may play a minimal causal role in this disorder. Thus, it is more likely that they form because of the lifestyle that is characteristic of mania patients (higher rates of substance abuse and cardiovascular risk) than because of a patient's susceptibility to bipolar disorder. However, further research is needed to clarify the role of white matter hyperintensities in bipolar disorder (Stoll et al., 2000).

Lower whole-brain glucose metabolic activity has been observed across the brains of bipolar patients experiencing bipolar depression than in patients experiencing bipolar mania (Baxter et al., 1985). Although one study has shown higher whole-brain blood flow during mania (Rush et al., 1982), many have failed to show blood flow differences in bipolar mania or depression compared with healthy controls (Strakowski et al., 2000). (See Figure 8.6).

Depressed state   Manic state   Depressed state

[Figure 8.6]
Brain activity and bipolar disorder. This PET scan shows a dramatic increase in the brain's metabolization of glucose when the patient goes from a depressed to a manic state.

COURTESY OF DRS. LEWIS BAXTER AND MICHAEL E. PHELPS, UCLA SCHOOL OF MEDICINE

[Box 8.5]

A Case in Point

Kay Redfield Jamison

Kay Jamison has written four successful books on mental illness/health and, in November 2001, she was awarded the prestigious MacArthur Genius Grant. Jamison could easily be this chapter's Investigator, but her struggle with bipolar disorder for most of her life is central to her identity as well.

Jamison's first book, *An Unquiet Mind: A Memoir of Moods and Madness* (1996), carefully documents the highs and lows of her emotional struggles with bipolar disorder. Her first feeling of emotional despair occurred at the vulnerable age of 15, when her father, an Air Force meteorologist and pilot, moved the family from their familiar home in Washington, D.C., to California. Being a military kid in a school where most of the students' parents worked in the film industry was a bit overwhelming.

Although she began to make friends over the next couple of years, Jamison also became aware that she had intensive levels of energy that seemed to exhaust people around her. During her first battle with mania, she felt a bit seduced by the seemingly positive symptoms of pleasure, promise, and a decreased need for sleep. But these periodic highs were followed by de-

pressed phases in which she was preoccupied with the notion of death.

As an undergraduate at UCLA, Jamison struggled with managing classes around her diverse mood swings. She found some solace when the professor of her personality theory class asked her to assist in his research. She loved the independence and flexibility in her work schedule that accompanied the research. During her junior year, she opted to escape from her tumultuous life at UCLA by going to study and conduct research at the University of St. Andrews in Scotland. Her brother, who was studying abroad, encouraged her to venture out of the United States; that and her admiration of the Scottish music and poetry that she associated with her Scottish ancestry contributed to her decision to make the trip.

During that year Jamison worked with a prominent neurophysiologist, making electrophysiological recordings of the locusts' auditory nerves. She found this research challenging, and she found the atmosphere in Scotland healing for the emotional wounds she had developed with her mental illness. On returning to UCLA, Jamison decided to pursue a career in psychology; she was especially interested in individual differences in emotional capacity. A reprieve in her illness enabled her to successfully complete graduate school, where she trained to become a clinician. Although she had been battling the highs and lows of bipolar disorder for years, she did not recognize herself as a manic-depressive

---

Treatment for Bipolar Disorder

lithium Chemical element approved in the 1970s as a drug for treatment of bipolar disorder. Although the specific biological mechanism is unknown, lithium is known to share ionic properties with some of the important ions maintaining neural functions such as magnesium and calcium.

Pharmacotherapy has been quite successful in treating bipolar disorder. Although the chemical element **lithium** was recognized over 150 years ago as having some potential for treating affective disorders, its potential efficacy as a treatment for bipolar disorder did not surface until the work of John Cade (1949). Cade, an Australian psychiatrist who reportedly had little research training, was working in a small hospital with minimal equipment when he became convinced that a toxic substance was contributing to the mood swings observed in mania and depression. Specifically, the presence of this hypothesized toxic substance contributed to mania and the absence of this substance contributed to the symptoms of depression.

Kay Redfield Jamison
ROYCE CARLTON

even after studying mental illness in graduate school.

On earning her doctorate, Jamison was hired in the Department of Psychiatry at UCLA where she enthusiastically set out in her new career. She felt "madness" approaching during her first summer as a professor; her manic behavior had progressed to behavior that raised suspicions in her colleagues and led to the demise of her first marriage. When she started to hallucinate, Jamison knew she had to get professional help.

Jamison was then introduced to lithium and was able to focus on her career once again. She wrote in *An Unquiet Mind,* "My work and professional life flowed. But nowhere did this, or my upbringing, or my intellect, or my character, prepare me for insanity" (p. 81). Through this time, her psychiatrist recommended aggressive pharmacotherapy and psychoanalysis. Not wanting to surrender to the idea that she needed lithium to maintain a normal existence, she decided to stop taking her medication just six months after beginning it. She continued an on-again, off-again pattern of lithium use and active illness, which led to a suicide attempt. Ironically, Jamison took an overdose of the very drug that was saving her life—lithium. Her suicide attempt was unsuccessful, but it left her comatose. On recovering, Jamison learned to ride with her emotions and accomplished enough professionally to get tenure at UCLA.

After receiving tenure, Jamison was devastated when the man she was seeing died of a heart attack. Jamison decided to take a year's sabbatical in England where she could focus on moods—mourning her friend and studying the relationship between mood disorders and eminent British writers and artists. This work later became the book *Touched with Fire* (1993).

Although many people with bipolar disorder struggle their entire lives and are unable to maximize their career potential, Kay Jamison has certainly thrived. She shared her mental illness with the world when she published *An Unquiet Mind.* Subsequently, she wrote a book on suicide entitled *Night Falls Fast,* and most recently she published a book exploring more positive emotions called *Exuberance: The Passion for Life* (2004). She is currently married to Richard Wyatt, a schizophrenia researcher and chief of neuropsychiatry at the National Institute of Mental Health. After moving back to Washington, D.C., she accepted an appointment in the Psychiatry Department at Johns Hopkins University. She still takes lithium to protect against drastic mood fluctuation, but her maintenance doses are lower than the doses she started taking years ago.

To test his idea, Cade took the urine from his mania patients (he thought the urine might contain this toxic substance) and injected it into guinea pigs. All urine is toxic to guinea pigs, and Cade initially observed that the urine from the manic patients killed the animals at a faster rate—only about one-third of the typical lethal dose of urine from nonmania patients was needed. At this point, Cade knew he was onto something. After elegantly separating the chemical components of the urine from the manic patients, he found that urea was the toxic substance leading to the faster death of the guinea pigs. When he injected only urea, the guinea pigs responded as if they had received a urine injection. The other components of urine, uric acid and creatinine, failed to produce any toxic effects, but uric acid mildly enhanced the toxicity of urea.

Cade wanted to investigate further the finding that uric acid facilitated toxicity but ran into a hurdle trying to dissolve the uric acid crystals in water for the injections. To address the insolubility problem he simply chose the most soluble urate, lithium, to combine with urea for injections. Subsequently, Cade injected a few guinea pigs with the urea that was saturated with lithium urate and waited to observe the toxic effects. He was very surprised to see that, instead of killing the guinea pigs, the urea's toxicity was reduced. Cade shifted his emphasis to the potential protective qualities of the lithium.

But how could lithium, which is found in nature in only small quantities compared with chemicals such as sodium, magnesium, potassium, and calcium, have such a striking effect? The answer was not clear, but Cade trusted his data and pursued his research. He switched from the lithium ion to lithium carbonate because it produced fewer troublesome side effects. Again, he found that lithium carbonate decreased the urea-induced mortality by 50%. And when Cade injected only lithium carbonate into the guinea pigs, he also observed interesting effects. Following injections, when he placed the guinea pigs on their backs, instead of the typical frantic attempts to return to their normal upright position, they just lay back and gazed at the experimenter.

Cade had seen enough to take his laboratory efforts to the clinic; he decided to try the lithium carbonate on mania patients. Following the old medical maxim "Primum non nocere" ("First do no harm"), he decided to be the first person to take the lithium pills. After observing no ill effects, he gave lithium pills to ten manic patients. The results seemed miraculous; patients who had been institutionalized were released from their manic episodes and given an opportunity to live outside the hospital. In 1949, Cade published his findings in the *Medical Journal of Australia.*

Cade's exercise in cool logic is one of the best examples of serendipity that can be found in the scientific literature. No theory current at the time suggested that lithium was beneficial in manic episodes, and it is unlikely that any scientist would have encountered its effectiveness in treating mania if Cade had not stumbled across it trying simply to find a salt that is more soluble than uric acid. Fortunately, Cade was informed enough to follow the intriguing findings he was reporting in this line of research and was able to improve the quality of life of hundreds of thousands of people suffering from manic episodes (Restak, 1994). Interestingly, Cade did not go on to research fame. He went back to his patients and never conducted research again.

Although Cade made his discovery in the 1940s, lithium was not approved in the United States until the early 1970s; until recently, it was the only drug available for treating bipolar disorder. Before reviewing the more recent drugs, let's take a look at the possible effects of lithium. At the outset, it is important to note that researchers still do not know the biological basis for its therapeutic efficacy. On a general level, the fact that lithium shares ionic properties known to regulate the nervous system with some of the heavy-hitting ions, such as sodium, magnesium, and calcium, may be very important. Its chemical similarity with these ions allows lithium easy access into cells, where it probably exerts an impact on a host of intracellular processes.

It is conceivable that the nonspecific aspect of lithium uptake in multiple types of cells may affect both poles of bipolar disorder. Additional studies suggest that lithium may influence protein kinase C, a ubiquitous enzyme in the brain that regulates both presynaptic and postsynaptic components of neural transmission (see Chapter Four). Research suggests that short-term lithium exposure enhances protein kinase C-related effects, and long-term exposure attenuates these responses.

Overall, lithium seems to enhance presynaptic activity in the serotonergic system, although this effect depends on the duration of treatment and the neuroanatomical site being tested. It has been suggested that the widespread nature of its effects leads to the reestablishment of homeostatic processing among the structures of the limbic system and its associated areas (this research was reviewed in Manji, McNamara, & Lenox, 2000).

Lithium's many unwanted side effects (including tremors, weight gain, gastrointestinal disturbances, frequent urination, memory problems, sedation, and decreased levels of thyroid hormones) have led researchers to search for less harmful pharmacological treatments (Strakowski et al., 2000). In fact, as delineated in the Jamison case study discussed earlier, if dosages are not closely monitored, lithium toxicity can lead to a host of devastating effects such as seizures, coma, and death.

During the past several years, it has become evident that anticonvulsant medications are also effective for the treatment of bipolar disorder. The anticonvulsant **valproate** looks very promising for bipolar patients. Although valproate appears to be as effective as lithium in the treatment of acute mania, it is not clear if this substance will have the protective effects of lithium for bipolar patients. Lithium also seems to offer some antidepressant effects for some bipolar patients, and this effect has not been observed with valproate. On a positive note, valproate produces fewer side effects, and a wider therapeutic margin, or range of doses, can be given without toxic side effects. Although lithium remains the tried and true treatment for bipolar disorder, substances such as valproate may offer significant benefits to patients who do not respond to lithium or to those whose disorder is characterized by rapid cycling.

valproate Anticonvulsant drug that shows promise as an effective treatment for bipolar disorder.

Summary

Mood Disorders: An Overview

The mood-related disorders, all with different intensities, durations, and patterns, differ from many clinical disorders: they follow an intermittent pattern instead of a progressively worsening course. Major depression is among the most common mental illnesses, affecting approximately 17% of the population. Several factors seem to influence susceptibility to mood disorders, including gender, diet, stress, and certain genetic predispositions.

Evolutionary psychologists hypothesize that moods evolved to facilitate successful responses to an ever-changing environment, with more positive moods attracting us toward stimuli associated with increased survival (for example, food) and more negative moods repelling us from stimuli associated with decreased survival (for example, predator attacks). Problems arise when mood does not modulate in response to the appropriate stimuli in the environment.

Tracing the Neurobiological Roots of Depression

An elaborate neuroanatomical circuit has been proposed to underlie the symptoms of depression. The prefrontal cortex lies at the heart of the circuit (multiple forms of data indicate a general atrophy of the PFC in depressed patients). The prefrontal cortex has intimate connections with other brain areas implicated in depression, such as the hippocampus, amygdala, anterior cingulate cortex, thalamus, and nucleus accumbens. Collectively, these neuroanatomical sites contribute to commonly observed symptoms such as profound sadness, fear, anxiety, anhedonia, and difficulty in cognitive tasks. This circuit is modulated by two brainstem systems: serotonin secreted by the raphe nuclei and norepinephrine secreted by the locus coeruleus.

The serotonin depletion hypothesis suggests that, because drugs that increase levels of serotonergic functions in the synapse are successful in the treatment of depressive symptoms, depressed patients have low levels of serotonin. Although decreased serotonergic functions in depressed patients have been observed, other evidence suggests that alterations in serotonergic activity fail to influence depressive symptoms. The convergence of evidence, however, suggests that alterations in the sensitivity of serotonergic receptors play the biggest role in reducing symptoms of depression.

The catecholamine hypothesis proposed in the 1960s suggests that depression is caused by decreased levels of norepinephrine whereas mania is caused by excessive levels of norepinephrine. This theory became less popular with the introduction of the serotonin depletion theory, but nonetheless it remains viable. When patients who are taking drugs that increase norepinephrine in the synapse are placed on a norepinephrine-deficient diet, their symptoms reemerge, as seen when patients taking SSRIs are placed on a serotonin-deficient diet. It is currently thought that norepinephrine, like other monoamines, has a modulating role on the systems involved with depression: any manipulation of these systems can conceivably influence depression symptoms.

Corticosteroids, released during the stress response, are present in high levels in depressed patients. For this reason, researchers are investigating the role of this hormone in depression as well as the potential value of drugs that block the release of corticosteroids.

An exciting area of research suggests that depression may result from decreased brain plasticity. Successful depression therapies such as ECT and SSRIs have been shown to influence brain plasticity; specifically, ECT results in an increased production of new brain cells and SSRIs increase the production of the neurotrophic factor, BDNF.

Stress and Depression

Environmental stressors play a significant role in the etiology of depression. An interrupted parental bond (separation or abuse) early in an animal's life can disrupt the stress response system and lead to an increased susceptibility to depression. Additionally, disruptions in environmental variables such as seasonal changes in light seem to increase susceptibility to depression.

Treatment for Depression

Although MAOIs and tricyclic antidepressants were the first pharmacological therapies for depression, SSRIs have generally replaced these drugs. SSRIs aren't necessarily more effective than the earlier drugs, but they have fewer threatening side effects. Because SSRIs are not free from side effects, new antidepressants are being investigated. New drugs such as reboxetine, a norepinephrine uptake blocker, anticorticotropin-releasing hormone drugs, and various SNUBs are being introduced as pharmacological therapies.

ECT is a long-standing somatic therapy for depression. Because this therapy requires the patient to be anesthetized and frequently results in memory loss, it is used only as a last resort. A newer somatic therapy, rTMS, involves placing a magnet on the scalp to alter the conductivity of underlying neurons. Preliminary evidence suggests that this therapy may be as effective as ECT without the dangerous side effects, but more research is necessary before informed conclusions can be made.

Cognitive-behavioral therapy—therapist-guided discussions about depression and how to cognitively and behaviorally respond to life situations to alter the likelihood of depressive episodes—often results in efficacy rates similar to antidepressants. An advantage to various forms of CBT is a reduced relapse rate compared to pharmacotherapy.

Bipolar Disorder

Approximately 1% to 1.5% of the population suffers from bipolar disorder, in which depression episodes are interspersed with episodes of mania. Neuroanatomical studies suggest that the neurobiological components are similar to that seen in depression with the additional involvement of the basal ganglia. Hyperintensities of the white matter have also been observed in bipolar patients; more research is required, however, to determine whether hyperintensities are a cause or effect of bipolar disorder.

Although the specific mechanisms remain unknown, the most successful treatment for bipolar disorder is the drug lithium. Other drugs, such as valproate, an anticonvulsant, are currently being explored as alternative pharmacological treatments for patients who are not able to take lithium because of severe side effects.

Key Terms

mood (affective) disorders (p. 264)
major depressive disorder (p. 264)
bipolar disorder (p. 264)
depression (p. 265)
prefrontal cortex (PFC) (p. 270)
anterior cingulate cortex (p. 273)
anhedonia (p. 275)
learned helplessness (p. 275)
corticosteroids (p. 284)

seasonal affective disorder (SAD) (p. 290)
iproniazid (p. 291)
monoamine oxidase inhibitors (MAOIs) (p. 291)
imipramine (p. 291)
tricyclic antidepressants (p. 291)
fluoxetine (p. 294)
reboxetine (p. 296)

antalarmin (p. 296)
SNUBs (super neurotransmitter uptake blockers) (p. 297)
repetitive transcranial magnetic stimulation (rTMS) (p. 299)
cognitive behavioral therapy (CBT) (p. 300)
manic episodes (p. 301)
lithium (p. 304)
valproate (p. 307)

For Further Consideration

Jacobs, B. L., van Praag, H., & Gage, F. H. (2000). Adult brain neurogenesis and psychiatry: A novel theory of depression. *Molecular Psychiatry, 5,* 262–269. Just when we thought that we had a pretty good understanding of the role of certain neurochemicals such as serotonin in depression, these authors propose that brain plasticity plays a significant role in depression. They specifically point to neurogenesis in the hippocampus as an important contributing variable in depression.

Jamison, K. R. (1996). *An unquiet mind: A memoir of moods and madness.* New York: Vintage Books. This book is written by a psychologist who has bipolar disorder. Jamison describes the highs and lows of her personal life with the unique perspective of a psychologist. She conveys the lure of the manic phases in the earlier stages of her disorder and how exhausting the disorder became at later stages. By disclosing the personal details of her life, the reader gets a clear picture of what it is like to live with biploar disorder.

Nemeroff, C. B. (1998). The neurobiology of depression. *Scientific American, 278,* 28–35. This classic article describes the disorder of depression and evaluates likely underlying causes of this disorder. In addition to disrupted neurochemical systems, Nemeroff suggests that early stress may predispose people toward depression when they become adults. He calls this phenomenon the stress-diathesis model of depression. Beautiful illustrations of relevant neurochemical involvement and brain-imaging scans are included in this article.

Ressler, K. J., & Nemeroff, C. B. (2000). Role of serotonergic and neoradrenergic systems in the pathophysiology of depression and anxiety disorders. *Depression and Anxiety, 12,* 2–19. This is a wonderful review of both serotonin and noradrenaline in depression and anxiety. Although drugs that are effective in treating depression generally increase serotonergic function and generally decrease noradrenaline, these authors suggest that there is more to the depression–neurochemical story. They suggest that serotonin and noradrenaline modulate some unknown system. This article also explores the specific brain areas responsible for specific symptoms observed in depression.

Richelson, E. (2001). Pharmacology of antidepressants. *Mayo Clinic Proceedings, 76,* 511–127. This article is a thorough review of depression and the specific efficacy and underlying pharmacology for each of the drugs currently used in the battle against this disorder. In addition to the efficacy of each drug, relevant issues are specific neurophysiological effect, adverse side effects, and interactions with other drug or neurochemical systems. A discussion of possible new antidepressants is included in the last section of the article.

Solomon, A. (2001). *The noonday demon.* New York: Scribner. Andrew Solomon is a journalist, not a scientist, but his investigative skills enable him to approach depression from several different angles. In addition to including interviews with scientists and individuals suffering from depression, he provides a painful analysis of his own bout with depression. Because of Solomon's skill in storytelling, the reader can begin to feel the misery associated with this dreaded disorder. This book helps the reader to view depression from the multiple perspectives endorsed in this textbook.

9
Schizophrenia

Connections

Home Movies, Childhood Behavior, and Schizophrenia

Walker's examination of home movies of children prior to their diagnosis of schizophrenia suggests early motor patterns such as atypical hand movements shown in this picture.

COURTESY OF ELAINE WALKER

One of the greatest challenges for scientists interested in schizophrenia is the observation that, on the surface, a child seems perfectly fine throughout childhood only to experience a drastic alteration in late adolescence or early adulthood that leads to a diagnosis of schizophrenia. How could a seemingly healthy child, a child perhaps excelling at school, be so suddenly taken hostage by a schizophrenic brain? Elaine Walker, working at Emory University, is investigating this question with an unlikely source of data. Walker is using family photographs and home movies to determine facial and motor abnormalities that may have been present in children who would subsequently be diagnosed with schizophrenia (Walker, Lewine, & Neumann, 1996;

Walker, Grimes, Davis, & Smith, 1993; Walker, Savoie, & Davis, 1994; personal communication, 2002).

Trying to collect photographs through the parent network of the National Alliance of the Mentally Ill, one of the parents suggested that Walker might want to look at home movies of their children. Walker immediately realized the richness of this source of data—home movies are filmed at times of emotional relevance such as birthday parties and holidays, and the occasions provide a wonderful backdrop for assessing the appropriateness of facial expressions/movements (e.g., smiles). Additionally, home movies are filmed at developmental landmarks in the child's life, such as the first time a child rolls over, sits up, and walks, and thus provide valuable data related to motor development.

Walker and her students proceeded to collect a sufficient number of home movies of preschizophrenic children and devised a strategy to systematically code the videotapes for any physical/motor, social behavior, or facial expression anomalies. Researchers scoring the tapes were blinded to whether they were assessing a preschizophrenic child or a nonschizophrenic sibling. Subtle neuromotor abnormalities were evident in the first two years of preschizophrenic children. For example, these children engaged in more abnormal involuntary hand movements than their nonschizophrenic siblings.

The studies have revealed differences in the expression of emotions, as well; specifically, preschizophrenic children exhibited more negative facial emotions, such as crying, during their first year of life than did nonschizophrenic children. These findings have been associated with abnormal development of certain brain structures. When magnetic resonance imaging (MRI) was conducted on schizophrenia patients, Walker found that neuromotor deficits and negative affect in early childhood were associated with larger ventricle size in the subsequently developed brain of the adult.

Elaine Walker (second from left) and her team of researchers
COURTESY OF ELAINE WALKER

Currently, Walker is working with her graduate students Lisa Keslter and Annie Bollini on an investigation of the development of *schizotypal* adolescents, a condition closely related to schizophrenia. Keslter is also working with postdoctoral fellow Rebecca Huot, exploring developmental markers in other forms of mental illness. For example, they are studying the behavioral and psychological responses to stress of infants of depressed mothers.

Walker's data suggest that certain behavioral and affective anomalies exist in children who eventually will probably manifest the symptoms of schizophrenia. Learning of such early markers provides little relief to parents of children who have increased risk of developing schizophrenia until there is some therapeutic intervention associated with early identification. This research is still in its infancy; however, Walker and her colleagues would like to identify therapeutic interventions in the future. In the meantime, clarifying exactly when the brain is experiencing alterations will probably contribute valuable information to the existing knowledge of this devastating disease.

Schizophrenia represents a brain divided. Although schizophrenia has likely existed since the dawn of humankind, it has been objectively described and studied only for a century or so. In that time, treatment has moved from mere institutionalization and hopelessness to dramatic reversal of symptoms by a variety of strong pharmacological agents. What began the revolution in treating schizophrenia was the recognition that it is a brain disorder, the result of malformation of structure and function. Like gazing at the stars but never being able to travel there, however, curing schizophrenia remains elusive yet tantalizingly within our grasp. Neuroscience is this century's best hope for conquering it.

The climb up the mountain of diagnoses, data, and subjectivity that make up the field of research into schizophrenia is arduous. This chapter begins with a general overview of the vast symptomology that characterizes the disorder. Next we present the neurobiology of schizophrenia, intertwined with theories of its etiology and potential causes. We conclude with an overview of treatments for schizophrenia, including pharmacological, psychosocial, and cognitive therapies.

hallucination An internal perception of a realistic sensory event in the absence of any external stimuli.

OVERVIEW OF SCHIZOPHRENIA

Prevalence rates for schizophrenia have been reported to range from 0.5% to 1.5% of the adult population. This disorder is generally diagnosed between the ages of 15 and 35 years and is estimated to afflict over 24 million people worldwide (about 19% of the 450 million estimated to suffer from some mental health condition). Of these millions, more than 90% live in developing countries and fewer than 50% are receiving care and treatment (APA, 2000; World Health Organization, 2003).

Causes of the cultural differences in this disorder are unknown. Higher prevalence is reported in areas of Sweden, Croatia, and Ireland and among the Tamils of Southern India and Canadian Catholics. Lower rates are observed in the American Amish and the aboriginal tribes of Taiwan and Ghana (Andreasen & Black, 2001). As described in Connections at the beginning of the chapter, schizophrenia can develop in childhood, but the mean age for women is 27 years, for men 21 years.

Although the worldwide incidence rate is low, the chronic conditions of individuals receiving no or inadequate care lead to a significant cost to the individuals and surrounding community; hence schizophrenia represents a prevalent cost to society. More important, however, is the cost to the individual diagnosed with schizophrenia: statistics suggest that they are less likely to marry and have children, are more likely to be in low social classes, exhibit high rates of violent behavior (probably due to impaired thoughts and hallucinations), and are high risks for suicide (33% attempt, 10% are successful; Andreasen & Black, 2001).

History, Descriptions, and Definitions

The beginning of modern schizophrenia research can be traced to Emil Kraepelin a century ago (see Chapter Two for a fuller discussion of Kraepelin's contributions). Kraepelin, a psychiatrist and researcher, was among the first to attempt to distinguish different forms of mental distress. From among the many mental patients Kraepelin and his colleagues treated, there emerged a selective group of patients with a cluster of partially overlapping symptoms:

- Auditory and visual **hallucinations**
- Motor tics

catatonia Absence of movement; often observed in the schizophrenic patient.

hebephrenia Inappropriate and uncontrollable form of laughter.

dementia praecox Older term for schizophrenia describing what was believed to be a progressive and incurable deterioration of mental functioning that typically began in adolescence.

schizophrenia Mental disorder characterized by disordered thoughts, delusions, hallucinations, and other bizarre behaviors.

- Poor regulation of speech or disordered thought
- **Catatonia,** absence of movement often observed in the schizophrenia patient, coupled with **hebephrenia,** an inappropriate and uncontrollable form of laughter

Kraepelin termed this constellation of behaviors, observed in the thousands of patients he had treated, **dementia praecox** (early dementia), with an emphasis on the relatively early onset he and others had observed among their patients.

As noted in Chapter Two, Kraepelin advanced the field by distinguishing between patients who got better, such as those with depression, and those who moved inexorably toward dementia as observed in schizophrenia patients. He was among the first to recognize the existence of dementia praecox, the precursor to schizophrenia. He saw something that others did not or had merely hinted at. Like the first paleontologist to interpret the shape of a newly uncovered bone as indicative of a new species of dinosaur, though, Kraepelin realized that he was seeing two separable phenomena.

With this basic observation in hand, Kraepelin set out to describe and catalog schizophrenia with the naturalist's eye. His rich descriptions are still consulted as much for their completeness as for their objectivity. Eugen Bleuler, a Swiss psychiatrist, then built on Kraepelin's observational foundation.

Contemporary Views of Schizophrenia

Bleuler renamed Kraepelin's dementia praecox **schizophrenia** to more accurately reflect the fracture among various psychological activities. This new name was derived from the Greek words *schizo,* meaning "splitting," and *phrene,* meaning "psychic functions." Bleuler intended this new term to emphasize the splitting of normal psychological processes: the emotional and cognitive processes were not operating in a logical and synchronized fashion. Blueler found no evidence that patients' abilities deteriorate, and he thought the emphasis on the splitting of normal processes would convey this observation. He had no intention of describing the even rarer "split personality" associated with dissociative identity disorder (DID), formerly called multiple personality disorder (Andreasen & Black, 2001; Green, 2001; see Chapter One).

Bleuler categorized the symptoms associated with schizophrenia into fundamental and accessory symptoms. The fundamental, or core, symptoms included ambivalence, affective disturbances, and alterations in association. Accessory symptoms were the product of the fundamental symptoms and included hallucinations, delusions, and speech and behavioral abnormalities.

Interestingly, for most of the twentieth century, the accessory symptoms, not the fundamental symptoms, received most of the clinical attention. According to Green (2001), the accessory hallucinations and delusions became the "elephant in the middle of the room" demanding all the attention of the clinical experts. Other symptoms began to be considered in the 1980s. Today, statistical procedures such as factor analysis have enabled the DSM to provide not two but three broad categories of schizophrenia symptoms (Table 9.1). This three-part categorization is especially valuable today as researchers and clinicians interpret the differential success of psychoactive drugs on each category of symptoms.

[Table 9.1]

Diagnostic Criteria for Schizophrenia

A. *Characteristic symptoms:* Two (or more) of the following, each present for a significant portion of time during a 1-month period (or less if successfully treated):

(1) delusions

(2) hallucinations

(3) disorganized speech (e.g., frequent derailment or incoherence)

(4) grossly disorganized or catatonic behavior

(5) negative symptoms, i.e., affective flattering, alogia, or avolition

Note: Only one Criterion A symptom is required if delusions are bizarre or hallucinations consist of a voice keeping up a running commentary on the person's behavior or thoughts, or two or more voices conversing with each other.

B. *Social/occupational dysfunction:* For a significant portion of the time since the onset of the disturbance, one or more major areas of functioning such as work, interpersonal relations, or self-care are markedly below the level achieved prior to the onset (or when the onset is in childhood or adolescence, failure to achieve expected level of interpersonal, academic, or occupational achievement).

C. *Duration:* Continuous signs of the disturbance persist for at least 6 months. This 6-month period must include at least 1 month of symptoms (or less if successfully treated) that meet Criterion A (i.e., active-phase symptoms) and may include periods of prodromal or residual symptoms. During these prodromal or residual periods, the signs of the disturbance may be manifested by only negative symptoms or two or more symptoms listed in Criterion A present in an attenuated form (e.g., odd beliefs, unusual perceptual experiences).

D. *Schizoaffective and Mood Disorder exclusion:* Schizoaffective Disorder and Mood Disorder with Psychotic Features have been ruled out because either (1) no Major Depressive, Manic, or Mixed Episodes have occurred concurrently with the active-phase symptoms; or (2) if mood episodes have occurred during active-phase symptoms, their total duration has been brief relative to the duration of the active and residual periods.

E. *Substance/general medical condition exclusion:* The disturbance is not due to the direct physiological effects of a substance (e.g., a drug of abuse, a medication) or a general medical condition.

F. *Relationship to a Pervasive Developmental Disorder:* If there is a history of Autistic Disorder or another Pervasive Developmental Disorder, the additional diagnosis of Schizophrenia is made only if prominent delusions or hallucinations are also present for at least a month (or less if successfully treated).

Classification of longitudinal course (can be applied only after at least 1 year has elapsed since the initial onset of active-phase symptoms):

Episodic with Interepisode Residual Symptoms (episodes are defined by the reemergence of prominent psychotic symptoms); *also specify if:*

With Prominent Negative Symptoms

Episodic with No Interepisode Residual Symptoms

Continuous (prominent psychotic symptoms are present throughout the period of observation); *also specify if:*

With Prominent Negative Symptoms

Single Episode in Partial Remission; *also specify if:* **With Prominent Negative Symptoms**

Single Episode in Full Remission

Other or Unspecified Pattern

APA, 1994, pp. 285–286.

positive symptoms
Characteristics or attributes that are added to a schizophrenia patient's nature, such as hallucinations.

negative symptoms
Characteristics or attributes that are absent from the nature of a person with schizophrenia, such as reduced desire for social interaction.

disorganized symptoms
Symptoms in a schizophrenia patient such as nonlogical thoughts and speech.

■ Hallucinations and delusions are **positive symptoms,** in the sense of adding a new symptom to the repertoire.

■ Behaviors that are "taken away" from the patient's normal functioning (e.g., a lack of appropriate emotional expression, reductions of speech and thoughts, and a decreased desire for social interactions) are **negative symptoms.** It is easy to see how negative symptoms of schizophrenia might be confused with symptoms of depression; however, such social withdrawal (Bleuler's core fundamental symptoms) might very well be contributing to the more distinctive positive (accessory) symptoms.

■ **Disorganized symptoms** (for example, disorganized speech and thought patterns) are Bleuler's "alterations in association," which he considered a core symptom (Green, 2001).

Views of a Schizophrenic Mind

One way to understand how the symptoms of schizophrenia are expressed is to talk with a patient. Following is a short conversation with a man who was diagnosed with chronic schizophrenia in his early twenties. Currently an outpatient at a Richmond, Virginia area clinic, he has been following a regimen of antipsychotic medication for the last decade.

Reportedly a happy and active child, he was smart, effusive (his word), and curious. As a teenager, he played the piano and loved to write music. On the day of the interview at the clinic, he had not yet taken his medication. Note especially the instant familiarity, as if he were practiced in talking about his schizophrenia; note also the sensual nature and focus of some of his descriptions, and perhaps most obvious, the interplay of lucidity and fantasy, as if his imagination is controlling his speech.

Interviewer: Tell me a little about your day.

Patient: I wake up and see the moons in the face of my mother. She loves me and God loves me and I have cereal for breakfast. I like to eat Cheerios sometimes because they remind me of the wheels on the road by my house. The cars and trucks go fast and they make me forget about my pains.

Interviewer: What does it feel like when you are having your pains?

Patient: I don't like it much. My head gets tight and I hear the cars talking and they tell me that I am going too fast, and that I need to watch over the smells. I smell dogs and dog poop and I have to smoke the trucks that drive by my house.

Interviewer: What do you dream about at night?

Patient: The night scares me. The devil comes sometimes and I can smell him and I can smell the smoke that sticks to him from hell. I drink my Coke and my hamburger and I wait to fall asleep with the walls that cover me.

Interviewer: What do you want to do in the future?

Patient: I want to think and to fly and have the devil go away. The pills I take help me and they keep the devil's talking away, and I can see my mom, so I can fly in my room.

In just 12 sentences, a vast array of schizophrenic symptomology is apparent. Auditory hallucinations are conveyed in his reports of hearing cars and the devil talking; disorganized thinking is apparent in sentences such as the ones about having to smoke the trucks going by his house and perceiving that walls cover him. The patient also reports olfactory hallucinations of smelling the devil. Thus, the positive and disorganized symptoms are easily seen in this conversation.

Negative symptoms are more difficult to detect in a conversation, but social withdrawal and inappropriate emotional expression are vividly portrayed in the movie *A Beautiful Mind,* based on the life of Nobel Prize–winning mathematician John Nash (Nasar, 1999). As described in Box 9.1, social isolation was one of the earliest symptoms the Nash family noticed.

NEUROBIOLOGY OF SCHIZOPHRENIA

From animal models and brain scans using functional magnetic resonance imaging (fMRI) to detailed genetic analyses, including newly acquired data from the Human Genome Project, we now have the means to examine schizophrenia comprehensively. Though a long way from a cure or even a treatment free from significant drawbacks, the neurobiological direction in which schizophrenia research is moving promises to yield a clearer understanding of the disease, its etiology, and most effective treatment options.

Genetic Factors

The observations of Franz Kallmann in the 1920s and 1930s suggested a possible role for heredity in the transmission, incidence, and severity of schizophrenia. After losing his university position in Berlin in 1935, Kallmann, a Jew, immigrated to New York, where he conducted an elaborate study of the relative roles of heritability and environmental influences in schizophrenia. Using an archival methodological strategy, he used the medical records of New York State mental hospitals to assess the

[Box 9.1]

A Case in Point

The Transformations of John Nash's Schizophrenic Mind

As a child, John Nash was bright and curious, but introverted. He preferred to stay inside and read rather than play with the other neighborhood children. In retrospect, there were signs that are now identifiable as evidence of the mental turmoil that would wrack the adult Nash's life. Elaine Walker's research, described in the chapter-opening Connections, suggests that signs of motor difficulties may presage the development of schizophrenia. Nash gripped his pencil like a stick, and his handwriting was illegible. Although he preferred his left hand, his father insisted that he use his right hand. A picture of Nash sitting among his high school peers shows a child with his eyes rolled back in his head, appearing bored. He was the recipient of endless teasing for his many social mishaps and nonsocial, weird behaviors.

Even his hopeful mother, Virginia, thought her son was a mere bookworm, and she was passionate about providing a stimulating, educational environment for him. Although labeled as a bit of a social misfit, he managed to find his niche in academe as he excelled in mathematics. In 1945 he commenced his college education at the Carnegie Institute of Technology in Pittsburgh with the goal of becoming a chemical engineer, and he found success in his studies. His achievements in the classroom did not, however, transfer to his social life. He continued to appear immature to his friends; additionally, after making a clumsy pass at a male friend, he was teased for this homosexual-oriented behavior.

In 1948, Nash began graduate studies in mathematics at Princeton University. By this time, he had assumed a cocky, arrogant persona, frequently boasting of his mathematical accomplishments. As evidence of his extreme self-confidence, he once visited Einstein and suggested some new ideas for amending quantum theory. In 1950, he proposed Nash's equilibrium, an idea suggesting that the outcome of a game depends on the strategies of all the players. Nash went on to accept his first teaching position at the Massachussets Institute of Technology.

On the personal side, Nash fathered a baby out of wedlock in 1953. As might be predicted by his social immaturity and arrogance, he refused to support the baby's mother, and his first son, John David, spent some time in foster care. In 1956, he met Alicia Larde, an MIT coed and aspiring physicist, who would have an intense influence in his life. After having Nash as a professor in her advanced calculus class, Alicia was smitten with the handsome and intellectual Nash. They were married in 1957 and had one son, John Charles.

In the spring of 1959, Nash's world started to change in dramatic ways. At 30 years of age and on the brink of becoming a full professor, he became increasingly convinced that he was being followed. Among other things, he claimed that he was able to decipher encrypted messages from aliens that were printed in various newspapers. After having a confusing conversation with a colleague, he was committed to McLean Hospital for treatment.

When later asked how such a logical mathematician could believe that extraterrestrial beings were sending him messages trying to recruit him to save the world, he replied, "Because the ideas I had about supernatural beings came to me the same way that my mathematical ideas did. So I took them seriously" (Nasar, 2001, p. 11). After this first episode of paranoid schizophrenia, Nash became obsessed with numerology and religious prophecy and symbols, believing that he was an important religious figure.

This schizophrenic episode was the starting point of a tumultuous relationship with a devastating mental illness. For the next 30 years, Nash would flee to Europe several times, be hospitalized involuntarily about six times, and would, sadly, become a phantom of the arrogant and brilliant Nash of Princeton University. Throughout his sickness he encountered a wide variety of treatments. During his first hospitalization, Nash was given an initial dose of thorazine to calm him down. Subsequently, due in the part to the prevailing influence of Freud, Nash was exposed to extensive psychoanalysis, curiously leading to (because of a breakdown coincident with Alicia's pregnancy) a diagnosis of "fetus envy" (Nasar, 1999).

John Nash
CHARLES REX ARBOGAST/AP PHOTO

Additionally, his repressed homosexuality was thought to be a culprit causing him to suffer from "homosexual panic." Although his second hospitalization was in a unit known for aggressive ECT therapy, there is no documentation that Nash received this type of treatment. When the family's money began to dwindle, Nash was forced to enter Trenton State Hospital (which is near Princeton) in 1961. At the time, Trenton had 2500 patients, ten times more than the private hospitals he had previously been in.

While at Trenton, Nash was transferred to the "elite" insulin unit, and for six weeks he received daily insulin treatments. After early-morning insulin injections, Nash's blood sugar would drop drastically, causing him to experience drowsiness followed by delirium. By about 9:30 A.M., Nash would become comatose as his body became rigid and his fingers curled. A nurse would then place a rubber hose in his nose and esophagus through which a glucose solution was administered. Nash would slowly and agonizingly awake around 11:00. Each afternoon, he would attend occupational therapy.

Nash described the insulin therapy, first introduced by Manfred Sakel (see Chapter Two), as "torture" (Nasar, 1999). Just as radiation treatments are administered to cancer patients in an attempt to kill the unhealthy tumor cells, insulin treatment was thought to kill the marginally functioning neurons. We now know that there is no empirical evidence to support such a claim, and insulin use has fallen into disfavor.

Nash managed to pull his life together. In the mid-1960s, he was offered a faculty position at Princeton, but he couldn't escape the crushing waves of schizophrenia long enough to rebuild his reputation as one of the country's most brilliant mathematicians. He was placed on antipsychotics while he was hospitalized but because he didn't like the side effects, he didn't take the drugs following his release.

Nash just couldn't maintain a functional life—his marriage ended in divorce, he had no consistent relationship with his sons, and he wasn't able to keep his job at Princeton. In 1967, he retreated to his hometown of Roanoke, Virginia, to live with his mother, where he remained for three years.

In the 1970s Nash migrated back to Princeton, not as a professor, but more as an eccentric fixture. Wearing high-top tennis shoes, he would write his "problems" on numerous blackboards throughout the department. Ironically, this intense cognitive effort and the neural resources devoted to stating these problems may have contributed to the eventual remission of his schizophrenia. Around 1990, glimpses of rationality started to be seen in Nash as he started asking insightful questions at some of the departmental seminars.

When Nash later described his remarkable transition from delusions to remission, he stated, "I emerged from irrational thinking ultimately without medicine other than the natural hormonal changes of aging" (Nasar, 1999, p. 353). In support of the cognitive training discussed later in this chapter, he credits willpower for his remission. He believes his intense cognitive activity may have played a role in his recovery.

To those who have seen the movie *A Beautiful Mind,* the dramatic ending to Nash's story is well known. In 1994, Nash was awarded the Nobel Prize in Economics for his game theory. Not knowing how Nash would endure the stress of travel and the excitement of receiving the award, Nash was perceived as a risk to receive the award. The ceremony, however, went well, and the award has had a powerful and positive effect on his life.

Nash currently has an office at Princeton where he continues to spend many of his days. He has since reconciled with Alicia, and together they take care of their son. John David, who received a Ph.D. in mathematics from Rutgers University, is presently incapacitated with schizophrenia. Nash has received a considerable amount of media attention because of the release of the Academy Award-winning film featuring his life's story. When Nash met Russell Crowe, the actor who portrayed him in the movie, he warned him, "You're going to have to go through all these transformations!" an apt term to describe Nash's life with schizophrenia.

heritability of schizophrenia. Kallmann's initial data recorded a concordance of 86% in identical twins and 15% in fraternal twins.

Seymour Kety, Irving Gottesman, and others have refined the genetic approach introduced by Kallmann to reliably demonstrate a high likelihood of inherited biological factors as the major contribution to developing schizophrenia (Gottesman, 1991; Suddath et al., 1990). Adoption studies in which data for twins reared apart are compared provide compelling evidence for the genetic contribution to the expression of schizophrenia. If one identical twin has schizophrenia, the other is much more likely to develop schizophrenia.

Today, no one questions the link between schizophrenia and genetics. As seen in Figure 9.1, however, more recent studies report lower concordance rates in monozygotic (identical) twins (i.e., a range of 41% to 65% with most studies reporting an average of about 48%) than originally reported by Kallmann (Barondes, 1993; Cardno & Gottesman, 2000; Torrey, Bowler, Taylor, & Gottesman, 1994).

Perhaps the most dramatic evidence of familial contributions to schizophrenia is the case of identical sisters, known as the Genain quadruplets, who were all diagnosed with schizophrenia. The environment, however, may also have had a role, for all the girls varied in the severity

[Figure 9.1]
Heritability in schizophrenia.
The genetic contribution in schizophrenia is determined by investigating concordance rates in relatives with varying degrees of genetic similarity.

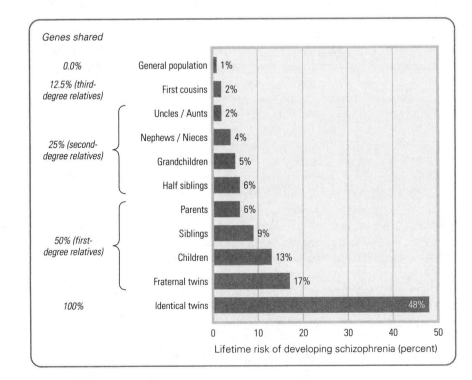

of schizophrenic symptoms. The variability in the expression of symptoms could have resulted from varied effects of early brain injury, low birth weights, and harsh punitive treatment as children.

As seen in Figure 9.2, the girls looked healthy and happy as young children; this changed, however, as they got older. They were diagnosed with schizophrenic symptoms between the ages of 22 and 24 years and have been repeatedly evaluated at the National Institute of Mental Health since the 1950s (Barondes, 1993). Most recently, at the 39-year follow-up examinations, at 66 years of age, the women were reported to exhibit improved cognition compared with previous tests—a finding supporting the notion that the cognitive impairment observed in schizophrenia is not due to degenerative processes (Mirsky et al., 1984; Mirsky et al., 2000).

[Figure 9.2]
Genain quadruplets
EDNA MORLOK

The concordance rate for identical twins only approaches 50%, so environmental influences are very important in the expression of schizophrenia. Studies have indicated that the most significant life differences in identical twins are birth complications; the twin suffering from birth complications is more likely to develop schizophrenia. It seems, though, that discordant twins carry the same genetic susceptibility for schizophrenia. Researchers find the same rates of schizophrenia in the families of discordant pairs of twins as observed in concordant pairs. Thus, if a twin is spared schizophrenia, the same risk of schizophrenia is found in his/her offspring as observed in the family of the twin who developed schizophrenia (Torrey, Bowler, Taylor, & Gottesman, 1994).

In what ways are the genetic factors expressing themselves? How does the brain go from normality to the depths of madness following the exquisitely timed orchestrations of genes being expressed, of turning on and off, as the brain plays the tune and the mind moves to it? It is a question as tangled as the neural organization of the schizophrenic brain.

At this time, no single gene has been identified as the "disease" gene for schizophrenia; rather, research suggests a growing list of genetic contenders that contribute moderate effects to the expression of the disease (McDonald & Murphy, 2003; Pulver, 2000). These genetic links are believed to reside on chromosomes 1, 6, 8, 10, 13, 15, 18 and 22 and the X chromosome (Bassett, 1989; Dawson & Robin, 1996; Heinrichs, 2001; Hyman & Nestler, 1993). The exact contribution of these genes in the healthy brain is still being determined through painstaking quantitative analyses and through application of the data from the Human Genome Project (whose promise so far is much greater than the data in hand).

[Box 9.2]

The Investigators

Daniel Weinberger

Daniel Weinberger told us that he always knew he wanted a career in medicine (personal commuication). Early on, he thought pediatrics would be the most interesting specialty—and then he encountered the brain. After graduating from Johns Hopkins University in 1969, Weinberger went on to medical school at the University of Pennsylvania.

During medical school, when Weinberger had an opportunity to observe brain cells under the microscope, he was hooked. He realized that, although practicing medicine seemed somewhat routine to him, a career of trying to understand the brain would be "infinitely intellectually challenging." Being in medical school during the Vietnam War, he was also attracted to the discipline of psychiatry and its humanistic views.

Once in the field of psychiatry, Weinberger became captivated with the devastating disorder schizophrenia. He was convinced that it is a brain disorder and his conviction provided him with the opportunity to be a

Daniel Weinberger
COURTESY OF DANIEL
WEINBERGER

brain investigator, a career he had been working toward since medical school. After graduating from medical school in 1973 and completing fellowships at UCLA Medical School and Harvard Medical School, Weinberger thought he was headed toward an academic career in Boston. But first he decided to take a brief professional detour to the National Institutes of Health to learn a few new skills that would be of help when he commenced his academic career.

In 1977, Weinberger was a Research Ward Director in the adult psychiatry branch at the National Institute of Mental Health (NIMH). This NIMH position was followed by an appointment as a staff psychiatrist and then in 1981 by an appointment as head of the Clinical Neuropsychiatry and Neurobehavior Unit at NIMH, as chief of the Section on Clinical Neuropsychiatry and Neurobehavior, and in 1986, as chief of the Clinical Brain Disorders Branch. Although he never made it to

Initial insights into the function of some of these genes are beginning to come to light; these functions at a few chromosomal locations are highlighted in Table 9.2.

Neuroscience research is a long way from understanding what goes wrong in the application pathways of these genes. Regardless, the genes are providing instructions, translating their commands into action by means of protein production. Whatever alterations might be present in the genetic code that leads to schizophrenia are manifested in the collection of proteins and subsequent structures and activities that are coded for.

Neuroanatomy

The etiology of schizophrenia is unknown. Though the existence of significant neuroanatomical alterations in the schizophrenic brain is undisputed, under what conditions or through what interaction these alterations occur are research questions of the greatest interest. The alterations reported in the neural architecture of the schizophrenic brain are large and obvious.

an academic position, Weinberger reports that he tried to make his research environments comparable with an academic environment.

Today, Weinberger is one of the world's leading schizophrenia researchers. Most of his approximately 350 publications address various research questions related to schizophrenia—the neuroanatomical, neuropharmacological, genetic, and behavioral perspectives of this unfortunate disorder. Indeed, he is using multiple windows to mental health in his attempt to solve the mysteries of schizophrenia.

According to Weinberger, one of the most important lessons he's learned as a researcher is the importance of flexibility—the ability to use several different techniques to answer questions related to mental illness. After all, Weinberger was initially trained to use psychoanalytic tools; currently, he is most excited about genetic tools. Although a cure for schizophrenia has still not been identified, he argues that genetic tools hold considerable potential for identifying the basic causes for this disease. Once the genetic factors are identified, the entry points into functional pathways will become more apparent, allowing for the development of more meaningful therapies.

But even before we have all the genetic mysteries solved, Weinberger is encouraged with today's treatments for patients suffering from schizophrenia. The drugs are much more refined than the initial pharmacological treatments, resulting in fewer side effects. He is also intrigued by the developmental work being conducted and feels that several clues to this disease lie in the late-maturing prefrontal cortex.

From a personal perspective, although schizophrenia still presents a monumental challenge to researchers trying to develop efficacious treatments, Weinberger is far from discouraged about the state of schizophrenia research and his choice to pursue this elusive disease as his career. He says that he never dreamed he would be able to work with such a stimulating, dedicated, creative team of scientists, and he wants to "kiss the ground" each day for having such a wonderful opportunity (personal commuication). He conveys that he can't imagine having more fun than he is currently having in his laboratory. He is extremely optimistic about bringing meaningful therapeutic interventions to patients suffering from schizophrenia in the near future.

Tuning in to the neural substrates of auditory hallucinations.

Nicole Gilbert's experience with "voices" began when she had difficulty reading, reporting that whatever she was reading was about her. The voices frequently suggested that Nicole was Jesus, only then to tell her that they were joking, suggesting that she was stupid to believe such comments. Now significantly recovered, Nicole reports that she couldn't

[Table 9.2]

Location of Putative Genes Involved in Schizophrenia

Chromosome	Function
1	G-protein regulation (important in synaptic functioning)
6	Protein associated with synaptic structure
8	Growth factor involved in formation of synaptic structure
13	Modulates NMDA glutamate transmission
15	Modulates acetylcholine transmission
22	Modulates dopamine transmission

Adapted from Freedman, 2003.

believe it when friends told her that the voices she had been hearing were not real (Goode, 2003).

The window into the brain that neuroimaging techniques provide could not even be dreamed of by early schizophrenia researchers. The window into the schizophrenic brain was opened by Silbersweig and colleagues (1995) when they examined in real time the brains of schizophrenia victims who were actually experiencing auditory hallucinations.

The belief—the certainty—of those affected with schizophrenia that they hear the voice of God, the CIA, their neighbor's dog, or some otherworldly figure authoritatively speaking directly, personally, to them is a positive symptom synonomous with schizophrenia. Although bizarre, as are many psychotic symptoms, auditory hallucinations represent an extreme form of a behavior observed in many individuals. For example, as a child, did you ever talk to an imaginary friend? Did your friend talk back? Shortly after her best friend moves away, a child may acquire a new, imaginary friend. In this case, hearing the voice of this imaginary friend provides comfort for her through the stressful time of losing her actual best friend.

Voices associated with imaginary friends can be quite adaptive as they reduce levels of stress in certain situations. In contrast, the voices characterizing the auditory hallucinations of schizophrenia command and compel their recipient, with unceasing regularity, to commit acts against their will. Those of us not so afflicted take for granted the thin curtain that separates our mind from our mind's voice; we *know* when we are having an internal dialogue and when we are simply talking to ourselves; this distinction is less obvious for people suffering from schizophrenia.

It is clear that, unlike the voice of an imaginary friend, the voices and commands conjured up out of the imagination of the schizophrenic brain constitute a severe liability. That these voices do not actually exist is irrelevant: they are real to the individual suffering from schizophrenia.

Where do the voices come from? How are they produced? Some compelling findings using fMRI imaging show excess neural activity in the temporal lobes of the individual experiencing auditory hallucinations (Silbersweig et al., 1995). The researchers recruited a number of chronic schizophrenia patients, placed them in an fMRI apparatus, and asked them to signal when they were experiencing vocal hallucinations. Their responses were compared to controls in whom the internal voices were absent. The data demonstrate significantly more activity in the thalamus, striatum, and hippocampus and in the cingulate, orbitofrontal, and auditory cortices during auditory hallucinations (Copolov et al., 2003; Silbersweig et al.). Researchers are currently exploring the role of Broca's area in the production of auditory hallucinations (Goode, 2003; Hoffman et al., 2003). With such extensive brain involvement in the production of auditory hallucinations, it is easy to understand how difficult it may be for the individual to differentiate between brain activation resulting from external voices and brain activation resulting from internal voices (Figure 9.3).

It is important to remember that to process any sounds, including real voices, physical stimuli must be transduced into neural impulses. Thus, the final pathway for the voice is in the brain. In the schizophrenic brain, the initial steps are absent, but the illusion of the voice is produced nonetheless. For example, activation in the thalamic nuclei, where audition is initially processed, is particularly interesting: perception without sensation. Therefore, the circuitry and its active engagement in these regions (including both afferents and efferents) must be very different in the schizophrenic brain relative to normally functioning brains. Following is a discussion of some of the general cellular and structural alterations observed in schizophrenic brains.

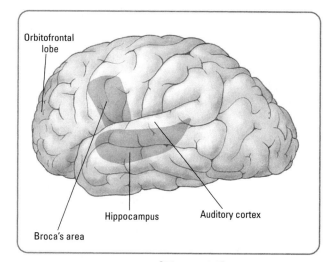

[Figure 9.3]
Investigating neuroanatomical areas contributing to auditory hallucinations. Current fMRI research suggests that orbitofrontal, temporal/auditory, and cingulate cortices, as well as limbic and striatal structures are activated during auditory hallucinations. (Striatal structures not shown; see Chapter Three.) Currently, research is focused on the role of Broca's area in auditory hallucinations.

Cellular disorganization and alterations. Several observed effects in the brains of patients diagnosed with schizophrenia suggest a significant problem with early brain wiring. Developmentally, their brains show marked neural disorganization. During development, the nascent brain cells in one region are destined to mature and grow and populate another, and thus they require the ability to migrate to their destination using a combination of chemical and glial paths. If these delicate migratory patterns are disrupted, the neurons fail to arrive at and align into precisely their correct locations.

As to what may cause the migratory patterns to be disrupted, some speculation centers on viral infection (discussed later in this chapter) and interference with the genetic instructions guiding the neuron-by-neuron assembly of the fetal brain. Regardless of the cause, the result can be disastrous for neuronal communication.

One area characterized by misaligned neurons is the hippocampus. Abnormal orientation of pyramidal cells in the hippocampus, as shown in Figure 9.4, is prevalent, where the displacement of the

[Figure 9.4]
Cellular organization in the schizophrenic brain. Orientation of *pyramidal cells* in the hippocampus is organized in the normal brain **(a)** and disorganized in the schizophrenic brain **(b)**.

normal "north–south" orientation is a feature of schizophrenia reported by many different researchers (Kovelman & Scheibel, 1984; Bunney & Bunney, 1999). Research has also indicated cytoarchitectural alterations in the entorhinal cortex, the cortex surrounding the hippocampal area. Specifically, some patients have differential densities of neuronal populations across the layers of the cortex (Bunney & Bunney, 1999). Though the awry patterning has been reported most often in postmortem analyses of cortex and hippocampus, where the neurons are rotated, like a hand waving from side to side, there may be other areas with poor neural organization and function.

Selemon and his colleagues at the Yale University School of Medicine found increased density of neurons in the prefrontal and occipital cortex of individuals with schizophrenia, yet the neuropil, or neuronal space that contains the axon and dendrites, was smaller compared with normal controls (Selemon, Rajkowska, & Goldman-Rakic, 1995). This study reminds us that a study focusing on just one piece of the neuroanatomy can be incomplete; the increased neuronal density was misleading until the decreased volume and neuropil in the cortical area were also identified.

Such effects, where the proper "populating" of a site with its quota of neurons is distorted, can result in poor or problematic transfer of information. Excessive numbers of neurons or connections may lead to ineffective information processing, either overprocessed and/or prematurely rerouted, whereas decreased numbers and/or connections may lead to alterations in the normal augmentation of neuronal signals as it moves from neuron to neuron or region to region.

A groundbreaking study conducted by Judith Rapoport and her colleagues at the National Institute of Mental Health identified early-onset schizophrenic patients (patients who met DSM criteria by the age of 13) and followed their neuronal loss over the next five years (Thompson et al., 2001). Each patient, along with normal controls and nonmedicated controls, was subjected to three MRI scans over the course of the study. As seen in Figure 9.5, the developmental trajectory of gray matter loss in these patients spread from the parietal cortices to the temporal and finally frontal regions of the cerebral cortex.

In individuals diagnosed with early-onset schizophrenia, gray matter loss occurred at about 5% per year in the areas of the frontal eye fields, and the parietal, temporal, and supplementary motor cortical areas in both hemispheres. Normal adolescents experienced subtle losses of about 1% per year, confirming that at least a low level of neuronal pruning exists through adolesence. To answer the question of whether the medication administered to the patients suffering from schizophrenia was the significant contributor to the neuronal loss, a group of patients who exhibited schizophrenialike symptoms but were never diagnosed with schizophrenia were used as medication-matched control subjects. These subjects received similar medications for their symptoms (for example, for control of aggressive outbursts) even though they were not as impaired as the schizophrenia patients.

The neuronal loss in this important control group fell between the normal controls and early-onset schizophrenic subjects, with the medication-matched subjects experiencing about half the loss of the schizophrenic patients, suggesting that, whereas the medication might contribute to neuronal loss, it was not the sole contributor. Finally, the extent of neuronal loss was significantly associated with the severity of both positive and negative symptoms. Therefore, a significant departure from normality in the nature or number of the brain's connections would be expected to result in aberrant neurotransmission and hence abnormal behavior.

Data also show that the size of neurons is smaller in the schizophrenic hippocampus (Arnold et al., 1995). A reduction in the size of the neuron, whether it is cell body, dendritic arborization, or length of the axon, may have a detrimental impact on its function, relative to a normal-sized neuron. This effect suggests underactivity and/or understimulation in the neuron. Additionally, alterations in the myelin surrounding the axons has been reported—an effect that could confound the signal being transmitted (Casanova & Lindzen, 2003; Davis et al., 2003).

Because we tend to contemplate the brain as a complex structure made up of enormous nests of neurons and connections, effects of the size or structure of a relative handful of neurons seem trivial. When placed in the context of the region where the effects have been reported in the schizophrenic brain (hippocampus, frontal lobes) and of the activities regulated there, such small alterations in neuronal size and number take on greater significance.

Focusing on the more microscopic neural landscape, the number of connections may also be compromised. One attempt to address this question is the assessment of synaptophysin, a membrane protein that plays a key role in neurotransmitter transmission. Schizophrenia patients have less synaptophysin-immunoreactive tissue in the prefrontal cortex than do control subjects (Eastwood & Harrison, 1995; Glantz & Lewis, 1997).

Single neurons are capable of influencing thousands of other, downstream neurons and thus can exert effects out of proportion to their

[Figure 9.5]
Mapping neuronal loss in the schizophrenic brain. These MRI scans indicate higher neuronal loss (indicated by brighter areas) in the schizophrenia brains. Because the medication-matched subjects had more bright areas, indicating cell loss, than the normal controls, it was concluded that medication taken for schizophrenia contributes modestly to neuronal loss.

THOMPSON ET AL., 2000, PNAS

absolute number. A neural signal is only as resonant as the last neuron(s) that carries it. As a Chinese proverb has it, the thousand-mile journey begins with a single step, and the neural signal must move from groups of neurons made up of individual neurons to other neurons in the circuit.

In the schizophrenic brain, misfiring or malfunctioning neurons (due to number, organization, and size) can produce a distorted and problematic signal. The net result is information that is "recognizable" neither by other malfunctioning neurons nor by unaffected ones. Thus hallucinations, distorted thinking, and paranoia—the terrible symptom array of schizophrenia—occur because of the inability of the processing units, the neurons, to operate properly.

Structural alterations in schizophrenic brains. One of the earliest discoveries suggesting structural alterations in brains afflicted with schizophrenia was the finding that the ventricles are larger than those of normal brains (Andreasen & Black, 2001). Recall from Chapter Three that the ventricles are well-defined, fluid-filled cavities in the brain where cerebrospinal fluid is made as part of an intrabrain circulatory system. In particular, the third and lateral ventricles are expanded, which suggests compression or loss of existing nervous tissue (Figure 9.6).

[Figure 9.6]
Ventricular size and schizophrenia. The brains of identical twins indicate different ventricular sizes. The twin on the right, diagnosed with schizophrenia, has a larger ventricle than his non-schizophrenic twin brother.

R. L. SUDDATH ET AL., *NEW ENGLAND JOURNAL OF MEDICINE 322* (1990): 789-94

In a study using identical twins, one of whom who developed schizophrenia while the other was unaffected, Suddath and colleagues (1990) showed that ventricular enlargement might be considered a reliable factor in the diagnosis of schizophrenia. Although it is difficult to ascribe a cause to the enlarged ventricles, the correlational effect is a persistent one, reported in many studies on schizophrenia (Bunney & Bunney, 1999).

The ventricles play a role in the development of the anatomical relationships of the brain. The ventricles form a kind of template or guide around which the nascent brain develops (see Chapter Six). From the outset, the proliferating cells pour onto each other and into areas around the ventricles, using them as a pressure-filled field of resistance. The new and migratory neurons inch their way along these spaces. It is interesting to speculate about deficits that might occur in areas such as the hippocampus and the temporal lobe in general as a result of disruptions of cellular migration patterns.

Although ventricular enlargement is the most commonly reported neuroanatomical alteration, other consistent differences have been observed in schizophrenic brains. The sulci that make up the convolutions of the immense cerebral cortex are enlarged (Andreasen & Black, 2001). Lower in the brain, the total volume of the midportion of the cerebellum is smaller in individuals diagnosed with schizophrenia (Okugawa, Sedvall, & Agartz, 2003).

A growing body of evidence suggests frontal lobe involvement in the development and expression of schizophrenia, including neuronal loss in the frontal lobes as described earlier. The overlapping symptom set includes apathy, inattention, motor deficiencies, lack of spontaneity, and a reduction in general motivation. Interesting parallels exist between patients with frontal lobe damage and patients with schizophrenia.

There are some indications that executive function, the oversight of brain and behavioral activity that is accorded frontal lobe regulation, is impaired in schizophrenia patients. Deficits have been observed in the Wisconsin Card Sorting Test and the Controlled Oral Word Association task, both reliable indices of frontal lobe activity (Heinrichs, 2001; Heinrichs & Zakzanis, 1998). Additionally, the Stroop Test, which gauges impulsivity by asking patients to recite color names printed on different-colored backgrounds, also presents greater problems for schizophrenia patients (Heinrichs & Zakzanis, 1998). When combined with complementary anatomical and brain activation evidence that supports the behavioral testing, there is a further suggestion of frontal lobe deficits (Andreasen et al., 1986, 1994, 1997; Goldman-Rakic, 1999).

In an interesting study aimed at identifying structural areas underlying cognitive alterations in schizophrenia, Nancy Andreasen and her colleagues compared blood flow patterns associated with random episodic silent thought in schizophrenic patients and healthy volunteers (Andreasen & Black, 2001; Kemether et al., 2003). Blood flow abnormalities were found throughout the frontal cortex and temporal cortex, as well as in the cerebellar and thalamic areas. The thalamus is smaller in schizophrenia patients. Thalamic involvement is especially interesting since it's a relay station that could easily play a role in the accuracy with which sensory messages are routed to the cortex.

In summary, although a single salient structure or circuit has not emerged as the indicative substrate of schizophrenia, the literature suggests the involvement of several structures in the frontal and temporal cortex, the hippocampus, cerebellum, and thalamus. The structural abnormalities characteristic of the schizophrenic brain appear to be robust but any individual effect may be small. Heinrichs (2001) has examined the effect size of studies reporting neuronal effects. He states, "If the postmortem studies from both hippocampal and frontal cortex are considered together, it is evident that no findings are large and consistent enough to argue for a *single* cytoarchitectural anomaly in schizophrenia. . . . No neurological 'smoking gun' has been found so far" (p. 201).

It is true that no "smoking gun" has been found, but there are certainly plenty of fingerprints all over the "gun" that is there. What the data do demonstrate is that the schizophrenic brain is clearly and reliably different, anatomically and functionally, from a nonschizophrenic brain. The difficulty lies in defining and documenting the finer-level responses of such myriad brain events in the human and in accounting for the extraneous variables and confounds that are lurking about.

Before we leave the discussion of neuroanatomical alterations in the schizophrenic brain, it is important to remember that the long-term neuroanatomical effects on the brains of schizophrenia patients who have taken a lifetime of powerful antipsychotic drugs can only be guessed at. The effects of these powerful drugs on the neuronal machinery bring us to an examination of the neurochemistry of schizophrenia.

Neurochemistry

It seems self-evident now that the neurochemistry of the schizophrenic brain is different from a normal brain. But the discovery of a concomitant neurochemical abnormality came about, if not by accident, by chance. As is true of so many clinical disorders, early treatment with some drugs was found to be effective without much being known about their action within the brain.

Dopamine hypothesis of schizophrenia. Working backward from the encouraging results in schizophrenia patients who were dosed with these early drugs subsequently led to examinations of the drugs' neurochemical bases. Thus, observations that the powerful antihistamine drug *chlorpromazine* (Thorazine) could mollify delusional patients led to widespread treatment of schizophrenia patients with different forms of these *phenothiazines*. Only after establishing that these drugs were effective did research commence into why. The finding that they affect a specific neurotransmitter (dopamine) system gave rise to a better understanding of the neurochemistry of schizophrenia.

A key finding that drove this new dopamine hypothesis of schizophrenia was the observation that the clinical efficacy of the early drugs correlated with their ability to block dopamine in vitro, not necessarily in a living human being (Byne, Kemether, Jones, Haroutunian, & Davis, 1999). Because of this seemingly powerful relationship between mitigation of positive symptoms of schizophrenia and a drug's ability to block dopamine, serious attention was focused on dopamine (DA). It was hypothesized that in schizophrenia, DA present in the synapse could not be cleared adequately or quickly enough, resulting in additional firings of the downstream neurons. Although aspects of this theory are correlational in nature and subject to cause and effect confusion, the DA hypothesis has driven much research into brain–mental illness relationships.

The mesocortical and the mesolimbic DA systems are believed to play a role, at least indirectly, in schizophrenic symptomology. The mesolimbic system arises from cell bodies in the ventral tegmental area (VTA) with projections that run into many limbic structures. The mesocortical system, like the mesolimbic, also arises from cell bodies in the VTA, but the projections run to the neocortex (the frontal lobes; in particular). Given the especially higher cognitive functions assigned to the areas innervated by mesolimbic and mesocortical DA projections, activities that are diminished and modified in the schizophrenic patient, attention has been devoted to DA regulation in general, and to those regions in particular.

Also supporting the dopamine hypothesis of schizophrenia was the observation that drugs that resulted in temporary excessive levels of DA led to schizophrenic symptomology. For example, an individual experiencing a cocaine-induced high is reacting to the drug's action blocking the DA transporter, thereby inhibiting reuptake. Similarly, a person under the influence of amphetamine, another DA agonist, experiences psychotic ideations that include schizophrenialike hallucinations and paranoia. Even seemingly benign substances such as L-DOPA can produce schizophrenia-related behaviors in a nonschizophrenic person. These data demonstrate that enhancing DA levels through manipulations that save endogenous DA from degradation or increase its release leads to the appearance of schizophrenic symptoms (Barondes, 1993).

Further support for the notion that the DA system is involved in the production of schizophrenic symptoms lies in research investigating binding densities of DA receptors. The effects on endogenous levels of DA work in combination with the receptor systems to which the DA binds. Six types of DA receptors have been identified and described. For instance, the D_2 receptor subtype is inhibitory in the second-messenger cascade. It inhibits adenylyl cyclase, which, as we learned in Chapter Five, normally catalyses adenosine triphosphate (ATP) to cyclic adenosine monophosphate (cAMP). The D_1 receptor, on the other hand, does the opposite: it activates adenylyl cyclase, thereby facilitating the production of cAMP. Abi-Dargham and coworkers (2000) found increased receptor-binding densities for D_1 DA receptors in the dorsolateral prefrontal cortex of schizophrenia patients with poorer cognitive function in working memory tasks. They hypothesized that the increased receptors may be a compensatory effect for cognitive impairments, however; the compensatory mechanism did not improve cognition.

Understanding more about the distribution of the DA receptors may help to elucidate the aforementioned receptor-binding density study. In schizophrenia, symptoms involve altered functioning of areas regulated by brain regions that contain specific DA receptor subtypes. For example, rich concentrations of D_2 receptors populate the nucleus accumbens, caudate, and putamen, as well as the cortex, hippocampus, and amygdala—areas that receive DA projections from the mesolimbic DA system. Surprising, though, is the high concentration of D_1 receptors in the caudate, cortex, and hippocampus—areas that receive DA projections from the mesocortical and mesolimbic DA systems. The sprinkling of D_2 and D_1 receptors in regions associated with emotion, memory, and thought provide dopaminergic dominion over those processes. Hence, when considering the functions associated with areas of the brain involved in dopaminergic transmission, the dopamine hypotheses received further confirmation.

As compelling as the dopamine hypothesis is, however, more recent research has highlighted inconsistencies in this theory. Consider the following conflicting evidence recently described by Robert Freedman of the University of Colorado (2003):

- When dopamine transmission is blocked, the symptoms of schizophrenia are not fully alleviated.

- The reduction in positive symptoms that is observed following antipsychotic medications is not accompanied by observed reductions in levels of dopamine receptors and metabolites—both of which remain in the range of normal values.

- The role of dopamine is extremely complex in the brain and is not likely to simply serve as a switch for the activation of psychotic symptoms.

- The new antipsychotics discussed in the treatment section do not solely target DA receptors the way the earliest drugs did (they also target other neurotransmitters, such as serotonin and glutamate), yet they are successful in treating schizophrenic symptoms.

So where does this evidence leave us? After spending a considerable amount of time learning about the potential role of dopamine in schizophrenia, do we just throw that idea out the window after considering the refuting evidence? Contemporary schizoprenia researchers have responded to this confusion with two research strategies. First, as suggested by Kenneth Davis and coworkers of the Mt. Sinai School of Medicine in New York (Davis, Kahn, Ko, & Davidson, 1991), the original hypothesis that schizophrenic symptoms were due to excessive levels of dopamine is being reconceptualized to suggest that decreased DA activity exists in the prefrontal cortex (perhaps leading to negative effects) and increased DA activity exists in the mesolimbic system (perhaps leading to positive symptoms). Second, increased attention is being placed on other neurochemicals that may be involved in the production of schizophrenic symptoms. Serotonin, glutamate, and acetylcholine are all being considered as potential neurochemical players in schizophrenia. Thus, whereas dopamine has not been abandoned as a neurochemical target of schizophrenia, the investigation has extended beyond DA to other neurochemicals. It is becoming increasingly clear that the dopamine theory of schizophrenia is much more complicated than originally thought.

Nondopaminergic neurochemical involvement in schizophrenia. Serotonin has been considered an influential neurochemical in schizophrenia for several reasons. Theoretically, serotonin seems like a logical candidate as a result of its involvement in the hallucinogenic effects of psychedelic drugs such as LSD. Although these drugs typically induce visual hallucinations instead of auditory hallucinations, researchers still perceive a role of this neurotransmitter in the positive effects of schizophrenia (Aghajanian & Marek, 2000).

Serotonin is intimately linked to DA transmission. Specifically, serotonin inhibits dopaminergic function in both the midbrain and forebrain areas. Thus, drugs that antagonize serotonin ultimately release dopamine from inhibition, an effect that may be particularly helpful in the forebrain where dopamine activity appears to be low. As discussed in the next section, drugs such as clozapine have focused on the interaction between serotonin and dopamine (Kapur & Remington, 1996).

Another drug, phencyclidine (PCP), has led researchers to focus on yet another neurotransmittor system. PCP was originally developed as an anesthetic, but the drug was later abandoned when it was discovered that patients being treated with PCP experienced adverse effects. Given at high doses, PCP can mimic much of the symtomology of schizophrenia including delusions, hallucinations, and disordered thinking. Because PCP works by serving as a glutamate receptor antagonist, research has focused on glutamate. Generally, levels of glutamate are lower in the cortex of schizophrenic patients, but interestingly, increased numbers of glutamatergic axons have been observed (Byne et al., 1999). Recently, decreased levels of a glutamatergic enzyme were observed in postmortem analyses of the dorsolateral prefrontal cortex of schizophrenic patients. Subsequent analysis indicated increased expression of messenger RNA for this particular enzyme (Ghose et al., 2004). Thus, whereas glutamate seems to be altered in schizophrenia, the direction of this effect remains confusing.

Finally, a drug that patients with schizophrenia voluntarily consume provides another clue to the neurochemistry of schizophrenia. About 80% of individuals diagnosed with schizophrenia smoke cigarettes. Two behaviors characteristic of schizophrenia, sensory-gating deficits (discussed later) and deficient smooth pursuit eye movements are corrected by the

minor physical anomalies (MPAs) Minor structural abnormalities located in various areas of the body; they are typically investigated in accessible areas of the body including the head, mouth, ears, eyes, hands, and feet.

nicotine (McEvoy & Allen, 2002). Thus, smoking cigarettes may provide transient improvement for schizophrenia patients and may be viewed as a form of self-medication (Freedman et al., 1994). Because the nicotinic receptors in the brain are activated by the neurotransmitter acetylcholine, research has focused on its role in schizophrenia. Providing further evidence for the role of acetylcholine in general is the observation that the atypical antipsychotic clozapine interacts with another cholinergic receptor, the muscarinic receptor (Raedler et al., 2003).

In sum, the once simplistic dopamine theory of schizophrenia is becoming increasingly more complex as we now entertain the reconceptualized theory of schizophrenia. It has become increasingly apparent over the past several decades that several neurotransmitter systems are probably involved in schizophrenia. As seen in Figure 9.7, all four neurochemical candidates discussed (dopamine, serotonin, glutamate, and acetylcholine) ultimately affect the pyramidal neurons of the cortex—an area significantly altered in schizophrenia.

DEVELOPMENTAL MARKERS OF SCHIZOPHRENIA

Thus far we have discussed neuroanatomical and neurochemical aspects of schizophrenia. To gain insight into the onset and developmental trajectory of this multifaceted brain disease, we now consider clues to schizophrenia's triggering stimuli and broader organization. We evaluate contributing factors from physical development, sensory-gating deficits, stress, and the controversial viral theories as they relate to the onset and development of schizophrenia.

Evidence from Minor Physical Anomalies

Recall from this chapter's Connections that early motor and anomalous emotional signs are apparent in preschizophrenic children. In addition, some scientists report that subtle and not-so-subtle physical deformities—**minor physical anomalies (MPAs)**—are part of the makeup of the schizotypal individual. We all have small minor neurodevelopmental mishaps—perhaps our ears are not perfectly aligned, our eyes are a bit too far apart, our hairline starts too far back—that make us unique. Usually these all-too-human conditions are nothing to be alarmed about, but as is evident in Down's syndrome, numerous MPAs may represent significant misalignment in development, both external and internal.

Some research indicates that MPAs characteristic of schizophrenia shed visible light on disruption of the development of the brain (Green,

2001; Green, Satz, Ganzell, & Vaclav, 1992). For example, our fingerprints are unique. But did you know that developmental researchers value these distinctive skin designs as much as criminologists do? They can be used as another record of neurodevelopment. In the human, our distinct fingerprints are established between the fourteenth and twenty-second week of gestation. Thus, any alterations in these prints may indicate a concurrent developmental disturbance. Reports indicate that schizophrenia patients manifest fingerprint abnormalities, including more and fewer ridges. This observation may shed light on the variability that underlies the differences in schizophrenic incidence between identical twins. The fingerprints in Figure 9.8 show that the twin with schizophrenia has roughly half the ridge count of the normal twin (Bracha, Torrey, Bigelow, Lohr, & Linington, 1991; Bracha, Torrey, Gottesman, Bigelow, & Cunniff, 1992; Green, 2001).

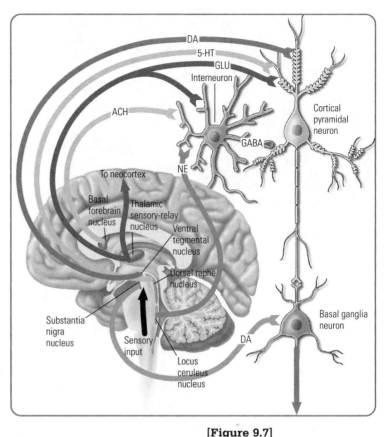

[Figure 9.7]
Proposed neural circuits of schizophrenia. Cortical pyramidal neurons, seemingly so important in the development of schizophrenia, receive neurochemical input from ventral tegmental nucleus (DA), dorsal raphe nucleus (serotonin) and thalamic (Glutamate) afferents. Additionally, interneurons in the cerebral cortex receives ACh input from the basal forebrain nucleus, NE input from the locus coeruleus, and glutamatergic input from the thalamus. These interneurons influence the cortical pyramidal neurons via GABA release. The cortical pyramidal neurons, along with additional DA input from the substantial nigra nucleus, influence the basal ganglion neurons involved in motor output.
AFTER FREEDMAN, 2003

Hand preference may provide further confirmation of a disruption in neurodevelopment. Schizophrenia patients seem to shift away from an established handedness to a more ambiguous hand preference. They switch hands for different tasks and, when asked to repeat a task, may switch hands to perform the same task. In the normal population only about 2% of individuals adopt such atypical handedness; in the schizophrenic population, about 20% adopt such handedness strategies (Green, 2001; Satz & Green, 1999).

Sensory-Gating Deficits as a Common Denominator

Have you ever played a game with a small child who repeatedly tried to scare you? Even though the child might have been quite successful on the first attempt, after a few sneak attacks you are completely habituated to this stimulus and you may feel boredom or a desire for the child to cease playing this game—but you certainly don't feel fear anymore. In a sense, you were able to *gate* this sensory stimulus in a way that diverted it from fear.

[Figure 9.8]
Fingerprint patterns in schizophrenia. The total finger ridge count is almost twice as high in the healthy twin (left) as compared with the twin with schizophrenia.

BRACH, ET AL., AMERICAN JOURNAL OF PSYCHIATRY, 1992

Individuals with schizophrenia find it difficult to show habituation to auditory stimuli—a phenomenon known as **sensory-gating deficits.**

Research on sensory gating involves the unexpected presentation of a loud auditory stimulus typically followed by a startle response in the subject. This startle response is accompanied by an easily identifiable eye blink. In the next phase, a less threatening tone is presented prior to the loud noise. In normal individuals the startle response is diminished by the presentation of the less threatening tone; however, in individuals with schizophrenia, the startle response never diminishes. Subjects with schizophrenia cannot suppress their startle response to the auditory stimulus even though they know that the stimulus poses no threat (Green, 2001). Another version of this laboratory test can be done with EEG patterns in which the P50 brain wave response is assessed following the auditory stimuli. In normal subjects the P50 wave is suppressed following the repeated presentation of the auditory stimulus (Adler et al., 1999).

Sensory-gating deficits are very interesting when we consider the current knowledge about alterations in the thalamus in schizophrenia. As the thalamus routes sensory information to the cortex for interpretation, it is easy to speculate that this structure may play a role in sensory-gating deficits. The inability to "filter" out irrelevant stimuli can easily be viewed as a simple model of what is going on in the brain of the patient with schizophrenia. The inability to filter out irrelevant auditory stimuli, past memories, or inner voices may all be the result of sensory-gating deficits.

This effect also has interesting heritability as it is found not only in patients with schizophrenia but also in first-degree relatives who do not have schizophrenia symptoms. Further, Freedman and his colleagues (1997) identified a gene for sensory-gating deficit on chromosome 15, and this gene is also involved in the cholinergic nicotinic receptor. As described in Box 9.3, this phenomenon is important in schizophrenia research using animal models.

Stress and Developmental Predisposition

Why does it take so long for schizophrenia to develop if the conditions are extant in childhood or before birth? Strong theoretical evidence points to stress as a significant player in the expression of schizophrenia symptoms. Some researchers suggest that stress, broadly defined, may play a role in

sensory-gating deficits The inability of schizophrenia patients to habituate the startle response to somewhat expected stimuli.

the physical anomalies linked to the disorder. Koenig, Kirkpatrick, and Lee (2002) report that stress hormones, particularly the glucocorticoids released from the adrenal cortex during periods of perceived stress, may interfere with normal development and lead to deleterious changes in the developing brain. This **neural diathesis–stress model** of schizophrenia assumes, first, that individuals possess a certain predisposition (a diathesis) toward schizophrenia and, second, that a subsequent significant stressor can foster later expression of schizophrenia symptoms.

In their work on schizotypal factors described at the beginning of this chapter, Elaine Walker and her colleagues suggest that adolescence is a critical developmental phase for schizophrenia because of the altered processing of steroid hormones (e.g., gonadal and HPA axis hormones). Specifically, adrenal steroid hormones enhance DA functioning—an effect that could easily influence schizophrenia (Walker & Diforio, 1997; Walker, Logan, & Walder, 1999). Corticosterone has been found to increase DA synthesis across the brain; further, some evidence suggests that HPA activation alters DA receptors, and, interestingly, these effects are more prevalent in adulthood (Walker & Diforio, 1997; Henry et al., 1995).

In a review of the relevant stress literature, Norman and Malla (1993a, 1993b) found little evidence supporting the observation that schizophrenia patients experienced more severe postnatal stressors than nonschizophrenic individuals. But these researchers also recognized a correlation between stressful events and the severity of schizophrenia symptoms. And increased stressful life events have been found to occur in the months preceding relapse (Walker & Diforio, 1997).

Read, Perry, Moskowitz, and Connolly (2001) examined the hypothesis that stress of another and later form—childhood abuse and harm—may play a role in the multidetermination of schizophrenia. They report that many observations of the home life of schizophrenia patients document a history of abuse and argue that developmental exposure to such difficult conditions may hypersensitize sensory and stress-responsive systems in the adult, thereby contributing to the display of schizophrenia symptoms. It is an intriguing idea that is difficult to test experimentally.

In a detailed study of German schizophrenia patients and their families, Holzinger, Kilian, Lindenbach, Petscheleit, and Angermeyer (2003) report that psychosocial stress is regularly observed in the background of adults with schizophrenia. These correlations are thought provoking, but they require empirical confirmation. Additionally, it is important to consider that many schizophrenia patients report no such significant stressors in their childhood.

neural diathesis–stress model of schizophrenia
Updated adaptation of the classic diathesis–stress model that emphasizes the role of alterations in steroidal hormones in the expression and severity of schizohrenic symptoms. Because of the dramatic changes in these hormones at puberty, Elaine Walker and colleagues have proposed that adolescence should be considered a critical phase in the development of schizophrenia.

[Box 9.3]

Brain Matters

Animal Models of Schizophrenia

Like thieves, diseases that affect the mind rob a piece of humanity from the afflicted person, be it thought, consciousness, or self-control. As detailed in Chapter Eight, animal models of disease or of treatment have accelerated the pace of research on mental disorders, particularly in the development of drug treatments. For schizophrenia, serendipity played a large role, but the real progress in antidopaminergic medications and other antipsychotics was pioneered in animal models.

The evidence that disturbances in the prefrontal cortex were a significant part of the cognitive deterioration of schizophrenia was confirmed in nonhuman primates. And future neurobiological therapies and treatments will be tested for efficacy in animals en route to their application to the schizophrenic brain.

El-Khodor and Boksa (2001) have extended in rats an interesting association observed in schizophrenia. Schizophrenia is correlated with increased birth compli-

cations (which affects mesolimbic dopamine levels), and stress has been shown to mediate schizophrenic symptoms. In the rat, Caesarean birth alters adult levels of dopamine (DA) D_1 receptors and the stress-induced regulation of brain D_3 and D_4 receptors as well. The authors conclude that "interactions between an individual's experience of stress at adulthood, together with other environmental events in their history, such as birth complications, can be important determinants of brain DA receptor levels" (p. 423). The data are intriguing because of the link between the role of DA and its receptors and early experiences in the expression of schizophrenia.

One application for schizophrenia comes from the research on knockout mice, which lack a variety of substances known to be involved in schizophrenia. Gainetdinov, Mohn, and Caron (2001) advocate and support the use of transgenic knockout mice lacking, respectively, for example, the DA transporter and the NMDA receptor (which binds glutamate, the brain's major excitatory neurotransmitter). In general, they make the point that selective knockout mice make powerful animal models for the study of schizophrenia and its treatment, especially its neurochemical underpinnings.

Viral Theory Controversy

Research has revealed that the schizophrenic brain is wired differently and malfunctions as a consequence. How do such effects come about? One novel explanation that has received empirical support suggests that the fetus is exposed to a virus during a critical stage of prenatal development (Karlsson et al., 2001). Support for this idea started with the observation of an interesting correlation. Helsinki, Finland, fell victim to a pandemic of influenza in the late 1950s, infecting scores of pregnant women in the last two trimesters. The offspring of the flu-exposed mothers were reported to be more likely to display schizophrenic symptoms compared with the rates of schizophrenia normally observed per 1000 live births in the city of Helsinki at other time periods.

Other explanations for the data have been suggested, and the evidence that the subjects were actually infected with the flu is indirect, but the association is compelling. Subsequent work investigating the viral theory produced mixed results (Mednick, Machon, Huttunen, & Bonett 1988),

Another research direction of interest and one that represents overlap between humans with schizophrenia and animal models is prepulse inhibition (PPI). The presentation of a signaling stimulus has the usual effect of diminishing a response to a larger, subsequently presented stimulus, much like an immunization creates a buffer against the subsequent disease. As described in this chapter, hearing a briefly presented tone reduces a startle response to another sound presented more loudly milliseconds later. Schizophrenia patients display a reduced PPI, suggesting a significant sensory -gating deficit (Parwani et al., 2000). In other words, more data can intrude on their brains.

Modeling this sensorimotor-gating phenomenon in animals, Black, Selk, Hitchcock, Wettstein, and Sorensen (1999) implicate the gaseous neurotransmitter nitric oxide (NO) in the development of schizophrenia and effects on prepulse inhibition. They treated young rats with the NO antagonist L-nitroarginine, which depletes NO by acting on its enzyme, NO-synthase. They report that in adulthood, treated males showed hypersensitivity to DA agonists and deficits in PPI and that females showed a similar effect for phencyclidine (PCP) but not PPI. The effects on the neurochemical systems are interesting, as is the report of the sex difference, both of which bear on observations made in humans with schizophrenia.

The use of PPI as a bridge between humans and animals has been investigated further. Paylor and Crawley (1997) reported on the feasibility of using inbred mice for the modeling of schizophrenia symptoms and treatments, especially sensorimotor gating and PPI responses. Their detailed parametric work paved the way for many animal studies investigating the link between a well-observed phenomenon in human schizophrenics and an empirical and replicable behavioral response in animals, that of PPI. Crawley and coworkers (1997) also demonstrate that the use of selective inbred strains may provide useful animal models for many psychiatric or neurobiologic conditions, such as anxiety, drug abuse, aggression, and social behaviors. Therefore, the use of animal models can go a long way to providing the necessary "neuroscience" that eventually unites to the "clinical," thereby speeding the delivery of treatments and cures to those afflicted with a variety of disorders.

but a 2003 investigation of the effects of influenza was conducted on nearly 1000 adults with schizophrenia (Limosin, Rouillon, Paron, Cohen, & Strub, 2003). When compared with nonschizophrenic siblings, siblings with schizophrenia were more likely to have been exposed to influenza—especially during the fifth month of his mother's pregnancy.

The data point to a critical prenatal period during which the fetal brain is especially susceptible to viral insults that might disrupt the delicate processes of neurogenesis and migration, described in Chapter Six. But it may be the timing, not the infection, that derails brain development and predisposes the infant to dementia down the line. At a time when the brain is actively developing, literally dividing itself over and over again, the virus, with its DNA-altering ramifications, may affect brain structure and function. During the latter months of fetal growth, brain development occurs swiftly. In fact, the brain begins to resemble the human version, with its multilayered complexity, involutions, and characteristic appearance, only during the last few months of gestation.

TREATMENTS FOR SCHIZOPHRENIA

Therapy for schizophrenia symptoms exists in multiple forms. Several different types of antipsychotics exist, and awareness of the importance of psychosocial intervention and neurocognitive training is increasing. Now that researchers are gaining a more accurate picture of the neuroanatomical, neurophysiological, and neurochemical alterations in the schizophrenic brain, alternative treatments with enhanced success and limited side effects are sure to emerge. Currently, about 40% of patients diagnosed with schizophrenia show improvement over time; although encouraging to physicians and researchers, this number is discouraging for the millions of individuals coping with this unwelcome "brain guest" (Green, 2001).

Contemporary treatment regimens include a diverse array of pharmacological agents that change continually as we learn the diverse underlying chemical currents associated with schizophrenic symptoms. Additionally, as the concept of the plasticity of the brain across the lifespan is increasingly accepted, neurocognitive training programs are becoming more prevalent. Certain psychosocial approaches benefit the schizophrenic patient by modifying and training behaviors that enable the individual to function in society; these programs emphasize the importance of treatment from many valuable sources such as family, peers, and medical practitioners.

Somatic Therapies

In Chapter Two we described some historic—and drastic—treatments of schizophrenia, such as insulin comas, frontal lobotomies, and the most prevalent form of therapy for schizophrenia during the first half of the twentieth century, *hydrotherapy*. Patients were exposed either to wet packs or to continuous baths, where they were placed in a hammock submerged in a tub. A sheet was placed over the top of the tub with only the patient's head showing, mummylike. Treatments could last up to several hours, an interminable amount of time for the "dunkee."

Doctors who administered this treatment, with little empirical support, saw hydrotherapy as an authentic strategy that influenced the brain via the body; the damp and shriveled patients, however, were not as enthusiastic. It was perceived as torturous by some, especially when extreme water temperatures were used (Green, 2001).

A recent treatment, repetitive transcranial magnetic stimulation (rTMS), discussed in Chapter Eight, appears to suppress auditory hallucinations in medication-resistant patients, with the effects lasting up to 15 weeks (Hoffman et al., 2003). Although still in its infancy, rTMS is viewed as a milder form of electroconvulsive therapy (ECT), which also influences the firing patterns of large populations of neurons within the brain. Today, though its mechanism is unknown, ECT is viewed as a treatment option for schizophrenia patients who have not responded to the standard therapies described in this section. Additionally, ECT is successful for catatonic schizophrenia patients (Chanpattana & Kramer, 2003; Suzuki, Awata, & Matsuoka, 2003).

Pharmacological Therapy

A cornucopia of drugs represents the peril and the hope of the biological treatment of schizophrenia. Treating deficiencies using a chemical strategy that focuses on dopaminergic transmission has been effective in restoring the schizophrenia patient to society, albeit incompletely and with a separate set of problems, or side effects, brought on by the very drugs that are supposed to help. Even though schizophrenia is becoming better understood, the practical drug treatment regimen lags behind the theorizing and data that support its use.

Drugs do work, but they merely manage the symptoms of schizophrenia; they do not cure the disease. Like the diabetes for those patients who require a daily regimen of insulin, without medication, the disease will overtake the patient. Drug therapy generally does wonders for some forms of schizophrenia, but side effects can be horrendous and intrusive and force the patient (or the doctor) to decide between two evils: the degradation of the disease or the debilitating effects of the pharmaceuticals designed to treat it.

The several classes of drugs we describe all share one insidious feature: they act all over the brain, including regions that are not deficient, and interfere with perfectly normal neurochemical activity. In particular, as mentioned earlier, are the extrapyramidal effects, in which the anti-dopaminergic actions of the drugs cause a range of motor/movement problems. In addition to doing what is intended, inadvertent effects create parallel problems, reducing the patient's motivation to continue taking the drugs. The vicious cycle of symptoms/drug/side effects is a condition from which today's patient cannot as yet be rescued. The drugs do much good, but they do harm as well.

Interestingly, certain drugs affect certain categories of schizophrenic symptoms. Recall that positive symptoms are symptoms that are displayed by the schizophrenia patient but not observed in normal individuals (Andreasen, 2001). These symptoms include delusions, irrational beliefs, and hallucinations, most of which interact to create vivid symptoms. Negative symptoms are behaviors displayed by nonschizophrenic individuals but not typically observed in schizophrenic patients

antipsychotics Psychoactive
drugs that reduce psychotic
symptoms but have long-term
side effects resembling symptoms of neurological diseases.

(Andreasen, 2001). For example, a flattening of affect results in decreased emotional communication and is displayed by schizophrenia patients as they stare relentlessly outward, failing to respond to others or to the environment.

Four major groups of drugs known as **antipsychotics** are used to treat schizophrenia. Three of the groups are further characterized as *typical antipsychotics*—these groups are older and hence called typical or classic— and one as *atypical antipsychotics*. Typical antipsychotic drug groups include the butyrophenones (haloperidol), the phenothiazines (chlorpromazine), and the thioxanthenes and are generally more effective against positive symptoms. The atypical antipsychotics include the drugs clozapine, olanzapine, and risperidone, and are generally more effective against negative symptoms.

The first drug shown to have a significant positive effect on the schizophrenic patient—quite inadvertently—was chlorpromazine (Thorazine). Originally developed as an antihistamine and later used as a tranquilizer to mollify postsurgical patients, chlorpromazine was extended from the surgical ward to the psychiatric clinic by observant and innovative physicians who realized its potential. Heinrichs (2001) presents a brief and interesting history of this first antipsychotic, which demonstrates that serendipity is sometimes as valuable as deduction.

The cascade of bizarre behaviors that categorizes schizophrenia—the auditory and visual hallucinations, the staccato *word salad,* the disordered thought patterns—is becalmed by chlorpromazine (Thorazine). This calming effect gives rise to an undesirable symptom, a motor condition in which the patient slowly and haltingly skates along an imaginary track from point to point, giving this side effect its derisive and well-known nickname of the "Thorazine shuffle."

Following the success of Thorazine and the discovery of its DA-antagonistic properties, new drugs with an increased ability to antagonize DA receptors were developed. Haloperidol (Haldol), for example, was 100 times more potent than chlorpromazine. The increase in potency came with a price: an increase in side effects. The increased DA blockage in the basal ganglia led to Parkinsonlike symptoms, including the development of the haunting, uncontrollable facial and tongue movements of *tardive dyskinesia.*

Today, these earlier antipsychotic medications are known as first-generation antipsychotic agents. Generally, only about 20% of patients experience a complete remission following treatment with these drugs. Most patients, however, experience a reduction in symptoms. These drugs also significantly decrease relapse rates: about 30% experience relapse compared with an 80% relapse rate in unmedicated patients.

As mentioned earlier, the first-generation antipsychotics produced many unwelcome side effects. In addition to the involuntary extrapyramidal effects (for example, tardive dyskinesia and tremor), these agents produced symptoms such as severe restlessness, decreased voluntary movement, and temperature dysregulation. Consequently, a second generation of antipsychotic drugs was later introduced in an attempt to decrease the side effects associated with the earlier drugs. Additionally, enhancing efficacy was a priority in the development of these drugs.

Clozapine (Clozaril) was the first drug introduced in the second wave of antipsychotics. Clozapine was considered an atypical antipsychotic because it possessed more efficacious antipsychotic effects with minimal movement effects. This drug was not perfect—it introduced the new, dangerous side effect *agranulocytosis,* an acute diminution in infection-fighting white blood cells (leukocytes). Because this condition was observed in 0.39% of users, it is important that all patients taking this medication have their white blood cell counts closely monitored by a physician. Interestingly, clozapine successfully treated schizophrenic symptoms in about 30% of the patients who did not respond to the other pharmacological treatments.

How do the mechanisms of the first atypical antipsychotic drug differ from that of the typical antipsychotics? Clozapine results in antagonist effects at a more diverse array of DA receptors, including D_1, D_2, and D_4 receptors. Additionally, it anagonizes serotonin and noradrenaline receptors. Finally, clozapine increases the amount of acetylcholine released at the synapse, which is interesting considering that patients who had been heavy smokers prior to medication reduce smoking once clozapine treatment commences.

The differential D_2 DA receptor binding can be seen in Figure 9.9. Notice that the brain to the left, which is a nonmedicated brain, has an abundance of activity in the basal ganglia. In contrast, the middle brain is medicated with halperidol and consequently shows no available D_2 receptors. The third brain is medicated with clozapine and shows a moderate amount of D_2 DA receptor availability (Barondes, 1993).

[Figure 9.9]
Dopaminergic Receptor Activity in Medicated Schizophrenia Patients. PET scans of these brains indicate D_2DA receptor binding and are used to learn more about the activity of successful schizophrenia medications. As seen in the unmedicated brain on the left, extensive binding in the basal ganglia is observed in the absence of pharmacological interventions. The brain medicated with haloperidol (in middle), a D_2DA ligand, exhibits no binding due to receptor cites already occupied by the drug. The brain on the right is mediated with clozapine and exhibits moderate D_2 receptor binding.

With the success of clozapine, additional second-generation agents were introduced. These newer drugs, including risperidone (Resperdal), olanzapine (Zyprexa), quetiapine (Seroquel), and ziprasidone (Geodon), capitalized on the dual serotonergic/dopaminergic action of clozapine. Generally, these second-generation antipsychotics are as successful or more successful than the first-generation drugs in treating the symptoms of schizophrenia with fewer motor side effects, including decreased occurrences of tardive dyskinesia.

Whereas the first-generation antipsychotics effectively treated the positive symptoms, the newer drugs also successfully treated negative symptoms. Regarding the disadvantages, the second-generation drugs can cause significant weight gain, as well as diabetes mellitus (Freedman, 2003; Tamminga, 1999). See Table 9.3 for a summary of popular antipsychotic drug effects and their physiological effects.

[Table 9.3]

Antipsychotic Drugs and Their Mechanisms

Pharmacological target	Drug	Physiological result
Dopamine D_2 antagonist	Haloperidol	Blocks DA-facilitated pyramidal neuron activation
DA D_2 and serotonin$_{2A}$ antagonism	Olanzapine, resiperidone, quetiapine, ziprasidone	Blocks DA-facilitated pyramidal neuron activation, as well as serotonin facilitation of glutamate secretion
Diverse actions	Clozapine	DA and sertonergic antagonism resulting in decreased pyramidal neuronal activation; increased ACH release, norepinephrine antagonism resulting in increased interneuron communication with pyramidal neurons
Dopamine agonism/antagonism	Aripiprazole	Activates low-level stimulation of DA receptors; suppresses high-level stimulation
DA D_2 and D_3 antagonism	Amisulpride	Blocks cortical DA receptors with no effect on basal ganglia

Adapted from Freedman, 2003.

Because the perfect antipsychotic has yet to be introduced, the search for more effective medications continues. Treating schizophrenia with agents that target the neurotransmitter glutamate is being explored. Blockade of the N-methyl-D-aspartate (NMDA) receptor for glutamate in control subjects can produce clinical symptoms very similar to those of schizophrenia (Krystal et al., 1994; Malhotra et al., 1996). Further, NMDA agents such as D-cycloserine and D-serine, taken in combination with existing antipsychotics, have been shown to ameliorate schizophrenia symptoms (Goff, Tsai, Manoach, & Coyle, 1995; Tsai, Yang, Chung, Lange, & Coyle, 1998). Finally, a few of the newer antipsychotics are focusing strictly on the dopaminergic receptor again—but to varying degrees in different receptors. For example, amisulpride (Solian) antagonizes D_2 and D_3 DA receptors in the cortex but not in the basal ganglia, and aripiprazole (Abilify) facilitates only low-level DA receptor stimulation (Freedman, 2003).

In sum, antipsychotic drugs were—and remain—a boon to the treatment of schizophrenia. Before their introduction, patients were a mass of symptoms. The tradeoff between cognitive improvement and significant side effects was in favor of the patient, who showed marked progress. The shortcoming of the antipsychotic drugs is that they treat only the symptoms of schizophrenia, not the cause. Like taking aspirin for a headache caused by a fractured skull, once the drug's effects wear off, the system remains unchanged. Furthermore, after the assault on the existing malfunctioning neurochemistry, the inundation by these powerful drugs further alters the chemistry of the brain, making a formerly sensitive system increasingly resistant, thereby increasing the dosage required to achieve the same effect.

This reciprocity demonstrates the delicate balance that is steamrolled by the aggressive antipsychotic chemicals used in the medical treatment of schizophrenia. Thus, although these pharmacological agents provide a priceless respite from the voices and cognitive derailments associated with schizophrenia, they should be used with extreme caution under the close supervision of an appropriate practitioner. In fact, it is usually recommended that pharmacological treatment accompany other forms of treatment such as neurocognitive training and psychosocial therapy, which can reinforce the effects of the drugs.

Neurocognitive Training

Therapeutic interest has recently turned to attempts at enhancing the cognitive abilities of the schizophrenia patients. When a person suffers an accident and loses the ability to move, a physical therapist exercises the afflicted muscles to restore their flexibility, mobility, and strength. Mental health researchers wonder if cognitive exercises could act similarly, restoring full cognitive function to schizophrenia patients.

Though in its infancy, the research is promising, suggesting that schizophrenia patients do show improvement in cognition after intense and focused cognitive training. For example, gains have been observed in card sorting and vigilance (Green, 1993; Green, Satz, Ganzell, & Vaclav, 1992; Medalia, Aluma, Tryon, & Merriam, 1998). More research is necessary to determine the most effective modes of cognitive training, the required duration, and modes of action. According to Andreasen (2001), cognitive programs are "designed to help patients learn to focus attention more precisely, to solve problems more efficiently or more rapidly, to monitor ideas and speech more effectively, and to improve both motor and mental coordination" (p. 214).

Psychosocial Therapy

In the book *Of Two Minds,* Luhrmann (2001) makes the point that a large divide separates therapists who would treat the schizophrenia patient and therapists who would treat the schizophrenic brain. Reinforcing the notion that a multifaceted approach is effective, a strategy that combines the cognitive/social and the biochemical approaches appears to be preferable to a single approach. Variations of the psychotherapy approach recognize that schizophrenia is a disease that has inputs (stressors, intrusive thoughts, and so on) from many different areas of the patient's life. Emphasizing the layers that contribute to the totality of the schizophrenia patient's thoughts and actions, the therapeutic approaches utitlized by the clinic focuses many forces on the patient's recovery.

The multitiered approaches are able to combine different aspects of the individual treatments available to the patient. For instance, outpatient facilities are available for schizophrenia patients; these services allow for the observation and treatment of the person in times of crisis and help and support at other times. The interaction with other clinic inpatients adds support and shared experiences to the cognitive load of the patient. This treatment plan, though more challenging to quantify and assess than more narrow treatment approaches, is reported to have some efficacy (Cozolino, Goldstein, Nuechterlein, West, & Snyder, 1988; Heinrichs, 2001).

The outpatient clinic also has the advantage of having medical intervention close by, if needed, and access to more complete psychiatric services. Further, the structure afforded by the regimentation of the hospital environment may be beneficial to the schizophrenia patient on a need-to basis for brief periods (weekends, for instance). The patient in these clinics is less a patient and more an individual; greater attention has benefits that translate into success rates for the schizophrenia patient.

When combined with support from family members and friends outside the clinic (who themselves require some training and education in how to live and interact with an individual diagnosed with schizophrenia), there is marked reduction in recurrence and severity rates (Lenroot, Bustillo, Lauriello, & Keith, 2003). Again, the familial and personal resources brought to bear on combating the illness ensure that the patient will benefit from one or more of the tacks being offered. Some of the ways in which social support networks can work is by extending the clinic to the home setting. There the patient can be exposed to a "best of both worlds" combination of family/friend support and professional guidance.

Summary

Overview of Schizophrenia
Bleuler chose *schizophrenia* as the name for the cluster of symptoms consisting of social withdrawal, delusions, hallucinations, and disorganized cognition because he felt that the cognitive abilities were "splitting" from the normal functions of the mind. Today, positive, negative, and disorganized symptoms are associated with this disorder.

Neurobiology of Schizophrenia
The strong genetic relationship in schizophrenia is revealed by a concordance rate of nearly 50% in identical twins reared apart. It is well established that schizophrenia is associated with significant neural architectural anomalies, including malformations in the arrangement of neurons in the cortex and hippocampus, together with gross effects such as enlargement of the ventricles and consequent loss of gray matter.

Schizophrenia has classically been defined, neurochemically, by dysregulation of dopamine. The so-called "dopamine hypothesis" states that an excess of dopamine interferes with normal neurotransmission. Today, however, other neurochemicals such as glutamate, serotonin, and acetylcholine have been associated with schizophrenia symptoms.

Developmental Markers of Schizophrenia
Several developmental theories have been proposed to help us understand the initial trigger and trajectory of the expression of schizophrenia symptoms. Certain minor physical anomalies in individuals who develop schizophrenia suggest that neuronal misalignment occurs in the earliest stages of development of the schizophrenia patient. Impairment observed in schizophrenia patients' ability to habituate to certain tones suggests that an ineffective processing of nonthreatening stimuli may be a common denominator in the schizophrenic brain. Other research suggests that stress may trigger the schizophrenia cascade in predisposed individuals. Finally, immunological challenges such as virus exposure may also serve as a trigger for the development of schizophrenia.

Treatments for Schizophrenia
Pharmacotherapy is currently the most pervasive form of therapy for schizophrenia. The first generation of drugs used to combat the schizophrenia symptoms targeted the dopaminergic system. More recently, second-generation drugs have targeted other neurochemicals such as serotonin, glutamate, and various dopamine receptors. With attention focused on neuroplasticity, it is now thought that certain forms of cognitive training may benefit the disorganized cognitive symptoms associated with schizophrenia. Finally, attention is also focused on integrative psychosocial treatment approaches in which life-functioning strategies, the support of family and friends, and outpatient medical services are all considered significant components of the treatment strategy.

Key Terms

hallucinations (p. 313)
catatonia (p. 314)
hebephrenia (p. 314)
dementia praecox (p. 314)
schizophrenia (p. 314)

positive symptoms (p. 316)
negative symptoms (p. 316)
disorganized symptoms (p. 316)
minor physical anomalies (MPAs) (p. 334)

sensory-gating deficits (p. 336)
neural diathesis–stress model of schizophrenia (p. 337)
antipsychotics (p. 342)

For Further Consideration

Andreasen, N. C. (2001). *Brave new brain: Conquering mental illness in the era of the genome.* New York: Oxford University Press. Andreasen set out to produce a book that captures the excitement of neuroscientists who are looking toward the future when "mental illness" will move into the realm of serious cures. She succeeds. Furthermore, this volume captures the anticipation of the forthcoming results from the nascent human genome project. However, one thing to remember is that promise is one thing, results quite another. We have a long way to go.

Black, M. D., Selk, D. E., Hitchcock, J. M., Wettstein, J. G., & Sorensen, S. M. (1999) On the effect of neonatal nitric oxide synthase inhibition in rats: A potential neurodevelopmental model of schizophrenia. *Neuropharmacology, 38,* 1299–1306. There are some well-documented sex differences in the expression of schizophrenia. The authors extend the observation that, during early brain development, schizophrenia patient may experience disruptions in the migration of nicotinamide-adenine dinucleotide phosphate-diaphorase (NADPH-d) neurons. Since this enzyme is involved in the synthesis of nitric oxide (NO), and since NO modulates early developmental processes in the brain, it is a logical candidate for study. Using a rat model, the authors interfered with NO activity early in life. They report that there were sex differences in the sensitivity to the manipulation, demonstrating that NO regulation of the development of the nervous system may be sexually dimorphic. Therefore, sex differences in schizophrenia may be related to the manner in which NO expression is managed during critical stages of nervous system construction.

Freedman, R. (2003). Schizophrenia. *New England Journal of Medicine, 349,* 1738-1749. If you're interested in a review of the past and present drugs used to treat schizophrenia, this article will take you on a journey through the development of the typical and atypical antipsychotics. Freedman subsequently presents an argument against the traditional dopaminergic theory of schizophrenia. Additionally, current research investigating several different neurotransmitter systems such as glutamate, serotonin, and acetylcholine is discussed with an emphasis placed on the emerging apparent importance of glutamate involvement in schizophrenia. Readers will walk away from this well-written article with healthy appreciation of the complex nature of the neurochemistry underlying schizophrenia symptoms.

Green, M. F. (2001). *Schizophrenia revealed: From neurons to social interactions.* New York: Norton. Green is a professor in the UCLA Department of Psychiatry and Biobehavioral Sciences and is chief of the treatment unit of the Department of Veterans Affairs Mental Illness Research clinical center. Therefore, Green writes from the double perspective of clinician and researcher and is able to present a full, multifaceted perspective of schizophrenia and potential treatments. This book is written for the lay person, so there is more breadth than depth in his narrative. The book includes many recent references, however, that interested readers can consult.

Heinrichs, R. W. (2001). *In search of madness: Schizophrenia and neuroscience.* New York: Oxford University Press. As the title suggests, this book focuses on the place that neuroscience can and will hold in understanding and treating schizophrenia. Heinrichs plays the skeptic throughout, critically examining and evaluating the multifaceted study of this terrible disease. It is not an easy task, but his use of meta-analyses and his application of effect sizes keep the data in perspective for the reader. One is less likely to be wowed by grandiose claims about new treatments and effects when one sees that the difference between experimental and control groups is marginally significant. He keeps the field grounded and tied to its critical roots.

Karlsson, H., Bachmann, S., Schröder, J., McArthur, J., Torrey, E. F., & Yolken, R. H. (2001) Retroviral RNA identified in the cerebrospinal fluids and brains of individuals with schizophrenia. *Proceedings of the National Academy of Sciences, 98,*

4634–4639. In this very detailed and technologically advanced study, the authors investigate the hypothesis that retroviruses play a significant role in the pathogenesis of schizophrenia. In 29% of the recent-onset schizophrenic or schizoaffective disorder patients, the authors found evidence of retroviral genes (human endogenous retroviral/HERV-W family) in the sampled cerebrospinal fluid (CSF); 5% of chronic schizophrenics' CSF contained virus. Further, evidence of the virus was found in the frontal cortex in the schizophrenics. In contrast, no evidence of the retroviruses was observed in control patients (those with noninflammatory neurological disease or nonpsychiatric subjects). The authors conclude that "the transcriptional activation of certain retroviral elements within the central nervous system may be associated with the development of schizophrenia in at least some individuals. Correlation does not infer causation, but these data strongly support the virus theory of schizophrenia development."

Silbersweig, D. A., Stern, E., Frith, C., Cahill, C., Holmes, A., Grootoonk, S. et al. (1995). A functional neuroanatomy of hallucinations in schizophrenia. *Nature, 378,* 176–179. This is a seminal paper. It shows for the first time the inner workings of the schizophrenia brain, shedding a sober scientific light on a mental illness. Furthermore, it goes a long way to removing the stigma of schizophrenia and should reduce any argument any skeptic has that schizophrenia is not a brain/biological malady.

Thompson, P. M., Vidal, C., Giedd, J. N., Gochman, P., Blumenthal, J., Nicolson, R., et al. (2001) Mapping adolescent brain change reveals dynamic wave of accelerated gray matter loss in very early-onset schizophrenia. *Proceedings of the National Academy of Sciences, 98,* 11650–11655. This paper attempts to reconcile the nature-versus-nurture debate that surrounds the study of schizophrenia. The authors applied a clever brain-mapping technique that utilizes fMRI technology in a population of early-onset schizophrenics. The patients were scanned every two years for a period of six years. The data showed a shifting pattern of tissue loss in schizophrenia that was correlated with a variety of symptom sets (for example, a mirroring "of the neuromotor, auditory, visual search, and frontal executive impairments in the disease," p. 11650, and subsequent loss of gray matter). For the first time, as if watching a time-lapse video of an event unfolding, the neuroscientists were able to observe the progression of this disorder in the brains of the subjects.

[Chapter Ten]
Drug Addiction

Connections

Vulnerability to Addiction: Threatened Territories in North America and in the Laboratory

Chief Joseph and his Nez Percé tribe were ordered off lands in the Pacific Northwest by the U.S. government in 1873. Joseph's refusal to relinquish his land prompted a series of battles between his tribe and U.S. Army troops. Eventually, Joseph and 750 Nez Percé tribal members were forced to retreat toward Canada. Just outside the Canadian border, U.S. troops surrounded Joseph and his people, forcing the chief to surrender. The bold leader seemed helpless and defeated as he made his famous speech: "Hear me, my chiefs! I am tired; my heart is sick and sad. From where the sun now stands I will fight no more forever."

Chief Joseph's story is one among countless examples (the Cherokee's Trail of Tears is another) of the severe, chronic stress suffered by the Native Americans as their familiar worlds and ways of life were stripped from them. Today, compared with Americans of all other races and ethnicities, Native Americans die more often from suicide, homicide, and accidents—most related to alcohol addiction. In fact, epidemiological data suggest epidemic levels of alcohol-related deaths, especially motor vehicle crash fatalities, among Native Americans (Campos-Outcalt, Prybylski, Watkins, Rothfus, & Dellapenna, 1997; Chang, Lapham, & Barton, 1996; Christian, Dufour, & Bertolucci, 1989; Lamarine, 1988).

More than a century after Chief Joseph was forced toward Canada to escape the threat of the U.S. Army, Canadian Suzane Erb, then a doctoral student at Concordia University, investigated the relationship between chronic stress and relapse in the addiction syndrome. To explore the relationship, she trained rats to press a lever for cocaine administration.

Once the rats were addicted to cocaine, the drug was removed from the lever. After a while, the rats caught on and stopped trying to self-administer the nonexistent drug. When the rats were later exposed to stress in their home cages, however, they would run back to the lever, suggesting that the stress prompted a craving response in the rats. In an elegant series of experiments, Erb showed that the stress neurochemicals corticotropin-releasing hormone (CRH) and noradrenaline contribute to stress-induced relapse (Erb, Salmaso, Rodaros, & Stewart, 2001).

Could the chronic stress experienced by the Native Americans be connected to their high rates of addiction? Are other populations faced with such powerlessness and hopelessness at risk for high rates of addiction? Is stress a valuable issue to address when treating addiction patients? Do any therapies incorporate stress reduction into their treatment regime? These questions—and many more—are addressed in this chapter.

drug addiction Strong desire to consume a drug accompanied by a diminishing capacity to limit the intake of the drug.

addiction syndrome Vast array of variables, sometimes difficult to tease apart, typically associated with drug addiction, including one's predisposition to consume drugs, the development of tolerance to a drug, withdrawal symptoms on the removal of a drug, craving for a drug, and the likelihood of relapse after ceasing consumption of a drug.

tolerance Characteristic of drug addiction in which the individual becomes increasingly less sensitive to the drug, requiring higher doses to obtain the initial effect of the drug.

withdrawal Defining feature of drug addiction in which the individual experiences either physiological or psychological symptoms after ceasing the consumption of a particular drug.

negative reinforcement Cessation of an aversive stimulus on the presentation of a particular response. Relapse into drug use is reinforced because it reduces the negative experience of withdrawal.

"Gotta have it" is the driving thought of an addict. A drink, a drag, a hit, a line, a pill, another piece of chocolate. "Gotta have it." Getting it is all that matters. Scrounging in the garbage for cigarette butts, stealing pills from a friend's medicine chest, driving into a dangerous neighborhood at night to meet a drug dealer, wiping out a child's bank account. Nothing is more important than smoking, swallowing, snorting, shooting, somehow securing and consuming it, and feeling its effects, *now*. Not health or physical safety. Not love or work or sex or money or relationships or responsibility. Not commitment or common sense or self-respect. Not the law or the truth. This urgent inner demand overrides all others, undermines reason, resolve, and will. It is relentless. It does not stop until it is satisfied. And then, it starts again. "Gotta have it!" What drives this madness? (Ruden, 1997, pp. 1–2)

What does drive the madness of drug addiction? In this chapter we discuss the general nature of this syndrome and the influences of variables such as sex, culture, and genetic profile. We also struggle with the question of how such a seemingly maladaptive behavior evolved.

Although specific drugs of abuse are introduced, the chapter focuses on drug addiction in a more general sense—supposing common predispositions, symptoms, and causes for most forms of addiction, whether cocaine addiction or alcoholism. Once we consider the neuroanatomical and neurochemical mechanisms related to addiction and subsequent craving, we consider the potential role of environmental context by focusing on stress in the addiction syndrome. Finally, we review various therapies, old and new, for addiction.

DRUG ADDICTION IN CONTEXT

Drug addiction is generally defined as an uncontrollable desire to take a drug accompanied by diminished control in limiting intake (Koob & Nestler, 1997). Because of the multiple factors related to addiction (e.g., predisposition, acquisition, craving, withdrawal, relapse), we sometimes use the term **addiction syndrome** to convey the expansive nature of this condition. Considering the prevalence of drug addiction and the threats it poses to our society, drug addiction, as opposed to other behavioral addictions or compulsions (as emphasized in Chapter Seven), is the focus of this chapter.

The maladaptive pattern of drug use often leads to the individual desiring more and more of the drug to re-create the first encounter. Reduced responsiveness, or **tolerance,** to a drug may result from several mechanisms, such as the body and brain's increased efficiency in breaking down the drug.

Addicts also experience **withdrawal** during times of abstinence (when the drug is not being consumed). Many times the patient is motivated to resume taking drugs to avoid aversive symptoms, an elegant example of **negative reinforcement.** As the individual's life becomes increasingly consumed with searching for and obtaining a particular drug, other important aspects of a fully rounded existence, such as those related to health, family, friends and work, are usually compromised.

Once tolerance and withdrawal are experienced, the person is generally thought to be dependent on the drug. **Dependence** can be viewed as either *physiological,* as demonstrated by modifications in the individual's physiology due to repeated use of the drug, or *psychological,* shown by a person's perception that he or she requires the drug to function normally or to just get through the day. The different types of dependence may occur simultaneously or individually; regardless, each can be a powerful, motivating pull toward acquiring a drug. See Table 10.1 for diagnostic criteria for substance dependence and Table 10.2 for diagnostic criteria for substance abuse.

[Table 10.1]

DSM Criteria for Substance Dependence

A maladaptive pattern of substance use, leading to clinically significant impairment or distress, as manifested by three (or more) of the following, occurring at any time in the same 12-month period:

(1) tolerance, as defined by either of the following:

    (a) a need for markedly increased amounts of the substance to achieve intoxication or desired effect

    (b) markedly diminished effect with continued use of the same amount of the substance

(2) withdrawal, as manifested by either of the following:

    (a) the characteristic withdrawal syndrome for the substance (refer to criteria A and B of the criteria sets for withdrawal from the specific substances)

    (b) the same (or a closely related) substance is taken to relieve or avoid withdrawal symptoms

(3) the substance is often taken in larger amounts or over a longer period than was intended

(4) there is a persistent desire or unsuccessful efforts to cut down or control substance use

(5) a great deal of time is spent in activities necessary to obtain the substance (e.g., visiting multiple doctors or driving long distances), use the substance (e.g., chain-smoking), or recover from its effects

(6) important social, occupational, or recreational activities are given up or reduced because of substance use

(7) the substance use is continued despite knowledge of having a persistent or recurrent physical or psychological problem that is likely to have been caused or exacerbated by the substance (e.g., current cocaine use despite recognition of cocaine-induced depression, or continued drinking despite recognition that an ulcer was made worse by alcohol consumption)

Specify if:

With Physiological Dependence: evidence of tolerance or withdrawal (i.e., either Item 1 or 2 is present)

Without Physiological Dependence: no evidence of tolerance or withdrawal (i.e., neither Item 1 nor 2 is present)

APA, 2000, p. 197.

Prevalence of Addiction

Addiction can afflict anyone who is capable of consuming a drug. In 1999, the National Institute on Drug Abuse (NIDA) reported that surveys in 21 major U.S. metropolitan areas showed an estimated 14.8 million Americans were using illicit drugs. In this report, users were defined as

dependence Development of tolerance and withdrawal following chronic use of drug; physical and psychological problems arise upon cessation of drug use.

[Table 10.2]

DSM Criteria for Substance Abuse

A. A maladaptive pattern of substance use leading to clinically significant impairment or distress, as manifested by one (or more) of the following, occurring within a 12-month period:

    (1) recurrent substance use resulting in a failure to fulfill major role obligations at work, school, or home (e.g., repeated absences or poor work performance related to substance use; substance-related absences, suspensions, or expulsions from school; neglect of children or household)

    (2) recurrent substance use in situations in which it is physically hazardous (e.g., driving an automobile or operating a machine when impaired by substance use)

    (3) recurrent substance-related legal problems (e.g., arrests for substance-related disorderly conduct)

    (4) continued substance use despite having persistent or recurrent social or interpersonal problems caused or exacerbated by the effects of the substance (e.g., arguments with spouse about consequences of intoxication, physical fights)

B. The symptoms have never met the criteria for substance dependence for this class of substance

APA, 2000, p. 199.

having used the drug at least once during the past month. The report also indicated that 3.5 million Americans were dependent on illicit drugs, whereas an additional 8.2 million reported being dependent on alcohol (NIDA, 2000).

Addiction is found in both men and women, but it is more prevalent in men than in women (American Psychiatric Association, 2000). For example, in a comprehensive study that investigated sex differences in alcohol consumption across several cultures, men were more likely to identify themselves as current drinkers and report more frequent heavy-drinking episodes. Focusing on Canada, Israel, the Czech Republic, and the United States, in most cases, men were more than twice as likely to be identifed as "drinkers," whereas women were more likely to be lifetime abstainers (Wilsnack, Vogeltanz, Wilsnack, & Harris, 2000).

It is important to remember that drug abuse does not exclude children and adolescents. In 1998, 10 percent of adolescents in one study reported illicit drug use sometime during the past month (Comerci & Schwebel, 2000). Even more daunting are recent data from a survey of 45,000 high school students. Of the students, who were tenth graders in the year 2000 in this study, 45% reported using an illicit drug; specifically, 40% reported using marijuana, 7% reported using cocaine, and 55% reported smoking cigarettes in their lifetime. Additionally, 23% reported being drunk in the month prior to the survey (NIDA, 2000).

One drug that is on the rise in adolescent circles is MDMA, or ecstasy (see Box 5.1), a drug that has both stimulant and hallucinogenic properties and is at this writing the most popular "club drug" for teens. In fact, the 18- to 25-year-old age group is the heaviest using group of ecstasy (NIDA, 2000). Thus, drug addiction can begin as early as 12 or 13 years of age (and earlier in some cases) and persist as long as the drugs are available for consumption.

As with any disorder, there are costs associated with addiction. In the United States alone, the total cost associated with drug abuse is estimated at $67 billion per year (NIDA, 2000). This figure includes both social and medical costs associated with the drugs of abuse and does not include nicotine-related costs. The social cost is high—more than half of the cost accrues to drug-related crime. Not only does drug abuse cost society, it affects the economic status of the individual users as well—it is estimated that Americans spent $57.3 billion on drugs between 1988 and 1995—$38 billion going to cocaine (NIDA, 2000).

Addiction Across Cultures

Addiction is found virtually everywhere. It is impossible, however, to compare and contrast rates of addiction across cultures because of the vast range of perspectives about what actually constitutes an addiction. For example, within the United States, different religious affiliations vary in their acceptance of alcohol consumption; some condemn its use in any context and others celebrate its use in various religious ceremonies.

Stepping outside the United States, the issue becomes terribly complex. If you are sitting down to dinner in Greece, little attention is paid to the amount of alcohol consumed, but drinking alcohol during meals is not considered normal in India (Gureje, Vazquez-Barquero, & Janca, 1996). One common perspective observed across cultures, however, is that most people are more accepting of alcohol than other addictive substances. For example, in most cultures, a person classified as suffering from a drug use problem typically exhibits less impairment than that required for a diagnosis of an alcohol use problem. This distinction is probably related to the illegal status of most drugs compared with the legal status of alcohol (Gureje, Vazquez-Barquero, & Janca, 1996).

Hereditary Influences on Addiction

Evidence amassed from alcoholism research suggests that addiction has a significant genetic component (APA, 2000). For example, boys and girls who are adopted have a greater risk of being an alcohol user if their biological parents are alcoholics. Alcohol abuse in the adoptive parents has no real predictive value for determining alcoholism in their adoptive children;

only low occupational status (a likely stressor) of the adoptive father seems to put the child at risk for becoming an alcohol abuser (Bohman, Cloninger, Sigvardsson, & von Knorring, 1987).

Research with rodents provides further support for the role of genetics in predisposing an individual for drug abuse. Certain strains of rats and mice have been bred for susceptibility to drug abuse and/or preference for certain drugs. When two different strains of rats are raised in the same environment, they exhibit differences in the amount of drugs consumed in a particular amount of time. Because differences in drug consumption cannot be explained by differences in the environment, the drug-preferring strains of rodents offer powerful evidence that genetics provide a meaningful piece of the addiction puzzle. Another confusing piece in this puzzle is the notion that a behavior that is so devastating to the species can have such a strong genetic component. Understanding more about the potential evolutionary role of the neurobiological system underlying addiction brings some clarity to this confusion.

Considering Addiction in the Context of Evolution

The rules of the evolution game have always focused on one important goal—*survival*. Our neuroanatomy was established hundreds of millions of years ago as nature was designing a hardwired system that would drive the organism to survive—to eat, drink, and copulate. The neurobiology that underlies addiction evolved in the brain long before the "mind" emerged. This older part of our brain—the part we have in common with other animals such as rodents—is the extended limbic system (see Figure 3.13). Our brian ensures that we engage in the appropriate behaviors, such as sex and eating at the appropriate time, to ensure survival of the species (Ruden, 2000).

Have you ever felt as if you would do anything for your favorite dessert? Bart Hoebel at Princeton University has demonstrated that it is possible to become "addicted" to certain foods. Hoebel has shown that rats (as well as humans) feel that way about sugar. Knowing what we do about the value of a strong initial "high" in the addiction syndrome, he designed the study so that the rats would initially binge on sugar. Each day he deprived them of food and then presented them with an appealing glucose drink. The animals quickly consumed the sweet drink each day for a week. When the glucose was removed, the rats showed signs of withdrawal such as chattering their teeth, fanning their paws, and shaking their heads.

It appears that this natural reward system can lead to addictions to certain foods that were of prime importance during the evolution of the mammalian species. Hoebel's research lends a certain amount of validity to our cravings for sugar (the proverbial sweet tooth) and salt (not being able to eat just one potato chip), which makes sense considering the important roles of glucose and sodium in physiology and neurological processing (Hoebel, Rada, Mark, & Pothos, 1999).

Humans, however, have learned to bend the rules a bit in this survival game. By introducing external substances—drugs of abuse—that stimulate reward, we have devised a system in which we experience a handsome perceived payoff without engaging in the necessary behavior. Once you are aware of how the system evolved, it is easy to see how quickly a person can slip from a normal level of motivation to an intense desire when consuming psychoactive drugs. This is why simple recreational use of the drug develops into a more serious condition—addiction or compulsive drug seeking (Wise, 1999).

Most of our knowledge about the neurobiology of addiction has come from animal models, but true addiction seems to be unique to humans. Animals become addicted only when humans help out a bit (as with the binging program designed by Hoebel). Animal models encompass some characteristics of the addiction syndrome, but they do not represent the true condition of human addiction (Wise, 1999). Some of the key ammunition against the war on drugs, such as commercials in which celebrities tell us that drugs kill, cannot be tested on an animal model. The influence of peer pressure is also a challenge to evaluate with animal models. Addiction seems to be driven by basic animal processes, but the highly evolved cortex of humans makes the addiction puzzle more complex.

In an attempt to evaluate the role of higher cerebral functioning in survival, evolutionary theorists have introduced **evolutionary game theory,** quantitative models derived from strategies used by animals to optimize survival and reproductive fitness. When considering the survival strategies of humans, the psychological structural system *self-perceived fitness (SPFit),* has been introduced. In essence, this system suggests that human behaviors and accompanying feelings related to survival and reproductive fitness are saved on the motivational hard drive and are habitually repeated even though the behavior may be maladaptive. For example, after consuming alcohol, many report a feeling of "power" and "sexual energy," even though alcohol severely compromises actual strength and sexual vigor. It is the *perception,* or feeling—which may or may not be an accurate reflection of the actual effect—that people equate with taking the drug.

According to evolutionary game theory, drugs of abuse send the deceptive message to the brain that the individual has just experienced a huge fitness benefit. This theory addresses a central paradox of substance

evolutionary game theory
Quantitative models used by evolutionary theorists to understand strategies used by animals to maximize survival (e.g., mating).

abuse, a paradox exemplified in Box 10.1. Why do people and animals become addicted to something that harms them? The artificially inflated SPFit becomes associated with the drug that is actually contributing to the demise of the individual's nervous system (Newlin, 1999).

TRACING THE NEUROBIOLOGICAL ROOTS OF ADDICTION

In the 1950s, James Olds and Peter Milner designed a study to determine whether stimulating the reticular formation in the brainstem would influence a rat's choice to turn a different way in a maze (Olds & Milner, 1954; Reeve, 1992). Quite serendipitously, the scientists observed interesting behavior in the animals receiving electrical stimulation—they seemed to like it! Also to their surprise, on autopsy of the brains, they discovered that the electrodes were not implanted in the brainstem as desired; they were accidentally placed in the septal nucleus of the limbic system.

 [Box 10.1]

A Case in Point

Running from Addiction

As Frank completes his leg of the 4-by-800 relay, he experiences pure joy. He feels his body cut through the air, his arms pumping his legs at a faster and faster pace, and a serene sense of pleasure. At 44, he wins the Men's National Masters Championship Relay by running at a 4:32/mile pace. Even more thrilling to Frank is that he is able to experience this pleasure by doing something he is proud of—not by the drug abuse that plagued him for years.

Frank was born to a blue-collar family in Chatham, New Jersey. His childhood days were filled with climbing trees, building forts, exploring the woods, and watching TV. He preferred reading to sports during middle school but discovered that running offered an escape from the pain and insecurity typical of the adolescent years. After his younger brother was fatally injured in an automobile accident, Frank discovered another escape from the pain—alcohol.

As Frank progressed through high school he also started smoking marijuana. He tried to moderate his marijuana and alcohol use so that he could continue to run, but moderation turned into uncontrollable addiction as he graduated from high school. Frank refused the many college scholarships offered to him and chose, instead, to stay at home and work for a landscaping company. A coworker introduced him to heroin and cocaine and all the rituals, and Frank began to love driving to New York City to buy drugs.

Two years out of high school, Frank found himself using heroin up to four times a week and decided to enroll in a methadone program to help curb his cravings. Methadone supposedly relieves symptoms of heroin withdrawal without producing its psychological effects, but Frank quickly learned from other patients how methadone's effects can be boosted with cocaine or Valium.

Finding that he liked the high even better than heroin, Frank maintained his new methadone habit for the next five years. He bought methadone from other patients in his program and supported his habit by turning to crime—stealing household items and then selling them to buy more drugs. He was eventually arrested and spent four agonizing months in jail detoxifying the natural way, without medication.

The day he was released, Frank bought a bottle of

They designed further studies that allowed the rats to deliver their own stimulation to this limbic area, and it became apparent that the animals were activating some type of reward circuit. Animals that received electrical stimulation to a general area of the brain known as the **medial forebrain bundle,** a large collection of axons that extend from the hypothalamus to the septum, could not get enough stimulation. They would press the bar continuously, sometimes as many as 2,000 times per hour, until they passed out from exhaustion (Olds, 1958). This research was an important step toward understanding that certain brain areas are specifically involved with the phenomenon of reward.

Today, we know that the nucleus accumbens, one endpoint of the medial forebrain bundle, plays a key role in brain reward. For example, if the nucleus accumbens is damaged, animals no longer self-administer the rewarding drug cocaine. It is as if the animal needs a healthy, working nucleus accumbens to experience the pleasures associated with cocaine (Pettit, Ettenberg, Bloom, & Koob, 1984).

medial forebrain bundle
Large collection of axons that extend from the hypothalamus to the septum, a structure in the limbic system. Animals respond continuously to receiving electrical brain stimulation in this area; consequently, it is considered the most prevalent brain reward system of the nervous system.

---

methadone and some pills. Little did he know that his body had lost tolerance to the drugs during his drug-free stay in prison. Consequently, he overdosed and was rushed to the hospital where he lay comatose for days. His family intervened and sent him to a therapeutic community to recover. This community emphasized strict discipline in a highly structured environment. Things started to look up for Frank. He completed the program, started running again, and was eventually offered a job as a trainee counselor.

Frank ignored recommendations to attend a social support group such as Narcotics Anonymous (NA) during this time; he felt he had the strength to maintain abstinence on his own. Then, after an impressive 10 years of sobriety, he made the mistake of having a glass of wine. When nothing catastrophic happened, it gave Frank the confidence to start experimenting with drugs once again. It wasn't long before he found himself buying methadone, taking pills, and shooting heroin.

This downward spiral prompted Frank to enroll in another rehabilitation program. He was assigned to a competent, friendly counselor and was required to attend NA meetings. He fell in love with the woman whom he would later marry but was still not able to

remain clean very long. After a year, he was back in the familiar downward spiral fueled by heroin, methadone, marijuana, and pills.

At the insistence of his girlfriend, he checked himself into a detox unit at a local hospital where he underwent medical withdrawal from the Valium. A couple of weeks later, he was discharged and referred to another methadone clinic where he was watched closely for additional drug use. Things started to look up again for Frank but, before he could be completely sober, he had to undergo two more detox cycles.

In 1995, Frank was completely free of drugs—this time paying close attention to aftercare treatment. He attended NA meetings daily, continued with a sponsor, and started regaining his physical strength. Today, he remains sober and is building a business, enjoying spending time with his wife. He gets high only the natural way—by running very fast!

Adapted from Fernandez, 1998.

ventral tegmental area (VTA)
Cluster of cell bodies in the midbrain that synthesize dopamine; extends to the nucleus accumbens and is involved with reward circuits of the brain.

bed nucleus of the stria terminalis (BNST) Subcortical limbic structure considered part of the extended amygdala that plays a role in the stress/anxiety response.

extended amygdala Brain structures continuous with and sharing morphological similarities with the amygdaloid nuclei, including the nucleus accumbens, BNST, and olfactory lobe.

Neural Circuits Involved in Establishing Addiction

The seminal work of Olds and Milner was just the beginning of an active area of research investigating the role of the nucleus accumbens in addiction. A half century later, the nucleus accumbens continues to be considered a key brain structure driving addiction. This structure doesn't work in isolation, however, it communicates with other influential brain areas. One brain area interacting with the nucleus accumbens is the OFC (orbitofrontal cortex), a more recently evolved cortical structure implicated in the maintenance of craving. These two key structures, the nucleus accumbens and OFC, are discussed in the following section.

Role of the nucleus accumbens. The nucleus accumbens is part of a larger brain circuit that determines whether a response (in this case, the consumption of a drug) is important enough to repeat. The nucleus accumbens receives messages directly from the **ventral tegmental area** in the midbrain, where a majority of dopamine is synthesized. The nucleus accumbens receives input, or projections, from other areas in the brain including the amygdala, hippocampus, and medial prefrontal cortex, as shown in Figure 10.1 (Robbins & Everitt, 1999).

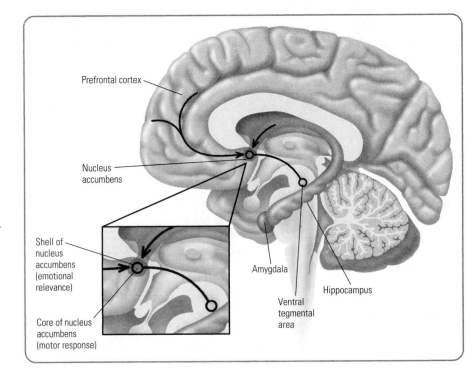

[Figure 10.1]
Extended amygdala. The ventral tegmental area projects to the nucleus accumbens, the neuroanatomical structure that plays a central role in addictive behavior. This structure, however, does not work alone; the amygdala, hippocampus, and medial prefrontal cortex send excitatory projections to the nucleus accumbens, shown in detail in the inset.
ADAPTED FROM ROBBINS & EVERITT, 1999.

Now that the structure of the nucleus accumbens has been studied extensively, it is known to consist of a core and a shell (Figure 10.1 inset). The *core* has characteristics of the caudate and putamen (recall from Chapter Three that these movement structures are collectively known as the striatum), and the *shell* seems to be an extension of the emotionally charged central amygdala (Everitt, Parkinson, Olmstead, Arroyo, Robledo & Robbins, 2000). Because the nucleus accumbens shell has morphological similarities with other structures, including the **bed nucleus of the stria terminalis (BNST)**, a subcortical limbic structure involved in the stress/anxiety response, and portions of the amygdala, the area diagrammed in Figure 10.1 is sometimes referred to as the **extended amygdala** (Koob & Nestler, 1997).

The two different components—the core and the shell—allow the nucleus accumbens a very important function in governing behavior. It serves as a mediator between the limbic structures that evaluate the emotional relevance of a particular environmental stimulus and the striatum, which can actually generate a motor response. As Hoebel suggests, the nucleus accumbens is the brain's sensory–motor interface, in which an environmental stimulus is processed, along with the animal's plans to respond to this stimulus (Hoebel, Rada, Mark, & Pothos, 1999). Hence, the nucleus accumbens plays a critical role in initiating and maintaining an animal's motivation toward stimuli relevant to its survival and propagation such as eating, drinking, and sex (Carelli & Deadwyler, 1994; Mermestein & Becker, 1995). If a behavior seems particularly relevant, the nucleus accumbens places the important variables associated with the behavior in the brain's version of boldface type and then saves it to the brain's long-term memory stores so that the animal will respond similarly when faced with the same stimulus in the future.

The process of emphasizing certain variables in the environment enables the animal to become more efficient at either avoiding danger (not entering a field in which a predator lives) or gaining rewards (entering a field that contains an abundance of food). This adaptive learning system, however, can lead to behavior that is not important for survival. The phenomenon is illustrated beautifully in the case of two literature professors who became addicted to gambling after succumbing to the lure of the riverboat casinos lining the banks of the Mississippi. In their essay published in *The New Yorker*, the professors convey how every blip in the environment thrives with meaning when they are playing blackjack and the game is going either especially good or especially badly.

In the brain's reward circuitry, bad gambling attempts are processed as threatening stimuli and good attempts are processed as potential rewards. Consequently, many frivolous associations are formed during the games.

For example, a certain number of ice cubes may be associated with bringing bad luck while a particular song may relate to bringing good luck (Barthelme & Barthelme, 1999). The abundance of these strong associations in their memory stores makes it difficult for these gamblers to forget even the most trivial information. As described in this example, it is easy to see how the nucleus accumbens plays a role in forming perceptions of many cues in an addict's environment (such as money, drug paraphernalia, or certain friends) as extremely relevant.

Hans Breiter and colleagues at Massachusetts General Hospital in Boston provide evidence that the brain responds to gambling in a similar fashion to the way it responds to drugs of abuse. Using a creative protocol, Breiter had subjects participate in a game of chance in which an arrow was spun on a disk to determine whether they won or lost money. Functional MRI scans indicated that, as the arrow was whirring around on the disk, the extended amygdala, nucleus accumbens, and hypothalamus were activated—as observed in subjects consuming cocaine. Consequently, Breiter reported that this circuitry is fundamental for processing information about rewards and losses, an endeavor that is central to most anything we do (Breiter, Aharon, Kahneman, Dale, & Shizgal, 2001).

Although this system may sometimes lead to faulty responding, for the most part, the nucleus accumbens circuitry is an efficient executor of responses. When an appetizing food is consumed, the nucleus accumbens may register the food so that the next time it is encountered the animal will be motivated to approach and consume it. In the day-to-day living of the typical animal, it experiences small doses of nucleus accumbens-induced pleasure as it engages in these survival-related behaviors (building relationships, caring for offspring, grooming, resting). Perversely, this beautifully adaptive system makes our brains vulnerable to addictive substances found in nature (Hyman, 1999). As described in the gambling professors example, sometimes an animal discovers that a drug or activity is the emotional equivalent of robbing the nucleus accumbens pleasure bank (Elster, 1999). The following passage conveys such an experience for a rat:

> The rat rapidly acquires the lever-pressing "habit"—giving itself approximately 5,000–10,000 pleasure/reward "hits" during each one-hour daily test session. During these test sessions, the rat is totally focused on obtaining the desired electrical stimulation—lever pressing at maximum speed and ignoring other attractions within the test chamber (food, water, playthings, sexually receptive rats of the opposite sex). After several weeks, the rat suddenly faces a new and unexpected behavioral contingency. An electrified metal floor grid has been placed in the test chamber between the entrance and the wall-mounted lever. This floor grid delivers intensely painful foot-

shocks. The rat enters the chamber, receives a footshock, and jumps back off the floor grid. It stands in the entrance, looking alternately at the aversive floor grid and the appealing wall-mounted lever. After some minutes of indecision, it crosses the floor-grid, receiving intensely painful footshocks with every step (and flinching and squealing in pain), to reach the lever and once again self-administer the pleasurable brain stimulation (Gardner & David, 1999, p. 94).

But, you say, this is a rat—an animal that has a cortex the size of a postage stamp. Surely, a human would not succumb to such ridiculous behavior. Well, we would all like to think that, but one look at the life of a drug-addicted person—a life in which the individual does anything to acquire a drug—suggests that humans are not too different from our rodent friends in this regard. The nineteenth-century American psychiatrist Benjamin Rush observed such addiction-driven frenzy in a chronic alcoholic who made the following statement: "Were a keg of rum in one corner of a room, and were a cannon constantly discharging balls between me and it, I could not refrain from passing before that cannon, in order to get at the rum" (cited in Elster, 1999, p. x).

Terry Robinson at the University of Michigan and Bryan Kolb at the University of Lethbridge provided even more evidence that the nucleus accumbens is intricately involved with addiction. These researchers were intrigued by the fact that chronic drug abuse seems to create long-lasting changes in brain and behavior, even after the drug is no longer being consumed. For example, when a previously addicted rat is exposed to an environment in which it once received the drug, the nucleus accumbens may become activated, accompanied with a behavioral change of hyperactivity or orientation toward the lever.

This observation prompted Robinson and Kolb to wonder if the drug may have permanently altered the structure of the neurons in the nucleus accumbens. They tested their idea by administering cocaine, amphetamine, or no drug to animals. Because these drugs result in increased levels of activity, another control group in which animals were housed in activity wheels (but received no drug) was utilized to control for the possibility that increased activity may alter the structure of accumbens neurons.

Following four weeks of injections or running wheel experience, the animals were left alone for twenty-five days. Animals treated with either amphetamine or cocaine had increased dendritic branches and spine density in the medium spiny neurons of the nucleus accumbens shell (Figure 10.2). These results suggest that addiction, or chronic drug use, may produce long-lasting or even permanent changes in the morphology of the brain.

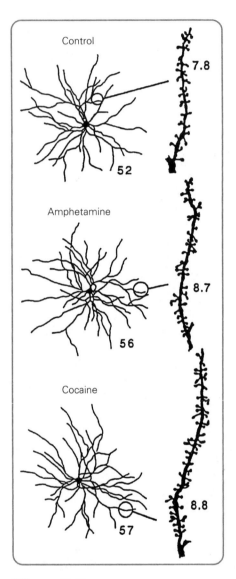

[Figure 10.2]
**Drugs modify neuronal struc-
ture.** Drawings of representative
medium spiny neurons from the
shell of the nucleus accumbens in
rats exposed to amphetamine,
cocaine, or wheel running (a control for increased activity). The
numbers at the lower right side of
each cell represent the number of
branches, whereas the number by
the spine segments represents
the number of dendritic spines, per
specified unit. ROBINSON & KOLB, 1999

Role of the orbitofrontal cortex. It is well established that
the nucleus accumbens plays an important role in acquiring an
addiction, but other evidence suggests that there is more to the
picture than simple pleasure. For example, an animal will still
self-administer a drug after it has developed tolerance to it and at
times continue to self-administer in the presence of adverse
effects of the drug. Nora Volkow and Joanna Fowler at the State
University of New York have proposed that a more recently
evolved brain structure, the orbitofrontal cortex (OFC), may also
play a role in maintaining addictions (Volkow & Fowler, 2000).

Several lines of evidence point to the involvement of this
structure, which is part of the OCD neuroanatomical circuit
(see Figure 7.1). When rats are placed in an environment previously associated with cocaine, the OFC becomes activated,
not the nucleus accumbens (Brown, Robertson, & Fibiger,
1992). Additionally, if electrodes are placed in the OFC of both
rats and rhesus monkeys, they will also press the bar to deliver the stimulation to their brains (Phillips, Mora, & Rolls,
1979). As we discuss later in the chapter, orbitofrontal activation is observed when human addicts report drug craving
(Volkow & Fowler, 2000).

Recall from Chapter Seven that the orbitofrontal cortex plays
a key role in maintaining the persistent thoughts and behaviors
associated with obsessive-compulsive disorder. Actually, it is
easy to see the relationship between OCD and the drive and
perseverance of behaviors typical of drug addiction (Volkow &
Fowler, 2000). Neuroanatomically, the OFC is a likely accom-
plice to drug addiction because the nucleus accumbens projects
to the orbitofrontal cortex by way of the mediodorsal nucleus of
the thalamus. To keep the lines of communication open, the
orbitofrontal cortex sends messages back to the nucleus accumbens. Finally, the OFC also receives input from limbic areas
such as the amygdala and hippocampus. Thus, a picture of the
OFC as an extension of the nucleus accumbens is emerging, providing
researchers with an explanation of how, once an animal hits the pleasure
lottery by activating the nucleus accumbens, it will continue to search
for the big payoff again and again—at any cost.

Neurochemistry of Addiction

Most drugs of abuse either directly or indirectly activate the dopaminergic (DA) system, which is intimately involved with the extended
amygdala. Serotonin may also play a role in addiction. Another

neurochemical of the nucleus accumbens, acetylcholine, is implicated as well but in aversive rather than pleasurable behaviors.

Dopamine: Primary fuel of addiction. A technique called **microdialysis** enables experimenters to implant probes into the brains of animals and measure levels of a neurotransmitter in freely moving animals. During cocaine self-administration, microdialysis studies reveal that dopamine is released in the nucleus accumbens and maintained above baseline levels (Pettit & Justice, 1991). Also, if rats receive a drug that antagonizes dopamine, they will respond longer than nontreated animals in the self-administration task (Corrigall & Coen, 1991). One interpretation of these data is that the reinforcing property of cocaine is diminished by the antagonist, prompting the rats to work harder to receive any amount of reward (Carelli, King, Hampson, & Deadwyler, 1993).

Most researchers hypothesize that the **mesolimbic dopaminergic pathway** is the quintessential reward circuit in the brain. As you'll remember from Chapter Five, the DA pathway extends from the cell bodies containing dopamine in the ventral tegmental area to the nucleus accumbens, prefrontal cortex, and dorsal striatum. Figure 10.3 depicts the

microdialysis Neurochemical technique in which the level of a neurotransmitter from a particular area of the brain is assessed. This technique is unique because the researcher can extract the neurotransmitter while the animal is engaging in a particular behavior.

mesolimbic dopamine pathway Neurons extending from the midbrain to the forebrain produce and release dopamine into the forebrain. Two pathways make up this system: (1) the mesocorticolimbic (reward circuit) system extends from the ventral tegmental area to the nucleus accumbens; (2) the nigrostriatal pathway, involved in neuromuscular functions, extends from the substantia nigra to the corpus striatum.

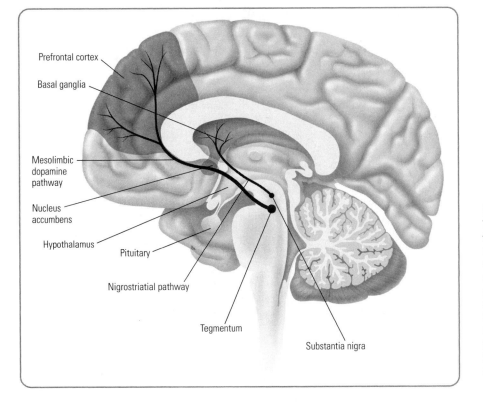

Prefrontal cortex

Basal ganglia

Mesolimbic dopamine pathway

Nucleus accumbens

Hypothalamus

Pituitary

Nigrostriatial pathway

Tegmentum

Substantia nigra

[Figure 10.3]
Two dopamine pathways in the brain. The nigrostriatial pathway, which is related to movement, originates in the substantia nigra and projects to the basal ganglia. The second pathway is critical for reward. This mesolimbic DA pathway originates in the ventral tegmentum area, projects to the nucleus accumbens, and then to the prefrontal cortex.
ADAPTED FROM RUDEN, 2000.

mesolimbic DA pathway and a second more motor-related nigrostriatal pathway projecting from the substantia nigra into the basal ganglia.

This dopamine hypothesis is strengthened by the fact that most abused substances (except for the anxiolytics called benzodiazepines) increase dopamine release somewhere along the mesolimbic pathway (Betz, Mihalic, Pinto, & Raffa, 2000). Cocaine, for example, increases the availability of dopamine in the synapse by inhibiting the *dopamine transporter (DA-T)*, described in Chapter Five, which is responsible for absorbing the dopamine molecule back into the synaptic vesicle (reuptake). See Table 10.3 for effects of other commonly abused drugs.

Neuroimaging studies with humans add another interesting twist to the dopamine–reward story. These studies suggest that the psychological high experienced by cocaine users is more closely associated with the *rate* at which cocaine enters the brain and antagonizes dopamine transporters than with the actual amount of the drug in the brain. Reductions in the number of dopamine receptors in the cingulate gyrus and the orbitofrontal cortex have been observed in cocaine abusers. This reduction probably contributes to a less efficient occupancy rate of receptors and an accompanying tolerance to the psychological effects of cocaine (Volkow, Fowler, & Wang, 1999). In other words, addicts lose the previously experienced high following drug consumption.

[Table 10.3]

Effects of Common Drugs of Abuse

Drug	Neurochemical action	Psychological effects
Cocaine	Inhibits dopamine transporters, resulting in increased dopamine in synapse	Pleasure; hyperactivity
Opiates	Stimulate opioid receptors; inhibit release of GABA, resulting in increase in dopamine	Relief from pain; pleasure
Amphetamines	Stimulate release of monoamines (including dopamine)	Pleasure; hyperactivity
Ethanol	Increases GABA receptor function; inhibits NMDA glutamate receptor function; increased dopamine release	Reduced anxiety; euphoria; disinhibition
Nicotine	Facilitates nicotinic acetylcholine receptors; increases release of dopamine	Relaxation; pleasure
Hallucinogens	Partially stimulate 5-HT2A receptors; thought to indirectly affect dopamine	Relaxation; hallucinations; pleasure
Cannabinoids	Stimulates cannabinoid receptors; triggers release of dopamine	Relaxation; mild hallucinations; pleasure
Ecstasy	Increases synaptic serotonin levels; leads to prolonged serotonin depletion due to blocked serotonin uptake; high affinity for noradrenaline receptors; promotes dopamine release and subsequent decreases in reuptake	Heightened pleasure; boost in self-confidence; feelings of extroversion

Adapted from Nestler, 1999.

It is unclear whether the reduced number of dopamine receptors in cocaine addicts is a cause or an effect of their condition. There is evidence that a person with fewer D_2 receptors is more likely to find psychostimulants reinforcing—in this case methylphendiate (ritalin)—than individuals with higher levels of receptors (Volkow et al., 1999). Making the dopamine receptor story even more complicated, *increased* D_3 receptor messenger RNA and binding have been observed in cocaine addicts' brains at autopsy (Staley & Mash, 1996).

If you wanted to determine the value of the dopamine transporters in the addiction syndrome, wouldn't it be interesting to "engineer" a mouse that does not have these transporters? Recent advancements in molecular biology enable neuroscientists to systematically turn off (or "knock out") genes that perform certain functions. Rocha and colleagues at the University of North Texas looked at the effect of cocaine and amphetamine on these **knockout mice** (*DA-T knockouts*) and reported that they did not appear to be affected by the drug because it failed to increase their activity (Rocha et al., 1998). These mice did, however, develop a place preference for the drug, suggesting that they were somehow experiencing pleasure from the drug without the services of the dopamine transporters (Figure 10.4).

Another type of knockout mouse was developed in which the brain vesicular monoamine transporter is inactivated. This knockout mouse

knockout mice Product of recently developed technique in behavioral neuroscience in which certain genes are eliminated (knocked out) so that their function can be determined in the genetically modified animal.

[Figure 10.4]
Conditioned place preference.
After receiving repeated injections in one distinct compartment, the drug-free rat is later given a choice between it and another compartment. If place preference is established, the rat will quickly go back to the drug compartment. The observation of conditioned place preference suggests that the animal finds the drug pleasurable because it chooses an environment that is associated with administration the drug. Addicts who repeatedly visit the same street corners or clubs in which they previously obtained drugs are also demonstrating conditioned place preference (Pinel, 2000, p. 366).

(VMAT2 knockout) lacks the ability to have its transmitter synaptic vesicles accumulate, or recycle, monoamines (dopamine and serotonin) from the cytoplasm. Such a genetic effect results in less efficient packaging of dopamine and may prolong its activity. The VMAT2 knockouts were less likely to develop a place preference for amphetamine than were their control mouse counterparts (Caron, 1997).

The finding that the VMAT2 knockout mice did not develop a place preference suggests that serotonin may also be a neurochemical player in addiction. Cocaine decreases the reuptake of serotonin as well as dopamine; additionally, serotonin neurons connect with the mesolimbic dopamine system. Low serotonin levels are related to depression, impulsive behavior, and alcoholism (Gamberino & Gold, 1999). Rats selectively bred to prefer alcohol have low levels of serotonin in the cortex, striatum, nucleus accumbens, hippocampus, and hypothalamus (Gongwer, Murphy, McBride, Lumeng, & Li, 1989). There is also evidence that some human alcoholics have low levels of serotonin in their cerebrospinal fluid (Cloninger, 1987).

What do these knockout studies mean? Do we throw the dopamine hypothesis out because of the place preference in the DA-T knockout animals? Certainly not. We should be cautious about drawing definitive conclusions from these studies because we are not certain how this genetic manipulation influences other physiological systems.

In Dr. Seuss's book *Because a Little Bug Went Ka-Choo,* a simple sneeze sets off a cascade of subsequent rhyming events in the bug's environment. A little bug sneezing causes a seed to drop on a worm's head, which prompts the worm to kick a coconut tree, which results in a coconut falling on a turtle's back—you get the picture. The point is that events do not occur in a vacuum. If a particular gene that makes a certain protein is turned off, the animal is very likely to compensate for the loss in some way. For example, other systems may produce a substitute for the protein, or another protein may serve a similar function. Thus, although fascinating, we have to be careful about interpreting the results of the knockout studies.

Potential role of acetylcholine. Hoebel and his colleagues have proposed a provocative theory: the acetylcholine neurons that reside in the nucleus accumbens along with dopaminergic neurons might serve the opposite function of dopamine. Let's consider some evidence for their theory.

Normally, rats drink large quantities of water sweetened with saccharin. The rate of drinking, however, decreases when the saccharin water is paired with high levels of acetylcholine in the nucleus accumbens (Taylor, Davidson, Mark, Rada, & Hoebel, 1992). This research suggests that the structure that has become an icon in behavioral neuroscience for pleasure seeking may also be involved in aversion. The notion that acetylcholine may stop the behavior triggered by the dopaminergic mesolimbic system may help us understand why, even when a behavior (eating, drinking, having sex) feels so good, we eventually stop engaging in the behavior.

Perhaps exogenous drug use fails to tap into the acetylcholine system and creates a situation similar to driving a car that has no brakes. Hoebel's research is important because it suggests that manipulation of acetylcholine in the nucleus accumbens may help form limits on the high rates of addictive behaviors. Just as something tells us to stop eating that third helping of pie, a brain mechanism such as the cholinergic system may reduce the number of times a drug is consumed in a particular time period. As seen in Box 10.2, some natural behavior–reward systems, such as the sexual drive of the squirrel, are difficult to restrain and appear to be in need of a boost from the cholinergic system.

Craving Response

Once an addiction is established, many individuals report a psychological **craving response,** a strong desire to experience the effects of a psychoactive drug that the user previously consumed (Diana, 1996). Craving for specific drugs may vary. For instance, craving for cocaine is characterized by some of the same symptoms of actually consuming cocaine (light-headedness, chest tightness, ear ringing, generalized arousal, euphoria, and even the taste of cocaine in the back of the mouth). This suggests that craving and actual drug use may be driven by some of the same biological mechanisms (Childress, Mozley, McElgin, Fitzgerald, Reivich, & O'Brien, 1999).

Craving as a conditioned response. Craving is a key problem in the fight against addiction. Not only does craving sustain an addiction—even after a person has abstained for months or years—but craving might also cause the individual to start using again, which is called *relapse,* as Frank did in Box 10.1. Craving and relapse are as maddening to the therapists working with addicts as they are to the addicts themselves, but these states are not surprising to researchers aware of conditioned responses (see Chapter Two for discussion of Pavlov's work).

Quickly and effortlessly, the nervous system starts to make associations between the conditioned stimuli—sight of the drug, the drug paraphernalia, even the décor of a room in which a person frequently uses— and the physiological and psychological effects of the drug. Once this predictive power is established with the conditioned stimuli, the cues can trigger a drug-related response in the individual. The response, whether aversive or inviting, is likely to lead to further drug use.

craving response Persistent, intense desire to consume a drug.

[Box 10.2]

Brain Matters

Substance Abuse and Behavioral Compulsion: Two Expressions of the Same Neurobiological System?

In the sweltering heat of the summer of 1997, Army Sergeant Gail Baker drove to a convenience store in Jasper County, South Carolina, and commenced a 7-hour binge of video poker. When Gail finally returned to her steaming car, she discovered that her 10-day-old baby she had left in the car had not survived her video-poker overdose. Her husband later argued that he did not hold her responsible for the death of their child because she had an addiction (Bragg, 1998). Is he right? Are substance abuse addictions and behavioral compulsions tapping in to the same neurobiological systems?

The fact that Baker continued to engage in her behavioral compulsion when the consequences were so great (a child's life) suggests that gambling was highly rewarding to her. The intensity of her drive to gamble certainly resembles the drives or cravings of drug addicts who continue their habit with no regard to the consequences. We've already discussed how the mesolimbic dopaminergic system and extended amygdala are involved in motivating animals to engage in certain behaviors related to survival. Is it possible for these natural behaviors to activate the system to the degree that drugs do? When you consider the sexual behavior of the squirrel, you will probably conclude that, at least temporarily, the male squirrel is as addicted to sex as the most addicted of drug users.

John Koprowski in the Wildlife Department at the University of Arizona has been observing the sexual lives of squirrels for years. It just so happens that the female goes into heat for a mere 6 hours during breeding season—6 hours for the entire year—which occurs in the dead of winter to assure the arrival of the young squirrels in the spring. To impregnate females in this short time period, the males have to be extremely driven to engage in sexual behavior—at the cost of everything else.

Koprowski has observed females emerging from their nest with as many as 22 male callers "looking for love." At this time, the great chase begins. Males continue to chase the female to copulate, and, if a squirrel is fortunate enough to have such an opportunity, other impatient males often try to displace the copulating male. When the female's 6 hours are up, the males direct their attention toward the next female in heat.

Koprowski observes that these squirrel Casanovas look very much like drug addicts. Males will continue the pattern for days—chasing females without even stopping to eat. A few times he even observed males emerge from their nest only to fall over dead—probably due to exhaustion and a depletion of resources (autopsies reveal that they don't have an ounce of body fat on them). As with drug addicts who engage in risky behavior (such as crime) to get a hit, this behavioral addiction of squirrels continues in the face of danger. As seen in the photo below, a male squirrel is continuing to copulate even though the branch has broken and he is about to plummet to the ground!

COURTESY JOHN KOPROWSKI

Given this information, the occurrence of relapse following a lengthy abstinence is disappointing, but considered a logical step in the conditioning process (Robbins & Everitt, 1999). A rehabilitated drug user may actively avoid strong cues related to prior drug use, but it is impossible to step into a world devoid of all potential triggers. For most people, it is only a matter of time before they encounter a powerful cue and become physiologically overwhelmed, testing the strongest of wills.

Neural components of the craving response. Anna Rose Childress and her colleagues at the University of Pennsylvania have designed clever experiments to determine the brain areas that are activated during craving (Box 10.3). In one study, 20 men who regularly used cocaine but who reported that about 13 days had passed since last using, were brought into the lab and shown a drug-related video (with all the drug triggers) and a nondrug-related video. PET scans indicated that the addicts showed increased activity in the amygdala, anterior cingulate, and dorsolateral frontal cortex during the drug-related video. (Unfortunately, the nucleus accumbens is too small for adequate resolution with the PET scan.) Lifelong abstainers failed to show limbic activation in response to the drug video (Childress, Mozley, McElgin, Fitzgerald, Reivich & O'Brien, 1999).

Other neuroimaging studies have been conducted utilizing PET, SPECT, and fMRI scans on patients experiencing craving. In addition to the areas mentioned in the foregoing paragraph, the thalamus, caudate, orbital cortex, and insular cortex have been implicated in craving in humans. Except for the thalamus, all these areas receive neural messages from dopamine-releasing neurons in the midbrain. Collectively, these brain areas are related to the basal ganglia–thalamocortical circuits (described in Chapter Three) that play an important role in making decisions about the appropriate behavior for a particular context (Hommer, 1999).

Focusing on rat models of craving, Barry Everitt, working with his colleagues at Cambridge University, reports that the basolateral area of the amygdala is a key component of the neural circuitry that contributes to drug craving and subsequent relapse. His research has shown that damaging this brain area switches off the rats' conditioned cravings for morphine (Schulteis, 2000). Hence, robust evidence in both humans and rodents suggests the critical role of the amygdala in the production of cravings.

After abstaining from a drug, long-lasting changes in the dopaminergic system may also play a role in craving and relapse. Studies have shown that in rats dependent on either morphine or ethanol the mesolimbic neurons fired less often than their nonaddicted counterparts. If a certain baseline

[Box 10.3]

The Investigators

Anna Rose Childress

As a child, Anna Rose Childress was fascinated with a few of her aunts who suffered from bipolar disorder. She was intrigued by the fact that their moods would change without apparent environmental triggers. These early observations prompted Childress to think about the role of the brain in psychology. She attended Virginia Tech and studied Skinnerian psychology, but she was not able to return to the role of the brain until she attended graduate school at Bryn Mawr College. Her doctoral dissertation focused on mapping rat brain self-stimulation reward sites.

As a postdoctoral fellow at the University of Pennsylvania, Childress finally got an opportunity to work with humans. By focusing on addiction, she was able to study the brain's involvement in reward and motivation in chronic drug use. Childress was finally in a setting that enabled her to investigate the brain's role in moods and behavior—the area that interested her so much as a child.

Currently, Anna Rose Childress is a professor of psychology in the Psychiatry Department at the University of Pennsylvania School of Medicine and a clinical psychologist in the Drug Dependence Unit at the VA Medical Center in Pennsylvania. She is also the director of an imaging laboratory at the University of Pennsylvania, where she is working diligently to understand the biological components of cue-induced craving. Her diverse training and experience as an experimental behaviorist, a behavioral neuroscientist, a clinician, and a neuroimaging researcher have prepared her to design an impressive line of research.

Childress's creative approach takes her to the streets where drugs are sold and used on a regular basis. Guided by her addict subjects, she captures the drug-relevant cues—the specific street corner, the exact amount of money, the drug itself—on video. Back in her laboratory, she exposes her subjects, who are either current or former addicts, to the visual triggers and records their responses. Control subjects have the

---

level of firing in the mesolimbic system is necessary for normal levels of motivation, then a marked decrease in neuronal activity may lead to the dysphoric, or depressed, state sometimes typical of withdrawal. Certainly, a lack of pleasure may also lead to craving or relapse (Diana, 1996).

In withdrawal from cocaine addiction, cells in the nucleus accumbens are less responsive. This means that more stimulation than is typically required to achieve action potentials in these neurons must be encountered to elicit a response. For example, if a single-scoop ice cream cone used to make a person excited, it may take a triple-scoop cone to do the trick under these circumstances. This inactivity of the area of the brain involved in coordinating motivation and response patterns (the nucleus accumbens) may be related to withdrawal-induced **anhedonia** (lack of pleasure) and depression (Wise, 1982; Zhang, Hu, & White, 1998). The fact that these modifications in the mesolimbic DA system continue to exist even after the more physical withdrawal symptoms disappear may prompt a person to feel as if something were not quite right—making him

anhedonia Lack of desire or pleasure; drugs that interfere with the mesolimbic dopaminergic system produce this state.

pleasure of watching nature videos. Whereas she began with more modest physiological measures such as heart rate, today Childress uses the latest neuroimaging techniques, such as functional magnetic resonance imaging (fMRI), to capture the brain areas that are activated when the subject experiences the drug cues, or triggers.

Childress's neuroimaging studies have pointed to the role of limbic activation in the craving response. Currently, she is exploring the release of dopamine in the limbic region during craving, as well as the potential ability of GABA blockers to blunt the craving response. Most recently, she has explored possible mechanisms of individual differences in susceptibility to addiction. Initial data indicate that cocaine addicts have less gray matter in their orbitofrontal, anterior cingulate and temporal cortices, ranging from 5% to 11% reductions. She argues that it may be more difficult for these addicts to consider the negative, long-term consequences of drug use than it is for subjects with larger cortical areas. In other words, it may be more difficult for these subjects to "just say no" (Franklin et al.,

COURTESY ANNA ROSE CHILDRESS.

2000). Whether a compromised frontal/temporal cortex is a cause or effect of chronic drug use is a question that remains to be answered.

Childress's research combines the best aspects of experimental technique, field-work, and clinical investigation to reveal the critical brain areas maintaining the craving responses that haunt so many recovering addicts.

or her more likely to return to drug use if an opportunity arises (Diana, Muntoni, Pistis, Melis, & Gessa, 1999).

Researchers also think that serotonin may play a role in craving. Many of the psychiatric symptoms associated with drug withdrawal, such as irritability/aggression, insomnia, and depression, may be caused by altered functioning of the serotonergic system. Similar to the unpleasant feelings associated with the low-dopamine-induced anhedonia, a disruption of the serotonergic system may also contribute to the psychological distress experienced by many patients during drug withdrawal.

Relapse is likely to occur as a person attempts to self-medicate by reintroducing the drug into the body. The former user is quite familiar with obtaining and ingesting the drug to feel better, a task that seems quicker and easier than seeking out expensive or even painful medical treatment. Further, low levels of brain serotonin have been implicated in a decrease of impulse control. Obviously, abstaining from drug use when a person encounters trigger after trigger takes a healthy amount of impulse control.

Any compromise in this system is related to increased relapse rates (Ciccocioppo, 1999).

A group of researchers recently investigated potential predictive factors that may be related to an animal's vulnerability to relapse during a period of abstinence from chronic drug administration. Whereas behavioral responses to drugs or stressors failed to predict whether an animal would relapse during abstinence, the *amount* of the drug consumed during early drug use was influential in predicting relapse (Sutton, Karanian, & Self, 2000). This finding is interesting if you consider research conducted by Volkow and her colleagues (1999) indicating that more than 50% of the DA-T blockade is required for a person to report experiencing a "high." In other words, a significant amount of dopamine must be allowed to circulate through the mesolimbic system before it becomes intensely pleasurable.

Additionally, as previously mentioned, the *rate* at which the drugs enter the brain contributes to a more intense high (Volkow, Fowler, & Wang, 1999). Perhaps the higher amounts of drugs consumed by the rats leads to relapse because of the more intense high experienced during early drug use. These findings suggest that the intensity of the high experienced with the first use of the drug plays a powerful role in determining the magnitude of the subsequent craving responses.

STRESS AND ADDICTION

People faced with stress are susceptible to addiction. Research suggests that previous stress experiences might predispose an individual to becoming an addict. Further, as you learned in Connections on pages 351 and 352, extensive research on the stress response has identified the key neurochemicals (for example, corticotropin-releasing hormone, cortisol) in the stress response that underlie drug addiction.

A little over a decade ago, Pier Piazza at the University of Bordeaux conducted research indicating that an animal's stress response and stress history may be important in determining whether the animal will self-administer (or abuse) amphetamine. Simply observing how an animal reacted to being placed in a new environment provided important clues about its predisposition to become an addict. Specifically, the more reactive the animal was in this new situation, the more likely it would be to acquire amphetamine self-administration (Piazza, Deminiere, Maccare, Mormedi, Lemoal, & Simon, 1990.)

Further exploring the possibility that susceptibility to amphetamine self-stimulation was somehow related to a more reactive stress response, other researchers exposed animals to footshock and subsequently monitored activity in the nucleus accumbens. Dopamine levels increased in the shell of the nucleus accumbens, the area related to reward (Kalivas & Duffy, 1995). This study is a beautiful example of how the nucleus accumbens is thrown into action when a threatening stimulus is encountered. Hence, stress and amphetamine administration both tap into the same dopaminergic system. In some cases, stress may serve as a primer for the mesolimbic dopaminergic system, making an individual more likely to self-administer psychoactive drugs in the future (Wise, 2000).

Does this research mean that stress can be pleasurable? That's difficult to answer, but the data does indicate that the same reward system is activated in both situations. Perhaps these findings explain why some people actually pay money to be stressed—to engage in behaviors such as skydiving, watching scary movies, and riding roller coasters. If the notion that the mesolimbic DA system is important in translating relevant environmental stimuli into appropriate actions is true, then it makes sense that it would be turned on during these stressful times. As expressed in John Mellencamp's song "Hurts So Good" (a song your parents may remember), it seems that, in some situations, the emotional responses of stress and reward may be blurred to some extent and may exhibit some crossover effects.

Jane Stewart of Concordia University in Montreal thinks that stress might help to answer a question that has baffled addiction researchers: Why do certain individuals who are addicts abstain for a while only to relapse during a stressful period in their lives? The relapse doesn't seem to be due to negative factors related to withdrawal because these individuals seem to be doing fine—until they encounter stress.

Stewart designed an animal model in rats to explore stress-induced relapse. In this model, rats were trained to press a lever to self-administer a drug. Once the rats were addicted, Stewart suddenly removed the drug so that pressing the bar no longer resulted in a drug hit. The rats, however, were free to keep trying to administer the drug, but after a while they tired and stopped responding to the drug lever. After approximately six weeks, the animals did not seem to be motivated to administer the drug, the presentation of brief footshocks sent them running to the bar—not unlike humans running to a bar when their lives become complicated!

Of course, Stewart and her team wanted to know why stress caused the animals to relapse. Their research points to corticotrophin-releasing hormone (CRH), the initial step in the hypothalamic-pituitary-adrenal (HPA) axis cascade described in Chapter Five, which triggers the release of adrenocorticotropin hormone (ACTH) from the anterior pituitary gland. Just delivering CRH into the brains of rats reinstates heroin seeking; giving the animals a drug to antagonize the CRH receptors in the animal's brain suppresses the relapse.

Where does CRH work to produce this form of relapse? CRH receptors are located in the central amygdala and the bed nucleus of the stria terminalis—two structures involved in the limbic/reward system. Further work, however, has indicated that the BNST seems to play a more important role here than the central amygdala. Hence, this line of research suggests that stress or anxiety may trigger CRH receptors in the BNST, which activates the HPA axis. Stress hormones released by the HPA axis activation prompt the animal to search for a way (e.g., drug administration, behavorial compulsion) to reestablish hormonal homeostasis (Stewart, 1999).

What if researchers could conduct a study in which people were placed in a stressful situation, allowed to develop an addiction, and then promptly removed from the stressful situation? Do you think the addiction would stop on cessation of the stress? If the intensity of the addiction changed after the cessation of stress, the hypothesis that addiction is facilitated by stress and its accompanying HPA activation would be supported.

It would certainly be unethical to conduct such a study, but returning U.S. soldiers from the Vietnam War were subjected to this set of conditions. During the summer of 1971, the military began screening the urine of servicemen as they were preparing to return to the United States. Even though the soldiers knew of the drug screening, 5% of the enlisted men tested positive for drug use.

About this time the military effort was being rapidly reduced, and thousands of men were returning to the United States each month amid great concern about treating the large number of addicts and about possible criminal actions that might accompany their drug use. Consequently, a study was conducted by the White House Special Action Office for Drug Abuse Prevention to follow these men. On returning to the United States, 45% of the servicemen reported narcotic use in Vietnam and half of them perceived themselves as addicts. Once these men reestablished themselves in the United States—away from the trauma of warfare—only 7% reported being addicted to narcotics.

When you get to the therapy section of this chapter, you will not read about any therapies that have been as effective as simply taking these servicemen out of Vietnam and the chronic stress of war (Robins, Davis & Nurco, 1974; Ruden, 2000). Drug companies dream of developing drugs with such successful effects. Of course, one cannot rule out the fact that, with the drastic environmental change accompanying the move back to the United States, many of the drug-related cues were also changed. A reduction in these environmental triggers might have reduced the cue-induced craving and led to decreased use of the drug.

As you read on pages 351 and 352, stressful situations, such as Native Americans fighting for their land or rats trying to avoid footshock, disrupt the internal milieu, or neurobiological homeostasis, of the organism. In an attempt to reduce this aversive state, new habits may be formed or old habits may be reinstated to help the animal feel physiologically balanced once again.

After reading about the influence of stress and environmental cues on craving, it is apparent that several factors are related to the production of craving that leads one to relapse into drug use. See Table 10.4 for a summary of these factors.

[Table 10.4]

Possible Reasons for Craving that May Lead to Relapse

Reason	Description
Drug priming	When animals are reexposed to a drug during a period of abstinence, they show interest in self-administering the drug.
Stress/Anxiety	Research suggests that CRH triggers an animal to engage in drug seeking during a period of abstinence.
Dysphoria	During drug withdrawal, some individuals report a distinct lack of pleasure that is aversive and motivates them to seek pleasure—i.e., consume the drugs once associated with a pleasurable feeling.
Physical distress	When users stop taking drugs, some experience physical discomfort such as nausea and headaches. Because these individuals are aware that these aversive feelings are due to the removal of the abused drug in their body, they self-medicate by seeking the drug.
Strong initial high	Both human and animal research indicates that the high experienced during initial drug use is a powerful factor determining whether the user will continue to seek out the drug during periods of abstinence.
Environmental triggers	Associations are formed between drugs and their related stimuli (needles, money, etc.), but the stronger these associations are, the more likely it is that a person will experience craving during periods of abstinence when these cues in the environment are encountered.

detoxification Initial step in the treatment of drug addiction that involves clearing a patient's system of the abused drug. This process can be accomplished by requiring a patient to abstain from drug use, or it may be facilitated by certain pharmacological agents.

methadone Opiate drug that is given to heroin addicts to help wean them from opiate addiction because it minimizes withdrawal symptoms and is not thought to produce a high that is comparable to that induced by heroin or morphine.

naloxone Drug that blocks opiate receptors in the brain; counteracts drugs such as morphine. Naltrexone has a similar function.

THERAPY FOR DRUG ADDICTION

Multiple factors influence one's predisposition and susceptibility to addiction. It should come as no surprise, then, that there is no single treatment for this complex condition. For the most part, therapy is an individual process. The clinician must find the most effective combination of therapies for effectively treating each patient.

This section introduces the process of **detoxification,** the initial step of the recovery process that involves clearing one's system of the abused drug. It would be wonderful if the problems of addiction ended with the exit of the drugs from the patient's body, but many addicts relapse after detoxification. Now that we know that relapse is due to the drug-induced changes in the brain that persist beyond the removal of the drug, focus is placed on trying to keep the detoxified user's brain from relapsing. The strategies for keeping a person clean of drugs include various medications (for example, antagonists and agonists) that interrupt the drug's ability to generate the desired response in the user, behavioral-cognitive therapies (for example, acupuncture and support groups), and the newest therapy on the drug research scene—vaccination.

Initial Step: Detoxification

A primary concern when tackling the addiction syndrome is the patient's physiological dependence on the abused substance. Knowing that the administration of the drug changes the individual's neurochemistry, the therapist must initially remove the drug to decrease the user's dependence on it. Detoxification can be achieved naturally by ceasing intake of the drug, or the process can be aided with various medications.

Typically, the type of drug abused determines the detoxification process. For example, the withdrawal syndrome for most cocaine addicts is far from fun, but the symptoms of fatigue and depression usually resolve themselves in a few days without the aid of other interventions. Heroin addicts, however, experience more serious symptoms typical of a bad case of the flu (sweating, nausea, cramps, diarrhea, tremors), and the detoxification phase of recovery can be made less aversive with an agonist. In this form of detoxification, an opiate agonist such as **methadone** is given to the patient. Methadone occupies the opiate receptors and decreases the negative effects of withdrawal from heroin, typically without producing the rewarding psychological effects of the drug. When used in the detoxification process, doses of methadone can be gradually decreased to help the body ease into a detoxified state.

In more extreme cases, rapid detoxification can be achieved by putting a person under general anesthesia and then administering an opioid antagonist such as **nalaxone** or *naltrexone,* a drug with similar function.

The patient wakes up hours later in a detoxified state. Rapid detoxification is an expensive new strategy in great need of research to identify its advantages and disadvantages. Finally, antianxiety drugs such as *benzodiazepines,* discussed in Chapter Seven, are used during detoxification from alcohol to decrease the sometimes life-threatening symptoms experienced during alcohol withdrawal (O'Brien, 1999).

buprenorphine Recent drug approved by the FDA to treat opioid addiction; works as a partial agonist for mu-opioid receptors.

Maintaining Abstinence

In most cases, detoxification is the simple part of the recovery process: the challenge lies in keeping the individual from consuming drugs after leaving the detoxification facility. Relapse rates vary with different drugs but can be as high as 80% during the first year (Wickelgren, 1998). This is why the addiction syndrome should be approached as a chronic rather than acute condition that persists beyond detoxification.

In addition to use in the detoxification process, methadone is also used to maintain abstinence from opiates. Even after detoxification, methadone stabilizes opioid addicts, making them less likely to suffer from negative withdrawal symptoms and craving for heroin (Dole & Nyswander, 1965). This finding opened the door for medical approaches to prevent a previous user from relapsing. Currently, about 115,000 patients in the United States are being maintained on methadone to reduce their cravings for heroin (O'Brien, 1999).

In the fall of 2002, the Food and Drug Administration approved the use of **buprenorphine** for people suffering from a dependency on heroin, prescription painkillers, or other opioids. (It is estimated that in the United States, 800,000 of these individuals are currently not receiving any treatment.) Buprenorphine is a partial agonist for mu-opioid receptors that exhibits mechanisms similar to those of pure agonists such as heroin but with only about 40% of the agonist's potency. And buprenorphine likes to occupy the mu-opioid receptors because of its high affinity for these receptors—making it impossible for a heroin addict to experience a high from another opiate agonist for an extended period of time, sometimes lasting for days. The hope is that this new drug will enable clinicians to slowly wean patients off the opiate agonists without the abrupt crash observed in most detoxification procedures. This drug, however, is still quite new and more research is necessary to establish its true value as a tool for treating addictions to various opioids (Benson, 2003).

The first medication used to prevent relapse in alcoholics was *disulfiram.* This drug blocks the metabolism of alcohol, resulting in the buildup of the chemical acetaldehyde. This substance is very unpleasant to those suffering from alcoholism because it nauseates them. The hope was that the patients would associate the sickness with the alcohol—transforming

sensitization Process by which an animal or person becomes increasingly responsive to a particular stimulus following repeated presentation.

alcohol from a desired substance to an avoided substance—a conditioned taste aversion. The theory was sound in practice, but it has been understandably very difficult to get patients to comply and take a drug that they know will make them sick (O'Brien, 1999).

Because previous research had established a relationship between opioids and alcohol consumption, opioid therapy has also been used successfully to prevent relapse in alcoholism. Naltrexone, the previously mentioned opioid antagonist, suppresses craving for alcohol. In addition, a recently discovered drug, *bremazocine*, that antagonizes certain opioid receptors while serving as an agonist for others, is proving even more effective than naltrexone in animal studies (Nestby et al., 1999).

Researchers have had less success identifying a substance that will facilitate cocaine abstinence. Certain antidepressant and anticonvulsant drugs have been used with limited success (O'Brien, 1999). Recently, however, research with BP897, the first D_3 receptor agonist, shows that it appears to successfully reduce drug-seeking behavior in rodents. This drug is interesting because, similar to bremazocine, it has both agonist and antagonist qualities. Of course, the drug will have to be tested on humans before it is offered as a medicinal therapy for cocaine addicts.

We have already discussed the critical role conditioning plays in the acquisition and maintenance of an addiction. One line of attack is to try to diminish the strong associations between environmental cues and drug effects. Given the role of glutamate in learning processes, researchers started to investigate the possibility of reducing craving for drugs in general by altering glutamatergic levels. In addition to its role in learning, glutamate has been shown to be critical for an animal's sensitization to amphetamine or cocaine (Wickelgren, 1998). **Sensitization** is the process by which an animal or person becomes increasingly responsive to a particular stimulus following repeated presentation.

To appreciate the behavioral ramifications of sensitization, imagine the behavior of young children on Christmas morning. As they are waiting for their parents to stumble out of bed, find their robes, and start the video camera, they find it impossible to remain still. In anticipation of the pleasure they have previously associated with opening presents, they jump up and down, run around in circles, and laugh with delight. These children are sensitized to the rewards of presents.

Similarly, rats, when placed in conditions reminiscent of receiving psychostimulants, will run around, move their heads back and forth, and engage in what appears to be purposeless behavior in anticipation of their next hit of the drug. MK-801, an antagonist for one of the glutamatergic receptors, NMDA, inhibits cocaine self-administration in rats. Pilot data in humans demonstrate diminished withdrawal symptoms in opiate addiction (Bisaga & Popik, 2000; Wickelgren, 1998). Because of glutamate's general role in learning, it is probably involved in associations that drive most cravings for drugs. Thus, glutamatergic antagonists may help abusers of many types of drugs.

Stanley Glick and Isabelle Maisonneuve, working in the Department of Pharmacology and Neuroscience at Albany Medical College, have literally been beating the bushes for a novel medication for drug addiction. The African shrub known as *Tabernanthe iboga* (Figure 10.5) has a long medicinal history: African hunters have used it for years to help them stay awake yet motionless while stalking prey. Studies in France at the turn of the century indicated that iboga has hallucinogenic and stimulant properties.

Interest in iboga as an antiaddictive substance emerged in the 1980s when patents addressing this shrub's potential antiaddiction properties started to be requested. Iboga was thought to abolish craving for drugs, an effect that supposedly lasted for months. Interestingly, animal studies corroborated these findings, but the initial reports of this miracle cure were too good to be true. It turned out that, in addition to the hallucinogenic and stimulant properties, iboga also induced body tremors in rats.

Going back to the chemistry bench, researchers discovered that the antiaddiction properties of the compound could be separated from the tremor properties. Further work produced a new compound, known as 18 methoxycoronaridine (18-MC). This compound suppressed craving for morphine, cocaine, and alcohol by reducing drug-induced dopamine release in the nucleus accumbens. This evidence suggests that the iboga-related alkaloid may be an effective therapy for addiction to multiple drugs (Glick & Maisonneuve, 1999.)

[Figure 10.5]
Herbal cure for addiction. The *Tabernanthe iboga* shrub has been shown to be effective in preventing drug relapse. Because of serious side effects, research is currently being conducted on various compounds found in the leaves of the iboga that will have clinical efficacy with fewer side effects. DAN LIEBERMAN

Vaccination: Therapeutic Shot in the Dark?

Imagine yourself in the year 2015. You take your infant to the pediatrician for vaccinations. In addition to the traditional immunizations, the doctor asks your permission to vaccinate your child against cocaine, heroin, and alcohol addiction. The scenario sounds like something out of a science fiction movie, but may be closer to reality.

Research into vaccination therapy actually began in 1974 when Charles Schuster, formerly director of the National Institute of Drug Abuse and currently at Wayne State University, observed that heroin-addicted monkeys found heroin no more alluring than salty water after they were injected with a heroin-immunosensitive protein conjugate (Bonese, Wainer, Fitch, Rothberg, & Schuster, 1974). This reduction in craving, however, came at a cost. The inoculation regime was intense, causing lesions at the injection sites, and the effects were short-lived.

Nevertheless, this study was groundbreaking in that it introduced the notion of immunotherapy for addiction. The *active immunity* vaccination rationale is as follows. Injecting individuals with a specific drug fitted with a protein leads the body's immune system to make antibodies to this compound (Figure 10.6). Some time later, when our fictional child experiments with a particular drug, the antibodies rush to the drug as it enters the body, making it difficult for the drug to cross the blood-brain barrier and enter the brain ("No More Kicks," 2000).

[Figure 10.6] Vaccination therapy for drug abuse. In active immunotherapy, a rat is injected with a combination of the drug, in this case cocaine, and certain immunoreactive compounds so that the rat's immune system will actively generate antibodies to the drug, should cocaine be introduced into the body at a later time.
ADAPTED FROM NIDA, 1996.

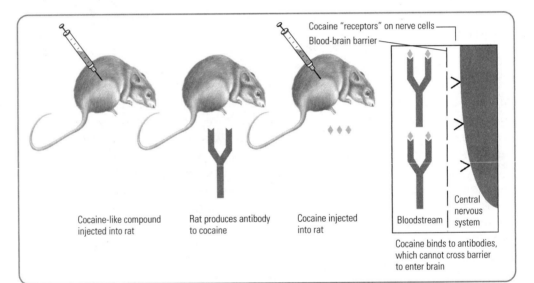

Cocaine-like compound injected into rat

Rat produces antibody to cocaine

Cocaine injected into rat

Cocaine "receptors" on nerve cells

Blood-brain barrier

Bloodstream

Central nervous system

Cocaine binds to antibodies, which cannot cross barrier to enter brain

As previously described, modest success was achieved in the initial attempt to immunize animals against drugs of abuse, but the costs were considered too great to continue this line of research. More than 20 years later, scientists revisited the potential of an addiction vaccine in a desperate attempt to secure at least one victory in the grueling war on drugs. Kim Janda and his colleagues at the Scripps Research Institute in LaJolla, California, developed a refined active immunity vaccination that dramatically decreases the psychoactive effects of cocaine in rats. The revised addiction vaccinations are currently being tested in human trials (NIDA, 1996; "No More Kicks," 2000).

In a recent report by Janda's team, *passive immunity* was tested (Carrera et al., 2000). The researchers tested the effect of merely injecting animals with antibodies designed to bind tightly to the drug, making it impossible for it to cross the blood-brain barrier. In passive immunity, the body plays no role in the antibody production. Thus, Janda believes that the active, or natural, immunity, combined with the super strength of the passive immunity strategy offers a double line of defense against addiction.

As impressive as these findings are, recent research has indicated a passive immunity strategy that might be even more effective. Researchers report that a catalytic antibody that facilitates the transition of cocaine to a psychologically inactive compound greatly diminishes animals' responsivity to cocaine. For example, rats injected with a catalytic antibody were protected against cocaine-induced seizures and sudden death. This protection was not observed in animals receiving a noncatalytic antibody (Mets et al., 1998). Seeing how quickly immunotherapy has advanced suggests that it is just a matter of time before it is used in some addiction treatment regimes. More information about how the immune system is currently viewed as an integral factor in clinical neuroscience is discussed in Chapter 12.

Behavioral Therapies for Addiction

In an attempt to prevent relapse, it is typically recommended that patients see a therapist on an individual basis and/or join a support group to facilitate abstinence. We use the term *behavioral therapy* to refer to such diverse treatments as support groups, incentive programs, and acupuncture. (However, in addition to the perception that attending a support group is a *behavioral therapy,* this approach may be considered as *psychosocial therapy* because of the social component or *cognitive therapy* because of the attempts to change addicts' perceptions and thoughts.) Generally, behavioral therapy is recommended as an additional protection even if medicinal therapies are being used. Whereas medicinal therapy directly influences the patients' physiology, behavioral/cognitive therapy helps patients build a psychological collection of coping mechanisms (also resulting in altered physiology) to help assure a drug-free life.

Alcoholics Anonymous, a popular support group created in 1935, encourages cognitive awareness of the addiction by requiring frequent attendance at meetings. The requirement keeps this awareness in the forefront of the patients' thinking. Other types of support groups exist. Rational Recovery, a therapy based on the work of the rational-emotive psychologist Albert Ellis, encourages self-analysis as a key step to recovery. This philosophy is less religious than Alcoholics Anonymous, requires fewer meetings, and expects the patient to no longer need the therapy after six months to a year (Ruden, 2000). Although empirical evidence is hard to obtain, these groups probably work for some patients because they help to diminish stress, provide an environment with fewer drug-related cues, and offer cognitive strategies for responding to the constant temptations to relapse. These groups are generally more effective when combined with supervised medical treatment (O'Brien, 1999).

Researchers at the Yale University School of Medicine tried a creative behavioral therapy when faced with the difficult issue of treating patients addicted to both heroin and cocaine (Avants, Margolin, Holford, & Kosten, 2000). These patients are placed on methadone for their heroin addiction, and because there is no currently approved medical treatment for cocaine, they continue to use cocaine. The Yale researchers tested the efficacy of acupuncture by inviting the users to come in daily for 45 minutes. During this time, the experimental subjects had needles inserted into the ear, a procedure typical of traditional acupuncture, while the control subjects either had the same number of needles placed in random places along the ear or experienced a mere relaxation period. Urine screens were used to determine whether the subjects had metabolized cocaine during the testing period. The results indicated that the acupuncture group was more likely to submit cocaine-negative urine. However, a more recent study suggests that acupuncture therapy is not effective as a stand-alone therapy and holds more potential as an ancillary treament (Margolin et al., 2002).

Some behavioral programs have been designed to offer rewards for drug-free urine. Working under the supervision of Hendree Jones, the Johns Hopkins Center for Pregnancy and Abuse uses an incentives program to keep women from using drugs during their pregnancies. As with the acupuncture therapy, this nondrug therapy is safe for the developing fetus. Women in the Hopkins program frequently submit urine for screening to determine whether they are using drugs. Clean urine results in rewards such as vouchers for food and baby supplies. This program is successful during the time of close scrutiny of the investigators, but it is not likely to lead to long-term results unless it is combined with other therapies (Jones, personal communication, 2000).

In his book *The Craving Brain*, Ronald Ruden (2002) acknowledges the importance of the dopaminergic system in motivating an individual toward a drug and the serotonergic system in reducing the craving-related anxiety following the consumption of the drug. This is the brain's natural system for survival-related rewards, so it is important for everyone to strive to balance the dopaminergic and serotonergic systems for adaptive, nonaddictive responding. Ruden encourages his patients to engage in various activities and/or pharmacological therapies to bring these systems to a healthy homeostasis. For example, the avoidance of stress may decrease dopaminergic activity in the accumbens area, and participation in a support group may reduce anxiety and result in raised serotonin levels.

Thus, according to Ruden, the craving brain is one that has either a sensitized mesolimbic dopaminergic system (leading to a prevalent drive to seek drugs) or a compromised serotonergic system (leading to a search for ways to reduce the uncomfortable feelings associated with anxiety). Empirical support for Ruden's theory can be found with the recent investigation of ondansetron, a drug previously used to fight nausea in cancer patients. This drug reduced the number of drinks consumed each day and increased the number of abstinent days in challenging alcoholism cases. It is believed that the drug works by regulating interactions between the dopaminergic–serotonergic systems—perhaps turning the craving brain into a homeostatically balanced brain (Johnson et al., 2000).

Ruden also advocates the use of **neurofeedback,** a biofeedback technique in which patients are trained to maintain certain electrical brain wave rhythms to achieve relaxation and brain homeostasis. Intensive training sessions enable patients to maintain *alpha brain waves* (8- to 13-cycle-per-second waves typically observed in relaxed states) and *theta brain waves* (slower, 4- to 7-cycle-per-second waves typically observed during information processing or learning). Preliminary research suggests that neurofeedback results in less frequent relapse in alcoholics (Peniston & Kulkowsky, 1989; Saxby & Peniston, 1995). Further research, however, is required to determine the true value of this approach.

You should be familiar enough with the brain by now to realize that it is doubtful that a person's propensity toward addiction and relapse depends on the balance of just two neurotransmitters. We have discussed several other neurotransmitters that seem to be involved in withdrawal. Thus, it is likely that the recipe for increasing a patient's resistance to relapse comprises several different ingredients. See Table 10.5 for a review of the various neurochemicals involved in this process.

neurofeedback Form of biofeedback in which patients learn to maintain certain electrical brain wave rhythms to achieve relaxation and brain homeostasis.

[Table 10.5]

Neurochemicals Involved with Withdrawal Phase of Addiction Syndrome

Neurochemical	Relative change during withdrawal	Withdrawal symptom
Dopamine	Decrease	Dysphoria
Opioids	Decrease	Pain, dysphoria
Serotonin	Decrease	Pain, dysphoria, depression
GABA	Decrease	Anxiety, panic attacks
Corticotropin-releasing hormone	Increase	Stress
Norepinephrine	Increase	Stress
Glutamate	Increase	Hyperexcitability

Adapted from Koob, 2000.

Ethical Questions About New Addiction Therapies

We have discussed several therapeutic approaches to help people remain free from drugs. But it is important to keep in mind that ethical considerations arise as scientists develop new treatments for addiction.

Is it ethical to immunize a child against a particular drug? Or is it a person's right to decide if drugs are worth trying? Is it ethical to make a person very ill when they take a drug—a response over which many addicts say they have no control? Is it responsible to require addicts who have committed a crime to serve time in prison—an enormous economic cost—only to be released without treatment to the same environment that prompted the addiction in the first place?

An example of the symbiotic relationship between therapy and ethics is evident in the discovery of a novel treatment introduced to the scientific community in 1986. Chemists at the Hoffmann-LaRoche drug company synthesized a substance, Ro15-4513, that had the potential of solving the problem of drunk driving. Alcohol stimulates the GABA receptor and this drug blocks alcohol's ability to activate the receptor. Rats given a large dose of alcohol could be dramatically sobered up with this drug (Figure 10.7). Also, if given the drug prior to consumption, the rats could consume a toxic level of alcohol with no apparent intoxication or threat to their health (Kolata, 1986).

[Figure 10.7]
Masking effects of addiction?
These two rats had the same dose of alcohol. The one on the right is obviously passed out while the one on the left, which was given Ro15-4513, is quite sober.

STEVEN PAUL/NATIONAL INSTITUTE OF MENTAL HEALTH.

These findings were exciting and provided further information about the mechanisms related to alcohol intoxication, but ethical concerns thwarted the commercial development of this drug. Would such a medication encourage more drinking? If for some reason the medication did not work and the intoxicated driver caused an accident, would the blame lie with the individual, the drug company, or the establishment that served the drinks? Obviously, such decisions about the development of addiction therapies should be approached with a great deal of scrutiny and caution.

Summary

Drug Addiction in Context

Physiological components of the addiction syndrome include tolerance, withdrawal, and dependency. Views about drug use differ in various cultures, but virtually every culture is plagued by drug addiction. The aggregation of drug addiction in families and across cultures provides further evidence of common genetic and neurobiological contributions to the acquisition and maintenance of drug addiction.

It appears that the reinforcement experienced by drug users is a product of the brain area that evolved to make survival-related behaviors rewarding. In drug addiction, humans bypass these natural rewards and trigger a flood of activity in this evolutionarily old limbic brain region.

Tracing the Neurobiological Roots of the Addiction Syndrome

Brain structures surrounding and continuous with the nucleus accumbens—known as the extended amygdala—have been implicated in addiction. The nucleus accumbens, the brain's sensory–motor interface, is divided into two parts: the shell that is continuous with certain limbic structures such as the amygdala and the core that is continuous with the striatum. Evidence is accumulating that the orbitofrontal cortex, an area that projects to the nucleus accumbens, plays a role in maintaining addiction—perhaps related to recurring thoughts and associations related to drug use.

Dopamine, with its involvement in reward and movement, is a critical neurotransmitter in addiction, but acetylcholine, serotonin, and glutamate also influence the syndrome. Once an addiction is established, craving is typically experienced by individuals and leads to relapse. The intense emotions associated with drug use produce strong conditioning; consequently, environmental triggers often lead to craving and relapse.

Stress and Addiction

Stress has been identified as a significant factor contributing to the acquisition and maintenance of drug addiction and to relapse. Laboratory studies suggest that previously addicted animals search for drugs when stressors are introduced, even after exhibiting for an extended duration no interest in self-administration of the drug. It is thought that cortiocotropin-releasing hormone interacts with two limbic structures, the amygdala and the bed nucleus of the stria terminalis, to reinstate drug-seeking behavior at times of stress.

Therapy for Drug Addiction

Because the addiction syndrome is multifaceted, several therapeutic approaches have shown moderate success. Following detoxification, medicinal therapies may be used to maintain abstinence (for example, methadone). In addition to detoxification, behavioral/cognitive therapies include aversive conditioning, incentives, and relaxation techniques.

Psychosocial approaches are seen in support programs such as the pervasive Alcoholics Anonymous. Pharmacological therapies are also used in the battle against drug addiction to facilitate reduction in drug consumption or to reduce anxiety to minimize temptation and prevent relapse. New approaches on the therapeutic horizon include vaccinations against specific drugs.

With the advent of innovative therapies such as aversion therapies and vaccinations, questions arise concerning the ethics of imposing such approaches on addicted individuals. Trying to balance certain rights of individuals with the prospect of successful treatment is a challenge for our society.

Key Terms

drug addiction (p. 352)
addiction syndrome (p. 352)
tolerance (p. 353)
withdrawal (p. 353)
negative reinforcement (p. 353)
dependence (p. 353)
evolutionary game theory (p. 357)
medial forebrain bundle (p. 359)

ventral tegmental area (VTA) (p. 360)
bed nucleus of the stria terminalis (BNST) (p. 361)
extended amygdala (p. 360)
microdialysis (p. 365)
mesolimbic dopamine pathway (p. 365)
knockout mice (p. 367)

craving response (p. 369)
anhedonia (p. 372)
detoxification (p. 378)
methadone (p. 378)
naloxone (p. 378)
buprenophrine (p. 379)
sensitization (p. 380)
neurofeedback (p. 385)

For Further Consideration

Barthelme, F., Barthelme, S. (1999. March 8). Good losers. *The New Yorker*, 46–61. If you have ever wondered how intelligent people find themselves in the throes of addiction, risking everything they have worked so hard to achieve, you will find this article fascinating. The Barthelme brothers obtained their graduate degrees from Johns Hopkins and are currently professors at the University of Mississippi. Initially attracted to the gambling casinos on the banks of the Mississippi out of sheer boredom, they quickly found themselves on an addiction ride that was controlling their lives. Although they knew the risks, these men lost their savings and their inheritance and continued to be seduced by the casino riverboats. They vividly describe their sensitivity to every event in the environment as their brains were desperately trying to make associations between environmental events and winning. After reading this article, it is easy to understand the notion that all addictions—even behavioral addictions—probably share the common denominator of mesolimbic reward.

Childress, A. R., Mozley, P. D., McElgin, W., Fitzgerald, J., Reivich, M., & O'Brien, C. P. (1999). Limbic activation during cue-induced cocaine craving. *American Journal of Psychiatry*, 156, 11–18. This research article captures the innovative research of this chapter's investigator, Anna Rose Childress, and her colleagues. In this study, cocaine users and naive control subjects were exposed to videos with potent cocaine-related cues while the researchers used positron emission tomography to measure their regional blood flow. During the video, the cocaine users reported that they were experiencing cravings, and the researchers found that they also displayed a pattern of increased cerebral blood flow in the limbic areas and decreased blood flow in the basal ganglia. No such patterns were observed in the control subjects. These data suggest that limbic activation accompanies psychological craving in addicted subjects.

Koob, G. F. & Nestler, E. J. (1997). The neurobiology of drug addiction. In S. Salloway, P. Malloy, & J.L. Cummings. *The neuropsychiatry of limbic and subcortical disorders*. Washington, DC: American Psychiatric Press. Exceptional overview of the literature related to the neurobiology of addiction, written by two highly respected researchers in this area. The role of the extended amygdala as the common denominator for drug reward is discussed. Additionally, the specific neurochemical events associated with individual drugs of abuse such as cocaine, amphetamine, opiates, and alcohol are covered. Finally, the molecular mechanisms associated with drug tolerance, withdrawal, and relapse are presented and enhanced with helpful figures. This chapter is a wonderful reference for an overview of the neurobiological mechanisms associated with all components of the addiction syndrome.

Ruden, R. (2000). *The Craving Brain* (2nd ed.). New York: HarperCollins. Ron Ruden is the medical director of an addiction clinic in New York City where he interacts with dozens of patients suffering from various forms of addiction every day. Consequently, this book gives the reader a more clinical perspective on addiction. More specifically, Ruden articulates the delicate balance between the dopaminergic and the serotonergic neurochemical systems and how a disruption in this balance can lead to cravings that ultimately result in addiction. He describes how he attempts to reduce cravings by helping patients reestablish neurochemical homeostasis. This edition discusses the intriguing field of neurofeedback and the possibility of reducing craving by teaching subjects to produce alpha and theta brain waves. Because of its interesting combination of clinical and neurochemical perspectives, this is a worthwhile book to use as a supplement to the more traditional neurobiological references.

Wise, R. A. (2000). Addiction becomes a brain disease. *Neuron, 26,* 27–33. Wise is an expert on motivation in animals and presents a nice overview of the past and present research in the field of addiction. He describes the importance of the environmental setting, neuroplasticity, and the role of genetics (assessed by numerous studies with drug-seeking strains of rats) in the addiction syndrome. Finally, the roles of stress and learning in the acquisition and maintenance of addiction are addressed. Written at the end of the 1990s, the decade of the brain, Wise identifies the challenges of the next decade as scientists continue to try to understand addiction.

11
Stress and Coping

Connections

Pacing and Prozac

Imagine that you are waiting for your best friend to arrive at your apartment after a long multistate trip. By your best estimate, he should have arrived two hours ago. Why hasn't your friend phoned you or answered your calls? After all, he always has a cell phone with him and is typically very responsible about letting you know if he was going to be late. You start thinking about why your friend may not have contacted you. An accident? An abduction? Gotten lost?

You feel so anxious and full of worry that you can't stop pacing back and forth in the kitchen. Finally you think it's best if you try to sit down and relax. After a few minutes you notice more movement. This time it's your fingers; they're tapping a pencil against a book you are holding in your lap. After making these observations, you stop to consider why it is so difficult for you to remain *motionless* as you wait anxiously for your friend to arrive. You find it difficult to explain your uncontrollable drive to *move*.

Research conducted by Barry Jacobs and Casimir Fornal at Princeton University reveals that this repetitive movement may be just what the doctor ordered for stress (Jacobs, 1994; Casimer Fornal, personal communication, 2002). More specifically, the Princeton laboratory has been looking closely at the activity of serotonergic neurons in cats. Increased serotonergic activity results in diminished depression symptoms in many patients (Chapter Eight).

Generally, the research team found that the cats' serotonergic neurons exhibit the highest rates of firing when they are engaging in frequent, repetitive movement such as walking on a treadmill. Firing of the serotonergic neurons decreases during slow-wave sleep, a time when there is little if any body movement. Additionally, virtually no serotonergic activity is observed during REM sleep, a time when there is no muscle tone. Further, patients suffering from depression sometimes benefit from reduced REM sleep, perhaps because of the decreased exposure to the sleep stage in which no serotonergic activity occurs.

More recently, Jacobs and Fornal have been investigating the activity of serotonergic neurons during times of fatigue. When cats have been placed on a treadmill for an extended time and they become visibly fatigued, the serotonergic neurons stop firing. Thus the convergence of evidence suggests that the serotonergic activity underlying movement may be related to mood fluctuations. When animals encounter stressful stimuli and become increasingly emotional, or stressed, it might be adaptive to engage in behavior that results in the secretion of serotonin. If this is the case, then chewing gum, riding a bicycle, jogging, and bouncing your leg up and down when you're seated may all be methods of administering the physiological equivalent of tiny doses of Prozac into your own brain!

Back to your missing friend. Once he arrives, your stress response subsides and you are able to sit perfectly still as you catch up on the last several months. At this point, there is no need for the brain or body to search for behavioral coping strategies that will reduce the amount of stress being experienced—or prepare you to respond to the impending danger associated with that stress. So what explains the fact that when your friend announces that he is getting married—a nonthreatening happy event—you can't stop jumping up and down?

Any event that interrupts homeostasis is stressful. Typically, we consider stress to be threatening, similar to the fear you have about losing your missing friend, but the physiological waters are also roiled during happy, exciting events such as finding out your friend is getting married. The interactions among your nervous system, emotions, cognitions, and coping responses determine the neurobiological impact of these events and how you cope with stress.

Unless you've been living in a protective bubble somewhere, you have had a lot of personal experience with stress. It seems as much a part of our world as breathing, yet there is so much about this complex response that we do not know. Why do some people embrace challenges whereas others avoid them? Why do some people survive horrendous events whereas others seem to crumple at the first sign of trouble? How can a psychological phenomenon such as stress cause physiological damage to our bodies and brains?

Although researchers do not have all the answers to these questions, they have made considerable progress toward solving the many mysteries surrounding our ubiquitous stress response. We begin this chapter by recounting classic research on stress and reviewing the neurobiological roots of the stress response as we discussed in Chapters Five and Six. Next we examine factors that influence responsiveness to stress over the lifespan. Then we apply this knowledge to strategies for coping with stress and mitigating the severity of the stress response. At the end of the chapter, we consider the symptoms, causes, and current treatments for post-traumatic stress disorder.

REVISITING THE STRESS RESPONSE

In 1925 Hans Selye was completing his studies in medicine at the University of Prague. After attending numerous lectures on anatomy, physiology, and biochemistry, he was thrilled to be allowed to visit patients. On that momentous day, he was introduced to several patients displaying the earliest stages of various infectious diseases. Although the patients were suffering from different forms of infection, young Selye was struck by the similarity of their symptoms—they all felt ill and complained of diffuse aches and pains in their joints and of gastrointestinal problems. He also noted that most had enlarged spleens and inflamed tonsils and were running fevers.

Selye thought this commonality was an important observation but his professor did not think it noteworthy. On the contrary, the professor was more interested in the specific characteristics of the various illnesses even though most details could not be seen until a disease was at an advanced stage. The fact that the symptoms displayed by all the patients at the onset of an illness were general made them less valuable to the professor—nonspecific symptoms were of no use to physicians at that time. Selye agreed with his professor that identifying certain symptoms was important for prescribing the most effective drugs, yet he was struck by the fact that only a few specific symptoms are characteristic of any particular disease, whereas most general symptoms are common to many or even all diseases (Selye, 1964).

Although Selye's observations remained in the back of his mind, he didn't revisit his initial revelation concerning sickness until he was an assistant professor in the Biochemistry Department of McGill University in the midst of investigating a new ovarian hormone from cattle ovary extracts. Selye discovered that all the ovarian extracts, regardless of their preparation, produced the exact same syndrome in the animals—a *sickness syndrome* consisting of an enlarged adrenal cortex, gastrointestinal ulcers, and atrophied, or shrunken, thymus and lymph nodes. Initially he was discouraged that there was nothing particularly interesting about the work; then he realized that he had produced an experimental model of the sickness syndrome that so intrigued him when he was a medical student (Selye, 1964).

Selye's discovery marked the dawn of an exciting new era in biomedical research. As he embarked on a research journey focusing on this sickness syndrome, he borrowed a term from engineering terminology—*stress*. Stress seemed to convey the idea of wear and tear on the human machinery that is a prevalent feature of our lives. It appears, however, that the physiologist Walter Cannon had used the term in the same general sense in the medical literature in the 1920s (Sapolsky, 1998; see Figure 2.10).

general adaptation syndrome Syndrome originally described by Hans Selye; he felt that stressed individuals undergo three phases during the stress response; alarm, in which the individual's body registers the threat of the imposing stressor; resistance, in which the body mobilizes its forces to fight off the stressor; if the stressor persists, exhaustion as the body runs out of energy to fight off the stressor.

Selye referred to the stress response as the **general adaptation syndrome.** He proposed that this syndrome consists of three stages: (1) the *alarm reaction* in which the body mobilizes its defensive forces to respond to the stressor, (2) *resistance,* which reflects full adaptation to the stressor, and (3) *exhaustion,* which occurs when the stressor is severe and chronic and leads to depletion of energy and, if continued, to death (Selye, 1936, 1976).

Selye went on to test the general nature of his stress syndrome. He exposed animals to multiple physical stressors—cold, noise, the boiler room in his building—all the animals developed the same symptoms observed with Selye's original ovarian extract injections. Selye likened the stress response to a home alarm system: no matter how the system is initiated, the same response occurs. Regardless of whether a threat occurs at a window or a door, the house alarm is activated and the authorities are called; accordingly, the stress alarm is activated on any type of threat to the body.

Selye was an extremely productive scientist who made many contributions to the field of stress. Throughout this chapter, however, we will address a few questions that challenge at least two assumptions proposed in his earlier theories about stress: Does an animal have the same response to all stressors? Does an animal die from stress because of the depletion, or wearing down, of certain defense forces?

Some stressors are like ships passing in the night: they come and they go, and they don't have a significant impact on our lives once they are gone. Other stressors, however, tie up to our physiological docks for an extended stay. Our bodies seem to be designed for the stress-ships-passing-in-the-night scenario—we can respond sufficiently to such threats—but our physiological systems are severely threatened when the stress is prolonged.

Acute Stress Response

Have you ever felt terrified? At what moment of your life were you most afraid? Perhaps you narrowly escaped a serious car accident when you were trying to change radio stations or you got dangerously close to a poisonous snake on a camping trip or you showed up in a class realizing that the professor was distributing an exam that you knew nothing about. Sometimes just remembering such moments re-creates the stressful response inside your body. Can you feel it? Your heart starts racing, your palms get sweaty, you feel a rush of energy running through your body.

As Stanford University biologist Robert Sapolsky describes so eloquently in his book *Why Zebras Don't Get Ulcers* (1998), this response makes perfect evolutionary sense when we think about surviving an *acute*, or short-term, stressor. Many physiological processes enable the zebra to escape the pursuit of a lion: increased focus on the task of escaping; increased breathing rate, heart rate, and blood pressure to get glucose and oxygen to the muscles so that the zebra can run faster; the rapid conversion of stored energy into usable energy for the escape response; and a temporary shutdown of reproductive, digestive, immunological, and growth processes.

Why shut down valuable physiological processes during the stress response? As described by Sapolsky, these are long-term investments of energy that mean nothing if the zebra is eaten by the lion and doesn't survive to the next day to reproduce, digest a meal, grow, or build up antibodies for the next sickness to pass across the African plains. In an apt analogy, he suggests that if you know a hurricane is about to hit your house, your time is better spent boarding up windows than hanging wallpaper in the guest bathroom.

If a wild animal is about to attack another animal, is it really smart for the prey to turn off its immune system? Maybe immunological energy directed toward surveillance of tumors or exotic diseases that may develop and kill the prey animal in the next several months is probably better spent contributing to escape (Sapolsky, 2000). But what if the zebra is wounded by the lion and survives the attack? It is likely to be left with a gaping wound filled with foreign antigens. Did that scenario factor into the evolution of this response?

Firdaus Dhabhar and his colleagues in the Department of Oral Biology at Ohio State University have conducted some interesting research addressing immune functioning during the stress response (Dhabar, Satoskar, Bluethmann, David, & McEwen, 2000). Dhabar's research has shown that, contrary to original thought, acute stress significantly *enhances* the movement of pathogen-fighting white cells from the blood to the skin—the exact place the lion's claws will invade the zebra's body. We consider the effect of stress on the specific activity of the immune system more thoroughly in Chapter Twelve.

A final aspect of the acute stress response is its consistency. Does an animal always have the same response upon the presentation of a stressful stimulus—as stated by Selye in his general adaptation syndrome? The best answer is probably yes and no. Yes, animals have the same general response of stress hormone release and the suppression of a few long-term, optimistic processes (growth, reproduction, and so on). But there are differences as well. For example, the stressful stimulus of social defeat in rats produces increases in mean arterial blood pressure whereas electric foot shock decreases blood pressure (Adams, Lins, & Blizard, 1987). Fear of foot shock produces both immobility and bradycardia (slowness

ecologically relevant Term used to describe stressors that an animal may find in its natural environment. Example: Social defeat is a more ecologically relevant stimulus for hamsters than cold or restraint.

species-specific stressor Stressor that is specific for a particular species. Example: Weasel urine is a natural stressor for rats but is not stressful for dogs.

of heart rate) in most rats whereas fear of a dominant rat results in half the rats demonstrating bradycardia and the other half immobility (Roozendaal, Koolhaas, & Bohus, 1990).

Given these different responses to various stressful stimuli, Robert Blanchard of the University of Hawaii argues that experimenters should be careful to use stressors that are biologically relevant across species—such as social stress that affects both rats and humans (Blanchard, McKittrick, & Blanchard, 2001). Certainly, the type of stressor should be carefully chosen and should have **ecological relevance** (likely to be found in the animal's natural environment). Some may argue that, whereas foot shock and cold restraint result in a stress response, these stimuli are not **species-specific stressors** for rats. If stress responses vary, even in subtle ways, on the presentation of different stimuli, then the use of more artificial stimuli may result in a distorted picture of the stress response.

It is also interesting to consider that the same stimulus presented repeatedly can produce different stress responses (at least different in intensity) as the animal either habituates (becomes less responsive) or sensitizes to the stimulus. As children learn what the smiling nurse is really going to do with that glistening needle, their stress response heightens. On the other hand, as the sensation seeker parachutes out of the plane for the twentieth time, his stress response is diminished compared with the initial jump. Thus, it seems that we've come a long way from Selye's claim that the stress response is universal.

Chronic Stress Response

The acute stress response is well orchestrated and critical to survival. When this response is not cut off, however, our survival can be threatened by the very system designed to keep us alive. It was the chronic effects of stress that Hans Selye originally described as the general adaptation syndrome.

It's been reported that Selye was not the most skilled researcher when it came to injecting rats, and after numerous days of being handled, dropped, chased, and injected, the rats in his lab started to develop the sickness symptoms previously described—gastric ulcers, hypertrophied adrenal glands, and atrophied thymus glands (Sapolsky, 1998). And when he was trying to stress his animals, Selye exposed them to the designated stressors (boiler room noise, cold temperatures) for extended periods of time. Clearly, his rats were chronically stressed.

When the stress response cannot be turned off, the immune system is suppressed, which obviously leads to an increased vulnerability to sickness (Raison & Miller, 2001). If you've ever gotten sick immediately following a stressful week of final exams you can relate to this observation. In addition to a higher susceptibility to disease or sickness, the cardiovascular system is also threatened by chronic stress. The heightened activity of the cardiovascular system is very effective for a short period of time, but having an increased heart rate and blood pressure for extended durations simply wears out the heart muscle.

To add insult to injury, residue from the transfer of stored energy substances (sugars and fats) into available energy for a quick response starts to build up in the blood vessels after a while, leading to a condition called **atherosclerosis.** This condition is exacerbated if chronic high blood pressure produces plaques, small tears, and pits in the internal lining of the blood vessels where the glucose and fatty acids can find a place to accumulate. Finally, chronically high levels of gluticocortoids alter the body's energy resources and subsequently influence eating strategies in humans. In many people who increase their consumption of certain foods (especially high-fat and high-carbohydrate "comfort food"), fat is more readily deposited around the midsection for energy availability (Dallman et al., 2003). See Box 11.1 for further discussion on stress and eating.

It's easy to envision a blood vessel that is already clogged becoming smaller and smaller during an acute stress response—getting dangerously close to forming an occlusion, or blockage, in the blood vessel. Jay Kaplan, a physiologist, and his colleagues at Bowman Gray Medical School showed this effect in monkeys (Manuck, Marsland, Kaplan, & Williams, 1995). When placed in a stressful, unstable social group, the low-ranking animals—those that had little control over their environment and probably experienced more stress—were more likely to develop atherosclerotic plaques than the higher-ranking animals. In response to the question posed earlier regarding illness resulting from a worn-down stress response, it is important to note that this stress-induced heart disease is a result not of an exhausted stress response but of chronic activation of the stress response.

Stress and personality traits. In the 1960s, two cardiologists, Meyer Friedman and Ray Rosenman, conducted research exploring the relationship between certain personality profiles and cardiovascular disease (Rosenman, Brand, Jenkins, Friedman, Straus & Wurm, 1975). They found that the subjects who were high achievers, very competitive, and always conscientious of the time were more likely to suffer cardiovascular disease than their more laid-back counterparts. Friedman and Rosenman used the label *Type A* for the competitive personality style and *Type B* for the more relaxed style. Before you press your parents' phone number on your speed dial to justify your relaxed performance in some of your classes, it's important to keep reading; there's an interesting twist to this story.

atherosclerosis Buildup of lipid substances in lesions in the blood vessels; can eventually lead to hardened arteries and disrupted blood flow.

[Box 11.1]

Brain Matters

Eating and Stress

Does stress influence how you eat? Some people respond to stressful situations by heading straight to the refrigerator; others tend to avoid food during anxiety-laden times. Elissa Epel and her colleagues in the Health Psychology Program at the University of California at San Francisco recently investigated the influence of psychological and physiological variables in determining the eating response to stress (Epel, Lapidus, McEwen, & Brownell, 2001).

They found that women who responded to stress with high cortisol levels were more likely to consume more calories on the days they were exposed to stress. These high-cortisol reactors also ate more sweet food throughout the experiment. So if you find yourself eating more during stressful times, it is possible that you respond to stress with high cortisol secretions.

Stress may also influence the pattern of fat distribution in individuals. Have you ever noticed that some people seem to have a disproportionate amount of fat in their mid-section? Central body fat is an indicator of greater visceral fat, which is extremely susceptible to cortisol's influence on fat accumulation and transfer in the bloodstream. Thus, increased central body fat is a risk factor for diseases such as hypertension, diabetes, stroke and coronary heart disease (Kissebah & Krakower, 1994).

In one study that attempted to identify the types of individuals most at risk for the increased midsection fat, women were exposed to stress sessions consisting of 45 minutes of psychological tests and challenges (e.g., speech tasks, serial arithmetic) for three days followed by a day of rest. Throughout this time the women's salivary cortisol levels and coping responses were measured. When these researchers correlated cortisol level with body type, they found that women with high levels of central fat reported being more threatened by the stress tests and secreted significantly more cortisol than the women with less central body fat. Another interesting finding in this study is

that lean women with central body fat are less likely to habituate to the stress tests than any other group; that is, their cortisol responses were still significantly increased on the third day of testing.

Why does this relationship between eating and stress exist? Perhaps the rats can tell us. Kevin Laugero (2001), at the University of California-San Francisco's School of Medicine, recently reported the surprising finding that mere sucrose ingestion stabilizes eating, energy balance, and CRH in rats that have received an adrenalectomy. Remember that the adrenal glands secrete glucocorticoids and adrenaline, so the removal of this organ drastically alters an animal's ability to respond to stressful stimuli.

Laugero argues that the relationship between eating and the HPA axis response to stress makes sense when the stress response is thought of as a response to reestablish energy levels in the organism following the initial threat and subsequent sympathetic response. Laugero's argument is strengthened by the observation of the simultaneous emergence of HPA axis receptivity and adult glucose sensitivity during an organism's development (Widmaier, 1990). Thus, the HPA axis may have evolved for the more general purpose of maintaining energy levels in the body. In fact, during nonstressful times, HPA axis function follows circadian rhythms, peaking just prior to times of increased energy expenditure, namely waking, increased activity, and foraging (Dallman, Viau, Bhatnagar, Gomez, Laugero, & Bell, 2002).

Just being mindful that during times of significant stress we're going to be motivated to eat high-calorie, "comfort" foods may make us more aware of our eating patterns during these times (Dallman et al., 2003). Of course, in the short run, a candy bar makes us feel better, but repeated coping in this manner can increase midsection fat and make us vulnerable to a host of cardiovascular-related diseases. As we will see in Chapter 13, which addresses eating regulation and associated disorders, any drastic changes in eating patterns can also become a detrimental threat to our homeostasis by making us susceptible to conditions such as anorexia, bulimia, diabetes, and obesity.

This work was very influential, and a Duke University physician, Redford Williams, has attempted to replicate some of the findings of Freidman and Rosenman (Dahlstrom & Williams, 1983). Williams's work suggests that *hostility* is a more powerful personality predictor for cardiovascular disease than a more general Type A personality. This is especially true if a person has been chronically stressed.

As described previously, the chronic stress response will often leave a person's blood vessels clogged with substances absorbed for the utilization of energy in the fight-or-flight response. This is an especially high price to pay because we really don't need the extra energy most of the time—these days many people experience crises and solve them without even getting up from their office desk. So when this person has a subsequent full-blown stress response, the constriction of the blood vessels might result in a blockage, leading to either a heart attack or a stroke.

As depicted in Figure 11.1, the outrageous fits of hostility demonstrated by the successful basketball coach Bobby Knight may lead his team to a winning season but at significant cost to his health. Adding fuel to the fire, many hostile individuals carry their stress response around with them for longer periods of time, finding it hard to let go of their anger (Fredrickson, Maynard, Helms, Haney, Siegler, & Barefoot, 2000). Sustaining a dangerous condition for longer periods of time also increases susceptibility to cardiovascular disease.

Stress ulcers. Lesions in the lining of the stomach called **peptic ulcers** are a common consequence of chronic stress. As you recall, ulceration was one of the original symptoms Selye observed in chronically stressed rats. The cause of peptic ulcers was a mystery until a revolutionary finding in the 1980s. Up until this time most people were comfortable with the belief that ulcers were caused by an excessive amount of hydrochloric acid in the stomach because, sure enough, antacid medications were a rather effective treatment. However, because the relapse rate was high, it was apparent to the clinicians in the field that antacid medication was a mere peptic Band-Aid and there was more to the story. If chronic stress led to a reduction of gastric activity—and acid secretion—how could an ulcer form? That dry mouth you develop as you try to give an oral presentation is an early sign of the decreased digestive juices secreted during stress. It appeared contradictory to our knowledge of what was happening during the stress response; if anything, it appeared that a person should be *protected* against ulceration during a stressful period.

But study after study showed that animals exposed to stress developed stress ulcers. As detailed in Chapter Seven, the

peptic ulcers Lesions that occur in the stomach lining; usually caused by a bacterium, but they are exacerbated by stress.

[Figure 11.1]
Toxicity of hostility. Basketball coach Bobby Knight may be leading his team to victory, but his coaching style could score a real loss for his cardiovascular system.

ROD AYDELOTTE, WACO TRIBUNE HERALD/ AP/ WIDE WORLD PHOTO

[Figure 11.2]
Stress ulceration. A rat's stomach removed after five days of being housed in an activity cage and fed one hour per day. The necrotic tissue (black streaks) in the corpus of the stomach show the ulcerations.

KELLY LAMBERT, RANDOLPH-MACON COLLEGE BEHAVIORAL SCIENCE LABORATORY

activity-stress paradigm, which consists of exposing animals to a restricted feeding regimen and free access to a running wheel, produced severe ulcers in just four days (Figure 11.2). It was thought that the mucosal lining of the stomach became compromised during the digestive-acid, glandular-secreting–deficient period—leading to an ulcer as soon as the digestive acids resumed their activity. Again, though, a piece of the puzzle was missing.

A creative twist to this ulcer drama came in the 1980s when Barry Marshall, an Australian pathologist, announced at a conference that he had found a bacterium, *Helicobacter pylori,* in the stomach lining of humans suffering from peptic ulcers and gastritis (Sapolsky, 1998; Warren & Marshall, 1983). At that time, it was thought that bacteria could not survive in the acidic lining of the stomach; even more damning was the fact that numerous studies had shown a connection between stress and peptic ulcers. Consequently, Marshall's hypothesis was not warmly welcomed.

This reception prompted Marshall to take drastic measures. He actually ate some of the bacteria, waited, and documented the genesis of his very own peptic ulcer—perhaps the world's first planned and anticipated human peptic ulcer. This result was successful in attracting the interest of other researchers who went on to confirm Marshall's findings. Even more exciting was the realization that, if ulcers are caused by a bacterium, then antibiotics will be an effective treatment. This hypothesis turned out to be the case. Many patients suffering from ulcers are able to obtain longer-lasting relief from antibiotics than from antacid treatments.

After the *Helicobacter* theory of ulceration gained acceptance, it seemed for a while that the door was shut to this area of investigation in psychology (Melmed & Gelpin, 1996). But researchers could not deny the fact that stress was still an important factor since so many studies had shown that stress exposure exacerbates ulceration. It appeared that we might have evolved a defense mechanism protecting us against the destructive actions of the bacteria, but this defense system is compromised in some way when we have to endure chronic stress.

Today, researchers are trying to understand how stress makes an individual more vulnerable to bacteria-induced ulceration. Several possibilities exist—a compromised immune system may enliven the bacteria, a compromised mucosal lining may degrade the barrier that protects the stomach lining from the bacteria, or decreased blood flow during sympathetic arousal may create an optimal environment for the bacteria. Regardless, researchers and clinicians are once again convinced that stress plays an important role and that the bacteria are a necessary but not sufficient cause of ulceration.

Thus, whereas the acute stress response is a wonderful adaptation to survive an impending threat, chronic stress, whether real or imagined, is a different story. In fact, going back to the title of Sapolsky's book, this point addresses the question of *Why Zebras Don't Get Ulcers*. Once the lion gets tired of chasing the zebra and the zebra is safely out of harm's way, the zebra's stress response is terminated, so all the digestive acids start to flow again, creating a more hostile environment for the bacteria and inhibiting their ability to create ulcers.

Considering this information, you may think that it does not appear that we were designed to undergo chronic stress and, for that reason, we get sick. It almost seems like an evolutionary mistake. However, life isn't that simple. As certain bodily systems evolved, there was no guarantee that others would not be compromised. In other words, we are not always able to eat our evolutionary cake and have it too. For humans, as our neocortex became larger and larger, holding the capacity to store stressful memories, share others' pain, and generate anxiogenic thoughts and scenarios, it was inevitable that we enter the world of chronic stress. Don't close your book now in frustration—after we review the effects of nature and nurture on the stress response, we'll consider ways to cope with chronic stress.

Brain's Stress Circuit

Not long after Cannon described the role of the sympathetic nervous system in re-establishing physiological homeostasis, as detailed in Chapter Five, Hans Selye described the sickness syndrome associated with stress. One of the general symptoms is an enlarged adrenal gland. This symptom pointed to another important stress circuit in the brain, the hypothalamic-pituitary-adrenal (HPA) axis, that isn't quite as immediate as the sympathetic response but is just as valuable.

At the heart of the HPA circuit are the glucocorticoids, or stress hormones, released by the adrenal cortex. Selye theorized that the adrenal glands were enlarged because they were pumping out so many glucocorticoids because of the chronic stress (Sternberg, 2000). Today we know considerably more about the HPA axis mechanisms related to the release of cortisol in humans. As Table 11.1 reveals, cortisol influences the hippocampus, an area rich with glucocorticoid receptors.

Bruce McEwen, a noted neuroscientist at the Rockefeller University, has conducted considerable research delineating the effects of chronic glucocorticoid secretion on the functioning and structure of the hippocampal neurons. In 1990, McEwen and his collaborators Catherine

(a)   **(b)**

[Figure 11.3]
Stress-induced restructuring of hippocampal neurons. CA3 pyramidal neurons from (a) a control rat and (b) a rat that received 21 days of injections of glucocorticoids. The control rat's dendritic processes are both longer and have more connections than does the neuron from the animal receiving exogenous stress hormones.

BRAIN RESEARCH, 531 (1990) 225-231, ELSEVIER. COURTESY OF CATHERINE S. WOOLLEY, ET AL., LABORATORY OF NEUROENDOCRINOLOGY, THE ROCKEFELLER UNIVERSITY. (SHAM-INJECTED (a) AND CORT-INJECTED (b) ANIMAL BRAIN CELLS)

Woolley and Elizabeth Gould examined neurons in the CA3 area following 21 days of injections of exogenous glucocorticoids (Figure 11.3) (Woolley, Gould, & McEwen, 1990). This three-week period may be similar to many of our own chronic stress phases—worrying about an upcoming exam or a relationship or suffering from a prolonged bout with the flu.

To the researchers' surprise, significant dendritic restructuring occurred in CA3 neurons after this seemingly short duration (Figure 11.3). As you can see, neuron (b) has fewer and less elaborate dendritic branching than its control counterpart (a). This finding was also confirmed in rats that were exposed to 6 hours of restraint (psychological stress) for 21 days (Watanabe, Gould, & McEwen, 1992).

To date, no single mechanism has been identified as being the chief factor that leads to the damaged CA3 pyramdial cells. Because cellular damage and death have been linked to excessive levels of glutamate and activation of associated NMDA receptors, this process is sometimes known as **excitotoxicity**. The inhibitory neurotransmitter GABA also seems to play a role in the stress-induced hippocampal damage. Benzodiazepine, a GABA agonist, blocks stress-induced dendritic restructuring (Magarinos, Deslandes, & McEwen, 1999). Additionally, serotonin may play a role in the demise of the hippocampal neurons during stress. An atypical antidepressant drug, tianeptine, which enhances serotonin uptake resulting in decreased extracellular levels of serotonin, has been found to reduce stress-induced dendritic alterations in tree shrews undergoing severe chronic stress (Czeh et al., 2001).

[Table 11.1]

Effect of Cortisol on Various Tissues in the Body

Tissues	Effect
Neuron	Increased catecholamine synthesis
Hippocampus	Enhanced memory formation
Thalamus	Increased sensitivity to incoming stimuli
Adrenoreceptors	Increased alpha and beta receptor sensitivity
Adrenal medulla	Increased synthesis of catecholamines
Immune system	Both excited and inhibited
Inflammation	Inhibited
Glucose	Increased production
Fatty acid	Increased release from energy stores
Kidney	Water diuresis and retention of sodium

After Lovallo, 1997, p. 49.

Although it is not clear whether a reduction in neurogenesis might be related to these hippocampal effects, psychosocial stress has been reported to reduce the production of new neurons in the tree shrew hippocampus (Gould, McEwen, Tanapat, Galea, & Fuchs, 1997). What effect might reductions in hippocampal dendritic branching have on our brains and memory processes? McEwen (2000b) suggests that the structural changes are reversible following the termination of the HPA axis activation. Thus, if the stress subsides before the cells atrophy (die), there is hope for their recovery. As for the effect of the altered neurons on cognitive processes, stress produces deficits in both episodic and spatial memory systems in animals and humans. If the stress is chronic (lasting several years), it is likely that the hippocampus will be smaller in the most severely impaired individuals and recovery will be more of a challenge than in more acute stress situations (Lupien et al., 1998; McEwen, deLeon, Lupien, & Meaney, 1999).

One measure of the value of the stress response can be assessed by the sheer number of brain areas devoted to carrying out some aspect of stress responsivity. The sympathetic nervous system's fight-or-flight response to an impending threat such as a loud noise is one of the earliest responses observed in the stress-response cascade. The auditory stimulus associated with the loud noise will also activate the amygdala and its associated fear circuit (see Chapter Seven). Neurochemicals important for sustaining the increased activity necessary to escape the stressor are triggered by the HPA axis (glucocorticoids) as well as by the locus coeruleus (noradrenaline).

The hippocampus and forebrain are also part of the brain's stress circuit, as animals are required to place stressful stimuli in appropriate contexts to determine the most effective response or must problem solve to determine possible escape routes from various stressors. Later in this chapter, we'll discuss the transition from *reaction* to *action*—how an animal evaluates emotional information from the basic stress circuits in the brain and then makes voluntary decisions about how to respond. Such planned responses require the forebrain and hippocampus to a greater extent than the more basic stress responses such as freezing in place or running.

excitotoxicity Process that probably occurs in CA3 neurons of the hippocampus. This effect is caused by excessive glutamate activity in the neurons, which may lead to neuronal death; prolonged exposure to stress hormones may trigger the process.

STRESS RESPONSIVITY OVER THE LIFESPAN

Although Selye advocated the generalized adaptation syndrome in which different stressors led to standard responses, increasingly the research shows that significant individual differences exist in responding to stress. In Chapter Six, for example, we noted how parental involvement, aging, and sex differences can affect a person's response to stress. Now we expand on the relevance of developmental research in explaining differing behavioral responses.

Role of Mother-Infant Interactions

[Figure 11.4]
Effects of maternal separations. Rhesus monkeys raised in separation from their mothers show anxious behavior when placed with same-age peers. Juvenile rhesus monkeys raised with their mothers typically engage in rough-and-tumble play when introduced to peer monkeys.

HARLOW PRIMATE LABORATORY, UNIVERSITY OF WISCONSIN

Harry Harlow's classic work investigating the effects of extended maternal separation in rhesus monkeys provided convincing evidence that mother-infant interaction is critical to the development of the stress response as well as to other aspects of development. Harlow reported that the animals were agitated in the beginning and then entered a lethargic stage for the rest of the three-week separation (Suomi, 1983).

The hyperresponsive stress response was also seen when the motherless animals were allowed to play with other motherless infants. As seen in Figure 11.4, whereas other healthy monkeys would probably be engaging in bouts of rough-and-tumble play, these animals huddled together in a cautious, tense posture (Harlow & Harlow, 1962). Confirming Michael Meaney's findings, reported in Chapter 6, that rodent maternal attention directed toward pups plays a significant role in the development of the animal's response to challenges as adults, Harlow reported that these motherless primates were not good mothers themselves—their behavior ranged from indifference to abuse.

Of course, it would not be ethical to conduct maternal deprivation studies in humans; unfortunately, some natural circumstances provide opportunities to collect relevant data. Early studies conducted by Spitz (1946) and Bowlby (1960) suggested that human children respond to prolonged separation with initial protest followed by a phase characterized by dejection and social withdrawal (Mineka & Suomi, 1978). More recently, economic problems and social policies in Romania during the 1980s resulted in over 65,000 children being placed in orphanages; 85% were placed in the orphanages during their first month of life.

The Romanian orphanages were grossly understaffed; child-caregiver ratios were 10:1 for infants and 20:1 for children over 3 years of age. Consequently, infants were kept in their cribs unattended for up to 20 hours per day (Ames & Carter, 1992; McMullan & Fisher, 1992). Generally, these children developed behavioral abnormalities typically seen in maternal and socially deprived primates, characterized by self-stimulatory behaviors, various motor stereotypies (a stereotypy is an almost mechanical repetition of posture or speech; rocking back and forth is an example), and insecure attachments (Chisholm, Carter, Ames, & Morison, 1995; Suomi, 1997). As expected, they also developed a host of physical deficits due to malnutrition (Chugani et al., 2001).

Mary Carlson and Felton Earls (1997) of Harvard University had an opportunity to measure cortisol levels in 2- to 3-year old Romanian orphans. They took advantage of an intervention program in which orphans were placed in enriched social conditions starting at an average of 6 months of age. After about 13 months of the intervention program, cortisol levels of the children raised in the neglected conditions of the orphanage were compared with those of home-raised children.

Cortisol was assessed several times throughout the day. Overall, the home-reared children had higher cortisol levels in the morning than the intervention and orphanage-raised children, but the home-raised children had lower levels throughout the rest of the day than the other children. Cortisol levels typically peak prior to times of increased activity, so the lack of an increase in the orphanage group denotes a deficiency in the HPA axis.

As described earlier in this chapter, sustained increased levels of cortisol throughout the day can be harmful to the pyramidal cells of the hippocampus (see Figure 11.3 inset). Indeed, Carlson and Earls (1997) have noted that the children with the highest cortisol levels have the lowest scores in motor and mental development. In another study, PET scans of adopted Romanian orphans were compared with those of normal adults and children with refractory focal epilepsy. The Romanian orphans showed decreased rates of glucose metabolism in several limbic structures including the frontal gyrus, the amygdala, hippocampus, and temporal cortex (Chugani et al., 2001).

Thus, HPA axis development in humans is vulnerable to the stress of maternal separation. Certainly events as stressful as parental separation have a severe impact on the developing stress response system. Research also suggests that, even when children grow up with parents, acute and chronic stressful conditions alter the stress response. One study indicated that undergraduate students who described their parents as cold and detached were four times more likely to develop chronic illness, including depression and alcoholism, in midlife (Russek & Schwartz, 1997). As described in Chapter Eight, girls who were sexually abused had increased cortisol responses to mild stress as adults (Heim & Nemeroff, 2002).

Socioeconomic status (SES), too, can affect HPA responsiveness in children. As seen in Figure 11.5, salivary cortisol levels taken during the first hour of school were lowest in children with high SES. The most drastic effect was seen in 10-year-old children; low SES children had cortisol values that were twice that of the high SES children (Lupien, King, Meaney, & McEwen, 2000).

[Figure 11.5]
Cortisol levels and SES.
Morning basal cortisol levels measured in children 6, 8, and 10 years old. Children of high socioeconomic (SES) status had lower levels in each age group. Among children of low SES, the 10-year-old group recorded the highest levels.
ADAPTED FROM LUPIEN ET AL., 1998, P. 978.

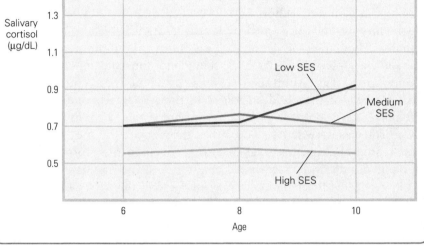

[Figure 11.6]
Cortical-induced hippocampal shrinkage. The hippocampus in two elderly subjects are indicated by arrows in these images. The subject on the left secreted normal levels of cortisol, whereas the subject on the right secreted high levels. The hippocampus on the right is 14% smaller than the hippocampus of the normal-secreting elderly subject.
FROM EMBER, 1998, CHEMICAL AND ENGINEERING NEWS, P. 21

Aging-Related Effects of Stress

Sonia Lupien of McGill University studied elderly subjects who secrete high levels of cortisol and found a 14% reduction in hippocampal volume and accompanying cognitive impairment (Figure 11.6) compared with subjects of similar age who secreted lower levels of cortisol (Lupien et al., 1998; McEwen et al., 1999). These high levels of glucocorticoids produce cognitive deficits in hippocampal-dependant learning in just a few days (McEwen & Sapolsky, 1995). These human data corroborate Meaney's findings, discussed in Chapter Six, that nonhandled rats that secrete high levels of corticosterone perform more poorly in the hippocampal-dependent swim task than the handled, stress-response-efficient animals (Meaney et al., 1985; Meaney, Aitken, & Sapolsky, 1987).

As we age, it becomes increasingly difficult to turn off the stress response, perhaps because of the decreased number or sensitivity of receptors in the hippocampus. The resulting increases in stress hormones for longer durations can lead to aging-related pathologies (Porter, Herman, & Landfield, 2001; Sapolsky, 2000). Figure 11.7 diagrams the glucocorticoid hypothesis of cognitive impairment observed in elderly subjects.

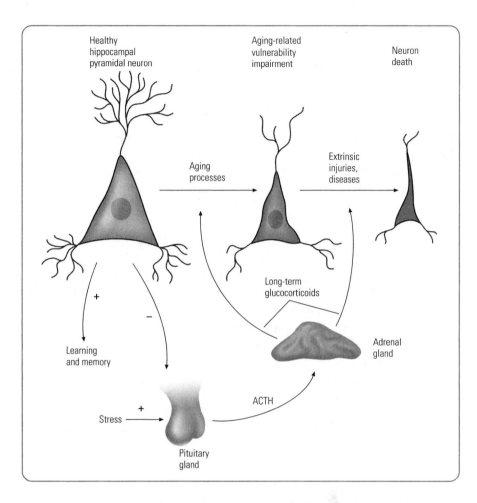

Healthy
hippocampal
pyramidal neuron

Aging-related
vulnerability
impairment

Neuron
death

Aging
processes

Extrinsic
injuries,
diseases

Long-term
glucocorticoids

+

−

Learning
and memory

Adrenal
gland

ACTH

+

Stress

Pituitary
gland

[Figure 11.7]
The aging HPA axis and hippocampal neurons. Healthy pyramidal neurons in the hippocampus facilitate learning and memory and provide appropriate feedback to the pituitary to moderate stress hormone secretion. After prolonged, excessive ACTH and glucocortoid release, pyramidal neurons become more vulnerable to threats such as oxygen free radicals and disease.
ADAPTED FROM MCEWEN & GOODMAN, 2001, P. 297

Effects of Sex Differences on Responses to Stress

William Pare and his colleagues at the Veterans Affairs Medical Center in Perry Point, Maryland, emphasize the importance of looking at both acute and chronic stress when assessing sex differences in the stress response (Pare, Blair, Kluczynski, & Tejani-Butt, 1999). When they exposed rats to either an acute session or repeated sessions (chronic condition) of restraint stress, a more complete picture of sex differences in the stress response began to emerge. Although females were more active in the open field test after one session of stress, the sex differences disappeared after five sessions. In a test of simple learning, female rats were impaired following acute and chronic stress whereas males were impaired only following acute stress.

Food consumption progressively decreased for female rats whereas males regained baseline levels after five days. Males were more likely to develop stress ulcers than females, but females had heavier adrenal glands, suggesting more activity of the HPA axis. As shown by the varying sex effects for different variables, one must be careful when only one measure is used. Pare concluded that female rats seem to be more vulnerable than males to the effects of chronic stress.

Pare's conclusion sheds light on the observation suggested by most epidemiological studies that women are more likely to develop psychiatric disorders, such as depression, in which HPA axis dysregulation is a likely causal factor (Wolf, Schommer, Hellhammer, McEwen, & Kirschbaum, 2001). When studies have focused on the age of men and women, increased HPA axis activation is more commonly observed in older women (Seeman, Singer, Wilkinson, & McEwen, 2001).

In addition to differences in physiological responsivity, Shelley Taylor and her colleagues at the University of California in Los Angeles have proposed an evolutionary hypothesis highlighting the adaptive significance of men and women having different behavioral response strategies (Taylor, Klein, Lewis, Gruenwald, Gurung, & Updegraff, 2000). They propose that the typical *fight-or-flight* response is actually a more representative male style, and the female stress response is more accurately described as a *tend-and-befriend* style. In particular, Taylor's team argues that the male response may be more influenced by sympathetic arousal (and fight-or-flight) and the female response more by physiological factors related to caregiving (tend-and-befriend). More empirical evidence, however, is needed before the ultimate value of this intriguing hypothesis can be determined.

COPING WITH STRESS

How do you combat the stressors in your life? Are you more likely to take charge of the situation, or do you retreat and just wait for the stressor to pass? Do you run to the support of your family and friends during stressful times or do you prefer to be alone? The transition from a *reaction* to a stressor to a decision about the most appropriate voluntary *action* is a complex, multifaceted process.

Researchers, however, are starting to look at the nature of the behavioral stress response as well as the physiological response. The research is painting a picture in which the behavioral response that an animal makes when presented with a stressor has important implications for the physiological response and subsequent health-related consequences. Sense of control, social support, and level of activity in the behavioral stress response strategy all offer significant ways to mitigate the dangerous effects of an unrelenting stress response.

Perception of Control

In the Italian film *La Vita e Bella (Life Is Beautiful)*, the main character, Guido, is a bookseller in the Tuscan town of Arezzo during the stressful time of the German occupation of Italy in World War II. In this fable, Guido falls in love with the beautiful Dora and they have a son, Joshua. The fairy tale turns into a tragedy when the family is taken to a Nazi death camp.

A significant part of the movie recounts Guido's attempt to alter the stressful nature of this horrific experience for his precious son. He does this by convincing Joshua that the day-to-day horrors imposed by the Nazis are part of an exciting game. He explains that three scenarios will result in losing the game—crying, asking to see his mama, and whining about being hungry. The winner of the game, Guido tells Joshua, will receive an army tank. If you've seen the movie, you know that Joshua eventually gets to ride in the tank because he was able to follow his father's rules. But more important, this story illustrates the potent effect of perceived control in stressful situations.

In the film *Life Is Beautiful,* Guido instructs his son Joshua in the rules of "the game," his attempt to minimize the terror of imprisonment in a Nazi death camp.

This award-winning film is controversial because some argue that it makes light of the terrifying conditions of the Nazi concentration camps. Political and cultural implications of the film aside, the strategy Guido chooses to cope with an almost unimaginably stressful experience is extremely adaptive. He is able to create a world for his son in which he has some sense of control—if he follows the rules, he will win a tank! Juxtaposed to the reality of being held prisoner by a group that has no concern for their welfare, Guido's scenario is certainly preferable.

Research on control. This theatrical anecdote is persuasive in demonstrating that perception of control is important in mitigating the stress response, but what does the research suggest? The empirical story of the impact of coping responses came to light with a famous study conducted by Joseph Brady in 1958. In this study, known as the *executive monkey study,* Brady selected four pairs of rhesus monkeys. One of each pair he dubbed the *executive* monkey and the other was the *yoked* monkey. The paired monkeys were placed in a restraint chair and subjected to periodic bursts of unsignaled electrical shock. The executive monkey was able to postpone the shock for 20 seconds by pressing a lever. Failure to press the lever resulted in a shock for both the executive and yoked monkey.

Thus, both monkeys received the same number of shocks but only the executive monkey had control over the shock. When the first two executive monkeys died in the apparatus, Brady examined their stomachs and discovered duodenal ulcers. The yoked animals did not develop ulcers. At this point, Brady realized that this shock-avoidance procedure was successful in producing ulcers. He continued to examine the remaining monkeys, and the remaining executive monkeys developed ulceration as well.

You may be wondering whether this is the most appropriate study to convince you that having control over stress is a *good* thing, given that all the executive monkeys developed ulcers. In fact, for several years, Brady's data were interpreted to mean that being "in charge" or an "executive" may mean a larger salary, but it also means more stress-associated health problems. But there is more to this monkey business.

For the next decade, researchers attempted to replicate Brady's study, but they had difficulty producing ulcers in the executive monkeys. In fact, one study reported that the only ulcers observed were in one of the yoked animals (Foltz & Millett, 1964). The emphasis continued to shift to the yoked animals in 1977 when Jay Weiss reported that rats with the ability to control shock by turning a wheel—executive rats—developed less severe gastric ulcers (as opposed to duodenal ulcers in Brady's executive monkeys) than the yoked control rats. In this experimental design, a signal was presented to all rats (including a no-shock control group) 10 seconds prior to the shock.

Weiss was very interested in why his research produced results that differed so significantly from Brady's. After conducting a series of studies, he concluded that two important aspects of Brady's study contributed to the opposing results. First, Brady selected the executive monkeys on the basis of how *active* the monkeys were on a preliminary task; additionally, he did not use signaled shock. Thus, Brady probably chose the most reactive of the monkeys to serve as the executives, which served as a confounding variable in a study designed to assess stress responses. The lack of a signal before the electric shock also contributed to higher rates of ulceration (Weiss, 1972, 1977).

Another famous series of experiments conducted in the 1960s emphasizes the importance of perception of control over a stimulus. Using dogs as subjects, Martin Seligman and Steven Maier, then at the University of Pennsylvania, conducted a study in which one group was exposed to foot shock in an experimental compartment with no possibility of escape (Seligman, 1990). Another group experienced the shock, but had an opportunity to escape.

Interestingly, when the dogs that were initially provided no escape route were subsequently exposed to shock in a compartment that had an escape route, the majority failed to attempt escape—they literally sat and accepted the stress. On the contrary, dogs that had experienced their initial shock session in the area with an escape route proceeded to escape in subsequent shock sessions. It was as if the dogs in the initial inescapable shock condition had *learned* that their behavioral responses had no consequences—that they had no control over the stressor. As you learned in Chapter Eight, Seligman and Maier called this phenomenon *learned helplessness*. This animal model has been used extensively as a model of human depression.

Since these seminal studies, subsequent research has confirmed the importance of having control—or at least the *perception* of control—over stressful stimuli. A chronic stress paradigm developed by Jean Kant and Sally Anderson at the Walter Reid Army Institute of Research in Maryland attempted to simulate chronic stress experienced by soldiers in combat (Anderson, Saviolakis, Bauman, Chu, Ghosh, & Kant, 1996). In this paradigm, rats received *signaled* foot shock every 5 minutes, 24 hours per day for 2 weeks. Although this program would seem extremely stressful, rats adapt easily to this design. After a few days of increased glucocorticoid production, the animals maintain their body weight, manage to obtain sleep durations comparable with controls (although in more frequent bouts), and the females' normal estrus cycle persists. The presentation of signals that predict the shock seems to decrease the magnitude of the stress response in these chronically stressed animals.

Although researchers have refrained from shocking humans to test the idea of perception of control, Carl Lejuez and Michael Zvolensky of Brown University designed a similar study to test the idea of control over a noxious stimulus (in Carpenter, 2000). In this study, subjects were given a breathing mask to wear and told that air enriched with 20% carbon dioxide would be delivered to them. Carbon dioxide is considered a noxious stimulus because it produces feelings of panic or anxiety in subjects. Half the subjects in this study were told a tone would warn them of the upcoming carbon dioxide bursts; the remaining subjects received no such warning. The researchers measured skin conductance activity and breathing patterns. All the subjects found the stimulus stressful, but overall they preferred that its administration be preceded with the signal.

Coping with lack of control. More recently, research has focused on low SES as an ecologically relevant form of chronic stress in which people have little control over their environments. Moving down the SES scale, life choices become more limited; hence, the perception of control over environment is probably lower than that of individuals with higher SES. In support of this hypothesis, low SES children up to age 16 have increased cortisol levels compared with high SES subjects; fortunately,

decatastrophizing Any attempt to minimize the impact of a stressor, likely to result in a decreased allostatic load. Some people may decatastrophize by gaining an increased perception of control or employing active coping strategies to minimize the negative impact.

affiliative social contact Non-threatening social contact. This type of social contact probably increases oxytocin, which subsequently triggers a cascade of responses that maximize growth and minimize stress.

paraventricular nuclei A collection of neurons located in the hypothalamus; the processes extend into the posterior pituitary, where oxytocin and vasopressin are released.

supraoptic nuclei Hypothalamic nuclei that produce oxytocin.

though, this difference subsides during the high school years (Lupien, King, Meaney, & McEwen, 2001).

Research with rodents, dogs, and primates shows that having a sense of control offers protection against the damaging effects of chronic HPA axis activation. Whereas Selye emphasized the dangerous effects of physical stress, the studies conducted by Weiss and others highlight the importance of *psychological* stress. In these studies, the amount of physical stress, or shock, was held constant between groups, yet the amount of control over the stressors, a psychological variable, determined the stress-induced pathology.

These studies also opened the door for research to focus on the value of modifying psychological variables in situations in which it is not possible immediately to remove the stressful conditions (for example, poverty, living in an unpredictable world). After being asked at a conference why a few dogs do attempt to escape after being placed in the inescapable condition, Martin Seligman focused his research attention on why some people demonstrate persistent coping responses even when they're not always reinforced. He calls this phenomenon *learned optimism*. Seligman (1990) claims that psychological strategies such as attempting to minimize the impact of a stressor, or **decatastrophizing** stressful events, as Guido did in the death camp, can be a valuable weapon in our coping arsenals.

Social Support

There is an old saying that misery loves company: when you're down and out, the best strategy is to have someone experience the stressful situation with you. It's not clear that having a social partner actually reduces the stress in any way—it just seems to reduce our responsiveness to the stressor. In this section we'll address just how important **affiliative social contact** is in reducing the stress response.

Let's start in the **paraventricular nuclei** and **supraoptic nuclei** of the hypothalamus, where, as you learned in Chapter Five, the neuropeptide oxytocin is produced and transported to the posterior pituitary prior to its release into the bloodstream. In addition to being responsible for milk ejection, nursing mothers also experience lowered blood pressure, decreased cortisol levels, and increased gastrointestinal hormones resulting from increased oxytocin. The neurotransmitter GABA is also increased in the mother during suckling; this inhibitory neurotransmitter decreases noradrenaline activity in the locus coeruleus (Carter, Altemus, & Chrousos, 2001; Kendrick, Keverne, Hinton & Goode 1992). Psychologically, women who are breast-feeding report being calmer than women who are not breast-feeding; the degree of calmness correlates with the oxytocin levels. Table 11.2 summarizes the stress-related benefits of nursing on the mother and the child.

A subsequent exploration on the effects of lactation on personality traits was conducted by Uvnas-Moberg and her colleagues at the Swedish University of Agricultural Sciences (Sjogren, Widstrom, Edman, & Uvnas-Moberg, 2000). The researchers found that, during the first three to six months following childbirth, women who had been breast-feeding for at least eight weeks had lower anxiety, muscular tension, monotony avoidance, and suspicion scores and higher scores on the socialization scale. The team concluded that pregnancy and lactation prepare women for a lifestyle that is more relaxed and tolerant of monotony (e.g., being quiet while the baby rests).

The effects of oxytocin are not limited to lactating mothers. Oxytocin is produced in both males and females, and in general, its repeated administration results in decreased sympathetic nervous system activation, lowered activity in the HPA axis, increased activity of the vagal nerve, enhanced digestive activity, and a feeling of calmness. Hence, Uvnas-Moberg (1998) argues that oxytocin has an antistress effect on both physiological and psychological processes.

[Table 11.2]

Neurobiological Effects of Nursing on Mother and Infant

Mother	
Physiological effects	**Psychological effects**
Decreased HPA responsivity	Decreased anxiety
Increased oxytocin	Decreased muscle tone
Increased GABA	Increased positive interactions with infant (e.g., smiles)
Decreased cardiovascular reactivity	Reduced vulnerability to depression
	Increased tolerance of monotony
	Decreased suspicion
	Increased socialization

Infant	
Physiological effects	**Psychological effects**
Increased oxytocin	Development of strong social bonds
Increased growth	Decreased vulnerability to developing depression
Decreased HPA responsivity	

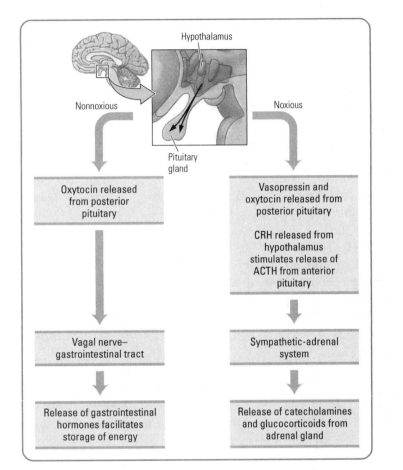

[Figure 11.8]
Hypothalamic responses to noxious or nonnoxious stimuli.
During nonnoxious social stimulation (left), oxytocin is released, facilitating an antistress response pattern that conserves energy. During noxious social stimulation (right), CRH triggers the stress hormonal cascade that mobilizes the body to expend energy very quickly to survive the impending threat.

ADAPTED FROM UVNAS-MOBERG, 1998, P. 25.

You may be thinking that it would be nice to bottle oxytocin and take a healthy dose when we're feeling stressed. In fact, the solution to self-administering this valuable neuropeptide may be as simple as reaching out and touching someone. In one study, rats were stroked, or massaged, for 5 minutes. Following this stimulation, a decrease of 20 mm of mercury (Hg) in blood pressure and 60 beats per minute in heart rate were observed in the animals for up to 4 hours.

The control animals that were held but received no stroking had a 20 mm Hg increase in blood pressure and an increase in heart rate of 60 beats per minute for up to 1 hour following the handling (Lund, Lundeberg, Kurosawa, & Uvnas-Moberg, 1999). In addition to touch several forms of nonnoxious stimuli, such as vibration, warm temperature, and electroacupuncture have been associated with oxytocin increases in the plasma and cerebrospinal fluid. Figure 11.8 shows the possible divergent routes of noxious and nonnoxious stimuli in the brain.

As shown in Figure 11.9, grooming may provide another form of nonnoxious stimulation—especially considering the relaxed posture of one of the primates. If primate grooming is calming, it is interesting to speculate why going to the hair salon is a popular endeavor for many of us for the same reasons. As evidence, when Andrew Solomon (2001), the journalist featured in Box 8.1, went to Cambodia to interview survivors of the horrible atrocities suffered at the hands of the Khmer Rouge, he was especially struck by the story of Phaly Nuon, a nominee for the Nobel Peace Prize. Nuon told Solomon that she had attempted to facilitate healing in Cambodian women who had suffered unspeakable atrocities by setting up something akin to a psychotherapy hut, incorporating a host of different therapies from traditional Khmer medicine to antidepressants to cognitive therapies.

Nuon was desperate to find some way to reach these debilitated women, many of whom were unable to talk or even take care of their children following their "utterly incapacitating post-traumatic stress" (Solomon, 2001, p. 36). Following some cognitive exercises to help the women forget the pain, she would try to distract them with music or knitting (perhaps releasing serotonin because of the repetitive movements) and finally, she attempted to reestablish their ability to form affiliative relationships, or to love. Together with the relaxing effects of social contact previously discussed, Nuon used grooming behavior to restore the social bonds of these isolated women.

[Figure 11.9]
Grooming-induced relaxation.
These Java macaques at Monkey Jungle (in Miami, Florida) spend much of the day grooming each other. Recipients typically display a range of relaxed postures, from seated positions to the totally relaxed loss of muscle tone shown here.
KELLY LAMBERT

And then when they have mastered work, at last, I teach them to love. I built a sort of lean-to and made it a steam bath. . . . I take them there so that they can become clean, and I teach them how to give one another manicures and pedicures and how to take care of their fingernails, because doing that makes them feel beautiful, and they want so much to feel beautiful. It also puts them in contact with the bodies of other people and makes them give up their bodies to the care of others. It rescues them from physical isolation, which is a usual affliction for them, and that leads to the breakdown of the emotional isolation. While they are together washing and putting on nail polish, they begin to talk together, and bit by bit they learn to trust one another, and by the end of it all, they have learned how to make friends, so that they will never have to be so lonely and so alone again. Their stories, which they have told to no one but me—they begin to tell those stories to one another (Solomon, 2001, p. 36).

The interplay between oxytocin and the HPA axis contributes to the formation of social bonds in the prairie vole. This mouselike rodent has serum corticosterone concentrations that are about ten times higher than levels observed in rats. As opposed to other mammals that respond to the negative feedback of the activated HPA axis, social cues seem to be a primary factor that influences corticosterone secretion in prairie voles. Prairie voles are unique in that they are monogamous, and glucocorticoid levels drop in the pair-bonding process, suggesting that the HPA axis may contribute to this process in some way. Providing further support that oxytocin is involved in the formation of the pair bonds in these animals, prairie voles fail to form social bonds when oxytocin is disrupted (Carter & Getz, 1993; DeVries, 2002).

Forming strong pair bonds offers evolutionary advantages for this mammal including enhanced pup survival and development and a buffer against the harmful effects of stress (Carter, 1998; Getz & Lindstrom,

1992). It is not clear whether oxytocin plays a central role in human pair-bonding, but it is known that oxytocin is released during human sexual contact. Because sexual contact is neither necessary nor sufficient to maintain human pair bonds, the role of oxytocin in human pair-bonding remains unclear. Further, the distribution of human oxytocin receptors is different from that observed in the prairie vole, so we need to be cautious before we apply the prairie vole model of pair-bonding to humans (Insel & Winslow, 1999).

It is important to note that the pair bond doesn't have to have a sexual foundation to serve as a buffer against stress. In another monogamous species, the California deer mouse, same-sex siblings raised together since birth exhibit fewer behavioral signs of stress when tested in the *chronic unpredictable stress paradigm*. In this paradigm, animals are exposed to annoying and unpredictable stimuli such as a tilted cage, predator odors, and altered light-dark schedules. The paired deer mice exhibit fewer signs of emotionality when tested in an open field and have lower levels of corticosterone following exposure to a predator odor (Lambert et al., 2001). This social buffering effect has been observed in multiple species—ranging from guinea pigs to humans (in DeVries, 2002).

Once established, though, the disruption of social bonds can be stressful. We have already discussed the consequences of prolonged durations of mother-infant separation on the developing infant. Several primate species, such as titi monkeys, marmosets, and cotton top tamarins, also exhibit increased cortisol concentrations in response to being separated from an established partner (Mendoza & Mason, 1986; Norcross & Newman, 1999; Smith, McGreer-Whitworth, & French, 1998).

Social contact can play a beneficial role in combating another form of stress: the recovery from trauma, sickness, or disease. Courtney DeVries and her colleagues at the Ohio State University recently showed the importance of social contact during recovery from experimentally induced stroke (DeVries, 2002). Male mice housed with females had less damaged brain tissue and less severe cognitive impairment than mice housed in isolation.

Research conducted by Tiffany Field (1993, 2002) at the Touch Research Institute at the University of Miami School of Medicine has shown that another form of social contact, massage, benefits premature infants. Specifically, massaged infants have lower levels of cortisol and grow at a significantly faster rate than same-age infants who do not receive a massage (the two groups did not differ in food consumption). Thus, it is likely that touch- or contact-related health benefits can be attributed to the interaction of social contact with the HPA axis. As you will learn in Chapter Twelve, complex interactions exist among the level of social contact, stress responsivity, health, and immune functioning.

As we leave this section on social contact, it is important to point out that the *type* of contact is very important when considering its impact on the stress response. When DeVries exposed brain-injured mice to social stimuli of an aggressive nature, the contact exacerbated the brain injury (DeVries et al., 2001). In fact, social contact, the variable that we have been describing as having a significant stress-mitigating effect, can be deleterious if the nature of the relationship is agonistic. Box 11.2 describes the work of Eberhard Fuchs at the German Primate Laboratory in Göttingen. Fuchs has demonstrated that tree shrews become so stressed being housed in another tree shrew's territory that they die—not from being attacked but from the effects of the potent psychological stressor of being housed with a more dominant, resident animal (Fuchs et al., 2001).

Research with Syrian hamsters has shown that social stress can be long-lasting. Kim Huhman at Georgia State University uses a **social defeat paradigm** in which a hamster is placed in the home cage of a larger, more aggressive hamster (Huhman, Banks, Harmon, & Jasnow, 2002; Huhman, Mougey, & Meyerhoff, 1992). Following the defeat of the intruder hamster by the resident hamster, the defeated animal will no longer attempt territorial aggression. Even when smaller hamsters are placed in their home cages, the defeated animal fails to defend its home territory. This conditioned defeat effect lasts for at least a month following the initial defeat. Because corticotropin-releasing hormone (CRH) exacerbates conditioned defeat and conversely a CRH receptor antagonist diminishes the submissive behavior, it is clear that this agonistic social encounter is intimately integrated with HPA responsivity.

Paul MacLean (1998) wrote that mammals differ from reptilian vertebrates in three distinguishing forms of behavior: audiovocal communication, parenting, and play. In most mammals, these behaviors involve social contact and/or interaction. An extreme portrayal of the human desire for contact was seen in the film *Cast Away*. The protagonist, Chuck, played by Tom Hanks, developed a close affiliative bond with a companion named Wilson after being stranded on a deserted island. If you've seen the movie, you know that Wilson was a unique companion—he was a Wilson volleyball with a blood-painted face and grassy hair. Perhaps our intense predisposition to seek out and maintain affiliative social contact explains why audiences willingingly accepted the idea of developing a close friendship with a ball. Because of the evolutionary relevance of affiliative contact, it is likely that even more biologically relevant consequences of social contact will be uncovered in the future.

social defeat paradigm
Animal model of chronic stress in which an animal is exposed to a larger, more aggressive animal and is defeated in a single aggressive encounter. For up to a month or longer, the defeated animal will not exhibit defensive behavior when an animal—even a smaller animal—is placed in its cage.

[Box 11.2]

The Investigators

Eberhard Fuchs

In the late 1960s when Eberhard Fuchs was a biology and chemistry student at the University of Munich, he sometimes found himself thinking about psychological processes. In the midst of his studies, he became intrigued by a passage written by the prolific Wilhem Reich, suggesting that "it would be good to learn more about human behavior to understand more about the chemistry of anxiety." Young Fuchs asked his biology and chemistry professors about such academic pursuits, and they sent him down one floor to a professor in the Zoology Department, Alchim Raab, who opened the door to a whole new world for Fuchs—the world of behavioral neuroscience.

After hearing that male tree shrews become aggressive if several are housed in the same enclosure, Raab established what is thought to be only the second tree shrew colony in the world. Tree shrews (*Tuapia belangeri*) are about the size of a squirrel and are viewed as a kind of intermediate species (order Scandentia) between insectivores and primates. In their native Southeast Asia,

these animals are intensely territorial. Fuchs was intrigued by Raab's work with the shrews and, under his mentorship, got his Ph.D. in zoology in 1977.

Fuchs is now group leader for the Division of Neurobiology at the German Primate Center in Göttingen. He is a prolific scientist and scholar in the field of chronic stress and continues to use the same animal model that intrigued him as a student. Currently, the standard social stress protocol with tree shrews includes housing a submissive male with a more dominant male that can establish his dominance over the territory. Once this relationship is established, the males are separated by a wire mesh panel for up to four weeks. During this time the animals are monitored closely. The subordinate animals exhibit more interruptions in sleep, increased metabolic rate, increased secretion of stress hormones, and reduced gonadal activity than do their dominant counterparts.

Fuchs has focused most recently on the effects of this form of chronic social stress on the brain, specifically the hippocampus. Generally, he has found that, although the stressed animals have the same number of neurons, they are more likely to have increased apoptosis (programmed cell death) and decreased neurogenesis

Active versus Passive Coping

When confronted with the bad news that your car is going to cost thousands of dollars to repair, do you remain motionless as you contemplate what you are going to do with the car? Or do you go immediately to the nearest garbage can and give it a swift kick? As we discussed earlier in this chapter and in Chapter Six, some people develop active responses to stressful stimuli whereas others prefer a more passive response. But what do these differences in behavioral responding really mean? Researchers are just beginning to ask this question in a systematic fashion, but the literature is far from providing definitive answers.

Whereas the physiological response to stress is well documented, many questions remain about the nature of behavioral responses to stressful stimuli. For example, increased cortisol levels are generally viewed as an index of stress in animals, but increased behavioral responsiveness is not always considered an indication of stress. In a defensive

Eberhard Fuchs
COURTESY OF DR. EBERHARD FUCHS

(production of new neurons) in the dentate gyrus. But *decreased* levels of apoptosis are observed in the CA1 area of the hippocampus (Gould et al., 1997; Ohl, Michaelis, Vollmann-Hansdorf, Kirshbaum, & Fuchs, 2000).

Fuchs is currently investigating hippocampal volume in the intact animal by using an MRI device adapted for small animals. Using this technology, he sees a pattern of a decreased hippocampal volume in stressed males. He has also recently started testing the animals in a working memory task and is finding that the stressed animals experience a delayed impairment in their learning about seven weeks after the termination of the stress paradigm (Fuchs et al., 2001).

By using an animal species closely related to primates, Fuchs's work is valuable for the assessment of chronic stress in humans. He doesn't limit his research to tree shrews, though; he also uses marmosets (a small primate) and rats in his laboratory. His approach to the study of stress is comprehensive. He focuses on both microstructure (cells in dentate gyrus) and macrostructure (volume of hippocampus); includes a behavioral assessment of the effects of stress on the brain; investigates the effects of various neurochemical influences on the stress response (Boldizsar, Michaelis, Watanabe, Frahm, Biurrun, et al., 2001); focuses on both short-term and long-term effects of stress; and uses a naturalistic form of chronic stress (territorial-based aggression).

The convergence of all of Fuchs's measures contributes greatly to the complex literature of stress physiology. His practical approach to understanding the stress response incorporates his realization that short-term specific stress-induced neurochemical fluctuations are probably less important than long-term effects on an animal's health and learning ability. Throughout his research, Fuchs remains aware that individual differences are so pervasive in short-term responses to stress that it is the more global, long-term changes that will help researchers understand the ultimate effects of stress on an animal's ability to adapt and survive in its natural environment. Neuroscience has benefited greatly from Fuchs's many contributions, thanks to his undergraduate professors who steered him in the right direction—to the tree shrew colony in the basement!

burying task, prolonged digging is generally viewed as evidence of increased anxiety or stress, but increased activity in the open field test is generally considered a sign of decreased stress or anxiety (Palanza, Gioiosa, & Parmigiani, 2001; Pinel, Mumby, Dastur, & Pinel, 1994). So it is interesting to consider whether an animal's behavioral response to a stressor is specific to that particular stressor or if animals develop certain pervasive response strategies to a diverse array of stressors.

Some research supports the notion that a general active response strategy is beneficial. Jay Weiss (1972), now at Emory University, conducted a simple experiment in which he shocked rats in their cages; one shock group was placed in their home cages with another rat in the cage, whereas the other group was placed in their home cage with no other animal. Weiss investigated the ulceration of these animals' stomachs. Interestingly, the rats that had another rat in the cage developed fewer ulcers than the isolated controls.

coping style Persistent
response strategy in the presence of stressful stimuli. An
animal may have an active,
passive or flexible style.

Weiss attributed these differences to the observation that the shocked
rats would routinely and vigorously bite the other rat in the cage. Likewise,
when a piece of wood was placed in the cage as an alternative biting target, less ulceration was observed. Thus, in this case, a more active response
resulted in reduced stress-induced ulceration (Weiss, 1972).

Jaap Koolhaas and his colleagues at the University of Groningen in the
Netherlands have analyzed extensively the nature of coping styles in animals (Koolhaas et al., 1999). They define **coping style** as a persistent,
consistent collection of physiological and behavioral responses to stressful stimuli. Instead of speaking of active and passive coping styles,
Koolhaas prefers the terminology *proactive* and *reactive*. For example, a
male rat that is consistently aggressive toward other males is categorized
as proactive, whereas a less aggressive rat is considered more flexible, or
reactive, in his responses because he responds only when absolutely necessary.

Generally, physiological differences exist between the proactive and
reactive animals. Proactive coping styles are characterized by low HPA
axis activity (shown by low cortisol levels) and high sympathetic activity
(such as high catecholamine levels). More passive reactive coping styles
are characterized by higher HPA axis reactivity and higher parasympathetic activity. These differences also persist for baseline levels of hormones; aggressive mice have low levels of corticosterone during baseline
conditions when compared with their nonaggressive counterparts
(Koolhaas et al., 1999). The benefits of hitting a punching bag for reducing the stress response suddenly makes sense!

More evidence for divergent coping styles in animals can be gained
from a visit to a farm where researchers have established a test to assess
individual coping styles in pigs. This *backtest* involves placing the animal
on its back and keeping it in a supine position for a minute (Figure 11.10).
When this is done, some pigs struggle to escape and are classified as resistant pigs, while others do not show any signs of struggle. Pigs exhibiting
few escape attempts are known as nonresistant copers. Interestingly, pigs
that are tested at a couple of weeks of age retain their coping style
throughout their lives.

In keeping with the rodent data, the more active pigs are also more
exploratory in an open field and have lower baseline levels of cortisol
than the less active pigs (Schouten & Wiegant, 1997). The backtest can
even be done with hens. Two lines of hens differing in their propensity to
feather-peck have been tested. When the birds are kept on their side for
8 minutes, the high-feather-pecking line was more resistant, or active,
whereas the low-feather-pecking line was less resistant. Corticosterone
levels were higher in the low-pecking birds and sympathetic repsonsivity

was highest in the high-feather-pecking birds (Koolhaas et al., 1999; Korte, Beuving, Ruesink, & Blokhuis, 1997). (Neuroscientists have yet to establish whether birds of a high-feather-pecking line flock together. Do birds of opposite feather-pecking lines attract? We'll leave that question to the social psychologists.)

Additional support for the notion that more active responding leads to a diminished stress response comes from the research conducted by Barry Jacobs's laboratory at Princeton University (Jacobs, 1994). As described in the chapter-opening Connections, the serotonergic neurons are most active during repetitive movement. Using cats as subjects, Jacobs has shown that the felines have high firing rates of the serotonergic neurons in the raphe nucleus when walking and virtually no firing in REM sleep when the animal has no muscle tone.

[Figure 11.10]
Profiling the stress response of piglets. Pigs are used as subjects at the University of Groningen to establish varying styles of behavioral coping. During the backtest they are simply held on their backs and the researchers record the number of times the animal struggles to escape.
COURTESY WILLEM SCHOUTEN

Because most antidepressants enhance serotonergic levels, it is possible that repetitive movements such as chewing gum or pacing the floor are comparable to the effects of SSRIs (Jacobs, 1994). Even the stereotypies sometimes observed in captive animals have been reported to lower cortisol and arousal levels; if this is the case, this seemingly abnormal behavior of pacing back and forth in a cage might be quite adaptive in reducing the amount of stress responsivity experienced by the animals (Koolhaas et al., 1999).

Thus, whereas more active coping strategies seem most adaptive in general, it is important to remember that specific circumstances require appropriate responses. There are certainly times when an animal frozen in movement will survive when an animal making noises in proximity to a predator will not. Do you remember the guppies described in Chapter One? In this study, all the bold guppies became lunch for the predator bass in the tank, whereas 40% of the timid, nonresponsive guppies survived the predator.

There may also be cases when having the capacity to respond in a variety of styles proves more adaptive. A study focusing on rats' coping strategies in response to many different stressors identified three categories: low reactivity, variable reactivity, and high reactivity. Interestingly, the variable reactivity group exhibited more hypothalamic and amygdala activation in the face of stress, perhaps leading to enhanced vigilance in the animals.

In the human's large brain, perhaps a coping style that employs more of the brain might lead to the more adaptive response. Knowing when to react and when to be passive may also be a critical factor in adaptive

allostasis Literally, maintaining stability through change; the active process of maintaining physiological homeostasis in the face of any challenge.

allostatic load Wear and tear on the body that results from repeated activation of the processes that maintain homeostasis.

coping (Campbell, Lin, DeVries, & Lambert, 2003). In support of this idea, Japanese college students who possess more flexible coping strategies exhibited fewer signs of depression than more rigid responders (Kato, 2001).

Allostatic Load

We have established that the stress response can be significantly modified by the coping strategy adopted by the stressed individual. Generally, incorporating social support, active behavioral responses, and a sense of control over our lives enables us to respond to stress more effectively and efficiently. Actually, the method of minimizing the stress response is less important than the fact that it is being diminished in some way.

According to Bruce McEwen, once faced with a stressor, a person's physiological homeostasis is threatened (McEwen & Lashley 2002). Fortunately, as described earlier in this chapter, we have an arsenal of responses to help us escape the stressor; these responses include activation of the HPA axis, the sympathetic nervous system, and the engagement of various brain centers. McEwen points out that responses triggered in the face of a stressful stimulus are important: they reestablish homeostatic balance.

These stress-induced responses are allostatic. The term **allostasis** is derived from the Greek root *allo,* which means *variable,* and is used in this context to emphasize the point that dynamic physiological systems keep the body stable (McEwen & Lashley, 2002). To maintain homeostasis, or internal balance, the body must exhibit a wide range of changes, such as varied heart rate, hormonal secretions, and energy storage. It is ironic that change (allostasis) is required to maintain balance (homeostasis) in the body.

Homeostasis thus may not be the norm for our bodies. Other than a few variables, such as body temperature, which must be maintained within a narrow range, our physiological systems—heart rate for example—are characterized by a varied response range. Appropriate for this chapter, allostasis more accurately describes our dynamic physiological responses that are directed toward optimal responding in times of threat. According to Jay Schulkin (2003), "Allostasis also highlights our ability to anticipate, adapt to, or cope with impending future events" (p. 17).

If the allostatic processes have to work extensively to maintain homeostasis, the added work may contribute to wear and tear in the system—or **allostatic load.** Let's consider an analogy to make it clearer: Suppose that your car breaks down. You take it to a local mechanic for a diagnostic workup and when you return, the mechanic describes in agonizing and uninteresting detail what the problems are. Your mind wanders—until he gets to the point of telling you what it will cost to repair. You snap to attention. On hearing the price, you have to quickly determine how you will handle it. Will it interfere with purchasing basics, such as room and board, that trip you had been planning, or even keep you from paying your tuition?

Never good news, and depending on your current financial situation, car repairs can be a real hardship. In this example, though, we have created stress for both you and your car. A particular event(s) resulted in your car breaking down and was thus the stressor for your car. The repairs that the mechanic will perform (provided you can pay) will bring it back to baseline condition: This is allostasis. The allostatic load was the wear and tear on the car that led to the breakdown. Determining how to reduce your car's allostatic load (e. g., regular maintenance, oil changes, etc.) may mean less money out-of-pocket to you—which ultimately reduces your own allostatic load.

In this analogy of homeostasis and allostasis, *you* have to assume the responsibility of your car's allostatic load; in reality, no one can pay that cost for your body—you always have to pay the allostatic bill following every threat to homeostasis. Thus, any coping strategy, regardless of its specific nature, is effective if it reduces your allostatic load. Although journalist Terry Anderson (Box 11.3 on page 424) was held hostage for seven hellish years, he was able to employ effective coping strategies to keep his brain and body from entering terminal allostatic overload.

POST-TRAUMATIC STRESS DISORDER

Once a stressful stimulus is removed, in most cases, the stress response subsides so that it is ready for activation when the person is faced with the next stressor life has to offer. On rare occasions, however, the stress response recurs or does not diminish; it persists to the point that it interferes with day-to-day activities. In 1980, a diagnostic category was created in the DSM-III for such a condition, **post-traumatic stress disorder (PTSD).**

Generally, PTSD is defined as an anxiety disorder characterized by the reexperiencing of a traumatic event, accompanied by both enhanced arousal and avoidance of trauma-related stimuli (APA, 2000). Because the traumatic trigger results in a severe stress response, we feature PTSD here in our discussion of stress and coping.

PTSD is currently thought to affect between 1% and 9% of the population (Mezey & Robbins, 2001). These rates, however, can be considerably

post-traumatic stress disorder (PTSD) Disorder characterized by symptoms such as memories and dreams related to a traumatic event that recur up to months or years following the event. Individuals with this disorder feel as if they are reexperiencing the trauma and have the accompanying physiological arousal to enhance their belief of impending danger.

[Box 11.3]

A Case in Point

How Terry Anderson Survived as a Hostage

Early on a Saturday morning in 1985, Terry Anderson, 38, a talented journalist working for the Associated Press in Beirut, Lebanon, got up, kissed his fiancée, who was then six months pregnant with their child, and headed for the tennis courts to meet his colleagues. On the way back, Anderson's car was pulled over, his glasses were snatched from his face, and he was instructed to kneel down in a small space between the front and back seats and hidden under a blanket. As fear spread throughout his body, his captor calmly told him, "Don't worry. It's political" (Anderson, 1993, p. 7). The date was March 16, the beginning of a 2454 day nightmare for Terry Anderson.

Anderson's ankles were chained to a cot in a very small room with no windows and, for most of his nearly seven years of captivity, no companionship. He was forced to wear a blindfold while guards were in his room or when he left his quarters. The food was barely fit to eat and, most humiliating for this accomplished correspondent, he was at the mercy of his young, immature, aggressive captors for the privilege of even going to the bathroom.

No music, no conversation, no outdoor scenery, nothing to read, no freedom to control any aspect of his life characterized his days. Anderson described this time as "long nights, squirrel-in-a-cage nights. Mind spinning, thoughts, emotions whirling. Anger. Frustration. Pain. Guilt" (p. 89). How does anyone cope with such stress? Is there any way for the human mind to survive such torment?

Terry Anderson took advantage of every possible factor to strengthen his chances of surviving. A basic physical need that he addressed about a month into his captivity was washing off all the filth that his body had accumulated. Smelling like a mixture of sweat and urine, his hair caked with dirt and oil, he decided to strip and bathe himself with a hose attached to a water tap on the wall during one of his short bathroom trips. A guard blasted through the door and threatened him, but Anderson knew from his military training how important hygiene is to avoiding illness and staying alive.

One of the biggest threats to Anderson's sanity was isolation. He didn't speak Arabic, so he couldn't even understand the conversations of the guards outside his door. Anderson tried ceaselessly to recall the image of his fiancée and to feel the presence of his loved ones. In the midst of such loneliness he craved any companionship. Whenever he was placed in rooms with other hostages he maximized the social exchange by having extensive conversations with his new "roommates."

Even without the company of other hostages, Anderson attempted to develop social relationships with any guards who seemed remotely sympathetic. When he knew hostages were being kept in adjacent rooms he devised elaborate ways to communicate, such as tapping on the walls between the rooms. A mouse that made regular stops in his room during the middle of the night even became his companion, and he faithfully saved a bread crumb on his pillow each evening. During times when it might have been easier to retreat within himself, Anderson's concerted efforts to maintain social contact probably contributed greatly to his continuing sanity.

Almost impossible to tolerate was complete lack of control. Yet again, Anderson coped. He gained control whenever he could—even if it was minimal. Taking the initiative to bathe himself, even though he risked retaliation, was one great success in regaining some control over his seemingly hopeless situation. He kept track of the passing days to gain a sense of control over the passing of time. And although many hostages would have been too fearful to challenge the guards, Anderson persisted in asking for things that were critical to his sanity. He asked for books, a radio, for his chains to be loosened when they were cutting off his circulation, and for medical care for another hostage who was very ill.

Anderson also gained a sense of control by relying on religion, reciting biblical passages that he had committed to memory, asking for a Bible and reading it over and over, talking about religion when fellow hostages were present. In painfully small increments, he was able to see that some of his attempts to change his predicaments resulted in minor changes—an observation that was important for maintaining psychological health.

(left) Terry Anderson in 1985, before captivity
(right) Terry Anderson in 1991, five months prior to release AP/ WIDE WORLD PHOTOS

Another aspect of maintaining his health during this time was getting some exercise—even trying to let his muscles move. After several years he developed an automatic pacing pattern that enabled him to make the best use of his five-foot chains without jerking them or tripping. He asked to go to a larger space for a few minutes on some days to exercise. At one point, he used filled water jugs as free weights.

You now know enough about the brain to know that it did not evolve to exist in a sea of nothingness for seven years. Anderson had to fight to keep his mind functioning and disciplined. Early in his captivity, he wrote a daily journal, but after a time he realized that its mere existence made him even more vulnerable to his captors. Once he had persuaded a guard to bring him anything at all to read, he quickly reveled in these books, reading them over and over.

When others were in his room he made games such as chess or cards out of leftover paper, or played 20 questions. He designed elaborate buildings in his mind, decided what he would do if he had a million dollars, and thought about his loved ones. When he was housed with Tom Sutherland, a former professor at Colorado State University, Anderson persuaded Sutherland to go over all his lectures in all his classes. At one point he even started studying Arabic.

Although Anderson was amazingly successful at maintaining his sanity during this time, he admits to having some experiences with depression, describing it as "enormous, a thick, black blanket smothering me" (p. 179). At another point, he described losing control and beating his head against the wall until a guard stopped him. All in all, however, he survived the ordeal with his mental faculties intact. In fact, toward the end of his captivity a guard picked up his Bible, gesturing that he wanted to learn the English word for it. Anderson responded by saying "cup," and each time he picked up the Bible, he slowly said "cup" as if teaching the guard the correct word for Bible. This event actually sparked a bout of laughter among Terry and the other hostages—another sign of mental health.

On December 4, 1991, Anderson was released to the American government. He was reunited with his fiancée and met his 6-year-old daughter for the first time. He has continued to engage in responses beneficial to his mental health. He married his fiancée and accepted a teaching position at the School of Journalism at Ohio University. He fought back at the Iranian government officials whom he suspected of sponsoring his captors by suing them as an attempt to hold them responsible for their actions. His current activities include working for and supporting several charities, raising and training horses on his ranch, pursuing political causes and offices, and owning several restaurants and a blues bar. If he's tapping his foot to the music, he may be assuring that his serotonergic neurons are always functioning in concert with this rhythmic movement and, as discussed in the Connections section, perhaps relieving residual anxiety.

higher under extreme conditions. A sample of Cambodian refugees in the United States was recently found to have an 86% prevalence rate (Carlson & Rosser-Hogan, 1991; Paunovic & Ost, 2001). The typical duration of PTSD varies, whereas some victims experience relief after a year, others report persistant symptoms for much longer. For example, 19 years following combat exposure in Vietnam, 15% of male veterans suffered from PTSD (Kulka et al., 1990).

PTSD is characterized by symptoms such as recurring memories and dreams related to the traumatic event (Table 11.3). At times, people

[Table 11.3]

DSM-IV-TR Diagnostic Criteria for Post-Traumatic Stress Disorder

A. The person has been exposed to a traumatic event in which both of the following were present:

 (1) the person experienced, witnessed, or was confronted with an event or events that involved actual or threatened death or serious injury, or a threat to the physical integrity of self or others

 (2) the person's response involved intense fear, helplessness, or horror. Note: In children, this may be expressed instead by disorganized or agitated behavior

B. The traumatic event is persistently reexperienced in one (or more) of the following ways:

 (1) recurrent and intrusive distressing recollections of the event, including images, thoughts, or perceptions. Note: In young children, repetitive play may occur in which themes or aspects of the trauma are expressed

 (2) recurrent distressing dreams of the event. Note: In children, there may be frightening dreams without recognizable content.

 (3) acting or feeling as if the traumatic event were recurring (includes a sense of reliving the experience, illusions, hallucinations, and dissociative flashback episodes, including those that occur on awakening or when intoxicated). Note: In young children, trauma-specific reenactment may occur.

 (4) intense psychological distress at exposure to internal or external cues that symbolize or resemble an aspect of the traumatic event

 (5) physiological reactivity on exposure to internal or external cures that symbolize or resemble an aspect of the traumatic event

C. Persistent avoidance of stimuli associated with the trauma and numbing of general responsiveness (not present before the trauma), as indicated by three (or more) of the following:

 (1) efforts to avoid thoughts, feelings, or conversations associated with the trauma

 (2) efforts to avoid activities, places, or people that arouse recollections of the trauma

 (3) inability to recall an important aspect of the trauma

 (4) markedly diminished interest or participation in significant activities

 (5) feeling of detachment or estrangement from others

 (6) restricted range of affect (e.g., unable to have loving feelings)

 (7) sense of a foreshortened future (e.g., does not expect to have a career, marriage, children, or a normal life span)

D. Persistent symptoms of increased arousal (not present before the trauma), as indicated by two (or more) of the following:

 (1) difficulty falling or staying asleep

 (2) irritability or outbursts of anger

 (3) difficulty concentrating

 (4) hypervigilance

 (5) exaggerated startle response

E. Duration of the disturbance (symptoms in Criteria B, C, and D) is more than 1 month.

F. The disturbance causes clinically significant distress or impairment in social, occupational, or other important areas of functioning

Specify if:

Acute: if duration of symptoms is less than 3 months

Chronic: if duration of symptoms is 3 months or more

Specify if:

With delayed onset: if onset of symptoms is at least 6 months

APA, 2000, pp. 467–468.

affected by the disorder feel that they are reexperiencing the trauma, and the accompanying physiological arousal enhances their belief of impending danger. As patients try to avoid stimuli that will trigger these memories, their ability to function day to day is diminished.

Tracing the Neurobiological Roots of PTSD

The triggering stimulus for PTSD is obvious—a traumatic event. Less obvious is why a majority of people experience an appropriate stress response that subsides when the traumatic stimulus is removed, whereas, as observed in PTSD patients, others have problems suppressing the stress response for months or years following the event. As described earlier in the section on social contact, extreme stress such as experienced by the Cambodian women results in a much higher rate of PTSD-like symptoms; thus severity of the stressor is an important factor in determining the likelihood of PTSD. Although it appears that the PTSD patient is experiencing a heightened stress response, cortisol levels are actually decreased. It has been proposed that the significant trauma enhances the negative feedback components of the HPA axis (Anisman, Griffiths, Matheson, Ravindran, & Merali, 2001), making it more sensitive to lower levels of cortisol.

A recent study explored the areas of the brain that might be involved in perpetuating the PTSD symptoms. The investigators conducted a functional MRI scan of PTSD patients as they were recalling the traumatic event associated with their PTSD symptoms. The fMRI scans were compared with those of nine patients who had been exposed to a traumatic event but had not met the criteria for the diagnosis of this disorder. Their results suggest that the PTSD patients have lower activity in the thalamus, medial frontal cortex, and the anterior cingulate gyrus (Figure 11.11).

Disruptions in these areas may inhibit the PTSD patient's ability to interpret memories of the traumatic event as memories rather than impending dangers. This study is interesting, however, because the brain area that is most often associated with fear—the amygdala—was not found to be more active in PTSD patients. The results do suggest, however, that altered brain functions underlie traumatic recall in PTSD patients (Lanius et al., 2001).

[Figure 11.11]
Brain activation in PTSD patients. A comparison of fMRI scans of a non-PTSD patient *(top)* and a PTSD patient *(bottom)* reveals less activity (shown as brighter areas) in the thalamus, anterior cingulated cortex, and prefrontal cortex.

AMERICAN JOURNAL OF PSYCHIATRY, 158, 1920-1922, 2001. (C) 2004, AMERICAN PSYCHIATRIC ASSOCIATION HTTP://AJPPSYCHIATRYONLINE.ORG. REPRINTED BY PERMISSION.

Thalamus   Anterior Cingulate   Anteromedial Prefrontal Cortex

exposure therapy Type of therapy sometimes used with PTSD patients in which the facilitator exposes the patient to the stimulus/event that is most feared in an attempt to have him/her see that exposure isn't always associated with a negative outcome.

Treatment for PTSD

Current treatments for PTSD include cognitive-behavioral therapies and various pharmacological treatments. Most of these therapies are associated with modest improvements; however no cures for this disorder currently exist. As shown by the recent popularity of the novel treatment known as eye movement desensitization and reprocessing (EMDR) described below, patients and clinicians should approach new therapies with caution and skepticism.

One cognitive-behavioral therapy that may be used to treat PTSD is **exposure therapy,** where patients are encouraged to experience gradually increasing representations of the original trauma. The idea is that the strong association between actually experiencing the event and having memories of it should dissolve as the patient realizes that that memory is not predictive of the traumatic event. In another type of cognitive-behavioral therapy, the patient is taught to avoid catastrophizing following intruding memories. Patients are also encouraged to practice controlled breathing to counteract the irregular breathing that typically accompanies a recollection. The efficacy of these two therapies was recently assessed; results suggest that both are more effective than a placebo and that the two therapies are equally effective for PTSD patients (Paunovic & Ost, 2001).

Pharmacological treatments include drugs that may reduce arousal or anxiety, such as tricyclics and selective serotonin reuptake inhibitors (SSRIs). Although there is still a need for controlled studies testing the efficacy of various drugs on PTSD symptoms, a recent double-blind, placebo-controlled, long-term study that investigated the SSRI *sertraline* provided evidence of its value for treating PTSD. Sertraline was shown to enhance sustained improvement in symptoms and protect the patients against relapse (Davidson et al., 2001). Relapse, however, is likely to occur on the termination of the pharmacological treatment, so a combination of behavioral and pharmacological therapies is likely to offer the patient the most protection against relapse.

Eye movement desensitization and reprocessing (EMDR), a novel and controversial treatment for PTSD and other anxiety disorders, was introduced by Shapiro in 1989. Using EMDR, a patient is instructed to induce rapid and rhythmic eye movements by following the therapist's finger back and forth for about 20 seconds. During this time the patient is instructed to elevate the negative emotions and cognitions associated with the trauma to the "forefront of the mind" where they can be replaced with positive emotions. According to the protocol, this procedure continues until the traumatic emotions and memories are significantly reduced (Shepherd, Stein, & Milne, 2000).

In the last 10 years, EMDR has become very popular: over 25,000 trained clinicians regularly use this procedure. James Herbert and his colleagues at Hahnemann University in Philadelphia, Pennsylvania, warn us that we need to be cautious when evaluating the validity and efficacy of this treatment (Herbert, Lilienfeld, Lohr, Montgomery, O'Donohue, 2000). It seems that the majority of research articles suggesting that EMDR is successful consists of vivid case studies or studies lacking the appropriate control groups. In fact, Herbert provides convincing evidence to suggest that this treatment is built on pseudoscientific techniques. Such techniques may prove helpful, but critical therapists are encouraged to wait for empirical evidence of efficacy before incorporating EMDR into their treatment regime for trauma-related anxieties.

eye movement desensitization reprocessing (EMDR)
Type of therapy introduced for the treatment of PTSD; consists of having the patient follow the therapist's finger back and forth for about 20-second intervals to produce a rapid and rhythmic pattern of eye movements, while thinking about the negative aspects of the trauma experience associated with the PTSD.

Summary ▬

Revisiting the Stress Response

There are generally two stress responses: (1) the sympathetic fight-or-flight response originally described by Cannon (see Chapter Five) and (2) the hypothalamic-pituitary-adrenal axis response described by Selye. Both systems are designed to help the body mobilize adequate resources to be able to defend itself in an acute stress response. When a stress response enters the chronic phase, the body and brain face numerous health risks.

Although Type A personality traits were originally associated with chronic stress-induced cardiovascular disease, research has identified hostility as a more powerful personality predictor for cardiovascular risk. Another health risk associated with chronic stress is gastric ulceration. A type of bacteria, *Helicobacter pylori,* has a causal role in the creation of ulcers; however, chronic stress exacerbates ulceration.

The glucocorticoids released by the adrenal glands in HPA axis activation interact with the brain's stress circuit, namely the hippocampus. Researchers have found that neuronal restructuring following chronic stress leads to a reduced hippocampal volume. Further, as the brain has evolved, the frontal cortex probably works with the hippocampus to interpret the context of a challenging event so that the most adaptive response will be produced.

Stress Responsivity over the Lifespan

A plethora of research indicates that an animal's experiences early in life have a significant impact on the development of the stress response. For example, Meaney's work suggests that maternal interactions result in a more efficient stress response, whereas, maternal neglect, as seen in Harlow's monkeys, leads to increased anxiety when the infants mature.

As an individual ages, the brain becomes less sensitive to circulating glucocorticoid levels and becomes vulnerable to hippocampal damage and cognitive impairment. Thus, effective coping strategies throughout a lifetime enhance hippocampal and cognitive function in old age. Although both sexes experience stress, there may be subtle differences in their responses. For example, males may be more susceptible to ulceration and females to stress-related mental illness following chronic stress.

Coping with Stress

A sense of control is important when responding to stress. Research with animals suggests that having control or even the perception of control over a stressor is significantly better than having no perception of control over the stimulus.

During affiliative social contact, oxytocin is released and likely results in an "antistress" effect of lowering blood pressure. Lactating women report less stress, and anesthetized rats that received massages demonstrated lower blood pressure. Oxytocin plays a role in the establishment and maintenance of pair bonds in the prairie vole (a rodent with very high circulating levels of glucocorticoids). Agonistic social contact, on the other hand, can be one of nature's most potent stressors.

Generally, animals that respond to stress with more active styles have lower levels of glucocorticoids and stress-related illness. Also repetitive movement is associated with increased activity of the serotonergic neurons in the raphe nucleus. Any coping response that reduces allostatic load, the wear and tear on the body, is an effective strategy.

Post-Traumatic Stress Disorder

PTSD, characterized by a persistent stress response that extends well beyond the duration of the actual stressor, sometimes develops in people who have experienced severe stress or trauma. Although a normal response initially, recurring memories and dreams make it difficult to function normally. Lower than normal levels of cortisol are typically found in PTSD patients. Antidepressants are sometimes used for treatment along with behavioral and cognitive therapies. Eye movement desensitization reprocessing is an interesting therapy but lacks empirical support for the successful treatment of PTSD.

Key Terms

general adaptation syndrome (p. 394)

ecological relevance (p. 396)

species-specific stressor (p. 396)

atherosclerosis (p. 397)

peptic ulcers (p. 398)

excitotoxicity (p. 402)

decatastrophizing (p. 412)

affiliative social contact (p. 412)

paraventricular nuclei (p. 412)

supraoptic nuclei (p. 412)

social defeat paradigm (p. 417)

coping style (p. 420)

allostasis (p. 422)

allostatic load (p. 422)

post-traumatic stress disorder (PTSD) (p. 422)

exposure therapy (p. 428)

eye movement desensitization reprocessing (EMDR) (p. 428)

For Further Consideration

Koolhaas, J. M., Kortec, S. M., DeBoer, S. F., Van Der Vegt, B. J., Van Reenen, V., Hopster, H., et al. (1999). Coping styles in animals: Current status in behavior and stress physiology. *Neuroscience and Biobehavioral Reviews, 23,* 925–935. This article is a comprehensive review of behavioral and physiological responses to stressors across a wide array of species. The authors consider the validity of assuming two coping styles in animals: proactive and reactive strategies. These coping strategies are observed in both laboratory and farm animals and have predictive potential for the identification of disease susceptibility.

McEwen, B. (with Elizabeth Norton Lasley) (2002). *The end of stress as we know it.* Washington, DC: Joseph Henry Press. In this book, Bruce McEwen suggests that we need to modify our perceptions of the stress response. Specifically, he suggests that stress is not always the uncontrollable villain in life; in fact, we can do a lot to decrease the negative effect of stress on our bodies. After covering the fundamentals of the stress response, McEwen highlights strategies to minimize allostatic load in chapters entitled "How Not to Be Stressed Out," "Positive Health," and "Where We Could Go from Here." This is an interesting, informative review of stress research.

Sapolsky, R. M. (1998). *Why zebras don't get ulcers: An updated guide to stress, stress-related diseases, and coping.* New York: Freeman. This book is a "must read" for anyone interested in the stress response. Sapolsky's expertise as a leading neuroscientist assures an informed coverage of the most influential studies in the stress literature. In addition to his expertise and knowledge, Sapolsky uses the perfect blend of wit, historical cases, personal insight, popular culture, and human interest stories to make this book read more like a novel than a scientific book. Topics such as the fundamentals of the stress response, stress-related diseases, stress and memory, stress and depression, and managing stress are among the many covered in the book.

Schulkin, J. (2003). *Rethinking homeostasis: Allostatic regulation in physiology and pathology.* Cambridge, MA: MIT Press. For those of you who enjoy musing over theories, this book reviews basic theoretical approaches proposed to explain an individual's response to a threat. The accuracy of viewing homeostasis as a representative characterization of our physiological responses is questioned as the value of allostasis is considered a more accurate description of effective responding. In the context of allostasis, Schulkin focuses on the general notion of motivation considering that motive states such as cravings are engaged to maintain energy demands of the body.

[Chapter Twelve]
Psychoneuroimmunology

Connections

Species, Scents, and Sex

In the mostly forgettable science fiction movie *Species II,* a hybrid "human" female is created from DNA obtained from a mission to Mars. This high-priority science project, named Eve, grows up in a tightly guarded laboratory. Once she reaches sexual maturity, Eve, a tall, beautiful young woman, is isolated from males and any presence of testosterone in order to suppress her sexual motivation. Of course, this gender isolation can last only so long. Later, a second American mission to Mars results in an astronaut's being infected with Mars DNA which retroactively changes his genetic constitution (while apparently keeping his human form and personality intact).

In the film, evolution on Mars follows the same general principles as evolution on Earth (with reproductive fitness the priority); the astronaut's altered DNA drives him to seek out human females to impregnate them with the Mars DNA. Eventually, Eve is exposed to the male space traveler with the mutated Mars DNA (similar to her own) and her sex drive develops to such intense levels that it becomes very difficult to restrain her in the laboratory.

Her enhanced sex drive, however, is very selective. When another male astronaut approaches Eve's living enclosure, she moves toward the glass wall with interest and then walks away, suggesting that she has no sexual interest in this male. At that point, the scientist in the film remarks that, since this African-American man is a carrier for sickle cell anemia, Eve's DNA could not cope because it has no defense against our diseases. Consequently, because of genetic incompatibility, she had no desire to have sex with this man.

The notion that our genetic composition influences our romantic inclinations is an intriguing idea for a science fiction movie, but obviously it has no influence on our romantic preferences in real life. After all, genetic profiles are not the topics of conversation in singles bars or Internet chat rooms. Sabra Klein, a researcher in the Department of Molecular Microbiology and Immunology at the Johns Hopkins School of Public Health, is conducting research that is providing empirical evidence that certain immunological characteristics can indeed be sexy to certain animals.

Sabra Klein COURTESY OF DR. SABRA KLEIN

Klein's research supports the notion that the secondary sex characteristics that we find so visually appealing (for example, enlarged biceps in males and breasts in females) may be important because they advertise our immunocompetence. Both secondary sex characteristics and immune functioning are intimately related to sex hormones. Conducting research with a little rodent known as a meadow vole, Klein has found that when given the choice between bedding with the odor of males infected with the *Trichinella spiralis* parasite or uninfected males, females prefer the scent of uninfected, or healthier, males. Additionally, when male prairie voles (which are monogamous) contract a bacterial infection, the females spend less time with them than with their noninfected counterparts. Klein's ongoing research investigating how different aspects of the immune system influence mating strategies suggests that our

immune system's ability to resist disease, probably detected through olfaction or secondary sex characteristics, is a powerful factor in the romantic lives of rodents (Klein, Gamble, & Nelson, 1999; Swonguer, Lambert, & Klein, 2003).

Rodents have extremely sensitive olfactory systems, so it is easy to understand how olfaction may play a role in their sexual attractions, but is there a connection between immune functioning and romance in humans? Could body odor possibly override dancing eyes, warm personality, or sense of humor? As mentioned previously, it is possible that physical and even behavioral characteristics in humans are related to immunocompetence and thus attraction; research also suggests that humans, like other animals, do not ignore the power of odor.

As you will discover in this chapter, humans produce chemicals with associated odors, and research suggests that when given an opportunity to sniff out smelly T-shirts, subjects prefer the T-shirts of individuals with a more diverse genetic profile to T-shirts of people with more similar genetic profiles. This reproductive choice makes adaptive sense when you consider that more diverse immunological abilities, serving as a form of insurance policy for resisting certain diseases, translate into enhanced survival in the offspring. Thus, exciting new discoveries in the field of psychoneuroimmunology are informing us that the immune system certainly influences both what we do and with whom we do it!

The emerging field of **psychoneuroimmunology (PNI)** explores the relationships among the brain, behavior, and the immune system. Although formally introduced as a field of scientific inquiry in the early 1980s, the notion that emotions influence health has been around for thousands of years.

psychoneuroimmunology (PNI) Exploration of the relationships among the brain, behavior, and the immune system.

To the ancient Greeks, the god of healing, Asclepius, along with his daughters, Hygeia and Panacea, symbolized the importance of maintaining the proper balance of healthy diet, pure waters, social support, and exercise. The ancient Greeks also thought that one's emotions were critical to one's health; they advocated soothing emotions by music, sleep, and prayer. The idea that the mind was an important factor in the healing of the body was so revered that the image of Asclepius carrying a wooden staff (representing the body) with a serpent wrapped around it (representing the mind) became an established symbol of the relationship between the mind and the body. In fact, today this image, the caduceus, is the universal symbol for medicine (Sternberg, 2000).

Considering these early thoughts about the intimate relationship between body and mind, it is curious that Western medicine has focused primarily on the physiological causes and cures for diseases instead of how psychological processes may play a role in making an individual more or less susceptible to disease. In fact, the notion that a relationship exists between psyche and body has been more often seen in cartoons and jokes (for example, the cartoon depicting a tombstone that reads, "See, it wasn't psychosomatic") than in medical textbooks. We are moving toward an era, however, in which health professionals can no longer deny that the ancient Greeks were on to a meaningful theory.

It has taken a few millennia, but the notion that psychological processes such as emotions influence both the brain and the immune system is being acknowledged by formal health-related disciplines once again. In fact, ancient Asian healing practices (meditation, yoga, and tai chi, for example) are now being subjected to Western-style clinical tests to establish medical validity. Comparing the efficacy of Asian healing traditions, however, with the efficacy of traditional Western medicine is no small methodological feat. The Asian emphasis on emotional, cognitive, spiritual, and cultural influences presents a challenge to researchers as they attempt to establish clinical efficacy over the placebo response, which also draws from cognitive and emotional factors (Fabrega, 2002).

After reading this chapter, you'll begin to understand how the three areas of PNI—psychological, neural, and immune factors—can work together to maintain health. Basic knowledge about how the immune system operates is critical for understanding how it interacts with the nervous system, so we describe immune functioning first. Next we review neuroanatomical and neurochemical evidence that supports a relationship between the nervous system and immune functioning. The last section of this chapter considers research on how psychophysiological processes such as stress and sense of control influence immune functioning.

FUNDAMENTALS OF THE IMMUNE SYSTEM: THE BODY'S FEDERAL BUREAU OF INVESTIGATION

Just as the primary goal of the FBI is to protect the citizenry against any form of criminal enterprise or threat, the goal of the immune system is to protect the body against any threat to its homeostatic balance.

The Body's Most-Wanted Invaders

When an individual poses a threat to public safety, a picture of the person is distributed across the country—especially in post offices—so that he or she will be recognized when encountered. In fact, the FBI regularly publishes the ten most-wanted fugitives list. The body also has a most wanted list. The putative criminals of the body are infectious agents known as **pathogens** that have the ability to replicate in host cells to cause tissue damage and disease. Humans' most wanted pathogen list includes four groups: *viruses, bacteria, fungi,* and *parasites.* The monumental task assigned to the immune system is to protect against these invaders (Westermann & Exton, 1999).

The best protection against pathogens is offered by the physical barriers of the body. Just as countries have immigration checks to make sure that undesirables do not cross their boundaries, our bodies are covered with skin—two square meters of borders. This physical barrier keeps the majority of potential invaders from entering our bodies. More resourceful invaders, however, seek out alternative entry points into the body, such as our respiratory, digestive, or reproductive tract.

The pathogens that enter these tracts are not home free; they encounter a mucosal lining similar in texture to syrup in which the motility, or movement, of the pathogens is compromised (Jacobs & Schmidt, 1999). The total area covered by the mucosa-lined tracts in our bodies measures on average 400 square meters (Sompayrac, 1999). In case the physical barriers of the skin and mucosal tracts are not sufficient to ward off invaders, a host of specialized cells is stationed in and around these areas to make sure the pathogens are terminated before causing damage.

Innate Immunity: The Immune System's Front-Line Defense

If a pathogen breaches the physical barriers of the skin or mucosa, it has yet more defenders awaiting it—the cells of the **innate immune system.** These cells take immediate action at the first sign of an invasion, but although powerful and effective, they are typically one-trick ponies: they respond similarly to all pathogens.

pathogen Microorganism (a virus or bacterium) that can cause disease.

innate immune system Components of the immune system, such as skin, phagocytic cells (e.g., macrophages), NK cells, the complement system, and cytokines that exist prior to an invasion by a pathogen; also known as the *front-line defense.*

[Figure 12.1]
Macrophage attack.
This macrophage has detected
the presence of a pathogen via
chemical signals and is engulfing
the foreign substance. The
macrophage will wrap the captured bacterium in a pouch, or
vesicle, and then escort the vesicle into its intracellular compartment, where the vesicle will
meet with destructive chemicals,
leading to its demise. This
process is known as phagocytosis. MICROWORKS/PHOTOTAKE.

phagocytes Cells, such as
macrophages, that protect the
body from invaders by engulfing them.

macrophage Phagocytotic cell
of the immune system that is
activated by chemicals
released from foreign microorganisms and T-cell
cytokines. In addition to
engulfing microorganisms,
they may secrete proinflammatory cytokines and serve as
antigen-presenting cells.

lysosome Package of special
chemicals found inside phagocytotic cells that degrade proteins; these organelles also
play a role in the MHC II molecule pathway.

A prominent early-response cell is the **phagocyte** ("eating
cell") that can ingest foreign material that invades the body.
If a pathogen manages to sneak past the physical barriers of
the skin or mucosal tracts, it is likely to encounter a type of
phagocyte known as a **macrophage,** or "big eater." Suppose
you get a splinter in your finger; the splinter serves as a
transportation system for a host of bacteria to enter your
body. Once the bacteria have entered the system, the
macrophages are able to detect foreign chemical messages
emitted by the invading pathogen. As seen in Figure 12.1,
once the macrophages are activated by the chemicals, they
start reaching out to capture the bacteria. Upon contact, the
macrophage then moves in for the kill. It engulfs a bacterium so that it
can expose the pathogen to internal **lysosomes,** specialized organelles
containing chemical weapons (enzymes) that inactivate and destroy the
bacterium by degrading its constituent proteins.

As the macrophage voraciously consumes the bacterium, it periodically "burps" some of the pathogen, or its remnants, back into the tissue;
these poor table manners are actually beneficial because the bacterial
debris alerts other immune cells to a potential battle. Also, as the
macrophage is battling the bacterium, it releases a protein messenger, or
cytokine, to other cells so that other components of the system are abreast
of its activities. Once the invader has been neutralized, the macrophage
goes back to its other favorite activity, being a garbage collector—that is,
consuming everything it encounters (Sompayrac, 1999).

Focusing again on your sore finger, you may wonder why it typically
swells and turns red. As seen in Figure 12.2, you can thank your
macrophages for that effect as well. To confine the invader to the finger,
the macrophages send another chemical to constrict any outgoing blood
vessels, leading to a buildup of blood in the area around the splinter. The
cells in the skin of your finger also constrict and, as they do, some of the
cellular fluid leaks into the tissue around the splinter. This is the cause of
the swelling.

As impressive as the versatile macrophage is, the **neutrophil** may be
the most important phagocyte. About 70% of the white blood cells (also
called *lymphocytes* or *leukocytes*) in circulation are these specialized phagocytes. Lymphocytes are characterized by their dense nucleus and small
amount of cytoplasm relative to other cells.

The body manufactures on average 100 billion neutrophils each day.
The life span of these cells is only a few days, so they have but a short
time to conduct their sentinel activity. Interestingly, the neutrophils die
by committing cellular suicide (also known as apoptosis; see Chapter Six)

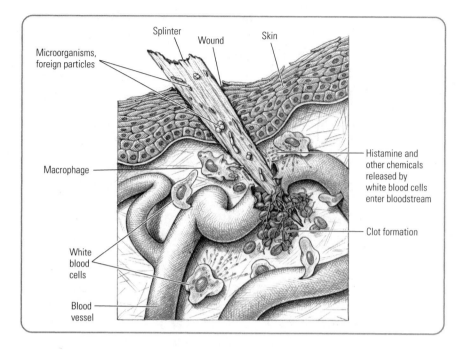

Splinter
Wound
Skin
Microorganisms, foreign particles
Macrophage
Histamine and other chemicals released by white blood cells enter bloodstream
Clot formation
White blood cells
Blood vessel

[Figure 12.2]
The innate immune system in action. The foreign invaders, or microbes, transported into a wound by this splinter activate macrophages to approach and destroy the unwelcome pathogens. The macrophages also emit chemical signals to constrict the blood flow so that pathogens managing to survive the macrophage attacks can't escape to infect other areas of the body.
ADAPTED FROM STRAUB, 2002, P. 106.

after diving into a mound of pus (Sompayrac, 1999). In a military analogy of the immune system, the neutrophils would be World War II kamikazi pilots. They search out a battle with a pathogen and move in, ready to kill. Most neutrophils contain lysosomes that they release at the invasion site (Abbas, Lichtman, & Pober, 2000).

A third type of cell making up the innate immune system is the **natural killer (NK) cell.** NK cells travel through the blood to the site of infection, where they can kill many types of cells, including tumor cells, parasites, fungi, bacteria, and virus-infected cells. What is the killing method these special agents use? One option is to drill a hole in the infected cell by secreting a cocktail of damaging enzymes. This cocktail is known as **perforin,** and when released, it forms a channel to the cell's vulnerable interior chamber. Once the cell interior is exposed, the NK cells deposit enzymes that cause the cell to die. NK cells can also use another weapon: a protein is expressed on the surface of the NK cells when in contact with a protein on the target cell and triggers apoptosis—programmed cellular death—in the unwelcome cells (Sompayrac, 1999).

A fourth component of the innate immune system is the cytokines, low-molecular-weight proteins that regulate immune functions and facilitate communication among the various cells of the immune system. Cytokines are manufactured as they are needed and stored in granules in the various innate immune cells (Jacobs & Schmidt, 1999). Cytokines are

neutrophil Most abundant white blood cell circulating in the blood; these cells are recruited to inflammation sites where they utilize either phagocytosis or enzymatic digestion of pathogens.

natural killer (NK) cells Cells in bone marrow that are a component of the innate immune system. On recognizing a microbe, these cells move in for the kill, using techniques such as secreting toxic substances and creating fatal damage to the invading cell.

perforin Protein used as a weapon by killer T cells and NK cells that drills a hole in the infected cells so that other enzymes can continue the destruction of the cells.

cytokine "Messenger" protein secreted by many cells that regulate immune functions and mediate communication among the cells of the immune system; also called immunotransmitters or interleukins.

complement complex Group of nonimmune proteins that combines to form an important part of the immune system, which can damage threatening cells by quick responses such as cutting holes in the pathogen cells.

acquired immune system B cells and T cells that following exposure to infectious pathogens are stimulated to develop a selective immunity that results in a faster response should the same type of pathogen invade the body again; also known as *adaptive immunity*.

vaccination Preparation of a specific antigen that is administered to an individual to stimulate the acquired immune system to protect against actual, natural exposure to the antigen, should it occur.

B cells or B lymphocytes Cells that originate in the bone marrow and migrate to lymphoid tissue, bone marrow, and in low numbers, the blood. These are the only immune cells with the capability of producing antibodies.

bone marrow Located in the center of the bone; serves as the site of the generation of all blood cells (e.g., lymphocytes and B cells).

antibodies or immunoglobulins (Ig) Glycoprotein molecules produced by B lymphocytes that bind to specific antigens. The four types are IgA, IgE, IgG, and IgM.

antigen Molecule that binds specifically to either an antibody or a T-cell receptor.

sometimes referred to as immunotransmitters or *interleukins* (literally, between white blood cells).

In an emergency situation, the immune system relies on a group of nonimmune proteins in the blood and other organs known as the **complement complex** that can combine to damage threatening pathogens by literally boring holes in them. Similar to situations in which the FBI needs to rely on the local police because the latter can respond quickly to a crisis, a distinguishing characteristic of the complement component of the innate system is the speed at which it can respond to an intruder (Sompayrac, 1999).

Acquired Immunity: Cells That Plan for the Future

Although the innate immune system is powerful, it cannot successfully protect us from infectious pathogens such as viruses because these responses do not enable us to develop resistance. Therefore, in addition to the body's physical barriers and innate immunity, a third line of defense, the **acquired immune system,** evolved to provide further protection against these formidable invaders. The adaptive capabilities of this system were identified in the eighteenth century when Edward Jenner discovered that he could condition what would later be called the immune system to build defenses against deadly viruses.

Jenner made this discovery in 1790 when he was trying to develop a way to protect people against the deadly smallpox virus. Hundreds of thousands of people died from this disease; if they did not die, they were often horribly disfigured from the skin lesions produced by the virus. Jenner noticed that milkmaids often developed a few minor skin lesions due to a related virus, cowpox. Interestingly, the milkmaids who contracted the cowpox virus never seemed to develop smallpox. It was as if the cowpox protected the women from contracting the deadly smallpox.

This observation of the milkmaids gave Jenner an idea for an experiment. What would happen if you collected pus (dead neutrophils and virus) from cowpox lesions in the milkmaids and injected it into a person? Would that person be protected against subsequent exposure to smallpox?

Jenner injected the cowpox pus into a little boy named Phipps and then injected him with smallpox pus—not an experiment that would pass an institutional review board today. Amazingly, Phipps did not contract smallpox—he had developed immunity. Today we would say that Phipps was vaccinated against smallpox. The word **vaccination** is derived from the Latin word *vacca*, which means "cow" (as in cowpox). Phipps, however, was able to contract measles and mumps, indicating that his acquired immunity was specific (Sompayrac, 1999).

Phipps's immune system had acquired a memory of the smallpox virus and therefore was prepared to respond immediately on a subsequent exposure to the virus. How can the immune system accomplish such an amazing feat? It depends on the actions of two specialized lymphocytes that serve as "special agents" for the acquired immune system: B cells and T cells.

Antibodies and B cells. B cells originate from undifferentiated stem cells in the **bone marrow,** located in the center of bones, where all blood cells are generated. While still in the bone marrow, young B cells acquire gene segments that enable them to develop specialized weapons against pathogens called antibodies. **Antibodies,** or **immunoglobulins (Ig),** are small proteins that circulate in the blood following the invasion of a foreign substance and systematically search for specific pathogens to destroy.

Once mature, B cells become antibody factories. Although each individual B cell produces only one kind of Ig, the total collection of B cells produces enough different types of antibodies to be able to recognize virtually any organic molecule that crosses its path. And how many potential invasive molecules do the B cells need to be ready to encounter? Immunologists estimate about 100 million. This diversity is a product of an elaborate DNA-shuffling scheme that goes on as the young B cells are developing.

In general, the Igs formed by the B cells have a prototypical Y shape formed by two pairs of different proteins, a heavy chain on the inside and a light chain on the outside (Figure 12.3). This is a very effective structure designed for grabbing an **antigen** (a molecule that activates an antibody) with either "arm" and binding to another immune cell with its "feet." In fact, the feet, or the receptor-binding region of the antibody, determines the type of cell it binds to and the class category of the antibody.

A good security system such as the FBI needs weapons specially designed for various threats. For example, the FBI trains agents specifically for chemical, terrorist, computer, and espionage threats to our security. The immune system has a comparable strategy in that it evolved at least four classes of antibodies produced by the B cells. Each Ig class has a unique structure making it well-suited to target certain antigens. See Table 12.1, on page 440, for a description of classes of antibodies.

T cells. A second type of lymphocyte contributing to the acquired immune system is the **T cell** or **T lymphocyte.** T cells originate in the bone marrow but mature in the **thymus,** an organ of the immune system located near the heart; hence the name T cell. T cells develop receptors

T cells or T lymphocytes
Mature in the thymus, travel in the blood, and populate secondary lymphoid tissue; make up cell-mediated immunity and function by exposing receptors that recognize foreign particles.

thymus Immune system organ (containing epithelial cells, dendritic cells, macrophages, and precursor cells) that becomes maturation site of T lymphocytes from bone marrow-derived precursor cells.

[Figure 12.3]
The immunoglobulin G (IgG) antibody. This Y-shaped antibody molecule consists of two different proteins—a heavy chain and a light chain. The antibody is multifunctional: it can bind to antigens with its two "hands," found in the antigen-binding regions, and bind to various receptors on cells with its "feet" region. IgG antibodies make up approximately 75% of the blood's antibodies. The binding region of the antibody determines the type of cell it binds to and the class category of the antibody.
ADAPTED FROM SOMPAYRAC, 1999

[Table 12.1]

Classes of Antibodies

Antibody class	Description
IgA	Secreted in milk; helps build resistance to stomach acid; protects the body's mucosal lining
IgE	An organism's protection against parasites; involved in allergies
IgG	Involved in blood's complement system; facilitates the ability of NK cells to kill; known to cross the placenta
IgM	Involved in blood's complement complex; first antibody produced in the body

helper T cells Type of T lymphocyte that activates macrophages and stimulate the release of antibodies from B lymphocytes.

killer T cell (also known as *cytotoxic T cell*) T cell that recognizes and kills virus-infected host cells; utilizes the protein perforin, which enables them to drill holes in cells, leaving them to die.

antigen-presenting cell (APC) Cell that displays fragments of protein antigens, along with MHC molecules, on its surface in order to activate T cells.

dendritic cells Serve as antigen-presenting cells for naïve T cells; important for acquired immunity. Originate in the bone marrow but eventually end up in the skin and lymphoid tissue.

lymph nodes Small nodules made up of lymphocyte-rich tissue found along the lymphatic channels in the body. Location of the origin of acquired immune functioning.

(*T-cell receptors,* or *TCRs*) that can recognize a foreign protein, or antigen, whereas B cells recognize any organic molecules such as peptides, lipids, and polysaccharides. TCRs are diverse, like the antibodies produced by the B cells, but whereas the B-cell receptors detach from the B cells and form antibodies, TCRs are permanent fixtures of T cells.

When an antigen is recognized by a TCR, a cloning process begins in which the T cell proliferates to respond to a particular antigen. This, however, takes a bit of time—the B-cell antibody response is relatively fast and the T-cell response is slower. Whereas the antibody response is analogous to purchasing more specialized weapons for existing special agents, the T-cell response is equivalent to recruiting and hiring additional special agents to capture a particular fugitive.

Although there may be more, two types of T cells have received a lot of attention. **Helper T cells** are "helpful" because they produce cytokines and help B cells produce antibodies; **killer T cells** kill pathogens. On being exposed to an antigen, the T cells send, via cytokines, communications (perhaps comparable with e-mail mass mailings) to all appropriate cells in the organs of the immune system.

Whereas the antibodies of the B cells recognize a pathogen on their own, helper T cells require a proper chemical introduction by another immune cell, an **antigen-presenting cell (APC).** Macrophages, for example, serve as APCs. The macrophages eat the antigen, and after accompanying signals from certain "battle" cytokines, they "burp" up certain amounts of the specific antigen (as described earlier) so that it is presented on the surface of the macrophage. Once the antigen has made its way to the surface, the macrophage can present the antigen to the helper T cell, with the appropriate exchange of chemical signals. Sending a message to commit significant energy into cloning a type of T cell is serious, so the macrophages also present a second type of protein on the surface, which has to be matched in addition to the antigen-receptor match. This security system helps protect against faulty activation of the helper T-cell response.

Another APC is the **dendritic cell,** akin to an FBI undercover agent because it resides on the front lines of the immune system, such as the skin, acting like a typical phagocyte, consuming large amounts of extracellular fluids in order to monitor any intruders in the area. Along with lymphocytes, dendritic cells make up a network of **lymph nodes** through the body. Fluid derived from blood plasma, also known as lymph, flows through these filtering "field stations." Figure 12.4 shows the locations of the lymph nodes as well as other immune structures in the body.

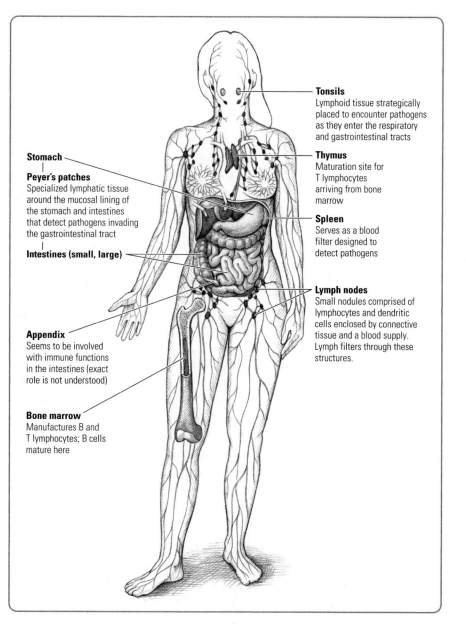

Tonsils
Lymphoid tissue strategically placed to encounter pathogens as they enter the respiratory and gastrointestinal tracts

Thymus
Maturation site for T lymphocytes arriving from bone marrow

Spleen
Serves as a blood filter designed to detect pathogens

Lymph nodes
Small nodules comprised of lymphocytes and dendritic cells enclosed by connective tissue and a blood supply. Lymph filters through these structures.

Stomach

Peyer's patches
Specialized lymphatic tissue around the mucosal lining of the stomach and intestines that detect pathogens invading the gastrointestinal tract

Intestines (small, large)

Appendix
Seems to be involved with immune functions in the intestines (exact role is not understood)

Bone marrow
Manufactures B and T lymphocytes; B cells mature here

[Figure 12.4]
Components of the immune system.
ADAPTED FROM STRAUB, 2002, P. 104

When an invader ends up inside the body, the dendritic cell leaves its field assignment and travels to a nearby lymph node to "deliver the goods," acting as an antigen-presenting cell to virgin T cells (Figure 12.5, on page 442). Thereafter the T cells will be activated to respond to this particular antigen (Rabin, 1999; Schedlowski & Tewes, 1999; Sompayrac, 1999; Westermann & Exton, 1999).

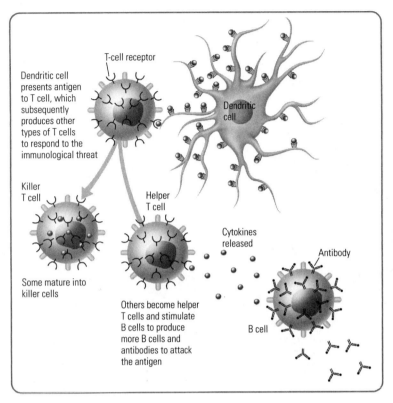

T-cell receptor

Dendritic cell presents antigen to T cell, which subsequently produces other types of T cells to respond to the immunological threat

Dendritic cell

Killer T cell

Helper T cell

Cytokines released

Antibody

Some mature into killer cells

Others become helper T cells and stimulate B cells to produce more B cells and antibodies to attack the antigen

B cell

[Figure 12.5]
Covert operations of the dendritic cells. Disguised as run-of-the-mill phagocytes, dendritic cells reside on the front lines of the immune system, monitoring intruding antigens and traveling to the lymph nodes to present the intruder to T cells that will mount an attack against the specific antigen.

ADAPTED FROM WEISSMAN & COOPER, 1993, P. 23

humoral immune system
Primarily antibodies released by B lymphocytes.

Although the antibodies produced by B cells are quite successful at identifying pathogens outside the cell, how would the body's acquired immune system defend itself against a virus that has penetrated the genetic code embedded in cells and is busy making copies of itself? Killer T cells, or *cytotoxic lymphocytes,* are designed to handle just this type of threat to the body's homeostasis. Playing a similar role as the innate immune system's NK cells, after receiving the appropriate cytokine message, the killer T cells are primed to start manufacturing the protein perforin.

As discussed previously, perforin is like an assassin's weapon in an immunological James Bond thriller that enables killer T cells to drill a hole in and kill the virus-infected cells. Just like any well-trained secret agent, the killer T cells have other means of destruction. They may pass off a package of enzymes to the target cell. After the target cell accepts the pouch of enzymes, it is escorted inside the cell via carrier proteins on the cell's surface. Once inside, the enzymes trigger apoptosis in the infected cell. Subsequently, the potentially damaging chemicals are stored in pouches that are systematically consumed by macrophages.

Contrasting acquired immune defense strategies. To summarize, consider the differences we have discussed between the acquired immune defense's B cells and T cells. Both types originate in the bone marrow, but B cells mature there while T cells migrate to the thymus to mature and differentiate.

B cells act as first responders to virtually any potentially threatening molecules. Once their receptors identify a pathogen, B cells become antibody factories. These antibodies are released into the bloodstream, where, like "smart" missiles, they search out specific pathogens. Because antibodies exist in the blood, the B-cell defense is known as the **humoral immune system** (*humoral* refers to the body's fluids, such as blood).

T cells take a little longer to respond to a particular antigen. They mature following programmed sets of activities designed to build effective defenses against pathogens inside as well as outside cells. Once the antigen is presented to immature T cells, the cells start cloning either helper T cells that release cytokines to stimulate the intracellular action of B cells or killer T cells that can recognize and destroy pathogens that have hijacked genetic material inside the cell to reproduce themselves (see Figure 12.5). Killer T cells operate by drilling holes in the affected cells, leaving them to die. Because killer T cells actually destroy other cells, this defense is known as the **cellular immune system** (Jacobs and Schmidt, 1999; Sompayrac, 1999).

Major Histocompatibility Complex (MHC) and Information Dissemination

For any security organization to be effective, it must be keenly aware of what is happening both inside and outside. Like the FBI, the immune system disseminates vital information about its ongoing activities and known invaders in the body. We can think of the cytokines as the body's immunochemical communications system. Another information system, the **major histocompatibility complex (MHC)**, works by displaying two groups of glycoproteins on the surface of cells. **MHC I molecules** advertise what is going on inside the cell, and **MHC II molecules** advertise what is going on outside the cell. Here's how the MHC works.

MHC I molecules serve as a kind of billboard system for displaying fragments of all the proteins being manufactured by the cell. If the cell has been invaded by a virus and is producing proteins encoded by the virus, this activity will also be displayed on the surface of the cell. Class I MHC molecules are found on virtually every cell in the body and help the immune system distinguish between its own material and something foreign. Killer T cells travel around to monitor the MHC I signals to determine whether a virus has invaded the cell's protein factories and to destroy any infected cells.

MHC II molecules are produced only by cells of the immune system because their purpose is to monitor the activity of the various immune cells and broadcast the information so that helper T cells can be recruited if danger is in the vicinity. Consequently, you need only enough cells expressing MHC II molecules to sample the environment outside the cell.

As stated in this chapter's opening Connections, the MHC may play a role in mate selection in some animals. For example, it is in the best interest of the animal to find a mate with MHC genes that are somewhat variable from its own complex to offer the offspring more diverse protection

cellular immune system Component of adaptive immunity composed of T cells that defend the body by either activating B-cell release or proliferating so that the T cells themselves can attack the antigen.

major histocompatibility complex (MHC) In humans, a genetic locus on chromosome 6 that encodes the peptides recognized by T lymphocytes; additionally, this genetic code influences cytokines and antigen proteins.

MHC I molecule MHC glycoproteins found on all cells of the body that display information related to the invasion of the cells by viruses.

MHC II molecule MHC glycoprotein produced in the immune cells; shares information only with the immune cells.

against pathogens. Variability and diversity are key characteristics of the MHC system; mice have up to 100 different alleles (or versions) at each locus, which contributes to an extreme level of heterozygosity, or genetic diversity, in MHC genes.

Claus Wedekind at the University of Edinburgh has conducted fascinating research on the role of MHC in human mating preferences. In addition to finding that humans can detect MHC variability through olfaction, Wedekind shows how such a mechanism can inhibit inbreeding (Wedekind & Penn, 2000). For example, he reports that a study of married couples in a reproductively isolated community of Austrian-German ancestry (the American Hutterites) suggested that the married couples had a more diverse MHC genetic profile than individuals chosen by chance.

If our MHC influences our attraction to our mates and even the immunological fitness of our offspring, then some of our more recent cultural behavior seems to go against the use of this selection system. For example, it has been reported that contraceptive pills alter women's olfactory preferences and the cologne and body hygiene industry prides itself on covering up our body odors. With this information it is easy to speculate about the tentative nature of human marriages. Perhaps this masking of important genetic information contributes to the high divorce rate—once women stop taking their contraceptive pills and spouses stop being so vigilant about using nice-smelling products, it may become apparent that the formerly attractive odor of an individual is now unpleasant—for MHC reasons.

Humans are complex organisms and many factors contribute to mate selection, but olfaction may be one among several significant factors. Further, a lack of MHC variability may contribute to fertility problems among couples; those experiencing problems conceiving a child may share more MHC genes than those who conceive more easily. Perhaps the Eskimos, who rub noses—and consequently engage in mutual sniffing—have a genetic advantage in mate selection over those of us in the Western world who use artificial odors and the nonsniffing version of a kiss (Furlow, 1996).

Finally, MHC has another very important implication. If you are going to receive an organ transplant, you need to find a donor who has very similar MHC I genes so that your immune system will identify the transplant as "self" and not reject it. Researchers experimenting with transplanting tumors in mice quickly saw the results of attaching skin and tumor on an animal with a different MHC I genetic profile. It turns out that killer T cells are just waiting for foreign MHC molecules and quickly attack the cells when they encounter them. The killer cells especially like to attack the blood cells of the foreign tissue; once the blood supply is cut off the tissue usually dies.

Immunologists started working with "inbred" strains of mice so that they would not have to worry about tissue rejection. Today, before patients receive an organ transplant, genetic screening is done to make sure the tissue is compatible and will not be rejected by the donor. Now you understand why this system is known as the major histo*compatibility* complex (Eggert & Ferstl, 1999; Sompayrac, 1999).

When Good Cells Turn Bad

Training of an individual or system is rarely perfect. For instance, despite all the effort that goes into the selection, instruction, and support of FBI agents, sometimes internal or external pressures compromise the functioning of an individual. An agent may be persuaded to work for the "other side," giving in to temptations from members of the criminal element, the very constituency the agent was trained to identify and destroy. Likewise, the immune system may become overactive at seemingly inappropriate times, as seen with allergies and arthritis. It may even contribute to self-destruction by killing healthy body tissue, as is seen in **autoimmune diseases** such as **multiple sclerosis,** in which glial cells making up the myelin sheath of the nerves are destroyed.

Another threat to the smooth functioning of the FBI is an ambitious agent who tries to sabotage the organization because of some personal designs to gain power. In a sense, this agent is analogous to cancer. Although cancer may be triggered by an external event, such as exposure to a particular pollutant or virus, it is in fact part of our own bodies, a genetic code that undergoes a mutation and then starts producing an excessive number of cells. Eventually, if not squelched by the immune system, the cancer cells lead to the body's demise.

For the most part, the etiology of cancer remains a mystery. Aside from understanding that it is the product of genetic mutation, researchers have yet to identify the definitive event that causes cancer. In a creative hypothesis, Michael Ruff and Candice Pert (1984) proposed that lung cancer in cigarette smokers might be due to macrophages that have been recruited in mass numbers to clean up the tar left from the cigarette smoke. The toxins from smoking may lead to a mutation in the macrophages whereby these cells, originally sent to rid the lung of pollutants to maintain its health, are altered by the pollutant and subsequently start growing and destroying the very organ they were originally sent to defend.

autoimmune disease Disease that results when the mechanisms designed to preserve self-recognition in the immune system are compromised so that the adaptive immune system responds to self-antigens in the same manner as it responds to foreign antigens—leading to cellular and tissue damage.

multiple sclerosis Neurodegenerative autoimmune disease in which T cells are thought to destroy the myelin sheath of the neurons. Leads to nausea, vertigo, bladder dysfunction, depression, and memory deficits.

In support of their controversial hypothesis, Ruff and Pert found macrophage antibodies bound to the cancerous lung cells. The observation that macrophages can travel around the body with such ease offered new explanations of the rapid growth of tumors, the lack of rejection of tumor tissue, and the ease with which tumor tissue can metastasize, or spread, to other parts of the body (Pert, 1999). This idea was illustrated in a rather unlikely venue, an animated movie entitled *Osmosis Jones* in which a "killer virus" attempts to recruit existing cells of the host to "take him down." To do this, the deadly virus travels to the armpit and throbbing ingrown toenail to persuade the immune cells to work for the "other side."

A final example of the immune system itself leading to a person's demise can be seen once an individual is infected with HIV (human immunodeficiency virus), which leads to acquired immune deficiency syndrome (AIDS). This virus attacks the individual's most important weapon in the fight against illness—the immune system. In the early, or acute, stage of infection, the immune system brings out the usual defense cells—B cells, helper T cells, and killer T cells. Usually, this reaction is enough to rid the body of the virus. In the case of AIDS, the virus manages to survive the initial immunological attack and enters a chronic phase that can last 10 or more years. After a while, the helper T cells start to diminish, leading to decreased activation of important killer T-cell response. At this point the immune defenses become overwhelmed, leaving the patient in a state of immunosuppression and increased vulnerability to any future immunological challenges.

It probably shouldn't be a surprise that a system as multifaceted and intricate as the immune system can malfunction in response to several different mechanisms. Table 12.2 summarizes the origins and symptoms related to several examples of *immunopathology,* when the immune system itself leads to tissue damage or sickness.

INTEGRATIVE OPERATIONS: IMMUNE AND NERVOUS SYSTEM COMMUNICATION

As powerful and effective as the FBI is on its own, it is important that there is some integration between the FBI and other agencies such as the Central Intelligence Agency (CIA). Working together, these organizations share their expertise, making it less likely that the nation's security will be breeched. It can be argued that the nervous system is the the body's CIA. We now know that the immune system and the nervous system collaborate and communicate in multiple ways.

[Table 12.2]

Examples of Immunopathology: When the Immune System Malfunctions

Disease	Symptoms	Cause
Cancer	Depend on affected organ. Although the disease may begin in a specific organ, it will metastasize if not stopped.	Mutations in normal genes of the body's own cells.
AIDS (acquired immune deficiency syndrome)	Flulike symptoms early and then symptoms associated with particular opportunistic infections that occur much later.	Human immunodeficiency virus (HIV) that leads to the destruction of T cells.
Multiple sclerosis	Multiple neurological deficits involving different components of the nervous system, including brainstem dysfunction leading to nausea and vertigo, bladder dysfunction, depression, and memory deficits.	Usually thought to be a T cell-mediated autoimmune condition; evidence that it is autoimmune is based on rodent models, but it is possible that the cause may be a virus; chronic inflammation destroys the myelin sheath.
Myasthenia gravis	Muscle weakness, fatigue. This disease is life-threatening if respiratory system is involved.	T cells attack postsynaptic nicotinic receptors in the neuromuscular junction, making skeletal muscles unable to contract.
Rheumatoid arthritis	Crippling inflammation of joints, particularly hands, wrists, and knees. The patient has difficulty moving affected joints.	Autoantibodies called rheumatoid factors act against a portion of the normal self-IgG in most but not all cases.

Adapted from Song & Leonard, 2000, and Sompayrac, 1999.

Conditioning the Immune System: A Serendipitous Discovery

In 1974, Robert Ader (Box 12.1) was working on a conditioning study with mice at the University of Rochester. Borrowing from the behavioral techniques introduced by Pavlov (see Chapter One), he was using the drug cyclophosphamide, which nauseates rodents, as the unconditioned stimulus (UCS). Ader presented water sweetened with saccharine and then injected the drug. As is the case with all classical conditioning studies, Ader's mice quickly learned to avoid water that tasted like saccharine.

The interesting observation came when Ader stopped injecting the drug, a known immunosuppressant, but kept the sweet water in the cages: the animals started dying. Why would an animal die when the drug that influenced the immune system was no longer being used? Further, why would the animals that consumed the most saccharine be the first to die?

Ader, an observant psychologist, quickly surmised that in addition to conditioning the mice to avoid the sweet water, he had conditioned their immune systems to become suppressed whenever the animals were exposed to the saccharine water. Thus, the more times an animal came in contact with the water, the more suppressed the immune system became and the less likely it was that the immune system could defend itself from foreign pathogens. Although this observation made perfect sense to Ader,

[Box 12.1]

The Investigators

Robert Ader

When Bob Ader, as an undergraduate student at Tulane University, registered for a course in experimental psychology, he had no idea of the impact the course would have on his education, career, and life. His professor adopted an unorthodox strategy of not using a textbook—declaring simply on the first day of the semester that he was going to teach the students to ask the research questions and then seek the most informed answers. Ader had taken traditional science courses and was underwhelmed by the usual recipe- or cookbook-version laboratories, in which students were told exactly what research problem to address, how to solve it, and what the correct solution should be. The ability to pose his own questions was liberating for Ader, and he was hooked on experimental psychology from that point on, taking every psychology course Tulane offered (personal communication, 2003).

Because of Ader's enthusiasm for psychology and his passion for research, his professors advised him to attend graduate school at Cornell University. His self-confidence took a hit, however, when he failed every one of his psychology placement exams. He continued to put in long hours in the laboratory, still convinced that he wanted a career as a behavioral scientist. By the end of his first year in graduate school, unbeknownst to Ader, one of his professors observed that he had never seen a student who knew so few facts about the discipline yet was such a sophisticated researcher. Despite his rocky start, Ader completed his Ph.D. in 1957 and began his distinguished career at the University of Rochester School of Medicine and Dentistry. An impressive 230 publications later, it is safe to say that his graduate professor was correct in identifying Ader's talent as a behavioral scientist.

his conclusion was not readily accepted in the field of immunology because, at that time, the dogma was that there were no connections between the immune system and the nervous system. After all, an immunologist can observe immune responses in cells in a test tube in the absence of a nervous system. Ader's proposed conditioning of the immune system meant that the nervous system interpreting the presence of the sweet water was somehow communicating with the immune system.

At that point, Ader started collaborating with Nicholas Cohen, an immunologist at the University of Rochester, and using all the proper experimental control groups, they confirmed the immunoconditioning and have been working together ever since (Ader & Cohen, 1975; Moyers, 1993). In 1981, Ader coined the term *psychoneuroimmunology* (PNI) for both a conference and a book.

Although the term *PNI* was introduced only in 1981, a little digging in the literature reveals that observations suggesting possible conditioning of the immune system were made many years prior to Ader's mouse studies. For example, in 1896, Mackenzie published an article describing a case in which an allergic patient would sneeze upon the presentation of an artificial rose. It has also been reported that Russian investigators used Pavlovian conditioning to pair a neutral stimulus with

On beginning his career as an instructor in the Department of Psychiatry, Ader focused his research interests primarily on behavioral conditioning and emotional responsivity—mostly in rodent models. Although the relationship between the brain and the immune system was not recognized to exist, Ader boldly took up the long campaign to convince the research community otherwise. In his 1980 presidential address to the American Psychosomatic Society, Ader introduced the term *psychoneuroimmunology*. A year later, an edited volume entitled simply *Psychoneuroimmunology* was published under Ader's supervision.

Just as psychopharmacologists know that drug effects depend on the physiological state of the subject and neuroendocrinologists know that the effect of hormones depends on their interactions with the nervous system, Ader (2000) argues that "we cannot fully understand immunoregulatory processes without considering the organism and the internal and external milieu in which immune responses take place" (p. 167).

Robert Ader
COURTESY OF DR. ROBERT ADER

The field of PNI, launched by Ader, has made significant progress in defining the nature of this integrative approach.

After almost a half century in the laboratory, Ader's passion for research continues unabated. Currently director of the Division of Behavioral and Psychosocial Medicine in the Department of Psychiatry at the University of Rochester Medical School, he is cautiously optimistic that the data will prevail and health professionals and immunologists will adopt more intergrative views of immune functions. Along these lines, Ader (2000) states that "the clinical implications of psychoneuroimmunology will be better appreciated when we are able to identify and manipulate the interacting variables that govern immunoregulatory processes" (p.174).

injections of foreign proteins, resulting in conditioned antibody production. (Metal'nikov & Chorine, 1926, 1928).

These initial observations were not formally interpreted as examples of cross talk between the immune and nervous systems until the landmark work of Ader and Cohen. Obviously, this formal introduction into the scientific literature prompted researchers to think about some exciting possibilities. If immunosuppression is possible, can one demonstrate immunoenhancement? Is immunoconditioning related to the fascinating phenomenon known as the placebo effect? Could results with mice generalize to humans? Since the initial reports in this field, abundant research has been conducted, but many questions concerning the boundaries and mechanisms of immunoconditioning remain (Ader & Cohen, 1991).

Additional Pieces of the Neuroimmune Puzzle

A serendipitous discovery by David Felten, also at the University of Rochester, provided evidence of a neuroanatomical link between the immune and nervous systems. One day in the 1980s, when observing spleen cells under the microscope, Felten observed nerve fibers. (The

spleen Filtering organ, located in the abdomen, that plays a large role in defending the body against blood-borne antigens.

interleukin-1 (IL-1) Cytokine produced primarily by activated phagocytes that activates B and T cells, influences NK and macrophage activity, and induces fever.

spleen, a filtering organ located in the abdomen and shown in Figure 12.4, plays a large role in defending the body against blood-borne antigens.) Surprised by the finding of nerve tissue in immunological tissue, Felten pursued the discovery. He and his colleagues subsequently found that not only do nerve fibers weave throughout the spleen, they extend to virtually every immune organ—laying the foundation for an extensive communication system (Felten, Ackerman, Wiegand, & Felten, 1987; Moyers, 1993; Sapolsky, Rivier, Yamamoto, Plotsky, & Vale, 1987).

In 1984, a publication by Edwin Blalock, who is currently at the University of Alabama at Birmingham, provided another interesting piece of the nervous system/immune system communication puzzle. His work pointed to the nature of the messages being sent between the nervous and immune systems. Specifically, he reported that when exposed to a viral infection, leukocytes produce endorphins and the stress hormone antecedent adrenocorticotropic hormone (ACTH). This line of research suggested that leukocytes produce numerous neuropeptides and, sealing the partnership between these systems, have receptors for most of the neuroendocrine hormones. Thus, immune tissue can both produce and receive neural messages.

Completing the picture, Robert Sapolsky, currently at Stanford University, demonstrated that the nervous system could also respond to cytokines, specifically **interleukin-1 (IL-1)**, a cytokine produced primarily by activated phagocytes that activates B and T cells, influences NK and macrophage activity, and induces fever (Sapolsky et al., 1987). When Sapolsky injected IL-1 into the veins of rats, a rise in ACTH was found, an increase that he determined was mediated by corticotropin-releasing hormone (CRH) secreted by the hypothalamus. Thus, it appears that the brain has receptors for cytokines of the immune system.

Stress: Mediator Between the Immune and Neural Agencies

As discussed in Chapters Five, Six, and Eleven, stressors prompt an elaborate cascade of physiological events, including immunological responses. In a sense, the stress and immunological responses are the body's key systems for warding off any event or pathogen that may threaten homeostasis. Without realizing it, you are already aware of the interaction between these two systems—when you have a nasty rash that is swollen and painful (evidence that your immune system is actively trying to oust the invading infection), you probably put a cortisone cream on the rash in an attempt to help reduce the swelling. The active ingredient in this cream is the glucocorticoid cortisol, a substance recognized as a principal neurochemical in the stress response. Cortisol treatments are also used for the inflammation associated with arthritis and for certain medical situations such as organ transplants (Rabin, 1999).

Aside from being involved in skin rashes and joint inflammation, do glucocorticoids or other neurochemical components of the stress response play a more central role in immune functioning? Esther Sternberg and Philip Gold (1997), working at the National Institute of Mental Health, have taken a serious look at the relationship between the stress and the immune responses. Starting with neuroanatomy, as seen in Figure 12.6, the hypothalamic neurons that secrete CRH send fibers to the brainstem. Some of these fibers regulate the sympathetic nervous system, which ultimately innervates immunological organs such as the thymus, spleen, and lymph nodes. Other fibers in the brainstem activate the locus coeruleus, a neural circuit discussed in Chapter Five involved in general arousal—including fear and enhanced vigilance.

Recall that the amygdala is a primary brain area involved with fear responses. The amygdala also features CRH-secreting neurons that communicate with the hypothalamus (which also secretes CRH) and the locus coeruleus. And adding even more "relations" to this immuno-neuronal family, the CRH neurons are activated by the immune cells during an immune response.

Sapolsky's finding that the injection of IL-1 results in a rise in stress hormones lends further support to the notion of an immune-CRH relationship. The relationship is beneficial because it enables the immune system to recruit the cortisol response to restrain the immune response a bit—as when you apply cortisol cream to your swollen rash. Additionally, as you will read later in the chapter, HPA activation induces behaviors that assist in helping the individual recover from the illness.

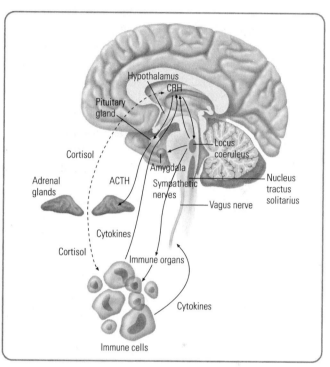

[Figure 12.6]

HPA axis and immune functions. The arrows in this diagram denote interactive pathways between the nervous and immune systems. Cytokines are produced from immune cells and activate the vagus nerve, which in turn activates various parts of the brain. The locus coeruleus in the brainstem activates the hypothalamus, which subsequently initiates the HPA axis, resulting in the release of ACTH. The locus coeruleus also projects to the amygdala, a brain area involved in fear and vigilance responses. Ending this feedback loop, the stress hormone cortisol influences immune and hypothalamic cells. ADAPTED FROM STERNBERG, 2000, P. 89

Sickness Behavior and Its Role in Maintaining Health

The heading above may strike you as oxymoronic, but recall from our discussion of the protection offered from being exposed to small amounts of antigens in vaccinations that being sick can be your insurance to a prolonged life. A little background information will clarify how the immune and nervous systems interact to produce sickness behavior.

Let's start with the "sick response." Have you ever noticed that, regardless of the type of sickness you may have, you experience the same general set of symptoms? It's very likely that the last time you were sick, you felt cold and feverish, you wanted to sleep all day, your joints ached when you tried to walk around, and you lost interest in food and sex. In fact, Benjamin Hart (1988), a veterinarian at the University of California at Davis, has identified over 60 common diseases that result in the same list of symptoms. Regardless of whether the animal has a respiratory or a digestive illness, the symptoms are quite similar.

The body works diligently to produce, not reduce, these behaviors (Sapolsky, 1997). Instead of being the result of an exhausted body in the midst of expending all its energy to fight off pathogens, sickness is more accurately viewed as an organized strategy that is necessary for the survival of the animal (Dantzer, 1999). To understand why the body orchestrates the multifaceted defense of sickness behavior, let's look at each general symptom a little more closely.

Fever. The key response to surviving a pathogen is the *fever*. Fevers, which occur even in primitive organisms, are adaptive because most of the microbial organisms flourish at temperatures comparable with the body temperature of the host (for us, 98.6°F). Once the body temperature is elevated, the pathogens are not able to reproduce and thus become compromised. Additionally, fevers enhance the immunological response to the infection. For example, white blood cells divide more quickly and phogocytes kill more efficiently at higher body temperatures (Maier & Watkins, 1998). Of course, few things come without a cost, and a fever exacts a huge metabolic cost.

For the body to increase its temperature, cytokines signal the hypothalamus to reset the body temperature *set point*, or ideal temperature point for optimal functioning, resulting in an organism that feels cold because its body temperature is below the new optimal temperature. The animal conserves heat by keeping the blood flow in the central part of the body and by seeking warm places to rest. The feverish animal also tries to produce heat by shivering and increasing the metabolic rate.

Although shivering seems like a mild response, it increases the metabolism about fourfold. Recognizing the value of a fever may contradict our usual practice of "treating" a fever with antipyretics, or fever-reducing medications such as acetaminophen. Some studies show that people take longer to get well when taking drugs to reduce their fever as the drugs interfere with the body's well-orchestrated responses (Neese & Williams, 1994).

Now that the role of the fever and its high cost to the body is understood, it is probably becoming apparent why you have a desire to sleep and are not motivated to be active or to engage in social activities when you are sick. These behaviors simply cost too much energy in a time when energy stores are critical for maintaining the fever. Achy joints may provide even more justification for taking it easy.

Loss of appetite. One behavior, anorexia, or decreased eating, does not seem to follow the logic of the other symptoms. At a time when your body has such high metabolic costs, why would you reduce your food intake? Scientists do not have the answer to this question but speculate that increased food intake may increase plasma levels of iron (which is not advantageous for a fever), that a reduced appetite decreases the possibility of the animal expending energy foraging for food, or that a sick and compromised animal out rummaging around in the environment may be extremely vulnerable to predators (Maier & Watkins, 1998).

Role of cytokines. We mentioned that cytokines play a significant role in inducing the sick response. Let's look a little closer at exactly how this happens. A group of Swiss scientists found that IL-1 was the key cytokine in inducing a fever. By injecting particles of bacteria known as *lipopolysaccharides,* or LPSs, into the stomachs of mice, these researchers showed indirectly that brain IL-1 was produced (Fontana, Weber, & Dayer, 1984).

In the fashion of true FBI agents, Steven Maier and Linda Watkins (1998) of the University of Colorado have conducted a detailed analysis of the role of cytokines in behaviors related to sickness. They stress the importance of the vagus nerve (a large cranial nerve that extends into the abdominal cavity) in the cytokine-mediated communication with the brain. If the vagus nerve is cut, the sickness response does not develop.

But how does IL-1 in the periphery stimulate the vagus nerve to activate critical areas in the brain? Maier and Watkins report that the macrophages initially release IL-1 on the presentation of a pathogen, and IL-1 binds to receptors on clusters of neurons known as *paraganglia* around the vagal nerve fibers. The paraganglia release a chemical message that travels back to the brain via the vagus nerve (afferent direction). The message activates the brainstem area known as the nucleus tractus solitarius (NTS), which is situated near the *area postrema*—the area of the brain involved in another sickness behavior that helps to rid your body of unwanted particles—vomiting.

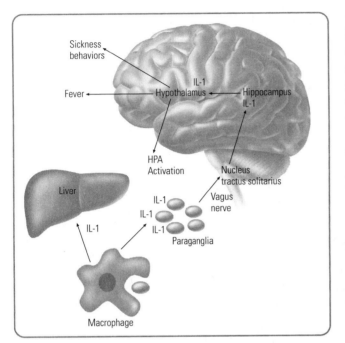

[Figure 12.7]
Inducing a sick response. LPS is consumed by a macrophage, triggering the release of IL-1 that subsequently stimulates the paraganglia of the vagus nerve. The vagus nerve stimulates the liver and the nucleus tractus solitarius which further activates the hippocampus and the hypothalamus, ultimately resulting in HPA axis activation, the production of a fever, and more IL-1 release in the brain.
ADAPTED FROM MAIER & WATKINS, 1998.

The NTS subsequently carries messages to the hypothalamus and hippocampus, triggering the secretion of IL-1 in the brain. Thus, IL-1 produced by the macrophages triggers a cascade of responses that ultimately result in the production of IL-1 in the brain. Figure 12.7 diagrams this process.

The intimate relationship between the two primary defense systems—the stress response and the immune response—helps assure an animal's survival. If a predator is approaching, the stress response helps the animal to escape; if a pathogen approaches, the immune system helps the body survive the invasion. Thinking further about these two protective systems, Maier and Watkins suggest that the fight or flight reaction is a recently evolved stress response that enables an animal to produce enough energy to survive a distal threat such as an approaching predator. The immune response is also a stress response to the pathogen interrupting the homeostatic balance of the body. This response requires only the animal's ability to distinguish self from nonself—even sponges contain phagocytes and can respond to this proximal stress.

PUTTING THE "PSYCH" IN PSYCHONEUROIMMUNOLOGY

How might the interplay between the immune and nervous systems lead to mental illness? Several researchers have pointed out the parallels between sickness behavior and depression. Depressed patients often suffer from hyperinsomnia (or other sleep-related problems), a loss of motivation to eat or engage in sex, and as mentioned in Chapter Eight, depressed patients exhibit a sustained hypersecretion of cortisol. In fact, one may view depression as an organized anxiety state as opposed to an inactive state. Depressed patients are hypervigilant about distal threats such as relationship failures or the inability to maintain a job. It may be that depression is less about a serotonin reduction and more directly influenced by a stress response that is stuck in the "on" position.

Imipramine, a drug known to help with depression symptoms, has been found to decrease CRH and HPA activity in healthy persons. The observation that patients suffering from rheumatoid arthritis, a condition brought on by an overactive immune system, develop depression at a higher rate than normally expected also provides evidence that an overactive stress response system may be involved in depression. Thus, viewing depression as an overactive vigilance system (activated by a more recently evolved component of the acquired immune system) that may be treated from an immunological perspective is drastically different from the perspectives currently used to approach this disorder.

We have spent considerable time discussing the fundamentals of the immune system and how it interacts with the nervous system. But this chapter is entitled "psychoneuroimmunology," not "neuroimmunology." If the *psycho* prefix denotes psychological processes, then how does psychology fit into the PNI domain?

We have already touched on a few psychological connections: sexual motivation and sickness-related behaviors may be influenced by the immune system. But at the heart of the question of the role of psychological processes in PNI is the question of individual differences, a central concern of much psychological inquiry. After you and your sweetheart spend the weekend with a niece who has a cold, why do you contract a cold the next week but your significant other does not? You were both exposed to the same stimuli: shouldn't both of you get sick? Why do you get sick after a grueling finals week and your best friend feels great? How can the immune system act so differently in two members of the same species?

The answers can be found in the variation in environments, social situations, and psychological profiles. As described in Chapter Eleven, when faced with a threatening stimulus, one person may express fear and aggression, another may run to the security of loved ones, and another may respond to the threat in solitude. Each of these responses has a very different influence on the immune system (Kemeny & Laudenslager, 1999).

In this section we consider how varying responses to stress and social relationships, as well as various environmental elements, influence the immune response. Beware, though, as we move from examining the immune system in the petri dish or the single organism in the lab to considering its activity in the integrated context we typically refer to as "real life," the studies become less controlled and the conclusions become a little more tentative. As discussed in Box 12.2, however, this line of research is imperative if the PNI field is going to lead to enhanced immune functioning outside the controlled laboratory setting (for example, in hospitals). Once we navigate through this interesting literature, the convergence of evidence will enable us to make some specific conclusions.

[Box 12.2]

A Case in Point

Evan Handler

At the age of 24, Evan Handler seemed to be right on track with his life and his career. His girlfriend, Jackie, had just moved in to his New York apartment and he was preparing to play a leading role in the Broadway production of Neil Simon's *Biloxi Blues*. And he had scheduled a meeting with Warren Beatty to finalize his part in a movie Beatty would soon be making with Dustin Hoffman.

Handler's world fell apart when he went to the doctor to check out a rash on his feet and why he had been feeling a little sick lately. Those innocent symptoms translated into a dreaded diagnosis—leukemia. Handler never made the movie with Beatty and Hoffman, which he didn't regret too much because it turned out to be the box office flop *Ishtar*. Instead, he took on the leading role in his own life drama, the drama of surviving leukemia.

Handler checked into New York's Memorial Sloan-Kettering Cancer Center because it had a reputation as a research hospital that could offer him the latest treatments to successfully attack the leukemia. From the time Handler entered the hospital and became patient 865770, he realized that, in addition to his immune system being in turmoil, his emotional world was about to enter a downward spiral. In a procedure typical of many leading research hospitals at the time, he was herded through corridors filled with dying, moaning patients. He was also made to wait long hours in miserable waiting rooms. Worst of all, he was treated as if he should accept the fact that his odds were dismal and that he should start to get used to the idea that he might not survive the disease.

At that point Handler realized that if he was going to recover, he could not put his fate in the hands of that hospital staff; he would have to take an extremely active role in his recovery process. Handler accomplished this goal by adopting what he called a strategy of *opportunistic optimism*, utilizing meditation, visualization, hypnotherapy, personal therapy, psychic sessions, nutritional therapy, massage, and aromatherapy, which are all strategies that helped him to relax as he endured his extended, tormenting

Psychological Factors Leading to Compromised Immune Function

We have already discussed the connection between the stress system and immune functioning. As a psychological factor that threatens the body's homeostasis, researchers have found that stressors have a significant impact on an animal's immune system.

Focusing on rodent models, scientists have employed a multitude of stressors including shock, forced swim, restraint, and rotational stress and have found that stress reduces lymphocyte-mediated cytotoxicity, diminishes stem graft rejection, and suppresses antibody responses (Shavit, 1991). Although these studies have produced interesting results, the stressors typically used are somewhat artificial. Most animals live in complex social structures, not individually in small territories (such as laboratory cages). Consequently, observations of animals in natural or seminatural conditions are necessary to understand how an animal might respond in a stressful situation and subsequently how the response influences the immune system.

Evan Handler
CARLO ALLEGRI/GETTY IMAGES

hospital stay. He also attempted to remove all doubt-provoking stimuli from his life. For example, his girlfriend screened his mail and books so that he could focus only on the positive. Finally, Handler became keenly aware of the value of the love and support of others and turned even more frequently to the support of his girlfriend.

Handler endured many months of chemotherapy and experienced a remission. Following his three rounds of chemotherapy, Handler went on to star in two movies and got a part in Neil Simon's *Broadway Bound.* Unfortunately, the leukemia returned; at this point he opted for a bone marrow transplant at Johns Hopkins University. He was amazed at the contrast between Hopkins and Sloan-Kettering. Hopkins's staff was extremely sensitive to the psychological needs of the patients, attempting to treat the entire person as opposed to a compartmentalized disease. The bone marrow transplant was successful and Handler is currently back in his acting life.

In addition to playing dramatic roles in films such as *Ransom* and *Natural Born Killers,* he has tried his hand at writing. In 1996, Handler wrote *Time on Fire: My Comedy of Terrors,* an autobiographical account of his journey from cancer to recovery. You might recognize Handler from one of his more recent roles as the lawyer Harry Goldenblatt in the popular television series *Sex and the City.*

Handler's story offers ample evidence that patients suffer not only from a particular disease but are barraged with emotional experiences as well. Current research suggests that stress and anxiety rob the immune system of much needed energy. But Handler used a very active coping strategy, including exercising a sense of control over his life-threatening condition. As discussed in Chapter Eleven, an increased perception of control leads to reduced stress responsivity. Thus, Handler's story reminds us of the wisdom of Asclepius mentioned earlier in this chapter—healing is about focusing on the relationship between psychological and physical factors. Ignoring either one leaves a patient more vulnerable to the disease.

An example of a seminaturalistic approach can be found in work done on *Antechinus stuartii,* a small insectivorous marsupial that resembles a mouse with a long pointed nose and that lives in the forests of Australia. Because of stress, the males rarely live past their first breeding season (less than a year) and females may live a little longer but never past two years. In fact, the males seem to have the more stressful existence. They enter an intense mating period in late winter when the weather conditions are harsh—consisting of low temperatures, rain, and occasionally snow. During the frenzy and stress of mating, males lose body weight and develop enlarged adrenal glands as well as increased production of corticosteroids and androgens. To add to the animals' stress, the males become extremely aggressive during this time as they attempt to defend their territories.

Does this extreme form of stress have an effect on the immune system? Absolutely. When examined, these animals are heavily infested with endo- and ectoparasites. If brought into the lab, the male antechinus produces very low levels of antibodies to sheep red blood cells (a commonly used laboratory immune challenge). In the wild, due to compromised immune systems, the animals die shortly after copulating as a result of both gastrointestinal hemorrhage and invasion of parasites and microorganisms. Thus, with all the animals' energy directed toward sexual behavior, little is left for the immune system. The cost of this sexual encounter is enormous for the individual antechinus male—death.

Do these effects generalize to humans? After all, although research suggests that human males are more motivated than females to engage in sexual behavior, few would probably risk their lives for one intimate encounter. Consequently, scientists do not go to singles bars to investigate the human stress experience; instead, they turn to another situation with which you, as a student, are very familiar. Scientists believe that the stress of taking exams is a useful model of naturalistic stress in humans. Researchers have found that medical students taking exams exhibit lower lymphocyte proliferation, IL-2 production, and NK-cell activity (Guidi et al., 1999; Kiecolt-Glaser & Glaser, 1991).

Academic stress also decreases apoptosis. It is thought that apoptosis is one mechanism that the body uses to protect against the growth of abnormal cells that may eventually result in cancer. Thus, prolonged stress may place the body in a situation where it cannot rid itself of cells containing DNA interruptions that may mutate into cancer cells (Kiecolt-Glaser and Glaser, 1999)

A troubled relationship is another stressful situation that has been explored in humans. Janice Kiecolt-Glaser and Ron Glaser of Ohio State University studied 90 newlywed couples (Kiecolt-Glaser, Glaser, Cacioppo, & Malarkey, 1998). The couples were instructed to discuss one or more areas of disagreement for 30 minutes. As the couples were engaged in this discussion, the researchers taped and scored the behaviors that occurred during the session.

Hostile behaviors such as raising one's voice were related to higher blood pressure and neuroendocrine increases as well as NK-cell and T-cell decrements. In wives, both norepinephrine and cortisol increased as the husbands exhibited withdrawal during the encounter. The researchers also found that separated or divorced men were more distressed and reported more illnesses than their married counterparts. When tested, these men had compromised immune systems (for example, lower antibody response to herpes viruses).

Another stressful situation that has been assessed is the chronic stress and despair experienced by individuals who are caregivers for Alzheimer's patients. Glaser and his colleagues gave an influenza virus vaccination to 32 caregivers and matched controls (Glaser, Sheridan, Marlarkey, MacCallum, & Kiecolt-Glaser, 2000). The caregivers had poorer antibody and activated T-cell responses. These researchers also gave a series of three hepatitis-B vaccinations to medical students on the third day of three-day exam period blocks (Glaser, Kiecolt-Glaser, Marlarkey, & Sheridan, 1998). Higher antibody responses were observed in students who reported greater social support and lower levels of anxiety.

Thus, the stressful situations of taking medical exams, experiencing marital discord, and taking care of a loved one suffering from Alzheimer's disease have all been empirically linked to compromised immune functioning. Knowing, as you do, the relationship between stress and the immune system, the findings that stress affects the immune system shouldn't come as a surprise. But in addition to pointing out factors that produce immunological deficits, researchers have also worked diligently to identify factors related to immunological enhancements.

Psychological Factors Leading to Enhanced Immune Function

After reading the previous section you may be tempted to think that a person can enhance immune functioning by just avoiding any type of stress. That may be true but life is rarely that simple. A few studies suggest that acute stress may actually result in *increased* immune system activation.

At the height of the Iraqi Scud missile attacks on the cities of Israel during the 1991 Persian Gulf War, for example, Weiss and his colleagues (1996) subjected 22 male volunteers living in Jerusalem to a battery of psychological tests as well as to various immunological and neuroendocrine assays. These subjects were tested again after the end of the war. The results suggested that anxiety and anger were higher during the war than after and that NK-cell activity was significantly elevated during the war. Neuroendocrine measures such as ACTH indicated that physiological stress levels were also highest during the war—a time in which Iraq's professed goal was to reduce Israel to ashes.

Some interesting work using actors as subjects confirms that negative emotions such as fear and sadness result in increases in immunological functioning. In the "actor" studies, subjects are asked to improvise a monologue that will produce either sad or happy emotions. Much to the researcher's surprise, during an intense sad state, NK cells were increased in the actor's bloodstream. As they expected (and as described in Box 12.3), intense happy states also produced immunological enhancement (Kemeny, 1993).

Recall that during times of stress the immune system is compromised because the body's energy is directed toward actions necessary for survival—

[Box 12.3]

Brain Matters

Humor's Influence on Health:
No Laughing Matter!

Among the pioneers who helped convince health professionals that the mind is indeed involved with health was a very unlikely figure—Norman Cousins, the editor of the influential magazine *The Saturday Review.* In 1964, Cousins became extremely ill with a severe connective tissue disease, ankylosing spondylitis. Cousins was less than impressed with the standard treatment offered by the hospital, complete with tasteless food, powerful medications with debilitating side effects, and a steady stream of interruptions.

Although Cousins had no prior medical training, he took an active role in his quest for recovery. He traded his hospital room for a motel room and began a treatment regime built on megadoses of vitamin C and Charlie Chaplin. He reported that a good 10-minute belly laugh had an anesthetic effect that allowed him to have at least a couple of hours of pain-free sleep (Cousins, 1976, 1979).

Cousins worked with an open-minded physician who valued his patient's views about recovery. About a decade after recovering from the illness, Cousins publicly told his story in 1976 in an article in the *New England Journal of Medicine,* followed by a book entitled *Anatomy of an Illness.* Toward the end of his life, Cousins worked with the UCLA School of Medicine to facilitate the study of more global and compassionate perspectives in the healing profession.

Evidence of Cousins's philosophy was seen by millions of Americans in a movie titled *Patch Adams,* based on a book entitled *Gesundheit: Good Health Is a Laughing Matter.* In the film, the actor Robin Williams portrays a real-life physician, Hunter "Patch" Adams, who became disillusioned during his training for a career in medicine with the apparent lack of compassion and attention toward a person's emotional state. In an attempt to treat the patient as well as the illness, Adams went on to incorporate laughter and compassion in his treatment strategies. He established the Gesundheit! Institute in West Virginia, where humor is regularly prescribed for patients who are offered treatment free of charge.

As you know, case studies, books, and movies are very interesting but offer a weak substitute for true empirical evidence of a particular effect. What does traditional science say about humor and the immune system? In one study (Berk, Tan, Napier, & Eby, 1989), experimental subjects watched the comedian Gallagher on a life-size screen while having their blood collected at various intervals during the hour-long video. Compared with the control subjects, the subjects exposed to the Gallagher video expressed less cortisol, epinephrine, and dopamine—or at least a metabolite of dopamine. Another study conducted by the same research group (Berk, Tan, Fry, et al., 1989) found that mirthful laughter also increased the NK-cell activity.

In another study (Newman & Stone, 1996), subjects were asked to view a silent, stressful film. One group was instructed to write a humorous monologue for the film whereas a second group was asked to write a serious monologue. Various measures were taken before, during, and after the film. Subjects who were instructed to generate a humorous monologue exhibited lower tension, a less negative emotional state, and less psychophysiological reactivity (heart rate, for example) than the serious monologue group .

Thus, although it is certainly not clear that laughter is the best medicine, mounting evidence demonstrates that it helps relieve stress, which many times restricts the efforts of the immune system. Akin to the humorous antics of the Gesundheit! Institute, an Australian hospital has created a laughter room in which patients augment their treatment protocol with a dose of humor (May, 1996).

the fight-or-flight response. How can it be adaptive, then, for the body to use some of its valuable energy to fuel the immune system during times of fear and stress? Firdaus Dhabhar (1998) of the Ohio State University has proposed that stress may have a bidirectional effect—in certain conditions stress may enhance immunological functioning, whereas other conditions may result in immunosuppression.

Further, acute stress may suppress certain functions while enhancing other immune actions. For example, during an acute stress episode (for example, being attacked by a lion) it is likely that should you survive, your body will be exposed to immediate immune challenges such as wounds. Dhabhar suggests that the body may direct blood leukocytes to migrate to certain immunological battle stations such as the skin to help the animal survive the attack and the impending immunological threat. This stress-induced enhancement is likely to occur only in acute rather than in chronic stress. If this theory is correct, there may be some value in trying to eliminate chronic stress in patients while periodically exposing them to acute stress to activate the immune system.

Aside from acute stress, researchers have found that social ties boost immunological protection. In one study, 276 healthy volunteers were given nasal drops that contained one or two rhinoviruses (cold viruses that invade the nasal passages). The scientists simply waited to see who developed coldlike symptoms. In the end, subjects with more types of social relationships (friends, family, coworkers, spouse) were less likely to develop coldlike symptoms (cough, runny nose). Additionally, the subjects with more social support generated less mucus with a lower viral count (Cohen, Doyle, Skoner, Rabin, & Gwaltney, 1997).

In a related study focusing on susceptibility to influenza, other researchers have provided evidence that flu infections are more likely to occur in families viewed as rigid or chaotic than in more engaged, balanced families (Clover, Abell, Becker, Crawford, & Ramsey, 1989). Thus, positive interpersonal relationships can have a strong impact on immune functioning.

In a study consisting of probably more subjects than any other experiment in this text, further evidence for health benefits of social ties were found. In Evans County, Georgia, 3,201 subjects were recruited for a study investigating life-style factors and longevity. In general, the researchers found that, at least in white subjects, increased mortality risk was found in those with few social ties. Additionally, they found that spending spare time in church benefited females (Schoenbach, Kaplan, Friedman, & Kleinbaum, 1986).

In another large study conducted a few years later, researchers at Duke University Medical Center collected blood samples from 1,718 subjects to assess specific immune regulators such as IL-6, the proinflammatory cytokine (Koenig, Cohen, George, Hays, Larson, & Blazer, 1997). The researchers also found a relationship, although subtle, between religious attendance and IL-6 production; specifically, attending religious services was related to decreased production of this inflammatory cytokine, which is related to aging processes. As described by Strawbridge, Cohen, Shema, and Kaplan (1997), the benefits of attending religious services may be partly explained by the life-style of many religious individuals, including more stable marriages, increased social contacts, and improved health practices (for example, a likelihood of decreased smoking and increased exercise).

James Pennebaker joined forces with Janice Kiecolt-Glaser and Ron Glaser (1988) to investigate another factor possibly related to enhancing one's immune defenses. In this study, 50 college students were randomly assigned to either a group instructed to write about a traumatic event or a group instructed to write about superficial topics for 20 minutes per day for 4 days. The subjects in this study agreed to have their blood drawn the day before writing, the day of the last writing session, and 6 weeks later.

During the writing phase, subjects in the traumatic event group poured out their hearts in their writing—disclosing instances of rape, suicide attempts, death, child abuse, and family conflict. Each day, the subjects writing about traumas reported feeling more upset than the group writing about superficial topics. Once the blood was collected, white blood cells were isolated and their reactions to foreign substances were assessed. The results suggested that people who wrote about traumatic events had a more heightened immune response to foreign invaders than did the superficial group. This effect was more pronounced on the last day of writing, but it persisted for the next 6 weeks.

Just a year later, another landmark study was published suggesting that "opening up" one's feelings or emotions may have therapeutic value for patients. David Spiegel and his colleagues at Stanford University School of Medicine (Spiegel, Bloom, Kraemer, & Gottheil, 1989), impressed with the emotional bonds that were created among cancer patients undergoing group psychotherapy, decided to look a little closer at any benefits experienced by women suffering from breast cancer who participated in this form of group therapy. They found that the life spans of the women in therapy were significantly longer than those of control subjects not participating in group therapy.

Concentrating on positive emotions, the relationship between immune factors and optimism in first-year law students was assessed by a group of researchers at the University of California in Los Angeles (Segerstrom,

Taylor, Kemeney, & Fahey, 1998). During the initial two months of law school, 50 students had their blood drawn and were instructed to complete questionnaires about their dispositions. The researchers found that optimism was associated with higher numbers of helper T cells and natural killer-cell cytotoxicity. In a more recent study conducted by David Snowden and his colleagues (Danner, Snowdon, & Friesen, 2001) at the University of Kentucky, nuns who expressed positive emotions (love, happiness, joy) in autobiographies written in their early twenties lived up to 10 years longer than nuns who expressed fewer positive emotions. If you're happy and you're aware of it, you just may live longer!

Additional evidence drawing relationships between disposition, or temperament, and immune responses is provided in a recent study focusing on a group of men with asymptomatic HIV infection. Following up on anecdotal observations that extroverted individuals were healthier and longer-lived than introverted AIDS patients, Naliboff and his colleagues (Cole, Kemeny, Fahey, Zack, & Naliboff, 2003) assessed personality profiles (for example, social inhibition, or shyness), stress responses, and HIV viral load and number of T cells (two immunological defenses destroyed by AIDS). The results were clear—the shy men with more reactive stress responses had higher viral loads, up to eight times higher than nonshy patients, indicating a compromised defense against HIV. These data provide perhaps the first clinical evidence that increased neural activity (for example, autonomic nervous system responsivity) is the mediating factor between psychological variables and infectious disease progression.

Finally, exercise has been associated with immune enhancement (Crist, Mackinnon, Thompson, Atterbom, & Egan, 1989; Simon, 1991). Although exercise may be viewed as a stressor because it disrupts the homeostasis of the body's physiology, exercise can relieve tension and promote relaxation. Focusing on immune functions, increased leukocyte, NK cell, and IL-1 levels have been found in subjects following exercise.

Now that a case has been made for the role of psychological processes in immune functions, it should be easier to see that the ancient Greeks' notion of health being the functions of both the mind and the body was right on target. The ancient Greeks even wrote about the mitigating effect of specific psychological processes such as despair and hopelessness on the immune system. Thucydides, an Athenian general who wrote about a devastating plague that struck Athens in 430 B.C., and who personally suffered from this dreaded plague, made some interesting observations about the disease:

> The most terrible thing of all was the despair into which people fell when they realized that they had caught the plague; for they would immediately

adopt an attitude of utter hopelessness, and, by giving in this way, would lose their powers of resistance (Clark, 1995).

Clearly, Thucydides was gathering anecdotal evidence on the relationship between psychological states and resistance to disease. Whether or not the hopelessness led to impaired resistance or was simply the product of the sickness behavior triggered by the activated immune system has yet to be clarified in the health arena. With the field of PNI becoming more and more visible, researchers and practitioners will extend the effort to view health as the multifaceted phenomenon that more accurately reflects its nature. As suggested by Sternberg and Gold (1997), classifying illnesses into medical and psychiatric specialties seems more and more artificial once we understand that the once demarcated boundaries between the mind and the body are themselves artificial.

Summary

The notion that one's health is influenced by a convergence of psychological, physiological, and immunological systems has been around for thousands of years. However, as Western medicine evolved, the role of psychological factors in one's susceptibility to illness took a back seat to an emphasis on physiological causes and cures for diseases. An increasing amount of literature supporting the role of psychological processes in health and the emerging field of psychoneuroimmunology are forcing researchers to once again embrace the integrative notions of the ancient Greeks and of many Asian traditions.

Fundamentals of Immune System Function: The Body's Federal Bureau of Investigation

The central threat to one's immune system is infectious agents known as pathogens, including viruses, bacteria, fungi, and parasites. The body's initial defense against pathogens is the skin and the mucosal lining of respiratory, digestive, and reproductive tracts. Once a pathogen breaches the barriers of the immune system, cells of the innate immune system (macrophages, neutrophils, and natural killer cells) provide a front-line defense.

The body's defense also involves an acquired immune system made up of antibody-producing B cells, as well as T cells that proliferate in response to the appearance of an antigen from the organism's past. The major histocompatibility complex (MHC) helps the body process the massive amounts of information related to responses to various antigens and ultimately helps the immune system distinguish between self and nonself.

The components of the immune system are distributed throughout the body and include the bone marrow, thymus, lymph nodes, spleen, tonsils, and Peyer's patches. With the massive amount of information being exchanged among the elements of the immune system, mistakes sometimes occur—pathogens sometimes slip through, and sometimes a body's own immune cells destroy healthy tissue.

Integrative Operations: Immunological and Nervous System Communication

Serendipitous studies confirming the conditioning of the immune system provided seminal empirical evidence that the nervous system communicates with the immune system. Following these studies, the field of psychoneuroimmunology was created. Subsequent to this finding, nerve fibers were observed in immunological tissue, and surprisingly, leukocytes were observed to produce neurochemicals.

The stress response mediates between nervous and immune systems—providing further evidence of the abundance of cross talk between these two systems. The "sick response" is a product of input from the nervous and immune systems to assure that an individual conserves energy while the body wages war against a pathogen.

Putting the "Psych" in Psychoneuroimmunology

Several so-called psychological factors have been demonstrated to influence susceptibility to illness. Chronically stressful situations such as troubled relationships, taking exams, and caring for sick loved ones may compromise immune functions, whereas positive social relationships, disclosure of painful emotions, decreased stress responsivity, humor and exercise have all been shown to enhance immune functioning.

Key Terms

psychoneuroimmunology (PNI) (p. 433)

pathogen (p. 435)

innate immune system (p. 435)

phagocyte (p. 436)

macrophage (p. 436)

lysosome (p. 436)

neutrophil (p. 436)

natural killer (NK) cells (p. 437)

perforin (p. 437)

cytokine (p. 437)

complement complex (p. 438)

acquired immune system (p. 438)

vaccination (p. 438)

B cells *or* B lymphocytes (p. 439)

bone marrow (p. 439)

antibodies *or* immunoglobulins (Ig) (p. 439)

antigen (p. 439)

T cells *or* T lymphocytes (p. 439)

thymus (p. 439)

helper T cells (p. 440)

killer T cell (p. 440)

antigen-presenting cell (APC) (p. 440)

dendritic cells (p. 440)

lymph nodes (p. 440)

humoral immune system (p. 442)

cellular immune system (p. 443)

major histocompatibility complex (MHC) (p. 443)

MCH I molecule (p. 443)

MCH II molecule (p. 443)

autoimmune disease (p. 445)

multiple sclerosis (p. 445)

spleen (p. 450)

interleukin-1 (IL-1) (p. 450)

For Further Consideration

Handler, E. (1997). *Time on fire: My comedy of terrors.* New York: Henry Holt. This autobiographical book provides an honest, realistic view of what it is like for the immune function to be taken over by a disease, in this case, leukemia. Handler, then a young, aspiring actor, describes his emotions, desires, fears, and strategies for survival. Several M.D.s have declared this book required reading for health practitioners as it provides an opportunity to glimpse into the world of the patient. Now that you have become acquainted with the PNI field, you will appreciate the impact of Handler's emotional ups and downs on his fragile immune system.

Nelson, R. J., Demas, G. E., Klein, S. L., & Kriegsfeld, L. J. (2002). *Seasonal patterns of stress, immune function, and disease.* Cambridge, UK: Cambridge University Press. If you enjoy considering how evolution shaped our physiological functions, this book focuses on how the natural fluctuations of seasons alter immune functioning. The question of the natural rhythms of the immune system is important and may lead to clinically relevant findings directing medical practitioners to consider how the current energy demands of the season might influence a patient's battle with a particular disease. A dramatic example of researchers assessing the functioning of the immune systems of bold individuals who live in Antarctica during the winter, enduring its −30°C daily temperatures, provides powerful evidence that seasonal fluctuations influence immune functions.

Schedlowski, M., & Tewes, U. (Eds.). (1999). *Psychoneuroimmunology: An interdisciplinary introduction.* New York: Kluwer Academic/Plenum. For those of you who want to read more original literature on the many topics in this chapter, the 27 chapters of this book are written by leading researchers on a diverse array of PNI-related topics ranging from the fundamentals of the immune system to exercise and immune functions and sleep and immune functions. The book is filled with the most relevant research in the field and many valuable illustrations.

Sternberg, E. M. (2000). *The balance within: The science connecting health and emotions.* New York: Freeman. This is a beautifully written story of how the mind/brain interacts with immune functions. It is fascinating to learn how Sternberg went from a child running around her father's laboratory in the same building as Hans Selye (the "father" of stress) to a respected researcher in the field of PNI. The book is about the science of mind-body interactions and how they influence health, but Sternberg's inclusion of real-life information makes the book read more

like a novel at times—it will surely keep your interest. Serving as the director of the Molecular, Cellular, and Behavioral Integrative Neuroscience Program and chief of the Section on Neuroendocrine Immunology and Behavior at the National Institutes of Health, Sternberg has a lot to say on the matter of neural-immune interactions in health issues.

Sternberg, E. M., & Gold, P. W. (1997). The mind-body interaction in disease. *Scientific American,* 7 (1), 8–15. This article lays the groundwork for the neuroanatomical and neurochemical connections between the nervous system and the immune system. It elegantly describes the relationship between the hypothalamic-pituitary-adrenal axis and immune functioning and then considers the effects of this interaction on psychological phenomena such as stress and depression. Additionally, the wonderful illustrations help guide the reader through the neural-immune integration pathways.

13

Eating Regulation and Associated Disorders

Connections

Increased Rates in Eating Out Accompany Increased Inches in Our Waistlines

Odds are that the fast food industry has so insidiously become part of the context of our lives that we don't notice it. As you drive across town singing along with their jingles on the radio, you will probably see several billboards advertising fast food specials; as you watch TV, you will see commercials showing lean, healthy people munching on high-fat burgers; as you walk through the children's clothing or toy departments, you think nothing of seeing McKids clothes or toys that make French fries out of playdough. And with the sheer density of the restaurants themselves lining America's main streets, it is convenient to pull into a drive-through at a minute's notice and order the meal deal of the week.

A recent book entitled *Fast Food Nation* by Eric Schlosser (2002) brings some startling facts about the fast food industry to the attention of American citizens. The industry with roots in Southern California has swept across the nation; fast food restaurants are found not only on the highways and byways of our society but in places such as airports, schools, Wal-

Marts, gas stations, cruise ships, and even hospital cafeterias. As a society, we are certainly responding to all these salient food cues: whereas in 1970 Americans spent around $6 billion on fast food, today we spend closer to $118 billion. Obviously, fast food is big business; in 1997, Burger King launched a whopper of an advertising campaign—$70 million—to simply promote the supremacy of their French fries over those of their competitors. It's a sobering fact that Americans now spend more on fast food than on higher education.

But it's not only fast food restaurants that are influencing our eating habits; more and more Americans are eating out at table-service restaurants, as well. The event of dining out has evolved from a rare occurrence in past generations to a common practice today. Whereas Americans spent about 19% of their "food" money eating out in some type of restaurant in the 1950s, today we spend closer to 41%, including $100 billion on nonfast food restaurants and cafeterias.

Another book written for popular consumption, titled *Restaurant Confidential* by Michael F. Jacobson and Jayne Hurley (2002) of the Center for Science in the Public Interest, illuminates the effective strategies utilized by the restaurant and fast food industry. In the past several decades, both plates and portions have become bigger, resulting in our waistlines getting bigger. An extreme example of increasing portions can be seen with soda size. In the 1950s, sodas were dispensed in 8-ounce servings; today 7-Eleven sells the Big Gulp, which is a hefty 32 ounces, and if that isn't large enough, their Double Big Gulp is 64 ounces and 768 calories. As the restaurants spend minimal resources making the food irresistible with extra-large portions, our fat consumption sky-rockets. Seemingly unaware of the caloric consequences, Americans are slurping up 1010-calorie vanilla milkshakes at McDonald's and wolfing down 2000-calorie fried onions at their favorite neighborhood restaurant.

In the recent documentary *Super Size Me,* Morgan Spurlock conducted an interesting experiment by placing himself on a diet consisting of only McDonald's food for one month and limiting his exercise to that of an average American. An expanding waistline was the least of his worries: in addition to gaining twenty-five pounds, he became lethargic, showed signs of depression and food addiction, significantly increased his cholesterol levels, and developed potentially serious liver problems.

Kelly Brownell, director of the Center for Eating and Weight Disorders at Yale University and along with Katherine Horgan, author of the recent book *Food Fight* (2004), is aware of the health consequences of our ever-increasing propensity to dine out in restaurants. He and his students are also trying to make the public aware of the consequences of unhealthy eating, claiming that in the absence of high-fat food and high rates of inactivity, there would

be virtually no obesity (Brownell, 2002a, 2002b). But while rates of food consumption are increasing, exercise is decreasing; the Surgeon General's report recently stated that 60% of American adults fail to get enough daily exercise. Consequently, according to the National Center for Health Statistics, about 60% of Americans are overweight. Brownell and his students are painfully aware that the increased portions costing merely pennies to the food vendors will result in billions of dollars in health-related costs as our overweight society ages. Additionally, psychological costs emerge as overweight individuals find themselves the targets of discrimination. The team observed that seemingly harmless "before and after" weight-reduction advertisements promoted the perception that overweight people are lazy or lack enough self-control to look like the "after" picture in the advertisements. Constant reminders of an inability to accomplish the weight loss demonstrated by all the smiling models in these ads promote low self-esteem in overweight people (Geier, Schwartz, & Brownell, 2003).

Because obesity is very difficult to treat, Brownell feels that the current eating crisis cries out for prevention, and he is attempting to change public policy concerning the eating industry. By doing so, Brownell is moving away from the medical model, in which the individual person is investigated for reasons for his or her obesity, to a public health model that considers why our nation is obese. This public health model has led him straight to the influence of the environment. Brownell and his colleagues and students are gearing up to fight the food industry. When asked about the daunting task of going head-to-head with such a powerful foe, Brownell explains: "Twenty years ago the same could have been said about challenging the tobacco industry—but look at how public opinion has changed about the health consequences of smoking" (Brownell, personal communication, 2003). Currently Brownell has six policy proposals in mind: (1) enhancing opportunities for physical activity, (2) regulating food advertisements targeted to children, (3) removing fast foods and soft drinks from schools, (4) restructuring school lunch programs, (5) subsidizing the purchase of healthy foods, and (6) taxing foods that have poor nutritional value.

Although some of the topics covered in this text may be difficult for you to relate to personally, this chapter discusses a behavior that is near and dear to us all—EATING. Eating is such a common daily occurrence that most of us do it almost unconsciously—food is there, we eat it, and that is that. This behavior, however, is anything but simple—a multitude of variables contribute to the likelihood that you will eat a particular food at a certain time. As you will learn in this chapter, several neurochemicals, such as leptin and neuropeptide Y, play a role in the amount of hunger we experience at any given moment as they interact with specific areas of the brain. Further, our environment and past learning history contribute significantly to this process.

How many times have you eaten because it was the established time to eat (not because you were hungry) or because it was courteous for you to eat a meal (even if you didn't especially like the food)? Certainly these environmental and cultural variables play a role in this important behavior. Not surprisingly, aspects of our well-established hunger regulation system can easily malfunction, producing a disruption of homeostasis and possibly severe sickness leading to death. Malfunctions come in many varieties—eating too much, not eating enough, and eating and then purging the body of the food. In this chapter we will discuss the current findings related to eating regulation and the evolutionary context in which these behaviors developed. Why include a chapter on eating regulation in a text about mental health? As discussed in Chapters Five and Eight, food affects moods and serves as dietary precursors for neurochemicals. You learned in the Connections section that obesity may be related to psychological problems (such as low self-esteem), and as we will discuss throughout this chapter, unhealthy eating behavior can lead to illness and even death. Thus, it is important to understand the most salient factors related to this life-sustaining behavior.

EATING REGULATION

Before we get to the variables related to eating disorders, it is important to understand the fundamental neurobiological factors that regulate eating in healthy animals. After describing the classic Washburn and Cannon investigation of stomach factors involved in hunger (and subsequent research), neuroanatomical, neurochemical, and environmental factors will be described.

Early Hunger Research Was Difficult to Swallow

The earliest research on hunger focused on the digestive system, an expansive network of storage organs and tubules situated inside the abdominal area. Once food enters the mouth, it travels down the esophagus to the stomach and then passes through the duodenum and small and large intestines before making its exit via the anus (Figure 13.1). At

[Figure 13.1]
Human digestive system.

AFTER PINEL, 2000

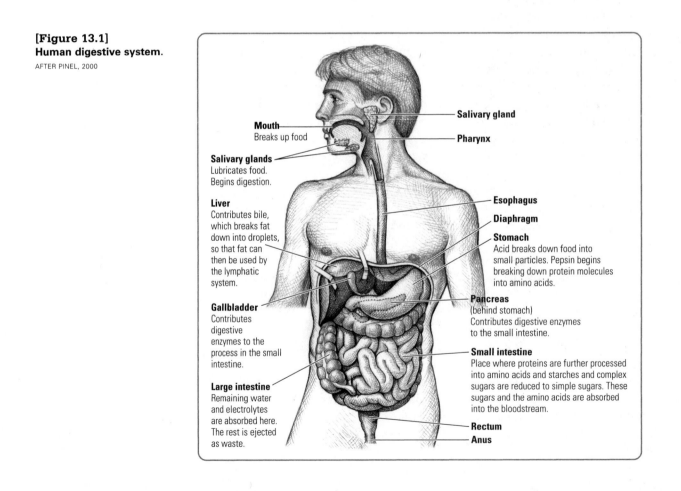

many of the digestive stops along the way, enzymes are mixed with the food to aid in the process. As the food passes through the digestive system, certain substrates, such as fats, proteins, simple sugars, electrolytes, and water, are absorbed at various sites before the excess food remnants are discharged from the body.

Without fail, when students are asked how they know they are hungry, their first responses are related to the stomach in some way. They report that their stomachs growl, grumble, or just feel empty. Thus, it is not surprising that one of the earliest hunger experiments focused on the role of the activity of the stomach in initiating hunger. In this creative experiment, conducted by W. B. Cannon and A. L. Washburn in 1912, the researchers investigated the notion that the activity of the stomach dubbed "stomach pangs" constituted the hunger signal. To support this notion, Washburn swallowed a balloon that was later inflated. As can be seen in Figure 13.2, the balloon was connected to a recording device that was sensitive to any movement of air or contractions within the stomach or balloon. Additionally, Washburn was instructed to press a button each time he felt a hunger craving. Sure enough, stomach pangs coincided with the movement of air in the balloon—when the stomach contracted, a hunger pang was felt.

For decades researchers felt that the mystery to hunger had been solved—it was the movement of the stomach that prompted us to go to the kitchen to make ourselves a snack. But there was a small problem with these conclusions. In 1959, another team of researchers used abdominal electrodes to record the stomach's activity and found that the

Subject swallows balloon, which measures stomach contractions.

Subject presses key each time he feels hungry.

Stomach contractions

Hunger pangs

0 1 2 3 4 5 6 7 8 9 10

Time in minutes

[Figure 13.2]
Hunger pains and stomach contractions. Diagram of Washburn and Cannon's crude experiment that involved swallowing a balloon that would be sensitive to the contractions of the stomach. As seen on the graph, the hunger pangs coincided with stomach contractions.
AFTER MYERS, 2004

ventromedial hypothalamus
Brain area which, when lesioned in rats, caused the rats to become hyperphagic. Initially dubbed the "satiety center," it is now believed to be involved in energy metabolism.

lateral hypothalamus Brain area which, when lesioned in rats, caused the rats to become hypophagic and to die unless the experimenter assisted with feeding. In addition to diminishing hunger, LH lesions also decrease general motivation.

dual-centers hypothesis of hunger regulation Proposed by Stellar in 1954, the VMH was considered the hunger center and the LH was the satiety center.

noradrenergic bundle Bundle of fibers originating in the locus coeruleus of the brainstem that travel to limbic and cortical structures. These noradrenergic fibers have been strongly associated with brain reward and arousal.

paraventricular nucleus
Nucleus of the hypothalamus thought to be more intimately involved in hunger regulation than the VMH and LH.

stomach is actually at its quietest when it is empty. Davis, Garafalo, and Kveim (1959) repeated Washburn and Cannon's experiment but replaced the step of swallowing a balloon with merely recording the movement of the stomach with electrodes positioned on the skin outside the stomach. In this situation, the stomach was found to be the least active during times of hunger or food deprivation. In retrospect, it was obvious that the movement of the stomach in Cannon and Washburn's experiment was an artifact of having a balloon placed in it—the stomach was merely trying to digest the balloon. Additional contradictory evidence was the observation that many human patients who had their stomachs removed due to medical problems still continued to report feelings of hunger and satiety (Pinel, 2003). Thus, it was concluded that the activity of the stomach played a minimal role in triggering hunger.

At this point you may be a bit confused. After hearing this historical review, most of our students throw their hands in the air and report that their stomachs do indeed become active when they are hungry; after all, most everyone has experienced the embarrassment of a growling stomach during an otherwise quiet moment. This is a good point that shouldn't be overlooked. Keep reading—we'll come back to this question later in the chapter.

Neurobiology of Hunger Regulation

In the 1940s, investigations of the brain's role in hunger began to occur. Researchers found that animals become hyperphagic (they eat too much) after receiving bilateral lesions in their **ventromedial hypothalamus** (VMH; Hetherington & Ranson, 1940). After a few weeks of eating everything in sight, known as the *dynamic phase,* their eating declines a bit as they enter the *static phase* of hunger alteration. In 1951, researchers found that delivering bilateral lesions to the **lateral hypothalamus** (LH) severely restricted hunger and thirst in an animal. Unless an experimenter intervened, the animal would die of starvation (Anand & Brobeck, 1951). Subsequently, an influential article written by Stellar (1954) proposed the **dual-centers hypothesis of hunger regulation;** specifically, one nucleus of the hypothalamus was the hunger center while another was the satiety center.

Although these roles of the VMH and LH are taught to virtually every general psychology student, it's becoming evident that the initial conclusions derived from the experiments have been a bit distorted from the actual truth. As Pinel (2003) points out, recent evidence suggests that, rather than being a satiety center, the hypothalamus plays a significant role in energy metabolism. It is now thought that the VMH-lesioned rats overate because the altered metabolism made them become obese. Specifically, the VMH lesion altered the amount of insulin levels in the blood, which increased the amount of body fat and decreased the number of usable forms of energy. Thus, the rat had to increase food consumption to maintain appropriate levels of energy. A side effect of the brain surgery, however, was increased body fat.

Additionally, a close investigation of the neuroanatomy of the hypothalamus reveals that a large fiber bundle known as the **noradrenergic bundle** passes through the VMH and is probably critical to maintaining hunger levels. A neighboring nucleus of the hypothalamus, the **paraventricular nucleus (PVN)**, is currently receiving more attention as the critical nucleus of the hypothalamus involved in hunger regulation. (Figure 13.3 shows the anatomical locations of the LH, VMH, and PVN). More information about the role of the PVN will be presented in the section on neurochemical factors. Current research on LH lesions suggests that there are so many deficits associated with these lesions—ranging from motor deficits to a lack of responsiveness—that concluding that the LH is specifically related to eating satiety is somewhat like suggesting that a person in a coma isn't responding due to a lack of interest.

Another classic line of research in hunger regulation was the consideration of the role of glucose in triggering the exact amount of motivation an animal should have to consume additional energy. After all, glucose is an important fuel for both the body and brain. The brain would be particularly sensitive to declining levels of this precious fuel. In accordance with this line of thinking, Jean Mayer (1953) proposed that the delivery of glucose to the body's cells was the key factor in hunger motivation. When insulin levels were high, animals did not eat, and when they were low, animals ate. After noting that individuals with diabetes, who had high circulating levels of glucose, were constantly hungry, Mayer modified his

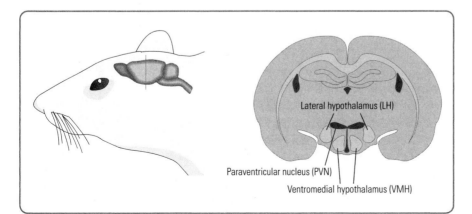

[Figure 13.3]
Hypothalamic feeding centers.
Coronal section of a rat brain showing the ventromedial, lateral, and paraventricular areas of the hypothalamus. AFTER PINEL, 2003

Lateral hypothalamus (LH)

Paraventricular nucleus (PVN)

Ventromedial hypothalamus (VMH)

glucose utilization theory of hunger regulation Proposed by Jean Mayer, this theory suggested that hunger was more influenced by the level of glucose metabolization in the cells than circulating levels of glucose.

cholecystokinin
Gastrointestinal peptide released following ingestion of a meal in order to coordinate different functions of the digestive system.

leptin Neurochemical produced in fat cells and detected by receptors in the brain. Genetically obese mice (*ob/ob*) deficient in leptin are extremely overweight and the obesity is diminished by exogenous injections of leptin.

theory to include the criterion that the glucose had to be metabolized in the cells before influencing hunger, or the **glucose utilization theory of hunger regulation** (Mayer, 1955). Once diabetics are given insulin, their glucose is utilized by their body's cells and their hunger subsides.

Neurochemical Factors

Today, the focus in hunger regulation research is on the neurochemical and neuroendocrine signals produced by various states of hunger and satiety. In the body's periphery, the actions of glucose and cholecystokinin (CCK) will be discussed. In the central nervous system, the influences of NPY and leptin will be covered.

Glucose. Although the initial excitement about the glucostatic theory waned as a result of research suggesting that glucose levels varied little during normal life conditions (LeMagnen, 1981), more recent research suggests that alterations in glucose may indeed be meaningful. In studies conducted by Campfield and Smith (1986, 1990), rats were housed individually in cages where they had free access to food and water. As previously described, the baseline glucose level rarely varies more than 1% to 2% over long periods of time, but prior to a spontaneous meal, the glucose level drops for about 12 to 20 minutes. Once the glucose level drops to about 12% below baseline, it starts to increase and within a matter of minutes, the rat approaches the food bin for a meal (Figure 13.4). Providing stronger evidence for these findings, Campfield and Smith have shown that rats also eat following pharmacologically induced decreases in glucose that mimic the natural pattern of fluctuation.

[Figure 13.4]
Fluctuations in glucose across feeding episodes.
Graph showing the time course of glucose declines in a rat and the initiation of a meal. As the glucose begins to rise following the initial drop, the animal moves to the food bin to begin a meal.
WOODS AND STRUBBE, 1994, FIGURE 3, P. 148

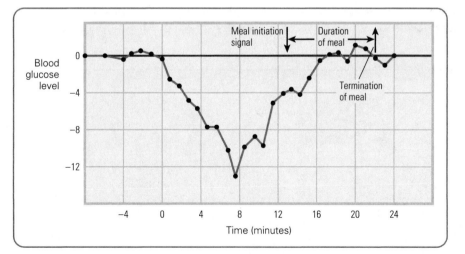

Cholecystokinin. **Cholecystokinin (CCK)** is a gastrointestinal peptide that is released following ingestion of a meal to coordinate different
functions of the digestive process. When administered to both humans
and animals, CCK reduces meal size (Leibowitz, 1992). Further research
suggests that the satiety effect of CCK is abolished when the vagal nerve
is cut (also known as vagal deafferentation) but remains intact in the
decerebrate rat model (the rat's cerebrum has been removed), suggesting
that the CCK effect is mediated by an interaction of the vagal nerve and
the brainstem. Additionally, two CCK receptors have been identified. The
specific nature of CCK's effects, however, is controversial; some
researchers have suggested that CCK's suppression of appetite may be
due to increased nausea rather than a decrease in feelings of hunger
(Baldwin, Parrott, & Ebenezer, 1998).

Leptin. Although a "satiety" signal had long been proposed, the neurochemical **leptin** seemed as if it might be the critical factor that prompts
an animal to feel full and cease eating. The leptin story goes back to the
1950s when a genetic mutation occurred that resulted in very obese mice
that weighed up to three times more than their normal-weight counterparts. The mutated mice were called *ob/ob mice* because they were
homozygous recessive for the mutant *ob* gene (Figure 13.5). These overweight mice, ate considerably more than their normal-weight siblings and
were very efficient at converting their calories into fat. After the *ob/ob*
gene was cloned, it became apparent that the fat cells produced the protein known as leptin, from the Greek word *lepos,* meaning "thin" (Blum,
1997; Pinel, 2003). When leptin was merely injected into *ob/ob* animals,
their weight decreased with no apparent side effects. Thus, in the leptin-
deficient mouse, the exogenous administration of leptin counters obesity.
In accordance with the original dual-centers theory of hunger regulation,
abundant levels of leptin receptors have been found in the VMH
(Williams et al., 2001). But what about humans? Although it is true that
leptin-deficient overweight patients would benefit from the administration of this fat regulator, very few such patients exist. In fact, most overweight individuals are far from leptin-deficient: they have high levels of
leptin. It has been suggested that these obese people have an impaired
sensitivity to leptin (Blum, 1997).

In one study, 23 overweight male and female subjects agreed to participate in a strict diet program for 10 weeks. After about 4 weeks, leptin levels dropped significantly and increased only slightly for the
duration of the program. If leptin works in humans as it does in the animal models, this reduction in leptin would stimulate appetite and
reduce the subjects' energy expenditures—two factors that would not

[Figure 13.5]
**Obese *ob/ob* mouse and con-
trol mouse.** PINEL, 2003, P. 319

neuropeptide Y (NPY)
Pancreatic polypeptide that is one of the most abundant neurotransmitters in the mammalian brain; NPY stimulates eating and reduces energy expenditure.

arcuate nucleus Nucleus of the hypothalamus where most of the NPY neurons are located.

orexins Neuropeptides that are secreted from the lateral hypothalamic neurons and involved in eating, arousal, and other motivated behaviors. Administration of orexins to the CNS results in increased food intake.

contribute to a successful diet. Perhaps leptin decreases are responsible for the many unsuccessful attempts people have with diets (Scholz et al., 1996). In the future, more information related to variables associated with leptin receptor sensitivity may be useful in the battle against obesity.

Neuropeptide Y. Neuropeptide Y (NPY) is a pancreatic polypeptide and is an abundant neurotransmitter in the mammalian brain. Most NPY neurons are located in the **arcuate nucleus** of the hypothalamus, which lies at the base of the third ventricle. Additionally, NPY has been found in the paraventricular area of the hypothalamus around the third ventricle, the suprachiasmatic nucleus, and the supraotic nucleus. In addition to its involvement in functions such as memory processing and the regulation of blood pressure, NPY is known for its ability to stimulate eating and reduce an animal's expenditure of energy—the perfect formula for obesity. Just a nanomolar dose of NPY into a rat's ventricles can stimulate eating, and multiple NPY injections induce obesity. Likely candidates for NPY's role in obesity include decreased nonshivering thermogenesis and enhanced formation of triglyceride deposits (Williams et al., 2001). Adding to the complexity of NPY's role in obesity is the observation that there are *six* types of NPY receptors (Balasubramaniam, 1997).

It appears that the NPY neurons are sensitive to depleted energy stores. Once an animal's energy reserves drop (as seen in starvation, lactation, and insulin-dependent diabetes), the neurons become overactive, apparently initiating feeding and more efficient metabolic responses to conserve energy. For example, animals with depleted energy reserves will engage in food-seeking behavior at the cost of other behaviors that may be related to regulating fat storage, such as thermogenesis (Williams et al., 2001). The observations that NPY gene expression increases prior to food intake and that diabetes-induced hunger is reduced by anti-NPY antibody injections provide support for the stated relationship between NPY and eating (Fuxe, Tinner, Caberlotto, Bunnemann, & Agnati, 1997; Sahu, Sninsky, & Kalra, 1997). Further, doses of leptin that reduce eating have been found to reduce mRNA production in NPY neurons in the PVN and ARC (Baskin et al., 1999).

Researchers at the Institute of Experimental Medicine in Budapest, Hungary (a fitting location for eating research!), found that in the human brain, the corticotrophin-releasing hormone neurons' perikarya and dendrites were coaligned with the axons of the NPY neurons in the hypothalamus (Mihaly, Fekete, Lechan, & Liposits, 2002). These data suggest that the NPY neurons are regulating CRH neurons in the human hypothalamus, implying that some of the effects of NPY on eating regulation are mediated through the CRH system.

Another study reported increased levels of NPY in diabetic women but no differences between obese women and controls (Milewicz, Mikulski, & Bidzinska, 2000). Corroborating these findings, Goldstone, Unmehopa, Bloom, and Swaab (2002) failed to find immunocytochemical evidence of altered NPY in obese autopsied subjects, suggesting that the subjects were responding appropriately to peripheral levels of NPY.

Thus, several neurochemicals have been associated with eating and hunger. The utilization of glucose and the release of leptin from the fat cells of the body generally suppress eating whereas NPY is associated with increases in eating. This chapter is by no means comprehensive in its coverage of possible neurochemical influences on hunger—other neurochemicals such as **orexins** and *ghrelin* are also receiving attention in the eating literature (Cai et al., 2002; Wu & Kral, 2004). On August 8, 2002, a *New York Times* headline proclaimed "Hormone That Causes Full Feeling Is Found." The article reported that a new hormone, peptide YY3-36, which is released from the small intestines in response to the presence of food, seems to stop the feeling of hunger—leading to smaller meals. This substance is currently undergoing early clinical trials as a nasal spray by Nastech Pharmaceutical Company. It will be interesting to see if the substance will be yet another in a long line of initially encouraging but ultimately disappointing potential weight loss substances.

Although the neurochemicals covered here appear to be intimately involved with hunger regulation in animal models (Table 13.1) their effect on human consumption is uncertain, a real challenge to the pharmaceutical industry. This industry continues to search for the panacea drug that will enable people to control their appetites. Because of the complexity of the interactions among these neurochemicals and the strong propensity for compensation in the brain and body, such a drug will undoubtedly require an ingredient that will interact with several neurochemicals. With so many factors involved in hunger regulation,

[Table 13.1]

Neurochemicals and Related Functions

Neurochemical	General function
Glucose	Animals tend to eat following a drop in glucose levels
Cholecystokinin	Reduces meal size; leads to satiety
Leptin	As levels decrease, eating is stimulated
Neuropeptide Y	Stimulates eating and reduces energy expenditure

set-point theory of hunger regulation Theory suggesting that animals are motivated to eat when food or energy levels drop below a particular level.

lipostatic theory of hunger regulation Early eating regulation theory that proposed that some fuel or form of adipose tissue circulated throughout the blood and was interpreted by the brain so that current energy levels could be detected. If lipostatic measures were too high, it was theorized, the animal would cease eating. The defining lipostatic measure was never discovered.

several hunger and satiety signals would have to be altered before a disruption of the process would occur.

Environmental Factors

In addition to levels of specific neurochemicals in the brain, factors in the environment can have a meaningful impact on hunger and satiety. In the obesity section, we will consider the importance of our contemporary life-styles, steeped in high-fat fast food and low activity levels. As you will read, these factors play a huge role in the amount and type of food we consume. Additionally, John de Castro at Georgia State University has conducted some interesting research on the role of social factors on one's appetite (de Castro & de Castro, 1989). His work generally suggests that we eat larger meals when we eat with others. Possible explanations for his findings include the following: friends (1) increase arousal and therefore food intake, (2) relax our vigilant monitoring of the amount of food we're consuming, and (3) increase competitiveness for the available food.

Prior associations influence our motivation to eat certain foods. A food always served by your grandmother as she showered you with her unconditional adoration may be appealing for the duration of your life. On the other hand, as discovered by John Garcia, foods associated with illness are likely to be avoided throughout life (Garcia, Kimmeldorf, & Koelling, 1995). When I (KGL) was a child, a neighbor made a casserole with water chestnuts in it. The crisp texture of water chestnuts in a casserole was foreign to me, so later when I got sick, I quickly attributed my sickness to the water chestnuts because they stood out so clearly in my mind. Three decades later, I'm still avoiding water chestnuts, even though I know it was a stomach flu—not the water chestnuts—that made me ill. Additionally, exposure to the foods of a culture has a strong influence on food preferences. Alaskan Eskimos perceive whale blubber as a tasty treat; Bedouins like the taste of camel eyes; with the exception of Europeans and North Americans, many cultures eat dog, rat, and horse meat (Myers, 2004).

These Alaskan Eskimo children are enjoying a whale blubber snack.

EVOLUTIONARY THEORIES OF HUNGER REGULATION

Now that we have covered some of the fundamentals of hunger research, in this section we will consider some of the theories concerning how eating behaviors and physiological systems evolved. As with most topics in this text, understanding the roots of the behavior may enhance our knowledge of hunger regulation.

Set-Point Theory

The **set-point theory of hunger regulation** is one of the most widely accepted hunger/satiety theories. This theory is similar to basic supply-and-demand theories: when the food or energy level drops, the demand for food increases. Researchers have spent decades trying to find set-point signals—glucose, insulin, or some hypothesized fat metabolite, the last of which was initially proposed in Kennedy and Mayer's **lipostatic theory of hunger regulation** (Kennedy, 1953; Mayer, 1955). As we discussed in the last section, more refined players such as leptin and NPY are currently being considered. Whereas this approach seems perfectly reasonable, set-point theory has serious flaws (Pinel, 2002). First, if our bodies were designed to respond to current energy supply, how do we explain the fact that over half our population is overweight? Or the fact that some individuals, such as anorexic patients, fail to respond to demand signals for increased food consumption? If there is a set-point signal, the reception seems to be more than a bit off because our society is plagued with a variety of eating disorders.

Second, if one considers the evolution of human eating, our ancestors did not have the luxury of easy food accessibility. In fact, the availability of food was quite unpredictable; consequently, to survive, it was important to consume food as it was available and to store it as fat—people never knew where the next meal would come from. The individuals who ceased eating to rub their bellies and let out their loincloths a notch once they had reached their set point would not have endured long winters or periods of drought. Warm-blooded animals require significant amounts of food to maintain thermoregulation, and it is illogical for our bodies to have evolved to respond only to deficits—once a real deficit is detected, the animal is in a critical state. A better design would be to use precautions against ever reaching the level of energy depletion.

A third weakness of set-point theory is that although it has been around for over half a century, credible evidence for it is still lacking. Yes, people are hungry after being deprived of food, but deprivation is more extreme than the normal day-to-day fluctuations of energy levels. Apparently, about half our population has an excess of fat deposits and their eating is certainly not deterred by any set point of some particular molecule.

preparatory response theory of hunger regulation Theory suggesting that the feeling of hunger may be more closely related to the body's preparation to eat than any deficit of food.

positive-incentive theory of hunger regulation Theory suggesting that people eat because it is a pleasurable, rewarding experience.

Preparatory Response Theory

Stephen Woods (University of Washington) and Jan Strubbe (University of Groningen in the Netherlands) wrote an interesting article in 1994 proposing the **preparatory response theory of hunger regulation.** Instead of thinking about hunger and all its associated cues as a system designed to *prompt* you to eat, the more immediate purpose may be to *prepare* your body for incoming food. Let's think about this for a minute. You're sitting there reading your textbook several hours after eating lunch. Everything is probably just fine with your digestive system and energy availability; however, if you should eat a large meal (a chunk of meat, several servings of vegetables, bread, and soda), your digestive system is suddenly thrown completely out of its resting state.

If a meal is invasively large—an all too common characteristic of our eating patterns—all the changes associated with it could threaten the body's physiological homeostasis. In fact, Woods (1991) views a large meal as a drug that is delivered to the body and, in the process of digestion, disrupts many precisely monitored homeostatic processes. A solution to this sudden turmoil of the digestive system is time to prepare for it. It makes perfect sense for the body to elevate its temperature to facilitate the digestive processes and decrease blood glucose levels prior to receiving a new energy load. The Russian physiologist Ivan Pavlov (1927) was one of the first to write about anticipatory responses of the digestive system. When his canine subjects perceived a cue that was associated with food, they started salivating—their mouths were preparing for the incoming food. The increase in insulin level prior to meals has also received a lot of research attention (Teff, Mattes, & Engelman, 1991). Strong support for the importance of premeal insulin secretion is the observation that, in the absence of the response, animals eat smaller meals, suggesting that this anticipatory function is necessary for the processing of food (Inoue, Bray, & Mullen, 1978). Also in support of this notion is a study in which the rats given food at a standard time each day ate more than the rats that missed their standard meal and were fed several hours later. The delayed feeding group had gone longer without food and, according to the traditional hunger theories, should have eaten more; ironically, they ate less and more slowly (Bousfield & Elliott, 1934). The fact that their bodies were not allowed to prepare for the incoming food seemed to result in less consumption.

Before we leave the preparatory response theory, let's revisit the growling stomach. If the stomach is at its quietest when it has no food to digest, then why does the stomach rumble at eating time? When food enters the stomach, the stomach engages in *peristalsis,* or the movement of the walls of the stomach to work the food down toward the intestines. In line with the preparatory response theory, we can propose that the empty, growling stomach is merely "warming up" in preparation for its next workout. The sound is present because the stomach is unfilled and the muscle walls make a noise as they rub against one another. In support of this preparatory growling hypothesis is the notion that the stomach has been conditioned to engage in this movement at a particular time every day. You can confirm this with your own gastric "vocalizations." Try an experiment on yourself: the next time your stomach begins growling preceding a time when you usually eat a meal, just skip the meal and record your stomach's activity. If your stomachs are like ours, instead of becoming increasingly intense as meal time passes (and your system becoming even more depleted), the growling typically subsides—until the next time you typically eat a meal. So you may feel hungry when your stomach is growling because, based on your routine, it is time to eat.

Positive Incentive Theory

How do you explain the fact that after just eating two portions of everything at the all-you-can-eat buffet at your favorite restaurant you salivate when the dessert tray comes around. In fact, the only factor that stops your consumption is the physical discomfort you experience as you finish your dessert. The **positive incentive theory of hunger regulation**—we eat because it is a pleasurable, rewarding experience—suggests that humans and other warm-blooded animals evolved to eat to their physiological capacity.

Historically, excessive eating behavior would have been adaptive in food-replete times. In these times of readily available food, however, this food strategy has had severe effects on weight and health. For example, as we have stated repeatedly, overeating and obesity have reached epidemic levels in many wealthy societies—one recent study reports that 64.5% of the population of the United States, that is 127 million people, are overweight (Brownell & Horgen, 2004). As food has become more plentiful in our environment, the rate of obesity has grown at an alarmingly rapid pace. Not only is eating in general a pleasurable response, but particular tastes that, in nature, promote human survival seem especially pleasing (Pinel, Assanand, & Lehman, 2000). For example, humans especially like foods that taste sweet, fatty, and salty; interestingly, these foods are naturally rich in energy and essential minerals and vitamins. We do not desire many bitter substances because that taste is often naturally associated with poison.

In a society in which there is a never-ending supply of sweet, fatty, and salty foods, it is easy to see why the rates of consumption are sky-rocketing. The empirical research suggests that animals also are strongly influenced by the positive incentive of taste. Rogers and Blundell (1980) placed laboratory rats on a diet in which two palatable foods, bread and chocolate, were available. According to depletion models of eating, the rats should have maintained their consumption rates, but that was not the case. The caloric intake of the rats increased by 84% resulting in a 50% weight gain over a period of four months. Alternatively, when Brandes (1977) diminished the positive incentive associated with eating by flavoring the rats' food with the bitter-tasting quinine, the rats decreased their eating, and even when made hypoglycemic with insulin injections, the rats continued to reduce their consumption rates. Clearly, the rats in these studies were responding not only to physiological need but to taste.

Why would nature do this to us? If the foods to which we are most attracted are rich in calories, fat, salt, and sugar, our battle of the bulge will be never-ending. It would be so nice to find foods such as carrots and broccoli irresistible—we'd be lean and loaded with lots of antioxidants for our aging brains! As previously suggested, our craving for foods such as movie popcorn and chocolate-covered raisins can be traced to our evolutionary roots. As warm-blooded animals, our ancestors needed to spend a large portion of the day making sure that they ate an adequate amount of food, especially sufficient amounts of sweet, fatty, and salty foods. Additionally, because they never knew when and where their next meal was going to be, it was adaptive for them to eat as much as they could to protect against some future food-scarce incident.

Those of us who live in times of feast as opposed to famine have ample opportunity to maximize our eating capacity. In fact, just to give you an idea about the degree of excess energy stores in contemporary humans, a lean human has enough stored energy to meet the body's energy requirements for a month, average-sized persons can store energy for up to two months, and overweight individuals are typically packing enough energy insurance for more than a year. Obviously, our evolutionary roots are at odds with our contemporary situation. If you are unhappy with the amount of excess weight you are carrying around, recall that obese people in today's society probably would have been the individuals most likely to survive in a more natural environment due to their ability to eat large amounts of food when it was available and to store it for further use. The restraint exercised by lean individuals probably would have prevented them from surviving the first period of low food availability.

Thus, the positive incentive theory helps to explain why, in an environment of readily available foods rich in fat and calories, our population is getting heavier and heavier. This theory also explains the findings from another study, which showed that, when faced with access to a large supply of a preferred food, 81% of the subjects typically ate until they felt ill (Assanand, Pinel, & Lehman, 1996).

Sensory-Specific Satiety

This theory addresses the types of food we consume. It is daunting to think that over the course of our eating, we need to make sure that we consume all the essential nutrients required for healthy living. Barbara Rolls of Johns Hopkins University proposed the **sensory-specific theory of satiety** to help us understand our eating habits when faced with food options (Rolls, 1986). Think about your favorite food for a moment. Is it French fries? Chocolate cake? Pizza? Filet mignon? You might eat a favorite food until you felt miserable, but would you do so if you could eat only your favorite food? If you're like most people, after just a few meals of your favorite food your consumption would decrease and your motivation to find another food would increase.

According to Rolls, another evolutionary pressure in eating regulation was consumption of a variety of foods to ensure the consumption of dietary nutrients required for survival. This theory helps explain why, after eating a large portion of your favorite food—to the point of refusing any more—your eyes light up when a different food is offered to you. It also explains why increased variation in food leads to enhanced consumption—to confirm this, just spend time at your local all-you-can-eat restaurant and observe the patrons' rate of consumption—and body weight.

Sensory-specific satiety seems to be influenced by the sensory properties of food rather than any gastric feedback from the food in the digestive system. Normal-weight subjects rated several commercially available foods prior to having the opportunity to eat one of these foods as a meal. After just 2 minutes of eating the food, its pleasantness rating started to decrease, whereas the pleasantness rating for the foods not being consumed remained unchanged. The pleasantness ratings were followed over the duration of an hour and the greatest decrease was 2 minutes following their consumption—when the sensory properties of the ingested food seem to diminish. Thus, in a meal, after eating a particular food for about 2 minutes, the subjects would be motivated to eat another type of food (Rolls, 1986). Perhaps this is the reason that some diets require the dieters to eat only a few types of food—or eat one type of food all day—all the grapefruit you can eat on

sensory-specific theory of satiety Theory suggesting that animals are motivated to consume a different taste after previously eating to satiety; this hypothesis explains why animals and humans placed on a diverse cafeteria diet frequently overeat.

[Box 13.1]

The Investigators

Paul Rozin

The brain wasn't Paul Rozin's first academic love; from the time he was about 9 years old he was certain he was going to be a nuclear physicist. Rozin was a bright child, and after completing the tenth grade at a high school in Brooklyn, he commenced his college education at the University of Chicago. After taking a few mathematical courses, however, he gravitated away from physics and toward biological science. Following graduation, Rozin began his graduate training in 1956 at Harvard University in the Psychology Department. At the time when B. F. Skinner was at Harvard and at the height of his career changing the direction of research in psychology toward behavior, Rozin was more interested in pursuing a biological route. Consequently, he took classes with Phil Teitelbaum—the researcher who first discovered the role of the ventromedial hypothalamus in eating behavior—and Jean Mayer, who, as previously described, proposed the glucostatic theory of hunger. Ultimately, Rozin received a joint Ph.D. in biology and psychology. After having the opportunity to work with two significant pioneers in eating research, it is no surprise that Rozin began a career delving into aspects of eating. He also contin-

Paul Rozin
COURTESY OF PAUL ROZIN

ued to be interested in the brain and took neurology courses as well.

Rozin began his teaching career at the University of Pennsylvania. Early in his career, Rozin was intrigued by the question of how animals choose their diets. Once he became bored working with rats, he began focusing on humans.

Characteristic of Rozin's diverse interests in multiple areas within the field of psychology, in the early 1970s he became interested in reading development in children, even consulting for the children's television show *Sesame Street*. But when Rozin's wife wrote a cookbook entitled *The Flavor Principle Cookbook*, Rozin's interest returned to eating. He became interested in cultural influences in taste preferences; for example, why does every child in Mexico like chili peppers whereas very few children in the United States will even try them? He also became interested in food preferences in general—and became intrigued by the role of the environment on their development. He considered questions such as why infants up to the age of 2 years have anything but a discriminating taste. These

Monday, all the pasta you can eat on Tuesday, and all the baked potatoes you want on Wednesday. After several bites, the desire—and consumption—diminish. On the other hand, Box 13.1 describes Paul Rozin's research with amnesic patients that suggests that the type and amount of recently consumed food has nothing to do with one's desire to continue eating.

DISORDERS OF EATING REGULATION

In this section we will consider three common disruptions of healthy eating patterns—obesity, anorexia nervosa, and bulimia nervosa. These conditions seem to be less about preexisting distortions of the neurobiological correlates of hunger/satiety than about the influence of a toxic eating environment and specific psychological variables. Hence, they might just as young eating machines put anything into their mouths and attempt to chew it up and swallow it. After this age, however, environmental influences become activated as children go from putting cat food in their mouths to avoiding everything but chicken tenders.

The variables playing significant roles in the development of a person's taste preferences remain an interest for Rozin. For example, do differences in the development of food preferences influence disruptions of eating regulation such as obesity? Additionally, Rozin has conducted research on the development of food aversions and feelings of disgust toward a particular food item. He feels that the origins of the emotion disgust lie in the response toward food that we find unappealing—or repulsive. In fact, disgust may play a role in the fight against obesity; in one of Rozin's talks, he displays an image of a new franchise of restaurants that he proposes for dieters—called the Used Food Café. Most people find the prospect of eating used food . . . you guessed it . . . disgusting.

Rozin has also embarked on a program of research focusing on cultural differences in eating patterns. Currently he is focusing on the differences between the United States and France. Rozin states that the French manage their eating patterns more effectively than do people in the United States. Obesity is lower in France—probably due to cultural differences, including smaller portion sizes, increased physical activity,

longer mealtimes, and decreased snacking. It is interesting that the French, with their famous high-fat sauces and pastries, remain a slimmer culture than the United States.

Paul Rozin has contributed many valuable ideas in the area of hunger regulation. His 200 articles have made a significant contribution to the psychological and medical literatures. One intriguing work is related to the issue of satiety. He found that patients with amnesia would eat up to three lunches when offered intermittently throughout the lunch period. This study is interesting because it suggests that these patients were making decisions unrelated to gastrointestinal factors about whether or not to eat a meal because they had no memory of previously eating lunch.

As you can ascertain from the diverse research approaches described, Rozin is a bit different from the typical neuroscientist, who chooses to focus on a specific problem during his or her whole career to gain credibility for the competitive grants necessary to fund expensive research. Rozin is a bit of a rebel—he is creative in his thinking about eating and doesn't hesitate to delve into a research project even though it may be different from the more traditional strategies in the field. Obviously, researchers such as Rozin are necessary to keep us thinking outside the box—in this case, the cookie box.

easily go into other chapters, such as the addiction or anxiety disorder chapters, but because they involve eating behavior, they are included in this chapter. There are no easy cures for these altered eating patterns, but we are learning more and more about them each day.

Obesity

Obesity is considered a general medical condition in the *International Classification of Diseases,* but it isn't included in the DSM-IV-TR because of the lack of evidence suggesting that obesity is associated with a psychological or behavioral syndrome. Because **obesity** involves the *behavior* of eating too much and is often associated with feelings of insecurity and self-consciousness (psychological effects), we include this condition as an eating disorder.

obesity A state of pathologically overweight due to both genetic and environmental factors. Technically one is considered obese if one's body mass index (BMI) is 30 kg/m^2 or greater.

Possible causes. If you type in the words "weight loss" in an Internet search engine, odds are you'll get over 2,000,000 hits. As you look through women's magazines, it is obvious that the female icon has become much slimmer than she was a half-century ago. Grocery stores are carrying many more fat-free and healthful food choices than they did a few decades ago. Fueled by a $30-billion dieting industry advocating the sales of diet books, videos, pills, and exercise devices, approximately 40% of women and 25% of men can be found to be dieting at any given time (Brownell & Rodin, 1994; Horm & Anderson, 1993; Serdula et al., 1993). So with a lot of general interest in losing weight, the social ideal or slim physique, and many options for fat-free food, a sociologist could conclude that our society was now much leaner than it was a half-century ago. How in the world could a culture so obsessed with thinness and weight control be so—well—fat?

The psychological well-being of overweight individuals may be more vulnerable than originally thought—research is currently indicating discrimination against overweight individuals. For example, 28% of teachers conveyed that obesity was the worst thing that could happen to a person; 24% of nurses confessed to being repulsed by obese patients, and also distressing, when grades and income variables are kept constant, parents provide less money for college for their overweight children than for their thin children (Puhl & Brownell, 2001). In addition to mental health costs, obesity is associated with a host of medical costs as well, including increased risk for diabetes type II, hypertension, cardiovascular disease, and some cancers (Brownell & Rodin, 1994). Thus, we feel that there is ample reason to consider obesity as a legitimate eating disorder in this chapter.

With 27% of U.S. adults classified as obese and another 34% classified as overweight, professionals in the field are describing the overweight condition of our society as an *epidemic*. In fact, the rates of obesity have doubled since 1900, and as can be seen in Figure 13.6, they are currently increasing at an alarming rate (Brownell & Rodin, 1994; Flegal, Harlan, & Landis, 1988; National Center for Health Statistics, 1999). Considering the attention and resources devoted to losing weight, it is imperative that researchers determine the factors contributing to our ever-increasing body weights. As described in the neurochemical section of this chapter, although neuropeptides such as leptin and neuropeptide Y are certainly involved in hunger regulation, researchers have fallen short of identifying a neurochemical magic bullet to reduce the hunger or fat storage in overweight individuals. And although genetic mutations have produced obese rats and mice, these mutations are not the underlying cause of obe-

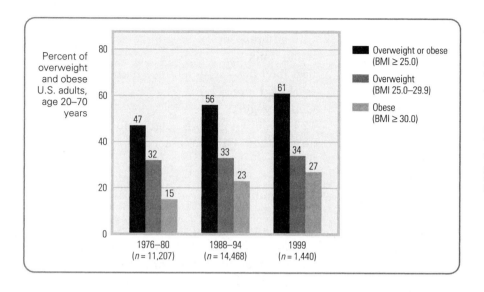

[Figure 13.6]
**Tracking rates of adult obesity
in the United States.** Age-
adjusted prevalence of overweight and obesity among U.S.
adults, ages 20 to 70 years. The
number of overweight and obese
individuals is slowly rising each
decade. Currently, more adults
than not fall in one of these
categories.

NATIONAL CENTER FOR HEALTH STATISTICS,
HTTP:WWW.CDC.GOV/NCHS/PRODUCTS/PUBS/
PUBD/HESTATS/OVER99FIG1.HTM

sity in humans. Past research on genetic factors, for example, has indicated that 25% to 40% of body weight variability in the population can be
attributed to genes that regulate factors usch as metabolic rate and number of fat cells (Brownell & Horgen, 2004). However, Eric Stice (2002) of
the University of Texas at Austin recently suggested that since obesity
rates have increased from 4% to 30% in the last century and genes do not
change that quickly, obesity must be behaviorally mediated. Even though genetic research may identify variables
that make individuals susceptible to obesity, Fairburn and
Brownell (2002) state:

> Searching for obesity genes in hopes of establishing cause may
> be akin to pursuit of a gene explaining lung cancer in smokers.
> True, the discovery might identify those most at risk and per-
> haps lead to ways to counteract the disastrous effects of tobac-
> co, but the cause of the cancer is environmental. Removal of
> the toxin would eliminate most of the disease.

In keeping with the aims of this textbook we will
emphasize the role of the brain in the epidemic of obesity and possible treatment and prevention of this condition. Instead of
focusing on reductionist neurobiology, however, we will focus on the
cognitive processing of information about eating behavior (which eventually influences neurobiological responses to food stimuli). For example, consider the following two examples of typical consumption in our
fast-paced world of eating out:

**Tracking psychological effects
of obesity.** Kelly Brownell (right)
and his undergraduate student at
Yale University, Andrew Grier, are
interested in delineating the
effects of obesity on psychological variables such as self-esteem
and self-control (see Connections).
COURTESY KELLY BROWNELL

Scenario A

Breakfast: Cinnamon scone and a grande cappuccino with whole milk

Lunch: Fast food meal with 6-ounce hamburger, large fries, and large Coke

Afternoon snack: Cup of yogurt

Dinner: 12 buffalo wings with celery and ranch dressing as appetizer, Oriental chicken salad, 12-ounce beer

Late-night snack: Chocolate chip cookie and 12-ounce glass of whole milk

Scenario B

Breakfast: Cereal with reduced-fat milk, orange juice, slice of toast, fruit, caffe latte with skim milk

Lunch: 6-ounce roasted chicken breast sandwich, baked chips, diet soda

Dinner: Minestrone soup, pasta with chicken and veg-etables, two slices of bread, ice water with lemon, 8-ounce glass of white wine

Late-night snack: Scoop of lowfat coffee fudge ice cream

As you consider each of the daily meal scenarios, it is obvious that Scenario B is the lower in calories, but by how much? After all, in Scenario A the person has a small breakfast, yogurt as a snack, and an appetizer and salad for dinner—that can't be too bad, can it? Well, brace yourself: there are more than twice the calories in scenario A than scenario B (Scenario A has an estimated 4830 calories whereas Scenario B has an estimated 2300 calories). Worse, scenario A has 86% more fat than scenario B—265 grams and 38 grams of fat, respectively. It is recommended that one consume only 65 grams of fat in a 2000-calorie diet (Jacobson & Hurley, 2002). This example shows that the toxicity of the eating environment in our society, coupled with the lack of rigorous exercise, produces a surefire recipe for obesity. Thus, changing these behaviors through education seems to be the most promising brain approach to the threat of obesity.

Treatment. As mentioned previously in this section, although several individual neurochemicals have been identified in the hunger/satiety literature, researchers have yet to develop a panacea drug to combat obesity. Several years ago, a drug known as fen-phen (a combination of fenfluramine and phentermine) hit the market and seemed to be a promising pharmaceutical agent against obesity. This drug increased the availability of both serotonin and noradrenaline and successfully increased weight loss, but it was withdrawn from the U.S. market in 1997 because of its association with abnormalities in the cardiac valves of adults (Jones et al., 2002; Volmar & Hutchins, 2001).

Although new neurochemicals are frequently identified in the literature as having promise for the pharmaceutical treatment of obesity, only a few drugs are currently approved for the long-term treatment of obesity. The drug sibutramine (Meridia) inhibits the reuptake of both norepinephrine and serotonin, and the drug Orlistat (Xenical) blocks the enzyme lipase and increases the fecal loss of triglyceride. Clinical trials indicate that these drugs produce a 5% to 10% decrease in body weight. These weight losses do not come without health costs—sibutramine has been associated with blood pressure increases and Orlistat has been associated with unappealing side effects such as wet flatulence, increased urge of bowel movement, incontinence of stool, and abdominal bloating (Bray, 2001). Others drugs such as fluoxetine and phentermine may be prescribed for obesity as well (Proietto, Fam, Ainslie, & Thorburn, 2000).

The behavioral interventions of reducing caloric and fat intake and increasing physical activity are additional options for treating obesity. Although early reports suggested that the effects of dieting were discouraging—only a small percentage of individuals could lose weight and keep it off (Stunkard & McLaren-Hume, 1959)—more contemporary studies offer more favorable results (Bjorvell & Rossner, 1992). It's probably no surprise that programs with low-calorie intake, a behavioral modification component, and an intensive education program offer very favorable long-term results (Beliard, Kirschenbaum, & Fitzgibbon, 1992; Nunn, Newton, & Faucher, 1992). As indicated by Brownell and Rodin (1994), it is important to consider the benefits of even modest success with weight loss programs; small weight losses have been associated with medical benefits such as improved blood pressure and blood glucose control. Dieting and exercise, however, are not as easy to swallow as a pill per day, so patient enthusiasm for such programs is not exceedingly high.

Drastic surgical measures are available for obese individuals. If a patient has a fat "trouble spot," the fat cells can literally be sucked out of the spot with the medical equivalent of a vacuum cleaner. This surgery, known as **liposuction,** became the most common procedure conducted by plastic surgeons (American Society of Plastic and Reconstructive Surgeons, 1990).

An even more drastic procedure, known as **gastric bypass surgery**, is becoming an attractive option for morbidly obese patients who have tried every weight loss technique with no success. In gastric bypass surgery, the stomach is reduced to a tiny pouch about the size of a thumb (approximately 1% of the size of the preoperative stomach) and is reconnected with the intestines. As described in Box 13.2, obese patients can lose

liposuction Surgical technique used to extract fat from the body.

gastric bypass surgery (also known as *bariatric surgery*) Surgery conducted in obese individuals to reduce the stomach to about 1% of its original capacity.

[Box 13.2]

Brain Matters

A Closer Look at Gastric Bypass Surgery

After trying various diets and exercise programs, Alberto Guerrero, a nurse in Miami, was at the end of his rope. His 5-foot, 9-inch frame was overburdened by the 358 pounds he was carrying around. The simple act of going to sleep was one of Alberto's biggest problems: his huge stomach would push against his diaphragm, making it difficult for him to breathe. He would go two or three nights before his body got so exhausted that he could sleep through the night. When faced with the option to have bariatric (gastric bypass) surgery, Alberto decided that it was necessary if he was ever going to live a normal life. In May of 2001, he had the Rouxen-Y procedure, which, as seen in the illustration, reduces the stomach to about 1% of its normal size. With such a reduced stomach size, patients feel sated more rapidly and for longer durations than with their larger stomachs. In a year, Alberto lost 150 pounds. He no longer has problems going to sleep at night and has adapted to his new eating strategy of avoiding high-fat food; today when he goes to a restaurant he splits an entrée with his wife and takes small bites. He says his new eating restrictions are worth it because he feels as if he has a whole new life (Contreras & Noonan, 2002).

More and more, we are reading about transformations following bariatric surgery, and with insurance companies paying for the surgery more frequently, the surgery will undoubtedly continue to be on the rise. In

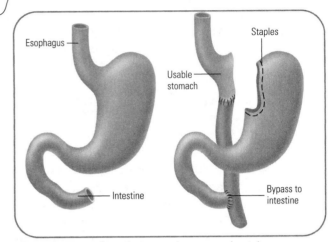

Procedure to reduce the stomach to approximately 1% of its normal size.

addition to being life-altering for gastric bypass patients, this type of surgery provides valuable information about hunger regulation. Although the empirical results are just beginning to appear in the literature and much of our information has been retrieved in case-study scenarios, we can learn a lot from this surgery. For example, we have discussed the role of many neuropeptides such as leptin and NPY in hunger regulation, but this surgery emphasizes a factor that falls outside the general vicinity of the brain—that is, the stomach. The primary modification in bypass patients is a reduction of the area of the stomach. With the smaller stomach, patients report feeling full after eating a very small meal. What does this tell us about the role of the stomach in hunger regulation? In

weight very quickly—generally 66% in one to two years—and the weight stays off in most patients (Holzwarth, Huber, Majkrzak, & Tareen, 2002). The surgery doesn't come without risks, however. Box 13.3 highlights details of gastric bypass surgery, which has been called life-saving by many health professionals.

A small group of health professionals remains cautious about submitting patients to such major surgery, especially considering some of the this preliminary stage of sifting through the gastric bypass data, it appears that the fullness of the stomach, or the tautness of the lining of the stomach, may play an important role in hunger and satiety. If this is the case, obese patients may find themselves in a never-ending battle because the more they eat the larger the stomach becomes—requiring more food to achieve a feeling of satiety.

From these initial observations, other means of decreasing the size of the stomach without undergoing traumatic bypass surgery are worth considering. Work by Allan Geliebter and his colleagues suggests that, when subjects were placed on a 600-kcal-per-day diet for four weeks, their gastric capacity decreased by about 30% (Geliebter, Schachter, Lohmann-Walter, Feldman, & Hashim, 1996). In another interesting study conducted by Geliebter and Hashim (2001), the gastric capacity was measured in normal-weight, obese, and bulimic women.

In case you're wondering how gastric capacity is measured, here are the details. Subjects are asked to fast overnight and report to the hospital around 10:00 A.M. the next day. After loosening any tight clothing and sitting in a relaxed position, the subjects are asked to swallow a 10-cm portion of a condom attached to a lubricated tube. Eventually, the condom is filled with water at a rate of 100 ml/min. After each 100 ml, subjects were asked to rate their hunger, fullness, nausea, and any discomfort. Intragastric pressure was also measured throughout this process. The process ended when the subjects expressed discomfort. From the tolerated volume data, bulimics had significantly larger gastric capacities; when another measure—the volume required to increase intragastric pressure by 5 cm of water—was used, the obese and bulimic groups were more likely to have larger stomach capacities than the normal-weight subjects. Hence, the bulimics may be able to tolerate the massive amounts of food consumed during binges because of a large stomach. On the other hand, if bulimics have a significantly larger stomach capacity, large amounts of foods may be necessary to produce a feeling of satiety.

Aside from reducing stomach capacity, gastric bypass surgery provides information about the importance of incentives in hunger regulation. Case study evidence suggests that, after having surgery, bypass patients no longer crave the high-fat foods that had been such a large part of their lives prior to surgery. On one level, this is easy to understand. As mentioned in the obesity treatment section, patients experience aversive consequences when they consume carbonated drinks, sugar, or high-fat foods. Generally, we avoid food that makes us sick, but the interesting point is that these patients don't even seem to *desire* eating the food. It appears that once these foods are associated with negative consequences, the patient no longer craves them. One gastric bypass patient conveyed that, after carrying a soda around with her every minute of the day for years and years, she doesn't even miss them. These preliminary observations about consequences associated with particular foods suggest that behavioral therapy may have unrealized potential.

As insurance companies are stepping up to pay for surgery in obese patients, we will undoubtedly learn more about the role of gastric capacity and incentives in the role of hunger regulation.

side effects experienced by a small percentage of patients (e.g., small-bowel obstructions, major leaks, and gall bladder disease; Blachar, Federle, Pealer, Ikramuddin, & Schauer, 2002; Fobi et al., 2002). Further, because of the reduced number of calories consumed by gastric bypass patients and the reduced size of the stomach, the ability and opportunity for the absorption of vitamins is greatly reduced. In order to reduce the chances of micronutrient deficiencies, patients must take vitamins and

dumping syndrome Side effect sometimes seen in patients following gastric bypass surgery; syndrome consists of nausea or general sickness following the consumption of fat or sugar.

supplements—especially to avoid deficiencies (Sugerman, 2001). Another annoying side effect is known as **dumping syndrome**—a feeling of nausea, vomiting, dizziness, and weakness that occurs if a bypass patient eats too much fat or sugar (Commonwealth Surgeons, Ltd., 2002). But the side effects are not all bad. Gastric bypass surgery significantly improves hypertension, type II diabetes, and hyperlipidemia; additionally, symptoms of sleep apnea and depression often subside following surgery (Holzwarth, Huber, Majkrzak, & Tareen, 2002). All in all, the benefits seem to outweigh the disadvantages, a fact noticed by health insurance companies, which are covering bypass surgery at an increasing rate. It is worth noting that new techniques such as the recently FDA-approved adjustable gastric banding system (also known as lap band) have been established to modify the volume of the gastric chamber with minimal surgical intervention (U. S. Food and Drug Administration, 2001).

Children and obesity. For an adult, losing weight is a long, involved process that involves life long changes in eating and rates of physical activity. Certainly the best way to treat obesity is to prevent it from occurring in the first place. This brings us to the children of our society. If 60% of the adults are facing weight problems, does the future look better for our children? Let's consider some observations. On average, children in the United States see about 10,000 food advertisements per year, 95% of which are advertising sugared cereals, candy, soft drinks, and fast foods (Brownell, 2002b). The children's menu at most restaurants perpetuates the consumption of high-calorie, high-fat foods, such as macaroni and cheese, chicken fingers, French fries, and grilled cheese sandwiches—it is difficult to find evidence of a green vegetable on a children's menu.

A favorite icon of children is Ronald McDonald, the spokesperson for McDonald's. The McDonald's corporation currently operates about 8000 playgrounds at its restaurants—cleverly increasing children's positive associations with the restaurant, incentives that are likely to persist throughout their adulthood as paying customers. But the cleverness doesn't stop there. The key positive incentive for kids seems to be toys. In a typical week McDonald's sells about 10 million Happy Meals; however, in April of 1997 after introducing a Teenie Beanie Baby with each purchase, Happy Meal sales skyrocketed to 100 million per week. And McDonald's is just one example; other restaurants have ways of luring kids as customers as well (Schlosser, 2002).

The habits depicted here are one reason why children in the United States, along with their adult counterparts, are facing an epidemic of obesity.
DONNA DAY/GETTY IMAGES

More distressing is what is happening in the schools. As parents, we had naively assumed that our children could purchase only the meal advertised on the school menu calendar that we keep posted on our refrigerators each month or a chef's salad. On the contrary, in our Virginia school district, students ages 5 to 11 make their own decisions about what they want to eat. As well as the traditional meal of a meat, vegetable, and fruit cup, children can purchase cookies, chips, Italian ice, and ice cream. A 5-year-old can choose between a traditional meal and a meal of cookies and chips. Additionally, over 5000 schools in the United States, have fast food "outlets" in their cafeterias. If the fast food isn't contracted out, many school cafeterias serve their own version of fast food—French fries, hamburgers, chicken nuggets—on a regular basis. Contracts between fast food and soft drink corporations are also appearing on the horizon. In 1993, a public school district in Colorado Springs became the first in the United States to distribute Burger King ads in the school's hallways and on the sides of school buses (Schlosser, 2002). In 1998, the Colorado Springs school district signed a multimillion dollar contract with the Coca-Cola Company. Fearful that the students were not buying enough Coke products, a letter was sent to all principals recommending that the soft drink machines be moved to locations more accessible to the students. Teachers were also encouraged to allow Coke products in the classroom (DeGette, 1998). Sadly, our children are receiving an abundance of information about eating habits, but most of it is coming from the food sales industry with virtually no formal educational programs about healthy eating habits.

It should come as no surprise at this point that children are as much at risk for obesity as adults. Unhealthy eating habits, coupled with increased viewing of television, playing of computer games, and decreased physical activity, lead to an unhealthy child population. As seen in Figure 13.7, increasing numbers of children are becoming overweight each year. From 1970 to 1999 the percentage of overweight children ages 6 to 11 increased from 4% to 13%. And these overweight children are going to become overweight adults with all the related health risks and costs—if they don't develop these health complications as children.

[Figure 13.7]
Tracking rates of childhood obesity in the United States.
Prevalence of overweight among children and adolescents ages 6 to 19 years. According to the National Center for Health Statistics, the percentage of obese children 6 to 11 years of age more than tripled from 1963 to 1999 (4% and 13%, respectively). *TIME*, JANUARY 21, 2002, P. 88

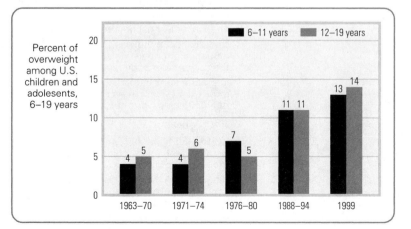

anorexia nervosa (AN) An eating disorder characterized by decreased food consumption and excessive physical activity. Although individuals with this disorder are severely underweight, they remain reluctant to eat to regain their health. If not treated, this condition may lead to the patient's death.

The increased number of adipose cells resulting from the children's weight gain can never decrease—unless liposuctioned out. Further, the increased number of adipose cells probably leads to more difficulty when the person attempts to lose weight since there are more adipose cells to try to satisfy with fat (Logue, 1991). Even children are beginning to have gastric bypass surgery (Morgan, Tanofsky-Kraff, Wilfley, & Yanovski, 2002).

It is frightening to consider how quickly our society is becoming obese. Increased awareness and appropriate social policy concerning healthy eating and increased exercise seem to be the key to reversing the trends to more reasonable body weights.

Anorexia Nervosa

Eating too much is a problem for many individuals, but for a small percentage of our population, the problem is an inability to eat enough to be healthy. As seen in Table 13.2, individuals suffering from **anorexia nervosa (AN)** lose excessive amounts of weight and fear gaining it back. Anorexia is more prevalent in industrialized societies, characterized by an abundance of food—especially societies in which thinness is considered attractive. Over 90% of anorexia cases occur in females, typically beginning in mid- to late adolescence and rarely in females older than 40 years of age (APA, 2000). Familial patterns exist for anorexia; in one study focusing on concordance rates in monozygotic and dizygotic twins, the

[Table 13.2]

DSM-IV-TR Diagnostic Criteria for Anorexia Nervosa

Refusal to maintain body weight at or above a minimally normal weight for age and height (e.g., weight loss leading to maintenance of body weight less than 85% of that expected or failure to make expected weight gain during period of growth, leading to body weight less than 85% of that expected).

Intense fear of gaining weight or becoming fat, even though underweight.

Disturbance in the way in which one's body weight or shape is experienced, undue influence of body weight or shape on self-evaluation, or denial of the seriousness of the current low body weight.

In postmenarcheal females, amenorrhea, i.e., the absence of at least three consecutive menstrual cycles. (A woman is considered to have amenorrhea if her periods occur only following hormone, e.g., estrogen, administration.)

Specify Type:

Restricting Type: during the current episode of Anorexia Nervosa, the person has not regularly engaged in binge-eating or purging behavior (i.e., self-induced vomiting or the misuse of laxatives, diuretics, or enemas).

Binge-Eating/Purging Type: during the current episode of Anorexia Nervosa, the person has regularly engaged in binge-eating or purging behavior (i.e., self-induced vomiting or the misuse of laxatives, diuretics, or enemas).

APA, 2000

MZ twins had a 55% concordance rate, compared to a 14% rate for DZ twins (Holland, Hall, Murray, Russell, & Crisp, 1984).

Possible causes. Up until the 1960s, AN was thought to be a defense against an anxiety related to sexual maturity; in a sense, because anorexia induces amenorrhea (cessation of menstruation), it can delay the onset of puberty. In the 1960s however, when thinness became fashionable, researchers made an observation about a disturbance of body image, and by 1970, it was accepted that it was a fear of fat that prompted women to starve themselves (Russell & Treasure, 1989). The association between lean fashion trends and the realization that young anorexic women seemed to be fearful of being fat has prompted researchers to consider another time during the twentieth century in which thinness was fashionable. During the 1920s, "flapper fashion" was the trend, characterized by noncurvaceous figures. Although it is hard to obtain adequate evidence, existing evidence suggests that there was a decrease in weight of college students during that time (Russell & Treasure, 1989; Silverstein, Peterson, & Perdue, 1986). Walter Kaye of the Department of Psychiatry at the University of Pittsburgh and Michael Strober of the Department of Psychiatry at UCLA (2001), in a recent review of the neurobiology of eating disorders, point out that although cultural attitudes about physical attractiveness constitute a relevant influence in the psychopathology of eating disorders, there seems to be more to this disorder. If dieting to look thin like the models (Figure 13.8 on page 496) is a primary cause of AN, then why don't more women develop AN? After all, dieting behavior is quite commonplace in our society, yet AN affects only about 0.5% of women. Further, descriptions of cases of AN have been found from the mid-nineteenth century—a time when it was not fashionable to be thin. Thus, it appears that although our thinness-crazed culture may form the backdrop for the development of AN, other factors determine who will develop this deadly disorder.

Aside from cultural influences, research suggests that AN patients have certain personality traits in common, including conformity, obsessionality, perfectionism, lack of affect and emotional expressiveness, and decreased social spontaneity. These traits do not seem to be mere correlates of the women going through the AN sickness; they persist once the AN patient has been in long-term recovery (Casper, 1990; Kaye & Strober, 2001; Strober, 1980).

It is likely that neurobiological correlates underlie these differences in personality traits. A hyperactive HPA axis has been documented in AN patients (Putignano et al., 2001); this effect normalizes after weight restoration (Kaye & Strober, 2001). Stress responsivity is probably expressed in personality traits—especially those related to anxiety.

[Figure 13.8]
Changing ideal physiques. A contemporary fashion model (Esther Canades) is considerably thinner than the ideal physique of the 1950s (for example, Marilyn Monroe).

LEFT: © EVAN AGOSTINI/LIAISON AGENCY
RIGHT: BETTMANN/CORBIS

Further, CSF B-endorphin levels are lower in underweight AN patients than in normal weight controls (Kaye, 1992; Kaye & Strober, 2001) but become normalized following recovery. The neuropeptides of the posterior pituitary are also affected in AN patients. CSF vasopressin, which regulates fluids in the kidney, is increased in AN patients. On the other hand, the other posterior pituitary neuropeptide, oxytocin, which is involved with uterine contractions and milk letdown following the birth process, along with other influences on stress reactivity, is decreased in the CSF (Demitrack et al., 1990). Again, these abnormalities stabilize following recovery (Kaye & Strober, 2001).

Among the neuropeptides related to eating behavior, NPY is elevated in underweight AN patients. As previously discussed, NPY is a powerful stimulant of feeding behavior, so you may wonder why it doesn't promote feeding in AN patients. Researchers don't know the answer to this question but speculate that the high NPY levels may contribute to the somewhat paradoxical obsession AN patients have with food (Kaye, Berrettini, Gwirtsman, & George, 1990). CCK has also been measured, but the results are mixed. Some studies report high levels of CCK in underweight AN patients. However, this effect stabilizes at recovery. It could be theorized, if this effect is indeed robust, that high CCK levels could contribute to levels of satiety in AN patients (Geracioti, Liddle, Altemus, Demitrack, & Gold, 1992). Finally, as one would suspect, the hormone leptin is significantly decreased in AN patients, suggesting that AN patients have a normal response to starvation (Grinspoon et al., 1996). Finally, another study focused on the neuropeptide **galanin,** which stimulates appetite and fat consumption. This study investigated galanin levels in recovered AN patients and healthy control women. The

galanin A neuropeptide that stimulates feeding behavior, particularly fat intake, when injected into the paraventricular hypothalamus results suggested that galanin levels were lower in the recovered AN patients than in the controls (Frank, Kaye, Sahu, Fernstrom, & McConaha, 2001).

Because of the established role of the monoamines in anxiety and emotionality systems, this system has been intensely studied as well. Generally, AN patients have low central and peripheral noradrenergic (NA) activity. This finding corroborates studies of normal-weight subjects undergoing a starvation regime (Pirke, 1996).

Walter Kaye at the University of Pittsburgh Medical Center has proposed a provocative theory related to serotonin levels and AN. Considering that serotonin generally is involved in mood regulation, impulse control, behavioral constraints, and obsessiveness, it is easy to contemplate the notion that serotonin may underlie the behavioral characteristics of AN. As mentioned previously, AN patients score high in obsessiveness, perfectionism, attention to detail, and/or harm avoidance—characteristics shared by the most successful scientists! More to the point of this discussion, however, is the observation that those characteristics occur in patients who have high levels of serotonergic activity. As seen in Figure 13.9, when one metabolite of serotonin, *5-hydroxyindolacetic acid (5-HIAA)*, is assessed in ill and recovered AN patients, it becomes apparent that the serotonergic system is involved in AN and perhaps a spectrum of eating disorders. Underweight AN patients have significantly decreased concentrations of 5-HIAA in the CSF, and CSF levels of 5-HIAA are elevated in recovered anorexics (Kaye & Strober, 2001). The 5-HIAA levels in recovered AN patients are thought to provide a window to the condition of the system prior to the onset of the illness; it appears that AN patients had high circulating levels of this metabolite and serotonergic activity prior to the onset of anorexia. Again, high levels of the monoamine might lead to the perfectionist behavior mentioned above, as well as feelings of satiety.

The anxiety caused by serotonin-induced perfectionism could be diminished, or medicated, by depleting the system of dietary precursors of serotonin. As discussed in Chapter Five on neurochemistry, tryptophan is a dietary precursor that leads to significant increases in brain levels of serotonin. Kaye and others are arguing that starvation may decrease the levels of tryptophan entering the CNS, resulting in lower levels of serotonin, and subsequently decreasing the anxiety caused by obsessing about having the perfect body weight (Kaye, 2001; Kaye, Frank, 2001). Also making this an

[Figure 13.9]
CSF 5-HIAA levels in sick and recovered AN and BN patients. As indicated in the figure, compared with healthy women, AN patients have decreased 5-HIAA activity while ill, and increased levels during recovery. BN patients only have altered (i.e. increased) 5-HIAA levels in recovery. AFTER KAYE & STROBER, 1999

interesting story is the observation that increased serotonin leads to feelings of satiety, possibly making it easy for the potential AN patient to restrict her eating in the early phases of the sickness. This finding is also supported by the finding that fluoxetine is not an effective treatment for underweight AN patients when the serotonergic system is hyporesponsive but following recovery can reduce relapse from 90% in the placebo group to just 30% in the fluoxetine group. Once recovered, the levels of serotonin are reestablished and are more likely to be responsive to SSRIs.

Researchers have also implicated dopamine in anorexia nervosa. Dopaminergic activity in the nucleus accumbens is associated with natural rewards such as eating. A group of researchers at the Instituto Scientifico Ospedale in Milan, Italy, have recently proposed that central dopamine function might play a role in anorexia nervosa. It appears that restricting their eating and engaging in excessive levels of exercise are rewarding to the AN patient. The Italian researchers found evidence of a downregulation of postsynaptic D_2 receptors and suggested that hypersecretion of dopamine was also a likely characteristic in the AN patients (Brambilla, Bellodi, Arancio, Ronchi, & Limonta, 2001). In fact, the decreased sensitivity of the D_2 receptors is probably a compensatory mechanism for the overactive dopaminergic system. In addition to being related to experiencing pleasure and rewards, dopamine suppresses the appetite—which might contribute to the ability to starve oneself. In fact, AN patients given pimozide, a D_2 receptor blocker, showed clinical improvement in AN symptoms (Chowdhury & Lask, 2001). Further, the decreased serotonin levels in ill AN patients may contribute to increased dopamine secretion—and the subsequent ability to exist on minimal food consumption (Brambilla, 2001).

Brambilla's proposal of dopaminergic involvement supports recent findings with the activity stress paradigm, also known as **activity-based anorexia.** As previously described, rats are housed in running wheels and fed one hour per day. Rats commence high running levels and fail to eat enough to remain healthy. As observed in the Chapter Five Connections box, these animals are very motivated to get to their wheel. Our students have observed increased c-*fos* activity in the nucleus accumbens of anorexic rats (Aurentz et al., 1999). Also, when activity-stress rats were given pimozide, the survival rate was increased by 50% (Lambert & Porter, 1992). Vandereycken and Pierloot (1982) found dopaminergic activity important in human anorexic patients after observing that patients given pimozide experienced a suppression of AN symptoms. The role of dopamine in A-S suggests that another cause of AN may be related to pleasure and/or control rather than trying to look like a supermodel or delaying puberty. Feeling a dopaminergic-induced "high"

activity-based anorexia An animal (rodent) model of anorexia nervosa in which animals that are food restricted increase activity levels to the point that they become very ill if the experimenter does not intervene.

after restricting food consumption could be rewarding enough for the AN patient to become addicted to the restrictive behavior and excessive exercise.

What about the data from brain-imaging studies of AN patients? These studies suggest that underweight AN patients have decreased gray matter volumes that sometimes but not always fully reverse following recovery (Chowdhury & Lask, 2001). One study reported that the ventricles of the AN patient are still small three years following recovery (Katzman, Christensen, Young, & Zipursky, 2001). In a study using magnetic resonance imaging of the hippocampus-amygdala formation in AN and control subjects, the results of AN patients showed a smaller volume of their hippocampal amydala formation than did the results of the control subjects (Giordano et al., 2001). Another study used single-photon emission computed tomography (SPECT) in women who were either sick or recovered AN patients. AN patients had obvious hypoperfusion of the temporal, parietal, occipital, and orbitofrontal lobes. In the recovered young women, hypoperfusion was observed in the tempoparietal and orbitofrontal region of the brain (Rastam et al., 2001). In an interesting positron emission tomography study conducted by Catherine Gordon and colleagues (2001), the researchers exposed AN patients to high-calorie food stimuli (bagel and cream cheese) and low-calorie food stimuli (lettuce salad with no dressing). AN patients reported elevated anxiety on exposure to the high-calorie diet compared to the responses of the normal weight subjects. Further, patients with AN responded with higher rates of elevated bilateral medial temporal lobe rCBF than did normal-weight controls. The elevated anxiety and activity in the temporal areas involved in the emotionality component of the brain suggest that food, a rewarding stimuli for most, elicits phobialike responses in AN patients.

In sum, many studies have been conducted in which some neurobiological variable is assessed in either sick or recovered AN patients and healthy control subjects. As described, many interesting differences have been observed. These findings, however, should be received with caution because they do not necessarily prove that the variables are causal in any way. In every case, the altered neurobiological variable could be the result of the starvation that the subject experienced either recently or several years ago. To get a better handle on actual causes, McHugh and colleagues have called for an emphasis on epidemiological research to identify risk factors for this disease (McHugh, Moran, & Killilea, 1989).

Treatment. Unfortunately, progress in the treatment of AN has been slow. Frequently, patients are hospitalized for extended durations to restore weight. AN patients are hospitalized at a higher rate than patients with any other psychiatric disorder other than schizophrenia and organic disorders (McKenzie & Joyce, 1992). Although this intervention is life-saving in the short term, it falls short of offering long-term benefits. In fact, this type of treatment can be very traumatic for the AN patient—hospitalizing and force feeding the patient so that she rapidly gains weight is the equivalent of throwing someone with a phobia of snakes into a snake pit. Hospital stays are expensive and insurance companies rarely cover the recommended inpatient and outpatient treatment sessions (DeAngelis, 2002). For these reasons, traditional hospitalization does not seem to be the most effective form of treatment.

Excitement is currently building around a form of family therapy that invites the parents to participate in their daughters' journey back to health. This therapy was developed by Christopher Dare and Ivan Eisler at the Maudsley Hospital in London. Although the preliminary results look promising, official endorsements of this form of therapy await the data from ongoing clinical trials (DeAngelis, 2002; Le Grange, 1999; Lock, Le Grange, Agras, & Dare, 2001). Residential treatment centers, with a more calming, relaxing, homier environment than hospitals, also provide alternative treatments for anorexic women (see Box 13.3 on page 502 for a description of one such program). As mentioned previously, in some cases the antidepressant fluoxetine has been found to lessen AN symptoms and is often incorporated into treatment strategies (Kaye & Strober, 2001; Kaye, Weltzin, Hsu, & Bulik 1991; Kaye et al., 1997).

Bulimia Nervosa

Another eating disorder, **bulimia nervosa (BN),** has also intrigued researchers and practitioners. Typically beginning during adolescence or early adulthood, BN frequently develops during a dieting episode. BN patients, often as obsessed with food as AN patients, frequently eat so much that they become uncomfortable. Because of their concern with weight, many BN patients compensate for the huge influx of calories by purging the system of food. BN patients may induce vomiting, use excessive amounts of laxatives, or exercise for extended durations to rid themselves of the calories. Bulimia nervosa affects approximately 1% to 3 % of women, and similar to AN, BN is one-tenth as prevalent in males. BN patients are more difficult to identify because they are more likely than anorexia patients to remain at a normal body weight. BN is seen in most industrialized countries that have been studied, including the United States, Europe, Canada, Australia, New Zealand, Japan, South Africa and the countries of Europe (APA, 2000). (See Table 13.3)

Purging is related to a host of medical problems. If excessive vomiting is used, the BN patient's teeth can be damaged due to a permanent loss

bulimia nervosa An eating disorder characterized by bouts of both overeating and self-induced vomiting/laxative use. Symptoms are often responsive to serotonergic treatments.

[Table 13.3]

DSM-IV-TR Diagnostic Criteria for Bulimia Nervosa

Recurrent episodes of binge eating. An episode of binge eating is characterized by both of the following:

Eating in a discrete period of time (e.g., within any 2-hour period) an amount of food that is definitely larger than most people would eat during a similar period of time and under similar circumstances.

A sense of lack of control over eating during the episode (e.g., a feeling that one cannot stop eating or control what or how much one is eating).

Recurrent inappropriate compensatory behavior in order to prevent weight gain, such as self-induced vomiting; misuse of laxatives, diuretics, enemas, or other medications; fasting; or excessive exercise.

The binge eating and inappropriate compensatory behaviors both occur, on average, at least twice a week for 3 months.

Self-evaluation is unduly influenced by body shape and weight.

The disturbance does not occur exclusively during episodes of Anorexia Nervosa.

Specify Type:

Purging Type: during the current episode of Bulimia Nervosa, the person has regularly engaged in self-induced vomiting or the misuse of laxatives, diuretics, or enemas.

Nonpurging Type: during the current episode of Bulimia Nervosa, the person has used other inappropriate compensatory behaviors, such as fasting or excessive exercise, but has not regularly engaged in self-induced vomiting or the misuse of laxatives, diuretics, or enemas.

APA, 2000, p. 594

of dental enamel. Increased cavities are also frequently observed. The abuse of laxatives may lead to a dependency on such products to stimulate bowel movement. Purging in any form may lead to fluid and electrolyte imbalances; further, on rarer occasions, severe medical complications such as cardiac arrhythmias, esophageal tears, and gastric rupture may develop (APA, 2000).

Possible causes. Because the concordance rates of BN for monozygotic twins is higher than it is for dizygotic twins (50% and 35%, respectively), genetic influences for this disorder are of particular interest to researchers. There also seems to be a strong relationship between AN and BN; research suggests that the twin of a twin suffering from AN is almost three times more likely to have BN than the twin of an unaffected twin (Kendler et al., 1995; Walters & Kendler, 1995). However, research also suggests a more general eating disorder phenotype as opposed to more specific AN and BN phenotypes. This research is confusing, though, because many individuals with eating disorders also suffer from other psychiatric symptoms such as depression, and conversely, many individuals suffering from psychiatric disorders develop eating disorders that are secondary to the primary disorder. Hence it is difficult to differentiate between the genetic chicken and egg in these studies (Kaye & Strober, 2001).

[Box 13.3]

A Case in Point

Sara Hunnicutt's Bout with Anorexia Nervosa

A few years ago, when Sara Hunnicutt heard her stomach growling as she went to bed, it brought a smile to her face and a sense of accomplishment, knowing that she had managed to defy nature and deny herself food yet one more day. Accomplishment and achievement were very important to her; she was valedictorian of her Pennsylvania high school class, and during her sophomore year at the University of Richmond, she maintained a 3.8 grade point average. But Hunnicutt was also becoming an overachiever on the dieting front. Typical of many freshmen who find themselves selecting food from what seems like an endless list of choices in the cafeteria each day—in addition to enjoying pizza late at night with friends—Hunnicutt's weight increased from 115 to 130 pounds (on a 5-feet-1-inch frame). She soon started a rigid diet of cereal with skim milk each morning, a cereal bar, fruit, or pretzels for lunch, and some type of pasta for dinner. Additionally, she exercised excessively. This rigor resulted in the loss of the weight she wanted to lose plus a lot more: about 40 pounds, as she dropped to a low of 90 pounds. Hunnicutt was proud of the self-discipline she used to deprive herself of food. Even though she wore a size 0 and bought some of her clothes in children's departments, she still didn't perceive herself as anorexic. In her mind, anorexics ate only lettuce and were the size of a stick, but she ate a little more. When she stopped menstruating for several months, her gynecologist knew that her massive loss of fat was the reason and recommended that Hunnicutt gain weight.

One of the intriguing questions about anorexia is how an intelligent person who has spent his or her life going from one impressive accomplishment to another can fail to engage in the one behavior necessary for survival—eating. Every young woman's story is different, but let's look at what brought Hunnicutt to this point. Primarily, while she was in high school, her father died after losing a battle with brain cancer, and although she tried to keep going, Hunnicutt was still in a lot of emotional pain as she entered college. Additionally, once she got to the University of Richmond, she was faced with not being a big fish in a little pond anymore—she was just one of a sea of valedictorians. Hence, emotional angst due to losing her father at a young age and anxiety about competing for grades at college set the stage for a drastic coping response. When she thought that she needed to lose weight, her coping response seemed obvious—gaining control over eating. As she felt more and more accomplishment with every pound she lost, she also knew that she was sending a message to her loved ones about the emotional pain she was still experiencing.

Once it was recommended that Hunnicutt gain weight, she was so far into the anorexia disorder that she couldn't gain weight on her own. She decided to enter the Renfrew Center for Eating Disorders in Philadelphia, which was close to her home. This residential facility provided a warm, cozy, homelike environment for patients and provided opportunities for both group and individual counseling each day. Although food consumption was monitored closely, patients weren't force-fed in any way. For each meal they had the opportunity to select the particular entrées they wanted to eat—a task that continued to give the patients control over their eating and enabled them to

Another possible cause of BN is related to overconcern about body shape and weight—a concern that may be related to cultural norms of body weight. Researchers find that even recovered BN patients have these concerns and continue to have abnormal eating habits and mood fluctuations. The persistence of these symptoms after recovery suggests that they were probably present before the development of BN; however,

COURTESY OF SARA HUNNICUTT

become active participants in their recovery process. If they didn't finish the appropriate amount of food during the daily meal sessions, they were required to make up the missed calories by drinking Ensure at the end of the day. Loaded with fat and calories, this product was a nightmare for AN patients, so they were motivated to avoid that consequence. At any point during the meals or during the day, there were plenty of counselors around to talk about anxieties. Accustomed to being an obedient student, Hunnicutt always ate her meals as she was told. As an additional component of her program, she met with psychologists and psychiatrists throughout her recovery period. She also was placed on Prozac as a pharmacological aid. Sara's insurance paid for only two weeks of inpatient therapy, so she moved out and continued as an outpatient at the center every day from 8:00 to 5:00. She subsequently weaned herself to three nights per week and then one group session per week.

After taking a year off from school to focus on her recovery, Hunnicutt was ready to go back and complete her major in sociology. Evidence of her confidence in her recovery is seen in her decision to study abroad in Scotland for her final semester—thousands of miles from her family and therapists. After graduation in 2001, Hunnicutt adopted healthy eating habits, and although she still loves to exercise, she keeps it to a reasonable amount. She currently works in the employee benefits department at a Philadelphia law firm. When she can get away, she travels around the country with her boyfriend. As she reflects on the whole ordeal with anorexia, she says that the time when she was sick seems like a blur but that her recovery has clearly been a miracle. When asked how she currently copes with anxiety, Sara admitted that she uses exercise as a coping response when she's feeling anxious—but she limits stress workouts to no longer than an hour. She also knows that it is okay to just relax and watch TV when she needs a mental break.

Thus, Hunnicutt is currently a healthy, happy, well-adjusted young woman. She has worked her way from a fragile 90-pound person who was dominated by thoughts of food to a college graduate with a career, supportive family, and boyfriend. And how much does she weigh now? She reports that her weight is in a healthy range—and that was good enough for us. It seems harmful to define her success in recovery by a number considering that her obsession with certain weight- and food-related numbers played an important role in the development of AN in the first place. As seen in the picture she sent us, Hunnicutt certainly seems to have moved beyond anorexia.

the development of the eating disorder probably exaggerates these symptoms—for example, concerns about thinness, symmetry, and perfectionism (Collings & King, 1994; Kaye & Strober, 2001).

As with AN, altered neuropeptide levels have been observed in BN. Similar to AN, decreased levels of CSF B-endorphin have been observed in sick BN patients and these levels normalize following recovery (Kaye,

peptide YY (PYY) Peptide closely related to NPY and also implicated in hunger stimulation.

1992). The research with the strong cousin of NPY, **peptide YY (PYY)**, presents an interesting scenario. Although levels of PYY are normal in acutely ill BN patients, they increase about a month following abstinence from binge eating and purging. It is unknown what role this postsickness increase might suggest: a compensatory response to the reduction in binge eating, some epiphenomenon of the pathologic eating in which the BN patient engaged during the sickness, or a preexisting condition that was normalized with the binge episodes (Kaye & Strober, 2001). The apparent satiety neuropeptide CCK is also reduced in BN patients, and intravenous CCK-8 was found to suppress a binge in BN patients (Brambilla, 2001).

Among neurotransmitters, the most significant findings have been found once again with serotonin, suggesting that this neurotransmitter may be related not just to one specific eating disorder but to the spectrum of eating disorders. Looking at the right half of Figure 13.9, you'll notice that whereas 5-HIAA levels are the same as healthy controls during recovery, recovered levels exceed 150% of normal levels (Kaye & Strober, 2001). Thus, in both recovered AN and BN individuals, levels of CSF 5-HIAA levels are high, which may contribute to the obsessions with symmetry and exactness and a tendency toward perfectionism, suggesting that high 5-HIAA levels may contribute to a spectrum of behavior characterized by behavioral overcontrol (Kaye & Strober, 2001). Other evidence of serotonergic involvement was recently found when serotonin 2A receptor activity was measured in recovered BN patients and normal control women. Whereas the normal controls had age-related decreases in 5-HT2A receptors, no age-related changes were observed in the recovered BN patients (Kaye, Frank, et al., 2001).

Treatment. Because altered serotonergic activity has been documented in BN patients, it is no surprise that one of the most effective pharmacological therapies is antidepressants—either tricyclic antidepressants or SSRIs (Brambilla, 2001). The pharmacologically induced benefits may fade over time however. Additionally, a recent multisite study testing the efficacy of two forms of psychotherapy reported encouraging results. Cognitive-behavioral therapy addressing the unrealistically negative thoughts related to body image that plague BN patients was compared to interpersonal psychotherapy addressing problems in current relationships. Both therapies were effective treatments, although a more immediate effect was observed with the cognitive-behavioral therapy (Agras, Walsh, Fairburn, Wilson, & Kraemer, 2000). Most of the research indicates that cognitive-behavioral therapy is effective for about 60% to 70% of BN patients with remission rates approaching 30% to 50% (Arnow, 1997).

DIGESTING THE CONFLICTING THEORIES OF EATING REGULATION

In this chapter we have taken a multifaceted approach to understanding the influential factors that determine the quantity and type of food we place in our mouths. Although we began this chapter thinking that the bulk of these factors would be the neurochemicals and neuroanatomical circuits involved with hunger regulation, an emphasis of this textbook, it quickly became obvious that two other factors, namely human evolutionary predispositions toward certain foods and the environment in which we live, play equally if not more significant roles in hunger regulation.

Trying to understand the mechanisms underlying eating disorders was considered in the last part of this chapter. Because obesity affects both brain and behavioral factors, it was included with the more traditionally observed eating disorders, anorexia nervosa and bulimia nervosa. The toxic food environment characterized by huge portions, high-fat foods, and unhealthy eating strategies all undoubtedly contributes to obesity. Anorexia and bulimia nervosa represent extremes of control and consumption in the spectrum of eating disorders. Although extensive research has been conducted on these disorders, there are more questions than answers related to effective treatment strategies. Genetics has been implicated as being a causal factor in several eating disorders, but, as Walter Kaye suggests, genetics probably only loads the eating disorders gun; it is the environment—complete with high-fat foods, super-thin models, and an abundance of stress—that actually pulls the trigger.

After an in-depth look at the historical and contemporary literature concerned with hunger regulation and related disorders, it is easy to feel confused about some of the conflicting ideas that emerge in these studies. Let us consider a few of these conundrums. If humans evolved to take advantage of eating opportunities leading to adequate intake of fat, sugar, and salt, how can certain individuals with anorexia override their evolutionary past and starve themselves? If the sensory-specific satiety theory is correct in suggesting that we also evolved to eat a diverse diet, why do so many parents have to fight with their children to get them to eat anything other than chicken nuggets? And what happened to turn those children from infants who would place anything in their mouths to kids with pathologically discriminating tastes? Why is it that parents don't hesitate to vaccinate their children against chicken pox, an admittedly annoying virus that lasts about a week, but seem to resist any type of inoculation against obesity, a condition that may cause significant lifelong health and psychological problems as well as a shorter life?

On another note, if positive incentives are related to increased consumption of certain foods, how do gastric bypass patients ignore a life's worth of positive associations related to excessive eating and lose even their desire to eat these foods after having surgery? And if gastric feedback about the contents of the stomach is so important—as indicated in the gastric bypass patients—how is it that experimental amnesic patients (discussed in Box 13.1) completely ignored the two lunches already occupying their stomachs and welcomed a third lunch? If cultural influences are so important in the development of eating disorders, why do only 0.5% of young women exposed to our cultural environment of abundant foods and thin female icons develop anorexia? If the stomach is mostly active during the digestion of food, why do our stomachs growl so much when we are hungry—and have no food to digest? If obesity involves unhealthy modifications of behavior (eating behavior), psychological processes (feelings of a lack of control, low self-esteem, and so on), and life functioning (possibly due to an inability to engage in certain tasks and activities because of body size and documented discrimination), why is it not recognized in DSM-IV-TR as an eating disorder? We've addressed some of these questions in the text of this chapter, but many of these conflicting theories and findings remain difficult to swallow, much less digest.

Summary

Eating Regulation

Washburn and Cannon conducted the classic study suggesting that the activity of the stomach was a critical criterion for experiencing hunger. Later studies suggested that the stomach is quietest when no food is present.

Several areas of the hypothalamus have been implicated in hunger regulation. The VMH was initially viewed as the satiety center and the LH as the hunger center—both contributing to the dual-centers hypothesis of eating. Today, the PVN is recognized as being more heavily involved in hunger regulation.

Several neurochemicals, such as glucose, leptin, neuropeptide Y, CCK, and insulin, have been shown to contribute to hunger regulation in the controlled settings of laboratories. To have a significant impact on hunger regulation, a pharmaceutical agent would probably have to influence more than one of these important substances.

Based on certain genetic variations leading to overweight rats and mice, such as the *ob/ob* mice and the Zucker rats, it is obvious that genetics is a contributing factor to an individual's susceptibility to obesity. Finding examples of these genetic mutations in humans, however, is a difficult task.

Evolutionary Theories of Hunger Regulation

Several evolutionary theories have been proposed to explain the eating strategies of animals and humans. In this chapter, the following evolutionary theories were described: set-point theory, preparatory response theory, positive incentive theory, and sensory-specific satiety.

Disorders of Eating Regulation

Obesity is on the rise and becoming a threat to the well-being of our society. Although the neurobiology of obesity is important, social policies related to consumption and environmental influences are also important pieces of the hunger regulation puzzle. Treatments for obesity are quite drastic; for example, bariatric or gastric bypass surgery is becoming more popular for the treatment of severe obesity. Rates of obesity in children are growing each year. It is important that children are informed about the hazards of obesity and that eating healthy foods and maintaining a healthy lifestyle are required to diminish the high rates.

Anorexia nervosa is seen in .5% of young women and has the highest death rate of all psychiatric disorders. Although societal values related to body ideals may set the stage for the development of these disorders, other factors such as stress, desire for control, and variations in neurochemicals such as serotonin and dopamine also contribute to susceptibility to the development of this disease.

Bulimia nervosa is slightly more prevalent than anorexia; this disorder responds to both pharmacological and cognitive-behavioral therapies.

Key Terms

ventromedial hypothalamus (p. 472)

lateral hypothalamus (p. 472)

dual-centers hypothesis of hunger regulation (p. 472)

noradrenergic bundle (p. 473)

paraventricular nucleus (p. 473)

glucose utilization theory of hunger regulation (p. 474)

cholecystokinin (p. 475)

leptin (p. 475)

neuropeptide Y (NPY) (p. 476)

arcuate nucleus (p. 476)

oxexins (p. 477)

set-point theory of hunger regulation (p. 479)

lipostatic theory of hunger regulation (p. 479)

preparatory response theory of hunger regulation (p. 480)

positive incentive theory of hunger regulation (p. 481)

sensory-specific theory of satiety (p. 483)

obesity (p. 485)

liposuction (p. 489)

gastric-bypass surgery (p. 489)

dumping syndrome (p. 492)

anorexia nervosa (p. 494)

galanin (p. 496)

activity-based anorexia (p. 498)

bulimia nervosa (p. 500)

peptide YY (PYY) (p. 504)

For Further Consideration

Brownell, K.D., & Horgen, K. B. (2004). *Food fight.* New York: Contemporary Books. Brownell, a respected researcher in the field of eating behavior and Director of the Yale Center for Eating and Weight Disorders, takes his academic gloves off as he attempts to wage a war against public health policies (or lack of them) that are encouraging our society to overeat. Considering that obesity has now surpassed smoking in terms of health-care costs, Brownell fears that the food industry's free access to children may lead to the current generation of children being the first to have shorter lives than their parents, Brownell is serious about bringing these issues to the public arena. He claims that, in a society in which pets are fed better diets than our children, public indifference toward the food industry, coupled with corporate opportunism, have to be addressed in order to get our society back on a healthy track. Brownell and Horgen also present potential public policy initiatives that may reverse the obesity trend.

Kaye, W., & Strober, M. (2001). The neurobiology of eating disorders. In Charney, D.S., Nestler, E. J., & Bunney, B. S. (Eds.), *Neurobiology of mental illness* (pp. 891-906). New York: Oxford University Press. This thorough chapter reviews the relevant empirical evidence addressing the neurobiological risk factors and clinical pathology of Anorexia Nervosa and Bulimia Nervosa. Atypicalities in numerous neurochemical systems (e.g., neuropeptide Y, B-endorphin, CCK, vasopressin, oxytocin, leptin, serontonin, norpinephrine), mood and cognitive characteristics, and medical physiology are discussed. Kaye and Strober advocate aggressive, sustained multifaceted treatment that encompasses nutritional, behavioral, and psychological elements of the syndromes. An emphasis is placed on the pharmacological normalization of monoaminergic and neuropeptidergic functions in treating these disorders.

Pinel, J.P.J., Assanand, S., & Lehman, D.R. (2000). Hunger, eating, and ill health. *American Psychologist, 55,* 1105-1116. This article evaluates our contemporary eating habits through an evolutionary window. Existing in an environment with limited food resources, the authors argue that our ancestors evolved the ability to consume as much food as possible when it was available to protect against future starvation. The problem comes, however, when that biological system is placed in today's environment (rich with food resources); contemporary humans still experience a strong motivation to consume to excess. Ironically, these authors point out that "...the individual who is most at risk in modern societies— the individual with an insatiable appetite who uses her or his energy efficiently and stores the excess— would be most suited to live in a natural environment." (p. 1112). The positive-incentive theory of food consumption is also discussed and presented as a potential explanation for anorexia nervosa with therapeutic implications.

Schlosser, E. (2002). *Fast food nation.* Perennial: New York. Schlosser acts as an investigative reporter to unearth the origins of our fascination with fast food and the immense success of this industry. Warning: if you enjoy fast food, go out and order your favorite meal before reading Fast Food Nation because your perception of that food will likely be permanently altered after reading this book. Among other disturbing societal changes, the author claims that the fast food industry has fueled the obesity epidemic and will continue to do so as our children are continuously bombarded with fun fast food messages through the media.

Clinical Neuroscience: Ethical Considerations and Future Directions

Connections

Superman, Stem Cells, and the Senate

Until the summer of 1995, Christopher Reeve was a successful actor, the embodiment of Superman, who he portrayed in a popular series of movies. A gifted athlete in real life, Reeve enjoyed many sports, including sailing, scuba diving, and horseback riding. After falling from a horse in May 1995 during a jumping competition, however, his life changed forever. When his horse balked at a jump, Reeve was pitched forward off the horse, landing on his head. His spinal cord was severed at the second cervical nerve and he was paralyzed below the shoulders.

In that split second, Reeve was transformed into, as he later described it, a "forty-two-year-old toddler" dependent on a ventilator for every breath and on the care of others for the most mundane daily activities. Even the most resilient among us would find it difficult to maintain sufficient cognitive and emotional energy to focus on recovering from such an accident. Reeve quickly realized, however, that he would have to focus on many more issues than his own medical regimen to recover. He soon learned that, contrary to his doctors' proclamation that his spinal cord would never regenerate, a few scientists thought such a feat could be accomplished.

These scientists faced many obstacles —money and political support among them—for pursuing exciting new embryonic stem cell research on restoring spinal function (see Chapter Six). Christopher Reeve soon realized that fund raising and politics were as important to his recovery as his daily rehabilitation therapy. With the energy and enthusiasm typical of his theatrical work, Reeve attacked each obstacle.

He lobbied for more funds to be directed toward the National Institutes of Health (NIH), especially for spinal cord injury projects. Next he tackled the NIH ban on funding for embryonic stem cell research by writing a letter to each member of the Senate as they were considering the Stem Cell Research Act of 2000. Today, NIH-funded researchers are severely limited by government restrictions on this research, which is critical to any hope of recovery for patients like Christopher Reeve. In response to this state of affairs, Reeve (2002) wrote:

> It is our responsibility to do everything possible to protect the quality of life of the present and future

generations. A critical factor will be what we do with human embryonic stem cells . . . . They have been called "the body's self-repair kit."

No obstacle should stand in the way of responsible investigation of their possibilities . . . In fertility clinics, women are given a choice of what to do with unused fertilized embryos: they can be discarded, donated to research, or frozen for future use . . . But why has the use of discarded embryos suddenly become such an issue? Is it more ethical for a woman to donate unused embryos that will never become human beings, or to let them be tossed away as so much garbage when they could help save thousands of lives?

While we prolong the stem cell debate, millions continue to suffer. It is time to harness the power of government and go forward. (p. 96)

The days of cutting-edge neuroscientists having to think only about their research are history; challenges such as ethical and faith-based issues related to the use of living tissue, validity of clinical trials, and availability of funds are here to stay. In 2000, Reeve again took the stage—this time as an informed and passionate speaker on the topic of spinal cord recovery—to address thousands of neuroscientists in New Orleans at the Society for Neuroscience. He was the first nonscientist ever to address this group.

Regretfully, as we completed final edits for this chapter, Christopher Reeve died of heart failure. Up until his death, the diversion from his actual rehabilitation therapy had not prevented his progress. Unable to rely on the promise of stem cells that have the potential of developing into nervous tissue, he sustained a rigorous physical therapy program and an intense mental focus. Five years after his injury he surprised himself and amazed his doctors and the scientific community by demonstrating that he could move his fingers and lift his arm. This accomplishment was difficult to explain, considering that the spinal cord nerves that move the fingers and arm are located below the place where the cord was severed. The medical textbooks teach future doctors that this is impossible; Reeve, however, seemed to enjoy rewriting the pages on spinal cord recovery.

Following Reeve's untimely death, the Christopher Reeve Paralysis Foundation is poised to continue supporting innovative research in the area of neural regeneration.

We have now come full circle. We began this book by arguing for the emerging discipline of clinical neuroscience and covering the historical, methodological, and fundamental science behind this exciting new field. We then discussed the relevance and therapeutic potential for treating a representative set of clinical disorders and considered the use of neuroscience information, incorporating strategies such as pharmacological and cognitive-behavioral interventions in treating and preventing mental illness. Here we consider some emerging ethical controversies springing from clinical neuroscience research, discuss additional evidence confirming the plasticity of the nervous system, and emphasize the importance of going forward in a responsible, ethical, and methodologically sound manner.

ETHICAL WAVES ON THE SEA OF NEUROSCIENCE

We've covered a lot of information about both the fundamentals and applications of neuroscience in this text. As the experience of Christopher Reeve makes clear, greater knowledge about the nervous system is accompanied by more questions and increased responsibilities concerning the morality and clinical efficacy of neuroscience findings and applications. **Neuroethics** is a convergence of disciplines as diverse as philosophy and religion, medicine and psychology, to recognize and address moral issues related to the rapidly growing and changing field of neuroscience.

In May 2002, the rising tide of ethical considerations was evident at a conference entitled Neuroethics: Mapping the Field (Marcus, 2002). More than 150 neuroscientists, psychiatrists, psychologists, bioethicists, philosophers, lawyers, and journalists convened in San Francisco for this landmark event. The neurobiology of criminal behavior, the neural basis of morality, medicalization of our minds, cloning, cell transplants, brain enhancement, and the role of religion in neuroscience were among the vast array of topics covered.

Neuroethics is quickly gaining recognition as a formal piece of the clinical neuroscience puzzle. Knowledge that has the potential to reduce suffering or enhance quality of life does not grow in a vacuum: gains in knowledge must coincide with a government willing to financially and legally support the research. More than ever before neuroscientists are required to leave their comfortable laboratory benches and speak to various political audiences and the general population about the benefits of their research. They must engage in lively interdisciplinary conversations with colleagues in fields that attempt to divine the social and economic costs and benefits of moving forward with certain lines of research.

Here we limit our coverage to several of the important controversies facing contemporary neuroscientists: (1) how neuroscience is influencing our thoughts about criminal behavior and relevant legal evidence and (2) how the hype surrounding psychopharmacology and behavioral engineering is influencing our minds and brains.

neuroethics Convergence of several disciplines, such as philosophy, religion, and medicine, to recognize the importance of ethical issues related to the rapidly changing field of neuroscience.

Neuroscience and Criminal Behavior

In Chapter One you learned about Phineas Gage, perhaps the first clinical neuroscience case study. Recall that damage to Gage's frontal lobe resulted in personality changes (namely, loss of impulse control and judgment problems) in the absence of other general medical problems (see Figure 1.3). How can disruptions of brain function exact a toll on personality? Can such disruptions actually cause criminal behavior? Could brain damage or malfunction lead a once moral, upstanding member of the community to a life of crime? If so, how does a jury assign responsibility for the crime in such cases?

Brain areas influencing criminal behavior: The usual suspects. Neurologists Jeffrey Burns and Russell Swerdlow, both at the University of Virginia, recently reported a case study suggesting that a brain tumor could lead to criminal behavior (Burns & Swerdlow, 2003). This case involved a schoolteacher who, contrary to his typical behavior, started soliciting prostitutes and visiting child pornography Web sites. Eventually his wife had him evicted from their home when she learned that he had made sexual advances toward children.

This case took a turn when the teacher checked himself into the hospital complaining of headaches and an increasing urge to rape his landlady. MRI scans showed an egg-sized tumor in the right orbitofrontal cortex, an "executive area" known to be associated with moral decision making. The pedophilia and rape tendencies subsided on the removal of the tumor. Eventually, however, his behavior reverted again, and sure enough, MRI scans confirmed the regrowth of the tumor.

This example suggests that brain abnormalities, in this case a tumor, can lead to amoral or criminal behavior, which may necessitate a reevaluation of legal terms such as *crime, motive,* and *punishment.* But, how does an assault on one's brain tissue lead to a specific effect on one's ethical thoughts and behaviors? Some "gambling" experiments have shed light on this question. Antonio Damasio, a neurologist at the University of Iowa College of Medicine, and his colleagues designed a program of research in which they observed subjects with frontal lobe damage playing a card game.

Prior to the game, the subjects were given $2000 in realistic-looking play money and told that the object of the game was to lose as little money as possible. The subjects soon learned that when cards from two of the four decks on the table were turned over, they might get a decent payment or occasionally be hit with a rather large monetary penalty. The other two decks generally paid less but did not have exceptionally high surprise penalties. When subjects in this experiment were monitored for skin conductance, a measure of emotionality that assesses subtle physiological events—such as sweating—differences were observed between patients with frontal lobe damage and normal subjects.

Damasio found that, prior to turning over a card from the high-risk deck, normal subjects exhibit significantly more electrodermal, or somatic, activity than the patients with frontal lobe damage. This research validates the "gut" feelings so many of us talk about when we're on the brink of making an important decision. In this case, prior to making a "gutsy" decision, we experience a **somatic marker** that typically makes us step back and reassess the situation before acting.

A person without this physiological response might be more likely to engage in risky behavior. In his book *Descartes' Error,* Damasio (1994) suggests that the prefrontal cortex is one of the few brain regions that can eavesdrop on virtually every activity occurring in our bodies and brains at a given time. Consequently, he's noticed more risk taking and uninhibited behavior in many of his patients suffering from damage to this important brain surveillance system.

Research conducted by Adrian Raine of the University of Southern California in Los Angeles supports Damasio's ideas about the importance of the prefrontal cortex (PFC) in ethical decisions. More specifically, his work suggests that a section of the PFC, the orbitofrontal cortex (OFC), is involved in the psychopathic condition leading to criminal acts. As seen in Figure E.1, PET scans suggest that convicted murderers have less OFC activity than noncriminal subjects. MRI scans suggest that PFC volume is reduced by 14% in men who have committed violent crimes.

In a related line of research, James Blair, at University College London, thinks the amygdala plays an influential role in criminal behavior (Abbott, 2001). His work has shown that this structure responds to sadness and anger in others—empathy, if you will—in normal subjects. He hypothesizes that amygdala dysfunction might lead to a lack of fear and empathy, making intrusive, aggressive social behavior more likely.

Further support for brain involvement in criminal behavior has been gathered by psychiatrist Dorothy Lewis and neurologist Jonathan Pincus. They have spent considerable time performing clinical interviews on juvenile offenders in Connecticut. Overwhelmingly, both investigators conclude that the most vicious criminals have experienced a combination of child abuse and brain injury. According to Lewis and Pincus, this toxic mixture results in an impediment in the individual's ability to follow the rules of society—a likely task for the executive function of the PFC.

Evidence of deficits in following rules are seen in a card-sorting task in which the juvenile offender has to change from using color as a sorting variable to using number—the subject simply keeps following the old rule that is no longer appropriate. Also, these subjects have difficulty when there are no structured rules. For example, when

somatic marker Body signal, such as altered electrodermal activity, that is interpreted by the brain as an indication of a relevant impending event.

[Figure E.1]
OFC activity in criminal behavior. Pet scans show that the OFC activity in the prefrontal cortex is much lower in convicted murderers than in noncriminals. This suggests an important role in ethical decision-making for the PFC.

RAINE, D., PHIL, ADRIAN *NATURE, 410,* MARCH 15, 2001

Normal   Murderer

Lewis and Pincus use the word-fluency task, they ask the subject to name as many words they can think of that begin with a certain letter, let's say F, in 1 minute.

People with a history of frontal lobe damage have trouble with this activity. This unstructured task requires the successful subject to make free associations as they mentally jump around from word to word. These subjects, however, get stuck on one root word—four, fourteen, forty, forty-four—using it over and over and not coming up with the normal number of about 14 words. If you give the same subject a more structured task—say, name 16 items in the grocery store in 1 minute, they perform at the same level as subjects without frontal lobe damage (Gladwell, 1997).

So how does this line of research affect society's thoughts about criminal behavior? It is certainly easier thinking that criminals are "bad" people who deserve to be punished. The thought that a malfunctioning brain might push someone to commit a crime, in a similar fashion as a malfunctioning nerve in the arm may lead to paralysis, is quite unsettling for many of us.

This research muddies the waters about personal responsibility, intent, and blame. Whereas defense lawyers are already bringing researchers into the courtroom to testify on behalf of their clients who may have suffered a form of brain injury, the jury is still out on this line of research. It is difficult to tease out the brain injury from chronic substance abuse in many of these studies; also, most of the imaging of the violent individual's brain is conducted after the person has been sitting in a jail cell for some time, and it is difficult to discern what effect such an altered environmental experience has had on the prisoner's brain.

Many of the young offenders studied by Lewis and Pincus exhibited a lifetime of bad decisions and violent behavior, making it difficult to pinpoint a single cause of the criminal behavior. However, if a person suddenly starts engaging in criminal behavior following a lifetime of adhering to the rules, as observed in the schoolteacher who suddenly developed a tendency for pedophilia, there may be a neural cause such as a brain tumor.

Another example of the brain causing an abrupt shift to a criminal act may be seen in the data collected by forensic psychiatrist Anneliese Pontius. After interviewing about 200 alleged murderers, she noticed a pattern in about 20 cases. All 20 were to some extent loners and very shy, and they experienced what seemed to be a psychotic break and committed a heinous crime. Many times the victim was unknown and there was no motive. After the event, each suspect was remorseful and did not hesitate to confess to the crime.

Pontius argues that the dysfunctional social behavior, years and years of loneliness and rumination about life's stresses and traumas, might lead to an eventual brain seizure in the limbic circuit. Although the specifics of these cases varied, they all reported experiencing strange hallucinations preceding the crime and no rage or feeling during the murder—appearing similar to the way an animal attacks its prey.

The perpetrators also reported certain visceral responses such as nausea, incontinence, and a racing heart during the violent act. Afterwards, the somatic feelings and hallucinations subsided, replaced with overwhelming remorse for the act. This **kindled limbic seizure** proposed by Pontius is, as you can imagine, very controversial. It is virtually impossible to gather evidence that an actual seizure occurred while the murder was taking place (LoPiccolo, 1996).

Neuroscience and the burden of proof. In addition to providing theories about the causes of criminal behavior, rigorous scientific methodology of neuroscience is also being used to identify people who have committed criminal acts. One way to ascertain guilt is to determine whether a person is lying about involvement in a crime. Throughout history it has been known that lying is associated with altered physiological functions such as nervousness, sweaty palms, and a dry mouth. In one of the early lie detector tests, the Chinese forced suspected liars to chew on rice powder and then spit it out. If the powder was dry (due to sympathetic arousal—see Chapter Four), the suspect was determined to be lying (Gayle, 1988).

The more modern lie detector, or polygraph, measures other indices of autonomic activity—galvanic skin response (electrodermal activity), blood pressure, heart rate, and respiration. The reasoning behind polygraph testing is that a person will be selectively emotional when asked about specific information related to a particular crime. For example, a suspect shouldn't show emotionality when asked to give his address but should be emotional when asked to identify the murder weapon (if that person indeed committed the crime). Although this seems like a reasonable test, most behavioral neuroscientists could spend hours describing its shortcomings.

David Lykken, a psychologist at the University of Minnesota, has written extensively about problems with the use of polygraphs for lie detection, including inadequate equipment and training, lack of statistical validity when analyzing the data, and perhaps most important, the ease with which the autonomic nervous system can be adjusted to fool the polygrapher. In his book *A Tremor in the Blood,* Lykken (1998) describes how criminals can do things like place a tack in their shoe or generate a provocative thought to evoke what looks like an "emotional" response to

kindled limbic seizure
Temporal lobe seizure thought to be related to the accumulation of chronic stress and loneliness; may be accompanied by uncharacteristic violent behavior.

many types of questions, making it impossible for the polygrapher to identify the crime-relevant emotional responses.

In fact, these concerns are so troubling that congressional action in 1988 severely limits the use of polygraph tests in employment situations (except, curiously, in the government). Further, because validity studies fail to show predictive value of this test, polygraph evidence is rarely accepted in the courtroom. Why, then do we still hear so much about polygraph tests being used in police investigations? If a test is found to lack validity for use in employment screening and courtroom evidence, how does it have enough validity to be used in important police investigations?

If a neurobiological response is involved in lying, how can we assess it in a valid way to determine the perpetrator of a crime or if someone has criminal intentions or plans to commit an act of terrorism? A recent test known as **brain fingerprinting** has received media attention. In December 2000, the television news show *60 Minutes* interviewed neuroscientist Larry Farwell from Iowa about this new technology that has caught the attention of the CIA and FBI (Farwell, 2000).

Essentially, Farwell's technique incorporates past research indicating that the brain responds in a certain brain wave pattern (that is, with a peak known as a p300 wave) when it recognizes information. Additionally, he reports that the p300 wave is a component of a large brain wave he patented and named a MERMER (memory and encoding-related multifaceted electroencephalographic response), Farwell's test requires subjects to observe words or images on a computer screen while brain wave activity is monitored. If a suspect fails to show the brain wave pattern in response to critical information that the perpetrator would have been exposed to and have stored in the brain, then the suspect would be determined innocent (Figure E.2).

The CIA has given Farwell $1 million in hopes that such a technique can detect potential terrorists. The final scientific validity for such a technique remains to be seen; currently Farwell is assessing individuals previously convicted of a crime. Although the approach is intriguing, the legal community has been slow to embrace this technology and its claims.

Daniel Langleben of the University of Pennsylvania, along with his colleagues, is currently using fMRI technology to get to the truth about the brain areas underlying decep-

[Figure E.2]

Brain fingerprinting. In one case study, Farwell conducted a Brain Fingerprinting test on convicted murderer Johnny Ray Slaughter (pictured on left). To conduct the test, Farwell identified three types of stimuli to be presented while monitoring EEG responses: target (information relevant to the crime that is known by Slaughter); irrelevant (information that may be related to a crime but has no specific relevance for the particular crime in question) and probe stimuli (information containing accurate information about the crime that the perpetrator denies knowing such as the position of the victim's body). Slaughter's EEG record showed the typical recognition response (i.e., p300 and MERMER) for the target stimulus but does not exhibit recognition of the irrelevant and probe stimuli; thus "information absent" was declared for Slaughter's test (at a statistical significance of 99%).

BRAIN FINGERPRINTING LABS

tion (Ross, 2003). The rationale is as follows. If a person is telling the truth, a certain area of the brain should be activated, but if a person is telling a lie, it's likely that the same area activated during truth telling would be activated in addition to another area that must be employed to suppress the true information and supply new, false information.

In short, telling the truth and telling a lie are two very different cognitive and neurobiological tasks. Langleben found that two areas are activated during lying—the anterior cingulate cortex and the left prefrontal cortex. Specifically, when subjects were shown a playing card, more activation was observed in these areas when asked to falsely deny that they were seeing, for example, the five of clubs than when they truthfully reported the identity of the card.

Practical applications of brain fingerprinting are still unknown, and it's not likely that police stations are all going to have fMRI scanners any time soon. Of course, there's the meta-ethical question that looms over this discussion—do we really want to decree a fail-proof technique to identify lying? It would undoubtedly create anxiety for politicians, promiscuous spouses, and spies!

In sum, clinical neuroscience is providing evidence that is causing legal professionals to rethink traditional ideas about guilt and innocence, valid evidence of truth-telling and lying, and the rights of individuals to protect their mental access to certain bits of information.

Designer Brains, Designer Disorders

Throughout this text we have considered a host of valid reasons for trying to change brain chemistry. This section is not about transforming a malfunctioning brain into a functional brain but rather about **euneurics,** or brain enhancement, including the increasing use of treatments, usually drugs, to change a healthy brain into a "better" brain (better as defined by the owner of the brain). One aspect of euneurics is **cosmetic pharmacology,** the use of psychoactive drugs for personality modification or lifestyle alterations unrelated to mental illness.

In the popular book *Listening to Prozac,* psychiatrist Peter Kramer (1993) describes his first patient to use Prozac to combat depression. This patient had a miserable childhood and early adulthood, characterized by child abuse, an alcoholic father, and the responsibility of caring for siblings and an aging mother. When Tess met with Kramer, he reported that she met the criteria for depression and he subsequently put her on the traditional medication imipramine. After a month of taking the drug, Tess reported that she was better—she was herself again.

Kramer wrote that after meeting with her for 15 minutes every month or two, he was not satisfied with her progress. About that time Prozac

brain fingerprinting Theory suggesting that specific brain-wave activity accompanies the identification of familiar stimuli. This technology may be used in criminal investigations.

euneurics Movement to design "better" brains.

cosmetic pharmacology Using psychoactive drugs for personality modification or lifestyle alterations unrelated to mental illness.

became available, and he recommended that she take the drug "to terminate her depression more thoroughly" (p. 7). The results were striking. Tess had more energy than ever before, had up to three dates a weekend, was laughing more, and had more self-confidence than ever before—what a transformation!

Eventually, Tess stopped taking Prozac. After about eight months off the drug, Tess told Kramer that she no longer felt like herself; she was slipping. Her company was undergoing union negotiations and she felt vulnerable and asked to go back on Prozac. Faced with the dilemma of placing a patient on a medication for personality rather than medical reasons, Kramer wrote: "I discussed the dilemma with her, but then I did not hesitate to write the prescription. Who was I to withhold from her the bounties of science? Tess responded again as she had hoped she would, with renewed confidence, self-assurance, and social comfort." (p. 10).

More recently, the antidepressant sertraline (Zoloft), was approved for treating social anxiety disorder (essentially, severe shyness). Although documented as a disorder in DSM-IV-TR, social anxiety may be more accurately viewed as a personality trait than a mental disorder (Restak, 2003). Pfizer Corporation, the manufacturer of Zoloft (2003), defines it on the Zoloft Web site:

> Social anxiety is a real medical condition. It affects over 16 million Americans. If you have social anxiety disorder, you often get very nervous around other people. It feels like everyone is watching you and judging you. You're afraid of making a mistake or looking like a fool. You will do all you can to keep that from happening. You may even avoid certain people, places or social events. Social anxiety disorder is a serious illness. It can cause real problems in your life. Like any health condition, it needs to be treated.
> *Social anxiety disorder can make you fear or avoid*
>   —meeting new people
>   —talking to your boss—or anyone in charge
>   —speaking in front of groups
>   —drawing any attention to yourself
> *If you have to do these kinds of things, you may*
>   —blush
>   —sweat
>   —tremble
>   —have a fast heartrate

To entice the potential Zoloft user, Pfizer sponsors an advertisement in popular magazines simplistically depicting how serotonin floats across the synaptic gap at a decreased level in a neuron with an unhappy, blushing face. After taking the drug, however, the neuron takes up less serotonin, allowing more to float across the junction, resulting in a neuron with a happy, more confident face. You may remember from the discussion in Chapter Eight that the physiological mechanisms of selective serotonin reuptake inhibitors (SSRIs) are a bit more complicated than depicted in this advertisement. You may also recognize the symptoms of social anxiety disorder listed on the Web site as important social and normal autonomic functions.

Social anxiety disorder is but one example of how the use of prescription drugs is moving from the treatment of severe mental dysfunctions such as major depression, obsessive-compulsive disorder, bipolar disorder, and schizophrenia to medicalizing certain perfectly normal reactions, personality styles, or lifestyles. From the perspective of pharmaceutical companies, the motivation to provide a pharmacological treatment for more people (normal people) is attractive because it drastically increases the number of potential users and profits.

Consider another example. The pharmaceutical company Cephalon sells **modafinil,** marketed as Provigil (abbreviation for "promotes vigilance") for the treatment of **narcolepsy,** a sleeping disorder characterized by irresistible urges to fall asleep at inappropriate times such as driving or speaking in public. Despite the fact that narcolepsy is rare, occurring in about 1 of every 2000 Americans (0.0005 percent), sales in 2001 totaled a whopping $150 million. Most of the purchasers—75%—did not have narcolepsy; they were perfectly normal and were taking the drug to combat drowsiness. Researchers have also explored other uses of the drug and report that modafinil can keep healthy individuals awake for more than two days without showing a deficit. This effect is another example of a drug treating a lifestyle rather than a disorder (Restak, 2003).

Thus, it appears that the increasing availability of certain drugs to treat various aspects of mental health and illness has increased the number of individuals taking drugs for lifestyle alterations. Also, according to David Healy at the University of Wales College of Medicine, the increased availability of psychopharmacological choices may also be influencing the number of individuals reported to be suffering from disorders. In his recent book *The Creation of Psychopharmacology,* Healy (2002) reports that in the 1950s, less than 0.5% of the population was diagnosed with a depressive disease. Prevalence rates for major depressive disorder in the 1990s had risen more than twentyfold to 10% of the population, and some studies reported rates up to 25%. He states that this significant increase in depressed patients provides a huge market for antidepressants.

Using drugs to influence lifestyle and normal emotional experiences may have a drastic effect on our emotional lives, as illustrated in Box E.1 on page 520. Richard Restak (2003), a neurologist and neuropsychiatrist at George Washington University Medical Center in Washington, D.C., warns that the same drugs that bring welcome relief to sufferers of severe mental illness may result in *social engineering* when enlisted to enhance normal functioning. He points to the example of psychiatrists frequently

modafinil Drug originally developed to keep narcoleptic patients from suddenly falling asleep. It is also being used by nonnarcoleptic patients to stay awake for extended periods of time.

narcolepsy A condition in which individuals succumb to irrestistible urges to sleep, even at such inappropriate times as while driving or speaking in public.

[Box E.1]

A Case in Point

Richard Restak's "Ted"

This hypothetical case from Restak's *The New Brain* (2003), included here in its entirety, exemplifies the growing concern in the neuroscience community about cosmetic psychopharmacology and how it may be changing our brains.

Our subject is a 54-year-old entrepreneur. Let's call him Ted. As a result of frequent business travel, Ted's sleep pattern tends to be irregular and affected by the different time zones he finds himself in from one day to another. After traveling across several time zones, Ted typically arrives too tired to function efficiently. But Ted has recently solved that problem with modafinil . . . whose exact mode of action remains unknown.

Two weeks prior to the current trip, Ted's younger brother, Jim, died in a car accident. Although Ted was initially upset when hearing the news, he quickly regained his composure by taking a tranquilizer. Three days later he took another tranquilizer so that he could remain calm and composed during the funeral service. Apparently the drug worked, since Ted didn't shed a tear at his brother's funeral. Immediately after the service Ted took a cab to the airport and resumed his business trip.

Now, after two weeks of travel, Ted is starting to find himself thinking of his brother. In the airport in Dallas he suddenly burst into tears "for no rea-

son." But Ted isn't going to give in to any "morbid" responses. Based on his reading he has correctly diagnosed himself as experiencing the onset of depression secondary to an aborted grief reaction. When he reflects briefly on whether he should have acted differently, he ends up regretting nothing. Sure, it might have been nice to cancel his business trip for a few days and make himself available to comfort Jim's widow and children, but what was there to say, really? Jim is gone and nothing is to be gained by morbidly dwelling on that fact.

Ted has in his possession some antidepressants left over from two years ago when he became, in his words, "nonfunctional" and "moped around the house" wondering what "my life was all about." The antidepressant worked and he soon stopped moping and asking himself such questions. Now Ted reasons that the antidepressant should work equally well in regard to his current "fixation" on his brother's death. Ted considers it best to "get over it" and to "move on."

*If the antidepressant "works" well Ted will soon stop thinking of his brother. He will operate at his maximum efficiency, completely free of grief or any morbid inclinations to dwell on the past. When he gets to his hotel room later he'll accustom himself to the five-hour time change by taking the modafinil. At the end of his business meetings he'll return to his room and take a sleeping pill. And in the morning he'll take his antidepressant and begin his new day **without any feelings at all**. (pp. 139–140)*

---

diagnosing people with pessimistic personalities as having *dysthymic disorder*.

We can all think of examples of negative situations leading to something positive—medicine, peace negotiations, a poem. What are the societal consequences of taking the edge off life situations? One letter to the editor of the *Washington Post* stated:

Human development is often stimulated in response to a perceived lack or need. Drugs that mask oppressive social conditions by increasing feelings of self-worth would effectively obscure the need for further social and material progress. A drug-induced euphoric haze can cloud human awareness to social realities and inure one to the inequality and inhumanity of existing world conditions. (Restak, 2003, pp. 137–138)

A satirical view of the medicalization of emotions was published in the *Onion,* a tabloid parody of societal events that reflects societal trends in a sometimes irreverent and humorous style. The *Onion*'s satire "Pfizer launches 'Zoloft for Everything' Ad Campaign" (2003) reports that the

> Zoloft for Everything campaign will employ print and TV ads to inform potential users about the "literally thousands" of new applications for Zoloft. Among the conditions the drug can be used to treat: anxiety associated with summer swimsuit season, insecurity over sexual potency and performance, feelings of shame over taking an antidepressant, and a sense of hollowness stemming from losing an online auction. . . . Do you find yourself feeling excited or sad? No one should have to suffer through those harrowing peaks and valleys.

This satirical account reflects how extensive the use of antidepressants has become in our society. We don't have the answers to all the questions, but you'll recall from Chapter Eight that our ability to experience a rich, varied emotional life is probably very important for our mental health.

LOOKING TO THE FUTURE THROUGH ALL THE WINDOWS OF CLINICAL NEUROSCIENCE

We end this book where we began, by elaborating on two issues we emphasized in Chapter One: (1) the value of viewing mental health from multiple perspectives as a balance between body and brain and (2) the importance of being vigilant about using empirical methodologies and research designs.

Integrating Mental Health Perspectives

Several windows on mental health were introduced in Chapter One, from neurobiology and genetics to environment and evolution. But as we discussed treatment strategies throughout this text, you probably noticed that the *neurochemical* window is the one most frequently used in clinical neuroscience. Psychopharmacology has provided much-needed relief for some severe symptoms associated with many mental disorders; however, this benefit has come at the cost of excessive use of drugs for medicalizing our lifestyles in addition to treating mental illnesses. As helpful as drugs can be when used appropriately and responsibly, it is also important to consider other effective treatment strategies.

cognitive/behavioral-induced neuroplasticity Changes in a person's neurobiology resulting from significant cognitive and/or behavioral training

In our coverage of therapeutic options to maintain mental health homeostasis, we have discussed exposure therapy for phobias, transcranial magnetic stimulation for depression, neurosurgical treatment for obsessive-compulsive disorder (OCD), cognitive training for schizophrenia, and relaxation therapies for addiction. Recently, increased attention has been focused on **cognitive/behavior-induced neuroplasticity,** our term for changes in neurobiology resulting from significant cognitive and/or behavioral training. We discussed one prime example in Chapter Seven—Jeffrey Schwartz's cognitive-behavioral therapy (CBT) for OCD. CBT results in brain changes measureable by PET scans. (See Box E.2 to learn more about Schwartz). Unlike neurosurgical treatments or psychoactive drugs that alter brain structure and functioning, CBT offers a far less invasive way to change the brain.

Although William James, the father of American psychology, wrote of the *plasticity* of the nervous system in his *Principles of Psychology* (1890), twentieth-century psychology was dominated by the view that the nervous system is fixed and amenable to change only at certain rigidly defined critical periods in development. Even though evidence of environmentally induced plasticity (for example, via enriched environments) was reported several times throughout the last century, neuroscientists did not begin to rethink the idea that the brain is immutable until the mid-1980s. Today, research conducted on rodents and humans provides convincing evidence that the brain changes in response to the changing demands of the environment.

Focusing on "normal" brains, experience has been found experimentally to have significant effects on neurobiological functions. For example, researchers in the United Kingdom investigated the brains of London taxi drivers and found their posterior hippocampus to be significantly larger than that of control subjects who were not taxi drivers. If you've ever wondered how taxi drivers negotiate such tight spaces and have such good memory for directions, now you know why. Their brains respond more sensitively and accurately to the traffic than a non-taxi-driving brain does (Maguire, Gadian et al., 2000; Maguire, Spiers et al., 2003).

A group of researchers in Germany found that when subjects commenced a juggling training program their brains developed increased gray matter in the middle temporal area of the visual cortex and the left posterior lobe at the point of demonstrating their highest skill. Even more interesting is the observation that, after abstaining from juggling for three months, the juggler's brains morphed back to the equivalent of the control group's brains. So when you feel as if you have too many balls in the air, don't worry. Your brain can change to accommodate your needs (Draganski et al., in press).

[Box E.2]

The Investigators

Jeffrey Schwartz

To keep up with Jeff Schwartz's fast-paced, multidimensional, multidisciplinary views of mental health, you need to strap on a cognitive seat belt. The values he places on multiple views and creative hypotheses, however, are just the criteria that make Schwartz the perfect Investigator for our discussion of the future of clinical neuroscience.

A native of New York State, Schwartz admitted that he had not always wanted to be a neuropsychiatrist—his initial career aspiration was to play for the New York Yankees. After a "mindful" reality check at about 14 years of age, however, he reassessed his situation; the father of one of his friends was a psychiatrist and that became the new perfect career for him. In fact, Schwartz reports that the rigorous religious training of preparing for his bar mitzvah also prepared his mind for the scientific and literary pursuits that characterize a career in psychiatry. He also values the discipline and preparation he developed through his training as a wrestler in high school. Even as an adolescent, Schwartz recognized the value of rigorous mental and physical training in the maintenance of mental health.

Schwartz attended the University of Rochester and studied the philosophy of mind as an honors exchange student at the University of Edinburgh. He attended the medical school of the State University of New York, where he devoutly read the journal *Archives of General Psychiatry* every month.

From the beginning of his medical education, Schwartz conducted research, initially at Columbia University and eventually in California at the Scripps Research Institute where he worked with Floyd Bloom and George Koob. Schwartz had his eye on going to UCLA, where the PET scanners were. He wanted to conduct a landmark study that would provide irrevocable evidence for his ideas about the therapeutic power of "mental effort," or cognitive training. His eventual research with the PET scans of OCD patients before and after CBT provided a platform for a book *Brain Lock* and several media appearances on programs such as *Oprah* and *60 Minutes*.

He continued to endorse his ideas about self-directed training in his book *The Mind and the Brain* (2002), written with Sharon Begley, in which he discusses the importance of topics as diverse as quantum physics, philosophy, psychology, and neuroscience. Schwartz also incorporates Buddhist philosophy into his ideas about mental health as well as in his personal life (he meditates 75 minutes each day).

Jeffrey Schwartz
COURTESY JEFFREY SCHWARTZ

Intertwined in his support for cognitive-behavioral therapy and increased mindfulness is a priority to give patients control over their recovery process. As part of describing the four-step method in his CBT OCD protocol, Schwartz informs his patients about the nervous system and identifies key brain structures leading to the OCD symptoms (see Box 7.2). The knowledge increases the patients' perception of control. One of his patients told us that she was extremely relieved after just listening to that single lecture and learning that there was a *physical* reason for her OCD—not some mystical demon that couldn't be controlled.

In an attempt to take OCD to an even larger audience, Schwartz agreed to coach actor Leonardo de Caprio in Martin Scorsese's movie *The Aviator,* depicting the life of Howard Hughes. Schwartz has studied accounts of Hughes's behavior and has retrospectively diagnosed him with OCD, a fascinating view of this eccentric billionaire's behavior.

Jeff Schwartz relies on a diverse array of contexts to gain a clearer understanding of the natural, bare, context of the mind and the brain. He has learned from his experiences with psychiatry, meditation, neuroscience research, readings in philosophy, religious practices, sports training, and perhaps most important, from listening carefully to his patients that there are many ways to access the brain and the mind (personal communication, Sept, 2003; Schwartz & Begley, 2002).

constraint-induced (CI) movement therapy Type of rehabilitation therapy requiring an individual to constrain his or her "good arm" to stimulate use of the "bad" arm

dyslexia Learning disability that results in slow reading and comprehension; it is thought that the exposure of affected subjects to repetitive auditory language facilitates recovery.

It is easy to discern that the brain changes in the normal individual to allow for more accurate responding. The more relevant question for us, however, involves the therapeutic value of cognitive/behavior-induced neuroplasticity for various nervous system dysfunctions. Recall Chrisopher Reeve's successful use of physical therapy to obtain partial movement in his fingers.

Edward Taub, now at the University of Alabama in Birmingham, and his colleagues have shown that **constraint-induced (CI) movement therapy** restores function in patients who have an impaired limb following a stroke (Morris & Taub, 2001; Page & Levine, 2003). When the functioning arm is constrained, significant gains are found in the impaired arm. Taub is most proud of his patient James Faust of Calera, Alabama. After a stroke damaged his left cortex, Faust's right arm was useless. In fact, he had thought about just having it removed since he had no control over the limp appendage.

After hearing about Taub's CI therapy, he signed up, figuring he had nothing to lose. Improvements were observed after just a few weeks of CI therapy. One evening at a restaurant, without even thinking about it, Taub's wife caught him using his right hand to try to cut his meat. Today, he is able to shave, tie his shoes, brush his teeth, and drive (Schwartz & Begley, 2002).

Cognitive/behavior-induced neuroplasticity is also being considered for individuals suffering from the reading disability **dyslexia.** Michael Merzenich of the University of California at San Francisco has investigated the effect of exposing children diagnosed with dyslexia to extensive training trials consisting of hours and hours of various sound repetition in an attempt to sensitize the brain to phonological processing. Recently, Merzenich's lab conducted fMRI scans on 20 children with dyslexia between the ages of 8 and 12, during and after phonological training (Temple et al., 2003). Although preliminary, a correlation was observed between improvement observed in oral language ability and the extent of increased activation of the left temporoparietal cortex. Consequently, Merzenich has begun the first neuroplasticity enterprise, Fast ForWord, to train children to be more efficient readers (Holloway, 2003; Schwartz & Begley, 2002).

Thus, it appears that intensive cognitive-behavioral training leads to significant therapeutic improvements in stroke and traumatic brain injury, as well as in certain sensory and language impairments such as dyslexia. We've already discussed its effectiveness in treating OCD, but what about other disorders? And, can cognition or thought alone lead to clinical changes?

In the book *The Brain and the Mind: Neuroplasticity and the Power of Mental Force* (2002), Jeffrey Schwartz and Sharon Begley report that a single study conducted in 1995 by Alvaro Pascual-Leone and his colleagues provides convincing evidence that thought exercises can indeed alter neuroanatomy and neurophysiology, just as repeated physical therapy helps restore bodily functioning (Pascual-Leone et al., 1995). In this study, one group of subjects practiced a five-finger piano exercise, and their brain's functional map was compared with a group that *mentally* practiced the exercise for the same amount of time. Interestingly, both physical and mental exercises resulted in an altered motor cortex, a result that probably doesn't surprise any sports psychologist who uses imaging to help client-athletes perfect their motor performance during competition.

In Chapter One, we discussed the effectiveness of behavioral conditioning in treating patients with phobias. In one study, when subjects with arachnophobia were exposed to a CBT, fMRI scans suggested that less prefrontal activity and parahippocampal activity were observed following treatment. These researchers state that "changes made at the mind level, within a psychotherapeutic context, are able to functionally 'rewire' the brain" (Paquette et al., 2003, p. 409).

In Chapter Eight, we discussed CBT's clinical efficacy with depressed patients, but does this therapy lead to actual changes in the brain? Related to depression is the ability to escort unwanted memories from one's thoughts. Recently a study reported that successful repression of unwanted memories was associated with increased dorsolateral prefrontal activation, reduced hippocampal activity, and an increased forgetting of the memories (Anderson et al., 2004). Such findings provide further support for the evidence that CBT is clinically effective in depressed patients.

Thus, it appears that cognitive, or mental, therapies have the potential to produce neuroplasticity sufficient for therapeutic improvement in an impaired nervous system.

The activity devoted to accomplishing this effect requires active participation of the individual as opposed to the passive nature of drug use. A recent study, however, reminds us that the use of psychopharmacology and CBT need not be mutually exclusive. Michael Davis and his colleagues at Emory University have reported that patients with a fear of heights respond to a form of CBT known as virtual reality therapy (i.e. virtual elevator rides) in eight sessions. The number of sessions required to procure clinical efficacy, however, decreases to only two sessions when the CBT virtual therapy is combined with the NMDA uptake blocker, d-cycloserine (a memory-enhancer) (Davis, 2004).

[Figure E.3]
Virtual reality therapy. Virtual reality therapy investigated by Michael Davis and colleagues consists of working with a virtual reality tour of an elevator shaft (pictured below) to desensitize patients to their fears of heights. View (a) looks up from a glass elevator, view (b) looks out at the fifth floor, and view (c) looks down. When this therapy is combined with an NMDA reuptake blocker, the number of therapy sessions required for efficacy drops.
RESSLER, ROTHBAUM, TANNENBAUM, ANDERSON, GRAAP, ZIMAND, HODGES, & DAVIS (IN PRESS)

(a)

(b)

(c)

self-directed neuroplasticity
Systematically altering one's brain via extensive mental and/or physical training

Although neuroscientists have not been comfortable with terms such as *volition, mental force,* and *mindfulness* because these states cannot be easily measured, with the recent onslaught of data showing that such activity alters neurophysiology, it is becoming increasingly difficult to ignore this therapeutic strategy. Recently, the term **self-directed neuroplasticity** has been proposed to convey the idea that focused training and mental and/or physical effort systematically alter the brain's function in a potentially therapeutic manner (Schwartz & Begley, 2002). This strategy, although requiring considerable effort on the part of the patient, seems especially powerful due to its multifaceted nature—behavioral, cognitive, and environmental manipulations alter psychological, neurophysiological, and neuroanatomical responses.

Cleansing Our Views with Empirical Evidence: Remembering Past Lessons

In the last section we emphasized the range of therapeutic approaches to the nervous system. As important as the range is, it is not nearly as important as making sure that the appropriate methodology is utilized to yield the most accurate, informed results. You may be on the right road to a desired destination, but if your mode of transportation isn't working, you're not going to get there.

We have discussed numerous therapeutic approaches in this text. It is probable that some will stand the test of time, yet others will be identified as faulty and misleading, methodological "lemons" that fall short of yielding accurate information. Obviously, clinicians and neuroscientists need to do everything possible to avoid making methodological mistakes in the haste to find "magic bullet" cures for various mental illnesses. As techniques become more molecular and biological, it appears that we are gaining methodological power, yet it is important to maintain high experimental standards. Living with a mental illness presents a significant challenge to those affected. They don't need the added burden of taking unnecessary detours on their therapeutic highways of life.

A few months ago, a colleague gave us an article from *Life* magazine, dated March 3, 1947 entitled "Psychosurgery: Operation to Cure Sick Minds Turns Surgeon's Blade into an Instrument of Mental Therapy." Reading through this article provided a powerful reminder of why we need informed students in the field of clinical neuroscience.

Life reported that, at that point, 2000 U.S. patients had received prefrontal lobotomies, and the article went on to celebrate the success of this then innovative therapy, claiming particular effectiveness in depression, and a mortality rate of "only" 3% (60 people out of 2000). The article also described the mechanisms involved with the success of prefrontal lobotomies. The depressed individual was thought to suffer from an overactive conscious (residing in the prefrontal cortex) that suppresses impulses (originating in the brainstem) and disrupts judgment (apparently residing in the occipital lobe) and executive function (around the parietal cortex). In a confusing, seemingly insensitive, and grossly inaccurate fashion, this article discusses topics such as the neuroanatomical location of the *superego* as if it were fact.

This misinformed article is only a half-century old—it's not describing techniques used by some ancient society. Rather, this Nobel-prize winning work is a recent piece of our history. Although we are applying 20/20 hindsight and it is true that the popularity of this technique was rather short-lived, certainly more accurate methodological techniques, including an in-depth analysis of the animal literature, more accurate presurgery assessments, more thorough postsurgical follow-ups, and meaningful control groups would have dampened the enthusiasm for the lobotomy technique.

In *The Trouble with Testosterone* (1997), Robert Sapolsky describes another unthinkable case of unnecessary invasive surgery. At the turn of the last century, it was unknown why some infants died in their sleep—a condition called "crib death" then but currently known as **sudden infant death syndrome (SIDS).** Today, it is thought that SIDS is caused by some malfunction in the medulla that is involved with breathing. At that time, however, when SIDS infants were autopsied, physicians noticed that the thymus gland was much larger than the glands of "control" infants who did not die of SIDS.

But it's important to know that the non-SIDS infants were typically from impoverished, stressful environments and had likely been chronically stressed prior to their unfortunate deaths. Recall what chronic stress does to structures of the immune system such as the thymus: it shrinks those organs. So as you have probably already figured out, the SIDS infants did not have abnormally large thymus glands; they were being compared to chronically stressed infants with abnormally small glands.

The pediatricians of a century ago were not as methodologically sophisticated as today and went on to hypothesize that the large thymus glands in SIDS infants pressed on the trachea while the infant was sleeping—leading to death. By the 1920s, a treatment was recommended in most pediatric textbooks for this disorder, known as *status thymicolymphaticus*. Until the 1950s, pediatricians recommended irradiating the throats of young infants to shrink the dangerous thymus gland. This treatment failed to help the nonexistent condition, and because the thymus is

sudden infant death syndrome (SIDS) Respiratory malfunction, perhaps influenced by an immature medulla, that results in an infant's death.

located next to the thyroid gland (involved in growth and metabolism), thousands of cases of thyroid cancer developed.

No one knows how many mistakes of this magnitude are being made today. What we do know is that appropriate empirical evidence is the best antidote. Working on a mental health problem from many perspectives helps ensure against taking an unwanted detour. Informed, dedicated, hard-working, compassionate practitioners and researchers will keep us on the best therapeutic paths in the future.

Summary

Ethical Waves on the Sea of Neuroscience

Clinical neuroscience research does not exist in a vacuum. Contemporary researchers are concerned with ethical considerations of new findings as they emerge in the field of clinical neuroscience. For example, researchers suggest that neuroanatomical areas, such as the prefrontal cortex and amygdala, are involved in violent behvior. As we learn more about brain structures involved in criminal behavior, the legal community is forced to consider the possibility that someone may commit a crime due to a malfunctioning brain area—perhaps similar to a medical condition. It is similar to the insanity defense, with a lowered bar related to more specific regulation of the act or behavior. How will such findings shape society's ideas about personal responsibility and conduct in the future?

Neuroscience information is also being used to identify truth telling and lying in criminal investigations. Although the polygraph test is thought to lack validity, new tests such as the brain fingerprinting test and fMRI scans show promise detecting lies.

Another important ethical issue in the field of clinical neuroscience is related to the field of psychopharmacology. Brain-altering drugs have been successful in the treatment of mental disorders such as depression and schizophrenia but currently drugs are being increasingly prescribed for the purpose of altering personality style, rather than regaining mental health. Imagine a life without the emotional ups and downs that characterize daily activities. It is very important to consider the long-term effects of medicalizing and homogenizing personality styles.

Looking to the Future Through All the Windows of Clinical Neuroscience

Throughout this text, many perspectives are used to examine the treatment of both mental illness and other conditions. The neurochemical perspective is a popular treatment approach; however, cognitive behavioral therapies are quickly gaining respect as effective therapeutic options. Many studies provide empirical evidence indicating that CBT leads to detectable brain changes and accompanying clinical improvement. Of course, the best way to determine clinical efficacy is through the use of appropriate research methodologies and their long-term evaluation. The history of clinical neuroscience—indeed, science and history—is rife with examples of misdirected therapies that were eventually shown to be ineffective. With well-designed and interpreted research, we are less likely to subject vulnerable patients to ineffective treatments. The future of the clinic must be informed by the rigor inherent to science and to neuroscience. Clinical neuroscience represents a valuable approach to providing effective care and treatment to the patient formerly fated to less effective diagnostic and management strategies. The student interested in psychology today will one day likely be the beneficiary of a science shaped by the future gains of clinical neuroscience.

Key Terms

neuroethics (p. 511)

somatic marker (p. 513)

kindled limbic seizure (p. 515)

brain fingerprinting (p. 516)

euneurics (p. 517)

cosmetic pharmacology (p. 517)

modafinil (p. 519)

narcolepsy (p. 519)

cognitive/behavioral-induced neuroplasticity (p. 522)

constraint-induced movement therapy (p. 523)

dyslexia (p. 523)

self-directed neuroplasticity (p. 526)

sudden infant death syndrome (SIDS) (p. 527)

For Further Consideration

Adolphs, R., Tranel, D., Damasio, H., & Damasio, A. (1994). Impaired recognition of emotion in facial expressions following bilateral damage to the human amygdala. *Nature, 372,* 669–672. The group from Iowa has done beautiful work showing the way in which the brain, in this case, the amygdala, regulates quintessentially human behaviors. In this paper they discuss the case of an adult female with a history of poor social relationships. Focusing on the amygdala, which processes visual information, primarily from faces, they report that this woman's poor social relationships may be due to her damaged amygdala (which underwent a type of calcification). Their data suggest that this brain region responds to fear (mainly) and other emotionally-laden visual stimuli from others' faces, but is not involved in the recognition of those same faces. That most human of social behaviors, responding to another's emotional state, appears to reside in this tiny almond-shaped temporal lobe region.

Barrash, J., Tranel, D., & Anderson, S.W. (2000). Acquired personality disturbances associated with bilateral damage to the ventromedial prefrontal region. *Developmental Neuropsychology. 18,* 355–381. If a general acceptance of the idea that basic regulation of complex human behavior is accomplished by prosaic biochemical activities in the brain is going to be accepted one day, more solid studies such as this one need to be done. These researchers closely examined individuals with prefrontal damage (two types of ventromedial lesions [bilateral v. unilateral]) compared to those without. They measured differences in personality related to the brain damage.

They concluded that damage to the prefrontal area, especially the ventromedial portion, is responsible for the poor decision-making, emotional regulation (both subjective experience and overt displays), and lack of "insight" characteristic of sociopaths. The connection between brain damage, subtle and otherwise, and a personality type associated with the worst kinds of crimes and behavior is intriguing. Other studies such as this will begin to assemble a data base showing how minor brain damage or malfunction can have major consequences.

Blight, A.R. (2002). Miracles and molecules—Progress in spinal cord repair. *Nature Neuroscience, 5* (supplement), 1051–1054. As anyone who has ever witnessed the devastating aftermath of a spinal cord injury knows, being able to find a way to reverse the damage would be a dream come true to the paralyzed individual and his family. Here Blight reviews the hopeful advances that have been made in the area of spinal cord injury (SCI) and its treatment. He discusses the strategies for treating SCI immediately afterwards, to minimize further damage, slowing down or preventing "hemorrhagic necrosis," a progressive loss of spinal cord tissue that inevitably spirals out of control, leading to more damage. It is shameful that these and other treatments go understudied or do not get applied because their commercial value (cost:benefit ratio) is so slim. Other work covered includes techniques to regenerate axons lost, through transplantation or directly treating the spinal demyelination that occurs. A molecular biological approach that includes new understanding of the Nogo molecule and its regulatory control of myelin formation also holds promise. He ends by discussing the basis of the scientific method for this field, hypothesis, test, reformulation of hypothesis, re-test, etc. It is because of and through this elegant procedure that the future holds promise for SCI.

Dennett, D. (2001). Are we explaining consciousness yet? *Cognition, 79,* 221–237. Dennett is the gadfly of current theorizing about consciousness. He buzzes around with new problems for the "wet" scientists (those who study the neurobiology of his favorite subject) to solve, creating new tasks that must be accomplished before consciousness can be satisfactorily explained or accounted for. He provides a necessary foil to the neuroscientists who are engaged in the search for the ultimate human character. In this paper, he poses the idea that the cause of consciousness is different from the state of consciousness, both of which are different than the "aftermath" of consciousness, presumably one's self awareness. It is a philosophical labyrinth best navigated carefully and with an eye out for the next, sudden turn. Dennett is a skillful polemicist but in this paper his language sometimes interferes with the points he is making. Overall, however, it makes for an important and necessary read for one interested in the larger picture about the humanness problem.

Goldberg, L. (2001). *The executive brain: Frontal lobes and the civilized mind.* New York: Oxford University Press. The frontal lobes of the brain have undergone a renaissance lately. They are being implicated in virtually everything the human does. When they work properly, life is rosy; when they malfunction, society is certainly to crumble. The simplistic extremes just represented mark the examination of the frontal lobes with equal parts curiosity and caution. Goldberg presents a sober examination of the frontal lobes and their roles in the complex behavior of the human. He takes new data, the latest, and discusses it. He explains well and is not prone to exaggeration. The reader comes away with respect for the complexity of the issue, and renewed understanding of the fragility of brain regulation of human behavior. It is a fine book to have to study when another atrocious human behavior rears itself or when you want to gaze in wonder at the difficulty controlling free will.

LeDoux, J. (2002). *Synaptic self: How our brains become who we are.* New York: Viking Press. A companion volume to another of LeDoux's interesting offerings (called *The Emotional Brain*), *Synaptic Self* explores some new territory and treads upon some well worn ones. First, the premise is one that is in need of expressing widely: That human consciousness is a result of complex, but prosaic nevertheless, interactions that neurons provide. Synapses are the critical unit for LeDoux, and he does a wonderful job of making the case for them. Because of their development and expression by endogenous biological mechanisms, and their sensitivity to environmental, real world like stimulation, the synapse represents the brain's window on the world and, hence, thought, self-awareness, learning, etc. LeDoux argues convincingly for these myriad, plastic sites (which number Francis Crick has stated exceeds that of charged particles in the known universe). It is a book well worth having and, appropriately enough, thinking about.

McLaren, A. (Ed.). (2002). *Cloning.* Strasbourg: Council of Europe Publishing. The need for this book was not apparent ten years ago. The cloning genie, however, is out of the bottle. This volume does a fine job of presenting the many arguments, for and against, the science of cloning. Legal, ethical, religious and other perspectives are represented from a wide variety of thinkers, scientific and other. Background on the science of cloning, its technical wizardry, and inherent difficulty also are highlighted by those in the thick of the work. The overall effect is one of a complex topic, presented fairly, that falls firmly in the gray area between beneficial and dangerous.

Parvizi, J., & Damasio, A. (2001). Consciousness and the brainstem. *Cognition, 79,* 135–160. In the same issue as Dennett's article described above, these authors attempt to reconcile consciousness with what is known about the neurobiology of consciousness. It is not unlike a philosophical Tower of Babel—many different languages attempting to build an edifice. They frame their discussion of consciousness into several regions of regulation (basal, vegetative, and internal and external sensory monitors).

The concept of consciousness must include all of these levels, summing as they do to produce and maintain the organism and, in the case of the human, his awareness of his activities. It is self-referential, but Parvizi and Damasio's arguments, and their understanding of the neural systems that underlie the activities they outline, are tight and reasoned. It is an important paper to help understand how the brain leads to the mind.

Warnock, M. (2002). *Making babies: Is there a right to have children?* New York: Oxford University Press. It is often said that it takes more training and education to obtain one's driver's license than it does to have a baby. Nature has simply made it too easy to get pregnant, without a guarantee that the woman and/or her mate will be adequate parents. Warnock, whose work has included recommendations that led to Great Britain's passage of the Human Fertilization and Embryology Act in 1990, weighs in with a pithy volume that addresses the applications that cloning, particularly human cloning, may have in the future. She presents reasoned arguments about reproduction in general that, nevertheless, will be controversial to some and downright heretical to others. Still, she makes points that need to be made and arguments that will be attractive to the thoughtful individual. Whether one agrees or not with her well-made points, there is no denying that the future will wrestle with the ethical and moral morass, the peril and hope, of human cloning. It is best to get a jump on he future by reading this small but concentrated book.

Glossary

absolute refractory period. A point during the action potential, while the cell is returning to its resting potential, when the neuron cannot respond to another action potential.

acetylcholine (ACh). Neurotransmitter in the somatic and parasympathetic nervous systems involved in cognition and at the neuro-muscular junction.

acquired immune system. B cells and T cells that, following exposure to infectious pathogens, are stimulated to develop a selective immunity that results in a faster response should the same type of pathogen invade the body again; also known as *adaptive immunity*.

action potential. Physical basis of the nerve impulse; the depolarization of an axon produced by a stimulation beyond threshold potential.

activity-based anorexia. An animal (rodent) model of anorexia nervosa in which animals that are food restricted increase activity levels to the point that they become very ill if the experimenter does not intervene.

activity-stress paradigm. Animal model of chronic stress and compulsive behavior in which rats are housed in activity wheels and exposed to restricted food resources. Rats typically increase running and exhibit multiple signs of stress-induced illness when faced with these conditions.

addiction syndrome. Vast array of variables, sometimes difficult to tease apart, typically associated with drug addiction, including one's predisposition to consume drugs, the development of tolerance to a drug, withdrawal symptoms on the removal of a drug, craving for a drug, and the likelihood of relapse after ceasing consumption of a drug.

adenosine triphosphate (ATP). Chemical the body uses as its primary way of delivering energy where it is needed; also used as a neurotransmitter.

adrenocorticotropic hormone (ACTH). A hormone released by the anterior pituitary which stimulates the adrenal gland to release glucocorticoids from the adrenal cortex. ACTH is a critical component of the hypothalamic-pituitary-adrenal-(HPA)-axis stress response.

adult stem cells. Undifferentiated cells located in a currently differentiated tissue; these cells have the ability to renew themselves and differeniate, within certain limits, to various specialized cell types characteristic of the tissue from which it was derived.

afferent information. Information carried inward toward the brain.

affiliative social contact. Nonthreatening social contact. This type of social contact probably increases oxytocin, which subsequently triggers a cascade of responses that maximize growth and minimize stress.

affinity. The strength of attraction that a neurotransmitter has for a particular type of receptor.

agonist. A drug that mimics the endogenous actions of the targeted neurotransmitter.

all-or-none law. Observation that, once the threshold is reached, all action potentials are the same size regardless of the intensity of the original stimulation.

allostasis. Literally, maintaining stability through change; the active process of maintaining physiological homeostasis in the face of any challenge.

allostatic load. Wear and tear on the body that results from repeated activation of the processes that maintain homeostasis.

alpha-amino hydroxy-methyl-isoxazolepropionate (AMPA) receptors. A subtype of glutamate receptor in which Na + influx causes an excitatory postsynaptic potential (EPSP).

amino acids. The so-called building blocks of proteins, composed of an amino group (NH2) and a carboxylic acid (COOH). These are essential components of proteins and the basis for organic life.

amygdala. Almond-shaped structure at the tail end of the basal ganglia within the temporal lobe; functions as part of the limbic system involved in regulation of emotion and sexual urges.

anhedonia. Lack of desire or pleasure. Drugs that interfere with the mesolimbic dopaminergic system produce this state.

anorexia nervosa (AN). An eating disorder characterized by decreased food consumption and excessive physical activity. Although individuals with this disorder are severely underweight, they remain reluctant to eat to regain their health. If not treated, this condition may lead to the patient's death.

antagonist. A drug that blocks the actions of an endogenous neurotransmitter.

antalarmin. New drug that inhibits the release of corticotropin-releasing hormone and has been found in animal models to reduce anxietylike behaviors in animals. Researchers are hopeful that this drug may be used as an antidepressant in humans in the future.

anterior cingulate cortex. Front portion of the older lobe of the cerebral cortex that surrounds the corpus callosum. Decreased activity in this area has been found to accompany profound sadness; thus, this area has been implicated in the symptoms of depression.

anterograde amnesia. Ability to recall long-ago events but not recent events, and a general inability to incorporate recent events into memory.

antibodies or **immunoglobulins (Ig).** Glycoprotein molecules produced by B lymphocytes that bind to specific antigens. The four types are IgA, IgE, IgG, and IgM.

antigen. Molecule that binds specifically to either an antibody or a T-cell receptor.

antigen-presenting cell (APC). Cell that displays fragments of protein antigens, along with MHC molecules, on its surface in order to activate T cells.

antipsychotics. Psychoactive drugs that reduce psychotic symptoms but have long-term side effects resembling symptoms of neurological diseases.

anxiolytics. Drugs such as the benzodiazepines that work to reduce anxiety.

apoptosis. Programmed cellular death characterized by fragmentation of the cell; prompted by nuclear or other related signals from within the cell or from signals outside the cell. Serves as a form of neuronal sculpting in the developing brain.

arcuate nucleus. Nucleus of the hypothalamus where most of the NPY neurons are located.

arginine vasopressin. A neuropeptide that is secreted by the posterior pituitary gland and also by nerve endings in the hypothalamus. It affects learning functions and water resorption in mammals.

association cortex. Areas of the cortex that integrate information to produce cognition.

astrocyte. Relatively large, star-shaped glial cell found in the CNS.

atherosclerosis. Buildup of lipid substances in lesions in the blood vessels; can eventually lead to hardened arteries and disrupted blood flow.

attention deficit hyperactivity disorder (ADHD). A condition observed in children and adults characterized by inattention, hyperactivity, and impulsivity.

autoimmune disease. Disease that results when the mechanisms designed to preserve self-recognition in the immune system are compromised so that the adaptive immune system responds to self-antigens in the same manner as it responds to foreign antigens—leading to cellular and tissue damage.

autonomic nervous system (ANS). Maintenance component of the nervous system, composed of sympathetic and parasympathetic divisions.

axon. Fiberlike outgrowth from the cell body of a neuron that is cylindrical until the very end, when it breaks into numerous small branches; the "sending" fiber of the neuron, it carries the nerve impulse.

axon hillock. Swelling of the soma of the neuron, the point where the axon begins and an action potential "firing decision" is made.

B cells or **B lymphocytes.** Cells that originate in the bone marrow and migrate to lymphoid tissue, bone marrow, and in low numbers, the blood. These are the only immune cells with the capability of producing antibodies.

barbiturates. Psychoactive drugs that act as CNS depressants, producing a wide array of effects ranging from relaxation to coma. They are highly addictive.

basal ganglia. Subcortical cluster of nuclei in the telencephalon that forms a circuit with the cortex, thalamus, and midbrain to coordinate body movements and links to the limbic system via the amygdala.

bed nucleus of the stria terminalis (BNST). Subcortical limbic structure considered part of the extended amygdala that plays a role in the stress/anxiety response.

behavioral addiction. Notion that an animal or human may develop a physiological addiction (similar to drug addiction) to engaging in certain behaviors such as compulsions.

behaviorism. Theory advocated by J. B. Watson calling for a shift of emphasis in the field of psychology from unconscious processes to the empirical manipulation of environmental stimuli and observable responses.

benzodiazepines. A class of drugs (usually of the tranquilizer variety) that increases the frequency of chloride channel openings in the presence of GABA.

biomedical model. Therapeutic approach using mostly medical diagnoses and drug prescriptions.

bipolar disorder. Mood disorder characterized by episodes of mania interspersed with episodes of depression. This disorder occurs in about 1% to 1.6% of the population and is sometimes referred to as manic depression.

blastocyst. The 150 cell preimplantation embryo comprising an outer layer, a fluid-filled cavity, and a cluster of interior cells

blood-brain barrier. Protective environment formed by tightly packed capillaries and neutroglia that prevents passage into the brain of most substances circulating in the blood.

bone marrow. Located in the center of the bone; serves as the site of the generation of all blood cells (e.g., lymphocytes and B cells).

brain-derived neurotrophic factor (BDNF). A stimulating factor localized in the CNS that promotes the growth and survival of neurons.

brain fingerprinting. Theory suggesting that specific brain-wave activity accompanies the identification of familiar stimuli. This technology may be used in criminal investigations.

bulimia nervosa. An eating disorder characterized by bouts of both overeating and self-induced vomiting/laxative use. Symptoms are often responsive to serotonergic treatments.

buprenorphine. Recent drug approved by the FDA to treat opioid addiction; works as a partial agonist for mu-opioid receptors.

catatonia. Absence of movement; often observed in the schizophrenic patient.

catecholamines. A group of three different amine neurotransmitters that contain catechol. These three neurotransmitters are dopamine, norepinephrine, and epinephrine (also called adrenaline).

cell adhesion molecules (CAM). Glycoproteins located on the cell surface that play a role in guiding growing axons as they move toward their final destinations in the brain.

cell body (or soma). Structure of the cell that contains the nucleus, cytoplasm, and various organelles used in cell metabolism.

cell membrane. Membrane that maintains the cell's shape and contains the cytoplasm, nucleus, and assorted organelles. The membrane is a bimolecular leaflet with semipermeable properties.

cellular immune system. Component of adaptive immunity composed of T cells that defend the body by either activating B-cell release or proliferating so that the T cells themselves can attack the antigen.

central canal (also called **spinal canal**). Pathway through the vertebral column for cerebral spinal fluid and the vertebral arteries.

central nervous system (CNS). One of the two main divisions of the human nervous system, consisting of the brain and spinal cord; the main coordinating and controlling center of the body that processes information to and from the peripheral nervous system.

central sulcus. Deep sulcus that separates the frontal lobe (motor cortex) from the parietal lobe (sensory cortex).

cerebellum. Hindbrain structure concerned with the coordination and control of voluntary muscular activity and movement.

cerebral aqueduct. Narrow tube interconnecting the third and fourth ventricles of the brain, located in the center of the mesencephalon.

cerebral cortex. Most recently evolved part of the brain that envelops the midbrain; also associated with complex cognitive functions.

cerebrospinal fluid (CSF). Normally clear, salty liquid produced in the ventricles, filling them and circulating around the brain in the subarachnoid layer of the meninges and central canal to nourish and protect the brain and spinal cord.

cholecystokinin. Gastrointestinal peptide released following ingestion of a meal in order to coordinate different functions of the digestive system.

cingulum. Latin for *belt;* an association tract located in the cingulate gyrus that projects to the entorhinal cortex; stimulation of this area results in a desire to engage in repetitive behaviors.

classical conditioning. Basic form of associative learning originally studied by Ivan Pavlov; involves pairing a neutral stimulus with an unconditioned stimulus known to automatically evoke a response so that, eventually, the neutral stimulus will lead to the behavior originally produced by the unconditioned stimulus.

clomipramine. SRI that prevents the reuptake of serotonin and norepinephrine from the synapse, ultimately increasing the availability of serotonin; similar in structure to imipramine, a tricyclic antidepressant; used as therapy for OCD.

cognitive/behavioral-induced neuroplasticity. Changes in a person's neurobiology resulting from significant cognitive and/or behavioral training

cognitive-behavioral therapy (CBT). Therapy developed in the 1960s that involves the therapist working with the depressed patient to educate him or her about the disorder so that they can eventually alter behaviors and cognitions to reduce the symptoms of depression.

coma therapy. Physical therapy in which an insulin coma was induced to treat mental illness in a patient. After the 1960s the use of this therapy decreased because of rising popularity of electroconvulsive therapy and psychoactive drugs.

comorbidity. Presence of two or more health problems in the same individual.

complement complex. Group of nonimmune proteins that combines to form an important part of the immune system, which can damage threatening cells by quick responses such as cutting holes in the pathogen cells.

compulsions. Ritualistic acts that accompany obsessions in OCD patients; typically include hand washing, checking, repeating actions, ordering, praying, and counting.

computerized tomography (CT). Neuroimaging technique developed in the 1960s that is the equivalent of taking an X ray of the brain.

concentration gradient. In diffusion, the attraction of a region of high concentration for one of low concentration.

concordance rate. Frequency with which two individuals express the same condition. For example, the rate at which identical twins both develop schizophrenia is the concordance rate for schizophrenia.

constraint-induced (CI) movement therapy. Type of rehabilitation therapy requiring an individual to constrain his or her "good arm" to stimulate use of the "bad" arm.

coping style. Persistent response strategy in the presence of stressful stimuli. An animal may have an active, passive, or flexible style.

correlation. Statistical technique used to determine how strongly two variables are related; two variables may change in a similar pattern (positive correlation) or a different pattern (negative correlation).

cortex (neocortex). Phylogenetically the newest cortex, the outermost layer of cerebral gray matter, including the sensorimotor and association cortices.

corticosteroids. Hormones secreted by the adrenal cortex during stress. These neurochemicals influence the brain and are thought to be a trigger for depressive symptoms. Some drugs targeted at reducing corticosteroids reduce symptoms of depression.

corticotropin-releasing hormone (CRH). A releasing hormone produced in the hypothalamus that travels to the anterior pituitary where it triggers the release of ACTH from the anterior pituitary.

cortisol. The stress hormone secreted by the adrenal cortex in primates.

cosmetic pharmacology. Using psychoactive drugs for personality modification or lifestyle alterations unrelated to mental illness.

cranial nerves. Twelve pairs of nerves, each pair having sensory and/or motor functions, extending to and from the brain without passing through the spinal cord.

craniotomy. Early physical therapy in which a section of a patient's skull was removed in an attempt to restore balance to the four humors, leading to recovery from mental illness.

craving response. Persistent, intense desire to consume a drug.

culture-bound syndrome. Condition that appears to be culture specific, for example, anorexia (United States), latah (Malaysia), koro (Malaysia), and brain fag (Nigeria). The DSM categorizes these disorders in this broad classification.

cytokine. "Messenger" protein secreted by many cells that regulate immune functions and mediate communication among the cells of the immune system; also called immunotransmitters or interleukins.

decatastrophizing. Any attempt to minimize the impact of a stressor, likely to result in a decreased allostatic load. Some people may decatastrophize by gaining an increased perception of control or employing active coping strategies to minimize the negative impact.

dementia. Progressive loss of mental functioning atypical of normal aging processes.

dementia praecox. Older term for schizophrenia describing what was believed to be a progressive and incurable deterioration of mental functioning that typically began in adolescence.

dendrites. Thin, widely branching fibers that emanate from the cell body of a neuron and "collect" information from adjacent neurons and other cells.

dendritic cells. Serve as antigen-presenting cells for naïve T cells; important for acquired immunity. Originate in the bone marrow but eventually end up in the skin and lymphoid tissue.

dendritic spines. Short, plastic outgrowths along the dendrites that increase surface area and where the majority of synapses are found.

deoxyribonucleic acid (DNA). Molecule that composes the chromosomes.

dependence. Development of tolerance and withdrawal following chronic use of drug; physical and psychological problems arise upon cessation of drug use.

depolarization. The actual change in the resting charge of the neuron, from slightly negative (polarized) to less negative/more positive (i.e., less polarized).

depression. Mood disorder characterized by feelings of sadness, diminished pleasure, alterations in sleep, fatigue, difficulty concentrating, and feelings of worthlessness; several variations exist (for example, major depression, dysthymic disorder).

detoxification. Initial step in the treatment of drug addiction that involves clearing a patient's system of the abused drug. This process can be accomplished by requiring a patient to abstain from drug use, or it may be facilitated by certain pharmacological agents.

diencephalon. "Between" area of the forebrain that surrounds the third ventricle; includes the thalamus, hypothalamus, and pineal gland, structures that synthesize sensory information and regulate motivated behaviors.

diffusion. Tendency for dissolved ions or molecules to move from areas of high concentration to areas of low concentration.

disorganized symptoms. Symptoms in a schizophrenia patient such as nonlogical thoughts and speech.

dopamine (DA). The resulting neurotransmitter when dopa reacts with the enzyme dopa decarboxylase. This is an important neurotransmitter involved in movement and brain reward systems.

drug addiction. Strong desire to consume a drug accompanied by a diminishing capacity to limit the intake of the drug.

dual-centers hypothesis of hunger regulation. Proposed by Stellar in 1954, the VMH was considered the hunger center and the LH was the satiety center.

dualism. Philosophical position taken on the mind–body problem suggesting that the mind and body/brain are separate entities; Descartes proposed interactionism in which the two entities interacted in the physical brain, specifically in the pineal gland.

dumping syndrome. Side effect sometimes seen in patients following gastric bypass surgery; syndrome consists of nausea or general sickness following the consumption of fat or sugar.

dyskenesias. Abnormal involuntary motor movements and difficulty in carrying out voluntary movements.

dyslexia. Learning disability that results in slow reading and comprehension; it is thought that the exposure of affected subjects to repetitive auditory language facilitates recovery.

ecologically relevant. Term used to describe stressors that an animal may find in its natural environment. Example: Social defeat is a more ecologically relevant stimulus for hamsters than cold or restraint.

ectoderm. The outer layer of the fertilized egg, or zygote, that eventually gives rise to the skin, nerve cells, and most of the neuroglia.

efferent information. Information carried outward from the CNS to the periphery.

efficacy. The capacity to produce a desired effect with a drug or treatment.

electroconvulsive therapy (ECT). Physical therapy used for mental illnesses such as major depression and schizophrenia; involves the delivery of electrical current to an anesthetized patient in an attempt to reconfigure neural functions for normal mental functioning.

electroencephalography (EEG). One of the earliest methods of recording activity of the living brain; involves placing electrodes on an individual's scalp and recording the activity of large populations of neurons. This technique has been valuable in diagnosing epilepsy and in delineating the various stages of sleep.

electrostatic pressure. Electrical attraction and repulsion (+/− and +/+, −/−, respectively); complement to diffusion.

embryonic stem cells. Undifferentiated cells derived from the embryo that have the potential to develop into a wide variety of cell types.

empirical evidence. Evidence that can be confirmed by systematic observations. This evidence should play a critical role in a researcher's or practitioner's opinion of causes and treatments for certain disorders.

endoderm. The innermost layer of the fertilized egg, or zygote, that eventually gives rise to the developing fetus's internal organs.

endogenous opioids. Naturally occurring neurotransmitter-like substances found in the brain that produce analgesic and euphoric effects similar to heroin and morphine.

endoplasmic reticulum. Network of thin tubes within a cell that transport newly synthesized proteins to other locations.

endorphin. An opioid-like substance produced in the hypothalamus and elsewhere that is related to pain reduction and reward, but also facilitates the release of epinephrine from the adrenal medulla during the stress response.

entorhinal cortex. Cortical structure on the medial surface of the temporal lobe that surrounds limbic structures such as the amygdala and has rich interconnections with the hippocampal formation.

enzymes. Proteins that facilitate chemical reactions and are intimately involved in the regulation of activity inside the neuron.

epinephrine. One of the three catecholamine neurotransmitters that is also called adrenaline; epinephrine neurons contain phentolamine.

episodic memory. Autobiographic memory for personal experiences (episodes) pinpointed to specific place and time contexts.

euneurics. Movement to design "better" brains.

evolutionary game theory. Quantitative models used by evolutionary theorists to understand strategies used by animals to maximize survival (e.g., mating).

excitatory postsynaptic potential (EPSP). Graded depolarization of a neuron.

excitotoxicity. Process that probably occurs in CA3 neurons of the hippocampus. This effect is caused by excessive glutamate activity in the neurons, which may lead to neuronal death; prolonged exposure to stress hormones may trigger the process.

exocytosis. Release of chemicals from cells into the extracellular fluid (release by the axon terminal of a chemical neurotransmitter into the synaptic cleft).

experiment. Research technique in which variables are purposively manipulated in a systematic way to test or establish a hypothesis.

exposure and response prevention (ERP). Behavioral therapy for OCD; patients are encouraged to remain in contact with a feared stimulus while simultaneously suppressing the rituals they typically use to decrease anxiety.

exposure therapy. Type of therapy sometimes used with PTSD patients in which the facilitator exposes the patient to the stimulus/event that is most feared in an attempt to have him/her see that exposure isn't always associated with a negative outcome.

extended amygdala. Brain structures continuous with and sharing morphological similarities with the amygdaloid nuclei, including the nucleus accumbens, BNST, and olfactory lobe.

external locus of control. Component of a theory proposed by Julian Rotter that emphasized the importance of one's perception of his or her source of control in life—either within the individual (internal) or in the environment (external).

eye movement desensitization reprocessing (EMDR). Type of therapy introduced for the treatment of PTSD; consists of having the patient follow the therapist's finger back and forth for about 20-second intervals to produce a rapid and rhythmic pattern of eye movements, while thinking about the negative aspects of the trauma experience associated with the PTSD.

fight-or-flight response. The sympathetic branch of the autonomic nervous system triggers this response that prepares the animal to either fight the stressor, or flee from the stressor.

filopodia. An extremely fine tubular shaped extension that emerges from the neuron's growth cone.

fissures. Deep grooves covering the outer surface of the brain.

5-hydroxyindole acetic acid (5-HIAA). Metabolite of serotonin (5-HT), found in the cerebrospinal fluid, 5-HIAA; levels are reduced in sick anorexics and elevated in recovered anorexic patients.

fixed action pattern (FAP). Motor program that seems to develop automatically in particular species of animals (e.g, the courting displays of many birds); once triggered, these rigid, consistent, and predictable responses are continued to completion.

fluoxetine. Selective serotonin reuptake inhibitor (SSRI) produced by Eli Lilly pharmaceutical company in 1985;

this drug had the specific effect of blocking the reuptake of serotonin.

frontal lobe. Part of the cerebral cortex in either hemisphere of the brain found directly behind the forehead; helps to control voluntary movement and is associated with the higher mental activities and with personality.

functional magnetic resonance imaging (fMRI). MRI that provides information about activity of the brain by quantifying cerebral blood flow during a cognitive challenge.

G proteins. Membrane-bound proteins that bind GTP when activated by a membrane receptor. Active G proteins can stimulate or inhibit other membrane-bound proteins.

galanin. A neuropeptide that stimulates feeding behavior, particularly fat intake, when injected into the paraventricular hypothalamus.

gamma-aminobutyric acid (GABA). An amino acid that acts as an inhibitory neurotransmitter in the central nervous system.

gastric bypass surgery. (also known as *bariatric surgery*). Surgery conducted in obese individuals to reduce the stomach to about 1% of its original capacity.

general adaptation syndrome. Syndrome originally described by Hans Selye; he felt that stressed individuals undergo three phases during the stress response; alarm, in which the individual's body registers the threat of the imposing stressor; resistance, in which the body mobilizes its forces to fight off the stressor; if the stressor persists, exhaustion as the body runs out of energy to fight off the stressor.

generalized anxiety disorder (GAD). Vague sense of anxiety not directly related to an anxiety-provoking event.

glia (or glial cells). Nonneuronal cells in the nervous system that provide, among other things, support for neuronal structures and insulation of neuronal messages.

glucocorticoids. Compounds that belong to the family of substances called corticosteroids. They affect metabolism and have anti-inflammatory and immunosuppressive effects.

glucose utilization theory of hunger regulation. Proposed by Jean Mayer, this theory suggested that hunger was more influenced by the level of glucose metabolization in the cells than circulating levels of glucose.

glutamate (Glu). A principle excitatory neurotransmitter that regulates cortical and subcortical functions.

glycine (Gly). An excitatory amino acid that mediates most CNS synapses along with glutamate and GABA.

Golgi apparatus. Set of membranes in the cytoplasm that wraps around chemicals released by secretory cells. In neurons this structure manufactures the synaptic vesicles.

graded potential. Series of incoming electrical signals that have little or no effect on the neuron depolarizing or firing.

gyri (sing. **gyrus**). Convolutions of the surface of the brain, caused by the infolding of the cerebral cortex.

hallucination. An internal perception of a realistic sensory event in the absence of any external stimuli.

haloperidol. Neuroleptic drug that blocks dopaminergic activity; used in the treatment of schizophrenia and Tourette's syndrome.

hebephrenia. Inappropriate and uncontrollable form of laughter.

helper T cells. Type of T lymphocyte that activates macrophages and stimulate the release of antibodies from B lymphocytes.

hippocampus. Arching limbic structure within the temporal lobe important in learning, memory, and navigating the environment.

histology. Systematic preparation of brain or other physiological tissue for microscopic study to be used for experimental and diagnostic purposes.

homeostasis. Internal balance and regulation of physiological systems in an organism.

humoral immune system. Primarily antibodies released by B lymphocytes.

humoral theory. Early physical theory of mental illness proposed by Hippocrates. Four humors, or liquids, were thought to contribute to mental illness when they became unbalanced.

Huntington's chorea. Hereditary neurodegenerative disorder of motor control characterized by ongoing involuntary jerky movements and progressive dementia; associated with hyperactivity of the dopaminergic system.

hyperpolarization. A shift in the membrane potential to more negative (i.e., more polarized and farther apart). Neuron is inhibited from firing and must receive more insistent electrochemical signals to be undone.

hypothalamic-pituitary-adrenal axis (HPA axis). The stress response originally described by Hans Selye, in which the hypothalamus secretes a releasing factor (CRH) which travels to the anterior pituitary and triggers the release of ACTH. ACTH then travels to the adrenal cortex where it stimulates the release of glucocorticoids.

Generally an adaptive response (in short bursts), this sequence and its aftermath help the animal produce enough energy to survive the impending stressor.

hypothalamus. Brain nuclei that control the endocrine system and regulate motivated behavior.

hysteria. Early characterization of mental disturbance described in women who had no known accompanying brain damage. Charcot thought that only hysterical women could be hypnotized.

imipramine. Synthesized originally for treatment of schizophrenic patients, this drug was observed to have antidepressant qualities. Researchers found that it influenced the synapse by blocking the reuptake of monoamine transmitters back into the terminal.

immediate early genes. Class of genes that exhibit rapid responses to certain extracellular stimuli by producing proteins that prompt the release of such neurochemicals as corticotropin releasing hormone (CRH), which is involved in the stress response.

inferior colliculi. Nuclei in the mesencephalon that take part in localizing sounds, integrating hearing reflexes, and orienting the body toward auditory stimuli.

inhibitory postsynaptic potential (IPSP). Temporary hyperpolarization of a membrane.

innate immune system. Components of the immune system, such as skin, phagocytic cells (e.g., macrophages), NK cells, the complement system, and cytokines that exist prior to an invasion by a pathogen; also known as the *front-line defense.*

interleukin-1 (IL-1). Cytokine produced primarily by activated phagocytes that activates B and T cells, influences NK and macrophage activity, and induces fever.

internal locus of control. Component of a theory proposed by Julian Rotter that emphasized the importance of one's perception of his or her source of control in life—either within the individual (internal) or in the environment (external).

interneurons. Nerve cells that associate sensory and motor activity in the central nervous system.

ion channels. Membrane-spanning proteins that form a pore allowing passage of ions from one side of the membrane to the other. The process results in either depolarization or hyperpolarization of the cell.

ionotropic receptors. Receptors with a binding site for neurotransmitter and a pore that regulates ion flow.

iproniazid. Drug developed in the 1950s as an antibacterial agent but later found to have antidepressant effects in patients. Researchers later showed that this drug was a monoamine oxidase inhibitor, which prolonged the presence of monoamines in the synapse.

kainite receptor. A subgroup of glutamate receptors whose functional role is not clearly understood but has been related to hippocampal plasticity.

killer T cell (also known as *cytotoxic T cell*). T cell that recognizes and kills virus-infected host cells; utilizes the protein perforin, which enables them to drill holes in cells, leaving them to die.

kindled limbic seizure. Temporal lobe seizure thought to be related to the accumulation of chronic stress and loneliness; may be accompanied by uncharacteristic violent behavior.

knockout mice. Product of recently developed technique in behavioral neuroscience in which certain genes are eliminated (knocked out) so that their function can be determined in the genetically modified animal.

lateral fissure. Prominent groove that separates the temporal lobe from the frontal and parietal lobes.

lateral hypothalamus. Brain area which, when lesioned in rats, caused the rats to become hypophagic and to die unless the experimenter assisted with feeding. In addition to diminishing hunger, LH lesions also decrease general motivation.

lateralization. The observation that different functions have been assigned, or lateralized, to each hemishpere of the brain.

learned helplessness. Usually resulting from several bouts with failure, the acquired belief that no effort can remove an individual from a stressful environment. Seligman suggests that this phenomenon may be a basis for clinical depression.

leptin. Neurochemical produced in fat cells and detected by receptors in the brain. Genetically obese mice *(ob/ob)* deficient in leptin are extremely overweight and the obesity is diminished by exogenous injections of leptin.

limbic system. Collection of brain regions (amygdala, mammilary bodies, hippocampus, fornix and cingulated gyrus) that collectively produce, respond to and regulate emotional responses.

lipostatic theory of hunger regulation. Early eating regulation theory that proposed that some fuel or form of adipose tissue circulated throughout the blood and was interpreted by the brain so that current energy levels could be detected. If lipostatic measures were too high, it was theorized, the animal would cease eating. The defining lipostatic measure was never discovered.

liposuction. Surgical technique used to extract fat from the body.

lithium. Chemical element approved in the 1970s as a drug for treatment of bipolar disorder. Although the specific biological mechanism is unknown, lithium is known to share ionic properties with some of the important ions maintaining neural functions such as magnesium and calcium.

lobotomy. Faddish operation to treat mental illness used in the 1930s and 1940s. The procedure involved separating sections of the frontal lobe from the rest of the brain.

localization of function. Notion that specific functions are localized in specific brain areas as suggested by the eighteenth-century theory of phrenology.

longitudinal fissure. Deep groove that separates the left and right cerebral hemispheres of the brain.

lymph nodes. Small nodules made up of lymphocyte-rich tissue found along the lymphatic channels in the body. Location of the origin of acquired immune functioning.

lysosomes. Neuronal organelles that engage in cellular cleansing and similar "house-cleaning" activities to maintain neuronal function by degrading proteins; these organelles also play a role in the MHC II molecule pathway.

macrophage. Phagocytotic cell of the immune system that is activated by chemicals released from foreign microorganisms and T-cell cytokines. In addition to engulfing microorganisms, they may secrete proinflammatory cytokines and serve as antigen-presenting cells.

magnetic resonance imaging. Technique that provides pictures of the brain by sending a magnetic field through a person's head so that the scanners can absorb radiation from hydrogen ions so that a three-dimensional, high-resolution picture of brain tissue is generated.

major depressive disorder. One of the most common psychiatric illnesses, occurring in about 17% of the population, with females suffering at about twice the rate of males and characterized by one or more major depressive episodes of at least two weeks and at least four additional symptoms of depression (for example, sleep disturbances, loss of concentration, decreased energy, guilt).

major histocompatibility complex (MHC). In humans, a genetic locus on chromosome 6 that encodes the peptides recognized by T lymphocytes; additionally, this genetic code influences cytokines and antigen proteins.

manic episodes. Hyperactivity characterized by euphoria and impaired judgment; exists with depression in bipolar disorder.

mecamylamine. Drug that acts as a chonlinergic receptor antagonist; currently being tested for use with Tourette's symptoms.

medial forebrain bundle. Large collection of axons that extend from the hypothalamus to the septum, a structure in the limbic system. Animals respond continuously to receiving electrical brain stimulation in this area; consequently, it is considered the most prevalent brain reward system of the nervous system.

medulla oblongata. Lowest part of the brain stem;, an extension into the skull of the upper end of the spinal cord; regulates basic vegetative functioning.

meninges. Three connective tissue membranes (arachnoid, dura, pia mater) that protect and enclose the brain and spinal cord.

mesencephalon. Midbrain joining the brainstem and forebrain and serving as a passageway for impulses to higher brain centers.

mesoderm. The middle layer of the fertilized egg, or zygote, that eventually gives rise to many muscles, the skin, skeleton, and connective tissue.

mesolimbic dopamine pathway. Neurons extending from the midbrain to the forebrain produce and release dopamine into the forebrain. Two pathways make up this system: (1) the mesocortico-limbic (reward circuit) system extends from the ventral tegmental area to the nucleus accumbens; (2) the nigrostriatal pathway, involved in neuromuscular functions, extends from the substantia nigra to the corpus striatum.

messenger RNA (mRNA). RNA molecule transcribed from DNA and translated into amino acid sequence of a polypeptide.

metabotropic receptors. Receptor that, when stimulated, produces a relatively slow but long-lasting effect through metabolic reactions.

methadone. Opiate drug that is given to heroin addicts to help wean them from opiate addiction because it minimizes withdrawal symptoms and is not thought to produce a high that is comparable to that induced by heroin or morphine.

MHC I molecule. MHC glycoproteins found on all cells of the body that display information related to the invasion of the cells by viruses.

MHC II molecule. MHC glycoprotein produced in the immune cells; shares information only with the immune cells.

microdialysis. Neurochemical technique in which the level of a neurotransmitter from a particular area of the brain is assessed. This technique is unique because the researcher can extract the neurotransmitter while the animal is engaging in a particular behavior.

microfilaments. Intraneuronal flexible supporting elements associated with membranes.

microtubules. Proteins in the cell bodies and axons of neurons that transport nutrients within the cell, especially from the cell nucleus out to the axon and down to the terminal buttons.

mind–body problem. Philosophical question posed to determine the nature, either mental or physical, of the mind.

minor physical anomalies (MPAs). Minor structural abnormalities located in various areas of the body; they are typically investigated in accessible areas of the body including the head, mouth, ears, eyes, hands, and feet.

mitochondria (sing. **mitochondrion**). Structures in the cell that perform the metabolic activities that provide energy.

modafinil. Drug originally developed to keep narcoleptic patients from suddenly falling asleep. It is also being used by nonnarcoleptic patients to stay awake for extended periods of time.

monoamine oxidase inhibitors (MAOIs). Class of drugs that deactivate monoamine oxidase in the synaptic area so that the monoamines have a prolonged period of activity.

mood (affective) disorders. Disturbances of mood typically accompanied by inappropriate expression of pleasure or misery; some people experience vigorous swings between the two extremes.

motor neurons. Broad phrase referring either to the output neurons carrying-out the commands from sensory and interneurons, or to neurons at the interface of glands, muscles and blood vessels.

MPTP. A neurotoxin that causes a neural disorder resembling Parkinson's disorder in primates.

multiple sclerosis. Neurodegenerative autoimmune disease in which T cells are thought to destroy the myelin sheath of the neurons. Leads to nausea, vertigo, bladder dysfunction, depression, and memory deficits.

myelin sheath. Insulating material that covers many vertebrate axons.

N-methyl-D aspartate (NMDA) receptors. A subtype of glutamate receptor that uses both Na^+ and Ca^{2+} influx to mediate its effects.

N-methyltransferase (PNMT). PNMT is the enzyme that converts norepinephrine to epinephrine.

naloxone. Drug that blocks opiate receptors in the brain; counteracts drugs such as morphine. Naltrexone has a similar function.

narcolepsy. A condition in which individuals succumb to irresistible urges to sleep, even at such inappropriate times as while driving or speaking in public.

natural killer (NK) cells. Cells in bone marrow that are a component of the innate immune system. On recognizing a microbe, these cells move in for the kill, using techniques such as secreting toxic substances and creating fatal damage to the invading cell.

negative reinforcement. Cessation of an aversive stimulus on the presentation of a particular response. Relapse into drug use is reinforced because it reduces the negative experience of withdrawal.

negative symptoms. Characteristics or attributes that are absent from the nature of a person with schizophrenia, such as reduced desire for social interaction.

nerve. Cordlike collection of nerve fibers outside the brain and spinal cord; conveys information to and from the CNS and the periphery.

nerve growth factor. A neurochemical secreted by the postsynaptic neuron during the formation of synaptic connections between neurons; it is considered a trophic factor because it stimulates the growth of the presynaptic neuron's axon.

nerve impulse (action potential). Physiological basis of communication in the nervous system triggered by the exchange of certain ions across the nerve cell membrane.

nerve net theory. Early theory of the nature of the nervous system implying that the nervous system is made up of continuous extensions of nervous tissue.

neural crest. The tissue that starts to develop on each side of the neural tube that later becomes the peripheral nervous system.

neural diathesis–stress model of schizophrenia. Updated adaptation of the classic diathesis–stress model that emphasizes the role of alterations in steroidal hormones in the expression and severity of schizohrenic symptoms. Because of the dramatic changes in these hormones at puberty, Elaine Walker and colleagues have proposed that adolescence should be considered a critical phase in the development of schizophrenia.

neural folds. A portion of the ectoderm of the embryo develops into folds that form around the neural tube; eventually, these folds will give rise to the entire nervous system.

neural groove. The groove found between the neural folds in the developing embryo; once the neural folds join, the neural groove becomes the neural tube.

neural plate. A group of cells derived from the embryonic ectoderm that subsequently develop into the neural goove and neural tube, the origins of the mature nervous system.

neural tube. An early form of the nervous system observed during prenatal development: The rostral section develops into the brain and the caudal section eventually develops into the spinal cord.

neurodegenerative diseases. Conditions that are sometimes inherited or acquired due to some sporadic condition that result in the progressive deterioration of some portion of the nervous system.

neuroethics. Convergence of several disciplines, such as philosophy, religion, and medicine, to recognize the importance of ethical issues related to the rapidly changing field of neuroscience.

neurofeedback. Form of biofeedback in which patients learn to maintain certain electrical brain wave rhythms to achieve relaxation and brain homeostasis.

neurofilaments. Neuronal structural proteins involved in membrane protein transport.

neurogenesis. Creation of new neurons through mitosis. It was once thought that developed brains could no longer produce new neurons, but research has confirmed the production of new neurons across the life span.

neurohormones. Brain substances that act like hormones and are released by neurons into the circulatory system.

neuromodulator. A substance that modifies or regulates the effect of a neurotransmitter.

neuron. Fundamental unit, or cell, of the nervous system.

neuron doctrine. Theory that separate units, or neurons, as opposed to continuous units, made up the nervous system.

neuropeptide Y (NPY). Pancreatic polypeptide that is one of the most abundant neurotransmitters in the mammalian brain; NPY stimulates eating and reduces energy expenditure.

neuropeptides. Proteins that are released by neurons and act as intercellular messengers.

neuropil. The intricate network of interwoven glial and neuronal processes that lie between axons.

neuropore. An opening at each end of the neural canal that eventually give rise to the brain and spinal cord.

neurotoxicity. Neural damage due to some threat presented to the nervous tissue such as toxins, low oxygen, decreased glucose, etc.

neurotransmitter. Chemical such as dopamine and serotonin in the brain that is essential for communication between two neurons.

neurotrophic factors. Neurochemicals such as BDNF (brain-derived neurotrophic factor) that promote the growth and complexity of neurons.

neurotrophins. Neurochemicals secreted in an activity-dependent fashion that are thought to be involved in the restructuring of synaptic connections

neutrophil. Most abundant white blood cell circulating in the blood; these cells are recruited to inflammation sites where they utilize either phagocytosis or enzymatic digestion of pathogens.

noradrenergic bundle. Bundle of fibers originating in the locus coeruleus of the brainstem that travel to limbic and cortical structures. These noradrenergic fibers have been strongly associated with brain reward and arousal.

norepinephrine. An amine neurotransmitter that contains tyrosine hydroxylase, dopa decarboxylase, and the enzyme dopamine B-hydroxylase (DBH). DBH is responsible for converting dopamine into norepinephrine.

nuclei. Functional collections of neurons in specific brain regions; can be identified by histological techniques.

nucleus. Structure within the cell that contains the chromosomes.

nucleus accumbens. Limbic component of the striatum sometimes referred to as the "pleasure center" of the brain; involved in motivating behavior and reinforcing survival responses; linked to disorders ranging from anxiety and depression to addiction.

obesity. A state of pathological overweight due to both genetic and environmental factors. Technically one is considered obese if one's body mass index (BMI) is 30 kg/m^2 or greater.

obsessions. Recurring, upsetting thoughts typically observed in OCD patients; typically related to contamination, doubts, order, aggression, and sexual imagery.

obsessive-compulsive disorder (OCD). Chronic condition characterized by recurring upsetting thoughts (obsessions) and subsequent ritualistic acts (compulsions).

occipital lobe. Region of the cerebral cortex lying at the very back of the brain, caudal to the parietal and temporal lobes; site of the primary visual cortex.

OCD loop. Brain structures thought to be involved in the maintenance of OCD; loop includes the orbitofrontal cortex, cingulate gyrus and embedded cingulum, caudate, thalamus, and amygdala.

orbitofrontal cortex (OFC). Anterior area of the prefrontal cortex, involved in more advanced cognitions and associations.

orexins. Neuropeptides that are secreted from the lateral hypothalamic neurons and involved in eating, arousal, and other motivated behaviors. Administration of orexins to the CNS results in increased food intake.

organelles. "Organlike" structures in the cytoplasm of the cell membrane that help in the maintenance and metabolism of the cell.

oxytocin. A posterior pituitary neuropeptide involved in complementary activities such as bonding, sexual behavior, and childbirth.

PANDAS. Pediatric autoimmune neuropsychiatric disorders associated with streptococcal infection; thought to be the cause of Tourette's syndrome in some children.

panic disorder. Intense anxiety-stress response, typically without an actual fear stimulus present. Physical components, including chest pain, shortness of breath, and nausea, resemble the symptoms of a heart attack.

parasympathetic nervous system. Maintenance component of the autonomic nervous system.

paraventricular nuclei. A collection of neurons located in the hypothalamus; the processes extend into the posterior pituitary, where oxytocin and vasopressin are released. Thought to be intimately involved in hunger regulation

parietal lobe. Main division of each hemisphere of the cerebral cortex, located beneath the crown of the skull; interprets somatosensory information and spatial relationships.

pathogen. Microorganism (a virus or bacterium) that can cause disease.

peptic ulcers. Lesions that occur in the stomach lining; usually caused by a bacterium, but they are exacerbated by stress.

peptide YY (PYY). Peptide closely related to NPY and also implicated in hunger stimulation.

perforin. Protein used as a weapon by killer T cells and NK cells that drills a hole in the infected cells so that other enzymes can continue the destruction of the cells.

periaqueductal gray (PAG). Region of the midbrain surrounding the cerebral aqueduct; contains neural circuits involved in species-typical behaviors and pain perception.

peripheral nervous system (PNS). One of the two divisions of the human nervous system, consisting of the sensory and motor nerves outside of the brain and spinal cord (12 pairs of cranial nerves and 31 pairs of spinal nerves).

phagocytes. Cells, such as macrophages, that protect the body from invaders by engulfing them.

pharmacokinetics. The study of the action and reaction of and to drugs in the body.

phenotype. External expression of certain genetic influences. The phenotype for one genetic assortment may be long fingers; for another the phenotype may be brown hair.

phospholipid bilayer. Basis of neuron cell membranes. Each molecule has a water-soluble head (a protein compatible with water) and a water-rejecting tail (consisting of a lipid). The head faces a watery solution (cytoplasm or extracellular fluid between cells) while the lipid tail faces another lipid tail in the interior of the cell membrane.

phrenology. Term popularized to describe Gall's theory of localization of function. In this theory, bumps on the surface of the skull were deemed to predict certain mental capabilities.

pituitary gland. Master endocrine gland at the base of the hypothalamus; releases a variety of hormones that influence the activity of other glands throughout the body.

placebo effect. Term used to describe a therapeutic effect resulting from the consumption of a physiologically inactive substance (for example, a sugar pill or some other unrelated treatment); used as evidence for mind-body communication.

plasticity. Inherent flexibility of the brain in responding to environmental changes; for example, by learning or to compensate for loss of function to damaged areas.

pluripotent. The potential of a single stem cell to develop into many types of cells in the body.

pons. Large bulge in the brainstem immediately ventral to the cerebellum; relays information from the cerebral cortex to the cerebellum and contains a portion of the reticular formation, nuclei that appear to be important for sleep and arousal.

positive symptoms. Characteristics or attributes that are added to a schizophrenia patient's nature, such as hallucinations.

positive-incentive theory of hunger regulation. Theory suggesting that people eat because it is a pleasurable, rewarding experience.

positron emission tomography (PET). Functional neuroimaging technique that involves injecting the patient with radioactively tagged glucose and quantifying the patient's metabolization of the radioactive glucose when the patient is presented with an experimental challenge (e.g., a cognitive task or a certain stimulus).

post-traumatic stress disorder (PTSD). Disorder characterized by symptoms such as memories and dreams related to a traumatic event that recur up to months or years following the event. Individuals with this disorder feel as if they are reexperiencing the trauma and have the accompanying physiological arousal to enhance their belief of impending danger.

precursors. Constituent and elemental substances that serve as the initial components in a chain of chemicals. For instance, fats and sugars combine with oxygen to form cellular fuels.

prefrontal cortex (PFC). Area of the frontal cortex involved in many higher functions. Evidence suggests that atrophy of neurons or compromised activity in this area may lead to symptoms of depression.

preparatory response theory of hunger regulation. Theory suggesting that the feeling of hunger may be more closely related to the body's preparation to eat than any deficit of food.

prosencephalon. Forebrain controlling sensation, perception, emotion, learning, thinking, and other intellectual functions; includes the olfactory bulb and tracts, cerebral hemispheres, nasal ganglia, thalamus, optic tracts, and hypothalamus.

proteins. Complex organic chemicals that are the essential building materials of living cells.

proximate causation. Doctrine stating that the most direct cause of an event is the most important factor. In evolutionary theory, proximate questions are most often questions of mechanism and development of certain behaviors.

psychoactive drugs. Drugs that produce a noticeable change in mood or perception.

psychoanalysis. Therapeutic approach to mental illness developed by Freud. In this subjective theory, unconscious motives were thought to direct behavior and thoughts.

psychometric test. Paper-and-pencil test typically used by psychologists for diagnostic purposes. These tests need to pass reliability, validity and standardization assessment before use with patients and clients.

psychoneuroimmunology (PNI). Exploration of the relationships among the brain, behavior, and the immune system.

psychopharmacology. Discipline that explores the relationship between certain psychoactive drugs and behavior and/or mental processes.

psychosocial model. Therapeutic approach emphasizing the relationship between client, or patient, and therapist while using therapies such as behavioral therapy, interpersonal therapy, classical psychoanalysis, or group therapy.

psychotropic (psychoactive) drug. Medication that influences psychological processes.

Purkinje neurons. Neurons in the cerebellum that are responsible for all the output from the cerebellar cortex to cerebellar nuclei.

radial glia. Neuroglial cells characterized by very long branches that serve as a physical guide or road map for developing neuroblast cells as they migrate toward their final destinations; following the development of the brain, it is thought that these cells are develop into astrocytes.

reboxetine. Relatively new drug that selectively inhibits the reuptake of noradrenaline in the synapse. Used as an antidepressant, this drug is thought to be more effective than other antidepressants in restoring social functioning in depressed patients.

receptors. Areas on a neuron specialized to be highly sensitive to a specific type of stimulation or chemical.

reflex. Most basic form of behavior that involves an automatic response to an environmental event or stimulus, for example, sucking or blinking.

repetitive transcranial magnetic stimulation (rTMS) Relatively new antidepressant treatment that involves placing a powerful electromagnet or coil on the scalp. The magnet produces depolarization in the underlying neurons in the brain.

resting (or membrane) potential. Electrical potential across a membrane when a neuron is at rest.

reticular formation. Collection of nuclei and fiber pathways traversing the brainstem from midbrain to medulla; play a primary role in arousal, attention, and sleep and wakefulness.

reuptake. The return of spent neurotransmitter from the synapse to the presynaptic neuron by means of specialized receptors.

rhombencephalon. Hindbrain, or brainstem, that surrounds the fourth ventricle.

ribosomes. Bulbous structures in the nucleus that are the primary destination for mRNA and the location of translation and assembly of proteins.

saltatory conduction. The electrical movement or jumping of the action potential across gaps (called nodes of Ranvier) in the myelin sheath.

schizophrenia. Mental illness characterized by hallucinations, delusions, social withdrawal, and cognitive deterioration. Certain brain modifications such as a smaller hippocampus and disarrayed neurons have been observed to accompany this condition.

seasonal affective disorder (SAD). Form of depression that occurs in winter months when the duration of natural light decreases.

second messenger systems. A multiple-step and complex signal amplification process that occurs in the neuron that translates, for example, hormonal signals into long-lasting cellular events.

self-directed neuroplasticity. Systematically altering one's brain via extensive mental and/or physical training.

self-efficacy. Term proposed by Albert Bandura to describe a person's assessment of his or her competence in dealing with life's problems.

sensitization. Process by which an animal or person becomes increasingly responsive to a particular stimulus following repeated presentation.

sensory-gating deficits. The inability of schizophrenia patients to habituate the startle response to somewhat expected stimuli.

sensory neurons. Refers to the specialized cells that transmit, input, and interpret physical stimuli (light, sound, touch, etc.) from the external world and translate it into neuronal impulses.

sensory-specific theory of satiety. Theory suggesting that animals are motivated to consume a different taste after previously eating to satiety; this hypothesis explains why animals and humans placed on a diverse cafeteria diet frequently overeat.

serotonin (5-HT). A major neurotransmitter involved in mood, aggression, and appetite regulation.

set-point theory of hunger regulation. Theory suggesting that animals are motivated to eat when food or energy levels drop below a particular level.

sexual selection. Choosing a mate or competing for a mate.

sexually dimorphic nucleus of the preoptic area (SDN-POA). Region of the anterior hypothalamic preoptic area that has a larger volume in male rats than in female rats.

simple (specific) phobia. Disorder that involves an intense fear of a particular object (e.g., heights, spiders, germs) that disrupts a person's normal functioning as he or she attempts to avoid the feared stimuli.

SNUBs (super neurotransmitter uptake blockers). New drugs that are designed to block the reuptake of more than one monoamine transmitter. These drugs differ from the original tricyclics in their weaker nature and consequently fewer side effects.

social defeat paradigm. Animal model of chronic stress in which an animal is exposed to a larger, more aggressive animal and is defeated in a single aggressive encounter. For up to a month or longer, the defeated animal will not exhibit defensive behavior when an animal—even a smaller animal—is placed in its cage.

social learning theory. Theory proposed by Albert Bandura emphasizing the importance of observations of models in social situations and how observations can lead to learning without direct exposure to a reinforcer.

sodium-potassium pumps. Mechanisms that actively transport sodium ions out of the cell while simultaneously drawing potassium ions in.

somatic marker. Body signal, such as altered electrodermal activity, that is interpreted by the brain as an indication of a relevant impending event.

somatic nervous system (SNS). Voluntary part of the peripheral nervous system that controls the movement of skeletal muscles or transmits somatosensory information to the central nervous system.

spatial summation. Summation of excitatory or inhibitory synaptic effects on a postsynaptic membrane resulting from the simultaneous action of several synapses at one time on one local area of the cell.

species-specific stressor. Stressor that is specific for a particular species. Example: Weasel urine is a natural stressor for rats but is not stressful for dogs.

spinal cord. Tube of central nervous system tissue extending from the base of the brain through the central canal to the upper part of the lumbar spine; conducts sensorimotor impulses between the brain and the body and is a site of reflex activity.

spleen. Filtering organ, located in the abdomen, that plays a large role in defending the body against blood-borne antigens.

stem cells. Cells that, when nurtured in the appropriate chemical culture, have the ability to divide and develop into specialized cells for an indefinite time period.

stereological analysis. Unbiased optical method of counting cells by randomly sampling various areas and depths within neural tissue.

stereotaxic apparatus. Scientific device that enables the experimenter or surgeon to access any three-dimensional point in the brain; used for placement of electrodes and various forms of neurosurgery.

striatum. Terminal for all afferent fiber pathways forming the basal ganglia; dysfunction in this motor system is believed to be involved in OCD and Tourette's.

stroke. Loss of brain tissue caused by blockade of a blood vessel and resultant loss of blood and hence oxygen; can result in sudden loss of consciousness, sensation, and voluntary movement.

substantia nigra. Nucleus of the tegmentum; communicates with the caudate nucleus and putamen in the basal ganglia to initiate movement.

sudden infant death syndrome (SIDS). Respiratory malfunction, perhaps influenced by an immature medulla that results in an infant's death.

sulci (sing. **sulcus**). Small grooves or mounds on the surface of an organ.

superior colliculi. Nuclei in the mesencephalon that takes part in controlling the body's reflexes to visual stimuli.

superstitious behavior. Response resulting from random reinforcement; thought to explain some ritualistic behavior.

supraoptic nuclei. Hypothalamic nuclei that produce oxytocin.

sympathetic nervous system. Arousing component of the autonomic nervous system.

synapse. Tiny gap that separates two neurons and is the location of communication between the two cells.

T cells or **T lymphocytes.** Cells that mature in the thymus, travel in the blood, and populate secondary lymphoid tissue; they make up cell-mediated immunity and function by exposing receptors that recognize foreign particles.

tectum. Dorsal part of the midbrain; made up of the inferior and superior colliculi, control centers for auditory and visual stimuli.

tegmentum. Ventral part of the midbrain, composed of various nuclei related to movement and to species-typical behaviors.

telencephalon. "Endbrain" portion of the forebrain that includes the cerebral hemispheres, basal ganglia, olfactory bulb, and olfactory tracts.

temporal lobe. Division of the cerebral cortex lying at each side within the temple of the skull that responds to auditory inputs and contains areas related to language pro-duction and recognition; underlying areas regulate and maintain memory and emotional processes.

temporal summation. Additive effects of a single neuron firing in rapid succession onto a postsynaptic membrane. Each new depolarization builds on the dissipating graded postsynaptic potential to eventually result in the appropriate hyperpolarization or hypopolarization threshold.

terminal buttons. At the tip of an axon, the points from which the axon releases chemicals (neurotransmitters).

testosterone. A steroid hormone produced by the testes that is important in the differentiation of the male brain and body.

thalamus. Structure of the forebrain; main source of input to the cerebral cortex.

threshold potential. The electrochemical point at which a neuron will respond to incoming stimulation with an action potential.

thymus. Immune system organ (containing epithelial cells, dendritic cells, macrophages, and precursor cells) that becomes maturation site of T lymphocytes from bone marrow-derived precursor cells.

tics. Rapid, repetitive, stereotyped movements or vocalizations; characteristic symptom of Tourette's syndrome.

tolerance. Characteristic of drug addiction in which the individual becomes increasingly less sensitive to the drug, requiring higher doses to obtain the initial effect of the drug.

Tourette's syndrome. A neurological condition characterized by involuntary "tic" movements and vocalizations.

tract (also called **fiber pathway**). Bundle of axons within the CNS that traverses long distances and connects different parts of the brain (distal) or is relatively short (local) and connects close-in nuclei and groups of neurons.

transcription. The process by which DNA is "copied" and transferred to mRNA for subsequent protein synthesis.

transduction. Conversion of physical energy, such as light, to energy that can be used in the nervous system.

translation. The process by which messenger ribonucleic acid (mRNA) is "read" by ribosomes in the neuron and protein synthesis is initiated.

traumatic brain injury (TBI). Injury to a person's brain usually resulting from an accident.

trepanning. Medical process of drilling a hole in the skull in an attempt to correct a problem associated with the brain (for example, a buildup of pressure on the brain).

tricyclic antidepressants. Drugs such as imipramine that increase the activity of serotonin (along with other monoamines) in the synapse by blocking its reuptake into the presynaptic neuronal terminal.

tryptophan. The amino acid from which the neurotransmitter serotonin is derived. The availability of tryptophan in the extracellular fluid of neurons regulates the synthesis of serotonin.

tyrosine hydroxylase (TH). An enzyme found in all catecholaminergic neurons. TH is a catalyst in the conversion of tyrosine to dopa, which is the first step in catecholamine synthesis.

ultimate causation. Doctrine stating that the more long-term causes of a behavior are important for a thorough understanding of the behavior. In evolutionary theory, ultimate causation questions are questions related to how and why certain behaviors evolve.

vaccination. Preparation of a specific antigen that is administered to an individual to stimulate the acquired immune system to protect against actual, natural exposure to the antigen, should it occur.

vagus nerve (cranial nerve 10). Mixed cranial nerve pair; sensory portion transmits sensations of pain and nausea from the viscera, motor component exerts parasympathetic control of cardiovascular and abdominal function, as well as controlling the muscles of the throat.

valproate. Anticonvulsant drug that shows promise as an effective treatment for bipolar disorder.

ventral tegmental area (VTA). Cluster of cell bodies in the midbrain that synthesize dopamine; extends to the nucleus accumbens and is involved with reward circuits of the brain.

ventricles. Internal capsules in the medial part of the brain that contain cerebrospinal fluid.

ventromedial hypothalamus. Brain area which, when lesioned in rats, caused the rats to become hyperphagic. Initially dubbed the "satiety center," it is now believed to be involved in energy metabolism.

vertebral column. Firm, flexible bony column extending from the base of the skull to the coccyx; longitudinal axis and chief supporting structure of the human body.

vesicle. Tiny, nearly spherical packet at the axon terminal filled with the neurotransmitter.

voltage-gated channels. Passageways for ions through a neuron's cell membrane that are opened or closed in response to changes of the membrane potential.

withdrawal. Defining feature of drug addiction in which the individual experiences either physiological or psychological symptoms after ceasing the consumption of a particular drug.

References

Abbas, A. K., Lichtman, A. H., & Pober, J. S. (2000). *Cellular and molecular immunology* (4th ed.). New York: Saunders.

Abbott, A. (2001). Into the mind of a killer. *Nature, 410,* 296–298.

Abi-Dargham, A., Rodenhiser, J., Printz, D., Zea-Ponce, Y., Gil, R., Kegeles, L. S., et al. (2000). Increased baseline occupancy of D_2 receptors by dopamine in schizophrenia. *Proceedings of the National Academy of Sciences, USA, 97,* 8104–8109.

Abrams, R. (1992). *Electroconvulsive therapy.* New York: Oxford University Press.

Achenbach, J. (2001, October 1). The power of light. *National Geographic,* pp. 3–31.

Ackerman, D. L., Greenland, S., Bystritsky, A., & Datz, R. J. (1996). Relationship between early side effects and therapeutic effects of clomipramine therapy in obsessive-compulsive disorder. *Journal of Clinical Psychopharmacology, 16*(4), 324–328.

Acocella, J. (1998, April 16). The politics of hysteria. *The New Yorker,* pp. 64–79.

Acquas, E., Tanda, G., & DiChiara, G. (2002). Differential effects of caffeine on dopamine and acetylcholine transmission in brain areas of drug-naïve and caffeine-pretreated rats. *Neuropsychopharmacology, 27,* 182–193.

Adams, N., Lins, M. D., & Blizard, D. A. (1987). Contrasting effects of social stress and foot shock on acute cardiovascular response in salt-sensitive rats. *Behavioral Neural Biology, 48,* 368–381.

Ader, R. (2000). On the development of psychoneuroimmunology. *European Journal of Pharmacology, 405,* 167–176.

Ader, R., & Cohen, N. (1975). Behaviorally conditioned immunosuppression. *Pyschosomatic Medicine, 37,* 333–340.

Ader, R., & Cohen, N. (1991). The influence of conditioning on immune responses. In R. Ader, D. L. Felten, & N. Cohen (Eds.), *Psychoneuroimmunolgy* (2nd ed.). New York: Academic Press.

Adler, L. E., Freedman, R., Ross, R. G., Olincy, A, & Waldo, M. C. (1999). Elementary phenotypes in the neurobiological and genetic study of schizophrenia. *Biological Psychiatry, 46*(1), 8–18.

Adolphs, R., Baron-Cohen, S., & Tranel, D. (2002). Impaired recognition of social emotions following amygdala damage. *Journal of Cognitive Neuroscience, 14,* 1264–1274.

Adolphs, R., Tranel, D., & Damasio, A. R. (1998). The human amygdala in social judgment. *Nature, 393,* 470–474.

Adolphs, R., Tranel, D., Damasio, H., & Damasio, A. R. (1994). Impaired recognition of emotion in facial expressions following bilateral damage to the human amygdala. *Nature, 372,* 669–672.

Aghajanian, G. K., & Marek, G. J. (2000). Serotonin model of schizophrenia: Emerging role of glutamate mechanisms. *Brain Research: Brain Research Reviews, 31*(2-3), 302–312.

Agras, W. S., Walsh, B. T., Fairburn, C. G., Wilson, G. T., & Kraemer, H. C. (2000). A multicenter comparison of cognitive-behavioral therapy and interpersonal psychotherapy for bulimia nervosa. *Archives of General Psychiatry, 57,* 459–466.

Albers, H. E., & Bamshad, M. (1998). Role of vasopressin and oxytocin in the control of social behavior in Syrian hamsters (Mesocricetus auratus). *Progress in Brain Research, 119,* 395–408.

Aldrich, R. W., Dionne, V. E., Hawrot, E., & Stevens, C. F. (1985). Ion transport through ligand-gated channels. In T. E. Andreoli, J. F. Hoffman, D. D. Farestil, & S. G. Schultz (Eds.), *Physiology of membrane disorders.* New York: Plenum Press.

Allman, J. M. (1999). *Evolving brains.* New York: Freeman.

Altemus, M., Glowa, J. R., & Murphy, D. L. (1993). Attenuation of food-restriction-induced running by chronic fluoxetine treatment. *Psychopharmacology Bulletin, 29*(3), 397–400.

American Psychiatric Association. (1994). *Diagnostic and statistical manual of mental disorders* (4th ed.). Washington, DC: American Psychiatric Association.

American Psychiatric Association. (2000). *Diagnostic and statistical manual of mental disorders* (DSM-IV-TR). Washington, DC: American Psychiatric Association.

American Society of Plastic and Reconstructive Surgeons. (1990). Press release retrieved from http://www.plasticsurgery.org/news_room/PST-03-05.cfmby

Ames, E. W., & Carter, M. (1992). Development of Romanian orphanage children adopted to Canada. *Canadian Psychology, 33*, 503.

Anand, B. K., & Brobeck, J. R. (1951). Hypothalamic control of food intake in rats and cats. *Yale Journal of Biology and Medicine, 24*, 123–140.

Anderson, M. C., Ochsner, K. N., Kuhl, B., Cooper, J., Robertson, E., Gabrieli, S. W., et al. (2004). Neural systems underlying the suppression of unwanted memories. *Science, 303*, 232–235.

Anderson, S. M., Saviolakis, G. A., Bauman, R. A., Chu, K. Y., Ghosh, S., & Kant, G. J. (1996). Effects of chronic stress on food acquisition, plasma hormones, and the estrous cycle of female rats. *Physiology and Behavior, 60*, 325–329.

Anderson, T. (1993). *Den of lions.* New York: Ballantine Books.

Andreasen, N. C. (2001). *Brave new brain: Conquering mental illness in the era of the genome.* New York: Oxford University Press.

Andreasen, N. C., Arndt, S., Swayze, V., Cizaldo, T., Flaum, M., O'Leary, D., et al. (1994). Thalamic abnormalities in schizophrenia visualized through magnetic resonance imaging averaging. *Science, 266*, 294–298.

Andreasen, N. C., & Black, D. W. (1991). *Introductory textbook of psychiatry* (2nd ed.). Washington, DC: American Psychiatric Association.

Andreasen, N. C., & Black, D. W. (2001). *Introductory textbook of psychiatry* (3rd ed.). Washington, DC: American Psychiatric Association.

Andreasen, N. C., Nasrallah, H. A., Dunn, V., Olson, S. C., Grove, W. M., Ehrhardt, J. C., et al. (1986). Structural abnormalities in the frontal system in schizophrenia: A magnetic resonance imaging study. *Archives of General Psychiatry, 43*, 136–144.

Andreasen, N. C., O'Leary, D., Flaum, M., Nopoulos, P., Watkins, G. L., Boles Ponto, L. L., & Hichwa, R. D. (1997). Hypofrontality in schizophrenia: Distributed dysfunctional circuits in neuroleptic-naïve patients. *Lancet, 349*, 1730–1734.

Andrews, R. J. (2003). Neuroprotection trek—the next generation: Neuromodulation I. *Annals of the New York Academy of Sciences, 993*, 1–13.

Angelucci, F., Aloe, L., Vasquez, P. J., & Mathe, A. A. (2000). Mapping the differences in the brain concentration of brain-derived neurotrophic factor (BDNF) and nerve growth factor (NGF) in an animal model of depression. *NeuroReport, 11*, 1369–1373.

Anisman, H., Griffiths, J., Matheson, K., Ravindran, A. V., & Merali, Z. (2001). Posttraumatic stress symptoms and salivary cortisol Levels. *American Journal of Psychiatry, 58*(9), 1509–1511.

APA Online. (2002). New Mexico governor signs landmark law on prescription privileges for psychologists. Retrieved March 2004 from http://www.apa.org

Aravanis, A. M., Pyle, J. L., & Tsien, R.W. (2003). Single synaptic vesicles fusing transiently and successfully without loss of identity. *Nature, 423*, 643–647.

Arendt, T. (2001). Alzheimer's disease as a disorder of mechanisms underlying structural brain self-organization. *Neuroscience, 102*(4), 723–765.

Arnold, G. L., Hyman, S. I., Mooney, R. A., & Kirby, R. S. (2003). Plasma amino acids profiles in children with autism: Potential risk of nutritional deficiencies. *Journal of Autism and Developmental Disorders, 33*, 449–454.

Arnold, S. E., Franz, B. R., Gur, R. C., Gur, R. E., Shapiro, R. M., Moberg, P. J., & Trojanowski, J. Q. (1995). Smaller neuron size in schizophrenia in hippocampal subfields that mediate cortical-hippocampal interactions. *American Journal of Psychiatry, 152*, 738–748.

Arnow, B. (1997). Psychotherapy of anorexia and bulimia. In W. H. Kayne & D. C. Jinerson (Eds.), *Bailliere's clinical psychiatry.* London: Bailliere, Tindall & Cox.

Ascher, J. A., Cole, J. A., Colin, J. N., Feighner, J. P., Ferris, R. M., Fibiger, H. C., et al. (1995). Bupropion: A review of its mechanisms of antidepressant activity. *Journal of Clinical Psychiatry, 56*, 395–401.

Ashford, J. W., & Jarvik, K. L. (1985). Alzheimer's disease: Does neuron plasticity predispose to axonal neurofibrillary degeneration? *New England Journal of Medicine, 5,* 388–389.

Ashford, J. W., Mattson, M., & Kumar, V. (1998). Neurobiological systems disrupted by Alzheimer's disease and molecular biological theories of vulnerability. In V. Kumar & C. Eisdorfer (Eds.), *Advances in the diagnosis and treatment of Alzheimer's disease.* New York: Springer.

Ashford, J. W., & Schmitt, F. A. (2001). Modeling the time-course of Alzheimer dementia. *Current Psychiatry Reports, 3,* 20–28.

Ashford, J. W., Soultanian, N. S., Zhang, S. X., & Geddes, J. W. (1998). Neuropil threads are collinear with MAP2 immunostaining in neuronal dendrites of Alzheimer brain. *Journal of Neuropathology and Experimental Neurology, 57,* 972–978.

Assanand, S., Pinel, J. P. J., & Lehman, D. R. (1996). *Common misconceptions about the regulation of feeding.* Unpublished manuscript, University of British Columbia, Vancouver, British Columbia, Canada.

Aurentz, C. A., Felts, P. T., Lowry, C. A., Wartella, J. E., Miller, S. D., Amory, E. A., et al. (1999). *Increased c-fos and tyrosine hydroxylase activity in the extended amygdala of rats displaying compulsive-like running.* Poster presented at the International Behavioral Neuroscience Society, Nancy, France.

Austad, N., Scott, D. T., Janowsky, J. S., Jacobsen, C., Carroll, R. E., Montalto, M. B., et al. (2003). Visual, cognitive, and language assessments at 39 months: A follow-up study of children fed formulas containing long-chain polyunsaturated fatty acids to 1 year of age. *Pediatrics, 112,* 177–183.

Avants, S. K., Margolin, A., Holford, T. R., & Kosten, T. R. (2000). A randomized controlled trial of auricular acupuncture for cocaine dependence. *Archives of Internal Medicine, 160,* 2305–2312.

Avoli, M., & Gloor, P. (1987). Epilepsy. In G. Adelman (Ed.), *Encyclopedia of neuroscience.* Boston: Birkhaeuser.

Aylward, E. H., Harris, G. J., Hoehn-Saric, R., Barta, P. E., Machilin, S. R., & Pearlson, G. D. (1996). Normal caudate nucleus in obsessive-compulsive disorder assessed by quantitative neuroimaging. *Archives of General Psychiatry, 53,* 577–584.

Bachoud-Levi, A. C., Remy, P., Nguyen, J. P. Brugieres, P., Lefaucheur, J. P., Bourdet, C., et al. (2000). Motor and cognitive improvements in patients with Huntington's disease after neural transplantation. *Lancet, 356,* 1975–1979.

Bainbridge, D. (2001). *Making babies: The science of pregnancy.* Cambridge, MA: Harvard University Press.

Balasubramaniam, A. A. (1997). Neuropeptide Y family of hormones receptor subtypes and antagonists. *Peptides, 18,* 445–457.

Baldwin, B. A., Parrott, R. F., & Ebenezer, I. S. (1998). Food for thought: A critique on the hypothesis that endogenous cholecystokinin acts as a physiological satiety factor. *Progress in Neurobiology, 55*(5), 477–507.

Bales, K. L., & Carter, C. S. (2003). Developmental exposure to oxytocin facilitates partner preferences in male prairie voles (Microtus ochrogaster). *Biochemical Neuroscience, 117,* 854–859.

Bandura, A. (1997). *Self-efficacy: The exercise of control.* New York: Freeman.

Banich, M. T. (1997). *Neuropsychology.* Boston: Houghton-Mifflin.

Barker, A. T., Jalinous, R., & Freeston, I. L. (1985). Noninvasive magnetic stimulation of the human motor cortex. *Lancet, 1,* 1106–1107.

Barondes, S. H. (1993). *Molecules and mental illness.* New York: Freeman.

Barr, C. L., & Sandor, P. (1998). Current status of genetic studies of Gilles de la Tourette syndrome. *Canadian Journal of Psychiatry, 43,* 351–357.

Barthelme, F., & Barthelme, S. (1999, March 8). Good losers. *The New Yorker,* pp. 46–61.

Baskin, D. G., Schwartz, M. S., Seeley, R. J., Woods, S. C., Porte, D., Breininger, J. F., et al. (1999). Leptin receptor long-form splice-variant protein expression in neuron cell bodies of the brain and co-localization with neurpeptide Y mRNA in the arcuate nucleus. *Journal of Histochemistry and Cytochemistry, 138,* 196–202.

Bassett, A. S. (1989). Chromosome 5 and schizophrenia: Implications for genetic linkage studies. *Schizophrenia Bulletin, 15,* 393–402.

Battro, A. M. (2000). *Half a brain is enough.* Cambridge, UK: Cambridge University Press.

Baumann, B., & Bogerts, B. (2001). Neuroanatomical studies on bipolar disorder. *British Journal of Psychiatry, 178,* 142–147.

Baumann, B., Danos, P., Krell, D., Diekmann, S., Leschinger, A., Stauch, R., et al. (1999). Reduced volume of limbic system-affiliated basal ganglia in mood disorders: Preliminary data from a post mortem study.

Journal of Neuropsychiatry and Clinical Neuroscience, 11, 71–78.

Baxter, L. R., Phelps, M. E., Mazziotti, J. C., Schwartz, J. M., Gerner, R. H., Selin, C. E., et al. (1985). Cerebral metabolic rates for glucose in mood disorders. *Archives of General Psychiatry, 42,* 441–447.

Bazil, C. W. (2002). New antiepileptic drugs. *Neurologist, 8,* 71–81.

Bear, M. F., Connors, B. W., & Paradiso, M. A. (1996). *Neuroscience: Exploring the brain.* Philadelphia: Lippincott, Williams & Wilkins.

Beatty, J. (2001). *The human brain.* London: Sage Publications.

Begley, S. (1998, January 26). Is everybody crazy? *Newsweek,* p. 53.

Beliard, D., Kirschenbaum, D. S., & Fitzgibbon, M. L. (1992). Evaluation of an intensive weight control program using a priori criteria to determine outcome. *International Journal of Obesity, 16,* 623–625.

Benjamin, L. T. (1993). *A history of letters.* Dubuque, IA: Brown & Benchmark.

Bennett, E. L., Diamond, M. L., Krech, D., & Rosenzweig, M. R. (1964). Chemical and anatomical plasticity of brain. *Science, 206,* 649–654.

Benson, E. (2003). A new treatment for addiction. *Monitor on Psychology, 3*(6), 18–20.

Berk, L. S., Tan, S. A., Fry, W. F., Napier, B. J., Lee, J., Hubbard, R. W., et al. (1989). Neuroendocrine and stress hormone changes during mirthful laughter. *American Journal of Medical Science, 298,* 390–396.

Berk, L. S., Tan, S. A., Napier, B. J., & Eby, W. C. (1989). Eustress of mirthful laughter modifies natural killer cell activity. *Clinical Research, 37,* 115A.

Berman, R. M., Belanoff, J. K., Charney, D. S., & Schatzberg, A. F. (1999). Principles of the pharmacotherapy of depression. In D. S. Charney, E. J. Nestler, & B. S. Bunney (Eds.), *Neurobiology of mental illness.* New York: Oxford University Press.

Berns, G. S., Pagoni, G., Zink, C. F., Martin-Skurski, M. E., & Capuron, L. (2004). Reward system activity in adolescents: An fMRI study. Program No. 785.17. *2004 Abstract Viewer/Itinerary Planner.* Washington, DC: Society for Neuroscience.

Betz, C., Mihalic, D., Pinto, M. E., & Raffa, R. B. (2000). Could a common biochemical mechanism underlie addictions? *Journal of Clinical Pharmacology and Therapeutics, 25,* 11–20.

Bingley, T., Lekskell, L., Meyerson, B. A., & Rylander, G. (1977). Long-term results of stereotactic anterior capsulotomy in chronic obsessive-compulsive neurosis. In W. H. Sweet, S. Obrador, & J. G. Martin-Rodrigues (Eds.), *Neurosurgical treatment in psychiatry, pain, and epilepsy.* Baltimore: University Park Press.

Bisaga, A., & Popik, P. (2000). In search of a new pharmacological treatment for drug and alcohol addition, N-methyl-D-aspartate (NMDA) antagonists. *Drug and Alcohol Dependence, 59,* 1–15.

Bizon, J. L., & Gallagher, M. (2003). Production of new cells in the rat dentate gyrus over the lifespan: Relation to cognitive decline. *European Journal of Neurology, 18*(1), 215–219.

Bjorvell, H., & Rossner, S. (1992). A ten-year follow-up of weight change in severely obese subjects treated in a combined behavioural modification programme. *International Journal of Obesity, 16,* 623–625.

Blachar, A., Federle, M. P., Pealer, K. M., Ikramuddin, S., & Schauer, P. R. (2002). Gastrointestinal complications of laparoscopic Roux-en-Y gastric bypass surgery: Clinical and imaging findings. *Radiology, 223,* 625–632.

Black, J. E., Greenough, W. T., & Anderson, B. J. (1987). Environment and the aging brain. *Canadian Journal of Psychology, 41,* 111(130.

Black, M. D., Selk, D. E., Hitchcock, J. M., Wettstein, J. G., & Sorensen, S. M. (1999). On the effect of neonatal nitric oxide synthase inhibition in rats: A potential neurodevelopmental model of schizophrenia. *Neuropharmacology, 38,* 1299–1306.

Blakemore, S. J., Wolpert, D. M., & Frith, C. D. (1998). Central cancellation of self-produced tickle sensation. *Nature Neuroscience, 1,* 635–640.

Blalock, J. E. (1984). The immune system as a sensory organ. *Journal of Immunology, 132,* 1067–1070.

Blanchard, R. J., McKittrick, C. R., & Blanchard, D. C. (2001). Animal models of social stress: Effects on behavior and brain neurochemical systems. *Physiology and Behavior, 73,* 261–271.

Blier, P., & Abbott, F. V. (2001). Putative mechanisms of action of antidepressant drugs in affective and anxiety disorders and pain. *Journal of Psychiatry and Neuroscience, 26,* 37–43.

Blier, P., & Montigny, C. (1994). Current advances and trends in the treatment of depression. *Trends in Pharmacology, 15*, 220–226.

Bligh-Glover, W., Kolli, T. N., Shapiro-Kulnane, L., Dilley, G. E., Friedman, L., Balraj, E., et al. (2000). The serotonin transporter in the midbrain of suicide victims with major depression. *Biological Psychiatry*, 1015–1024.

Bloom, F. E., & Lazerson, A. (1988). *Brain, mind, and behavior* (2nd ed.). New York: Freeman.

Bloom, F. E., Nelson, C. A., & Lazerson, A. (2001). *Brain, mind, and behavior* (3rd ed.). New York: Worth.

Blum, W. F. (1997). Leptin: The voice of the adipose tissue. *Hormone Research, 48*, 2–8.

Bohman, M., Cloninger, C. R., Sigvardsson, S., & von Knorring, A. L. (1987). The genetics of alcoholism and related disorders. *Journal of Psychiatric Research*, 21, 447–452.

Boldizsar, C., Michaelis, T., Watanabe, T., Frahm, J., de Biurrun, G., van Kampen, M., Bartolomucci, A., & Fuchs, E. (2001). Stress-induced changes in cerebral metabolites, hippocampal volume, and cell proliferation are prevented by antidepressant treatment with tianeptine. *Proceedings of the National Academy of Sciences, USA, 98*, 12796–12801.

Bonese, K. F., Wainer, B. H., Fitch, F. W., Rothberg, R. M., & Schuster, C. R. (1974). Changes in heroin self-administration by a rhesus monkey after morphine immunization. *Nature, 252*, 708–710.

Bousfield, W. A., & Elliott, M. H. (1934). The effect of fasting on the eating behavior of rats. *Journal of Genetic Psychology, 45*, 227–237.

Bowlby, J. (1960). Grief and mourning in infancy and early childhood. *Psychoanalytic Study of the Child, 15*, 9–52.

Bracha, H. S., Torrey, E. F., Bigelow, L. B., Lohr, J. B., & Linington, B.B. (1991). Subtle signs of prenatal maldevelopment of the hand extoderm in schizophrenia: A preliminary monozygotic twin study. *Biological Psychiatry, 30*, 719–725.

Bracha, H. S., Torrey, E. F., Gottesman, I. I., Bigelow, L. B., & Cunniff, C. (1992). Second-trimester markers of fetal size in schizophrenia: A study of monozygotic twins. *American Journal of Psychiatry, 149*, 1355–1361.

Brady, J. V. (1958). Ulcers in "executive" monkeys. *Scientific American, 199*, 95–100.

Brady, S. T. (2000). Neurofilaments run sprints, not marathons. *Nature Cell Biology, 2*, 43–45.

Bragg, R. (1998, January 22). End video poker gambling, South Carolina chief urges. *The New York Times*, p. A14.

Brain Injury Association. (2002). *The costs and causes of traumatic brain injury*. Retrieved July 15, 2003, from: http://www.biausa.org

Brambilla, F. (2001). Aetiopathogenesis and pathophysiology of bulimia nervosa. *CNS Drugs, 15*, 119–136.

Brambilla, F., Bellodi, L., Arancio, C., Ronchi, P., & Limonta, D. (2001). Central dopaminergic function in anorexia and bulimia nervosa: A psychoneuroendocrine approach. *Psychoneuroendocrinology, 26*, 393–409.

Brandes, J. S. (1977). Insulin induced overeating in the rat. *Physiology and Behavior, 18*, 1095–1102.

Bray, G. A. (2001). Drug treatment of obesity. *Review of Endocrine Metabolic Disorders, 2*, 403–418.

Breiter, H. C., Aharon, I., Kahneman, D., Dale, A., & Shizgal, P. (2001). Functional imaging of neural responses to expectanch and experience of monetary gains and .losses. *Neuron, 30*, 619–639.

Bremner, J. D., Narayan, M., Anderson, E. R., Staib, L. H., Miller, H. L., & Charney, D. S. (2000). Hippocampal volume reduction in major depression. *American Journal of Psychiatry, 157*, 115–118.

Brown, E. E., Robertson, G. S., & Fibiger, H. C. (1992). Evidence for conditional neuronal activation following exposure to a cocaine-paired environment: Role of forebrain limbic structures. *Neuroscience, 12*, 4112–4121.

Brownell, A. L., Canales, K., Chen, Y. I., Jenkins, B. G., Owen, C., Livni, E., Yu, M., et al. (2003). Mapping of brain function after MPTP-induced neurotoxicity in a primate Parkinson's disease model. *NeuroImage, 20*(2), 1064–1075.

Brownell, K. D. (2002a). The environment and obesity. In C. G. Fairburn & K. D. Brownell (Eds.), *Eating disorders and obesity: A comprehensive handbook* (2nd ed.). New York: Guilford Press.

Brownell, K. D. (2002b). Public policy and the prevention of obesity. In C. G. Fairburn & K. D. Brownell (Eds.), *Eating disorders and obesity: A comprehensive handbook* (2nd ed.). New York: Guilford Press.

Brownell, K. D., & Horgen, K. B. (2004). *Food fight*. New York: Contemporary Books.

Brownell, K. D., & Rodin, J. (1994). The dieting maelstrom: Is it possible and advisable to lose weight? *American Psychologist, 49*, 781–791.

Bunney, W. E., & Bunney, B. S. (1999). Neuro-developmental hypothesis of schizophrenia. In D. S. Charney, E. J. Nestler, & B. S. Bunney (Eds.), *Neurobiology of mental illness* (pp. 225–235). New York: Oxford University Press.

Byne, W., Kemether, E., Jones, L., Haroutunian, V., & Davis, K. (1999). The neurochemistry of schizophrenia. In D. S. Charney, E. J. Nestler, & B. S. Bunney (Eds.), *Neurobiology of mental illness* (pp. 236–257). New York: Oxford University Press.

Byrnes, E. M., & Bridges, R. S. (2000). Endogeneous opioid facilitation of maternal memory in rats. *Behavioral Neuroscience, 114,* 797–804.

Byrnes, E. M., Rigero, B. A., & Bridges, R. S. (2000). Opioid receptor antagonism during early lactation results in the increased duration of nursing bouts. *Physiology and Behavior, 70,* 211–216.

Cade, J. F. J. (1949). Lithium salts in the treatment of psychotic excitement. *Medical Journal of Australia, 36,* 349–352.

Cai, X. J., Liu, X. H., Evans, M., Clapham, J. C., Wilson, S., Arch, J. R., Morris, R., & Williams, G. (2002). Orexins and feeding: Special occasions or everyday occurrence? *Regulatory Peptides, 104*(1-3), 1–9.

Caldji, C., Liu, D., Sharma, S., Diorio, J., Francis, D., Meaney, M. L., & Plotsky, P. M. (2001). Development of individual differences in behavioral and endocrine responses to stress: Role of the postnatal environment. In B. S. McEwen & H. M. Goodman (Eds.), *Coping with the environment: Neural and endocrine mechanisms* (pp. 271–292). New York: Oxford University Press.

Campbell, T., Lin, S., DeVries, C., & Lambert, K. (2003). Coping strategies in male and female rats exposed to multiple stressors. *Physiology and Behavior, 78,* 495–504.

Campfield, L. A., & Smith, F. J. (1986). Functional coupling between transient declines in blood glucose and feeding behavior: Temporal relationships. *Brain Research Bulletin, 17,* 427–433.

Campfield, L. A., & Smith, F. J. (1990). Transient declines in blood glucose signal meal initiation. *International Journal of Obesity, 14,* 15–33.

Campos-Outcalt, D., Prybylski, D., Watkins, A., Rothfus, G., & Dellapenna, A. (1997). Motor-vehicle crash fatalities among American Indians and non-Indians in Arizona, 1979 through 1988. *American Journal of Public Health, 87*(2), 282–285.

Cannon, W. B. (1935). Stresses and strains of homeostasis. *American Journal of Medical Sciences, 189,* 1–14.

Cannon, W. B., & Washburn, A. (1912). An explanation of hunger. *American Journal of Physiology, 29,* 441–454.

Caplan, P. J. (1996). *They say you're crazy: How the world's most powerful psychiatrists decide who's normal.* Reading, MA: Addison-Wesley.

Cardno, A. G., & Gottesman, I. I. (2000). Twin studies of schizophrenia: From bow-and-arrow concordances to star wars Mx and functional genomics. *American Journal of Medical Genetics, 97*(1), 12–17.

Carelli, R. M., & Deadwyler, S. A. (1994). A comparison of nucleus accumbens neuronal firing patterns during cocaine self-administration and water reinforcement in rats. *Journal of Neuroscience, 14,* 7735–7746.

Carelli, R. M., King, V. C., Hampson, R. E., & Deadwyler, S. A. (1993). Firing patterns of nucleus accumbens neurons during cocaine self-administration in rats. *Brain Research, 626,* 14–22.

Carlson, E. B., & Rosser-Hogan, R. (1991). Trauma experiences, posttraumatic stress, dissociation, and depression in Cambodian refugees. *American Journal of Psychiatry, 148,* 1548–1551.

Carlson, M., & Earls, F. (1997). Psychological and neuroendocrinological sequelae of early social deprivation in institutionalized children in Romania. In C. S. Carter, L. L. Lederhendler, & B. Kirkpatrick (Eds.), *The integrative neurobiology of affiliation.* New York: Annals of the New York Academy of Science.

Carlson, N. R. (1994). *Physiology of behavior* (5th ed.). New York: Allyn & Bacon.

Carlson, N. R. (1999). *Physiology of behavior* (6th ed.) New York: Allyn & Bacon.

Caron, M. G. (1997). Knockout of the vesicular monoamine transporter 2 gene results in neonatal death and supersensitivity to cocaine and amphetamine. *Neuron, 19,* 1285–1296.

Carpenter, M. B., & Sutin, J. (Eds.). (1983). *Human neuroanatomy* (8th ed.). Baltimore: Lippincott, William & Wilkins.

Carpenter, S. (2000). Preferring the predictable. *Monitor on Psychology, 31,* 42–43.

Carrera, M. R., Ashley, J. A., Zhou, B., Wirsching, P., Koob, G. F., & Janda, K. D. (2000). Cocaine vaccines: Antibody protection against relapse in a rat model. *Proceedings of the National Academy of Sciences, USA, 97,* 6202–6206.

Carroll, J. (1982). Clinical applications of the dexamethasome suppression test for endogenous depression. *Pharmacopsychiatry, 15,* 19–24.

Carter, C. S. (1998).The neuroendocrinology os social attachment and love. *Psychoneuroimmunology, 23,* 779–818.

Carter, C. S., Altemus, M., & Chrousos, G. P. (2001). Neuroendocrine and emotional changes in the post-partum period. *Progress in Brain Research, 133,* 241–249.

Carter, C. S., & Getz, L. L. (1993). Monogamy and the prairie vole. *Scientific American, 268,* 100–106.

Casanova, M. F., & Lindzen, E. C. (2003). Changes in gray-/white-matter ratios in the parahippocampal gyri of late-onset schizophrenia patients. *American Journal of Geriatric Psychiatry, 11,* 605–609.

Casper, R. C. (1990). Personality features of women with good outcome from restricting anorexia nervosa. *Psychosomatic Medicine, 52,* 156–170.

Castellanos, F. X., Lee, P. P., Sharp, W., Jeffries, N. O., Greenstein, D. K., Clasen, L. S., et al. (2002). Developmental trajectories of brain volume abnormalities in children and adolescents with attention-deficit/hyperactivity disorder. *Journal of the American Medical Association, 288*(14), 1740–1748.

Cavigelli, S. A., & McClintock, M. K. (2003). Fear of novelty in infant rats predicts adult corticosterone dynamics and an early death. *Proceedings of the National Academy of Sciences,USA, 100,* 16131–16136.

Champagne, F., & Meaney, M. J. (2001). Like mother, like daughter: Evidence for non-genomic transmission of parental behavior and stress responsivity. *Progress in Brain Research, 133,* 287–302.

Champoux, M., Hibbeln, J. R., Shannon, C., Majchrzak, S., Suomi, S. J., Salem, N., & Higley, J. D. (2002). Fatty acid formula supplementation and neuromotor development in rhesus monkey neonates. *Pediatric Research, 51,* 273–281.

Chang, I., Lapham, S. C., & Barton, K. J. (1996). Drinking environment and sociodemographic factors among DWI offenders. *Journal of Studies on Alcohol, 57,* 659–669.

Chanpattana, W., & Kramer, B. A. (2003). Acute and maintenance ECT with flupenthixol in refractory schizophrenia: Sustained improvements in psychopathology, quality of life, and social outcomes. *Schizophrenia Research, 63,* 189–193.

Cheetham, S. C., Katona, C. L. E., & Horton, R. W. (1991). Post-mortem studies of neurotransmitter biochemistry in depression and suicide. In R. W. Horton & C. L. E. Katona (Eds.), *Biological aspects of affective disorders* (pp. 192–221). London: Academic Press.

Chen, J. F., Xu, K., Petzer, J. P., Stal, R., Xu, Y. H., Beilstein, M., Sonsalla, P. K., Castagnoli, K., Castagnoli, N., & Schwarzschild, M. A. (2001). Neuroprotection by caffeine and a_{2a} adenosine receptor inactivation in a model of Parkinson's disease. *Journal of Neuroscience, 21,* RC143.

Chenn, A., & Walsh, C. A. (2002). Regulation of cerebral cortical size by control of cell cycle exit in neural precursors. *Science, 297,* 365–369.

Childress, A. R., Mozley, D., McElgin, B. A., Fitzgerald, J., Reivich, M., & O'Brien, C. P. O. (1999). Limbic activation during cue-induced cocaine craving. *American Journal of Psychiatry, 156,* 11–18.

Chiocca, E. A., & Martuza, R. L. (1990). Neurosurgical therapy of obsessive-compulsive disorder. In M. L. Jenike, L. Baer, L. Minichiello, (Eds.), *Obsessive-compulsive disorders: Theory and management* (2nd ed., pp. 283–294). Chicago: YearBook Medical Publishers.

Chisholm, K., Carter, M. C., Ames, E. W., & Morison, S. J. (1995). Attachment security and indiscriminately friendly behavior in children adopted from Romanian orphanages. *Developmental Psychopathology, 7,* 283–294.

Cholerton, B., Gleason, C. E., Baker, L. D., & Asthana, S. (2002). Estrogen and Alzheimer's disease: The story so far. *Drugs & Aging, 19,* 405–427.

Chowdhury, U., & Lask, B. (2001). Clinical implications of brain imaging in eating disorders. *Psychiatric Clinics of North America, 24*(2), 227–234.

Christian, C. M., Dufour, M., & Bertolucci, D. (1989). Differential alcohol-related mortality among American Indian tribes in Oklahoma, 1968–1978. *Social Science and Medicine, 28,* 275–284.

Chugani, H. T., Behen, M. E., Muzik, O., Juhasz, C., Nagy, F., & Chugani, D. C. (2001). Local brain functional activity following early deprivation: A study of postinstitutionalized Romanian orphans. *NeuroImage, 14,* 1290–1301.

Ciccocioppo, R. (1999). The role of serotonin in craving: From basic research to human studies. *Alcohol and Alcoholism, 34,* 244–253.

Clark, A., Kirdby, K. C., Daniels, B. A., & Marks, I. M. (1998). A pilot study of computer-aided vicarious exposure for obsessive-compulsive disorder. *Australian and New Zealand Journal of Psychiatry, 32,* 268–275.

Clark, W. (1995). *At war within: The double-edged sword of immunity.* New York: Oxford University Press.

Cloninger, C. R. (1987). Neurogenetic adaptive mechanisms in alcoholism. *Science 236,* 410–416.

Clover, R. P., Abell, T., Becker, L. A., Crawford, S., & Ramsey, C. N. (1989). Family functioning and stress as predictors of influenza B infection. *Journal of Family Practice, 28,* 535–539.

Cohen, S., Doyle, W. J., Skoner, D. P., Rabin, B. S., & Gwaltney, J. M., Jr. (1997). Social ties and susceptibility to the common cold. *Journal of the American Medical Association, 277,* 1940–1944.

Cohn, J. P. (1995). *FDA consumer special report: The beginnings: Laboratory and animal studies.* Accessed June 1, 2004, from http://www.fda.gov/fdac/special/newdrug/begin.html

Colapinto, J. (2001). *As nature made him: The boy who was raised as a girl.* New York: Harper Perennial.

Cole, S. W., Kemeny, M. E., Fahey, J. L., Zack, J. A., & Naliboff, B. D. (2003). Psychological risk factors for HIV pathogenesis: Mediation by the autonomic nervous system. *Biological Psychiatry, 54,* 1444–1456.

Collings, S., & King, M. (1994). Ten-year follow-up of 50 patients with bulimia nervosa. *British Journal of Psychiatry, 164,* 80–87.

Comerci, G. G., & Schwebel, R. (2000). Substance abuse: An overview. *Adolescent Medicine, 11,* 79–101.

Commonwealth Surgeons, Ltd. (2002). Surgical weight loss: Risks. Retrieved Oct. 1, 2002 from http://www.commonwealthsurgeons.com/surgicalweightlossbenefitsandrisks.htm

Conel, J. L. (1939–1967). *The postnatal development of the human cerebral cortex* (Vols. 1–8). Cambridge, MA: Harvard University Press.

Contreras, J., & Noonan, D. (2002, June 10). The diet of last resort. *Newsweek,* pp. 46–47.

Cook, I. A., & Leuchter, A. F. (2001). Prefrontal changes and treatment response prediction in depression. *Seminars in Clinical Neuropsychiatry, 6,* 113–120.

Coons, P. M. (1992). The use of carbamazepine for episodic violence in multiple personality disorder and dissociative disorder not otherwise specified: Two additional case studies. *Biological Psychiatry, 32,* 717–720.

Cooper, J. R., Roth, R., & Bloom, F. E. (1996). *Biochemical basis of neuropharmacology* (6th ed.). New York: Oxford University Press.

Copolov, D. L., Seal, M. L., Maruff, P., Ulusoy, R., Wong, M. T., Tochon-Danguy, H. J., & Egan, G. F. (2003). Cortical activation associated with the experience of auditory hallucinations and perception of human speech in schizophrenia: A PET correlation study. *Psychiatry Research, 122*(3), 139–152.

Corodimas, K. P., Pruitt, J. C., & Steig, J. M. (2000). Acute exposure to caffeine selectively disrupts context conditioning in rats. *Psychopharmacology, 152,* 376–382.

Corrigall, W. A., & Coen, K. M. (1991). Cocaine self-administration is increased by both D1 and D2 dopamine antagonists. *Pharmacology, Biochemistry and Behavior, 39,* 799–802.

Cousino-Klein, L., & Corwin, E. J. (2002). Seeing the unexpected: How sex differences in stress responses may provide a new perspective on the manifestation of psychiatric disorders. *Current Psychiatry Report, 4,* 441–448.

Cousins, N. (1976). Anatomy of an illness (as perceived by the patient). *New England Journal of Medicine, 295,* 1458–1463.

Cousins, N. (1979). *Anatomy of an illness.* New York: Norton.

Cowan, W. M. (1979). The development of the brain. *Scientific American, 241,* 106–117.

Cowan, W. M., Sudhof, T. C., & Stevens, C. F. (Eds.). (2000). *Synapses.* Baltimore: Johns Hopkins University Press.

Cozolino, L. J., Goldstein, M. J., Nuechterlein, K. H., West, K. L., & Snyder, K. S. (1988). The impact of education about schizophrenia on relatives of varying levels of expressed emotion. *Schizophrenia Bulletin, 14*(4), 675–687.

Crawley, J. N., Belknap, J. K., Collins, A., Crabbe, J. C., Frankel, W., Henderson, N., et al. (1997). Behavioral phenotypes of inbred mouse strains: Implications and recommendations for molecular studies. *Psychopharmacology, 132,* 107–124.

Crick, F. (1994). *The astonishing hypothesis: The scientific search for the soul.* New York: Scribner's.

Crist, D. M., Mackinnon, L. T., Thompson, R. F., Atterbom, H. A., & Egan, P. A. (1989). Physical exercise increases natural cellular-mediated tumor cytotoxicity in elderly women. *Gerontology, 35,* 66–71.

Czeh, B., Michaelis, T., Watanabe, T., Frahm, J., de Biurrun, G., van Kampen, M., et al. (2001). Stress-induced changes in cerebral metabolites, hippocampal volume, and cell proliferation are prevented by antidepressant treatment with tianeptine. *Proceedings of the National Academy of Sciences, USA, 98,* 12796–12801.

Dahlstrom, W., & Williams, R. (1983). Hostility, CHD incidence, and total mortality: A 25-year follow-up study of 255 physicians. *Psychosomatic Medicine, 45,* 59.

Dallman, M., Pecoraro, N., Akana, S., la Fleur, S., Gomez, F., Houshyar, H., et al. (2003). Chronic stress and obesity: A new view of "comfort food." *Proceedings of the National Academy of Sciences, USA, 100,* 11696–11701.

Dallman, M., Viau, V., Bhatnagar, S., Gomez, F., Laugero, K. D., & Bell, M. E. (2002). Corticotropin-releasing factor (CRF), corticosteroids, stress and sugar: Energy balance, the brain, and behavior. *Hormones and Behavior, 1,* 571–632.

Damasio, A. R. (1994). *Descartes' error: Emotion, reason, and the human brain.* New York: Avon Books.

Damasio, H., Grabowski, T., Frank, R., Galaburda, A. M., & Damasio, A. R. (1994). The return of Phineas Gage: Clues about the brain from the skull of a famous patient. *Science, 264,* 1102–1105.

Daniel, J. M., & Dohanich, G. P. (2001). Acetylcholine mediates the estrogen-induced increase in NMDA receptor binding in CA1 of the hippocampus and the associated improvement in working memory. *Journal of Neuroscience, 21,* 6949–6956.

Danner, D. D., Snowden, D. A., & Friesen, W. V. (2001). Positive emotions in early life and longevity: Findings from the Nun Study. *Journal of Personality and Social Psychology, 80,* 804–813.

Dantzer, R. (1999). Sickness behavior: A neuroimmune-based response to infectious disease. In M. Schedlowski & U. Tewes (Eds.), *Psychoneuroimmunology: An interdisciplinary introduction.* New York: Kluwer Academic/Plenum.

Dantzer, R., Bluthe, R., Koob, G., & Le Moal, M. (1987). Modulation of social memory in male rats by neurohypophyseal peptides. *Psychopharmacology, 91,* 363–368.

Dantzer, R., Koob, G., Bluthe, R., & Le Moal, M. (1988). Septal vasopressin modulates social memory in male rats. *Brain Research, 457,* 143–147.

Darwin, C. (1887). *The life and letters of Charles Darwin.* New York: Appleton.

Daumann, J., Schnitker, R., Weidemann, J., Schnell, K., Thron, A., & Gouzoulis-Mayfrank, E. (2003). Neural correlates of working memory in pure and polyvalent ecstasy (MDMA) users. *NeuroReport, 14,* 1983–1987.

Davidson, J., Pearlstein, T., Londborg, P., Brady, K. T., Rothbaum, B., Bell, J., et al. (2001). Efficacy of sertraline in preventing relapse of posttraumatic stress disorder: Results of a 28-week double-blind, placebo-controlled study. *American Journal of Psychiatry, 158,* 1974–1981.

Davidson, R. J., Irwin, W., Anderle, M. J., & Kalin, N. H. (2003). The neural substrates of affective processing in depressed patients treated with venlafaxine. *American Journal of Psychiatry, 160,* 64–75.

Davis, K. L., Kahn, R. S., Ko, G., & Davidson, M. (1991). Dopamine in schizophrenia: A review and reconceptualization. *American Journal of Psychiatry, 148,* 1474–1486.

Davis, K. L., Stewart, D. G., Friedman, J. I., Buchsbaum, M., Harvey, P. D., Hof, P. R., et al. (2003). White matter changes in schizophrenia: Evidence for myelin-related dysfunction. *Archives of General Psychiatry, 60,* 443–456.

Davis, M. (2004, June 16). *Facilitation of fear extinction in rats and exposure-based psychotherapy in humans with the functional NMDA agonist D-Cycloserine.* Talk presented to the International Behavioral Neuroscience Society in Key West, FL.

Davis, R. C., Garafalo, L., & Kveim, K. (1959). Conditions associated with gastrointestinal activity. *Journal of Comparative and Physiological Psychology, 52,* 466–475.

Dawes, R. (1994). *House of cards: Psychology and psychotherapy built on myth.* New York: Free Press.

Dawson, E., & Robin, M. (1996). Schizophrenia: A gene at 6p. *Current Biology, 6,* 268–271.

de Castro, J. M., & de Castro, E. S. (1989). Spontaneous meal patterns of humans: Influence of the presence of other people. *American Journal of Clinical Nutrition, 50,* 237–247.

de Groot, J. C., de Leeuw, F. E., Oudkerk, M., Hofman, A., Jolles, J., & Breteler, M.M.B. (2000). Cerebral white matter lesions and depressive symptoms in elderly adults. *Archives of General Psychiatry, 57,* 1071–1076.

DeAngelis, T. (2002). Promising treatments for anorexia and bulimia. *APA Monitor, 33,* 38–41.

Deckersbach, T., Gershuny, B. S., & Otto, M. W. (2000). Cognitive-behavioral therapy for depression. *Depression, 23,* 795–809.

DeGette, C. (1998, November 22). To ensure revenue: Coke is it: Schools urged to boost sales. *Denver Post,* p. B1.

Delgado, P. L. (2000). Depression: The case for a monoamine deficiency. *Journal of Clinical Psychiatry, 61,* 7–11.

Delgado, P. L., & Moreno, F. A. (2000). Role of norepinephrine in depression. *Journal of Clinical Psychiatry, 61,* 5–12.

Demitrack, M. A., Lesem, M. D., Listwak, S. J., Brandt, H. A., Jimerson, D. C., & Gold, P. W. (1990). CSF oxytoxin in anorexia nervosa and bulimia nervosia.: Clinical and pathophysiologic considerations. *American Journal of Psychiatry, 147*(7), 882–886.

Dencker, S. J. (2000). The need for new and better antidepressants: Reboxetine a new option. *Acta Psychiatrica Scandinavica, 101,* 6–11.

Deutch, A. Y., & Roth, R. H. (1999). Neurotransmitters. In M. G. Zigmond, F. E. Bloom, S. C. Landis, J. L. Roberts, & L. R. Squire (Eds.), *Fundamental neuroscience* (pp. 193–234). New York: Academic Press

DeVries, A. C. (2002). Interaction among social environment, the hypothalamic-pituitary-adrenal axis, and behavior. *Hormones and Behavior, 41*(4), 405–413.

DeVries, A. C., Joh, H. D., Bernard, O., Hattori, K., Hurn, P. D., Traystman, R. J., & Alkayed, N. J. (2001). Social stress exacerbates stroke outcome by suppressing Bel-2 expression. *Proceedings of the National Academy of Sciences, USA, 98*(20), 11824–11828.

Dhabhar, F. S. (1998). Stress-induced enhancement of cell-mediated immunity. *Annals of the New York Academy of Sciences, 840,* 359–372.

Dhabhar, F. S., Satoskar, A. R., Bluethmann, H., David, J. R., & McEwen, B. S. (2000). Stress-induced enhancement for skin immune function: A role for gamma interferon. *Proceedings of the National Academy of Sciences, USA, 97,* 2846–2851.

Di Carlo, G., Borrelli, F., Ernst, E., & Izzo, A. A. (2001). St. John's wort: Prozac from the plant kingdom. *Trends in Pharmacological Sciences, 22,* 292–297.

Diana, M. (1996). Dopaminergic neurotransmission and drug withdrawal: Relevance to drug craving. In C. Ohye, M. Kimura, & J. McKenzie (Eds.), *The basal ganglia V.* New York: Plenum Press.

Diana, M., Muntoni, A. L., Pistis, M., Melis, M., & Gessa, G. L. (1999). Lasting reduction in mesolimbic dopamine neuronal activity after morphine withdrawal. *European Journal of Neuroscience, 11,* 1037–1041.

Dolberg, O. T., Iancu, I., Sasson, Y., & Zohar, J. (1996). The pathogenesis and treatment of obsessive-compulsive disorder. *Clinical Neuropharmacology, 19*(2), 129–147.

Dole, V. P., & Nyswander, M. (1965). A medical treatment for acetylmorphine (heroin) addiction: A clinical trial with methadone hydrochloride. *Journal of the American Medical Association, 193,* 80–84.

Doty, R. L., Ford, M., Preti, G., & Huggins, G.R. (1975). Changes in the intensity and pleasantness of human vaginal odors during the menstrual cycle. *Science, 190,* 1316–1318.

Draganski, B., Gaser, C., Busch, V., Schuierer, G., Bogdahn, U., & May, A. (2004). Neuroplasticity: Changes in grey matter induced by training. *Nature, 427,* 311–312.

Drevets, W. C. (1999). Prefrontal cortical-amygdalar metabolism in major depression. *Annals of the New York Academy of Science, 877,* 614–637.

Drevets, W. C. (2000). Neuroimaging studies of mood disorders. *Biological Psychiatry, 48,* 813–829.

Duman, R. S. (1999). The neurochemistry of mood disorders: Preclinical studies. In D. S. Charney, E. J. Nestler, & B. S. Bunney (Eds.), *Neurobiology of mental illness* (pp. 333–347). New York: Oxford University Press.

Duman, R. S., & Nestler, E. J. (1995). Signal transduction pathways for catecholamine receptors. In F. E. Bloom & D. J. Kupfer (Eds.), *Psychopharmacology: The fourth generation of progress* (pp. 303–320). New York: Raven Press.

Dunn, J. R. (2001). Humor in the brain: New discoveries. *Psychology Online Journal* Retrieved in January 2004 from http://www.psychjournal.com.

Durston, S., Hulshoff Pol, H. E., Casey, B. J., Giedd, J. N., Buitelaar, J. K., & van Engeland, H. (2001). Anatomical MRI of the developing human brain: What have we learned? *American Journal of Child and Adolescent Psychiatry, 40,* 1012–1020.

Eastwood, S. L., & Harrison, P. J. (1995). Decreased synaptophysin in the medial temporal lobe in schizophrenia demonstrated using immunoautoradiography. *Neuroscience, 69,* 339–343.

Edelman, G. M. (1987). *Neural Darwinism: The theory of neuronal group selection.* New York: Basic Books.

Edelman, G. M. (1993). *Bright air, brilliant fire: On the matter of the mind.* New York: Basic Books.

Eggert, F., & Ferstl, R. (1999). Functional relationship between the olfactory and immune systems. In M. Schedlowski & U. Tewes (Eds.), *Psychoneuroimmunology: An interdisciplinary introduction.* New York: Kluwer Academic/Plenum.

El-Khodor, B., & Boksa, P. (2001). Caesarean section birth produces long-term changes in dopamine D_1 receptors and in stress-induced regulation of D_3 and D_4 receptors in the rat brain. *Neuropsychopharmacology, 25,* 423–439.

Elster, J. (1999). *Addiction: Entries and exits* (Introduction). New York: Russell Sage Foundation.

Ember, L. R. (1998, May 25). Surviving stress. *Chemical and Engineering News.*

Engert, F., & Bonhoeffer, T. (1999). Dendritic spine changes associated with hippocampal long-term synaptic plasticity. *Nature, 399,* 66–70.

Epel, E. S., Lapidus, R., McEwen, B., & Brownell, K. (2001). Stress may add bite to appetite in women: A laboratory study of stress-induced cortisol and eating behavior. *Psychoneuroendocrinology, 26,* 37.

Epperson, C. N., McDougle, C. J., Brown, R. M., & Price, L. H. (1995, May 22). *Obsessive-compulsive disorder during pregnancy and the puerperium* [Abstract No. NR 112, p. 84]. New Research poster session presented at the annual meeting of the American Psychiatric Association.

Epperson, C. N., McDougle, C. J., & Price, L. H. (1996). Intranasal oxytocin in obsessive-compulsive disorder. *Biological Psychiatry, 40,* 547–549.

Erb, S., Salmaso, N., Rodaros, D., & Stewart, J. (2001) A role for the CRF-containing pathway from central nucleus of the amygdala to bed nucleus of the stria terminalis in the stress-induced reinstatement of cocaine seeking in rats. *Psychopharmacology, 158,* 360–365.

Eriksson, P. S., Perfilieva, E., Bjork-Eriksson, T., Alborn, A. M., Nordborg, C., Peterson, D. A., & Gage, F. H. (1998). Neurogenesis in the adult human hippocampus. *Nature Medicine, 4*(11), 1313–1317.

Everitt, B. J., Parkinson, J. A., Olmstead, M. C., Arroyo, M., Robledo, P., & Robbins, T. W. (2000). Associative processes in addition and reward: The role of amygdala-ventral striatal subsystems. *Annals of the New York Academy of Sciences, 877,* 412–438.

Fabrega, H. (2002). Medical validity in Eastern and Western traditions. *Perspectives of Biological Medicine, 45,* 395–415.

Fairburn, C. G., & Brownell, K. D. (Eds.). (2002). Eating disorders and obesity: A comprehensive handbook (2nd ed.). New York: Guilford Press.

Farah, M. J., Savage, J. H., Shera, D., Brodsky, N. L., Giannetta, J. M., Malmud, E., & Hurt, H. (2004). Stress and hippocampal memory development in the inner city.

Program No. 596.14. *2004 Abstract Viewer/Itinerary Planner.* Washington, DC: Society for Neuroscience.

Farwell, L. (2000, December 10). *Interview with Mike Wallace on Highlights of CBS 60 Minutes featuring brain fingerprinting.* Retrieved January 8, 2004, from: http://www.brainwavescience.com/Highlights60Minutes.htm

Fava, M., & Kendler, K. S. (2000). Major depressive disorder. *Neuron, 28,* 335–341.

Fava, M., McGrath, P. J., & Sheu, W. P. (2003). Switching to reboxetine: An efficacy and safety study in patients with major depressive disorder unresponsive to fluoxetine. *Journal of Clinical Psychopharmacology, 23,* 365–369.

Feldman, J. L., Mitchell, G. S., & Nattie, E. E. (2003). Breathing: Rhythmicity, plasticity, chemosensitivity. *Annual Review of Neuroscience, 26,* 239–266.

Feldman, R. S., & Quenzer, L. F. (1984). *Fundamentals of neuropsychopharmacology.* Sunderland, MA: Sinauer.

Felten, D., Ackerman, K. D., Wiegand, S. J., & Felten, S. Y. (1987). Noradrenergic sympathetic innervation of the spleen: I. Nerve fibers associate with lymphocytes and macrophages in specific compartments of the splenic white pulp. *Journal of Neuroscience Research, 18,* 28–36.

Ferguson, J. N., Aldag, J. M., Insel, T. R., & Young, L. J. (2001). Oxytocin in the medial amygdala is essential for social recognition in the mouse. *Journal of Neuroscience, 21,* 8278–8285.

Fernald, D. (1997). *Psychology.* Upper Saddle River, NJ: Prentice Hall.

Fernandez, H. (1998). *Heroin.* Center City, MN: Hazelden.

Fernstrom, J. D., & Wurtman, F. J. (1974). Control of brain serotonin levels by the diet. *Advances in Biochemical Psychopharmacology, 11,* 133–142.

Field, H. L., Monti, D. A., Greeson, J. M., & Kunkel, E. J. S. (2000). St. John's wort. *International Journal of Psychiatry in Medicine, 30,* 203–219.

Field, T. (1993) The therapeutic effects of touch. In G. G. Brannigan & M. R. Merrens (Eds.), *The undaunted psychologist.* New York: McGraw-Hill.

Field, T. (2002). Massage therapy. *Medical Clinics of North America, 86,* 163–171.

Finger, S. (2000). *Minds behind the brain.* New York: Oxford University Press.

Fischl, B., & Dale, A. M. (2000). Measuring the thickness of the human cerebral cortex from magnetic resonance images. *Proceedings of the National Academy of Sciences, USA, 97,* 11050–11055.

Fisher, H. (1982). *The sex contract: The evolution of human behavior.* New York: William Morrow.

Flament, M. F., Rapoport, J. L., Murphy, D. L., Lake, C. R., & Berg, C. J. (1987). Biochemical changes during clomipramine treatment of childhood obsessive-compulsive disorder. *Archives of General Psychiatry, 44,* 219–225.

Flegal, K. M., Harlan, W. R., & Landis, J. R. (1988). Secular trends in body mass index and skinfold thickness with socioeconomic factors in young adult women. *American Journal of Clinical Nutrition, 48,* 535–543.

Fobi, M., Lee, H., Igwe, D., Felahy, B., James, E., Stanczyk, M., & Fobi, N. (2002). Prophylactic cholecystectomy with gastric bypass operation: Incidence of gallbladder disease. *Obesity Surgery, 12,* 350–353.

Fodstad, H., Strandman, E., Karlsson, B., & West, K. A. (1982). Treatment of chronic obsessive-compulsive states with stereotactic anterior capsulotomy or cingulotomy. *Acta Neurochirurgica, 62,* 1–23.

Foltz, E. L., & Millet, F. E., Jr. (1964). Experimental psychosomatic disease states in monkeys. 1. Peptic ulcer – "executive monkeys." *Journal of Surgical Research, 26,* 445–453.

Fontana, A., Weber, W., & Dayer, J. M. (1984). Synthesis of interleukin 1/endogenous pyrogen in the brain of endotoxin-treated mice: A step in fever induction. *Journal of Immunology, 133,* 1696–1698.

Francis, D. D., Diorio, J., Liu, D., & Meaney, M. J. (1999). Nongenomic transmission across generations of maternal behavior and stress responses in the rat. *Science, 286,* 1155–1158.

Francis, D. D., & Meaney, M. J. (1999). Maternal care and the development of stress responses. *Current Opinion of Neurobiology, 9*(1), 128–134.

Francis, D. D., Young, L. J., Meaney, M. J., & Insel, T. R. (2002). Naturally occurring differences in maternal care are associated with the expression of oxytocin and vasopressin (V1a) receptors: gender differences. *Journal of Neuroendocrinology, 14,* 349–353.

Frank, G. K., Kaye, W. H., Sahu, A., Fernstrom, J., & McConaha, C. (2001). Could reduced cerebrospinal fluid (CSF) galanin contribute to restricted eating in anorexia nervosa. *Neuropsychopharmacology, 24,* 706–709.

Franklin, T. R., Acton, P. D., Maldjian, J. A., Gray, J. D., Croft, J. R., Dackis, C. A., et al. (2002). Decreased gray matter concentration in the insular, orbitofrontal, cingulate, and temporal cortices of cocaine patients. *Biological Psychiatry, 15,* 134–142.

Fredrickson, B. L., Maynard, K. E., Helms, M. J., Haney, T. L., Siegler, I. C., & Barefoot, J. C. (2000). Hostility predicts magnitude and duration of blood pressure response to anger. *Journal of Behavioral Medicine, 23,* 229–243.

Freedman, R. (2003). Schizophrenia. *New England Journal of Medicine, 349*(18), 1738–1749.

Freedman, R., Adler, L. E., Bickford, P., Byerley, W., Coon, H., Cullum, M. C., et al. (1994). Schizophrenia and nicotinic receptors. *Harvard Review of Psychiatry, 2*(4), 179–192.

Freedman, R., Coon, H., Myles-Worsley, M., Orr-Urtreger, A., Olincy, A., Davis, A., et al. (1997). Linkage of a neurophysiological deficit in schizophrenia to a chromosome 15 locus. *Proceedings of the National Academy of Sciences, USA, 94,* 587–592.

Fried, I., Wilson, C. L., MacDonald, K. A., & Behnke, E. J. (1998). Stimulating laughter. *Nature, 391,* 650.

Friedman, S., Smith, L., Fogel, D., Paradis, C., Viswanathan, R., Ackerman, R., & Trappler, B. (2002). The incidence and influence of early traumatic life events in patients with panic disorder: A comparison with other psychiatric outpatients. *Journal of Anxiety Disorders, 16,* 259–272.

Fuchs, F., Flugge, G., Ohl, F., Lucassen, P., Vollmann-Honsdorf, G. K., & Michaelis, T. (2001). Psychosocial stress, glucocorticoids, and structural alterations in the tree shrew hippocampus. *Physiology and Behavior, 73,* 285–291.

Fujita, M., Charney, D. S., & Innis, R. B. (2000). Imaging serotonergic neurotransmission in depression: Hippocampal pathophysiology may mirror global brain alterations. *Biological Psychiatry, 48,* 801–812

Fulton, J. F. (1951). *Frontal lobotomy and affective behavior.* New York: Norton.

Fulton, J. F., & Jacobsen, C. F. (1935). Fonctions des lobes frontaux; Etude comparée chez l'homme et les singes chimpanzes. London: International Neurological Congress.

Furlow, F. B. (1996, March/April). The smell of love. *Psychology Today,* pp. 38–45.

Fuxe, K., Tinner, B., Caberlotto, L., Bunnemann, B., & Agnati, L. F. (1997). NPY Y1 receptor-like immunoreactivity exists in a sub-population of beta-endorphin immunoreactive nerve cells in the arcuate nucleus: A double immunolabelling analysis in the rat. *Neuroscience Letters, 225,* 49–52.

Fylan, R., Harding, G. F., Edson, A. S., & Webb, R. M. (1999). Mechanisms of video-game epilepsy. *Epilepsia, 40,* 28–30.

Gage, F. H. (2000). Structural plasticity: Cause, result, or correlate of depression. *Biological Psychiatry, 48,* 713–714.

Gainetdinov, R. R., Mohn, A. R., & Caron, M. G. (2001). Genetic animal models: Focus on schizophrenia. *Trends in NeuroSciences, 24,* 527–533.

Galea, L. A. M., Tanapat, P., & Gould, E. (1996). Exposure to predator odor suppresses cell proliferation in the dentate gyrus of adult rats via a cholinergic mechanism. *Society for Neuroscience Abstracts, 22,* 1196.

Gamberino, W. C., & Gold, M. S. (1999). Neurobiology of tobacco smoking and other addictive disorders. *Addictive Disorders, 22,* 301–312.

Garcia, J., Kimmeldorf, D. J., & Koelling, R. A. (1955). Conditioned aversion to saccharin resulting from exposure to gamma radiation. *Science, 122,* 157–158.

Gardner, E., & David, J. (1999). The neurobiology of chemical addiction. In J. Elster & O. Skog (Eds.), *Getting hooked: Rationality and the addictions.* Cambridge, UK: Cambridge University Press.

Garza, A. A., Ha, T. G., Garcia, C., Chen, M. J., & Russo-Neustadt, A. A. (2004). Exercise, antidepressant treatment, and BDNF mRNA expression in the aging brain. *Pharmacology, Biochemistry and Behavior, 77*(2), 209–220.

Gayle, A. (Ed.). (1988). *The polygraph test: Lies, truth, and science.* Newbury Park, CA: Sage.

Geier, A. B., Schwartz, M. B., & Brownell, K. D. (2003). "Before and after" diet advertisment escalate the stigma of obesity. *Eating and Weight Disorders, 8*(4), 282–288.

Geliebter, A., & Hashim, S. A. (2001). Gastric capacity in normal, obese, and bulimic women. *Physiology and Behavior, 74,* 743–746.

Geliebter, A., Schachter, S., Lohmann-Walter, C., Feldman, H., & Hashim. S. A. (1996). Reduced stomach capacity in obese subjects after dieting. *American Journal of Clinical Nutrition, 63,* 170–173.

George, M. S., Nahas, Z., Kozel, R. A., Goldman, J., Molloy, M., & Oliver, N. (1999). Improvement of depression following transcranial magnetic stimulation. *Current Psychiatry Reports, 1,* 114–124.

George, M. S., Nahas, Z., Molloy, M., Speer, A. M., Oliver, N. C., Li., X., et al. (2000). A controlled trial of daily left prefrontal cortex TMS for treating depression. *Biological Psychiatry, 48,* 962–970.

George, M. S., Stallings, L. E., Speer, A. M., Spicer, K. M., Vincent, D. J., Bohning, D. E., et al. (1999). Prefrontal repetitive transcranial magnetic stimulation (rTMS) changes relative perfusion locally and remotely. *Human Psychopharmacology, 14,* 161–170.

Geracioti, T. D., Liddle, R. A., Altemus, M., Demitrack, M. A., & Gold, P. W. (1992). Regulation of appetite and cholecystokinin secretion in anorexia nervosa. *American Journal of Psychiatry, 149,* 958–961.

Getz, L. L., & Carter, C. S. (1992). Prairie-vole partnerships. *American Scientist, 84,* 56–62.

Ghandi, S. P., & Stevens, C. F. (2003). Three modes of synaptic vesicular recycling revealed by single-vesicle imaging. *Nature, 423,* 607–613.

Ghose, S., Weickert, C. S., Colvin, S. M., Coyle, J. T., Herman, M. M., Hyde, T. M., & Kleinman, J. E. (2004). Glutamate carboxypeptidase II gene expression in the human frontal and temporal lobe in schizophrenia. *Neuropsychopharmacology, 29*(1), 117–125.

Giedd, J. N., Blumenthal, J., Jeffries, N. O., Castellanos, X., Liu, H., Zijdenbos, A., Paus, T., Evans, A. C., & Rapoport, J. L. (1999). Brain development during childhood and adolescence: A longitudinal MRI study. *Nature Neuroscience, 2,* 861–863.

Gilbert, S. (2000). *Developmental biology.* New York: Sinauer.

Giordano, G. D., Renzetti, P., Parodi, R. C., Foppiani, L., Zandrino, F., Giordano, G., & Sandanelli, F. (2001). Volume measurement with magnetic resonance imaging of hippocampus-amygdala formation in patients with anorexia nervosa. *Journal of Endocrinological Investment, 24,* 510–514.

Gjerris, A. (1988). Baseline studies on transmitter substances in cerebrospinal fluid in depression. *Acta Psychiatrica Scandinavica, 78,* 1–36.

Gladwell, M. (1997, February 24 and March 3). Damaged. *The New Yorker,* pp. 132–147.

Glantz, L. A., & Lewis, D. A. (1997). Reduction of synaptophysin immunoreactivity in the prefrontal cortex of subjects with schizophrenia: Regional and diagnostic specificity. *Archives of General Psychiatry, 54,* 943–952.

Glasper, E. R., Lambert, K. G., Aurentz, C., Amory, E., Griffin, G., Graber, A., & Kinsley, C. R. (2000). *An investigation of the neurobiological mechanisms of withdrawal in activity-stress rats.* Poster presented at the American Psychological Society, Miami, FL.

Glick, S. D., & Maisonneuve, I. M. (1999). Development of a novel medication for drug abuse. *Annals of the New York Academy of Sciences, 909,* 88–103.

Goel, V., & Dolan, R. J. (2001). The functional anatomy of humor: Segregating cognitive and affective components. *Nature Neuroscience, 4,* 237–238.

Goetz, C. G., Tanner, C. M., Wilson, R. S., Carroll, V. S., Como, P. G., & Shannon, K. M. (1987). Clonidine and Gilles de la Tourette syndrome: Double-blind study using objective rating methods. *Annals of Neurology, 21,* 307–310.

Goff, D. C., Tsai, G., Manoach, D. S., & Coyle, J. T. (1995). Dose-finding trial of D-cycloserine added to neuroleptics for negative symptoms in schizophrenia. *American Journal of Psychiatry, 152*(8), 1213–1215.

Goktepe, E. O., Young, L. B., & Bridges, P. K. (1975). A further review of the results of stereotactic subcaudate tractotomy. *British Journal of Psychiatry, 126,* 270–280.

Goldapple, K., Segal, Z., Garson, C., Lau, M., Bieling, P., Kennedy, S., & Mayberg, H. (2004). Modulation of cortical-limbic pathways in major depression: Treatment-specific effects of cognitive behavior therapy. *Archives of General Psychiatry, 61*(1), 34–41.

Goldman-Rakic, P. S. (1987). Circuitry of primate prefrontal cortex and regulation of behavior by representational memory. In F. Plum & V. Mountcastle (Eds.), *Handbook of physiology: The nervous system* (pp. 373–417). Bethesda, MD: American Physiological Society.

Goldman-Rakic, P. S. (1999). The physiological approach: Functional architecture of working memory and disordered cognition in schizophrenia. *Biological Psychiatry, 46,* 650–661.

Goldstone A. P., Unmehopa, U.A., Bloom, S. R., & Swaab, D. F. (2002). Hypothalamic NPY and agouti-related protein are increased in human illness but not in Prader-Willis syndrome and other obese subjects. *Journal of Clincial Endocrinological Metabolism, 87,* 927–937.

Gongwer, M. A., Murphy, J. M., McBride, W. J., Lumeng, L., & Li, T. K. (1989). Regional brain contents of serotonin, dopamine and their metabolites in the selectively bred high and low alcohol drinking line of rats. *Alcohol, 6,* 317–320.

Goode, E. (2003, May 6). Experts see mind's voices in new light. *New York Times.*

Gordon, C. M., Dougherty, D. D., Fischman, A. J., Emans, J., Grace, E., Lamm, R., et al. (2001). Neural substrates of anorexia nervosa: A behavioral challenge study with positron emission tomography. *Journal of Pediatrics, 139,* 51–57.

Gore, S. M. (1999). Fatal uncertainty: Death-rate from use of ecstacy or heroin. *Lancet, 354,* 2167.

Gottesman, I. I. (1991). *Schizophrenia genesis: The origins of madness.* New York: Freeman.

Gould, E., McEwen, B. S., Tanapat, P., Galea, L. A. M., & Fuchs, E. (1997). Neurogenesis in the dentate gyrus of the adult tree shrew is regulated by psychosocial stress and NMDA receptor activation. *Journal of Neuroscience, 17,* 2492–2498.

Grant, M. M., & Weiss, J. M. (2001). Effects of chronic antidepressant drug administration and electroconvulsive shock on locus coeruleus electrophysiological activity. *Biological Psychiatry, 49,* 117–129.

Green, E. J., Greenough, W. T., & Schlumpf, B. E. (1983). Effects of complex or isolated environments on cortical dendrites of middle-aged rats. *Brain Research, 264,* 233–240.

Green, M. F. (1993). Cognitive remediation in schizophrenia: Is it time yet? *American Journal of Psychiatry, 150,* 178–187.

Green, M. F. (2001). *Schizophrenia revealed: From neurons to social interactions.* New York: Norton.

Green, M. F., Satz, P., Ganzell, S., & Vaclav, J. F. (1992). Wisconsin Card Sorting Test performance in schizophrenia: Remediation of a stubborn deficit. *American Journal of Psychiatry, 149,* 62–67.

Greene, A. E., Todorova, M. T., & Seyfried, T. N. (2003). Perspectives on the metabolic management of epilepsy through dietary reduction of glucose and elevation of ketone bodies. *Journal of Neurochemistry, 86,* 529–537.

Greenough, W. T., Larson, J. R., & Withers, G. S. (1985). Effects of unilateral and bilateral training in a reaching task on dendritic branching of neurons in the rat motor-sensory forelimb cortex. *Behavioral and Neural Biology, 44,* 301–314.

Greeson, J. M., Sanford, B., & Monti, D. A. (2001). St. John's wort (*Hypericum perforatum*): A review of the current pharmacological, toxicological, and clinical literature. *Psychopharmacology, 153,* 402–414.

Grinspoon, S., Gulick, T., Askari, H., Landt, M., Lee, K., Anderson, E., et al. (1996). Serum leptin levels in women with anorexia nervosa. *Journal of Clinical Endocrinological Metabolism, 81,* 3861–3864.

Gross, C. (2000). Neurogenesis in the adult brain: Death of a dogma. *Nature Reviews Neuroscience, 1,* 67–73.

Guidi, L., Tricerri, A. Vangeli, M., Frasca, D., Errani, A. R., DiGiovanni, A., et al. (1999). Neuropeptide Y plasma levels and immunological changes during academic stress. *Neuropsychobiology, 40,* 188–195.

Gulledge, C. C., Mann, P. E., Bridges, R. S., Bialos, M., & Hammer, R. P., Jr. (2000). Expression of mu-opioid receptor mRNA in the medial preopdtic area of juvenile rats. *Developmental Brain Research, 119,* 269–276.

Gunnar, M. R. (1998). Quality of early care and buffering of neuroendocrine stress reactions: Potential effects on the developing human brain. *Preventive Medicine, 27*(2), 208–211.

Gur, E., Lerer, B., Dremencov, E., & Newman, M. E. (2000). Chronic repetitive transcranial magnetic stimulation induces subsensitivity of presynaptic serotonergic autoreceptor activity in rat brain. *NeuroReport, 11,* 2925–2929.

Gureje, O., Vazquez-Barquero, J. L., & Janca, A. (1996). Comparisons of alcohol and other drugs: Experience for the WHO collaborative cross-cultural applicability research (CAR) study. *Addiction, 91,* 1529–1538.

Haber, S. N., Kowall, N. W., Vonsattel, J. P., Bird, E. D., & Richardson, E. P., Jr. (1986). A postmortem neuropathological immunohistochemical study. *Journal of Neurological Sciences, 75,* 225–241.

Habib, K. E., Gold, P. W., & Chrousos, G. P. (2001). Neuroendocrinology of stress. *Neuroendocrinology, 30,* 695–728.

Habib, K. E., Weld, K. P., Rice, K. C., Pushkas, J., Champoux, M., Listwak, S., et al. (2000). Oral administration of a corticotropin-releasing hormone receptor antagonist significantly attenuates behavioral, neuroendocrine, and autonomic responses to stress in primates. *Proceedings of the National Academy of Sciences, USA, 97,* 6079–6084.

Hamaleers, P. A., Van Boxtel, M. P., Hogervorst, E., Riedel, W. J., Houx, P. J., Buntinx, F., & Jolles, J. (2000). Habitual caffeine consumption and its relation to memory, attention, planning capacity and psychomotor performance across multiple age groups. *Human Psychopharmacology, 15,* 573–581.

Hardman, J. G., Limbird, L. E., & Gilman, A. G. (2001). *Goodman and Gilman's the pharmacological basis of therapeutics* (10th ed.). New York: McGraw-Hill.

Harlow, H., & Harlow, M. K. (1962). Social deprivation in monkeys. *Scientific American, 207,* 136–146.

Hart, B. (1988). Biological basis of the behavior of sick animals. *Neuroscience and Biobehavioral Reviews, 12,* 123.

Hatzidimitrious, G., McCann, U. D., & Ricaurte, G. A. (1999). Altered serotonin innervation patterns in the forebrain of monkeys treated with (+/=)3,4-methylenedioxymethamphetamine seven years previously: Factors influencing abnormal recovery. *Journal of Neuroscience, 19,* 5096–5107.

Headless chicken. (1945, October 22). *Life,* pp. 53–54.

Healy, D. (1997). *The antidepressant era.* Cambridge, MA: Harvard University Press.

Healy, D. (2002). *The creation of psychopharmacology.* Cambridge, MA: Harvard University Press.

Healy, D., & Leonard, B. E. (1987). Monoamine transport in depressive: Kinetics and dynamics. *Journal of Affective Disorders, 12,* 91–103.

Heim, C., & Nemeroff, C. B. (2001). The role of childhood trauma in the neurobiology of mood and anxiety disorders. Preclinical and clinical studies. *Biological Psychiatry, 49,* 1023–1039.

Heim, C., & Nemeroff, C. B. (2002). Neurobiology of early life stress: Clinical studies. *Seminars in Clinical Neuropsychiatry, 7*(2), 147–159.

Heim, C., Newport, D. J., Bonsall, R., Miller, A. H., & Nemeroff, C. B. (2001). Altered pituitary-adrenal axis responses to provocative challenge tests in adult survivors of childhood abuse. *American Journal of Psychiatry, 158,* 575–581.

Heinrichs, R. W. (2001). *In search of madness: Schizophrenia and neuroscience.* New York: Oxford University Press.

Heinrichs, R. W., & Zakzanis, K. K. (1998). Neurocognitive deficit in schizophrenia: A quantitative review of the evidence. *Neuropsychology, 12,* 426–445.

Heinsbroek, R. P., van Haaren, F., & van de Poll, N. E. (1988). Sex differences in passive avoidance behavior of rats: Sex-dependent susceptibility to shock-induced behavioral depression. *Physiology and Behavior, 43*(2), 201–206.

Henry, S. C., Guegant, G., Cador, M., Arnauld, E., Arsaut, J., Le Moal, M., & Demotes-Mainard, J. (1995). Prenatal stress in rats facilitates amphetamine-induced sensitization and induces long-lasting changes in dopamine receptors in the nucleus accumbens. *Brain Research, 685,* 179–186.

Herbert, J. D., Lilienfeld, S. O., Lohr, J. M., Montgomery, R. W., O'Donohue, W. T., Rosen, G. M., & Tolin, D. F. (2000). Science and pseudoscience in the development of eye movement desensitization and reprocessing: Implications for clinical psychology. *Clinical Psychology Review, 20,* 945–971.

Herner, T. (1961). Treatment of mental disorders with frontal stereotaxic thermo-lesions: A follow-up study of 116 cases. *Acta Psychiatrica Scandinavica, 36*(Suppl. 158), 1–140.

Hetherington. A. W., & Ranson, S. W. (1940). Hypothalamic lesions and adiposity in the rat. *Anatomical Record, 78,* 149–172.

Hibbeln, J. R., & Salem, N. (1995). Dietary polyunsaturated fatty acids and depression: When cholesterol does not satisfy. *American Journal of Clinical Nutrition, 62,* 1–9.

Hibbeln, J. R., Umhau, J. C., George, D. T., & Salem, N. (1997). Do plasma polyunsaturates predict hostility and depression? *World Review of Nutrition and Dietetics, 82,* 175–186.

Hill, R. D., Storandt, M., & Malley, M. (1993). The impact of long-term exercise on training on psychological function in older adults. *Journal of Gerontology, 48,* 12–17.

Hobson, J. A. (1999). *Consciousness.* New York: Scientific American Library.

Hobson, J. A. (2003). *Dreaming: An introduction to the science of sleep.* New York: Oxford University Press.

Hobson, J. A., & Leonard, J. A. (2001). *Out of its mind: Psychiatry in crisis.* Cambridge, MA: Perseus.

Hoebel, B. G., Rada, P. V. Mark, G. P., & Pothos, E. N. (1999). Neural systems for reinforcement and inhibition of behavior: Relevance to eating, addiction, and depression. In D. Kahneman, E. Diener, & N. Schwarz (Eds.), *Wellbeing: The foundations of hedonic psychology.* New York: Russell Sage Foundation.

Hoffman, R. E., Hawkins, K. A., Gueorguieva, R., Boutros, N. N., Rachid, F., Carroll, K., & Krystal, J. H. (2003). Transcranial magnetic stimulation of left temporoparietal cortex and medication-resistant auditory hallucinations. *Archives of General Psychiatry, 60*(1), 49–56.

Holland, A. J., Hall, A., Murray, R., Russell, G. F., & Crisp, H. H. (1984). Anorexia nervosa: A study of 34 twin pairs and one set of triplets. *British Journal of Psychiatry, 145,* 414–419.

Hollon, S. D., De Rubeis, R. J., Evans, M. D., Wiemer, M. J., Garvey, M. J., Grove, W. M., et al. (1992). Cognitive therapy and pharmacotherapy for depression: Singly and in combination. *Archives of General Psychiatry, 49,* 774–781.

Hollon, S. D., Thase, M. E., & Markowitz, J. C. (2002). Treatment and prevention of depression. *Psychological Science in the Public Interest, 3,* 39–77.

Holloway, M. (2003). The mutable brain. *Scientific American, 289,* 78–85.

Holsboer, F. (1999). Animal models of mood disorders. In D. S. Charney, E. J. Nestler, & B. S. Bunney (Eds.), *Neurobiology of mental illness* (pp. 317–322). New York: Oxford University Press.

Holsboer, F. (2000). The corticosteroid receptor hypothesis of depression. *Neuropsychopharmacology, 23,* 477–501.

Holtz, R. L. (1997). Brain's 'God Module' may affect religious intensity. *Los Angeles Times.*

Holzinger, A., Kilian, R., Lindenbach, I., Petscheleit, A., & Angermeyer, M. C. (2003). Patients' and their relatives' causal explanations of schizophrenia. *Society for Psychiatry and Psychiatric Epidemiolology, 38,* 155–162.

Holzwarth, R., Huber, D., Majkrzak, A., & Tareen, B. (2002). Outcome of gastric bypass patients. *Obesity Surgery, 12,* 261–264.

Hommer, D. W. (1999). Functional imaging of craving. *Alcohol Research and Health, 23,* 187–196.

Horm, J., & Anderson, K. (1993). Who in America is trying to lose weight? *Annals of Internal Medicine, 119,* 672–676.

Hormone that causes full feeling is found. (2002, August 8). *New York Times.*

Hosoda, T., Nakajima, H., & Honjo, H. (2001). Estrogen protects neuronal cells from amyloid beta-induced apoptotic cell death. *NeuroReport, 12,* 1965–1970.

Hubel, D. H., & Wiesel, T. N. (1965). Binocular interaction in the striate cortex of kittens reared with artifical squint. *Journal of Neurophysiology, 28,* 1041–1059.

Hubel, D. H., & Weisel, T. N. (1970). The period of susceptibility to the physiological effects of unilateral eye closure in kittens. *Journal of Physiology, 206,* 419–436.

Huhman, K. L., Banks, M. C., Harmon, A. C., & Jasnow, A. M. (2002). Acquisition and maintenance of conditioned defeat in male and female Syrian hamsters. In preparation.

Huhman, K. L., Mougey, E. H., & Meyerhoff, J. L. (1992). Hormonal response to fighting in submissive hamsters: Separation of physical and psychological effects. *Physiology and Behavior, 51,* 1083–1086.

Hunt, E. J., Lester, C. E., Lester, E. A., & Tackett, R. L. (2001). Effect of St. John's wort on free radical production. *Life Sciences, 69,* 181–190.

Huxley, A. (1932). *Brave new world.* London/Garden City, NY: Chatto & Windus/Doubleday, Doran & Co., Inc.

Hyman, S. E. (1999). Substance abuse disorders. In D. S. Charney, E. J. Nestler, & B. S. Bunney (Eds.), *Neurobiology of mental illness.* New York: Oxford University Press.

Hyman, S. E., & Nestler, E. J. (1993). *The molecular foundations of psychiatry.* Washington, DC: American Psychiatric Press.

Inoue, S., Bray, G. A., & Mullen Y. S. (1978). Transplantation of pancreatic B-cells prevents development of hypothalamic obesity in rats. *American Journal of Physiology, 235,* E266–E271.

Insel, T. R. (1992). Oxytocin—A neuropeptide for affiliation: Evidence from behavioral, receptor autoradiographic and comparative studies. *Psychoneuroendocrinology, 17,* 3–35.

Insel, T. R., Gingrich, B. S., & Young, L. J. (2001). Oxytocin: Who needs it? *Progress in Brain Research, 133,* 59–66.

Insel, T. R., Mueller, E. A., Alterman, I., Linnoila, M., & Murphy, D. L. (1985). Obsessive-compulsive disorder and serotonin: Is there a connection? *Biological Psychiatry, 20,* 1174–1188.

Insel, T. R., O'Brien, D. J., & Leckman, J. F. (1999). Oxytocin, vasopressin, and autism: Is there a connection? *Biological Psychiatry, 45,* 145–157.

Insel, T. R., & Shapiro, L. E. (1992). Oxytocin receptor distribution reflects social organization in monogamous and polygamous voles. *Proceedings of the National Academy of Sciences, USA, 89,* 5981–5985.

Insel, T. R., & Winslow, J. T. (1999). The neurobiology of social attachment. In D. S. Charney, E. J. Nestler, & B. S. Bunney (Eds.), *Neurobiology of mental illness.* New York: Oxford University Press.

Iwase, M., Ouchi, Y., Okada, H., Yokoyama, C., Nobezawa, S., Yoskikawa, E., et al. (2002). Neural substrates of human facial expression of pleasant emotion induced by comic films: A PET study. *NeuroImage, 17,* 758–768.

Jacob, S., McClintock, M. K., Zelano, B., & Ober, C. (2002). Paternally inherited HLA alleles are associated with women's choice of male odor. *Nature Genetics, 30,* 175–179.

Jacobs, B. (1994). Serotonin, motor activity and depression-related disorders. *American Scientist,* pp. 456–463.

Jacobs, B. L., van Praag, H., & Gage, F. H. (2000). Adult brain neurogenesis and psychiatry: A novel theory of depression. *Molecular Psychiatry, 5,* 262–269.

Jacobs, R., & Schmidt, R. E. (1999). Foundations in immunology. In M. Schedlowski & U. Tewes (Eds.), *Psychoneuroimmunology: An interdisciplinary introduction.* New York: Kluwer Academic/Plenum.

Jacobsen, L. K., Mencl, W. E., Pugh, K. R., Skudlarski, P., & Krystal, J. H. (2003). Preliminary evidence of hippocampal dysfunction in adolescent MDMA ("ecstasy") users: Possible relationship to neurotoxic effects. *Psychopharmacology* (Berl.), *173,* 383–390.

Jacobson, M. F., & Hurley, J. (2002). *Restaurant confidential.* New York: Workman.

James, W. (1890). *The principles of psychology.* New York: Holt.

Jamison, K. R. (1993). *Touched with fire: Manic depressive illness and the artistic temperament.* New York: Free Press.

Jamison, K. R. (1996). *An unquiet mind.* New York: Vintage Books.

Jamison, K. R. (1999). *Night falls fast: Understanding suicide.* Collingdale, PA: Diane Publishing Company.

Jamison, K. R. (2004). *Exuberance: The passion for life.* New York: Knopf.

Jarrett, R. B., Kraft, D., Doyle, J. L., Foster, B. M., Eaves, G. G., & Silver, P. C. (2001). Preventing recurrent depression using cognitive therapy with and without a continuation phase. *Archives of General Psychiatry, 58,* 381–388.

Jenike, M. A., Baer, L., Ballantine, T., Martuza, R. L., Tynes, S., Giriunas, I., et al. (1991). Cingulotomy for refractory obsessive-compulsive disorder. *Archives of General Psychiatry, 48,* 548–555.

Jenike, M. A., Breiter, H. C., Baer, L., Kennedy, D. N., Savage, C. R., Olivares, M. J., et al. (1996). Cerebral structural abnormalities in obsessive-compulsive disorder. *Archives of General Psychiatry, 53,* 625–632.

Jenike, M. A., Rauch, S. L., Cummings, J. L., Savage, C. R., & Goodman, W. K. (1996). Recent developments in neurobiology of obsessive-compulsive disorder. *Journal of Clinical Psychiatry, 57*(10), 492–503.

Johannes, S., Wieringa, B. M., Nager, W., Rada, D., Muller-Vahl, K. R., Emrich, H. M., et al. (2003). Tourette syndrome and obsessive-compulsive disorder: Event-related brain potentials show similar mechanisms of frontal inhibition but dissimilar target evaluation processes. *Behavioral Neurology, 14,* 9–17.

Johnson, B. A., Roache, J. D., Javors, M. A., DiClemente, C. C., Cloninger, C.R., Prihoda, T.J., et al. (2000). Ondansetron for reduction of drinking among biologically predisposed alcoholic patients: A randomized controlled trial. *Journal of the American Medical Association, 284,* 963–971.

Jones, K. L., Johnson, K. A., Dick, L. M., Felix, R. J., Kao, K. K., & Chambers, C. D. (2002). Pregnancy outcomes after first trimester exposure to phentermine/fenfluramine. *Teratology, 65,* 125–130.

Julien, R. (2001). *A primer of drug action* (9th ed.). New York: Worth.

Julien, R. (2004). *A primer of drug action* (10th ed.). New York: Worth.

Kadish, I., & Van Groen, T. (2002). Low levels of estrogen significantly diminish axonal sprouting after entorhinal cortex lesions in the mouse. *Journal of Neuroscience, 22,* 4095–4102.

Kalivas, P. W., & Duffy, P. (1995). Selective activation of DA transmission in the shell of the nucleus accumbens by stress. *Brain Research, 675,* 325–328.

Kandel, E. R., Schwartz, J. H., & Jessell, T. M. (1995). *Essentials of neural science and behavior.* Stamford, CT: Appleton & Lange.

Kandel, E. R., Schwartz, J. H., & Jessell, T. M. (2000). *Principles of neural science* (4th ed.). New York: McGraw-Hill.

Kandel, E. R., & Squire, L. R. (2000). Neuroscience: Breaking down scientific barriers to the study of brain and mind. *Science, 290,* 1113–1120.

Kapur, S., & Remington, G. (1996). Serotonin-dopamine interaction and its relevance to schizophrenia. *American Journal of Psychiatry, 153*(4), 466–476.

Karlsson, H., Bachmann, S., Schröder, J., McArthur, J., Torrey, E. F., & Yolken, R. H. (2001). Retroviral RNA identified in the cerebrospinal fluids and brains of individuals with schizophrenia. *Proceedings of the National Academy of Sciences, USA, 98,* 4634–4639.

Kasteleijn-Nolst Trenite D. G., Martins da Silva, A., Ricci, S., Rubboli, G., Tassinari, C. A., Lopes, J., Bettencourt, M., Oosting, J., & Segers, J. P. (2002). Video games are exciting: A European study of video game-induced seizures and epilepsy. *Epileptic Disorders, 4,* 121–128.

Kato, T. (2001). The relationship between flexibility of coping to stress and depression. *Japanese Journal of Developmental Psychology, 72,* 57–63.

Katzman, D. K., Christensen, B., Young, A. R., & Zipursky, R. B. (2001). Starving the brain: Structural abnormalities and cognitive impairment in adolescents with anorexia nervosa. *Seminars in Clinical Neuropsychiatry, 6,* 146–152.

Kaye, W. H. (1992). Neuropeptide abnormalitites. In K. A. Halmi (Ed.), *Psychobiology and treatment of anorexia and bulimia nervosa* (American Psychopathological Association Series, pp. 169–192). Washington, DC: American Psychiatric Press.

Kaye, W. H. (2001). *The neurobiology of anorexia and bulimia nervosa: Does dieting help people with eating disorders fit in their genes?* Retrieved March 19, 2001, from Ground Rounds on the Internet at http://psychiatry.uchicago.edu/grounds010319

Kaye, W. H., Berrettini, W., Gwirtsman, H., & George, D. T. (1990). Altered cerebrospinal fluid neuropeptide Y and peptide YY immunoreactivity in anorexia and bulimia nervosa. *Archives of General Psychiatry, 47,* 548–556.

Kaye, W. H., Frank, G. K., Meltzer, C. C., Price, J. C., McConaha, C. W., Crossan, P. J., et al. (2001). Altered serotonin 2A receptor activity in women who have recovered from bulimia nervosa. *American Journal of Psychiatry, 158,* 1152–1155.

Kaye, W. H., & Strober, M. (2001). The neurobiology of eating disorders. In D. S. Charney, E. J. Nestler, & B. S. Bunney (Eds.), *Neurobiology of mental illness.* New York: Oxford University Press.

Kaye, W. H., Weltzin, T. E., Hsu, L. K., & Bulik, C. M. (1991). An open trial of fluoxetine in patients with anorexia nervosa. *Journal of Clinical Psychiatry, 52,* 464–471.

Kaye, W. H., Weltzin, T. E., Hsu, K. K. G., Sokol, M. S., McConaha, C. W., & Plotnicov, K. H. (1997). Relapse prevention with fluoxetine in anorexia nervosa: A double-blind placebo-controlled study, in 1997. In *Annual Meeting New Research Program and Abstracts.* Washington, DC: American Psychiatric Association,

Keck, M. E., Welt, T., Post, A., Muller, M. B., Toschi, N., Wigger, A., et al. (2001). Neuroendocrine and behavioral effects of repetitive transcranial magnetic stimulation in a psychopathological animal model are suggestive of antidepressant-like effects. *Neuropsychopharmacology, 24,* 337–349.

Kelley, W. M., Moran, J. M., Wig, G. S., Adams, R. B., Duval, M. G., & Magge, R. S. (2002). The neural funny bone: Dissociating cognitive and affective components of humor [Abstract]. *Society for Neuroscience Abstracts,* Program No. 517.6.

Kelly, D., Richardson, A., & Mitchell-Heggs, N. (1973). Stereotactic limbic leucotomy: Neurophysiological aspects and operative technique. *British Journal of Psychiatry, 123,* 133–140.

Kemeny, M. E., & Laudenslager, M. L. (1999). Beyond stress: The role of individual difference factors in psychoneuroimmunology. *Brain, Behavior, and Immunity, 13,* 73–75.

Kemether, E. M., Buchsbaum, M. S., Byne, W., Hazlett, E. A., Hazndear, M., Brickman, A. M., et al. (2003). Magnetic resonance imaging of mediodorsal, pulvinar, and centromedian nuclei of the thalamus in patients with schizophrenia. *Archives of General Psychiatry, 60,* 983–991.

Kempermann, G., Kuhn, H. G., & Gage, F. H. (1997). More hippocampal neurons in adult mice living in an enriched environment. *Nature, 386,* 493–495.

Kendrick, K. M., Keverne, E. B., Hinton, M. R., & Goode, J. A. (1992). Oxytocin, amino acid and monoamine release in the region of the medial preoptic area and the bed nucleus of the stria terminalis of the sheep during parturition and suckling. *Brain Research, 569,* 199–209.

Kennedy, G. C. (1953). The role of depot fat in the hypothalamic control of food intake in the rat. *Proceedings of the Royal Society of London: Biological Sciences, 140,* 578–592.

Kennedy, S. H., Evans, K. R., Kruger, S., Mayberg, H. S., Meyer, J. H., McCann, S., et al. (2001). Changes in regional brain glucose metabolism measured with positron emission tomography after paroxetine treatment of major depression, *American Journal of Psychiatry, 158,* 899–905.

Kerr, D. A., Llado, J., Shamblott, M. J., Maragakis, N. J., Irani, D. N., Crawford, T. O., Krishnan, C., Dike, S., Gearhart, J. D., & Rothstein, J. D. (2003). Human embryonic germ cell derivatives facilitate motor recovery of rats with diffuse motor neuron injury. *Journal of Neuroscience, 23*(12), 5131–5140.

Keuker, J. I., de Biurrun, G., Luiten, P. G., & Fuchs, E. (2004). Preservation of hippocampal neuron numbers and hippocampal subfield volumes in behaviorally characterized aged tree shrews. *Journal of Comparative Neurology, 468*(4), 509–517.

Kiecolt-Glaser, J. K., & Glaser, R. (1991). Stress and immune function in humans. In R. Ader, D. L. Felten, & N. Cohen (Eds.), *Psychoneuroimmunology* (2nd ed.). New York: Academic Press.

Kiecolt-Glaser, J. K., & Glaser, R. (1999). Psychoneuroimmunology and cancer: Fact or fiction? *European Journal of Cancer, 35,* 1603–1607.

Kiecolt-Glaser, J. K., Glaser, R., Cacioppo, J. J., & Malarkey, W. B. (1998). Marital stress: Immunological, neuroendocrine and autonomic correlates. In S. M. McCann, E. M. Sternberg, J. M. Lipton, G. P. Chrousos, & C. C. Smith (Eds.), *Neuroimmunomodulation: Molecular aspects, integrative systems and clinical advances.* New York: Annals of the New York Academy of Sciences (Vol. 840).

Kim, J. H., Auerbach, J. M., Rodriguez-Gomez, J. A., Velasco, I., Gavin, D., Lumelsky, N., Lee, S. H., Nguyen, J., Sanchez-Pernaute, R., Bankiewicz, K., & McKay, R. (2002). Dopamine neurons derived from embryonic stem cells function in an animal model of Parkinson's disease. *Nature, 418,* 50–56.

Kinsley, C. H., Madonia, L., Gifford, G. W., Tureski, K., Griffin, G. R., Lowry, C., Williams, J., Collins, J., McLearie, H., & Lambert, K. G. (1999). Motherhood improves learning and memory: Neural activity in rats is enhanced by pregnancy and the demands of rearing offspring. *Nature, 402,* 137–138.

Kirsch, I., & Sapirstein, G. (1998). Listening to Prozac but hearing placebo: A meta-analysis of antidepressant medication. *Prevention & Treatment,1,* Article 0002a. Accessed August 2, 2002, from journals.apa.org/prevention/volume-1/toc-jun26-98.html

Kissebah, A. H., & Krakower, G. (1994). Regional adiposity and morbidity. *Physiological Review, 74,* 761–811.

Kleim, J. A., Swain, R. A., Armstrong, K. A., Napper, R. M., Jones, T. A., & Greenough, W. T. (1998). Selective synaptic plasticity within the cerebellar cortex following complex motor skill learning. *Neurobiology of Learning and Memory, 69,* 274–289.

Klein, S. L., Gamble, H. R., & Nelson, R. J. (1999). *Trichinella spiralis* infection in voles alters female odor preference but not partner preference. *Behavioral Ecology and Sociobiology, 45,* 323–329.

Kluger, J. (2001, April 2). Fighting phobias. *Time,* pp. 52–62.

Knight, G. C. (1969). Stereotactic surgery for the relief of suicidal and severe depression and intractable psychoneurosis. *Postgraduate Medical Journal, 45,* 1–13.

Knivsberg, A. M., Reichelt, K. L., Hoien, T., & Nodland, M. (2002). A randomized, controlled study of dietary intervention in autistic syndromes. *Nutritional Neuroscience, 5,* 251–261.

Knivsberg, A. M., Reichelt, K. L., & Nodland, M. (2001). Reports on dietary intervention in autistic disorders. *Nutritional Neuroscience, 4,* 25–37.

Kobak, K. A., Greist, J. H., Jefferson, J. W., Katzelnick, D. J., & Henk, H. J. (1998). Behavioral versus pharmacological treatments of obsessive disorder: A meta-analysis. *Psychopharmacology, 136,* 205–216.

Koenig, H. G., Cohen, H. J., George, L. K., Hays, J. C., Larson, D. B., & Blazer, D. G. (1997). Attendance at religious services, interleukin-6, and other biological parameters of immune function in older adults. *International Journal of Psychiatry in Medicine, 27,* 233–250.

Koenig, J. I., Kirkpatrick, B., & Lee, P. (2002). Glucocorticoid hormones and early brain development in schizophrenia. *Neuropsychopharmacology, 27,* 309–318.

Kolata, G. (1986). New drug counters alcohol intoxication. *Science, 234,* 1198–1199.

Kolb, B., & Whishaw, I. Q. (1996). *Fundamentals of human neuropsychology* (4th ed.). New York: Freeman.

Kolb, B., & Whishaw, I. Q. (2004). *Fundamentals of human neuropsychology* (5th ed.). New York: Worth.

Koob, G. F. (1998). Neurobiology of addiction: Toward the development of new therapies. *Annals of the New York Academy of Sciences, 909,* 170–185.

Koob, G. F., & Nestler, E. J. (1997a). The neurobiology of addiction. *Journal of Neuropsychiatry, 9*(3), 482–497.

Koob, G. F., & Nestler, E. (1997b). The neurobiology of drug addiction. In S. Salloway, P. Malloy, & J. L. Cummings (Eds.), *The neuropsychiatry of limbic and subcortical disorders.* Washington, DC: American Psychiatric Press.

Koolhaas, J. M., Korte, S. M., De Boer, S. F., Van Der Vegt, B. J., Van Reenen, V., Hopster, H., et al. (1999). Coping styles in animals: Current status in behavior and stress-physiology. *Neuroscience and Behavioral Reviews, 23,* 925–935.

Korkotian, E., & Segal, M. (1999). Release of calcium from stores alters the morphology of dendritic spines in cultures hippocampal neurons. *Proceedings of the National Academy of Sciences, USA, 96,* 12068–12072.

Korte, S. M., Beuving, G., Ruesink, W., & Blokhuis, H. J. (1997). Plasma catecholamine and corticosterone levels during manual restraing in chicks from a high and low feather pecking line of laying hens. *Physiology and Behavior, 62,* 437–441.

Kovacs, G. L. (1987). The behavioral physiology of vasopressin and oxytocin. *Advances in Biochemical Psychopharmacology, 43,* 115–128.

Kovalev, V.A., Kruggel, F., & von Cramon, D. Y. (2003). Gender and age effects in structural brain asymmetry as revealed by MRI texture analysis. *NeuroImage, 19*(3), 895–905.

Kovelman, J. A., & Scheibel, A. B. (1984). A neurohistological correlate of schizophrenia. *Biological Psychiatry, 19,* 1601–1621.

Kramer, P. D. (1993). *Listening to Prozac.* New York: Viking Press.

Krause, K. H., Dresel, S. H., Krause, J., la Fougere, C., & Ackenheil, M. (2003). The dopamine transporter and neuroimaging in attention deficit hyperactivity disorder. *Neuroscience and Biobehavioral Reviews, 27*(7), 605–613.

Krishnan, K. R. R., McDonald, W. M., Escalona, P. R., Doraiswamy, P. M., Na, C., Husain, M. M., et al. (1992). Magnetic resonance imaging of the caudate nuclei in depression: Preliminary observations. *Archives of General Psychiatry, 49,* 553–557.

Krystal, A. D., West, M., Prado, R., Greenside, H., Zoldi, S., & Weiner, R. D. (2000). EEG effects of ECT: Implications for rTMS. *Depression and Anxiety, 12,* 157–165.

Krystal, J. H., Karper, L. P., Seibyl, J. P., Freeman, G. K., Delaney, R., Bremner, J. D., Heninger, G. R., Bowers, M. B., Jr., & Charney, D. S. (1994). Subanesthetic effects of the noncompetitive NMDA antagonist, ketamine, in humans: Psychotomimetic, perceptual, cognitive, and neuroendocrine responses. *Archives of General Psychiatry, 51*(3), 199–214.

Kuba, R., Brazdil, M., Novak, Z., Chrastina, J., & Rektor, I. (2003). Effect of vagal nerve stimulation on patients with bitemporal epilepsy. *European Journal of Neurology, 10,* 91–94.

Kulka, R. A., Schlenger, W. E., Fairbank, W. E., Hough, R. L., Jordan, B. K., Marmar, C. R., & Wiess, D. S. (1990). *Trauma and the Vietnam War generation: Report of findings from the National Vietnam Veterans Readjustment Study.* New York: Brunner/Mazel.

Kupfer, D. J., & Frank, E. (2002). Effect of *Hypericum perforatum* (St. John's wort) in major depressive disorder: A randomized controlled trial. *Journal of the American Medical Association, 287,* 1853–1854.

Kurlan, R. (1998). Tourette's syndrome and "PANDAS": Will the relation bear out? *Neurology, 50,* 1530–1534.

LaBar, K. S., & LeDoux, J. E. (2001). Coping with danger: The neural basis of defensive behaviors and fearful feelings. In B. S. McEwen (Ed.), *Handbook of physiology, section 7: The endocrine system, Vol. IV: Coping with the environment: Neural and endocrine mechanisms* (pp.139–154). New York: Oxford University Press.

Ladd, C. O., Owens, M. J., & Nemeroff, C. B. (1996). Persistent changes in corticotropin-releasing factor neuronal systems induced by maternal deprivation. *Endocrinology, 137,* 1212–1218.

Lamarine, R. J. (1988). Alcohol abuse among Native Americans. *Journal of Community Health, 13,* 143–155.

Lambert, G., Hohansson, M., Agren, H., & Friberg, P. (2000). Reduced brain norepinephrine and dopamine release in treatment-refractory depressive illness. *Archives of General Psychiatry, 57,* 787–793.

Lambert, K. G. (1993). The activity-stress paradigm: Possible mechanisms and applications. *Journal of General Psychology, 120,* 21–32.

Lambert, K. G., Buckelew, S. K., Staffiso-Sandoz, G., Gaffga, S., Carpenter, W., Fisher, J., & Kinsley, C. H. (1998). Activity-stress induces atrophy of apical dendrites of hippocampal pyramidal neurons in male rats. *Physiology and Behavior, 65*(1), 43–39.

Lambert, K. G., Meyer, M., Fischer-Stenger, K., Zanetti, D. J. C., DeVries, A. C., et al. (2001). *Social contact during chronic unpredictable stress modulates stress responsivity and immunological functioning in Peromyscus californicus.* Poster presented at the annual meeting of the Society for Neuroscience, San Diego, CA.

Lambert, K. G., & Porter, J. H. (1992). Pimozide mitigates excessive running in activity-stress paradigm. *Physiology and Behavior, 52,* 299–304.

Landfield, P. W. (1987). Modulation of brain aging correlates by long-term alterations of adrenal steroids and neurally-active peptides. *Progress in Brain Research, 72,* 279–300.

Landfield, P. W., Baskin, R. K., & Pitler, T. A. (1981). Brain aging correlates: Retardation by hormonal-pharmacological treatments. *Science, 214,* 581–584.

Landgraf, R., Malkinson, T. J., Veale, W. L., Lederis, K., & Pittman, Q. J. (2003). Vasopressin and oxytocin in rat brain in response to prostaglandin fever. *American Journal of Physiology–Regulatory, Integrative and Comparative Physiology, 259,* 1056–1062.

Langston, J. W., Ballard, P., Tetrud, J., & Irwin, I. (1983). Chronic Parkinsonism in humans due to a product of meperidine-analog synthesis. *Science, 219,* 979–980.

Lanius, R. A., Williamson, P. C., Densmore, M., Boksman, K., Madhulika, A. G., Neufeld, R. W., et al. (2001). Neural correlates of traumatic memories in posttraumatic stress disorder: A functional MRI investigation. *American Journal of Psychiatry, 158,* 1920–1922.

Laugero, K. D. (2001). A new perspective on glucocorticoid feedback: Relation to stress, carbohydrate feeding and feeling better. *Journal of Neuroendocrinology, 13,* 827–835.

Leckman, J. F., Goodman, W. K., North, W. C., Chappell, P. B., Price, L. H., Pauls, D. L., et al. (1994). Elevated cerebrospinal fluid levels of oxytocin in obsessive-compulsive disorder: Comparison with Tourette's syndrome and healthy controls. *Archives of General Psychiatry, 51,* 782–792.

Leckman, J. F., Pauls, D. L., Zhang, H., Rosario-Campos, M. C., Katsovich, L., Kidd, K.K., et al. (2003). Obsessive-compulsive symptom dimensions in affected siblings pairs diagnosed with Gilles de la Tourette syndrome. *American Journal of Medical Genetics, 116,* 60–68.

Leckman, J. F., Price, R. A., Walkup, J. T., Ort S., Pauls, D. L., & Cohen, D. J. (1987). Nongenetic factors in Gilles de la Tourette's syndrome [Letter to the editor]. *Archives of General Psychiatry, 44,* 100.

Leckman, J. F., Riddle, M. A., Berrettini, W. H., Anderson, G. M., Hardin, M. T., Chappell, P.B., et al. (1988). Elevated CSF dynorphin A[1-8] in Tourette's syndrome. *Life Sciences, 43,* 2015–2023.

LeDoux, J. E. (1994). Emotion, memory and the brain. *Scientific American, 270,* 50–57.

LeDoux, J. E. (2002). *The synaptic self.* New York: Viking Press.

LeDoux, J. E., Cicchetti, P., Xagoraris, A., & Romanski, I. M. (1990). The lateral amygdaloid nucleus: Sensory interface of the amygdale in fear conditioning. *Journal of Neuroscience, 10,* 1062–1069.

LeGrange, D. (1999). Family therapy for adolescent anorexia nervosa. *Journal of Clinical Psychology, 55,* 727–739.

Leibowitz, S. F. (1992). Neurochemical neuroendocrine systems in the brain controlling macronutrient intake and metabolism. *Trends in Neuroscience, 15,* 491–497.

LeMagnen, J. (1981). The metabolic basis of dual periodicity of feeding in rats. *Behavioral and Brain Sciences, 4,* 561–607.

Lemonick, M. D. (1997, October 1). The tumor war: A California brain surgeon wields formidable new weapons as he battles on the front lines of the tumor war. *Time, 150,* 46–53.

Lenroot, R., Bustillo, J.R., Lauriello, J., & Keith, S. J. (2003). Integrated treatment of schizophrenia. *Psychiatric Services, 54,* 1499–1507.

Lessons from Lorenzo. (2002, January 26). *New Scientist.*

LeVay, S. (1991). A difference in hypothalamic structure between heterosexual and homosexual men. *Science, 253,* 1034–1037.

Levine, S. (2001). Primary social relationships influence the development of the hypothalamic-pituitary-adrenal axis in the rat. *Physiology and Behavior, 73*(3), 255–260.

Lieberman, H. R., Tharion, W. J., Shukitt-Hale, B., Speckman, K. L., & Tulley, R. (2002). Effects of caffeine, sleep loss, and stress on cognitive jperformance and mood during U. S. Navy SEAL training. *Psychopharmacology, 164,* 250–261.

Lilienfeld, S. O., Wood, J. M., & Garb, H. N. (2000). The scientific status of projective techniques. *Psychological Science in the Public Interest, 1,* 27–66.

Limosin, F., Rouillon, F., Payan, C., Cohen, J. M., & Strub, N. (2003). Prenatal exposure to influenza as a risk factor for adult schizophrenia. *Acta Psychiatrica Scandinavica, 107,* 331–335.

Lin, S., Glasper, E., Lambert, K. G., Madonia, L., Gatewood, J., & Kinsley, C. H. (2001). *Behavioral and neurobiological correlates of the addiction syndrome: Effects of maternal experience on withdrawal-induced changes in mesolimbic activity.* Poster presented at the annual meeting of the International Behavioral Neuroscience Society, Cancun, Mexico.

Liotti, M., & Mayberg, H. S. (2001). The role of functional neuroimaging in the neuropsychology of depression. *Journal of Clinical and Experimental Neuropsychology, 23,* 121–136.

Liotti, M., Mayberg, H. S., Brannan, S. K., McGinnis, S., Jerabek, P., & Fox, P. T. (2000). Differential corticolimbic correlates of sadness and anxiety in healthy subjects: Implications for affective disorders. *Biological Psychiatry, 29,* 887–899.

Liotti, M., Woldorff, M. G., Perez, R., & Mayberg, H. S. (2000). An ERP study of the temporal course of the Stroop color-word interference effect. *Biological Psychiatry, 45,* 96.

Liu, B., & Hong, J. S. (2003). Role of microglia in inflammation-mediated neurodegenerative disease. *Journal of Pharmacology and Therapeutics, 304,* 1–7.

Lock, J., LeGrange, D., Agras, W. S., & Dare, C. (2001). *Treatment manual for anorexia nervosa: A family-based approach.* New York: Guilford Press.

Loewi, O. (1921). Uber humorale ubertragbartkeit der herzenvenwirkung. *Pfluegers Archiv, 189,* 239–242. [On the humoral propagation of cardiac nerve action. In I. Cooke & M. Lipkin, Jr. (Eds.), *Cellular neurophysiology: A source book* (pp. 460–466). New York: Holt, Rhinehart, & Winston, 1972].

Loftus, E., & Ketcham, K. (1994). *The myth of repressed memory.* New York: St. Martin's Press.

Logue, A. W. (1991). *The psychology of eating and drinking* (2nd ed.). New York: Freeman.

Long, J. M., Mouton, P. R., Jucker, M., & Ingram, D. K. (1999). What counts in brain aging? Design-based stereological analysis of cell number. *Journal of Gerontology, Series A: Biological Sciences and Medical Sciences, 54*(10), B407–B417.

LoPiccolo, P. (1996, October). Something snapped. *Technology Review,* pp. 52–61.

Lorberbaum, J. P., Kose, S., Dubno, J. R., Horwitz, A. R., Newman, J. D., Sullivan, L. K., Hamner, M. B., Bohning, D. E., Arana, G. W., & George, M. S. (2004). Regional brain activity in parents listening to infant cries. Program No. 752.18. *2004 Abstract Viewer/Itinerary Planner.* Washington, DC: Society for Neuroscience.

Lovallo, W. R. (1997). *Stress and health: Biological and psychological interactions.* Thousand Oaks, CA: Sage Publications.

Lucarelli, S., Frediani, T., Zingoni, A. M., Feruzzi, F., Giardini, O., Quintieri, F., Barbato, M., D'Eufemia, P., & Cardi, E. (1995). Food allergy and infantile autism. *Panminerva Medicine, 37,* 137–141.

Luhrmann, T. M. (2000). *Of two minds: The growing disorder in American psychiatry.* New York: Knopf.

Lund, I., Lundeberg, T., Kurosawa, M., & Uvnas-Moberg, K. (1999). Sensory stimulation (massage) reduces blood pressure in unanaesthetized rats. *Journal of the Autonomic Nervous System, 78*(1), 30–37.

Lupien, S. J., de Leon, M., de Santi, S., Convit, A., Tarshish, C., Nair, N. P. V., McEwen, B. S., Hauger, R. I., & Meaney, M. (1998). Increase in cortisol during human aging predicts hippocampal atrophy and memory deficits. *Nature Neuroscience, 1*(1), 69–73.

Lupien, S. J., King, S., Meaney, M. J., & McEwen, B. S. (2000). Child's stress hormone levels correlate with mother's socioeconomic status and depressive state. *Society of Biological Psychiatry, 48,* 976–980.

Lupien, S. J., King, S., Meaney, M. J., & McEwen, B. S. (2001). Can poverty get under your skin? Basal cortisol levels and cognitive function in children from low and high socioeconomic status. *Development and Psychopathology, 13,* 653–676.

Lupien, S. J., & McEwen, B. S. (1997). The acute effects of corticosteroids on cognition: integration of animal and human model studies. *Brain Research Review, 24,* 1–27.

Luria, A. R. (1968). *The mind of a mnemonist.* Cambridge, MA: Harvard University Press.

Luria, A. R. (1972). *The man with a shattered world.* Cambridge, MA: Harvard University Press.

Luxenberg, J. S., Swedo, S. E., Flamant, M. F., Friedland, R. P., Rapoport, J., & Rapoport, S. I. (1988). Neuroanatomical abnormalities in obsessive-compulsive disorder detected with quantitative x-ray computed tomography. *American Journal of Psychiatry, 145,* 1089–1093.

Lykken, D. (1998). *A tremor in the blood: Uses and abuses of the lie detector.* New York: Perseus.

Mackenzie, J. N. (1896). The production of the so-called "rose cold" by means of an artificial rose. *American Journal of Medical Science, 91,* 45–57.

MacLean, P. D. (1949). Psychosomatic disease and the "visceral brain." *Psychosomatic Medicine, 11,* 338–353.

MacLean, P. D. (1954). Studies on limbic system ("visceral brain") and their bearing on psychosomatic problems. In E. D. Wittkower & R. A. Cleghorn (Eds.), *Recent developments in psychosomatic medicine* (pp. 101–125). Philadelphia: Lippincott.

MacLean, P. D. (1990). *The triune brain in evolution: Role in paleocerebral functions.* New York: Plenum Press.

MacLean, P. D. (1998). Paul D. MacLean. In L. R. Squire (Ed.), *The history of neuroscience in autobiography* (Vol. 2, pp. 244–275). New York: Academic Press.

MacLean, P. D., & Hakstian, A. R. (1990). Relative endurance of unipolar depression treatment effects: Longitudinal follow-up. *Journal of Consulting Clinical Psychology, 58,* 482–488.

Macmillan, M. (2000). *An odd kind of fame: Stories of Phineas Gage.* Cambridge, MA: MIT Press.

Madhav, T. R., Pei, Z., Grahame-Smith, D. G., & Zetterstrom, T. S. C. (2000). Repeated electroconvulsive shock promotes the sprouting of serotonergic axons in the lesioned rat hippocampus. *Neuroscience, 97,* 677–683.

Madsen, T. M., Treschow, A., Bengzon, J., Bolwig, T. G., Lindvall, O., & Tingstrom, A. (2000). Increased neurogenesis in a model of electroconvulsive therapy. *Biological Psychiatry, 47,* 1043–1049.

Magarinos, A. M., Deslandes, A., & McEwen, B. S. (1999). Effects of antidepressants and benzodiazepine treatments on the dendritic structure of CA3 pyramidal neurons after chronic stress. *European Journal of Pharmacology, 371,* 113–122.

Maguire, E., Gadian, D., Johnsrude, E., Good, C., Ashburner, J., et al. (2000). Navigation-related structural change in the hippocampi of taxi drivers. *Proceedings of the National Academy of Sciences, USA, 97,* 4398–4403.

Maguire, E., Spiers, H., Good, C., Hartley, T., Frackowiak, R., & Burgess, N. (2003). Navigation expertise and the human hippocampus: A structural brain imaging analysis. *Hippocampus, 13,* 250–259.

Maier, S. F., & Watkins, L. R. (1998). Cytokines for psychologists: Implications of bidirectional immune-to-brain communication for understanding behavior, mood, and cognition. *Psychological Review, 105*(1), 83–107.

Maletic-Savatic, M., Malinow, R., & Svoboda, K. (1999). Rapid dendritic morphogenesis in CA1 hippocampal dendrites induced by synaptic activity. *Science, 28,* 1860–1861.

Malhotra, A. K., Pinals, D. A., Weingartner, H., Sirocco, K., Missar, C. D., Pickar, D., & Breier, A. (1996). NMDA receptor function and human cognition: The effects of ketamine in healthy volunteers. *Neuropsychopharmacology, 14*(5), 301–307.

Manji, H. K., McNamara R. K., & Lenox, R. H. (2000). Mechanisms of action of lithium in bipolar disorder. In U. Halbreich & S. A. Montgomery (Eds.), *Pharmacotherapy for mood, anxiety, and cognitive disorders* (pp. 111–142). Washington, DC: American Psychiatric Press.

Mann, P. E., Foltz, G., Rigero, B. A., & Bridges, R. S. (1999). The development of POMC gene expression in the medial basal hypothalamus of prepubertal rats. *Developmental Brain Research, 116,* 21–28.

Manuck, S., Marsland, A., Kaplan, J., & Williams, J. (1995). The pathogenicity of behavior and its neuroendocrine mediation: An example from coronary artery disease. *Psychosomatic Medicine, 57,* 275.

Marcus, S. (Ed.). (2002). *Neuroethics: Mapping the field.* New York: Dana Press.

Margolin, A., Kleber, H. D., Avants, S. K., Konefal, J., Gawin, F., Stark, E., et al. (2002). Acupuncture for the treatment of cocaine addiction: A randomized controlled trial. *Journal of the American Medical Association, 287,* 55–63.

Marino, R., & Cosgrove, G. R. (1997). Neurosurgical treatment of neuropsychiatric illness. *Neuropsychiatry of the Basal Ganglia, 20*(4), 933–943.

Marks, I. (1997). Behavior therapy for obsessive-compulsive disorder: A decade of progress. *Canadian Journal of Psychiatry, 42,* 1021–1027.

Martin, M. (1992). *Hostage to the devil.* San Francisco: HarperCollins.

Massou, J. M., Trichard, C., Attar-Levy, D., Feline, A., Corruble, E., Beaufils, B., et al. (1997). Frontal 5-HT 2A receptors studied in depressive patients during chronic treatment by selective serotonin reuptake inhibitors. *Psychopharmacology, 133,* 99–101.

Matthews, K. A., Gump, B. B., & Owens, J. F. (2001). Chronic stress influences cardiovascular and neuroendocrine responses during acute stress and recovery, especially in men. *Health Psychology, 20*(6), 403–410.

May, C. (1996, March 6). Moruya Hospital laughter room: An experiment. *The Lamp.*

Mayberg, H. S., Brannan, S. K., Tekell, J. L., Silva, A., Mahurin, R. K., McGinnis, S., & Jerabek, P. A. (2000). Regional metabolic effects of fluoxetine in major depression: Serial changes and relationship to clinical response. *Biological Psychiatry, 48,* 30–42.

Mayer, J. (1953). Glucostatic mechanism of regulation of food intake. *New England Journal of Medicine, 249,* 13–16.

Mayer, J. (1955). Regulation of energy intake and the body weight: The glucostatic theory and the lipostatic hypothesis. *Annals of the New York Academy of Sciences, 63,* 15–43.

Mayo, W., George, O., Darbra, S., Bouyer, J. J., Vallee, M., Darnaudery, M., Pallares, M., Lemaire-Mayo, V., Le Moal, M., Piazza, P. V., & Abrous, N. (2003). Individual differences in cognitive aging: Implication of pregnenolone sulfate. *Progress in Neurobiology, 71,* 43–48.

McClintock, M. K. (1998). On the nature of mammalian and human pheromones. *Annals of the New York Academy of Sciences, 855,* 390–392.

McConville, B. J., Fogelson, M. H., Norman, A. B., Klykylo, W. M., Manderscheid, P. Z., Parker, K. W., & Sanberg, P. R. (1991). Nicotine potentiation of haloperidol in reducing tic frequency in Tourette's disorder. *American Journal of Psychiatry, 148*(6), 793–794.

McDonald, C., & Murphy, K. C. (2003). The new genetics of schizophrenia. *Psychiatric Clinics of North America, 26*(1), 41–63.

McDougle, C. J. (1999). The neurobiology and treatment of obsessive-compulsive disorder. In D. S. Charney, E. J. Nestler, & B. Bunney (Eds), *Neurobiology of mental illness* (pp. 518–533). New York: Oxford University Press.

McEvoy, J. P., & Allen, T. B. (2002). The importance of nicotinic acetylcholine receptors in schizophrenia, bipolar disorder and Tourette's syndrome. *Current Drug Targets CNS Neurological Disorders, 1,* 433–442.

McEwen, B. S. (1998). Protective and damaging effects of stress mediators. *New England Journal of Medicine, 338,* 171–179.

McEwen, B. S. (2000a). Allostasis and allostatic load. *Encyclopedia of Stress, 1,* 145–150.

McEwen, B. S. (2000b). Effects of adverse experiences for brain structure and function. *Biological Psychiatry, 48,* 721–731.

McEwen, B. S. (2000c). The neurobiology of stress: From serendipity to clinical relevance. *Brain Research Bulletin, 886,* 172–189.

McEwen, B. S., deLeon, M. J., Lupien, S. J., & Meaney, M. J. (1999). Corticosteroids, the aging brain and cognition. *Trends in Endocrinology and Metabolism, 19,* 92–96.

McEwen, B. S., & Goodman, H. M. (2001). *Handbook of physiology: The endocrine system: Sec. 7. Coping with the environment: Neural and endocrine mechanisms* (Vol. 4). New York: Oxford University Press.

McEwen, B. S., & Lashley, E. A. (2002). *The end of stress as we know it.* Washington, DC: Joseph Henry Press.

McEwen, B. S., & Magarinos, A.M. (2001). Stress and hippocampal plasticity: Implications for the pathophysiology of affective disorders. *Human Psychopharmacology, 16,* S7-S19.

McGuire, M., & Troisi, A. (1998). *Darwinian psychiatry.* New York: Oxford University Press.

McGuire, P. K., Bench, C. J., & Frith, C. D. (1994). Functional anatomy of obsessive-compulsive phenomena. *British Journal of Psychiatry, 51,* 62–70.

McHugh, P. R., Moran, K. T. H., & Killilea, M. (1989). The approaches to the study of human disorders in food ingestion and body weight maintenance. In L. H. Schenider, S. J. Cooper, & K. A. Halmi (Eds.), *The psychobiology of human eating disorders.* New York: New York Academy of Sciences.

McKenzie, J. M., & Joyce, P. R. (1992). Hospitalization for anorexia nervosa. *International Journal of Eating Disorders, 11*(3), 235–241.

McMullan, S., & Fisher, L. (1992). Developmental progress of Romanian orphanage children in Canada. *Canadian Psychology, 33,* 504.

Meaney, M. J., Aitken, D. H., Bodnoff, S. R., Iny, L. J., Tatarewicz, J. E., & Sapolsky, R. M. (1985). Early, postnatal handling alters glucocorticoid receptor concentrations in selected brain regions. *Behavioral Neuroscience, 99,* 760–765.

Meaney, M. J., Aitken, D. H., & Sapolsky, R. M. (1991). Environmental regulation of the adrenocortical stress response in female rats and its implications for individual differences in aging. *Neurobiology of Aging, 12,* 31–38.

Medalia, A., Aluma, M., Tryon, W., & Merriam, A. (1998). Effectiveness of attention training in schizophrenia. *Schizophrenia Bulletin, 24,* 147–152.

Mednick, S. A., Machon, R. A., Huttunen, M. O., & Bonett, D. (1988). Adult schizophrenia following prenatal exposure to an influenza epidemic. *Archives of General Psychiatry, 45,* 189–192.

Melmed, R., & Gelpin, Y. (1996). Duodenal ulcer: The helicobacterization of a psychosomatic disease? *Israeli Journal of Medical Science, 32,* 211.

Mendoza, S. P., & Mason, W. A. (1986). Contrasting responses to intruders and to involuntary separation by monogamous and polygamous New World monkeys. *Physiology and Behavior, 38*(6), 795–801.

Menon, V., Rivera, S. M., White, C. D., Eliez, S., Glover, G. H., & Reiss, A. L. (2000). Functional optimization of arithmetic processing in perfect performers. *Brain Research and Cognitive Brain Research, 9,* 343(345.

Mermestein, P. G., & Becker, J. B. (1995). Increases in extracellular dopamine in the nucleus accumbens and the striatum of the female rat during paced copulatory behavior. *Behavioral Neuroscience, 109,* 345–365.

Mesulam, M. M. (2000). A plasticity-based theory of the pathogenesis of Alzheimer's disease [Abstract]. *Annals of the New York Academy of Sciences, 924,* 42–52.

Metal'nikov, S., & Chorine, V. (1926). Rôle des reflexes conditionnels dans l'immunité. *Annales de l'Institute Pasteur (Paris), 40,* 893–900.

Metal'nikov, S., & Chorine, V. (1928). Rôle des reflexes conditionnels dans la formation des anticorps. *Comptes Rendus des Séances de la Societé de Biologie et de ses Filiales, 102,* 1333–1334.

Mets, B., Winger, G., Cabrera, C., Seo, S., Jamdar, S., Yang, G., et al. (1998). A catalytic antibody against cocaine prevents cocaine's reinforcing and toxic effects in rats. *Proceedings of the National Academy of Sciences, USA, 95,* 10176–10181.

Mezey, G., & Robbins, I. (2001). Usefulness and validity of post-traumatic stress disorder as a psychiatric category. *British Medical Journal, 323,* 561–563.

Michaelis, T., de Biurrun, G., Watanabe, T., Frahm, J., Ohl, F., & Fuchs, E. (2001). Gender-specific alterations of cerebral metabolites with aging and cortisol treatment. *Journal of Psychiatric Research, 35*(4), 231–237.

Miguel, E. C., Rauch, S. L., & Jenike, M. A. (1997). Obsessive-compulsive disorder. *Neuropsychiatry of the Basal Ganglia, 20*(4), 863–883.

Mihaly, E., Fekete, C., Lechan, R. M., & Liposits, Z. (2002). Corticotropin-releasing hormone-synthesizing neurons of the human hypothalamus receive neuropeptide Y-immunoreactive innervation from neurons residing primarily outside the infundibular nucleus. *Journal of Comparative Neurology, 446,* 235–243.

Milewicz, A., Mikulski, E., & Bidzinska, B. (2000). Plasma insulin, cholecystokinin, galanin, neuropeptide Y and leptin levels in obese women with and without type 2 diabetes mellitus. *International Journal of Obesity-Related Metabolic Disorders, 24,* 152–153.

Miller, S. D. (1989). Optical differences in cases of multiple personality disorder. *Journal of Nervous and Mental Disease, 177,* 480–486.

Miller, S. D., Blackburn, T., Scholes, G., White, G. L., & Mamalis, N. (1991). Optical differences in multiple personality disorder. *Journal of Nervous and Mental Disease, 179,* 132–135.

Milo, T. J., Kaufman, G. E., Barnes, W. E., Konopka, L. M., Crayton, J. W., Ringelstein, J. G., & Shirazi, P. H. (2001). Changes in regional cerebral blood flow after electroconvulsive therapy for depression. *Journal of ECT, 17,* 15–21.

Mindus, P., & Jenike, M. A. (1992). Neurosurgical treatment of malignant obsessive-compulsive disorder. *Obsessional Disorders, 15*(4), 921–937.

Mineka, S., & Suomi, S. J. (1978). Social separation in monkeys. *Psychological Bulletin, 85,* 1376–1400.

Mirsky, A. F., Bieliauskas, L. A., French, L. M., Van Kammen, D. P., Jonsson, E., & Sedvall, G. (2000). A 39-year followup of the Genain quadruplets. *Schizophrenia Bulletin, 26,* 699–708.

Mirsky, A. F., DeLisi, L. E., Buchsbaum, M. S., Quinn, O. W., Schwerdt, P., Siever, L. J., et al. (1984). The Genain quadruplets: Psychological studies. *Psychiatry Research, 13,* 77–93.

MIT News Office. (2004, February 20). *Carbs are essential for effective dieting and good mood, Wurtman says.* Retrieved March, 2004, from http://web.mit.edu/newsoffice/2004/carbs.html

Modell, J. G., Mountz, J. M., Curtus, G. C., & Greden, J. F. (1989). Neurophysiologic dysfunction in basal ganglia/limbic striatal and thalamocortical circuits as a pathogenetic mechanism of obsessive-compulsive disorder. *Journal of Neuropsychiatry, 1*(1), 27–36.

Moghaddam, B., Boliano, M. L., Stein-Behrens, B., & Sapolsky, R. (1994). Glucocorticoids mediate the stress-induced extracellular accumulation of glutamate. *Brain Research, 655,* 251–254.

Montagu, A. (1965). *The human revolution.* Cleveland, OH: World Publishing.

Montgomery, S. A. (2000). Changing targets of antidepressant therapy: Serotonin and beyond. In U. Halbreich & S. A. Montgomery (Eds.), *Pharmacotherapy for mood, anxiety, and cognitive disorders* (pp. 199–212). Washington, DC: American Psychiatric Press.

Morgan, C. M., Tanofsky-Kraff, M., Wilfley, D. E., & Yanovski, J. A. (2002). Childhood obesity. *Child and Adolescent Psychiatric Clinics of North America, 11,* 257–278.

Morris, D. M., & Taub, E. (2001). Constraint-induced therapy approach to restoring function after neurological injury. *Top Stroke Rehabilitation, 8,* 16–30.

Moyers, W. (1993). *Healing and the mind.* New York: Doubleday.

Muller, S. V., Johannes, S., Wieringa, B., Weber, A., Muller-Vahl, K., Matzke, M., et al. (2003). Disturbed monitoring and response inhibition in patients with Gilles de la Tourette syndrome and comorbid obsessive-compulsive disorder. *Behavioral Neurology, 14,* 29–37.

Mullin, R. (2003). Drug development costs about 1.7 billion. *Chemical and Engineering News, 81,* 8.

Murray, M. (1998). *Boost your serotonin levels the natural way to overcome depression, obesity, and insomnia.* New York: Bantam Books.

Myelin Project Web site: http://www.myelin.org.

Myers, A., & Hansen, C. (1997). *Experimental psychology.* New York: Brooks/Cole.

Myers, D. G. (2004). *Psychology* (7th ed.). New York: Worth.

Nakazato, M., Murakami, N., Date, Y., Kojima, M., Matsuo, H., Kangawa, K., & Matsukura, S. (2001). A role for ghrelin in the central regulation of feeding. *Nature, 409,* 194–198.

Naranjo, C. A., Tremblay, L. K., & Busto, U. E. (2001). The role of the brain reward system in depression. *Progress in Neuro-Psychopharmacological and Biological Psychiatry, 25,* 781–823.

Nardi, A. E., Valenca, A. M., Nascimento, I., & Zin, W. A. (2001). Hyperventilation challenge test in panic disorder and depression with panic attacks. *Psychiatry Research, 105,* 57–65.

Nasar, S. (1999). *A beautiful mind: A biography of John Forbes Nash, Jr., winner of the Nobel Prize in Economics, 1994.* New York: Simon & Schuster.

Nathan, P. J. (2001). *Hypericum perforatum* (St. John's wort): A nonselective reuptake inhibitor? A review of the recent advances in its pharmacology. *Journal of Psychopharmacology, 15*(1), 47–54.

National Center for Health Statistics. (1999). *Percentage of overweight and obese U. S. adults, age 20–70.* Retrieved June, 2004, from http://www.cdc.gov/nchs/prducts/pubd/hestats/over99fig1.htm

National Institute of Drug Abuse. (2001, July 30). Hearing before the Senate Subcommittee on Governmental Affairs. *Ecstasy abuse and control,* Testimony by Alan I. Leshner.

National Institute of Mental Health. (2001). *Bipolar disorder.* Retrieved on April 8, 2004, from http://www.nimh.nih.gov/publicat/bipolar.cfm#intro

National Institute of Mental Health. (2004). *Autism spectrum disorders (pervasive development disorders).* Accessed June 2, 2004, from http://www.nimh.nih.gov/publicat/autism.cfm

National Institute on Drug Abuse (NIDA). (1996). Nationwide trends. No.13567.

Neese, R. M. (2000). Is depression an adaption? *Archives of General Psychiatry, 57,* 14–20.

Neese, R. M., & Williams, G. C. (1994a). *Darwinian medicine.* New York: Vintage Books.

Neese, R. M., & Williams, G. C. (1994b). *Why we get sick.* New York: Vintage Press. (Original edition published 1992)

Nemeroff, C. B. (1998). The neurobiology of depression. *Scientific American, 278,* 28–35.

Nemeroff, C. B., Owens, M. J., Bissette, G., Andorn, A. C., & Stanley, M. (1988). Reduced corticotropin-releasing factor binding sites in the frontal cortex of suicide victims. *Archives of General Psychiatry, 45,* 377–379.

Nemeroff, C. B., Widerlov, E., Bissette, B., Walleus, H., Karlsson, I., Eklund, K., et al. (1984). Elevated concentrations of CSF corticotropin-releasing factor-like immunoreactivity in depressed patients. *Science, 226,* 1342–1344.

Nestby, P., Schoffelmeer, A. N. M., Homberg, J. R., Warden, G., DeVries, T.J., Mulder, A.H., & Vanderschruen, L. J. M. J. (1999). Bremazocine reduces unrestricted free-choice ethanol self-administration in rats without affecting sucrose preference. *Psychopharmacology, 142,* 309–317.

Nestler, E. J. (1999). Cellular and molecular mechanisms of addiction. In D. S. Charney, E. J. Nestler, & B. S. Bunney (Eds.), *Neurobiology of mental illness.* New York: Oxford University Press.

Newlin, D. B. (1999). Evolutionary game theory and multiple chemical sensitivity. *Toxicology and Industrial Health, 15,* 313–322.

Newman, M. G., & Stone, A. A. (1996). Does humor moderate the effects of experimentally induced stress? *Annals of Behavioral Medicine, 18,* 101–109.

Nibuya, M., Morinobu, S., & Duman, R. S. (1995). Regulation of BDNF trkB mRNA in rat brain by chronic electroconvulsive seizure and antidepressant drug treatments. *Journal of Neuroscience, 15,* 7539–47.

No more kicks. (2000). Rats immunized against effects of cocaine. *New Scientist, 11*(2). Taken from Internet NIDA Notes (1996). http://www.drugabuse.gov/NIDA_notes/NNVol11N2/Immunize.html

Nobler, M. S., Oquendo, M. A., Kegeles, L. S., Malone, K. M., Campbell, C., Sackheim, H. A., & Mann, J. J. (2001). Decreased regional brain metabolism after ECT. *American Journal of Psychiatry, 158,* 305–308.

Nobler, M. S., Sackheim, H. A., & Devanand, D. P. (2000). Electroconvulsive therapy: Current practice and future directions. In U. Halbreich & S. A. Montgomery (Eds.), *Pharmacotherapy for mood, anxiety, and cognitive disorders* (pp. 167–187). Washington, DC: American Psychiatric Press.

Norcross, J. I., & Newman, J. D. (1999). Effects of separation and novelty on distress vocalizations and cortisol in the common marmoset (Callithrix jacchus). *American Journal of Primatology, 47*(3), 209–222.

Norman, R. M., & Malla, A. K. (1993a). Stressful life events and schizophrenia: I. A review of the research. *British Journal of Psychiatry, 162,* 161–166.

Norman, R. M., & Malla, A. K. (1993b). Stressful life events and schizophrenia: II. Conceptual and methodological issues. *British Journal of Psychiatry, 162,* 166–174.

Nunn, R. G., Newton, K. S., & Faucher, P. (1992). 2.5 years follow-up of weight and body mass index values in the Weight Control for Life! program: A descriptive analysis. *Addictive Behaviors, 17,* 579–585.

O'Brien, C. (1999). Principles of the pharmacotherapy of substance abuse disorders. In D. S. Charney, E. J. Nestler, & B. S. Bunney (Eds.), *Neurobiology of mental illness.* New York: Oxford University Press.

Ohl, F., Michaelis, T., Vollmann-Honsdorf, G. K., Kirschbaum, C., & Fuchs, E. (2000). Effect of chronic psychosocial stress and long-term cortisol treatment on hippocampus-mediated memory and hippocampal volume: A pilot-study in tree shrews. *Psychoneuroendocrinology, 25*(4), 357–363.

Okugawa, G., Sedvall, G. C., & Agartz, I. (2003). Smaller cerebellar vermis but not hemisphere volumes in patients with chronic schizophrenia. *American Journal of Psychiatry, 160,* 1614–1617.

Olds, J. (1958). Satiation effects in self-stimulation of the brain. *Journal of Comparative and Physiological Psychology, 51,* 675–678.

Olds, J., & Milner, P. (1954). Positive reinforcement produced by electrical stimulation of the septal area and other regions of the rat brain. *Journal of Comparative and Physiological Psychology, 47,* 419–428.

Onion. (2003, May 14). *Pfizer launches "Zoloft for Everything" ad campaign [Parody].* Retrieved January 8, 2004, from http://www.healthyskepticism.org/reports/2003/0514.htm

Osborne, L. (2001, May 6). Regional disturbances. *New York Times Magazine*, pp. 8–102.

Page, S., & Levine, P. (2003). Forced use after TBI: Promoting plasticity and function through practice. *Brain Injury, 17*, 675–684.

Pakkenberg, B., Pelvig, D., Marner, L., Bundgaard, M. J., Gundersen, H. J., Nyengaard, J. R., & Regeur, L. (2003). Aging and the human neocortex. *Experimental Gerontology, 38*(1-2), 95–99.

Palanza, P., Gioiosa, I., & Parmigiani, S. (2001). Social stress in mice: Gender differences and effects of estrous cycle and social dominance. *Physiology and Behavior, 73*(3), 411–420.

Panksepp, J. (1998). *Affective neuroscience: The foundations of human and animal emotions.* New York: Oxford University Press.

Panksepp, J. (2000). The riddle of laughter: Neural and psychoevolutionary underpinnings of joy. *Current Directions in Psychological Science, 9*, 183–186.

Papez, J. W. (1937). A proposed mechanism of emotion. *Archives of Neurology and Psychiatry, 38*, 725–743.

Paquette, V., Levesque, J., Mensour, B., Leroux, J.M., Beaudoin, G., Bourgouin, P., & Beauregard, M. (2003). "Change the mind and you change the brain": Effects of cognitive-behavioral therapy on the neural correlates of spider phobia. *NeuroImage, 18*, 401–409.

Pardo, J. V., Pardo, P. J., Janer, K. W., & Raichle, M. E. (1990). The anterior cingulate cortex mediate processing selection in the Stroop attentional conflict paradigm. *Proceedings of the National Academy of Sciences, USA, 150*, 713–719.

Pare, W. P., Blair, G. R., Kluczynski, J., & Tejani-Butt, S. (1999). Gender differences in acute and chronic stress in Wistar Kyoto rats. *Integrative Physiological and Behavioral Science, 34*, 227–241.

Park, J. M., Matrix-Cols, D., Marks, I. M., Ngamthipwatthana, T., Marks, M., Araya, R., & Al-Kubaisy, T. (2001). Two-year follow-up after a randomized controlled trial of self-and clinician-accompanied exposure for phobia/panic disorders. *British Journal of Psychiatry, 178*, 543–548.

Parrott, A. C. Lees, A., Garnhaml, N.J., Jones, M., & Wesnes, K. (1998). Cognitive performance in recreational users of MDMA or "ectasy": Evidence for memory deficits. *Journal of Psychopharmacology, 12*, 79–83.

Parwani, A., Duncan, E. J., Bartlett, E., Madonick, S. H., Efferen, T. R., Rajan, R., et al. (2000). Impaired prepulse inhibition of acoustic startle in schizophrenia. *Biological Psychiatry, 47*, 662–669.

Pary, R., Lewis, S., Matuschka, P. R., & Lippmann, S. (2002). Attention-deficit/hyperactivity disorder: An update. *Southern Medical Journal, 95*(7), 743–749.

Pascual-Leone, A., Nguyet, D., Cohen, L., Brasil-Neto, J., Cammarota, A., & Hallet, M. (1995). Modulation of muscle responses evoked by transcranial magnetic stimulation during the acquisition of new fine motor skills. *Journal of Neurophysiology, 74*, 1037–1045.

Paunovic, N., & Ost, I. G. (2001). Cognitive–behavior therapy vs exposure therapy in the treatment of PTSD in refugees. *Behavioral Research Therapy, 39*(10), 1183–1197.

Pavlov, I. P. (1927). *Conditioned reflexes.* London: Oxford University Press.

Payer, L. (1996). *Medicine and culture.* New York: Holt.

Paylor, R., & Crawley, J. N. (1997). Inbred strain differences in prepulse inhibition of the mouse startle response. *Psychopharmacology, 132*, 169–180.

Pendergrast, M. (999). *Uncommon grounds.* New York: Basic Books.

Penfield, W. (1941). *Epilepsy and cerebral localization.* Baltimore: Thomas.

Peniston, E. G., & Kulsosky, P. J. (1989). Alpha-theta brain wave training and beta-endorphin levels in alcoholics. *Alcoholism: Clinical and Experimental Research, 13*, 271–279.

Pennebaker, J. W., Kiecolt-Glaser, J. K., & Glaser, R. (1988). Disclosure of traumas and immune function: Health implications for psychotherapy. *Journal of Consulting and Clinical Psychology, 56*, 239–245

Perini, G. I., Tosin, C., Carraro, C., Bernasconi, G., Canevini, M. P., Canger, R., et al. (1996). Interictal mood and personality disorders in temporal lobe epilepsy and juvenile myoclonic epilepsy. *Journal of Neurological Psychiatry, 61*, 601–605.

Perse, T. (1988). Obsessive-compulsive disorder: A treatment review. *Journal of Clinical Psychiatry, 49*, 48.

Peters, A., Palay, S. L., & Webster, H. D. (1991). *The fine structure of the nervous system: Neurons and their supporting cells.* New York: Oxford University Press.

Peterson, B. S., Riddle, M. A., Cohen, D. J., Katz, L. D., Smith, J. C., Hardin, M. T., & Leckman, J. F. (1993). Reduced basal ganglia volumes in Tourette's syndrome using 3-dimensional reconstruction techniques from magnetic resonance images. *Neurology, 43*, 941–949.

Pettit, H. O., Ettenberg, A., Bloom, F. E., & Koob, G. F. (1984). Destruction of dopamine in the nucleus accumbens selectively attenuates cocaine but not heroin self-administration in rats. *Psychopharmacology, 84,* 167–173.

Pettit, H. O., & Justice, J. G. (1991). Effect of dose of cocaine self-administration behavior and dopamine levels in the nucleus accumbens. *Brain Research, 539,* 94–102.

Phillips, A. G., Mora, F., & Rolls, E. T. (1979). Intracranial self-stimulation in orbitofrontal cortex and caudate nucleus of rhesus monkey: Effects of apomorphine, pimozide, and spiroperidol. *Psychopharmacology, 62,* 79–82.

Piazza, P. V., Deminiere, J. M., Maccare, S., Mormedi, P., LeMoal, M., & Simon, H. (1990). Individual reactivity to novelty predicts probability of amphetamine self-administration. *Behavioral Pharmacology, 1,* 339–345.

Pinel, J. P. J. (2000). *Biopsychology* (4th ed.). Needham Heights, MA: Allyn & Bacon.

Pinel, J. P. J. (2003). *Biopsychology* (5th ed.). Needham Heights, MA: Allyn & Bacon.

Pinel, J. P. J., Assanand, S., & Lehman, D. R. (2000). Hunger, eating, and ill health. *American Psychologist, 55,* 1105–1116.

Pinel, J. P. J., Mumby, D.G., Dastur, F. N., & Pinel, J. G. (1994). Rat (Rattus norvegicus) defensive behavior in total darkness: Risk-assessment function of defensive burying. *Journal of Comparative Psychology, 108*(2), 140–147.

Pirke, K. M. (1996). Central and peripheral noradrenalin regulation in eating disorders. *Psychiatry Research, 62,* 43–49.

Pizzagalli, D., Pascual-Marqui, R. D., Nitschke, J. G., Oakes, T. R., Larson, C. L., Abercrombie, H. C., et al. (2001). Anterior cingulate activity as a predictor of degree of treatment response in major depression: Evidence from brain electrical tomography analysis. *American Journal of Psychiatry, 1589,* 405–415.

Plotsky, P. M., & Meaney, M. J. (1993). Early, postnatal experience alters hypothalamic corticotropin-releasing factor (CRF) mRNA, median eminence CRF content and stress-induced release in adult rats. *Brain Research and Molecular Brain Research, 18,* 195–200.

Porges, S. (2002). Polyvagal theory: Three neural circuits regulate behavioral reactivity. *Psychological Science Agenda, 15,* 9–11.

Porter, N., Herman, J. P., & Landfield, P. W. (2001). Mechanisms of glucocorticoid actions in stress and brain aging. In B. S. McEwen (Ed.), *Handbook of physiology: Coping with the environment* (Vol. 4, pp. 293–309). Oxford, UK: Oxford University Press.

Post, R., & Weiss, S. R. B. (1999). Neurobiological models of recurrence in mood disorders. In D. S. Charney, E. J. Nestler, & B. S. Bunney (Eds.), *Neurobiology of mental illness.* New York: Oxford University Press.

Price, R. A., Kidd, K. K., Cohen, D. J., Pauls, D. L., & Leckman, J. F. (1985). A twin study of Tourette syndrome. *Archives of General Psychiatry, 42,* 815–820.

Proietto, J., Fam, B. C., Ainslie, D. A., & Thorburn, A. W. (2000). Novel anti-obesity drugs. *Expert Opinion on Investigating Drugs, 6,* 1317–1326.

Provine, R. R. (2000). *Laughter.* New York: Viking Press.

Psychosurgery. (1947, March 3). Operation to cure sick minds turns surgeon's blade into an instrument of mental therapy. *Life.*

Puhl, R., & Brownell, K. D. (2001). Bias, discrimination, and obesity. *Obesity Research, 12,* 788–805.

Pulver, A. E. (2000). Search for schizophrenia susceptibility genes. *Biological Psychiatry, 47*(3), 221–230.

Purves, D. (1994). *Neural activity and the growth of the brain.* Cambridge, UK: Cambridge University Press.

Purves, D., & Lichtman, J. W. (1980). Elimination of synapses in the developing nervous system. *Science, 210,* 153–157.

Putignano, P., Dubini, A., Toja, P., Invitti, C., Bonfanti, S., Redaelli, G., et al. (2001). Salivary cortisol measurement in normal-weight, obese and anorexic women: Comparison with plasma cortisol. *European Journal of Endocrinology, 145,* 165–171.

Raadsheer, F. C., Hoogendijk, W. J. G., Stam, F. C., Tilders, F. H. J., & Swaab, D. F. (1994). Increased numbers of corticotropin-releasing hormone expressing neurons in the hypothalamic paraventricular nucleus of depressed patients. *Neuroendocrinology, 60,* 433–436.

Rabin, S. (1999). Stress, immune function, and health. In M. Schedlowski & U. Tewes (Eds.), *Psychoneuroimmunology: An interdisciplinary introduction.* New York: Kluwer Academic/Plenum.

Raedler, T. J., Knable, M. B., Jones, D. W., Urbina, R. A., Gorey, J. G., Lee, K. S., Egan, M. F., Coppola, R., & Weinberger, D. R. (2003). In vivo determination of muscarinic acetylcholine receptor availability in schizophrenia. *American Journal of Psychiatry, 160,* 118–127.

Raisman, G., & Field, P. M. (1971). Sexual dimorphism in the preoptic area of the rat. *Science, 173,* 731–733.

Raison, C. I., & Miller, A. H. (2001). The neuroimmunology of stress and depression. *Seminar in Clinical Neuropsychiatry, 6*(4), 277–294.

Rajkowska, G. (2000). Postmortem studies in mood disorders indicate altered numbers of neurons and glial cells. *Biological Psychiatry, 48,* 766–777.

Ramachandran, V. S. (1998). The neurology and evolution of humor, laughter, and smiling: The false alarm theory. *Medical Hypotheses, 51,* 351–354.

Rapoport, J. L. (1990). *The boy who couldn't stop washing: The experience and treatment of obsessive-compulsive disorder.* New York: Signet.

Rapoport, J. L., & Fiske, A. (1998). The new biology of obsessive-compulsive disorder: Implications for evolutionary psychology. *Perspectives in Biology and Medicine, 41*(2), 159–175.

Rasmussen, S. A. (1993). Genetic studies of obsessive-compulsive disorder. *Annals of Clinical Psychology, 5,* 241–248.

Rasmussen, S. A., & Eisen, J. L. (1990). Epidemiology of obsessive-compulsive disorder. *Journal of Clinical Psychiatry, 51*(2), 10–14.

Rastam, M., Bjure, J., Vestergren, E., Uvebrant, P., Billberg, I. C., Wentz, E., & Gillberg, C. (2001). Regional cerebral blood flow in weight-restored anorexia nervosa: A preliminary study. *Developmental Medicine and Child Neurology, 43,* 239–242.

Rauch, S. L., Jenike, M. A., Alpert, N. M., Baer, L., Breiter, H. C. R., Savage, C. R., & Fischman, A. J. (1994). Regional cerebral blood flow measured during symptom provocation in obsessive-compulsive disorder using oxygen 15-labeled carbon dioxide and positron emission tomography. *Archives of General Psychiatry, 51,* 62–70.

Rauch, S. L., & Savage, C. R. (1997). Neuroimaging and neuropsychology of the striatum. *Neuropsychiatry of the Basal Ganglia, 20*(4), 741–768.

Read, J., Perry, B. D., Moskowitz, A., & Connolly, J. (2001). The contribution of early traumatic events to schizophrenia in some patients: A traumagenic neurodevelopmental model. *Psychiatry, 64,* 319–345.

Redei, E. E., Ahmadiyeh, N., Baum, A. E., Sasso, D. A., Slone, J. L., Solberg, L. C., et al. (2001). Novel animal models of affective disorders. *Seminars in Clinical Neuropsychiatry, 6,* 43–67.

Reeve, C. (2002). *Nothing is impossible.* New York: Random House.

Reeve, J. (1992). *Understanding motivation and emotion.* New York: Holt, Rinehart, & Winston.

Reichelt, K. L., & Knivsberg, A. M. (2003). Can the pathophysiology of autism be explained by the nature of the discovered urine peptides? *Nutritional Neuroscience, 6,* 19–28.

Ressler, K. J., & Nemeroff, C. B. (2000). Role of serotonergic and noradrenergic systems in the pathophysiology of depression and anxiety disorders. *Depression and Anxiety, 12,* 2–19.

Ressler, K. J., Rothbaum, B. O., Tannenbaum, L., Anderson, P., Graap, K., Zimand, E., Hodges, L., & Davis, M. (in press). Cognitive enhancers as adjuncts to psychotherapy: Use of D-cycloserine in phobics to facilitate extinction of fear. *Archives of Psychiatry.*

Restak, R. M. (1994). *Receptors.* New York: Bantam Books.

Restak, R. M. (2001). *The secret life of the brain.* Washington, DC: Joseph Henry Press.

Restak, R. M. (2003). *The new brain: How the modern age is rewiring your mind.* Emmaus, PA: Rodale Press.

Richelson, E. (2001). Pharmocology of antidepressants. *Mayo Clinic Proceedings, 76,* 511–527.

Robbins, T. W., & Everitt, B. J. (1999). Drug addiction: Bad habits add up. *Nature, 398,* 567–570.

Robertson, M. M. (1996). D2 be or not to be? *Nature Medicine, 2*(10), 1076–1077.

Robins, L. N., Davis, D. H., & Nurco. D. N. (1974). How permanent was Vietnam drug addiction? *American Journal of Public Health, 64,* 38–43.

Robinson, D., Wu, H., Munne, R. A., Ashtari, M., Alvir, J. M., Lerner, G., Koreen, A., et al. (1995). Reduced caudate nucleus volume in obsessive-compulsive disorder. *Archives of General Psychiatry, 52,* 393–398.

Robinson, L. A., Berman, J. S., & Neimeyer, R. A. (1990). Psychotherapy for the treatment of depression: A comprehensive review of controlled outcome research. *Psychological Bulletin, 108,* 30–49.

Robinson, T. E., & Kolb, B. (1999). Alterations in the morphology of dendrites and dendritic spines in the nucleus accumbens and prefrontal cortex following repeated treatment with amphetamine or cocaine. *European Journal of Neuroscience, 11,* 1598–1604.

Rocha, B. A., Fumagalli, F., Gainetdinov, R. R., Jones, S. R., Ator, R., Giros, B., et al. (1998). Cocaine self-administration in dopamine-transporter knockout mice. *Nature Neuroscience, 1,* 132–137.

Rogers, P. J., & Blundell, J. E. (1980). Investigation of food selection and meal parameters during the development of dietary induced obesity [Abstract]. *Appetite, 1,* 85.

Rolls, B. J. (1986). Sensory-specific satiety. *Nutrition Reviews, 40,* 93–101.

Ronan, P. J., Steciuk, M., Kramer, G. L., Kram, M., & Petty, F. (2000). Increased septal 5-HIAA efflux in rats that do not develop learned helplessness after inescapable stress. *Journal of Neuroscience Research, 61,* 101–106.

Roozendaal, B., Koolhaas, J. M., & Bohus, B. (1990). Differential effect of lesioning of the central amygdala on the bradycardic and behavioral response of the rat in relation to conditioned social and solitary stress. *Behavioral Brain Research, 41,* 39–48.

Rosenberg, D. R., & Keshavan, M. S. (1998). Toward a neurodevelopmental model of obsessive-compulsive disorder. *Biological Psychiatry 43,* 623–640.

Rosenman, R., Brand, R., Jenkins, C., Friedman, M., Straus, R., & Wurm, M. (1975). Coronary heart disease in the Western Collaborative Group Study: Final follow-up experience of 812 years. *Journal of the American Medical Association, 233,* 872.

Rosenstein, L. D. (1994). Potential neuropsychologic and neurophysiologic correlates of multiple personality disorder: Literature review and two case studies. *Neuropsychology, Neuropsychiatry and Behavioral Neurology, 7,* 215–229.

Rosenzweig, M. R., Breedlove, S. M., & Leiman, A. L. (1999). *Biological psychology* (2nd ed.). Sunderland, MA: Sinauer.

Rosenzweig, M. R., Breedlove, S. M., & Leiman, A. L. (2002). *Biological psychology* (3rd ed.). Sunderland, MA: Sinauer.

Ross, G. W., Abbott, R. D., Petrovitch, H., Morens, D. M., Grandinetti, A., Tung, K H., Tanner, C. M., Masaki, K. H., Blanchette, P. L., Curb, J. D., Popper, J. S., & White, L. R. (2000). Association of coffee and caffeine intake with the risk of Parkinson's disease. *Journal of the American Medical Association, 283,* 2674–2679.

Ross, G. W., & Petrovitch, H. (2001). Current evidence for neuroprotective effects of nicotine and caffeine against Parkinson's disease. *Drugs & Aging, 18,* 797–806.

Ross, P. (2003). Mind readers. *Scientific American, 289,* 74–77.

Rothschild, A. J. (2000). Sexual side effects of antidepressants. *Journal of Clinical Psychiatry, 61,* 28–36.

Rotter, J. B. (1993). Expectancies. In C. E. Walker (Ed.), *History of clinical psychology in autobiography* (Vol. 2, pp. 273–284). Pacific Grove, CA: Brooks/Cole.

Rubin, R. T., Poland, R. E., Lesser, I. M., Winston, R. A., & Blodgett, A. L. N. (1987). Neuroendocrine aspects of primary endogenous depression. *Archives of General Psychiatry, 44,* 328–336.

Ruden, R. A. (1997). *The craving brain: The biobalance approach to controlling addiction.* New York: HarperCollins.

Ruden, R. A. (2000). *The craving brain* (2nd ed.). New York: Perennial.

Ruff, M., & Pert, C. B. (1984). Small cell carcinoma of the lung: Macrophage-specific antigens suggest hemopoietic stem cell origin. *Science, 225,* 1034–1036.

Rush, A. J., Schlesser, M. A., Stokely, E. M., Bonte, F. R., & Altshuller, K. Z. (1982). Cerebral blood flow in depression and mania. *Psychopharmacological Bulletin, 18,* 6–8.

Russek, L. G., & Schwartz, G. (1997). Feelings of parental care predict health status in midlife: A 35-year follow-up of the Harvard Mastery of Stress Study. *Journal of Behavioral Medicine, 20,* 1–11.

Russell, G. F. M., & Treasure, J. (1989). The modern history of anorexia nervosa. In L. H. Schneider, S. J. Cooper, & K. A.Halmi (Eds.), *The psychobiology of human eating disorders.* New York: New York Academy of Sciences.

Russo-Neustadt, A. A., Beard, R. C., Huang, Y. M., & Cotman, C. W. (2000). Physical activity and antidepressant treatment potentiate the expression of specific brain-derived neurotrophic factor transcripts in the rat hippocampus. *Neuroscience, 101,* 305–312.

Russo-Neustadt, A. A., Ha, T., Ramirez, R., & Kesslak, J. P. (2001). Physical activity-antidepressant treatment combination: Impact on brain-deprived neurotrophic factor and behavior in an animal model. *Behavioral Brain Research, 120,* 87–95.

Ryvlin, P. (2003). Beyond pharmacotherapy: Surgical management. *Epilepsia, 44,* 23–28.

Sacks, O. (1984). *A leg to stand on.* New York: Touchstone.

Sacks, O. (1985). *The man who mistook his wife for a hat.* New York: Touchstone.

Sacks, O. (1990). *Seeing voices.* New York: HarperCollins.

Sacks, O. (1995). *An anthropologist on Mars.* New York: Knopf.

Sacks, O. (1997). *The island of the colorblind.* New York: Vintage Press.

Sacks, O. (1999a). *Awakenings.* New York: Vintage Press. (Original work published 1973).

Sacks, O. (1999b). *Migraine.* Berkeley: University of California Press.

Sacks, O. (2001). *Uncle Tungsten: Memories of a chemical boyhood.* New York: Knopf.

Sahu, A. L, Sninsky, C. A., & Kalra, S. P. (1997). Evidence that hypothalamic neuropeptide Y gene expression and NPY levels in the paraventricular nucleus increase before the onset of hyperphagia in experimental diabetes. *Brain Research, 755,* 339–342.

Sanberg, P. R., McConville, B. J., Fogelson, H. M., Manderscheid, P. Z., Parker, K.W., Blythe, M. M., et al. (1989). Nicotine potentiates the effects of haloperidol in animals and inpatients with Tourette's syndrome. *Biomedical Pharmacology, 43,* 19–23.

Sanchez, M. M., Hearn, E. F., Do, D., Rilling, J. K., & Herndon, J. G. (1998). Differential rearing affects corpus callosum size and cognitive function of rhesus monkeys. *Brain Research, 812*(1-2), 38–49.

Sanders, A. R., Detera-Wadleigh, S. D., & Gershon, E. S. (1999). Molecular genetics of mood disorders. In D. S. Charney, E. J. Nestler, & B. S. Bunney (Eds.), *Neurobiology of mental illness* (pp. 299–316). New York: Oxford University Press.

Sandfort, T. G., de Graaf, R., Bijl, R. V., & Schnabel, P. (2001). Same-sex sexual behavior and psychiatric disorders: Findings from the Netherlands Mental Health Survey and Incidence Study (NEMESIS). *Archives of General Psychiatry, 58,* 85–91.

Sapolsky, R. M. (1996). Stress, glucocorticoids, and damage to the nervous system: The current state of confusion. *Stress, 1,* 1–19.

Sapolsky, R. M. (1997). *The trouble with testosterone.* New York: Touchstone.

Sapolsky, R. M. (1998). *Why zebras don't get ulcers.* New York: Freeman.

Sapolsky, R.M. (2000). Stress hormones: Good and bad. *Neurobiology of Disease, 7,* 540–542.

Sapolsky, R., Rivier, C., Yamamoto, G., Plotsky, P., & Vale, W. (1987). Interleukin-1 stimulates the secretion of hypothalamic corticotropin-releasing factor. *Science, 238,* 522–524.

Sasson, Y., Zohar, J., Chopra, M., Llustig, M., Iancu, I., & Hendler, T. (1997). Epidemiology of obsessive-compulsive disorder: A worldview. *Journal of Clinical Psychiatry, 58*(Suppl. 12), 7–10.

Satz, P., & Green, M. F. (1999). Atypical handedness in schizophrenia: Some methodological and theoretical issues. *Schizophrenia Bulletin, 25,* 533–542.

Saxby, E., & Peniston, E. G. (1995). Alpha-theta brain-wave neurofeedback training: An effective treatment for male and female alcoholics with depressive symptoms. *Journal of Clinical Psychology, 51,* 685–693.

Schacter, D. L. (1996). *Searching for memory: The brain, the mind, and the past.* New York: Basic Books.

Schacter, D. L. (Ed.). (1997). *Memory distortion: How minds, brains, and societies construct the past.* Cambridge, MA: *Harvard* University Press.

Schedlowski, M., & Tewes, U. (Eds.). (1999). *Psychoneuroimmunology: An interdisciplinary introduction.* New York: Kluwer Academic/Plenum.

Schildkraut, J. J. (1965). The catecholamine hypothesis of affective disorders: A review of supporting evidence. *American Journal of Psychiatry, 122,* 509–522.

Schlosser, E. (2002). *Fast food nation.* New York: HarperCollins.

Schoenbach, V. J., Kaplan, B. H., Friedman, J., & Kleinbaum, D. G. (1986). Social ties and mortality in Evans County, GA. *American Journal of Epidemiology, 123,* 577–591.

Scholz, G. H., Englaro, P., Thiele, I., Scholz, M., Klusman, T., Kellner, K., et al. (1996). Dissociation of serum leptin concentration and body fat content during long term dietary intervention in obese individuals. *Hormones and Metabolism Research, 28,* 718–723.

Schonknecht, P., Pantel, J., Klinga, K., Jensen, M., Hartmann, T., Salbach, B., & Schroder, J. (2001). Reduced cerebrospinal fluid estradiol levels are associated with increased beta-amyloid levels in female patients with Alzheimer's disease. *Neuroscience Letters, 307,* 122–124.

Schouten, W. G. P., & Wiegant, V. M. (1997). Individual responses to acute and chronic stress in pigs. *Acta Physiologica Scandinavica, 640*(Suppl.), 188–191.

Schulkin, J. (2003). *Rethinking homeostasis: Allostatic regulation in physiology and pathophysiology.* Cambridge, MA: MIT Press.

Schulteis, G. (2000). Abolition of conditioned opiate withdrawal. *Nature, 405,* 1013–1014.

Schultz, D. P., & Schultz, S. E. (2000). *A history of modern psychology* (7th ed.). New York: Harcourt College Publishing.

Schwartz, J. M., & Begley, S. (2002). *The mind and the brain: Neuroplasticity and the power of mental force.* New York: HarperCollins.

Schwartz, J. M., & Beyette, B. (1996). *Brain lock: Free yourself from obsessive-compulsive behavior.* New York: HarperCollins.

Schwartz, J. M., Stoessel, P. W., Baxter, L. R., Martin, K. M., & Phelps, M. E. (1996). Systematic changes in cerebral glucose metabolic rate after successful behavior modification treatment of obsessive-compulsive disorder. *Archives of General Psychiatry, 53,* 109–111.

Schwartz, R., Gunzelmann, T., Hinz, A., & Brahler, E. (2001). Anxiety and depression in the general population over 60 years old. *Deutsche Medizinische Wochenschrift, 126,* 611–615.

Schwarzschild, M. A., Chen, J. F., & Ascerio, A. (2002). Caffeinated clues and the promise of adenosine A (2A) antagonists in PD. *Neurology, 58,* 1154–1160.

Seeman, T. E., Singer, B., Wilkinson, C. W., & McEwen, B. S. (2001). Gender differences in age-related changes in HPA axis activity. *Psychoneuroendocrinology, 26,* 225–240.

Segerstrom, S. C., Taylor, S. W., Kemeny, M., & Fahey, J. L. (1998). Optimism is associated with mood, coping, and immune change in response to stress. *Journal of Personality and Social Psychology, 74,* 1646–1655.

Seksel, K., & Lindeman, M. J. (1998). Use of clomipramine in the treatment of anxiety-related and obsessive-compulsive disorders in cats. *Australian Veterinarian Journal, 76,* 317–321.

Selemon, L. D., Rajkowska, G., & Goldman-Rakic, P. S. (1995). Abnormally high neuronal density in the schizophrenic cortex. A morphometric analysis of prefrontal area 9 and occipital area 17. *Archives of General Psychiatry, 52*(10), 805–820.

Seligman, M. E. P. (1990). *Learned optimism.* New York: Pocket Books.

Seligman, M. E. P., & Beagley, G. (1975). Learned helplessness in the rat. *Journal of Comparative and Physiological Psychology, 88,* 5166–5170.

Seligman, M. E. P., Schulman, P., & DeRubeis, R. J. (1999). The prevention of depression and anxiety. *Prevention and Treatment, 2,* 1–22.

Selye, H. (1936). A syndrome produced by diverse nocuous agents. *Nature, 138,* 32.

Selye, H. (1964). *From dream to discovery.* New York: McGraw-Hill.

Selye, H. (1976). *The stress of life.* New York: McGraw-Hill.

Serdula, M. K., Collins, M. E., Williamson, D. F., Anda, R. F., Pamuk, E. R., & Byers, T. E. (1993). Weight control practices of U.S. adolescents and adults. *Annals of International Medicine, 119,* 667–671.

Seroussi, K. (2002). *Unraveling the mystery of autism and pervasive developmental disorder.* New York: Broadway Books.

Shapiro, F. (1989). Eye movement desensitization: A new treatment for post-traumatic stress disorder. *Journal of Behavior Therapy and Experimental Psychiatry, 20,* 211–217.

Shavit, Y. (1991). Stress-induced immune modulation in animals: Opiates and endogenous opioid peptides. In R. Ader, D. L. Felten, & N. Cohen (Eds.), *Psychoneuroimmunology* (2nd ed.). New York: Academic Press.

Sheline, Y. I. (2000). 3D MRI studies of neuranatomic changes in unipolar major depression: The role of stress and medical comorbidity, *Biological Psychiatry, 48,* 791–800.

Sheline, Y. I., Wang, P., Gado, M., Csernansky, J., & Vannier, M. (1996). Hippocampal atrophy in recurrent major depression. *Proceedings of the National Academy of Sciences, USA, 93,* 3908–3913.

Shepherd, J., Stein, K., & Milne, R. (2000). Eye movement desensitization and reprocessin in the treatment of post-traumatic stress disorder: A review of an emerging therapy. *Psychological Medicine, 30,* 863–871.

Sher, L., Matthews, J. R., Turner, E. H., Postolache, T. T., Katz, K. S., & Rosenthal, N. E. (2001). Early response to light therapy partially predicts long-term antidepressant effects in patients with seasonal affective disorder. *Journal of Psychiatry and Neuroscience, 26*(4), 336–338.

Shorter, E. (1997). *A history of psychiatry.* New York: Wiley.

Shytle, R. D., Silver, A. A., & Sanberg, P. R. (2000). Co-morbid bipolar disorder in Tourette's syndrome responds to the nicotinic receptor antagonist mecamylamine (Inversine). *Biological Psychiatry, 15,* 1028–1031.

Silbersweig, D. A., Stern, E., Frith, C., Cahill, C., Holmes, A., Grootoonk, S., et al. (1995). A functional neuroanatomy of hallucinations in schizophrenia. *Nature, 378,* 176–179.

Silva, I., Mor, G. , & Naftolin, F. (2001). Estrogen and the aging brain. *Maturitas, 38,* 95–100.

Silver, A. A., Shytle, R. D., Sheehan, K. H., Sheehan, D. V., Ramos, A., & Sanberg, P. (2001). Multicenter, double-blind, placebo-controlled study of mecamylamine mono-therapy for Tourette's disorder. *Journal of the American Academy of Child and Adolescent Psychiatry, 40,* 1103–1110.

Silverstein, B., Peterson, B., & Perdue, L. (1986). Some correlates of the thin standard of bodily attractiveness for women. *International Journal of Eating Disorders, 5,* 895–905.

Simon, H. (1991). Exercise and human immune function. In R. Ader, D. L. Felten, & N. Cohen (Eds.), *Psychoneuroimmunology* (2nd ed.). New York: Academic Press.

Singer, H. S., & Walkup, J. T. (1991). Tourette syndrome and other tic disorders: Diagnosis, pathophysiology, and treatment. *Medicine, 70*(1), 15–32.

Singh, R., Bhalla, A., Lehl, S. S., & Sachdev, A. (2001). Video game epilepsy. *Epilepsia, 49,* 411–412.

Sjogren, B., Widstrom, A. M., Edman, G., & Uvnas-Moberg, K. (2000). Changes in personality pattern during the first pregnancy and lactation. *Journal of Psychosomatic Obstetrics and Gynecology, 21,* 31–38.

Skinner, B. F. (1963). Behaviorism at fifty. *Science, 140,* 951–958.

Sloman, L., & Gilbert, P. (2000). *Subordination and defeat: An evolutionary approach to mood disorders and their therapy.* Mahwah, NJ: Erlbaum.

Smith, T. E., McGreer-Whitworth, B., & French, J. A. (1998). Close proximity of the heterosexual partner re-duces the physiological and behavioral consequences of novel-cage housing in black tufted-ear marmosets (Callithrix kuhli). *Hormones and Behavior, 34*(3), 211–222.

Snowden, D. (2001). *Aging with grace.* New York: Bantam Books.

Soldatos, C. R., & Bergiannaki, J. D. (1999). Sleep in de-pression and the effects of antidepressants on sleep. In

U. Halbreich & S. A. Montgomery (Eds.), *Pharmacotherapy for mood, anxiety, and cognitive disorders* (pp. 255–272). Washington, DC: American Psychiatric Press.

Solinas, M., Ferre, S., You, Z B., Karcz-Kubicha, M., Popoli, P., & Goldberg, S. R. (2002). Caffeine induces dopamine and glutamate release in the shell of the nucleus accumbens. *Journal of Neuroscience, 22,* 6321–6324.

Solomon, A. (1994). *A stone boat.* Winchester, MA: Faber & Faber.

Solomon, A. (2001). *The noonday demon: An atlas of depression.* New York: Scribner's.

Sompayrac, L. (1999). *How the immune system works.* Malden, MA: Blackwell Science.

Song, C., & Leonard, B. E. (2000). *Fundamentals of psychoneuroimmunology.* New York: Wiley.

Spiegel, D., Bloom, J., Kraemer, H., & Gottheil, E. (1989). Effect of psychosocial treatment on survival of patients with metastatic breast cancer. *Lancet, 2,* 888–891.

Spitz, R. A. (1946). Anaclitic depression. *Psychoanalytic Study of the Child, 2,* 313–347.

Stafstrom, C. E., & Bough, K. J. (2003). The ketogenic diet for the treatment of epilepsy: A challenge for nutritional neuroscientists. *Nutritional Neuroscience, 6,* 67–79.

Stahl, S. M. (2000). Blue genes and the monoamine hypothesis of depression. *Journal of Clinical Psychiatry, 61,* 77–78.

Staley, J. K., & Mash, D. C. (1996). Adaptive increase in D3 dopamine receptors in the brain reward circuits of human cocaine fatalities. *Journal of Neuroscience, 16,* 6100–6106.

Stanovich, K. E. (Ed.). (1998). *How to think straight about psychology* (5th ed.). New York: Addison-Wesley Longman.

Stein, D.G., Brailowsky, S., & Will, B. (1995). *Brain repair.* New York: Oxford University Press.

Stellar, E. (1954). The physiology of motivation. *Psychological Review, 61,* 5.

Sternberg, E. M. (2000). *The balance within: The science connecting health and emotions.* New York: Freeman.

Sternberg, E. M., & Gold, P. W. (1997). The mind-body interaction in disease. *Scientific American, 7*(1), 8–15.

Stewart, J. (1999). Pathways to relapse: The neurobiology of drug and stress-induced relapse to drug-taking. *Journal of Psychiatry and Neuroscience, 25,* 125–136.

Stice, E. (2002). The neglect of obesity. *American Psychological Association Monitor, 33*, 33.

Stoll, A. L., Renshaw, P. F., Yurgelun-Todd, D. A., & Cohen, B. M. (2000). Neuroimaging in bipolar disorder: What have we learned? *Biological Psychiatry, 48*, 505–517.

Strakowski, S. M., DelBello, M. P., Adler, C., Cecil, K. M., & Sax, K. W. (2000). Neuroimaging in bipolar disorder. *Bipolar Disorders, 2*, 148–164.

Straub, R. (2002). *Health psychology*. New York: Worth.

Strawbridge, W. J., Cohen, R. D., Shema, S. J., & Kaplan, G. A. (1997). Frequent attendance at religious services and mortality over 28 years. *American Journal of Public Health, 87*, 956–961.

Strober, M. (1980). Personality and symptomatological features in young, nonchronic anorexia nervosa patients. *Journal of Psychosomatic Research, 24*, 353–359.

Stuart, G., Spruston, N., & Hausser, M. (Eds.). (1999). *Dendrites*. New York: Oxford University Press.

Stunkard, A. J., & McLaren-Hume, M. (1959). The results of treatment of obesity: A review of the literature and report of a series. *Archives of Internal Medicine, 103*, 79–85.

Suddath, R. L., Christison, G. W., Torrey, E. F., Casanova, M. F., & Weinberger, D. R. (1990). Anatomical abnormalities in the brains of monozygotic twins discordant for schizophrenia. *New England Journal of Medicine, 322*, 789–794.

Sugerman, H. J. (2001). Bariatric surgery for severe obesity. *Journal of the Associative Academy of Minor Physics, 12*, 129–136.

Suomi, S. (1983). Models of depression in primates. *Psychological Medicine, 13*, 465–468.

Suomi, S. (1997). Early determinants of behavior: Evidence from primate studies. *British Medical Bulletin, 53*, 170–184.

Sutton, M. A., Karanian, D. A., & Self, D.W. (2000). Factors that determine a propensity for cocaine-seeking behavior during abstinence in rats. *Neuropsychopharmacology, 22*, 625–641.

Suzuki, K., Awata, S., & Matsuoka, H. (2003). Short-term effect of ECT in middle-aged and elderly patients with intractable catatonic schizophrenia. *Journal of ECT, 19*, 73–80.

Swonguer, L., Lambert, K. G., & Klein, S. L. (20013, June). *Lipopolysaccharide-activated immune function influences affiliative behaviors and mating preferences in Peromyscus Californicus*. Poster at the annual meeting of the Society for Behavioral Neuroendocrinology, University of Cincinnati, Cincinnati, OH.

Talairach, J., Bancaud, J., Geier, S., Bordas-Ferrer, M., Bonis, A., Szikla, G., & Rusu, M. (1973). The cingulate gyrus and human behavior. *Electroencephalographic Clinical Neurophysiology, 34*, 45–52.

Tamminga, C.A. (1999). Principles of the pharmacotherapy of schizophrenia. In D. S. Charney, E. J. Nestler, & B. S. Bunney (Eds.), *Neurobiology of mental illness* (pp. 272–285). New York: Oxford University Press.

Tanskanen, A., & Hibbeln, J. R. (2001). Fish consumption, depression, and suicidality in a general population. *Archives of General Psychiatry, 58*, 512–513.

Taylor, K. M., Davidson, K., Mark, G. P., Rada, P., & Hoebel, B. G. (1992). Conditioned taste aversion induced by increased acetylcholine in the nucleus accumbens. *Society for Neuroscience Abstracts, 18*, 1066.

Taylor, S., Klein, L., Lewis, B., Gruenwald, T., Gurung, R., & Updegraff, J. (2000). Biobehavioral responses to stress in females: Tend-and-befriend, not fight-or-flight. *Psychological Review, 107*, 411–429.

Teff, K. L., Mattes, R. D., & Engelman, K. (1991). Cephalic phase insulin release in normal weight males: Verification and reliability. *American Journal of Physiology, 261*, E430–E436.

Temple, E., Deutsch, G., Poldrack, R., Miller, S., Tallal, P., Merzenich, M., & Gabrieli, J. (2003). Neural deficits in children with dyslexia ameliorated by behavioral remediation: Evidence from functional MRI. *Proceedings of the National Academy of Sciences, USA, 100*, 2860–2865.

Thompson, P. M., Vidal, C., Giedd, J. N., Gochman, P., Blumenthal, J., Nicolson, R., et al. (2001). Mapping adolescent brain change reveals dynamic wave of accelerated gray matter loss in very early-onset schizophrenia. *Proceedings of the National Academy of Sciences, USA, 98*, 11650–11655.

Thompson, R. A. (2000). *The brain: A neuroscience primer*. New York: Worth.

Tiller, J. W. (1993). Clinical overview on moclobemide. *Progress in Neuro-Psychopharmacology and Biological Psychiatry, 17*(5), 703–712.

Time. (2002, January 21). Too heavy, too young. *Time*, p. 88.

Tomizawa, K. Iga, N., Lu, Y.-F., Moriwaki, A., Matsushita, M., Li, S.-T., Miyamoto, M., Itano, T., & Matsui, H. (2003). Oxytocin improves long-lasting spatial memory during motherhood through MAP kinase cascade. *Nature Neuroscience, 6,* 384–390.

Torrey, E. F., Bowler, A. E., Taylor, E. H., & Gottesman, I. I. (1994). *Schizophrenia and manic-depressive disorder.* New York: Basic Books.

Tourette Syndrome Association (UK). (2002, February 22). Article part of *The Sun,* an on-line newsletter. Retrieved January 15, 2003, from www.tsa.org.uk/the_sun.html

Trivedi, M. H. (1996). Functional neuroanatomy of obsessive-compulsive disorder. *Journal of Clinical Psychiatry, 57,* 26–36.

Tsai, G., Yang, P., Chung, L. C., Lange, N., & Coyle, J. T. (1998). D-serine added to antipsychotics for the treatment of schizophrenia. *Biological Psychiatry, 44*(1), 1081–1089.

Tsien, J. Z. (2000, April). Building a brainier mouse. *Scientific American,* pp. 62–68.

Turbott, J. (1997). The meaning and function of ritual in psychiatric disorder, religion and everyday behavior. *Australian and New Zealand Journal of Psychiatry, 31*(6), 835–843.

U.S. Food and Drug Administration. (2001). *New device approval: LAP-BAND® adjustable gastric banding (LAGB®) system, June 6, 2001.* Retrieved June 15, 2004, from http://www.fda.gov/cdrh/mda/docs/p000008.html

Underwood, M. D., Khaibulina, A. A., Ellis, S. P., Moran, A., Rice, P. M., Mann, J. J., et al. (1999). Morphometry of the dorsal raphe nucleus serotonergic neurons in suicide victims. *Biological Psychiatry, 46,* 473–483.

Uno, H., Tarrara, R., Else, J. G., Suleman, M. A., & Sapolsky, R. M. (1989). Hippocampal damage associated with prolonged and fatal stress in primates. *Journal of Neuroscience, 9,* 1705–1711.

Uvnas-Moberg, K. (1998). Antistress pattern induced by oxytocin. *News of the Physiological Sciences, 13,* 22–26.

Vakili, K., Srinivasan, S. P., Lafer, B., Fava, M., Renshaw, P. F., Bonello-Cintron, C.M., & Yurgelun-Todd, D. A. (2000). Hippocampal volume in primary unipolar major depression: A magnetic resonance imaging study. *Biological Psychiatry, 47,* 1087–1090.

Valenstein, E. S. (1998). *Blaming the brain: The truth about drugs and mental health.* New York: Free Press.

Valentine, G. (2002). MDMA and Ecstasy. *Psychiatric Times, 19*(2).

Van Bockstaele, E. J., Bajic, D., Proudfit, H., & Valentino, R. J. (2001). Topographic architecture of stress-related pathways targeting the noradrenergic locus coeruleus. *Physiology and Behavior, 73*(3), 273–283.

Vandereycken, W., & Pierloot, R., (1982). Pimozide combined with behavior therapy in the short-term treatment of anorexia nervosa. *Acta Psychiatrica et Neurologica Scandinavica, 66,* 445–450.

van Geel, B. M., Assies, J., Haverkort, E. B., Koelman, J. H., Berbeeten, B., Wanders, R. J., & Barth, P.G. (1999). Progression of abnormalities in adrenomyeloneuropathy and neurologically asymptomatic x-linked adrenoleukodystrophy despite treatment with Lorenzo's oil. *Journal of Neurology, Neurosurgery, and Psychiatry, 67,* 290–299.

Vogel, S. (1992). *Vital circuits.* New York: Oxford University Press.

Volkow, N. D., & Fowler, J. S. (2000). Addiction, a disease of compulsion and drive: Involvement of the orbitofrontal cortex. *Cerebral Cortex, 10,* 318–325.

Volkow, N. D., Fowler, J. S., & Wang, G. J. (1999). Imaging studies on the role of dopamine in cocaine reinforcement and addiction in humans. *Journal of Psychopharmacology, 13*(4), 337–345.

Volkow, N. D., Wang, G. J., Fowler, J. S., Logan, J., Gatley, S. J., Gifford, A., et al. (1999). Prediction of reinforcing responses to psychostimulants in humans by brain dopamine D2 receptor levels. *American Journal of Psychiatry, 156,* 1440–1443.

Vollmayr, B., Faust, H., Lewicka, S., & Henn, F. A. (2001). Brain-derived-neurotrophic-factor (BDNF) stress response in rats bred for learned helplessness. *Molecular Psychiatry, 6,* 471–474.

Volmar, K. E., & Hutchins, G. M. (2001). Aortic and mitral fenfluramine-phentermine valvulopathy in 64 patients treated with anorectic agents. *Archives of Pathology and Laboratory Medicine, 125,* 1555–1561.

Walker, E. F., & Diforio, D. (1997). Schizophrenia: A neural diathesis-stress mode. *Psychological Review, 4,* 1–19.

Walker, E. F., Grimes, K., Davis, D., & Smith, A. (1993). Childhood precursors of schizophrenia: Facial expressions of emotion. *American Journal of Psychiatry, 150,* 1654–1660.

Walker, E. F., Lewine, R. R. J., & Neumann, C. (1996). Childhood behavioral characteristics and adult brain morphology in schizophrenia. *Schizophrenia Research, 22,* 93–101.

Walker, E. F., Logan, C. B., & Walder, D. (1999). Indicators of neurodevelopmental abnormality in schizotypal personality disorder. *Psychiatric Annals, 29,* 132–136.

Walker, E. F., Savoie, T., & Davis, D. (1994). Neuromotor precursors of schizophrenia. *Schizophrenia Bulletin, 20,* 453–480.

Walkup, J. T., Leckman, J. F., Price, R. A., Hardin, M., Ort, S. I., & Cohen, D. J. (1988). The relationship between obsessive-compulsive disorder and Tourette's disorder and Tourette's syndrome: A twin study. *Psychopharmacological Bulletin, 24,* 375–379.

Walters, E. E., & Kendler, K. S. (1995). Anorexia nervosa and anorexic-like syndromes in a population-based twin sample. *American Journal of Psychiatry, 52,* 34–38.

Wang, L., Ho, C.-L., Sun, D., Liem, R.K.H., & Brown, A. (2000). Rapid movement of axonal neurofilaments interrupted by prolonged pauses. *Nature Cell Biology, 2,* 137–141.

Warren, J., & Marshall, B. (1983). Unidentified curved bacilli on gastric epithelium in active chronic gastritis. *Lancet, 1,* 1273.

Wartella, J., Amory, E., Lomas, L. M., Macbeth, A., McNamara, I., Stevens, L., Lambert, K. G., & Kinsley, C. H. (2003). Single or multiple dreproductive experiences attenuate neurobehavioral stress and fear responses in the female rat. *Physiology and Behavior, 79*(3), 373–381.

Watanabe, Y., Gould, E., & McEwen, B. S. (1992). Stress induces atrophy of apical dendrites of hippocampal CA3 pyramidal neurons. *Brain Research, 588,* 341–345.

Waxman, S. G., Kocsis, J. D., & Stys, P. K. (Eds.). (1995). *The axon: Structure, function and pathophysiology.* New York: Oxford University Press.

Wecker, L. (1986). Neurochemical effects of choline supplementation. *Canadian Journal of Physiological Pharmacology, 64,* 329–333.

Wedekind, C., & Penn, D. (2000). MHC genes, body odors, and odor preferences. *Nephrology Dialysis Transplantation, 15,* 1269–1271.

Weiss, D. W., Hirt, H., Tarcic, N., Berzon, Y., Ben-Zur, H., Breznitz, S., et al. (1996). Studies in psychoneuroimmunology: Psychological, mmunological, and neuroendocrinological parameters in Israeli civilians during and after a period of Scud missile attacks. *Behavioral Medicine, 22,* 5–14.

Weiss, E. L., Longhurst, J. G., & Mazure, C. M. (1999). Childhood sexual abuse as a risk factor for depression in women: Psychosocial and neurobiological correlates. *American Journal of Psychiatry, 156*(6), 816–828.

Weiss, J. M. (1972). Influence of psychological variables on stress-induced pathology. In R. Porter & J. Knight (Eds.), *Physiology, emotion and psychosomatic illness.* Amsterdam: Associated Scientific Publishers.

Weiss, J. M. (1977). Psychological and behavioral influences on gastrointestinal lesions in animal models. In J. D. Maser & E. P. Seligman (Eds.), *Psychopathology: Experimental models.* San Francisco: Freeman.

Weiss, J. M., & Kilts, C. D. (1995). Animal models of depression and schizophrenia. In A. T. Schatzberg & C. B. Nemeroff (Eds.), *Textbook of psychopharmacology* (pp. 81–123). Washington, DC: American Psychiatric Press.

Weissman, I. L., & Cooper, M. D. (1993). How the immune system develops. In *Life, death, and the immune system: A Scientific American special issue* (pp. 14–25). New York: Freeman.

Werman, R., Davidoff, R. A., & Aprison, M. H. (1968). Inhibitory of glycine on spinal neurons in the cat. *Journal of Neurophysiology, 31,* 81–95.

Westermann, J., & Exton, M. S. (1999). Functional anatomy of the immune system. In M. Schedlowski & U. Tewes (Eds.), *Psychoneuroimmunology: An interdisciplinary approach.* New York: Kluwer Academic/Plenum.

Whale, R., Clifford, E. M., Bhagwagar, Z., & Cowan, P. J. (2001). Decreased sensitivity of 5-HT 1D receptors in melancholic depression. *British Journal of Psychiatry, 178,* 454–457.

Whitten, W. (2000). Pheromones and regulation of ovulation. *Nature, 392,* 177–179.

Whitty, C. W. M., Duffield, J. E., & Tow, P. M. (1952). Anterior cingulectomy in the treatment of mental disease. *Lancet, 1,* 475–481.

Wickelgren, I. (1998). Teaching the brain to take drugs. *Science, 280,* 2045–2047.

Widmaier, E. P. (1990). Glucose homeostasis and hypothalamic-pituitary-adrenocortical axis during development in rats. *American Journal of Physiology, 259,* E601–E613.

Wilens, T. E., Biederman, J., & Spencer, T. J. (2002). Attention deficit/hyperactivity disorder across the lifespan. *Annual Review of Medicine, 53,* 113–131.

Williams, G., Bing, C., Cai, X. J., Harrold, J. A., King, P. J., & Liu, X. H. (2001). The hypothalamus and the control of energy homeostasis: Different circuits, different purposes. *Physiology and Behavior, 74,* 683–701.

Willner, P., Muscat, R., & Papp, M. (1992). Chronic mild stress induced anhedonia: A realistic animal model of depression. *Neuroscience Biobehavior Review, 16,* 525–534.

Wilmut, I., Schnieke, A. E., McWhir, J., Kind, A. J., & Campbell, K. H. (1997). Viable offspring derived from fetal and adult mammalian cells. *Nature, 385,* 810–813; erratum in *Nature, 386,* 200.

Wilsnack, R. W., Vogeltanz, N. D., Wilsnack, S. C., & Harris, T. R. (2000). Gender differences in alcohol consumption and adverse drinking consequences: Cross-cultural patterns. *Addiction, 95,* 251–265.

Wilson, M. A., & McNaughton, B. L. (1993). Dynamics of the hippocampal ensemble code for space. *Science, 261,* 1055–1058.

Wilson, M. A., & McNaughton, B. L. (1994). Reactivation of hippocampal ensemble memories during sleep. *Science, 265,* 676–679.

Winslow, J. T., Hastings, N., Carter, C. S., Harbaugh, C. R., & Insel, T. R. (1993). A role for central vasopressin in pair bonding in monogamous prairie voles. *Nature, 365,* 545–548.

Wise, R. A. (1982). Neuroleptics and operant behavior: The anhedonia hypothesis. *Behavioral Brain Science, 5,* 39–87.

Wise, R. A. (1999). Animal models of addiction. In D. S. Charney, E. J. Nestler, & B. S. Bunney (Eds.), *Neurobiology of mental illness.* New York: Oxford University Press.

Wise, R. A. (2000). Addiction becomes a brain disease. *Neuron, 26,* 27–33.

Woese, C. R. (2002). On the evolution of cells. *Proceedings of the National Academy of Sciences, USA, 99,* 8742–8747.

Wolf, O. T., Schommer, N. C., Hellhammer, D. H., McEwen, B. S., & Kirschbaum, C. (2001). The relationship between stress-induced cortisol levels and memory differs between men and women. *Psychoneuroendocrinology, 26,* 711–720.

Wolf, S. S., Jones, D. W., Knable, M. B., Gorey, J. G., Lee, K. S., Hyde, J. M., et al. (1996). Tourette syndrome: Prediction of phenotypic variation in monozygotic twins by caudate nucleus D2 receptor binding. *Science, 273,* 1225–1227.

Woods, S. C. (1991). The eating paradox: How we tolerate food. *Psychological Review, 98,* 488–505.

Woods, S. C., & Strubbe, J. H. (1994). The psychobiology of meals. *Psychonomic Bulletin and Review, 1,* 142–155.

Woolley, C. S., Gould, E., & McEwen, B. S. (1990). Exposure to excess glucocorticoids alters dendritic morphology of adult hippocampal pyramidal neurons. *Brain Research, 531,* 225–231.

Wright, T. J., & Huddart, H. (2002). The nature of the acetylcholine and 5-hydroxytryptamine receptors in buccal smooth muscle of the pest slug Deroceras reticulatum. *Journal of Comprehensive Physiology, 172,* 237–249.

Wu, C. W., & Kass, J. H. (1999). Reorganization in primary motor cortex of primates with long-standing therapeutic amputations. *Journal of Neuroscience, 19,* 7679–7697.

Wu, C. W., & Kass, J. H. (2002). The effects of long-standing limb loss on anatomical reorganization of the somatosensory afferents in the brainstem and spinal cord. *Somatosensory Motor Research, 19,* 153–163.

Wu, J. T., & Kral, J. G. (2004). Ghrelin: Integrative neuroendocrine peptide in health and disease. *Annals of Surgery, 239*(4), 464–474.

Wyles, J. S., Kunkel, J. G., & Wilson, A. C. (1983). Birds, behavior, and anatomical evolution. *Proceedings of the National Academy of Sciences, USA, 80,* 4394–4397.

Yamato, T., Yamasaki, S., Misumi, Y., Kino, M., Obata, T., & Aomine, M. (2002). Modulation of the stress response by coffee: An in vivo microdialysis study of hippocampal serotonin and dopamine levels in rat. *Neuroscience Letters, 332,* 87–90.

Yatham, L. N., Liddle, P. F., Dennie, J., Shiah, I. S., Adam, M. J., Lane, C. J., et al. (1999). Decrease in brain serotonin 2 receptor binding in patients with major depression following desipramine treatment: A positron emission tomography study with fluorine-18-labeled setoperone. *Archives of General Psychiatry, 56,* 705–711.

Yeragani, V. K., Srinivasan, K., Balon, R., Ramesh, C., & Berchou, R. (1994). Lactate sensitivity and cardiac cholinergic function in panic disorder. *American Journal of Psychiatry, 151,* 1226–1228.

Yonkers, K. A., Kando, J. C., Hamilton, J. A., & Halbreich, U. (2000). Gender differences in treatment of depression and anxiety. In U. Halbreich & S. A. Montgomery (Eds.), *Pharmacotherapy for mood, anxiety, and cognitive disorders* (pp. 59–72). Washington, DC: American Psychiatric Press.

Young, D., Lawlor, P., Leone, P., Dragunow, M., & During, M. (1999). Environmental enrichment inhibits spontaneous apoptosis, prevents seizures, and is neuroprotective. *Nature Medicine, 5,* 448–453.

Young, L. J. (2001). Oxytocin and vasopressin as candidate genes for psychiatric disorders: Lessons from animal models. *Neuropsychiatric Genetics, 105,* 53–54.

Yusim, A., Ajilore, O., Bliss, T., & Sapolsky, R. (2000). Glucocorticoids exacerbate insult-induced declines in metabolism in selectively vulnerable hippocampal cell fields. *Brain Research, 870,* 109–117.

Zachrisson, O. C. G., Balldin, J., Ekman, R., Naech, O., Rosengren, L., Agren, H., & Blennow, K. (2000). No evident neuronal damage after electroconvulsive therapy. *Psychiatry Research, 96,* 157–165.

Zald, D. H., & Kim, S. W. (1996a). Anatomy and function of the orbital frontal cortex: I. Anatomy, neurocircuitry, and obsessive-compulsive disorder. *Journal of Neuropsychiatry and Clinical Neurosciences, 8,* 125–138.

Zald, D. H., & Kim, S. W. (1996b). Anatomy and function of the orbital frontal cortex: II. Function and relevance to obsessive-compulsive disorder. *Journal of Neuropsychiatry and Clinical Neurosciences, 8,* 249–261.

Zec, R. F., & Travedi, M. A. (2002). The effects of estrogen replacement therapy on neuropsychological functioning in postmenopausal women with and without dementia: A critical and theoretical review. *Neuropsychology Review, 12,* 65–109.

Zhang, X. F., Hu, X. T., & White, F. J. (1998). Whole cell plasticity in cocaine withdrawal: Reduced sodium currents in nucleus accumbens neurons. *Journal of Neuroscience, 18,* 488–498.

Zhou, J. N., Hofman, M. A., Gooren, L. J., & Swaab, D. F. (1995). A sex difference in the human brain and its relation to transsexuality. *Nature, 378,* 68–70.

Zigmond, M. J., Bloom, S. E., Landis, S. C., Roberts, J. L., Squire, L. R., & Woolley, R. S. (1999). *Fundamental neuroscience.* New York: Academic Press.

Zivin, J.A. (2000, April). Understanding clinical trials. *Scientific American, 282,* 69–75.

Zohar, J., Judge, R., & OCD Paroxetine Study Investigators. (1996). Paroxetine versus clomipramine in the treatment of obsessive-compulsive disorder. *British Journal of Psychiatry, 169,* 468–474.

Zoloft. (2003). *What is social anxiety disorder?* Accessed January 8, 2004, from http://www.zoloft.com/index.asp?pageid = 52

Name Index

Subject Index